Germany
$3.00

ADS
7969

Date Loaned

WITHDRAWN

STUDIES IN GERMAN HISTORY

By the same Author

BEFORE THE WAR, 2 VOLS.

COURTS AND CABINETS

STUDIES IN DIPLOMACY
AND STATECRAFT

FREDERICK THE GREAT:
The Ruler, The Writer, The Man

STUDIES IN GERMAN HISTORY

by

G. P. GOOCH

D.Litt., F.B.A.

LONGMANS, GREEN AND CO
LONDON • NEW YORK • TORONTO

LONGMANS, GREEN AND CO LTD
6 & 7 CLIFFORD STREET LONDON WI
ALSO AT MELBOURNE AND CAPE TOWN
LONGMANS, GREEN AND CO INC
55 FIFTH AVENUE NEW YORK 3
LONGMANS, GREEN AND CO
215 VICTORIA STREET TORONTO I
ORIENT LONGMANS LTD
BOMBAY CALCUTTA MADRAS

First published . . 1948

Printed in England
SPOTTISWOODE, BALLANTYNE & CO. LTD.
London & Colchester

PREFACE

THE items in this collection are partly old and partly new, but most of the former have been expanded and revised. *German Political Ideas from Luther to Hitler* appeared in 1945 in a volume of lectures sponsored by the Sociological Society entitled *The German Mind and Outlook*. *Germany in the Eighteenth Century* formed the Introduction to the author's *Germany and the French Revolution*, now out of print. *Mirabeau's Secret Letters from Berlin* appeared in the *Contemporary Review*, June and July, 1947. *Mirabeau and the Prussian Monarchy* is new. *Prince Henry of Prussia: Statesman and Diplomatist* borrows some passages from chapter XI of the author's *Frederick the Great*, but the story of his activities after the death of his brother is new. *Goethe's Political Background* and *Germany's Debt to the French Revolution* are reproduced from the author's *Studies in Modern History*, now out of print. *Ranke's Interpretation of German History* is new. *Treitschke in his Correspondence* was published in the *Contemporary Review*, December, 1947, January and February, 1948. *The Study of Bismarck* and *Holstein: Oracle of the Wilhelmstrasse* expand the essays contained in *Studies in Modern History* and utilise the material which has accumulated since 1931. *Bismarck's Table Talk* is new.

Though the studies collected in this volume were written at different times, they derive a certain unity from the fact that they illustrate almost every phase of German history from the Reformation to the eve of the Second World War. No attempt has been made to prove or disprove a thesis in this controversial field, though the author's opinions have not been concealed. The primary task of a historian is interpretation; he should enable his readers so far as possible to form their own conclusions on men, movements and events. Large tracts of German history are still little known to the outside world; and though we are under no obligation to accept the verdicts even of the most eminent German scholars, it is useful to ascertain what they are. Our best chance of understanding complex historical problems is to approach them from various points of view.

My thanks are due to the editors and publishers who have kindly granted permission to reprint.

G. P. GOOCH

STUDIES IN GERMAN HISTORY

GERMAN POLITICAL IDEAS FROM LUTHER TO HITLER	1
GERMANY IN THE EIGHTEENTH CENTURY	37
MIRABEAU'S *Secret Letters from Berlin*	75
MIRABEAU ON THE PRUSSIAN MONARCHY	96
PRINCE HENRY OF PRUSSIA: STATESMAN AND DIPLOMATIST	119
GOETHE'S POLITICAL BACKGROUND	166
GERMANY'S DEBT TO THE FRENCH REVOLUTION	190
RANKE'S INTERPRETATION OF GERMAN HISTORY	210
TREITSCHKE IN HIS CORRESPONDENCE	267
THE STUDY OF BISMARCK	300
BISMARCK'S TABLE TALK	342
HOLSTEIN: ORACLE OF THE WILHELMSTRASSE	391
INDEX	513

GERMAN POLITICAL IDEAS FROM LUTHER TO HITLER

WHAT part has Germany taken in the long and difficult quest for ordered liberty, the greatest prize of civilised mankind? A smaller share assuredly than England, where political thought has tended to stress the rights of the individual rather than the power of the state, and where the citizen for the last hundred years has chosen representatives to execute his will. Is that difference of evolution to be ascribed to racial factors? Certainly not. England takes her name from the Angles, France from the Franks—Germanic intruders who brought with them wider conceptions of personal freedom and political responsibility than they found. Yet Herder, in a memorable phrase, described Germany, with a good deal of justification, as the land of obedience—a term never applied to England or France by friend or foe. If the Germans of the *Völkerwanderung* were in the van, why are their modern descendants to be found in or near the rear?

The fundamental cause of the different attitude of the average modern German to political authority must be sought in his place on the map. Geography is the mother of history. The central European plain, stretching without a break from the Bay of Biscay to the Urals, and inhabited by many different stocks, is a standing invitation to strife. Lacking well-defined frontiers of mountains and sea, Germanic tribes were continually at war with their neighbours and with one another. The Holy Roman Empire strove in vain to organise the territories inhabited by men of German race. The Reformation introduced a new source of discord between north and south. The devastation of the Thirty Years' War was the grim penalty of external and internal disunion, and the Austro-Prussian rivalry dating from Frederick the Great postponed the creation of a nation-state to a period centuries later than in England and France, Spain and Russia. Italy alone of the Great Powers had to wait so long for the fulfilment of her dreams, and then she was able to construct her edifice of unity behind the rampart of the Alps. If Germany was ever to become a nation-state like the rest it could only be through the medium of a powerful executive, a formidable army, and a disciplined people. A country with open frontiers, surrounded by unfriendly neighbours, was necessarily conscious of its dangers to a degree not easily envisaged by Englishmen who evolved the theory and practice of self-government in a leisurely way behind their wooden walls. National strength, not internal self-determination, was the watchword. This penetrating difference of atmosphere and historical experience must be firmly grasped if we are to understand the evolution of political ideas in Germany in the era of nationalism.

In his instructive volume *Political Liberty*, Dr. A. J. Carlyle, our greatest authority on the evolution of political ideas since the fall of the Roman Empire, reminds us that the Middle Ages knew nothing of the doctrine of unlimited sovereignty and the absolute state. All human authority, it was believed, was limited, and all political authority was derived from the community itself. In Bracton's famous formula, the King had two superiors—God and the law. The medieval order symbolised by the Papacy and the Holy Roman Empire, which was dying in the fifteenth century, collapsed in the sixteenth, and our familiar world of differentiated sovereign states took its place. Excessive concentration followed the paralysing division of power. A new era of political thinking was inaugurated by Machiavelli, whose gospel of an unfettered executive has dominated the practice of large portions of the world ever since. The supreme achievement of the Reformation, as Figgis observed long ago, was the modern state. The community continued to be pictured as an organic whole; but while medieval thinkers tended to regard society as essentially a church, a community bound together by a common faith, modern publicists envisaged it as primarily a secular state. The craving for prosperity and social peace facilitated the transition from loose-limbed feudalism. In Catholic as well as Protestant countries civil authority waxed and ecclesiastical authority waned. The so-called Reception of Roman law, which took place in Germany at this time, played into the hands of autocrats.

The claim of the prince to unchallengeable power put forward in most continental countries was an innovation, and, next to Machiavelli, Luther was its prophet. Not that he was in any sense a systematic political thinker: he was indeed so obsessed by problems of the religious life that he had little taste for politics except in so far as they helped or hindered the cause of the Reformation. It is one of the ironies of history that the man who was largely responsible for the growth of the power of the state in Germany had a low opinion of its place in human society. His views are to be found above all in his tracts *To the Christian Nobility* (1520) and *On Worldly Authority* (1523). The good, he believed, needed no state, no law, no punishment, since they steered by the light within; his ideal was a community ruled by the Word of God and natural law. Unfortunately real Christians were everywhere in the minority, while the majority required the law, the magistrate and the sword. Thus the state was a necessary evil, approved by God for the needs of erring man, and as such its orders had to be obeyed. Active resistance to constituted authority was condemned by Scripture and led straight to anarchy. Commands contrary to divine law, of course, could not be obeyed, for the magistrate possessed no authority over the Christian conscience, worship and belief, in regard to which Scripture was supreme; resistance, however, must be passive and unjust punishments must be patiently borne. *Leiden, leiden, Kreuz, Kreuz, ist das Christenrecht*! No wonder that the author of that flaming aphorism claimed that no one had written so finely of the Emperor and obedience as himself. It was a common error that he was driven to adopt this doctrine by the excesses of the Peasants' Revolt; he had always held it and only the emphasis increased. The individualist in religion was at all times an authoritarian in secular affairs. Caring nothing for political liberty he was satisfied with the rule of a virtuous prince like his patron Frederick the Wise, Elector of Saxony. Never for a moment did he advocate political responsibility for the common man.

Though his ideal was the Christian prince, Luther had no illusions as to the character and capacity of the majority of rulers, and there is none of the unction in his writings to be found in many English seventeenth-century divines. Princes, indeed, were far from divine; a clever prince was rare, a pious prince rarer still. 'Let no one think the Land and People are mine, I will do what I like.' Yet authority there must be, and where else could it be found? The rights of the secular ruler as against ecclesiastical pretensions had been vigorously asserted by Marsilio and other publicists in the lively controversies of the Middle Ages, but with the coming of the Reformation the doctrine of civil supremacy hardened into a system. The duty of the ruler was to protect the good and punish the wicked without respect of persons, whether popes, bishops, monks, nuns or anyone else. His power was fortified by wholesale confiscation of church property and by the exercise of ecclesiastical patronage. One law should prevail, and all must obey, for only by the abolition of competing authority could the unity and strength of the state be secured. The conception of Christendom faded away and a mosaic of sovereign states took its place. Yet the state was more than a purely secular institution, for among its tasks, as the Reformers saw it, was to protect true religion against its domestic and foreign foes. Indeed, while the Reformation was fighting for its life its defence became the ruler's supreme responsibility. That such monopoly of power involved grave danger of abuse was obvious, and the Lutheran leaders came to admit the right of self-defence against violence, just as a man would rightly defend wife and child against murderers. Melanchthon went further than his master in proclaiming that there was nothing on earth more noble than the state, and that obedience to the magistrate was a religious duty; yet even he declared that the rights of rulers were limited by natural law, Scripture and customary law. None of the Lutheran leaders anticipated the watertight absolutism of Hobbes. Yet Luther was as much the pioneer of political authoritarianism in Germany as was Calvin, *malgré lui*, of the democratic tradition of the Anglo-Saxon world. At last the Prince, untrammelled by Church or feudal nobility, could exclaim with satisfaction *L'État c'est moi*.

After the long anarchy of feudalism some strengthening of the power and prestige of governments was overdue, but the pendulum swung too far and the tyranny inherent in centralisation had to be jealously watched. Opinions on the nature and functions of the state have differed as widely in Germany as elsewhere, and there have been libertarian as well as authoritarian oracles. Indeed the former were the more numerous till the opening of the nineteenth century, when the detested Napoleonic yoke called German nationalism into life. The first of them was Althusius, whose significance was revealed to the modern world by Gierke in a classical monograph acclaimed by Lord Acton as the best book on modern political thinking. The *Politica methodice digesta*, published in 1607, reiterated the sound doctrine of the Middle Ages that political society is founded on consent. The conception of a Social Contract, which played such a vital part in the controversies of the seventeenth and eighteenth centuries, rested on what we call a legal fiction; and this useful formula, except in the paradoxical presentation by Hobbes, embodied the principles of agreement and limited power. The task of government, argued the Helmstedt Professor, was the execution of the law; the law was made by the community; the supreme magistrate, like the people, was bound by contract embodied in solemn oaths taken by both parties on his accession or election. The notion that a ruler could do exactly what he liked, that he ruled by Divine Right, that resistance to his commands was unlawful even if he broke the contract, was rejected with scorn. Power was a trust, not a right. No individual was wise enough to rule without supervision and advice. Althusius believed in representation as heartily as any Englishman, though no Parliament on the English model existed among his countrymen. It was the task of the Diets of the Empire to discuss and decide on important affairs. 'What concerns all should be determined by all, for the many are wiser than the few, and it is by such a form of government that the liberty of the people is protected, for they compel the officials to recognise that the people is their master.' He would have approved the definition of liberty as power cut up into little bits. His unit of authority was not the individual but the group—the family, the city, the province, the Estates, culminating in a federal state. The contention that the executive power is limited not only by contract but by the necessities of society was reiterated by Puffendorf and Leibnitz in their refutations of the slavish doctrines of Hobbes.

Between Althusius and the era of the French Revolution no German thinker of the first rank devoted serious attention to the theory of the state. During the seventeenth century and the first half of the eighteenth the stage was occupied by the Cameralists, who accepted the Absolute State as an axiom. In *The German Princes' State*, published in 1655, Seckendorf produced a handbook of government and administration based on the practice of his master, Duke Ernest the Pious of Gotha. Cameralism was the theory and practice of administration, and though its exponents hoped to raise the standard of autocracy, they suggested no check more effective than an appeal to the conscience of the ruler. Instead of proceeding from the needs of the community, the state, not the people, was their starting-point, its power and wealth their aim. Their teaching was brought up to date a century later by Justi, whose writings reflect and idealise the theory and practice of benevolent autocracy in the age of the Philosophic Despots. The common weal is presented sincerely enough as the goal of the state, and the happiness of the subject receives lip-homage, but he assumes that it is secured by the authority of the prince. He is aware that the growth of material needs and moral demands create a rising standard for rulers, but he never suggests that the people should enforce it. He begs the ruler to respect property and law, and not to overtax his subjects, but they may not co-operate in the making of laws or punish oppressors. Like all the Cameralists he assumes the wisdom and benevolence of the ruler, the might and majesty of the state. Such teaching, however, was a double-edged weapon, for it prompted the suffering subject to point out that the state was not performing the duties which Justi declared that it should.

Frederick the Great was not merely the most prominent and successful practitioner of the Benevolent Despotism postulated by the Cameralists, but the chief literary exponent of its ideology; for during his crowded life he found time to produce solid treatises on the theory and practice of government in addition to histories, poems and essays. His *Anti-machiavel*, written in 1739, revised by Voltaire and published anonymously in 1740, the year of his accession, denounces the Florentine tempter as a monster. 'I have always regarded *The Prince* as one of the most dangerous books in the world, for an ambitious young man, too immature to distinguish good from evil, may only too easily be led astray by maxims which flatter his passions. That is bad enough in a private individual; it is far worse in reigning princes, who should set an example to their subjects and by their goodness, magnanimity and mercy be the living images of Deity. The passions of kings are worse than flood, pestilence and fire, for their consequences are more lasting.' Accepting the popular doctrine of the Social Contract as an axiom, he asserts that rulers were instituted for the protection and welfare of the community. Thus the sovereign, far from being the absolute master, is merely the first servant of the peoples over whom he rules. To Machiavelli's argument that goodness in this wicked world spells discomfiture he rejoins that, on the contrary, to avoid disaster one must be good and prudent. Accepting the paramount claim of interest he gives the word a different interpretation. The good king will be well served and need have no anxieties about his throne; a cruel prince, on the other hand, is likely to be betrayed, for cruelty is insupportable. Perfidy, another instrument recommended by the oracle of tyrants, is equally unwise. At this point, however, the preacher removes his surplice and descends from the pulpit. There are painful occasions, he argues, when a ruler cannot avoid breaking treaties and alliances, and even offensive wars are justified when undertaken to ward off a threatened attack. In home affairs, in a word, he should apply the maxims of a Sunday School, but in dealing with other states he must be guided by the *raison d'état* which the Italian publicist felt it his duty to recommend.

Frederick's *Political Testaments* of 1752 and 1768, first published in full in 1920, survey the whole field of government at home and abroad—the administrative machinery, the army, finance, justice, foreign affairs. They are the testimony of a working king who asks nothing of his subjects which he has not himself performed. In a country without the traditions and institutions of representative government it was the duty of the monarch, he declared, to hold all the reins firmly in his hand—knowing everything, supervising everything, visiting every corner of his dominions, deciding everything promptly and justly. A well-conducted government must have a system as coherent as a system of philosophy, so that finance, policy and the army are co-ordinated to the same end, namely the consolidation of the state and the increase of its power. Such a system could only issue from a single brain, that of the sovereign, who must be the last refuge of the unhappy, a father to the orphans, the succour of widows, caring for the meanest as for the highest in the land. 'He must often remind himself that he is a man like the least of his subjects, the first judge, the first general, the first financier, the first minister. He is only the first servant of the state, obliged to act with probity, wisdom and entire disinterestedness, as if at every moment he had to render an account of his administration to the citizens.' It was a fine though static ideal at the time that it was formulated, and he strove unceasingly for forty-six years to carry it out. That his people should ever share in the responsibilities of government never crossed his mind or that of his subjects. The weakness of the system of Enlightened Autocracy is that its successful operation postulates an unbroken succession of supermen. Autocrats, dynastic or otherwise, are not always enlightened, as no one knew better than Frederick himself, who expressed the lowest opinion of nearly all his centemporaries. Though he bitterly complained that the idle and dissolute nephew who was to succeed him as Frederick William II threatened the work of his life, he never contemplated the possibility of another system in which the people, as in England, might be the partner of the prince. Twenty years after the death of the greatest European figure of the eighteenth century his machine state, so strong in outward appearance, proved to be as brittle as glass.

The main cause of stagnation in political thinking during the eighteenth century was the lack of a nation-state. Germany was a geographical expression, a political curiosity shop, a soul without a body. The political education of the citizen was first seriously undertaken in the third quarter of the eighteenth century by a handful of courageous men. The first of these tribunes of the people was Friedrich Karl Moser, whose treatise *Der Herr und der Diener* (Master and Servant) was published in the Free City of Frankfurt in 1759. This widely read political classic of the German *Aufklärung* begins by reminding princes how easy it is to make their subjects happy, and by lamenting how seldom they succeed. They are brought up to be soldiers, not statesmen, and to believe they are responsible to God alone. A capable ruler is a blessing, but even in such a case several eyes are better than a single pair. Hopes are usually entertained of the heir, who sometimes dreams of reform; and if one-tenth of these good resolutions were carried out, Germany would be living in the Golden Age. But the new pilot finds himself among men who chant the refrain, Your Highness has only to command! 'The great goal of all the motley throng at Court is to win the favour of the ruler, who is like a beleaguered city and is surrounded by spies and traitors. Even in small Courts you will find a multitude of them.' This outspoken book was a transcript from the author's experience as Minister of the Landgrave of Hesse Darmstadt. Some years later he was recalled to office, but, like Turgot, he was too radical to retain his post. His later experiences were embodied in *Rulers and Ministers*, published in 1784. What sinister memories lurk behind the maxim that for the success of his plans the Minister needs not only the consent of the Prince, but also of the 'Night Ministry,' the wife, the mistress, the confessor, the chamberlains! He denounces the glaring faults of the Proprietary State with passionate earnestness, but he does not look beyond its reform. It was not enough to denounce evil rulers: it was necessary to bring them under effective control. By refusing to call the people to his aid he deprived himself of the only weapon by which he could strike terror into guilty hearts.

A sharper note was struck by Schlözer, the earliest political journalist of Germany and the first systematic political instructor of his countrymen. As Professor of History at Göttingen, he helped to make the young University the national centre for political, legal and diplomatic studies. His journals became the terror of evil-doers and the delight of the oppressed. They were read throughout Central Europe, and Maria Theresa would sometimes support her opinion in Council with the words, 'This will never do; what would Schlözer say?' He was far more than a critic of abuses. The Electorate of Hanover was a sort of British *enclave* in Germany. His creed was constitutional monarchy, representative institutions, and a free press. He was a student of Montesquieu and shared his admiration for British models. The happiness of a prince, he declared, lay in ruling with his people, not over them. There should be a contract, so that if it were broken he might be deposed. Rejecting Divine Right and patriarchal omnipotence, he locates sovereignty in the people, though he detested mob rule. As a champion of the *juste milieu*, the Cobbett of Germany was equally opposed to autocracy, oligarchy and democracy.

Schlözer's advice to adopt certain English forms was supported by Justus Möser. The Osnabrück lawyer, a thoughtful conservative, had visited England and liked what he saw. 'He who is to act in common must deliberate in common,' he declared; 'that is the principal formula of German law.' Unhappily, this axiom of English history had been forgotten in the land of its birth. Detesting absolutism as much as the rest of his countrymen, he sought salvation not in political experiments but in continuity and the preservation of ancient ways. Our ancestors, he observed, were not fools, an aphorism which Burke might have taken for his text in his *Reflections on the French Revolution*. He was the first German publicist to recommend the maintenance of institutions which by the mere fact of their duration had proved their worth. Distrusting political theories and formulations of the rights of man, he preferred customs to laws. The idea of equality seemed to him ridiculous because it was contradicted by experience. The state was not the creation of a contract but the result of historical growth, every community having its unique personality of which it should be proud. The possession of land was the sole title to political rights. Landowners, large and small alike, should elect representatives to decide on taxation and other important problems. Only a state where the greater part of the population was rooted in the soil was secure against revolutionary change. The peasant was the cornerstone of the edifice, for the restless townsman was inclined to challenge the stability of social life. Möser was proud of the relatively prosperous little state whose history he wrote; and the notion of a united and centralised Germany, if it had ever entered his head, would have shocked him as a violation of historic rights. His widely read articles, collected under the title *Patriotische Phantasien*, expound the gospel of organic growth. His significance has been increasingly recognised in recent years, and he ranks with Herder among the discoverers and admirers of the Volk (folk) and the Volksseele (folk soul). They and their disciples were more interested in the group than in the individual or the state. This almost mystical cult of the folk was the main source, not only of the Romantic Movement, but of the historical school of law founded by Eichhorn and Savigny.

Few Germans asked for anything more than decent government till the challenge of the French Revolution compelled them to think. Goethe's view of the state was moulded by the lucky accident which made him the lifelong friend and colleague of one of the best princes of his time, just as the youthful Schiller's explosive dramas were inspired by the misrule of Karl Eugen, Duke of Württemberg. Karl August inherited a principality with a hundred thousand inhabitants and an infertile soil, but after sowing their wild oats the prince and the poet settled down to make the Duchy of Weimar a model for rulers. At this task Goethe, as President of the Council, laboured with unflagging energy for a decade, his master for half a century. He promoted the development of agriculture, industry, and mines, the reform of education and finance, the amelioration of the lot of the poor. Though he returned to literature, his experience of public life determined his political ideas. All he had done and all he wished to do had been or could be accomplished by the will of a benevolent autocrat. The elements of any political structure other than paternal government were absent. The people had a right to be well governed, not to govern themselves. He stood midway between the Legitimists, to whom dynastic authority was sacrosanct, and the democrats, to whom the voice of the people was the voice of God. He was a conservative reformer, convinced that the initiative must come from above, that changes must be gradual, that order was heaven's first law. He agreed with Frederick the Great that the ruler must be *le premier domestique de l'état*. When the storm broke over Germany in his middle years his simple political faith remained completely unchanged. 'I could be no friend to the Revolution,' he confessed to Eckermann, 'but I am as little a friend to arbitrary rule.' Since the masses could not save themselves, it was the duty and the privilege of their rulers to save them. To both parties the European earthquake brought a solemn warning. For the prince to do too little and for the people to do too much was to invite a catastrophe. Eckermann described his master in old age as a mild aristocrat, but Goethe preferred the title of 'a moderate Liberal, as all rational people are and ought to be.'

The universal significance of the French Revolution was recognised both by those who took part in it and by those who watched it from afar. Its influence on political thinking was greater in Germany than in any other country. It was as if a huge rock had been hurled into a stagnant pool. The opening scenes were watched with delight not only by the average citizen, but by the great majority of the spokesmen of opinion. The Declaration of the Rights of Man put into words the muffled aspirations of the masses and brought a new sense of human dignity in its train. The windows of the prison house seemed to fly open, and the common man felt that he had come of age. Schlözer exclaimed that the angels must be singing Te Deums in heaven, Gentz that mankind had awakened from its long sleep. The glittering pageant soon faded, and many voices which had swelled the chorus of thanksgiving, among them Klopstock, Schlözer, and Gentz, began to curse. Yet the leaven continued to work. At long last Germany produced treatises on the nature and functions of the state worthy to rank with the classics of other lands. The transition from the eighteenth century to the nineteenth, from the Age of Rationalism to the Age of Nationalism, from the old Germany to the new, is reflected in the political writings of Humboldt, Kant, and Fichte.

Wilhelm von Humboldt's treatise, *The Limits of State Action*, was finished in 1792 and portions appeared in the reviews; but no publisher was willing to risk a conflict with the censorship, and the book was published sixty years later by the author's brother Alexander. It is the German equivalent of Mill *On Liberty*, and Mill has expressed his indebtedness to his famous predecessor. There are two questions, he begins, involved in the attempt to frame a constitution. The first is, Who shall govern? The second relates to the sphere to which the Government shall extend its operations. The former problem was being discussed on all sides, while the latter, which was far more important, was utterly neglected. Constitutions are only machinery for ministering to the needs and developing the capacities of the individual. While France was demanding freedom for a nation, Humboldt, who cared nothing for the sovereignty of the people, pleads for freedom for himself. The most important of all political questions are those which affect the private life of the citizen. As civilisation advances there is less need of government, and the question of its form becomes of secondary importance. His demand is not for better but for less government. It is a modest request to address to a ruler, and can be granted without waiting for a revolution. 'If to behold a people breaking their fetters asunder is a beautiful and ennobling spectacle, how much better is it to witness a prince himself unloosing the bonds of thraldom and granting freedom to his subjects!'

The true end of man, proceeds Humboldt, is the harmonious development of his powers, and reason demands a condition of things in which every one enjoys the most abundant opportunities of self-realisation. The unceasing effort of the state to promote the welfare of its citizens is harmful, for it creates uniformity, suppresses spontaneity, discourages energy, and thereby hinders the natural growth of the individual. What a man does under instruction or guidance fails to enter into his being and remains alien to his true nature. Legislation necessarily bears a general character, and therefore fails to meet the need of particular cases. Moreover, the greater the activity of the state the greater the army of functionaries. In a sentence which has a twentieth-century flavour he complains that every decade the number of officials increases and the liberty of the subject proportionately declines. 'The state should not proceed a step further than is necessary for the protection of its citizens against foreign enemies. It should abstain from all solicitude for their positive welfare.' Voluntary association is better than any arrangements that the Government can make. Civilisation has reached a point beyond which it cannot aspire to still loftier heights save through the development of individuals; and therefore all institutions which in any way obstruct this development are now far more hurtful than in earlier and less advanced ages. National education turns out all its scholars on the same pattern. A State Church, by encouraging certain opinions, gives a bias to the citizen and discourages freedom of thought. National supervision of morals might produce a peaceable and prosperous community, but its members would be like a flock of sheep. No serious consequences need be apprehended from the abuse of liberty. 'The state is merely a means to which man, the true end, must never be sacrificed.'

This earnest and eloquent work, like most other pleas for individualism, assumes that human nature is on the whole good, just as champions of autocracy assume that it is on the whole bad. 'Man,' declares Humboldt cheerfully, 'is naturally more disposed to beneficent than to selfish actions.' He believes that the world is full of men like himself, who possess sufficient virtue and wisdom to make their life a thing of beauty without the guidance of authority. Many years later, when he became Minister of Education in Prussia, he realised that the alternative to bad government was not philosophic anarchy but good government, and that wise action by the state is one of the most powerful factors in the development of a rich and harmonious personality. Despite his exaggerated individualism, which sometimes anticipates the paradoxes of Nietzsche, the youthful Humboldt remains an impressive figure; and his teaching that a state must be judged, not by its power and riches, but by the spiritual quality of its citizens, shines like a ray of light in the stagnant days of Frederick William II. The treatise was carefully studied by his friend Schiller, and the doctrine that the perfecting of the individual is a more urgent and fruitful task than the search for new institutions reappears in the *Letters on the Aesthetic Education of Man.*

By his individualism and cosmopolitanism Kant, no less than Humboldt, belongs to the eighteenth century; but the greatest of philosophers was also one of the boldest and most suggestive of political thinkers. His interest in affairs was aroused by the American War of Independence, which won his whole-hearted sympathy. Though nearly seventy at the outbreak of the French Revolution, he welcomed it with enthusiasm, and for the rest of his life his talk was mainly of politics. His pen was as bold as his tongue. In his study of *Religion*, published in 1793, he counters the argument that the French are not ripe for liberty with the axiom that men become ripe for liberty when they are set free. 'We must be free in order to use our powers wisely in freedom. The first attempts will naturally be imperfect; but experience will show the way, for God has created mankind for freedom.' In his *Philosophy of Law*, published four years later, he declares that liberty, equality and personal independence are the inalienable attributes of the citizen, and that the highest criterion of legislation is that it represents the will of the people. Since man is a rational and moral being politics must be based on reason and morality.

In the most arresting of his political works, *Perpetual Peace*, we catch the highest notes ever struck by a German publicist. If law, based on reason and morality, was the foundation of the life of the state, it should equally regulate the relations of states to one another. Humanity needed a constitution not less than France or Prussia; for so long as each state recognised no authority above itself and no duty except to itself, wars would continue. He does not waste time in proving the evil of war. Writing in 1795 he takes it for granted, and plunges at once into a discussion how it may be avoided. He first enumerates what he describes as the preliminary articles of peace: (1) No treaty shall be valid if it contains a secret reservation of materials for a future war. (2) No state shall be acquired through inheritance, exchange, or purchase; for it is not a property, but a society of human beings. (3) Standing armies shall one day be abolished, for they are always threatening other states with war. Rivalry in armaments begins, and armed peace becomes so oppressive that war may seem a preferable alternative. (4) No national debt shall be incurred except for purely internal affairs. (5) No state shall forcibly interfere with the constitution and administration of another.

These injunctions and exhortations are merely counsels of perfection so long as the destinies of nations are in the hands of irresponsible autocrats. The second part of the little treatise, therefore, proceeds to establish the fundamental conditions of permanent peace. The first is that all states must become republican, a term in which he includes every kind of genuinely constitutional government. 'The only constitution which is rooted in the idea of the original contract, on which the lawful legislation of every nation must be based, is the republican.' It recognises the dependence of the state on law and on the equality of its members. It is also the only constitution which ensures peace; for if the consent of the community is needed for war, it will think twice before undertaking such a bad business. When selfish and capricious autocracies are replaced by representative institutions, a new system of relations between states will become possible. The second article therefore demands a federation of free states. By war and victory, remarks Kant, the question of right can never be decided. Anticipating a League of Nations, he declares that if some powerful and enlightened people should form a republic, that is, should become master of its own fate, it would serve as a nucleus for other states, and the federation would gradually increase in size and authority. The only absolute security for perpetual peace would be a world-republic, which he laments that the nations will not accept. 'Hence, if all is not to be lost, we must obtain the negative substitute for it, a federation averting war.' Even then there will be constant danger. The third article claims what he describes as universal hospitality for individuals in whatever State they may find themselves. The idea of cosmopolitan right, or, as we say, of world-citizenship, is the complement of the unwritten code of law for the public rights of mankind.

The political ideal of this lofty and lonely figure—rationalist, moralist, cosmopolitan—was neither the benevolent autocracy of philosopher-kings nor the fleeting triumphs of alternating majorities. It was the *Rechtsstaat*, the state based on the rule of law; and by law he meant the fusing of reason and morality. Like Rousseau and the perfectibility school, Kant believed in the instinctive goodness of mankind, and, like other optimists, he wished to impose on the citizen the minimum of constraint. The state was merely an association—and not the only one—created by the community for its needs, and its chief purpose was to secure justice. The final authority, alike for the state and the individual, was the categorical imperative of conscience, the moralised will.

While Humboldt and Kant express the loftiest ideals of the eighteenth century, Fichte represents the transition to the dominant principle of German thought in the nineteenth century. Attracted to politics by the French Revolution he made his début as a publicist in 1793 with an anonymous pamphlet entitled *A demand for freedom of thought presented to the Princes of Europe who have hitherto suppressed it*. In scathing terms he attacks the rulers of his country. 'One of the sources of our misery,' he cries, 'is our exaggerated estimate of these folk. Their minds are warped by false teaching and superstition. I reckon as virtues all the vices they do not possess, and I thank them for all the evil acts they do not commit. Let us rid ourselves of the notion that it is for the princes to secure our happiness. We shall now dare to ask those who claim to rule us: By what right? If they reply, By inheritance, we rejoin that man cannot be inherited like flocks and herds. He is governed by conscience alone. If he admits any other rule, he sinks to the level of the animals. The prince obtains the whole of his power from his contract with society. It is indecent for thinking men to crawl at the foot of the throne and beg leave to be the doormat of kings. The strength of our rulers lies in the ignorance of their subjects.' This passionate attack on autocracy and obscurantism combines Humboldt's cult of the individual with the full-blooded doctrine of the sovereignty of the people newly imported from France.

A longer and less rhetorical treatise appeared in the same year entitled *A Contribution to the formation of a correct judgment on the French Revolution*. The great event, declares Fichte, is of importance for the whole of mankind. Now is the time to make the people acquainted with freedom, which he who seeks will surely find. 'Things have become the subject of conversation of which no one had dreamed. Talk of the rights of man, of liberty and equality, of the limits of the royal power, has taken the place of fashions and adventures. We are beginning to learn.' While deprecating violent change he stoutly upholds the rights of revolution. As man is or ought to be subject to the moral law alone, every citizen may terminate his share in the contract at his own discretion. As the contract was freely made, so it may be freely changed. Neither power nor privileges can be handed down. Man is born with certain inalienable rights, and he is under no obligation to a government or a social system which fails to respect them. If the individual is thus master of himself, how much more is it the right and duty of a whole people to remove all obstacles to the pursuit of a free and elevated existence.

With such unbridled individualism at work the life of the state is like the flame of a candle, and Fichte, whose mind never stood still, quickly realised that his position was untenable. In *The Foundations of Natural Law*, published in 1796, he begins to construct breakwaters against the tide of popular passion. Though clinging to the sovereignty of the people and the social contract, he creates a small body of Ephors with the power to veto the decisions of the government and check the tendency to revolution, which, though justifiable, often produces greater evils than it cures. He was not long in perceiving that his Ephors were men of straw, but the proposal shows that he is feeling his way towards the necessity of stable government. In *The Closed Commercial State*, published in 1800, we note a further departure from his original standpoint. The state should monopolise trade, control wages and prices, secure work for all, and aim at economic autarchy within a territory large enough to supply its material needs. Since Mercantilism led to commercial wars, and the economic freedom recommended by Adam Smith would ruin Germany's backward agriculture and industry, autarchy seemed the wisest course. As the son of a Saxon weaver Fichte was particularly anxious to raise the standard of the manual worker, and he was the first German publicist to proclaim the right to work. In return for his services the state should give to each citizen his share. This was impossible without a planned economy, which in turn necessitated the maximum approach to a self-sufficing state. Though economic security was the immediate object of the plan, the ultimate goal was intellectual and moral self-realisation in a world at peace. In all his changes he never dreamed of sacrificing the individual to an omnipotent state.

The battle of Jena turned Fichte into the most fervent and eloquent champion of the national state; and the *Addresses to the German Nation,* delivered in 1807-8 within earshot of the French garrison in Berlin, proclaim the political gospel of which his countrymen were one day to become devotees. He no longer paints his princes black and their subjects white. All, he cries, are responsible for the great collapse, all had been slack and selfish, all must co-operate in the work of reconstruction. The nation must become self-conscious, the school system must be reformed, and the state must be strong enough to defend its citizens. It was not merely the state which he had learned to regard: he shed his cosmopolitanism like an old garment. The man who in his youth had desired to become a French citizen woke up to the fact that the Germans were a great people. Retaining his conception of the unity of mankind, he now proclaimed that it could only be served in one's own fatherland. Germans had a peculiarly important part to play, for they had retained their language untainted by alien influences, and could therefore give incomparable expression to the soul of the people. They had shown their moral earnestness by the Reformation, their enlightenment in the healthy life of the Free Cities, and were therefore best fitted to lead the regeneration of mankind. To carry out this lofty mission he recommended a federation of democratic units, not a centralised autocracy. Except in this extravagant exaltation of his race the German Mazzini has little in common with Nazi ideology.

The most imposing figure on the German political stage between

Frederick the Great and Bismarck distrusted political theories. As a student of Justus Möser, Burke and Montesquieu, and an admirer of English institutions, Stein dreamed of far-reaching reforms; rejecting alike monarchical absolutism, feudal privileges and the sovereignty of the people, he wished the middle classes to have their chance. 'If the nation is to be uplifted,' he declared, 'the submerged part must be given liberty, independence, property and the protection of the laws.' His chief monument, the creation of municipal self-government and his share in the emancipation of the serfs, links him with modern conceptions of equal rights and self-determination; yet as an Imperial Knight he was rooted in the past. He wished to revive the Empire, and envisaged the citizen rather as a member of some corporate body than as an isolated unit. These corporations, he believed, should advise the ruler in regard to legislation and give their consent to taxation. Even this shade of liberal conservatism was too bright for the princes and the Junkers, who through their mouthpiece Marwitz angrily denounced him as a Jacobin. Hardenberg, his successor, who carried forward the creation of a free peasantry, owed his inspiration not to England but to France, and may be classified as a conservative liberal. In a memorandum written in 1807 at the King's request, he advised the application to Prussia of the ideas of the French Revolution, since such was their power that any state which rejected them would collapse. 'Your Majesty, we must do from above what the French have done from below.' It was not his fault that Prussia had to wait for a constitution till 1848. The idea of limited monarchy on the English model was in the air, but there it remained.

While Kant and Humboldt failed to grasp the full significance of the state, and Fichte only realised it when Prussia lay prostrate before the invader, Hegel made it the starting-point of his philosophy. The High Priest of the Restoration era was the first German thinker to concern himself long and deeply with its nature, and no subsequent writer of the first rank, except Nietzsche, has belittled it. As a student at Tübingen he had coquetted with the French Revolution, but the sufferings of his country during the great war taught him to seek remedies for her weakness. In his remarkable book, *The German Constitution*, written about 1802 but not published till long after his death, he bitterly bewails the helplessness of his countrymen. He surveys the Holy Roman Empire and concludes that Germany can no longer be called a state, for only that country deserves the name which can defend its possessions. He speaks enviously of other nations which have created a state, and thereby entered upon a period of power, wealth and prosperity. Order is the first need of society. Europe, he declares, had become less sensitive to the cry of freedom since the horrors of the French Revolution. 'In this bloody drama there has melted the cloud of liberty in embracing which the peoples have fallen into an abyss of misery. A settled government is necessary for freedom.' He adds that the people must co-operate in the making of the laws and that representation is essential to liberty, and concludes with proposals for the reform of the constitution.

Hegel had reached the height of his influence and had been called to Berlin when he published his *Philosophy of Right* in 1821. Since the War of Liberation had rendered the German people fully self-conscious the demand for some measure of political liberty had become general, and the South German states were granted constitutions by their princes. In Prussia, on the other hand, reactionary influences combined with the King's timidity to retain autocracy unimpaired. The students' demonstrations on the Wartburg and the murder of Kotzebue had been followed by the Carlsbad decrees, which muzzled the Universities and the Press. At this moment, when Metternich was in command, the most influential philosopher in Germany issued what was in some quarters regarded as a manifesto of the reaction. A famous witticism affirmed that he had mistaken the kingdom of Prussia for the kingdom of heaven. The accusation was exaggerated, for he demanded representative institutions a generation before they were granted. He had championed the reforming king of his native Württemberg in his struggle with the feudal interests, and part of an article on the English Reform Bill, written just before his death, was suppressed by the Prussian censor. Hegel was a philosophic conservative, not a reactionary.

The state, we read in the *Philosophy of Right*, is the realised ethical idea, the divine on earth, and therefore a law to itself. A people must embody its sense of right in a constitution, which, however, is not a mere manufactured article but the work of centuries. The best form is hereditary monarchy, which guarantees unity and continuity, and is raised above faction by ruling through ministers. Montesquieu's ideal of the separation of powers, watching and checking each other, is rejected on the ground that it threatens the strength and solidarity of the state. A Legislature is essential, but ultimate decisions must not be made by the people, which does not know what it wants. 'To know what we want, and still more to know what reason wants, and what is good for the state, is the fruit of deep knowledge and insight, and is therefore not the property of the people.' The right of criticism is the most valuable that the community possesses. 'Public opinion deserves both to be esteemed and despised—despised in its concrete expression, esteemed in its essential basis.' His notion of government is that it is a very difficult task, requiring highly skilled operators for its success. The sovereignty of numbers and the abstract Rights of Man are emphatically repudiated. He lacked that confidence in the average citizen which inspired the French Revolution and lies at the base of the democratic faith. In his political not less than in his philosophical system the individual tends to be engulfed in the whole.

In his doctrine of the relation of states to one another Hegel represents a deplorable reaction from Kant. While the elder philosopher proclaimed the overlordship of humanity, the younger denied the existence of moral relations between states. International law is no real contract, and no state is legally or morally bound by it. Differences can only be settled by war, which is neither good nor evil but natural and inevitable. Indeed, it has its uses as a national scavenger and in emphasising the unimportance of material things. In deciding on war the state must consult nothing but its own interest. Yet Hegel's teaching differs from the militarism of a later age which glorifies aggression and thinks exclusively in terms of force. A state, he declared, is held together, not by force, but by a deep-rooted instinct of order. It is a spiritual structure, the highest embodiment of reason, the guardian of liberty. The most influential of German political thinkers surrounded the state with a halo which it has never entirely lost.

Hegel's doctrine of the state was too rigid for the large and growing body of men who clamoured for a constitution. South German Liberals, led by Rotteck and Welcker, Baden Professors, authors and Members of Parliament, looked for inspiration to France, while North Germans cast wistful glances across the North Sea. The expulsion of the Bourbons in 1830 and the passage of the English Reform Bill in 1832 increased the ferment. It was at this time that Dahlmann, the German Guizot, from his chair at Göttingen, proclaimed the virtues of constitutional government as practised in

England. His treatise on political science, published in 1835, for some years the Bible of North German Liberalism, judged ideas and institutions, not in abstraction, but in their evolution and operation. He realised that constitutions, like states, must rest on historical foundations, not on abstract principles. In this spirited plea for representative government the illustrations are drawn almost exclusively from English history. His nobility of character made him one of the most impressive figures of modern Germany. His ardent nationalism and his deep conviction of the rightness of the popular thirst for liberty influenced generations of University students. His manly protest against the revocation of the Hanoverian constitution in 1837, promptly followed by his expulsion from Göttingen, increased his authority with the bourgeoisie, which he described as the kernel of the population and the centre of gravity of the state. He had no eye for the Fourth Estate.

The substitution in 1840 of the brilliant and romantic Frederick William IV as King of Prussia for his insipid father aroused hopeful expectations, but he contented himself with summoning the eight provincial Diets to a joint meeting at Berlin in 1847. His opening address explained the limits of this cautious advance. No power on earth should persuade him to transform the natural relationship between Prince and people into a conventional and constitutional form. He would never allow a piece of paper, like a second Providence, to take the place of the old consecrated loyalty. It was the duty of the Crown to rule in accordance with the law of God and the state and his own unfettered discretion, not according to the will of majorities. He would never have summoned the United Landtag had he imagined that its members would lust after the rule of 'so-called representatives of the people.' Despite this admonition the Landtag, though mainly composed of the landed nobility, replied that it could not regard itself as fulfilling the promises of Frederick William III, and expressed the hope for wider powers.

In 1848, the year of revolutions, the German people were politically more advanced than their rulers. The educated bourgeoisie looked with envy on the constitutional monarchy of Victorian England. The Professors, the most influential factor in the formation of opinion, were almost all adherents of moderate Liberalism, for the party of radical republicans who looked to France was small. Without asking or securing permission from the princes, a band of reformers in different states summoned a preliminary Parliament to Frankfurt to prepare for the election of the National Assembly which met in the Paulskirche on May 18. Among the chief ornaments of the Frankfurt Parliament were the three veterans, Arndt, Dahlmann and Jakob Grimm, all passionately devoted not only to Germany but to liberty. 'We have to frame a Constitution for Germany,' declared the elected President, Heinrich von Gagern, in opening the proceedings, 'and we derive our authority for this purpose from the sovereignty of the nation.' Such ringing words had never been heard in a German political assembly, but the Professors' Parliament, as it was called, was living in a fool's paradise. They drew up a constitution, but without the consent of the two leading Powers in the German Confederation, Austria and Prussia, nothing could be done. The Imperial Crown was offered to Frederick William IV, whose mystical doctrine of Divine Right forbade him to receive it from the hands of the people. It was for the princes, he declared, not for the people, to choose their ruler. The hour had come, but not the man. The failure of the Frankfurt experiment was a tragedy, for the tender plant of German liberalism never recovered from the shock. The Prussian constitution grudgingly granted in 1850, with its three-class system, open voting, and indirect election, left the power of the ruler virtually unimpaired; yet the King, enslaved by his feudal romanticism, carried on the fight against 'the revolution' by a secret political testament urging his successor to revoke it. Prussia reverted to the sterile inertia which had followed the Carlsbad decrees, and the clerical conservatism of Stahl became the order of the day.

An early convert from Judaism to Lutheranism, Stahl was summoned from Munich to a chair at Berlin by the idealistic ruler who found in him a man after his own heart. His system of Christian authoritarianism had been set forth at length in his *Philosophie des Rechts* in 1830, and the publication of his pamphlet *Das Monarchische Prinzip* in 1845, which summarised his message in readable form, made him a national figure. The year of revolution lured him from his lecture-room to the political arena. Joining the Conservative party he set forth its aims in eloquent speeches in the Prussian Parliament and in articles in the newly founded *Kreuzzeitung*.

Stahl's gospel, based mainly on Burke, Haller and Savigny, stressed the importance of organic development, rejected the doctrine of the sovereignty of the people, denounced the theorists who appealed to the tribunal of reason, and anchored statecraft to the doctrines of Christianity. He vindicates what he describes as the Christian State against Liberalism in all its forms, demanding the return of the human mind from the arrogance of reason to the shelter of revelation. As the goal of the state is the realisation on earth of the Kingdom of God, it must be built, not on the law of nature, the source of all revolution, but on Christian principles. The royal prerogative, the sole effective rival to popular sovereignty, and the rule of man over man needs a religious consecration to render it palatable. In words which were music to his romantic master he declares that a divine radiance rests on the wearer of the crown. Rejecting the fantastic notion of Haller, an echo of the far-off days of our Filmer, that the country was the private property of the prince, he accepts the principle of representation, though only after the predominance of the conservative elements is as amply secured as in the Prussian Constitution. Yet he was more than a selfish reactionary, clinging tenaciously to vested interests and inherited rights. He was never a totalitarian, for the ruler, like lesser men, was strictly subject to the precepts of Christianity. A typical child of the Restoration era, he champions the ruling classes—the dynasties, the landed nobility, the clergy, the army; the bourgeoisie, the peasant and the urban worker are regarded as the natural prey of democracy, socialism and the revolution. The Crown remained supreme, impregnable in its hereditary authority, appointing Ministers, initiating legislation, combining dynamic leadership with a humble consciousness of a divine mission—in a word, a monarcho-constitutional, not a Parliamentary regime, which in his view gravitated towards a republic. Systems in communities with different backgrounds were no model for Prussia, and the 'ideas of 1789' were held in special contempt.

Stahl's turn came when the conception of popular sovereignty had been discredited by the dismal failure of the revolution of 1848–9. Now was the time for a trumpeter of throne and altar, of monarchy by divine right, of authority against majority, of God's ordering, not the will of unruly men, of social differentiation, not universal suffrage. His postulates, a Christian ruler and an obedient people, were ready to his hand. Now Metternich was gone he was the outstanding figure of European conservatism. Moreover, though Bismarck had formed his own conclusions independently, the fiery Junker was widely regarded as his disciple, and something of the philosophy of the 'Christo-Germanic state' passed into the Constitution of the German Empire.

A new era in the life of the German people and the Prussian State opened with the accession of William I and the summoning of Bismarck to the helm in 1862. The Minister explained his standpoint in the Budget Committee in a few challenging sentences which echoed through Europe like a thunderclap. 'Germany does not look to Prussia's Liberalism but to her power. Prussia must concentrate her power till the favourable moment, which several times already has been allowed to pass, for her frontiers are unfavourable to a healthy body politic. The great questions of the time will be decided not by speeches and resolutions of majorities but by blood and iron.' He had championed the royal prerogative in the United Diet of 1847 in a series of speeches which marked him out as the leader of the extreme Right, and the surrender of Frederick William IV to the Berlin mob in the 'March days' of 1848 filled him with angry contempt. He had no sympathy with the Frankfurt Parliament, whose failure confirmed his conviction of the futility of deliberative assemblies; and within nine years from his accession to power he had founded the German Empire in three successful wars. 'This year,' wrote Gustav Freytag in 1871, 'Germans have regained what to many had become as unfamiliar as the *Völkerwanderung* or the Crusades—their State.' What little was left of the Liberalism of 1848 melted away, and the bourgeoisie was converted to the doctrine that national power was far more important than self-determination. Not till the industrialisation of Germany created a militant socialist party in the closing years of the century was there a serious demand for democracy.

Bismarck's attitude to the state is explained in his *Reflections and Recollections* in the chapter on the North German Bund. Absolutism, he declares, is neither desirable nor successful in Germany in the long run—the absolutism of the Crown as little as that of Parliamentary majorities. Absolutism would be the ideal form of government if the King and his officials were endowed with superhuman wisdom, insight and justice. But even the most experienced and well-meaning absolute rulers are subject to human imperfections, such as overestimation of their own wisdom, the influence and eloquence of favourites, not to mention petticoat influences, legitimate and illegitimate. Monarchy and the most ideal monarch, such as the Emperor Joseph II, stand in need of criticism, which sets them right when in danger of losing their way; but this function is more efficiently discharged by a wise Minister than by elected assemblies. The grant of manhood suffrage in 1866, he explains, was merely a tactical manoeuvre in the war against Austria and a threat to use all weapons in a struggle against possible coalitions. The principle was sound if accompanied by open voting—a condition which he had reluctantly to omit. The masses are too easily moved by greed and flashy rhetoric. Every state which lost the prudent and restraining influence of the propertied classes was bound to come to grief. Revolution would be followed by a dictatorship, because in the end even the masses realise from bitter experience the need of order, and cheerfully sacrifice that justifiable amount of freedom which ought to be maintained. Here then was the Iron Chancellor's ideal state: hereditary monarchy, an invincible army, a prudent Chancellor with security of tenure, the preponderance of property, a representative assembly to let off steam, and social legislation for the working classes. He deserved the criticism that he had made Germany great and the German citizen small.

As Fichte had reflected the change from the individualistic humanitarianism of the eighteenth century to the nationalism of the Wars of Liberation, so Treitschke spans the transition from the aspirations of 1848 to the era of blood and iron. His magnetic personality, his passionate conviction, and his incomparable eloquence, of which I was one of the last hearers at Berlin, made him an educative force of the first magnitude. In 1860, at the age of twenty-six, he struck the dominant note of his political teaching in his little book *The Science of Society*, which he bluntly asserted to have no existence. The only science was that of the state, which was society organised as a unit. The state was as necessary as language, and no contract was needed to create or maintain it. Two years later, in an article on Liberty suggested by Mill's essay, he unfolds his ideal of a state both strong and constitutional. It has the right to dominate the individual because he cannot live a worthy life without its protection and guidance. Far from being a mechanical structure for strictly limited purposes, it is the supreme moralising agency of the world. It is bound, however, by no moral code: self-preservation, which is merely an instinct with the individual, is its supreme duty. But though the state is force, it is much more than force. 'We want free men in a free state.' He speaks of the rights of conscience and liberty of thought with scarcely less fervour than Mill. Moreover, the liberty of the individual can flourish only under the protection of political liberty. All that was new and fruitful in the nineteenth century was the work of Liberalism. Applying his doctrine to the problem of German politics, he contends that Prussia can only become a rallying point for all Germans as a genuinely constitutional state. This gospel, which bore the stamp of his beloved teacher Dahlmann, he continued to preach till the guns of Sadowa blew what was left of German Liberalism into thin air.

Treitschke's monumental work on the history of Germany in the nineteenth century grew under his hands to such an extent that he was unable to realise his lifelong dream of a systematic treatise on political science, but the lectures which he delivered for a generation to crowded audiences in Heidelberg and Berlin were published after his death. His message is the moral and spiritual grandeur of large and powerful states. The state stands high above the individuals who compose it, and it exists in order to realise ideals far above individual happiness. This it can achieve only if it is strong. It is no part of its duty to inquire whether its actions are approved or disapproved by its subjects. It is the guardian of the national tradition and a trustee for the interests of unborn generations. Hereditary monarchy buttressed by a vigorous aristocracy is most conducive to national strength, and the executive must be independent of the ebb and flow of opinion. In like manner the state owes no allegiance to any external authority. International law is a mere phrase, and no tribunal can arbitrate between sovereign states. Treaties are a voluntary self-limitation, and no state can hamper its freedom of action by obligations to another. It must ever be ready for war, which, when undertaken for honour or for some supreme national interest, is wholesome and elevating. For war is not a necessary evil but an instrument of statesmanship and a school of patriotism. Only in war for the Fatherland does a nation become spiritually united: it is indeed the only medicine for a sick people. It is idealism that demands war and materialism which rejects it. Dreams of perpetual peace are the mark of a stagnant and decadent generation, for conflict is the law of life. 'The hope of banishing war is not only meaningless but immoral, for its disappearance would turn the earth into a great temple of selfishness.' We catch the echo of Moltke's aphorism: 'Perpetual peace is a dream, and not even a beautiful dream.'

While Treitschke was at the height of his influence another voice was heard which sounded as strangely in Bismarckian Germany as that of Humboldt in the Prussia of Frederick William II. Both were individualists, but their message was utterly different. Humboldt, like every good Liberal, believed in the ordinary citizen and longed to give him his chance; Nietzsche was only interested in the superman. Creative activity, not renunciation, acquiescence or routine, is our duty and our right. Doctrines that stimulate vitality are good, those which discourage it are bad. Of the latter the worst is Christianity, a fiction for weaklings, a conspiracy of the feeble against the strong. The religion of pity is the religion of slaves. The man of genius is the creator of all values and therefore a law to himself. The many must be sacrificed to the few. This gospel of anarchy makes Nietzsche as much of a rebel in political theory as in ethics. He despises democracy as the cult of numbers, socialism as the superstition of equality. He abhors standardisation and the factors that produce it—custom, religion, law, public opinion, the state—for all of them tend to fetter the superman. The bureaucratic machine encourages the citizen to crave its aid instead of elbowing his way through the throng. The schools and universities teach mere erudition, the army is a great leveller, the Empire a huge machine. Zarathustra lacks the community sense, and patriotism makes no appeal. 'We good Europeans' know nothing of national differences, and what are kings to us? What, indeed, was anything to Nietzsche except the Superman? The state, the Fatherland and the army were too firmly entrenched in the generation of 1870 to be rattled by his random blows, yet he exerted an indirect political influence which cannot be ignored. The exaltation of the will to power, the emphasis on personal prowess, the contempt for compromise coloured the thought and hardened the heart of Bismarckian and post-Bismarckian Germany.

The most notable utterance during the reign of William II on the nature and duties of the state is to be found in Delbrück's *Regierung und Volkswille*—a course of lectures delivered in Berlin a few months before the first world war.[1] Democratic government, he argued, was a fraud and Germany possessed the best government in the world. Defining the ideal of democracy as the realisation of the will of the people, he points out that even with a liberal franchise the actual voters are but a small proportion of the community and that many

[1] An American translation of the second edition, entitled *Government and the Will of the People*, appeared in 1923.

qualified voters stay at home. Thus the whole body of representatives is elected by a mere fraction of the people, and the majority, often only a little more numerous than the minority, represents a still smaller proportion of the nation. Moreover, an election is not a *bona fide* expression of opinion, but a campaign in which victory often falls to the party with fewest scruples and the longest purse. Even were it otherwise, what reason is there to believe that the majority is right? Again, a popularly elected Legislature in possession of supreme power falls a ready victim to corruption, though the record of England is much better than that of France and America.

This resounding attack seems to point to enlightened autocracy as the ideal, but Delbrück rejects it as decisively as Parliamentary democracy. The weakness of the system of Frederick the Great, he declares, was revealed at Jena. Some connection between the Government and the people is essential, and it was their co-operation which rescued Prussia in 1813. Two generations later Bismarck created not only the German Empire but a constitution to match. The Reichstag enjoys less power than other Parliaments, but it has as much as any Parliament ought to possess. What would happen to the German Empire if it were ruled by changing majorities, a Socialist Government following a Catholic, and each party proscribing its enemies? Indignantly repudiating the elder Liebknecht's description of the Reichstag as a mere fig-leaf to cover the nakedness of absolutism, he pronounces it a mighty organ of criticism and control. Its members, he contends, influence and modify legislation far more than is the case at Westminster. His only criticism is that it does not attract the best talent in the country, since its members never rise to a position of authority. The capital fault of democratic states is that power is in the hands of a single body. The shining merit of the German constitution is that Princes and Reichstag play parts of equal importance, jointly representing the interests as well as the will of the nation.

The finality of the Bismarckian Constitution was reiterated by a more influential voice. 'The German Empire,' wrote Bülow in his *Imperial Germany*, published in 1913, 'situated in the middle of Europe and insufficiently protected by nature on its frontiers, is, and must remain, a military state; and strong military states have always required monarchical guidance. The Crown is the corner-stone of Prussia and the keynote of the Empire. The dividing line between the rights of the Crown and of Parliament is immutably fixed.' While recognising that a modern monarchy requires the co-operation of the people, he pronounces against alterations in the sphere of constitutional law. Lamenting the relative apathy of the people and the weak sentiment of responsibility shown by members of the Reichstag, he proposes to deal with these evils, not by enlarging popular rights, but through the spread of political education. Political talent, he declares, is not among the many great qualities of the German nation, and, in particular, the parties which would benefit by the extension of Parliamentary power are lacking in political judgment and training.

Though democratic ideas were scouted by the governing classes, traces of the ideas of 1848 were still to be found among the bourgeoisie, and the demand for a more liberal theory of the state was strengthened by the growth of the Socialist movement. In his lectures on German parties, delivered in 1910,[1] Friedrich Naumann, the most eloquent spokesman of the Freisinnige or Radical Party in the Reichstag, sharply challenged Bülow's estimate of the political capacity of the nation. 'The word self-government signified in the mouth of the old Liberalism not merely a scheme of franchise but the will of every individual in his parish, in his province, and in his nation to have his share in political activity. Thus arose in Germany the great idea of a political people in which each member possesses an importance of his own. We parties of the Left must hold fast to our conviction that the idea of nationality will only reach its full height if it is saturated with the conception of free, self-governing citizenship.' There is an immense capacity for development in the German people which only awaits the overthrow of the parties of the Right. 'We wish to enter into ennobling competition with the Englishman and the American as to which of our nations shall make the greatest contribution to the future civilisation of the world.' Four years later the voice of such reformers was drowned in the thunder of the guns.

The collapse of the Hohenzollern Empire encouraged the reappearance of ideas which had been submerged by the Bismarckian tide. On November 16, 1918, a week after the proclamation of the Republic, Tröltsch, scholar, thinker, publicist, saluted the dawn of a new democratic age. 'Militarism is ended, that is a construction of the state and society on the Prussian military system and the spirit which corresponds to it. German militarism did not consist in a powerful army or a taste for Imperialism, which were common to

[1] *Die Politischen Parteien.*

other states. It was rather a political institution, the deciding element in the Constitution, since it formed the essence of ruling society. The German Constitution was a dualism, for behind the civil government, consisting of the Reichstag, the Bundesrath and the Ministers, stood the military power of the King of Prussia and the General Staff. The system was rendered tolerable by general well-being and a model bureaucracy; but it had no roots in the people, and it was broken to pieces by defeat.'

German democracy, which was born in the trenches, found expression in the Weimar Constitution. 'The German Constitution is a Republic,' runs the first of the 181 articles; 'supreme power emanates from the people.' The first part creates a *Volksstaat*, the second a *Rechtsstaat*. The sovereignty of the People is supplemented and consecrated by the Rights of Man. In the clauses devoted to the *Grundrechte* are mirrored the changes of thought and feeling which produced or sprang from the Revolution, and in these philosophic axioms and categorical imperatives we are back to the generous inspiration of 1848. The spiritual worth of the individual is proclaimed, with all his obligations and his rights. If Hugo Preuss, the Professor of Constitutional Law, is its chief architect in its structural aspect, the insertion of the *Grundrechte* is mainly due to Friedrich Naumann. Unfortunately for Germany and the world, though the forms of democracy were there, they lacked the breath of life.

Rathenau, the ablest of the Weimar team, a convinced democrat and a successful industrialist, wrote pessimistically as early as June 1919, the month in which the Treaty of Versailles was signed. 'There is no longer any doubt that what we call the German Revolution is a disappointment. Our chains were not broken—they fell off. There was no preparation, no revolutionary theory. Only a second revolution can save us, the revolution of sentiment.' *The New Society*, published in 1921, expounded his social and political ideas. Society must be socialised and everyone must earn his living, but socialism in the economic sense was unnecessary. 'The goal is not any division of property or equality of reward. It is the abolition of the proletarian condition of lifelong and hereditary servitude, of the two-fold stratification of society, of the scandalous enslavement of brother by brother which vitiates all our acts, all our creations, all our joys. Nor is this the final goal. The final object of all endeavour is the development of the human soul.' The last sentence might have been copied from Humboldt. 'We must achieve a genuine democratisation of the state and of education. Only then will the monopoly of class and culture be overthrown. The cessation of unearned income will register the downfall of the last of the class-monopolies, that of the plutocracy.' No one in Germany between the two world wars wrote so thoughtfully about the sociological foundations of the state as the Jewish intellectual who was murdered in 1923.

The democratic experiment was attacked, not only by Communists and adherents of the Imperial regime, but by Intellectuals who belonged to no party and had no axe to grind. The weakness of the executive stared Germans in the face. If the Constitution could not produce a strong and stable state, ought it to be retained? The question was answered with an emphatic negative when it had existed no longer than a year. Spengler's *Decline of the West* had caught the fancy of a defeated nation, and when he passed from the morphology of history to the present discontents he found a large audience. In his incisive little book, *Prussianism and Socialism*, he urged the young to return to the ancient ways. Socialism must be rescued from the clutches of Marx and the old Prussian spirit must be revived. 'In the heart of the people the Weimar Constitution is already doomed. Its completion was received with utter indifference. They thought that Parliamentarism was on the upgrade, whereas even in England it is going downhill. This episode is assured of the profound contempt of posterity. In the Paulskirche sat honourable fools and doctrinaires: at Weimar we felt the pull of interest. We know what is at stake, not for Germany alone but for all civilisation—Shall trade rule the state? In relation to this issue Prussianism and Socialism are the same thing. They must present a common front against the philosophy which sterilises the inner life of our people, and their union means not only the fulfilment of the Hohenzollern idea but the salvation of the workers. They will be saved together or perish together. As a separate movement of the proletariat Socialism has had its day; as a system it is beginning. The Conservatives must equally cast away selfish aims, and choose between conscious socialism and annihilation. Let no one hold back who is born to rule. I appeal to the young. Become men! We want no more ideologues, no talk of cosmopolitanism and the spiritual mission of Germany. We need hardness and socialist supermen. Socialism means Macht, Macht and again Macht. And the way to reach it is clear—the combination of the *élite* of the workers with the best representatives of the old Prussian feeling for the state, both resolved on democratisation in the Prussian sense, both linked by a common sentiment of duty and consciousness of a great task.' In an essay entitled *Pessimism?*, published a year later, he declared that a Roman hardness was beginning, and soon there would be room for nothing else. 'We shall not make another Goethe, but we may make another Caesar.' Though Spengler thought in terms of civilisations rather than of races or countries, he agreed with the Nazis that Parliamentary democracy was disastrous to a country which desired and required a strong hand at the helm.

The attack on the liberal experiment was continued by Moeller van den Bruck, whose book, *Das Dritte Reich*, published in 1923, furnished the Nazis with a slogan for their campaign. His voluminous writings had attracted little attention, and the disconsolate invalid committed suicide before his last book began to sell with the accession of the Nazis to power. Though Hitler's name and movement are not mentioned, for it was written before the Munich *Putsch*, it played a notable part in the struggle for a totalitarian dictatorship. Instead of government by party he proposed the ideal of the Third Reich— the old German dream of a German age. The nation's worst enemy was itself. The French occupation of the Ruhr had compelled it to think and restored its will. The Germans had never had a revolution. Now was the time and it was the last chance. The Bismarckian Empire, the Second Reich, was militarily and industrially a success, politically a failure, for William II was a liberal, not a conservative. Liberalism and the Emperor lost the war. Since the catastrophe the whole nation had lain under an evil spell, which could only be banished when the whole of the last generation had passed away. Only a spiritual renewal could save the country, the evolution of a new type. The revolution of 1918 was a liberal enterprise, and therefore it had failed. Its authors thought they had done all that was needful when they imitated the constitutional democracy of the west, where the name of liberty was only a cloak for selfish interests. Moeller van den Bruck surveys and denounces all the parties, but his sharpest arrows are reserved for the so-called Liberals. 'Liberalism has undermined civilisation, destroyed religions, ruined nations. Primitive peoples know no liberalism.' It is defined as the gospel of selfishness, of every one for himself. The genius of the German people is not revolutionary, still less liberal; it is conservative. The Reichstag had always been despised under the Second Empire, and the new Weimar Reichstag was despised still more. Since there was no republican tradition in Germany, the Republic had no roots. Germany was perishing for lack of a leader, and none was in sight. 'If once the people feel that they have found a real leader, they will joyfully accept his leadership and send to the devil all the democratic and socialist party chiefs whose impotence and selfishness they have long suspected.'

The Third Reich of which Moeller van den Bruck had dreamed came into being on January 30, 1933. No Nazi equivalent exists to the elaborate instruments creating the Bismarckian and the Weimar regimes, for scraps of paper are superfluous in a totalitarian state. The new system was formally established by the Enabling Law (Ermächtigungsgesetz) approved by the Reichstag on March 24, 1933, for a period of four years. When Hindenburg died no successor in the Presidency was appointed, and after 1934 Hitler was head of the state, head of the government, and head of the army. 'His will is my law,' declared Göring in 1933. 'Our Constitution is the will of the Führer,' echoed Dr. Frank in 1936. The Reichstag survived, not as an assembly elected by and responsible to the people, but as a gathering of party nominees who ratified the Führer's decisions without debate. The chief novelty in Nazi political ideology is the Führerprinzip, which, if it is to work, assumes an uninterrupted succession of supermen.

In a thousand speeches Hitler defined himself as the representative, the champion, the embodiment, of the nation, so assured of its confidence and so instinctively loyal to its permanent interests that opposition to his will was unthinkable. 'Cromwell saved England in a crisis similar to ours,' he declared to an American journalist in 1933, 'and he saved it by obliterating Parliament and uniting the nation.' That Cromwell never united the nation and commanded less and less support every year of his dictatorship he was unaware. When asked if he foresaw the resumption of Parliamentary Government after four years or twenty years, he replied, after a pause, 'Yes, but with a Parliament of a better type, something like the Italian Corporative State. The principle of a single centralised authority must first be established and then at all costs preserved. I myself assume absolute responsibility.' Here is the core of his teaching—an omnipotent executive under a dynamic leader, able to make rapid decisions and to carry them out because everything is settled, not by coalitions and compromise, but by a single unchallengeable will. The weakness of the Parliamentary system with its competing parties, he explained, was that no one knew how long the pilot would be at the helm. With the creation of the totalitarian state the period of class and sectional struggles, of hesitation, of uncertainty, of divided responsibility was over. Germany had at last found real leadership. So long as the German nation in every walk of life subjected itself to a single will, all problems could be solved.

The totalitarian doctrine may be conveniently studied in a little book by the distinguished jurist, Professor Carl Schmitt, editor of a series of monographs entitled *Der deutsche Staat der Gegenwart*. His own contribution, *Staat, Bewegung, Volk* (State, Movement, People), published in 1935, contrasts the Nazi system with the Weimar Constitution. That creation of the liberal-democratic school of thought, with its multiplicity of parties, its neutrality between friends and foes of the state, between genuine nationals and alien racial elements, was incompatible with the Nazi regime. The essential change was the creation of the one-party state: the danger of national disintegration as the result of the multiplicity of parties, which he calls the pluralistic system, was thus overcome. Hitherto, in Germany and most other countries, there had been only two factors, the state and the people, often in conflict with one another. This latent rivalry was smoothed out by the introduction of a third element—the party, or, as he calls it, the movement, which represented the people and provided the government. Thus the political unity of the state and the source of its strength is to be found in the combination of state, movement, people. Though resembling Italian Fascism in certain particulars, the Nazi system, declares Carl Schmitt, could appeal to German precedents and publicists, particularly to Hegel. While the liberal nineteenth century believed in principles of general applicability, the Nazi emphasised the uniqueness of the individual community. All law (Recht) is the law of a particular people. The liberal-democratic state had always tried to clip the wings of the executive and to secure the citizen against its 'interference.' With the Nazi ideology this is a needless alarm, for the Leader shares the blood, understands the interests, and fulfils the wishes of the people. It is not a dictatorship of the usual pattern but a specifically German concept. Tyranny is prevented by the fact that the Leader and the people come from the same mould. Equally the Nazi judge is no longer bound to the automatic application of the law, but must bear in mind the fundamental principles of the regime and the practical needs of the community. The whole object and result of the Nazi revolution is to substitute a strong and homogeneous for a weak and divided state. The virtual unanimity of the German people in desiring this political and ideological revolution is assumed throughout. In any case Nazi publicists, like the Berlin Professor, had no use for minorities.

Among the lessons taught by the Nazi regime is that such an evil interlude is only rendered possible by the weakness of the government which it destroys. When Hitler was overthrown the problem of combining a strong executive with popular rights, which had defied the attempts of successive generations, remained to be solved. The restoration of German sovereignty, however, and even of German unity, is a long way off, and German publicists will have plenty of time to reflect on the painful lessons of the past. The prospects are not encouraging, for among the outstanding characteristics of German history is the political apathy of the mass of the people.

BIBLIOGRAPHICAL NOTE

Bluntschli, *Geschichte des allgemeinen Staatsrechts und der Politik seit dem sechszehnten Jahrhundert*, and McGovern, *From Luther to Hitler*, are useful surveys. The best brief analysis of Luther's political ideas is in Allen, *Political Thought in the Sixteenth Century*, Ch. II. Gierke's *Althusius* (translated) is a classic. Albion Small, *The Cameralists*, is indispensable for the prevailing theory of the seventeenth and eighteenth centuries. For the ideology of Frederick the Great see Meinecke, *Die Idee der Staatsräson*, and Gooch, *Frederick the Great*, Ch. XII and XIII. For the period of the French Revolution see Aris, *History of Political Thought in Germany, 1789–1815*, and Gooch, *Germany and the French Revolution*. For Hegel, see Rosenzweig, *Hegel und der Staat* ; for Dahlmann, Springer, F. C. *Dahlmann*, Treitschke, *Historische und Politische Aufsätze*, Vol. I, and Wilhelm, *Die Englische Verfassung und der Vormärzliche Deutsche Liberalismus*. Only the first volume of Masur, *F. J. Stahl*, coming down to 1840, has appeared ; the best summary of his teaching is in Marcks, *Bismarck und die deutsche Revolution, 1848–1851*, Ch. VII. Meinecke, *Weltbürgertum und Nationalstaat*, and Valentin, *Die Deutsche Revolution, 1848–9*, are needed for the first half of the nineteenth century. For Treitschke see H. W. C. Davis, *The Political Thought of Heinrich von Treitschke*. A translation of his *Politics*, with an Introduction by Lord Balfour, appeared in 1916. An American translation of Delbrück's treatise, entitled

Government and the Will of the People, was published in 1923; an English translation of Moeller van den Bruck, *Germany's Third Empire*, in 1934. *Hitler's Speeches, 1922–1939*, have been admirably translated and edited by Norman Baynes; those dealing with internal affairs are collected in Vol. I. The series entitled *Der Deutsche Staatsgedanke* contains some of the classics of German political literature; the volume on Bismarck is edited by Rothfels. Rohan Butler, *The Roots of National Socialism, 1783–1933*, is a thoughtful sketch.

GERMANY IN THE EIGHTEENTH CENTURY

I

DURING the years immediately preceding the French Revolution Germany presented a curious spectacle of political decrepitude and intellectual rejuvenescence. The Holy Roman Empire,[1] in regard to which Voltaire caustically inquired in what respect it was holy or Roman or an Empire, was afflicted with creeping paralysis. Its wheels continued to revolve; but the machinery was rusty and the output was small.

> The Holy Roman Empire,
> How does it hold together?

shouted Goethe's revellers in Auerbach's Keller. 'No Curtius,' remarked Justus Möser in 1781, 'leaps into the abyss for the preservation of the Imperial system'—a system which offered no security against foreign invasion or civil war, and which had long ceased to command the respect either of its own members or of the world. Germany, cried Friedrich Karl Moser in the bitterness of his heart, is a great but despised people. Every nation, he added, had a governing principle. In England it was liberty, in Holland trade, in France the honour of the King, while in Germany it was obedience. Many a pamphleteer lamented the anaemia of the Fatherland, but not one of them could produce a restorative. The Imperial system was the consecration of anarchy, and Germany was racked by an incurable particularism. 'In my childhood,' wrote Wieland, 'I was told a great deal about duties; but there was so little about the duty of a German patriot that I cannot remember ever hearing the word German used with honour. There are Saxon, Bavarian, Frankfurt patriots; but German patriots, who love the Empire as their fatherland, where are they?' The Empire was not even wholly German. The King of

---

[1] See Bryce, *The Holy Roman Empire*; Perthes, *Deutsches Staatsleben vor der Revolution*; Biedermann, *Deutschland im 18ten Jahrhundert*; Auerbach, *La France et le Saint Empire Germanique*; Häusser, *Deutsche Geschichte*, i. 64–132; Treitschke, *Germany*, vol. i; Wenck, *Deutschland vor hundert Jahren*, vol. i; Bruford, *German Social Life in the Eighteenth Century*.

England was a member as Elector of Hanover, the King of Denmark as Duke of Holstein, the King of Sweden as Lord of Pomerania, while Belgium participated as an appanage of the House of Hapsburg. 'Germany is a very fine country,' wrote Hume prophetically in 1748, 'full of industrious and honest people; were it united it would be the greatest power that ever was in the world.'

In theory the Imperial crown was elective; but in practice it was found impossible to override the traditional claims of the Hapsburgs, as Charles VII of Bavaria and his champions learned to their cost in the war of the Austrian Succession. The Empire appeared to revive for a moment in the coronation pageantry at Frankfurt, when the Emperor received the homage of the Estates on bended knee and the herald brandished his sword towards the four quarters of heaven in token that all Christendom was subject to his sway; but in the eighteenth century it was nothing but a picturesque survival. Though the Emperor was still the fount of honour, except for the grant of titles his prerogatives had disappeared. As a German jurist aptly remarked, to prevent him from doing harm he was prevented from doing anything. Such powers as he possessed he owed, not to the crown of Charlemagne and Barbarossa, but to the territories and resources of the House of Hapsburg. The Golden Bull of Charles IV limited the Electors to seven, three of whom were the Archbishops of Mainz, Cologne, and Trier. The secular princes were the rulers of the Palatinate, Bohemia, Saxony, and Brandenburg, to which Bavaria and Hanover were added in the seventeenth century. The first in rank was the Elector of Mainz, the Arch-Chancellor of the Empire, who crowned the Emperor at Frankfurt. The legislative power was exercised by the Diet at Regensburg, to which ambassadors were accredited and from which the army of the Empire took its orders. Since 1663 it sat in permanence, but this decreased instead of increasing its importance, as it was only attended by delegates and most members of the Empire never troubled to be represented. It consisted of three Colleges, the Electors, the Princes (ecclesiastical and secular), and the Free Cities, sitting separately. If two Colleges agreed, and their wishes were sanctioned by the Emperor, the resolution became an Imperial law; but its execution depended on the separate decision of each separate unit of which the Empire was composed. It was only at Regensburg that 'Germany' could be found, but the significance of the Diet had waned with the strength of the Empire, and its time was largely wasted in solemn trifling and hoary pedantries. While the Emperor resided at Vienna and the Diet sat at Regensburg, the Supreme Court of the Empire was moved in 1693 from Speyer to Wetzlar, which owes its fame rather to Werther and Lotte than to its Imperial associations. The Court had earned an unenviable reputation for venality and procrastination, and if a few petty tyrants were thwarted or punished by its decrees, it was too weak to strike at powerful offenders. Young jurists like Goethe spent a few months in the sleepy little town to learn the routine of the law of the Empire, but its prestige was impaired by the fact that most of the important cases were reserved by the Emperor for the Aulic Council at Vienna.

In addition to the Emperor, the Diet, and the Court of Appeal, the machinery of the Empire included ten Circles, or administrative districts, created to counteract the dangers of excessive particularism by the formation of large groups. Each Circle possessed a Diet and a Director, who commanded the troops, controlled the police, and provided for the execution of the Imperial laws. In the course of the centuries, however, great changes had occurred. The Circle of Burgundy had been swallowed up in France. Holland was free. Many territories had become subject to members of the Empire, such as Hungary and the Polish provinces annexed by Austria and Prussia, which were not incorporated in its framework. On the eve of the French Revolution there were nine Circles: Upper and Lower Saxony, Austria, Bohemia, Bavaria, Westphalia, the Upper Rhine, Swabia, Franconia. Differing widely in size and importance, they were alike in their invertebrate character. Prussia formed part of three Circles, while Swabia and Franconia presented a bewildering mosaic of petty principalities, ecclesiastical and secular. It was in these Circles of the lower and middle Rhine that the hundreds of Imperial Knights, who recognised no superior but the Emperor, exercised unfettered sway over their Liliputian territories. Western Germany was the classic land of duodecimo States, which afforded no foundation for healthy political life and offered a tempting prey to the ambitions of France.

Thus the Empire was a phantom, its machinery rotten and crumbling, its head a mere honorary president. Whatever shadowy sentiment of unity had survived the Wars of Religion and the Treaty of Westphalia was destroyed in the prolonged duel of Frederick the Great and Maria Theresa; and the short but stormy reign of Joseph II showed that the Imperial dignity had sunk into the tool and plaything of the House of Hapsburg. As Austria became stronger the Empire grew weaker, for Emperor and Empire were regarded as strangers if not enemies in the larger States, especially in the Protestant North. So long as the Holy Roman Empire existed, Germany was condemned to remain a geographical expression.

Frederick the Great defined the Empire as a Republic of Princes with an elective head, and the real political life of the country was in the States and principalities which composed it. Since the Peace of Westphalia, which accorded to them the right of making treaties with foreign Powers, they were independent in all but name, and one of them climbed rapidly to a position from which it challenged the overlordship of the Imperial house.[1] The Great Elector attracted the attention of Europe to Prussia by his victories and his diplomacy, created a standing army, and laid the foundations of the autocracy on which the Hohenzollerns reared one of the mightiest political edifices of the modern world. His son Frederick I placed the crown upon his head, and his grandson, Frederick William I, created an administrative machine the efficiency of which was unmatched in Europe. Finding a well-trained army and an overflowing treasury on his accession in 1740, Frederick the Great seized Silesia on the death of the Emperor Charles VI six months later, and held it against the combined efforts of half Europe. Goethe has recorded in his Autobiography how the victories of the great King awoke Germany from her slumbers and gave a theme and an inspiration to poets, describing him as the pole-star round which Prussia, Germany, and indeed the world, seemed to revolve. 'His victories,' records Niebuhr, 'gave confidence and a sense of nationality to all Germans, not to Prussians and Protestants alone. The whole country felt that it had a prince whom Europe admired.' His prowess was sung in verse by Kleist and Gleim, and in prose by Archenholz. The Swabian Abbt was inspired by the disaster of Kunersdorf to write his 'Death for the Fatherland,' 'in order to stir up citizens to save the country, to fill them with noble patriotic sentiments, and above all to show my admiration for Frederick the Great.' It was not only to the successful warrior that all eyes were turned, but to the exponent of a new theory and prac-

[1] See Droysen, *Geschichte der Preussischen Politik*; Ranke, *Zwölf Bücher Preussischer Geschichte*; Koser, *König Friedrich der Grosse*. For more summary treatment, see Hintze, *Die Hohenzollern*; Treitschke, *Germany*, vol. i; Marriott and Robertson, *The Evolution of Prussia*; Fay, *The Rise of Brandenburg-Prussia*; Gooch, *Frederick the Great*.

tice of government. The contrast between the simple and laborious life of the King of Prussia and the idleness and extravagance of many of his contemporaries enhanced the prestige of the state. The Sovereign, declared the Crown Prince in his 'Anti-Machiavel,' far from being the absolute master of the people under his sceptre, is only their first servant. This celebrated sentence overthrew divine right and 'proprietary' monarchy by substituting the doctrine of service. Enlightened autocrats were to guide and govern their peoples as a wise father directs the steps of his children. Frederick was not the first Philosophic Despot, but his brilliant performance popularised the rôle and founded a school.

His state was so small and his energy so unflagging that for forty-six years he governed Prussia like no Hohenzollern before or after him. The Sovereign, he declared, was bound to act as if he had every moment to render an account of his stewardship to his fellow-citizens.[1] He only slept for six hours. When his doctor ordered the old man of sixty-nine to cancel a journey of inspection, he replied, 'You have your duties and I have mine, and I will carry them out till my last breath.' But the burden of war and taxation was heavy, feudalism stood unchallenged, a short-sighted mercantilism kept the country poor, and the political education of the people was neglected. In the King's famous words, the tacit arrangement was that his subjects should say what they liked and he should do what he liked. While Calas and La Barre were being tortured in France, the Philosopher of Sans Souci was declaring that in his dominions everyone might find his way to heaven in his own way. This easy toleration, however, was confined to religion, for which he cared nothing. He commenced his reign by allowing uncensored liberty to the Berlin papers, but the privilege was quickly revoked.[2] 'Do not talk to me of your liberty of thought and the press,' wrote Lessing from Hamburg to Nicolai in 1769. 'It reduces itself to the liberty to let off as many squibs against religion as one likes. Let somebody raise his voice for the rights of subjects or against exploitation and despotism, and you will soon see which is the most slavish land in Europe.' The general feeling was expressed by Wieland, an ornament of the Court of Weimar, who

---

[1] 'Essais sur les formes de gouvernement et sur les devoirs des souverains'; *Œuvres de Frédéric le Grand*, vol. ix.

[2] See Consentius, *Friedrich der Grosse und die Zeitungs-Zensur*, *Preussische Jahrbücher*, Feb. 1904.

remarked that while he felt the greatest admiration for the King of Prussia, he thanked heaven that he did not live under his stick or sceptre. Next to the King the army was supreme. 'In my State,' wrote Frederick, 'a lieutenant stands higher than a chamberlain.' The nobility, which he described as the incubator of officers, occupied almost all the higher posts in the army and the State, while the peasantry supplied the requisite cannon fodder. The Civil Service was recruited from the bourgeoisie.

His successor had neither the power nor the will to stretch the bow of Ulysses.[1] Mirabeau, who had met them both, described Frederick as all mind, his nephew as all body; and he uttered the prophetic words, 'I foretell nothing but weakness and confusion.' His Open Letter to the new king sketched out a bold programme of reform, including the cessation of the privileges of the nobility, liberty of thought and the Press, and the abolition of monopolies; but he had no expectation of its fulfilment. At first there was a sigh of relief at the removal of the iron hand which had governed with the rigidity of a machine. Frederick William II was affable and kind-hearted, and the abolition of the hated monopoly of coffee and tobacco seemed to promise a less rigorous regime. But it was not long before the best minds in Prussia regretted the disappearance of the Master-Builder. While Frederick had scorned delights and lived laborious days, dictating letters, reviewing his troops, and making tours of inspection throughout his dominions, his nephew filled Potsdam with loose women and dabblers in occultism, married first one and then another of his flames while his wife was still alive, left letters unanswered, wasted the treasure which his uncle had stored, and revoked the religious toleration which had been the brightest feature of the system of the royal philosopher. Thus, after a brief interval of hopeful expectation, Prussia found herself on the downward path which led to the stricken field of Jena.

The state most closely allied to Prussia by personal ties and community of political ideas was Brunswick. Charles William Ferdinand, the son of Frederick's sister, Charlotte, won fame both in the arts of war and peace.[2] He distinguished himself in the Seven Years' War,

---

[1] See Philippson, *Geschichte des deutschen Staatswesens*, vol. i; Heigel, *Deutsche Geschichte*, 1786–1806, vol. i. ch. 3.

[2] See Fitzmaurice, *Charles William Ferdinand, Duke of Brunswick*. There is a good survey of the minor States in Heigel, *Deutsche Geschichte*, i. 79–116.

visited Voltaire at Ferney, and studied Rome with Winckelmann as his guide. On his accession to the Duchy in 1780, he proved himself a model ruler. Inheriting the debts incurred during the long reign of his extravagant father, he restored the financial equilibrium of his little state by rigorous public and private economy. He maintained a small army, improved the roads, humanised the poor law, encouraged Campe to reform education, and was only prevented by the clergy from introducing secular control of the schools. His wide culture and personal charm, his policy of toleration, which embraced the Jews, and the freedom which he granted to the Press, made him the second hero of the German *Aufklärung*. French travellers and savants visited his Court, and Mirabeau, who was never happy at Berlin, found the atmosphere of Brunswick exceptionally congenial. 'He delights greatly in France,' he reported, 'with which he is exceptionally well acquainted, and he likes everything which comes thence.' On the death of Frederick the Great the Duke succeeded to his position as the outstanding political figure of Germany, and his campaign in Holland in 1787 raised him to the summit of military fame.

The Electorate of Hanover, on the other hand, lacked the amenities of a Court and the initiative of a resident ruler.[1] But though the dominions of his ancestors were never visited by George III, the land was administered by an honest and reasonably efficient bureaucracy. Justice was pure, taxation moderate, the Press reasonably free; the dynasty was popular, and the nobility were not in exclusive control of the government. There was a higher respect for the rights of the subject, and, in the upper classes, a more widespread interest in the State than anywhere else in Germany. Yet the country was none the less inert and sterile, and was described by Stein as the German China. The one touch of colour in a rather drab picture was supplied by the University of Göttingen, the child of Münchhausen, the enlightened minister of George II. The new school of learning quickly supplanted Halle as the leading German University, and young men destined for the service of the state flocked from every part of the country to its eminent teachers of law, history, economics, and political science.

An inferior variety of 'enlightened despotism' was to be found in Saxony.[2] The Electors, Augustus II and III, who were also chosen

[1] See A. W. Ward, *Great Britain and Hanover*, Lecture VI; and Treitschke, iv. 351–81.
[2] See Treitschke, iv. 289–329.

kings of Poland, aided and abetted by Count Brühl, the evil genius of the country, had overtaxed its resources by their wars and their endeavours to make Dresden the most brilliant capital in Europe after Paris. Though the Sistine Madonna was purchased and Winckelmann was sent to Rome, the greater part of the money expended by the Court was wasted in riotous living. On the death of Augustus III in 1763, his grandson, Frederick Augustus, began his long reign at the age of thirteen, unencumbered by the burden of the Polish crown. A new spirit of order and economy was at once introduced. Debt was paid off and the Court became a school of virtue. Torture was abolished, an Academy of Mines was founded at Freiberg which Werner made the first school of geology in Europe, and the book trade of Leipsic flourished during the generation of peace which followed the Seven Years' War. Though his subjects deservedly called him the Just, he was no statesman and his conception of good government was abstinence from evil courses. While Frederick the Great and Ferdinand of Brunswick welcomed the rays of the *Aufklärung*, Frederick Augustus stood aloof from the challenging currents of rationalism and humanitarianism which were beginning to surge through Europe. Even more remote from the sweep of modern ideas were the two Mecklenburg Duchies, politically the most backward of all German States. 'The home of the Mecklenburg noble who crushes his peasantry,' wrote Stein indignantly, 'seems to me to be like the lair of a wild beast, who ravages the neighbourhood and surrounds himself with the silence of the tomb.' The Dukes were almost as powerless as the peasants, for the feudal oligarchy reigned supreme.

The small States of central Germany revealed a similar variety of merit and defect. The Landgrave Frederick II of Hesse-Cassel shared the prevailing taste for French culture, transformed Cassel into an imposing city, and enriched the picture gallery; but the Court was loose, and the sale of his subjects to England at £15 a head for service against the American rebels earned him the detestation of Europe. The plight of Hesse-Darmstadt, whose Landgrave, Ludwig IX, wasted his resources on military antics, was no better. His son Ludwig X, who spent some time at the Court of Berlin, shared Frederick's devotion to the *Aufklärung*, and counted Schiller and Goethe among his friends; but his accession was quickly followed by the outbreak of the revolutionary war. Among the Duchies ruled by the Ernestine branches of the Saxon dynasty of Wettin, Saxe-Weimar stood out as the model of small principalities. The regency of Anna Amalia laid the foundations of the enlightened administration which her son Karl August, with the aid of Goethe, practised for half a century. His maxims of government and intellectual interests were shared by Duke Ernst of Gotha and Franz of Anhalt-Dessau, the patron of Basedow's Philanthropinum. A still more minute principality, that of Schaumburg-Lippe, had the good fortune to be ruled for a few years by Count Wilhelm, the friend of Herder, a man who only needed a wider stage to have written his name on the history of his country.

Among South German States the largest and the most stagnant was Bavaria.[1] The outburst of energy in the Thirty Years' War had been followed by a rapid decline, which was accelerated by domestic misgovernment. A ray of light penetrated the darkness during the middle of the eighteenth century in the reign of Max Joseph, who founded the Academy of Sciences, waged war on the Jesuits, and encouraged Ickstatt to reform the system of education. But under his successor the country sank back into hopeless obscurantism and was described by Frederick the Great as an earthly paradise inhabited by animals. Karl Theodor had ruled the Palatinate for thirty-five years before the failure of the direct line of the Wittelsbachs called him to Munich in 1778. The early years of his reign at Mannheim had not been wholly without distinction. His knightly bearing procured him the name of the First Cavalier of the Holy Roman Empire, his generosity to foreign scholars that of the German Maecenas. He founded an Academy of Science in Mannheim, enriched the galleries, and built the first Court theatre in Germany, soon to witness the triumphs of Schiller and Iffland. But his faults increased with age, and his later years were disgraced by intolerance, immorality, and greed. Religious persecution drove thousands of his Protestant subjects to America, and he procured money for his mistresses and bastards by the sale of offices and the oppression of his people. He exchanged Mannheim for Munich with a heavy heart, and saw in his new Electorate little but a means of supporting his illegitimate children. He disliked the heavy, boorish Bavarians, and was only prevented by Frederick the Great from selling the country to Joseph II.

[1] See Döberl, *Entwickelungsgeschichte Bayerns*, vol. ii; Temperley, *Frederick the Great* and *Kaiser Joseph*; Döllinger, *Studies in European History*; Kluckhohn, *Vorträge u. Aufsätze*; Kluckhohn, *Westenrieder*.

For a year or two he allowed progressive tendencies some scope, and supported the reforms in agriculture and industry carried out by the gifted American adventurer, Benjamin Thompson, Count Rumford, still remembered at Munich as the creator of the 'English Garden.' But the discovery of the activities of the Illuminati frightened the ageing Elector into reaction, and the Court of Munich became a byword throughout the Empire for immorality and obscurantism. His confessor, Father Frank, reigned supreme, and the faith of the state was kept intact by a strenuous censorship while its mind slumbered. The streets of the capital were filled with beggars and the countryside was infested with robbers. Munich was a city of churches, monasteries, and religious processions, while seventeen wonder-working relics competed for the patronage of the faithful. Bavaria cut itself off from the rest of Germany, strangers were regarded as foreigners, and German was discouraged as the language of the Lutheran heresy. Though the army shrunk to half its size there was a large annual deficit. A luxurious Court increased the sufferings of an impoverished people, but the country suffered rather from anarchy than from tyranny. Even greater were the misery and misrule of the Palatinate, over which the Elector continued to stretch his nerveless hand.

The position of Württemberg was in some respects more favourable than that of Bavaria.[1] Alone among German principalities, its old constitution of Estates continued to possess at least the shadow of power; and Fox once declared that the only countries in Europe which possessed constitutional government were England and Württemberg. There was also far more civic spirit, and the land shared in the intellectual revival of the eighteenth century. Yet in other respects it was less favourably placed than its neighbour, for its rulers were as extravagant as the Wittelsbachs and far more despotic. For twenty years of the reign of Eberhard Ludwig the country was ruled by his mistress Wilhelmina von Grävenitz, whose costly monument is the palace of Ludwigsburg. But the sufferings of the State reached their height during the long reign of Karl Eugen, whose struggles with the Estates attracted the attention of Europe and whose tyranny drove Schiller abroad. The prince was educated at the Prussian Court, and Frederick the Great composed for his guidance

[1] See Eugen Schneider, *Württembergische Geschichte*; and Wohlwill, *Weltbürgertum u. Vaterlandsliebe der Schwaben.*

his little tract 'Le Miroir des Princes.' The good advice was unheeded, and the young ruler became the scourge of his people. He broke his oath to observe the constitution of the country; to a bold Senator, who protested in the name of the Fatherland, he replied, 'What is that? I am the Fatherland.' The Estates found a champion in the great lawyer, J. J. Moser, the Coke of Württemberg, who set up the few surviving relics of primitive Germanic liberty as a breakwater against the flood of absolutism and was punished by five years' imprisonment. The Standing Committee of the Estates presented protest after protest and brought an action against the ruler in the Imperial Court, while the Courts of Prussia, England, and Denmark intervened with remonstrance and advice. The Duke's private life was no less detestable than his public activities. His fierce temper and sensuality were the terror of his subjects, and his Court was modelled on that of Louis XV. The ruler lived like an Oriental potentate, adding palace to palace, and passing his time at Ludwigsburg in balls and operas, hunting and gambling. Like his brother despots, he procured money for his pleasures by the sale of his subjects to foreign Powers and by putting up posts in the public service to auction. At length his debts compelled him to seek a reconciliation with the Estates and to recognise the constitution, and in 1778 a message of repentance was read aloud in the churches on his fiftieth birthday. His extravagance was held in check and his good resolutions were strengthened by his latest mistress, Franciska von Hohenheim, who became his second wife. His intellectual attainments were recognised by Schiller, and he posed as the friend of education by founding the Karlsschule at Stuttgart; but though the closing years of his reign were very different from its opening, his yoke was never light, and he sent Schubart and other outspoken critics to rot for years in the gloomy dungeons of the Asperg.

Alone of South German States, on the eve of the French Revolution, Baden was blessed with a ruler of capacity and conscience.[1] Karl Friedrich, the outstanding member of the House of Zähringen, ascended the throne as a boy, and his long reign witnessed the birth of a flourishing community. 'My neighbour of Württemberg,' he used to say in jest, 'does his utmost to ruin his land, and I do my

---

[1] See Weech, *Badische Geschichte*; Kleinschmidt, *Karl Friedrich von Baden*; Windelband, *Die Verwaltung der Markgrafschaft Badens zur Zeit Karl Friedrichs*; *Karl Friedrichs Brieflicher Verkehr mit Mirabeau u. Dupont.*

utmost to raise mine, but neither of us succeeds.' At any rate, he did all that could be done in a tiny State by a wise and unselfish ruler. Keenly interested in agriculture, he embraced the doctrines of the Physiocrats, corresponded with the elder Mirabeau and Dupont de Nemours, and himself wrote on political economy. He accepted and applied the famous maxim of Quesnay, 'Pauvres paysans, pauvre royaume; pauvre royaume, pauvre roi.' Though sharing the physiocratic preference for agriculture, he did not overlook the claims of industry and trade. Burdensome taxes and tariffs were removed, justice fairly administered, and popular education provided. Himself a student of literature and a friend of Voltaire and Klopstock, Herder and Jung Stilling, he showed himself hospitable to all the enlightened ideas of his time. He grasped the manifold needs of a modern state, remarking that material well-being could never be firmly established where intellectual development was held in check. After a long sojourn at Karlsruhe, Klopstock described his host as 'a man with whom one could talk'; while Herder praised him as the only prince he knew without princely airs and as perhaps the best German ruler alive in 1770. A still weightier tribute came from Frederick the Great, who at the end of his life remarked that he respected Karl Friedrich beyond all his princely contemporaries. He found an ideal agent and counsellor in Edelsheim, one of the noblest political figures of the *Aufklärung*. Perfect harmony existed between ruler and people, and in 1783 a general expression of popular gratitude greeted the abolition of serfdom. Though the Court was outwardly French, Karl Friedrich was thoroughly German at heart. He discussed the Fürstenbund with Karl August of Weimar and Franz of Dessau before Frederick the Great intervened, and he instructed Herder to work out a plan for a 'Patriotic Institute for Germany,' which should emphasise and encourage the sense of national unity in intellectual pursuits. The union of Baden-Baden on the death of the last Margrave in 1771 with Karl Friedrich's own principality of Baden-Durlach joined lands which had been separated for more than two centuries, and afforded him the opportunity of showing that a pious Protestant ruler could respect the religion of his Catholic subjects.

If Karl Friedrich was the best of South-German rulers, Karl of Zweibrücken, the elder brother of the future first King of Bavaria, was the worst. His passion for the chase ruined the crops of his tiny principality, and his cruelties were those of a madman. The scathing denunciations of Schlözer called the attention of the Empire to his insane freaks beyond the Rhine, but were of no avail to rescue his subjects from the galling yoke. The Court was French, and the Duke received and squandered a French pension. Scarcely better was the plight of Ansbach-Baireuth, whose Margrave, Karl Alexander, nephew of Frederick the Great, dissipated the resources of his State first on the French actress Clairon and then on Lady Craven; sold his regiments to England for the American War; and finally, at the bidding of his English mistress, sold his principality for hard cash to Prussia and retired to England.[1] No more perfect illustration of the prevailing assumption that the state and its inhabitants were the private property of its ruler could be found than the story of the closing years of the little principality.

The rule of the Electors of Mainz, Trier, and Cologne, which gave the Rhine the name of the Pfaffengasse or Parsons' Lane, was seldom tyrannical, but it was lifeless, enervating, and generally obscurantist.[2] The ecclesiastical States, of which the three Electorates were the most important, were highly unpopular in Protestant circles, and their shortcomings were fiercely denounced in 1787 by Friedrich Karl Moser. In Schlözer's journal the question was raised why people were less happy in the ecclesiastical principalities than elsewhere, and the answer was that it was owing to the worldliness of the prelates. Secularisation was in the air, and even Pacca, the Papal Nuncio, was conscious of an atmospheric change.

The first in importance was the Electorate of Mainz, which embraced large territories on the Rhine and the Main, and included the outlying dependency of Erfurt. As Chancellor of the Empire, President of the Electoral College, and Consecrator of the Emperor, the occupant of the See of Boniface could not fail to be an important figure in the life of Western Germany; thus the strength of one of the chief outposts of the Empire was a matter of importance to all its members. But since Schönborn, the friend and patron of Leibnitz, none of the Electors had been men of distinction, and the frequent changes of ruler made continuity of policy impossible. The people, pious and conservative, desired the cautious removal of abuses, but

---

[1] See Broadley and Melville, *The Beautiful Lady Craven.*
[2] See Perthes, *Politische Zustände u. Personen in Deutschland zur Zeit der französischen Herrschaft*; and Schultheiss, *Die Geistlichen Staaten beim Ausgang des alten Reichs.*

their rulers oscillated between bold innovation and mindless reaction. Count Ostein (1743–63), a friend and admirer of Voltaire, was a child of the *Aufklärung*, reforming education and engaging in a sharp skirmish with the Jesuits; but his subjects were frightened, and he was forced to moderate his reforming zeal. His successor, Emmerich, continued the attempt to revive intellectual life by founding an *École normale* and summoning foreign scholars to replace Jesuit teachers at the University. But the clergy, backed by the ignorant masses, opposed the reform of education, attacked him as a freethinker, and compelled him, like his predecessor, to compromise.

The last of the Electors, Baron von Erthal, was chosen in 1774 as a champion of the old paths which his two predecessors had deserted.[1] His first step was to remove freethinkers from the schools and to restore the strict observance of religious forms, but he quickly tired of the ascetic's *rôle*. 'He leads a purely worldly life,' reported Pacca, as he surveyed the brilliant scene, with its balls, its feasts, and its hunting parties. The candidate of the obscurantists finally blossomed out into an unblushing champion of the *Aufklärung*. He summoned 'freethinkers' to the University, and appointed the Swiss Protestant, Johannes Müller, his Privy Councillor and the radical Georg Forster his librarian. In the houses of some members of the Cathedral Chapter were seen busts of Voltaire and the philosophers, works of classical art replaced statues of the Virgin and the Crucifix, and the writings of Helvétius and other French materialists lay on the table. At Court the Elector and his favourite, Countess Hatzfeld, listened without blushes to the licentious pages of 'Ardinghello' read aloud by Heinse, a Renaissance figure who preached the emancipation of the flesh and the religion of beauty to a master who compared himself with the Medici Pope Leo X. Most leaders of thought and society in Mainz were real or pretended adherents of the *Aufklärung*, and Dalberg, the Coadjutor who held his Court in Erfurt, emulated his chief. But this 'enlightenment' was to a great extent a pose and was never applied to the problems of government. Forster, who was both a scholar and a reformer, commented severely on the extravagance and self-indulgence of the nobles and higher clergy by whom the Electorate was governed. The old abuses and the old privileges remained. Materialism, thinly disguised under a veneer of culture, was supreme, and the graver tasks of administration and defence were neglected.

[1] See Herse, *Mainz vor der Revolution*.

The fortifications were turned into gardens under the control of the Court gardener. To those who had eyes to see it was obvious that when the tempest came the whole edifice would topple over like a house of cards.

The Electorate of Trier showed similar variations during the eighteenth century, the general character of its rulers being that of benevolent inefficiency. The state was smaller and poorer than Mainz and less in the public eye. While Erthal aped the fashions of Versailles at Mainz, Clemens Wenceslas, the last Elector of Trier, a lover of music and the domestic virtues, exercised a just and tolerant sway at Coblenz. Though an ex-officer in the Austrian army and a son of Augustus II of Saxony, the champion sinner of his age, the Elector won the testimony of the Nuncio to his irreproachable character. Pacca added that he had a weak will; but he showed considerable vigour in his support of Hontheim, Bishop of Trier, better known by his *nom de plume* of Febronius, and of the anti-curial movement which convulsed Catholic Germany on the eve of the Revolution.[1] Though his ecclesiastical policy and the controversies to which it led were not to the taste of the mass of his subjects, he was popular and respected; but the old abuses lingered on, and no steps were taken to strengthen the state against the internal and external dangers which were soon to overwhelm it.

The most backward of the three ecclesiastical Electorates was that of Cologne, whose rulers during the larger part of the seventeenth and eighteenth centuries were members of the Bavarian reigning house. Joseph Clemens refused to read mass or perform his episcopal duties if his confessor tried to separate him from his mistress, the mother of several children. His successor, Clemens August (1723-61), the last of the Wittelsbach Electors, observed the outward forms of religion, but led a life of wild dissipation, wasting the substance of his subjects on dancers and singers, balls, hunts, and palaces. The Count of Königseck ascended the Electoral throne with a good character, but the vicious traditions of the Court at Bonn were too much for him. Not till the accession of the Archduke Max, youngest son of Maria Theresa, in 1784, did the Electorate possess a ruler whom it could respect. The new Elector cleansed the Court and restored order to the finances, but his main task was to assist his brother the Emperor Joseph in his crusade against Ultramontanism.

[1] See O. Meier, *Zur Geschichte der römisch-deutschen Frage*, vol. i.

He transformed the Academy, founded by his predecessor at Bonn, into a University, which was intended to render him independent of Cologne, whence the Electorate had hitherto drawn its officials and clergy. So bitter was the feud that in 1789 the Elector decreed that in future no student from Cologne should obtain any ecclesiastical or civil post in his dominions. Max was justified in desiring to emancipate his State from the paralysing embrace of obscurantism, but his zeal outran his discretion. Though the nobles and officials were, as a rule, freethinkers or indifferent, the bourgeoisie and the peasantry remained devout Catholics, deeply resenting the attacks on the Church, monasticism and pilgrimages launched by Eulogius Schneider and other scoffers imported by the Elector. Not one of the three ecclesiastical Electorates possessed a ruler with the strength and resolution to sweep away the accumulated abuses of generations. The smaller ecclesiastical principalities, scattered at random over the west and south of Germany, reproduced the main features of the Rhine Electorates. Ecclesiastical only in name, most of their rulers were temporal princes whose worldly life vied with that of their secular neighbours. Their subjects suffered or vegetated in silence, but from time to time the curtain was lifted on some particularly gross scandal, and all Germany rang with the story of tyranny or caprice. Thus the rule of the Archbishop of Speier, the most forcible personality among the Prince Bishops on the eve of the Revolution, was held up to the obloquy of Europe by the stinging pen of Schlözer.

The smallest members of the Empire were the Free Cities and the Imperial Knights. The former, once the pride of the Empire, differed in size and vitality not less than the principalities. The Hansa towns in the north, Hamburg, Lubeck, and Bremen, were kept alive by their trade, and the largest of the three was the most cosmopolitan city in the Empire. Commercial intercourse with France and England brought liberal notions to the Elbe, and the wealth of the merchant class provided an opportunity for culture which was eagerly seized. In no city in Germany was there such a free and vigorous intellectual life, such a number of cultivated men and women, such hospitality to new ideas. Klopstock made it his home in middle life, Lessing rebuked theological obscurantism and reformed the German theatre from its stage. The notes of Hamburg were energy, prosperity, culture, political and religious liberalism. Next in wealth and superior in political prestige was Frankfurt, the Imperial city *par excellence*. The old town on the Main, with its prosperous bourgeoisie, makes a charming picture in the golden light of *Dichtung und Wahrheit*; but its pulse beat slower, and it was less liberal and modern than Hamburg. By far the greater number of the Free Cities had long fallen from their high estate and slumbered behind their crumbling walls. In many cases the population had shrunk since the Thirty Years' War almost to the dimensions of a rotten borough, and the government had become the hereditary monopoly of a tiny clique. Subject to the Emperor alone, they were at once independent republics and close corporations; their vice was stagnation rather than tyranny. The magistrates were bound to summon the citizens or the Great Council on important occasions, and the newly elected officials had to swear fidelity to the Statutes. These forms in some degree helped to keep alive the tradition of law and liberty, but the little republics incurred the wrath and ridicule of the satirists. Wieland utilised recollections of his native Biberach in his 'Abderites.' Weckhrlin, who had crossed swords with the citizens of Augsburg and Nördlingen, denounced the cities as spiders' webs hanging on the Empire. Schubart spoke of the moss-grown communities, 'in which inveterate abuses have deeper roots than the oldest oaks.' Towns with an even more illustrious pedigree than Hamburg and Frankfurt had sunk into objects of shame and derision. The old Imperial city of Aachen, the scene of coronations centuries before Frankfurt, had been ravaged by faction and had fallen to political and economic ruin. Still more tragic was the fate of Cologne, which drew a cordon round her walls by the fourfold censorship of the University, the Archbishop, the Nuncio, and the Dominicans. No Protestant could own a house, hold office, or meet for service; and the permission to build a church, reluctantly granted in 1787, was withdrawn in the following year. Whole streets fell into decay and beggars barred approach to the churches. Industry, trade, art, learning, politics, had fallen on evil days, and the once proud Roman Colonia was the abode of dirt, poverty, and superstition.

Like the Free Cities, the Imperial Knights had outlived their day. Subject to the Emperor alone and unrepresented in the Diet, they were undisputed lords of the tiny territory which they surveyed from the castle windows. Scattered by hundreds over the south and west of Germany, they were at best picturesque survivals of the Middle Ages, at worst the scene of petty tyranny when the patrimonial jurisdiction was exercised by men of boorish habits and vindictive temper. They, too, had few friends among the writers who voiced or created public opinion. 'If a place looks particularly derelict,' wrote Friedrich Karl Moser, 'we need not ask questions, for we know it to be the village of an Imperial Knight.' There were men like Stein who exercised their rights with restraint and took their duties seriously, but the Reichsritter was an anachronism, and his possessions hindered the formation of larger and more healthy political units. At the first shock of the armed Revolution they were fated to disappear like spectres before the rising sun.

Such was the Holy Roman Empire in its last stages of decline, an object of scorn and derision to mankind. Few competent observers believed that it could be reformed, and an increasing number turned their eyes to Prussia as to a possible saviour. The Fürstenbund, the last creation of the mighty King, was hailed in certain quarters as the dawn of a new and better age. In a pamphlet of 1787 Johannes Müller lauded it as a bulwark against the world-domination of the Emperor, a defence of the rights of every member of the Empire. On the failure of Hapsburg ambitions and the death of its founder it fell to pieces; and Johannes Müller again raised his voice in 1788. 'Without law or justice,' he cried in anguish, 'without security against capricious burdens, uncertain of maintaining our children, our liberties, our rights or our lives for a single day, the helpless prey of superior power, without national feeling—that is the *status quo* of our nation.' To stand still was to perish. The only alternative to revolution was reform of the Empire. 'I cannot understand,' he wrote, 'how we Germans have lost the courage and intelligence to advance from hoary pedantries to an effective Imperial constitution, to a true Imperial connection, to a common patriotism, so that we could at length say, We are a nation.' 'It is a rickety house,' echoed the Austrian diplomatist Thugut; 'one must either leave it alone or pull it down and build another.' It was, indeed, past mending, and only waited for the *coup de grâce*. 'To say that Frederick the Great destroyed the Empire,' remarks Niebuhr, 'is to say that the person who buried the corpse killed the man.' If it had possessed real vitality, neither Frederick nor Napoleon could have struck it down.

No less urgent was the need of reform in the majority of the component parts of the Empire. Nowhere in Europe was absolutism more crushing and repulsive than in the little Courts where

Frederick's doctrine of 'service' had never penetrated, where mistresses ruled supreme, where venality placed adventurers in office, where reckless ostentation stood out in glaring contrast to the poverty of the people. 'The peasant,' wrote a satirist grimly, 'is like a sack of meal. When emptied there is still some dust—it only needs to be beaten.' For the most part the victims suffered in silence; but discontent was to find some interpreters, and the intellectual revival, aided by powerful external influences, began to wake the country from its slumbers. 'Who does not foresee great revolutions?' asked the Hamburg Privy Councillor Creuz in 1767, after reviewing the evils of the time. The question was echoed by a growing chorus of voices in the next two decades, and when the Rights of Man were proclaimed from the banks of the Seine millions were ready to welcome the new creed.

II

While political life in eighteenth-century Germany was thus backward and anaemic, a vigorous intellectual activity in the middle decades held out the promise of better days.[1] Wolff and Lessing, Moses Mendelssohn and Nicolai, the leaders of the *Aufklärung*—a name derived from the frontispiece of one of Wolff's books depicting the sun breaking through clouds—exhorted their countrymen to use their reason without fear; and deeper notes were struck by Kant and Herder, Hamann and Jacobi. The Augustan Age of German literature opened with Klopstock, and the language quickly shed its crudity. Lessing and Wieland, Kleist and Gleim, Goethe and Schiller, Lenz and Klinger, Bürger and Voss, Kotzebue and Iffland, poured forth a flood of poems, satires, novels, and dramas, which created and delighted a reading public. Bach inaugurated the long supremacy of German music and Winckelmann migrated to Italy, whence he proclaimed to his countrymen the glories of Greek art. The new interest in things of the mind was stimulated by a crop of journals devoted to literature and philosophy, society and art. It was the thawing of the winter ice—an age of experiment, adventure, and rejuvenescence—

---

[1] See Hettner, *Deutsche Litteratur im* 18*ten Jahrhundert*, vols. iii–iv ; Scherer, *History of German Literature*; Lévy-Bruhl, *L'Allemagne depuis Leibnitz*; Kuno Fischer, *Geschichte der neueren Philosophie*; Haym, *Herder*; Justi, *Winckelmann*; J. G. Robertson, *Life of Goethe*; Haznack, *Geschichte der Preussischen Akademie der Wissenschaften*; Cassirer, *Die Philosophie der Aufklärung* ; *Aufklärung* in *Realencl. f. Prot. Theologie*.

when the arrows of criticism began to fly and the pent-up rills of emotion burst forth. The country was full of intellectual centres which offered a rich soil for the exchange and propagation of ideas. During the generation of peace following the Seven Years' War, Germany learned to read, think, and ask questions. The critical spirit, once aroused, spread rapidly, finding nourishment in the rank evils which overspread the land. The ideas of reason and humanity, the starting-point and the goal of the *Aufklärung*, won almost uncontested supremacy over the mind of the educated bourgeoisie. Nicolai's organ, the 'Allgemeine Deutsche Bibliothek,' and the 'Berliner Monatschrift,' founded by Biester and Gedike in 1783, taught their readers to use their own judgment.[1] Though the roots of the *Aufklärung* were philosophic, not political, the revolt against authority spread to ever wider regions. Private citizens, excluded from all share in government, felt no interest in the state, and saw only the individual and humanity, the august but invisible Church of which the humblest were members and in comparison with which the state was a trifle. In an age of obscurantism and repression every leader of thought was on the side of the opposition. Everywhere there was an ideal of better conditions without any clear idea as to the machinery by which they were to be secured.

The critical spirit assailed traditional religion before it grappled with political institutions.[2] As the sterile dogmatism of the century following Luther had been tempered by the pietism of Spener and Francke, so pietism in turn yielded to rationalism. A critical view of the New Testament was taught by Semler at Halle, and in the Wolfenbüttel Fragments Lessing offered to the world the negations of Reimarus half a century after his death. Lessing himself, in his 'Education of the Human Race,' set forth a deeper view of the religious evolution of mankind than any of his predecessors or contemporaries; in 'Nathan the Wise' he immortalised his friend Moses Mendelssohn and embodied the ideal of religious toleration. The challenge to tradition could not draw rein at the frontiers of religion, and, though the theological rebels lacked interest in politics, the habit of questioning authority spread through the educated bourgeoisie.

An increasing interest in public affairs was displayed by men of

[1] See Hay, '*Staat, Volk u. Weltbürgertum in der Berlinischen Monatschrift.*'
[2] See Dorner, *History of Protestant Theology*; Ritschl, *Geschichte des Pietismus*.

letters and their readers. 'It hardly occurred to anybody in my youth,' wrote Goethe in 1790, 'to envy the privileged class or grudge them their privileges. But knights, robbers, an honest Tiers État, and an infamous nobility—such are the ingredients of our novels and plays during the last ten years.' The arrogance and oppression to which it was necessary to bow during the day were denounced in the evening behind the footlights; and the declamations of Figaro were as milk compared to the strong meat of 'Emilia Galotti' and 'Love and Intrigue,' in which Lessing and Schiller depicted a society throttled by tyranny from which the only escape was death. Wieland sketched both a model prince and a despot by divine right. Kant declared that all history was a striving towards a just constitution for states and proper relations between them. Rousseau, Montesquieu, and Plutarch were read in every town, and Johannes Müller's picture of the struggles of the Cantons made the name of Switzerland a talisman of liberty. Even the gentle Claudius wrote:

> The King should be the better man,
> Else let the best be ruler.

Göcking regretted that Germany could not boast the execution of a monarch. Young men quoted Posa's outburst in 'Don Carlos,' 'Ich kann nicht Fürstendiener sein.' Schiller pronounced the success of 'Fiesco' at Berlin a sign that republican freedom was understood. Friedrich Stolberg sang to liberty and the overthrow of tyrants. Republicanism, of course, was purely academic, but the bitter attacks on princes and the nobility were meant to hurt.

Except for Althusius early in the seventeenth century there was no systematic thinking in Germany about the principles of politics before the French Revolution, for the class which in France and England reflected on the nature and duties of the state occupied itself with the machinery of the Empire and the practice of administration. From the middle of the seventeenth to the middle of the eighteenth century the stage is occupied by the Cameralists, a school which discussed how best to satisfy the fiscal needs of the ruler.[1] In 'The German Princes' State,' published in 1655, Seckendorf produced a handbook of government and administration based on the practice of his master, Duke Ernst the Pious of Gotha. Though its exponents endeavoured to raise the standard of autocracy, they suggested no

[1] See Albion Small, *The Cameralists*.

check more effective than religion and conscience. The state, not the people, was their starting-point, whereas later thinkers were to start with the good of the people and to work up to the government required to secure it. Cameralism was restated and brought up to date by Justi, whose writings reflect the theory and practice of benevolent despotism in the age of Frederick the Great. The common weal is presented as the goal of the state, and the happiness of the governed receives lip homage, but Justi assumes that absolute government secures it. As the contemporary of Montesquieu and Rousseau he is aware of the growth of moral demands which form a standard for rulers, but he never suggests that the people may enforce it. He urges that they should 'be something' in every State, and appeals to the ruler to respect property and law, not to overtax his subjects, and to refrain from war; but they may not share in the making of laws or punish unjust rulers or ministers. Like all the Cameralists, he assumes the ruler to be wise and benevolent. Though the school passed away when the breezes of political criticism began to blow vigorously in the latter half of the century, its influence remained. If Germany was the land of obedience, to borrow Herder's phrase, it was in part because for generations the Cameralists had preached without serious challenge the might and majesty of the state.

The political education of the German mind was seriously undertaken by a handful of courageous men who risked their liberty, if not their lives, in denouncing the evils under which the majority of their countrymen were groaning. The first of these brave tribunes of the people was Friedrich Karl Moser,[1] who inherited his reverence for law from his father, the champion of the Württemberg Estates. The treatise 'Der Herr und der Diener' (Master and Servant) was published at Frankfurt in 1759, after a few years of official life. The book begins by reminding princes how easy it is to make their subjects happy and by lamenting how seldom they succeed. 'The despotism of many of our German rulers, the harsh treatment of their subjects, the manifold breach of the most sacred promises to the Estates, the ignorance of most rulers of their duties, and many other signs of evil times, are usually due to the military character of government.' Rulers are brought up to be soldiers, not statesmen. A second and no less baneful mistake is the idea that a ruler is responsible to

[1] See Bluntschli, *Geschichte des Staatsrechts*; and Rosenstein's two articles in *Preussische Jahrbücher*, vol. xv.

God alone. A capable ruler is a blessing, but even in such a case several eyes are better than a single pair. Hopes are usually entertained of the heir who sometimes harbours the ambition to reform the State; 'but if one-tenth of these good resolutions were carried out, Germany would be living in the Golden Age.' The new ruler, for instance, is too often the slave of a favourite. 'If he has rioted in secret, he now declares his mistress and presents himself to his land as an adulterer.' Others waste the substance of their subjects on building or hunting, the table or jewels; and the prince is surrounded by those who chant the refrain, 'Your Highness has only to command.' A courtier will not shrink from exaggerating the wealth of the country in order to secure the fulfilment of his selfish projects, and then even a well-meaning prince becomes an extortioner. If he perceives the evils of the state and the faults of his advisers, shall he dismiss the whole band? He can neither condemn them to ruin nor support both them and their successors. So the building is patched up till it falls with a crash, when surprise is expressed that it has stood so long. 'The great goal of all the motley throng at Court is to win the favour of the ruler, who is like a beleaguered city and is surrounded by spies and traitors: even in small Courts you will find a multitude of them. The fewer servants a ruler possesses, the better is he served. If only he possessed the secret of securing real Christians for his councillors he would accomplish marvels. There must always be a First Minister, but what mischief these men have done! Certain things I dare not mention,' he adds ominously, 'for we live in dangerous times.'

Ten thousand copies were printed of this memorable book, the political classic of the German *Aufklärung*, and French and Russian translations appeared. Though it draws its historical examples rather from France than Germany, it is in reality an audacious transcript from the author's experience as Minister of the Landgrave of Hesse-Darmstadt. The State had been reduced by misgovernment to a pitiable condition and needed a firm hand. 'He got me out of the mud,' said the Prince; but Moser's tenure of office was brief. Some years later he was recalled, but, like Turgot, he was too radical to remain long in power. His new experiences were incorporated in his book 'Rulers and Ministers,' published in 1784. It is the same message as that of 'Master and Servant,' but with an added poignancy. What sinister memories lurk behind the maxim that for the success of the Minister's plans he needs not only the consent of the Prince but also of the 'Night Ministry'—the wife, the mistress, the confessor, and the chamberlains! Moser was a keen observer and an honest and capable statesman, but his writings are rather ethical than scientific. His best thoughts, remarks Bluntschli, come from the heart. Though interested in Rousseau and Montesquieu, he pronounced them too theoretical. With passionate earnestness he denounces the glaring faults of the 'Proprietary State,' but he does not look beyond its reform. He finds the root of the mischief in the evil education of princes, not in the principle of autocracy. He sees only the Prince and his servants. The people, despite his active sympathy, form only the background of the picture. The supreme problem of government, as it presents itself to his eyes, is to train a ruler to be worthy of his high calling. And yet his writings possess the honourable claim of being the only Mirror of Princes fashioned in Germany during the eighteenth century. He was the first subject to demand that the official should be the servant not of the Prince but of the State, and should oppose commands which he considers to be wrong. In theory the ruler was to remain absolute; in practice his power was to be limited by the vigilance of an honest and courageous bureaucracy. 'Moser,' declared Niebuhr many years later, 'was the first to raise the voice of political liberty in Germany, the first to speak of the great evils of the country and of some of its governments. His books are hardly read now, but they had then much influence, especially on officials. But the rulers were deaf.' The appeal failed because he fired with blank cartridge. It was not enough to denounce evil rulers; it was necessary to frighten them. By refusing to summon the people to his aid, he deprived himself of the only weapon by which he could strike terror into the hearts of evil-doers in high places.

A less systematic but far more effective critic of public abuses was Schlözer,[1] the earliest political journalist of Germany. He was an essentially modern man, and no German publicist before the Revolution could boast of such extended knowledge of foreign countries. After leaving Göttingen he spent his early manhood in Sweden and Russia, learning their languages, studying their institutions, and

[1] See Schlözer's *Leben*, by his son; Heeren, *Biographische und Literarische Denkschriften*; Bock, *Schlözer*; Frensdorff, '*Von und über Schlözer*,' in *Abh. d. Ges. d. Wissenschaften zu Göttingen*, 1909.

writing their history. Brief visits to France and Italy still further enlarged his horizon and laid the foundation of his comprehensive interest in the politics of Europe. Appointed Professor at Göttingen after his return from Russia, he lectured on history and the political sciences to large and eager audiences. With the aid of Pütter, the oracle on constitutional law, Achenwall, the first of German statisticians, and Spittler, the most brilliant historical teacher of his time, he made the young University the centre for political, legal, and diplomatic studies. On reaching middle life, he added to his labours as teacher and historian the foundation of a political journal. A visit to Paris in 1773, where he met d'Alembert and other leading men, suggested his first journalistic venture, the 'Correspondence chiefly relating to Statistics.' Statistics and despotism, he used to maintain, could not co-exist. The journal failed after a year, but reappeared in 1776 as 'New Correspondence, Historical and Political.' This time it struck root and quickly became the most powerful organ in central Europe. The editor's wide circle of friends in and beyond Germany secured a flow of interesting communications. While in theory a purveyor of news, it owed its popularity and power to its criticisms. He wrote comparatively little, but he added pungent comments to the communications of his contributors. The articles were as a rule anonymous, and full responsibility was taken by Schlözer, who was so careful of the safety of his contributors that in dangerous cases he copied the manuscript with his own hand and destroyed the original. Thus writers were encouraged to tell all they knew, and readers learned to trust their accuracy.

The 'Correspondence,' which changed its name in 1782 to the 'Staatsanzeigen,' became the terror of evil-doers and the delight of their helpless victims. Niebuhr compared the paper to the lion's mouth at Venice, ever open to complaints. Duke Karl of Saxe-Meiningen offered his co-operation. 'Your paper,' he wrote in 1781, 'is read everywhere. It is now the only one of its kind which is so universally useful and awakes so many good ideas in the bosom of a well-intentioned ruler. Oh, best of men, continue to enlighten us, and let nothing frighten you into abandoning your journal!' 'You, Herr Professor,' wrote his friend Count Schmettow, a Holstein diplomatist, in 1786, 'have benefited the world more than Luther himself. Believe me, bad ministers and princes are really afraid of you. Countless abominations have been prevented by you. You have made enemies, of course, just as no Monsignore or Abbé in Rome was Luther's friend; but God and honest men must wish you well, and few or none of your contemporaries will be able on their deathbed to look back on so much good accomplished.' Maria Theresa would sometimes support her opinion in Council with the words: 'That will never do; what would Schlözer say?' The fearless editor knew the limits of his liberty, and was careful not to overstep them. As a Hanoverian subject, he refrained from criticising the policy of his sovereign in the Electorate or beyond the seas; and the long arm of Prussia and Austria counselled circumspection in dealing with the dominions of the Hohenzollerns and the Hapsburgs. Yet he occupied a privileged position as the star of Göttingen and a favourite of the Hanoverian government. He once attacked the postal service of his own State, received a reprimand, and never repeated the offence; but when remonstrances reached Hanover from other rulers the answer came that the Press was free. In his boisterous tournaments with all Germany looking on he could count on the passive support of the only princes who had the power to silence or punish him. Jacob Grimm complained that he had one pair of scales for the great Powers and another for the small, but he had no real choice. Moreover, the petty tyrants were the worst offenders. One day he would attack the magistrates of a Free City, next an Imperial Knight who tyrannised over a village, following with a list of the mistresses of the Canons of Munster and anecdotes of the half-crazy Duke of Zweibrücken. He was born for conflict and rejoiced at the reverberation of his ringing blows. His strident tones broke the ban of secrecy and compelled young men to interest themselves in public affairs.

Unlike Moser, Schlözer was far more than a critic of abuses. His creed was constitutional monarchy, and the two main planks in his programme were representative institutions and a free press. He was the child of Montesquieu and shared his admiration for the British Constitution. The happiness of a prince, he declared, lay in ruling with his people, not over them. There should be a contract so that if it was broken he might be deposed. He will hear nothing of divine right or patriarchal omnipotence, for sovereignty resides in the people. His enemies complained that he could only talk of the duties of princes and of the rights of peoples, but the sneer was undeserved. He detested mob-rule no less than the extravagances of 'personal government.' As a champion of the *juste milieu* he was equally opposed to autocracy, oligarchy, and democracy. He scoffed at the 'Republiquettes' of Greece, and maliciously dubbed aristocrats 'kakistocrats.' Freedom, he declared, was safer with a hereditary ruler than with two hundred hereditary or other councillors. He disapproved of the revolt of the American colonists, holding that the provocation was insufficient to justify rebellion. His ideal was ordered liberty and he made its foes his own. 'His residence in Russia,' writes Heeren of his colleague, 'moulded his political and literary character. The classic land of despotism awakened the spirit of opposition in him. The foundation of his political creed was his hatred of despotic power, and he hated it even more in republics than in monarchies.' The Cobbett of Germany believed that the pen was mightier than the sword. Without a free press liberty could be neither attained nor preserved. The deadliest enemy of despotism was publicity. Tyrants who were too strong to be overthrown must be intimidated, scandals dragged into the light of day, public indignation aroused, till the evil-doer was forced to ask himself whether the gratification of his whims and lusts was worth the storm of obloquy.

Though exerting a less extended influence than Schlözer, two Swabian publicists accomplished the same work of outspoken criticism in South Germany. Schubart's[1] fame owes as much to his ten years of imprisonment as to his journalism and his poems. His biographer, David Friedrich Strauss, has truly said that he had more blood than bones, more temperament than character, more sap than force. But though his ability was not of the highest order and his life was loose, he encouraged his countrymen to think and to dare. He was warmer and deeper in feeling than his Swabian rival Wieland, though less refined and less instructed. He was, indeed, a man of the people, as Wieland's temperament made him a man of the salon. Though the chief purpose of his 'Deutsche Chronik' was to preach a vigorous nationalism, he strove with equal vigour to create a demand for internal reform. His sharpest darts were reserved for princes, and he regarded the nobility, 'which has prickles above as well as below,' as a potentially useful bulwark against crowned tyrants. Editing his paper first in Augsburg and Ulm, he was enticed to Württemberg in 1777, and immured in the fortress of the Asperg on the heights above Ludwigsburg. Freed in 1787 at the instance of Prussia, he emerged

[1] See Strauss, *Schubarts Leben in Briefen*.

a broken man, a martyr to the cause of his country's political regeneration.

When Schubart was silenced, his mantle fell upon Weckhrlin,[1] his fellow Württemberger. There was nothing of the patriot about the man who spent nine years in Paris, worshipped Voltaire, loved France as the source of the *Aufklärung*, and castigated the Holy Roman Empire; but in political criticism he was far more effective, and his biting wit quickly made him a power. Schlözer remarked that he rose like a comet over Germany. He edited a journal between 1778 and 1788 under three successive titles, in which he sharply attacked tyranny and obscurantism. Lacking the privileged position of Schlözer, he had to measure his words and preferred the rapier to the bludgeon. Tradition made no appeal to his sceptical mind; but he had a keen scent for the misdeeds of republics, and he attacked the mouldering Swiss oligarchies as vigorously as Schlözer himself. Yet he desired to retain the nobility as a separate Estate, and felt the scholar's contempt for the intelligence of the masses. His chief enemy was the Church, and with the Jesuits he waged a truceless war. Indeed, he cared less for political than for intellectual liberty. 'Give us our rights,' he exclaimed, 'freedom of thought, freedom of speech, freedom of the press, freedom of belief. With these four liberties any government will suffice.' But such privileges were not to be had in South Germany till a great conflagration had consumed a mass of antiquated tyrannies in its purifying flame.

While most of the leading publicists of the time sought guidance in the dictates of reason, Justus Möser[2] detested the levelling rationalism of the *Aufklärung* and anticipated Savigny's demonstration of the utility of tradition. 'This strong, rude German soul,' as Goethe named him, studied and wrote the history of his native Osnabrück, and based his political philosophy on his researches. A consistent and disinterested conservative, he rejected philosophic despotism and was no friend of aristocrats. Anchored in loving loyalty to the past, he supported the inherited rights and popular customs which sanctified the interests of common men. Entirely free from the sickly romanticism which loves or tolerates abuses for their antiquity, he tried to revive the spirit of old institutions in order to save them, and he had no objection to cutting down dead trees. The backbone of the state and the guarantee

---

[1] See Ebeling, *Weckhrlin*, and Böhm, *L. Weckhrlin*.
[2] See Hatzig, *Justus Möser*.

of continuity, he taught, was the peasantry. While the liberal reformer looks to the townsman, the conservative turns to the peasant, who alone can be trusted to resist the seduction of new-fangled ideas. 'They do not walk on all fours,' he remarked bitterly, 'for they too are human beings.' He deemed himself a friend of liberty, but it was a liberty founded on ancient rights and customs, not on an imaginary social contract. A visit to England in middle life strengthened his liberal conservatism. Though content with the Estates, he recommends the German states to adopt some of the English forms of government. 'He who is to act in common must deliberate in common—that is the primeval formula of Germanic law.' Liberty is only to be found in law, but law is the expression of the majority of qualified voices. Rights are the correlative of property. Serfdom must be reformed, not abolished. His ideal was a community of occupying owners. He sought his golden age in primitive Germany, not in the Middle Ages when the small man was strangled in the meshes of feudalism. Indeed, his vision was so fascinated by the petty freeholder that it had no room for the state, which, with its rulers, its rigidity, and its centralisation, seemed to him the enemy of liberty. 'The present tendency to laws and regulations,' he declared in the 'Patriotische Phantasien,' 'is dangerous to the common liberty. We are deserting the true scheme of nature, which displays its richness in variety, and thus smooths the way to despotism. Should not each little town have its own constitution? It is worth discussion whether it would not produce a greater variety of virtues and a stronger development of spiritual force if each little social group was more its own lawgiver and conformed less to the general type.' Möser's prescription was not what Germany required, for the patient was sick of the particularism which he exalted.

The widespread longing for a new and nobler age expressed itself not only in the writings of publicists but in the formation of secret societies.[1] The founder of the Illuminati, Weishaupt, was a mixture of scamp and idealist. Educated at a Jesuit school in Ingoldstadt, the precocious boy reacted violently against the clerical atmosphere and plunged into unbelief and materialism. On the suppression of the Society, he succeeded to the chair of Canon Law in the University,

---

[1] See Kluckhohn, *Vorträge und Aufsätze*, '*Die Illuminaten u. die Aufklärung in Bayern*'; Le Forestier, *Les Illuminés de Bavière*; and Wolfram, *Die Illuminaten in Bayern*.

which a Jesuit had held; he also lectured on history and moral science. His eloquence and audacity, which fascinated the students, scandalised the partisans of the old order. He spoke with horror of the mind-killing education of the Jesuits, but he admired their iron discipline, and resolved to create an organisation on similar lines for the defence of the principles which they attacked. Masonry had been imported from England in 1737, when the first lodge was founded in Hamburg, and Frederick the Great joined the Brunswick lodge shortly before his accession. Scores of lodges were quickly formed in Protestant Germany by men of culture who desired religious liberty. The better side of the movement was the notion of a brotherhood of enlightenment, emancipated from cramping local prejudices. But the love of the marvellous, never more widespread than in the Age of Reason, led to the practice of magic and alchemy; and Masonry, the offspring of the *Aufklärung*, became in many places associated with childish superstition and obscurantism. It had already fallen from its high estate when Weishaupt heard of it in 1774, and resolved to borrow its outward forms for the new republic of his dreams.

Weishaupt's Order of Perfectibles—'a name which shows the object of my foundation'—soon became the Order of the Illuminati. The first members were drawn from his Ingoldstadt pupils, and instructions were issued to enrol clever young men in Munich and other cities of Bavaria. Several grades were instituted, elaborate processes of initiation were designed, and members were sworn to secrecy and obedience. A cipher language was constructed, and classical names were employed to heighten the mystery and for purposes of concealment. Bavaria was Greece, Munich was Athens, and the founder was Spartacus. 'My aim,' he declared, 'is to help reason to gain supremacy. The ideal of the Order is to diffuse light. We are fighters against darkness.' His creed was philosophic anarchism. The existence of States and the subjection of man to man were only temporary concessions to imperfection. The divine plan had been to give liberty and equality, but the leaders had turned tyrants. The *Aufklärung*, or spread of reason, would render princes and nations superfluous. The race would become a single family, the world the abode of reasonable beings. Nationalism, like despotism, was the enemy of humanity. Patriotism meant enlarging your country by force and fraud, the ruler sharing the booty with a few of his subjects by a compact known as the feudal system. Every evil arose from deserting cosmopolitanism, every effort must be made by a new Order to return to it. A few princes, diplomatists, and scholars in Bavaria and other parts of Germany became members, but only a handful joined in the first three years. The vague programme and childish ceremonies repelled more than they attracted, and Weishaupt was no Loyola. His personal morality was lax and his scanty following resented his autocratic ways. Spartacus was not a Mason; but in 1778 one of his chief disciples joined a lodge, and the idea suggested itself that the Illuminati might present themselves as members of a higher grade of Masonry, which had long established its position. It was at this moment of critical transition that the second founder of the Illuminati was enrolled at Frankfurt by an itinerant recruiter.

Adolph, Freiherr von Knigge,[1] a member of an old Hanoverian family, had heard much in early youth of Masonry and occultism, and had dabbled in alchemy. At twenty he entered a Masonic lodge, half sceptical, half credulous. Like Weishaupt, he was part enthusiast and part impostor, but he was superior to the Bavarian Professor in character and knowledge of the world. The dream of founding a new Order had taken root in his mind; but when he was told that such an Order was already in existence, he asked to be initiated, and brought a number of disillusioned Masons with him. Admitted at first only to the lower grade, Philo, as he was now called, desired to be seised of the mystery in its entirety. Weishaupt reluctantly confessed that the Order had no existence except in his head, and begged forgiveness for the fraud. Knigge rejoined that in that case the whole Masonic movement might be brought under their joint direction. Philo taught his new associates the different Masonic systems, and was commissioned to work out a scheme for the higher mysteries of which the Illuminati were to be the guardians.

Knigge insisted on a promise of cautious steering in the danger zones of religion and politics. The highest ranks of the new Order, he argued, should be informed of its political and religious attitude, which he proceeded to elaborate. Like Weishaupt, he exalts the stateless condition and claims for civilised man the privilege of liberty once enjoyed by the savage. When a nation reaches its majority, the need of tutelage ceases. 'Morality is the art which teaches man to enter on manhood and to do without princes. Morality alone can secure liberty.' Liberty and equality form the secret kernel of Christ's

[1] See Gödeke, *Knigge*.

teaching, and Christianity is therefore the foundation of the Illuminati. Religion and authority should be preserved and respected. The aim of the Order is not to overthrow the State and establish institutions by force, but to aid the processes of evolution, to keep monarchs from the path of evil, and to plant its members not only in the chief places of government but in schools and bookshops. A corresponding Order should be formed by women. Under his inspiration the Illuminati soon ranged from Paris to Warsaw, from Denmark to Italy. Since public life offered few opportunities secret societies became popular, and their cosmopolitan character gave their members a sense of release from the stifling influences of particularism. The prospects of the Order seemed bright, but its strength was sapped by quarrels between its leaders. To Knigge, as the soul of the movement, its members turned for help and advice, but he quickly discovered that there was no room for two heads. 'An Order,' he wrote angrily, 'which tyrannises over men as Spartacus aspires to do would be a heavier yoke than that of the Jesuits.' He therefore resigned, magnanimously declining to expose the founder, and he resolved never again to have dealings with secret societies. Almost at the same moment clerical denunciations began to reach the Elector of Bavaria, though without naming the Order. Weishaupt vainly demanded an audience at Munich to demonstrate the innocence of his Order, omitting some dangerous points—such as the words, 'Parsons and evil princes stand in our way.' Resignations followed, and on realising that the game was up the founder revealed the whole story to the Government. An edict was issued against Masons and Illuminati, Weishaupt was deprived of his chair, and documents were published revealing his character and activities. The Elector, now thoroughly alarmed and convinced that his throne and life had been in danger, imposed heavy penalties; and when the French Revolution broke out, the Bavarian Government saw the spectre of its old enemy behind every bush.

Liberal cosmopolitanism was not confined to the members of secret societies, for the disunion and impotence of the country led inevitably to a philosophy which, though in other lands to some extent a pose, was in Germany the sincere conviction of many of the strongest and most generous minds. It was not, indeed, universal.[1] Klopstock's odes and dramatic epics endeavoured to revive interest

[1] See Meinecke, *Weltbürgertum u. Nationalstaat*, ch. ii.

and pride in primitive Germany. 'The cosmopolitan,' wrote Herder, 'is among citizens like the polyhistor among scholars. The one belongs to every state and does nothing for any one of them, while the other takes all knowledge for his province and achieves no result. The savage who loves his wife and child and burns with zeal for his tribe is a truer being than the educated shadow who is filled with zeal for his race, which, after all, is a mere name. The heart of a cosmopolitan is a shelter for nobody.' In his book, 'Death for the Fatherland,' Abbt denied that patriotism existed only in republics, and demanded an education in civic duties from which patriotism would result. In his 'National Spirit,' Friedrich Karl Moser deplored the pitiable state of the Fatherland, adding, 'My heart trembles at the sight of our chains.' If political unity was impossible, unity of feeling might at least be encouraged. In his 'Deutsche Chronik,' Schubart preached a virile nationalism and castigated the aping of Versailles. 'He who does not fling a curse across the frontier from the ruins of Heidelberg is no true German. And yet what is there that my countryman does not fetch from beyond the Rhine? Fashions, cuisine, wine, even the language. What he might learn from the Frenchman with advantage is patriotism.' He envies England her liberty, but finds her too commercial, and never loses hope of a better future for his countrymen. 'Weep not,' he cries, 'over the flabbiness of thy people. The lions are waking, they hear the cry of the eagle. They rush forth and seize lands that the foreigner has torn away. A German Imperial throne will arise.'

The Nationalists, however, were voices crying in the wilderness. Particularism was the instinct of the masses, cosmopolitanism the creed of the *élite*. There was so little to be proud of in most German states that the eyes of their more reflective citizens turned abroad. Excluded from power and responsibility, men of liberal views felt themselves in closer association with reformers in other lands than with their own countrymen. 'German nationalism,' declared Nicolai bluntly, 'is a political monstrosity.' To such minds patriotism meant stagnation, a mulish antagonism to the stimulating challenge of foreign influences. 'I write as a citizen of the world who serves no prince,' remarked Schiller in 1784; 'I lost my Fatherland to exchange it for the great world.' Sonnenfels' 'Love of Fatherland' provoked Goethe in 1773 to a confession of unblushing cosmopolitanism. 'If we find a place where we can rest with our belongings, a field to support us, a house to shelter us, have we not a fatherland? And do not thousands in every State possess it? Wherefore, then, the vain striving for a feeling which we cannot and indeed do not desire to entertain, which is the result of special circumstances in certain peoples and at certain times?'

The noblest cosmopolitan of his time has been described by Heine as 'our literary Arminius, who freed our theatre from the foreign yoke,' but in politics Lessing knew nothing of national boundaries.[1] 'In one of your poems,' he complains to Gleim, 'the patriot outcries the poet. Perhaps the patriot is not wholly overlaid in me, though to be praised as a zealous patriot is the last thing I crave—a patriot, that is, who would teach me to forget that I must be a citizen of the world. I have literally no conception of the love of the Fatherland (I am sorry to confess my shame), and it appears to me a heroic failing from which I am glad to be free.' 'Nathan the Wise,' 'The Education of the Human Race,' and 'Ernst and Falk' embody his dream of a grand association of men, regardless of religious and political differences, for the higher work of the world. His views on the State are contained in the three exquisite dialogues in which Ernst and Falk discuss the character and possibilities of Masonry.[2] Lessing, himself a disillusioned Mason, speaking through Falk, declares that the highest duties of the Order can be fulfilled without being a member. The state is made for men, not men for the state, and society also is nothing but a means. The duty of the individual is to develop his capacities, to join hands with men who are engaged in the same task, whoever and wherever they be. The ideal Masonry would discard its childish tricks and work for the solidarity of mankind, offering itself as a counterpoise to the isolating influences of class and nation. 'Would that there were men in every state who knew exactly when patriotism ceases to be a virtue, who did not believe that only their own religion is good and wise, who rise above class! What if the Masons made it part of their duty to reduce these barriers, which make people such strangers to one another, to the smallest dimensions?' There speaks the authentic voice of the *Aufklärung*, passionately convinced of the rationality of man, of the unity of civilisation, of the fruitfulness of co-operative effort. Here was an alluring task for men of ability and goodwill, a rich compensation for their

---

[1] See Baumgarten, *Reden u. Aufsätze*, '*War Lessing ein Deutscher Patriot?*'
[2] Cp. Erich Schmidt, *Lessing*, ii. 582–604.

exclusion from the tasks of government. Humanity was the religion of the eighteenth century, and Lessing was among the loftiest of its prophets.

The political education of the German people was not more indebted to its own bolder spirits than to the kindling impact of foreign influences. The writings of Rousseau took the country by storm.[1] 'His influence was immense,' records Niebuhr, 'far greater than that of Voltaire. He was the hero of most clever people in my youth.' Lessing was among the earliest of his admirers. Kant declared that Rousseau first discovered the deep-hidden nature of men, and forgot his daily walk over a new volume. Herder fed on him. Klinger never freed himself from the spell. Schiller wrote an ode to him. Jacobi pronounced him the greatest genius who had written in French. Campe called him his patron saint. Arndt read 'Émile' with rapture at the age of fifteen, and Gentz pronounced parts of it to be sanctified for the whole human race. 'Rousseau, the friend of mankind and of virtue,' wrote Anselm Feurebach, the Bavarian jurist, 'I thank thee for thy good services to my heart; receive my gratitude in this holy resolve to love the good as thou lovedst it. I have warmed my heart at thy glow and strengthened myself to virtue through thy strength.' Lenz placed his statue beside Shakespeare. Adam Lux composed his own epitaph in the words 'Here lies a disciple of Jean Jacques Rousseau.' Nowhere did the teachings of 'Émile' find disciples so earnest and practical as Basedow and Campe. The 'Contrat Social' pronounced on some fundamental issues which no German thinker had dared to raise. While Montesquieu appealed to students and thinkers, Jean Jacques became the guide, philosopher, and friend of men and women, young and old. The dramas and novels of the Romantic school from 'Werther' to 'The Robbers' were pure Rousseau, and Niebuhr attributed to the Swiss philosopher the appearance in German literature of 'the silly notion' that virtue was only to be found in the lower classes. The doctrines of the sovereignty of the people and the social contract, a very charter of revolt, filtered in and encouraged the victims of misgovernment to criticise and to complain.

A second foreign influence of a stimulating character was the American War of Independence, in which the sympathy of almost

---

[1] See Fester, *Rousseau und die Deutsche Geschichtsphilosophie*; Lévy-Bruhl, *L'Influence de Rousseau en Allemagne*, in *Annales de l'École libre des sciences politiques*, 1887.

every writer outside Hanover was with the colonists and every defeat of the British troops was hailed as a victory for liberty. Extracts from debates at Westminster and speeches in Congress circulated in the German papers, and even the Declaration of Independence was allowed to appear by princes who were not in the pay of the English King. Klopstock wrote an ode celebrating 'this war of noble heroes, the dawn of a great day to come,' and invited visitors to kiss his cane from Boston. Goethe testifies that Franklin and Washington were the names which shone in the German firmament. The revolt against oppression, the success of the daring adventure, and finally the establishment of a democratic republic free from courts and armies, feudalism and poverty, leavened the fermenting thought of Europe. It was at once a warning to rulers that there was a limit to tyranny, and an inspiration to down-trodden peoples all over the world.

But Germany was far from being a mere spectator of the drama. Though no one of the stature of Lafayette or Kosciusko crossed the ocean to join in the crusade for liberty, Steuben, a Prussian noble, and other volunteers hurried to the standard of revolt. Yet for each German fighting of his own accord by the side of Washington there were hundreds fighting against him.[1] The traffic in human flesh carried on by German princes drew down fierce indignation on their heads and scarcely less on that of their British paymaster. That peaceable citizens were dragged from their homes and sold like cattle at so much a head to a foreign ruler engaged in trying to stamp out the liberties of small communities of his own children was the concrete argument which rallied German opinion in support of the colonists. 'I cannot remember anybody in my father's circle or mine on the English side,' records Henriette Herz. 'The idea of full equality before the law exerted perhaps an even greater spell then than now, and was embraced even by the young nobility in our circle; and the sale of Hessians and Brunswickers was felt as a disgrace to every German. Washington was the hero of the day.' Failing to obtain mercenaries in Holland and Russia, the King of England turned to the home of his race, and in spite of a few refusals succeeded in purchasing 29,000 soldiers at a price of £7,000,000. Of these no fewer than 17,000 were drawn from Hesse-Cassel, the rest being provided by the Duke of Brunswick, the Margrave of Anspach and one or two other petty rulers. The infamous traffic was denounced by German

[1] See Kapp, *Der Soldatenhandel deutscher Fürsten nach Amerika.*

writers outside the borders of the States that were implicated, and by none more passionately than by the youthful Schiller who wrote the scene in 'Love and Intrigue' with the Anspach mutiny in his mind. The priceless necklace presented to Lady Milford has been bought with blood-money. 'Yesterday,' says the Chamberlain, 'seven thousand of our boys started for America, and I have two sons among them. They pay for all this.' 'None of them were forced to go?' queries the favourite. 'My God, no,' cries the stricken father in bitter irony, 'they are all volunteers.' The most resounding protest was uttered by a foreign voice. In 1777 there appeared at Cleves an anonymous pamphlet entitled 'Avis aux Hessois et autres peuples de l'Allemagne, vendus par leurs Princes à l'Angleterre.' 'Will the brave Germans who defended their liberties against Rome now shed their blood in the interest of tyrants?' cried the author, who was none other than Mirabeau. The Landgrave of Hesse-Cassel bought up every copy of the stinging pamphlet on which he could lay hands, and issued a reply contending that it was his feudal right to sell his subjects. The anger of the people was increased by the knowledge that the blood-money was spent not on the needs of the State, but on the personal expenses of extravagant and degenerate rulers. But with indignation there was mingled another sentiment. As the surviving mercenaries drifted home, they brought stories of promise and opportunity, and Steuben wrote of the country where there were no kings or idle nobles, where all were happy and poverty was unknown.

Thus the lethargy which had weighed on Germany in the first half of the eighteenth century was passing rapidly away in the second. The personality and victories of Frederick the Great, the American War of Independence, the influence of Voltaire, Rousseau, and Montesquieu, the challenge of the *Aufklärung*, the radicalism of the dramatists, the arrows of Schlözer and Moser—these influences and experiences set the mind of the nation in a ferment. To borrow the words of Kant, written in 1784, it was not an enlightened age, but an age in process of enlightenment. Change was in the air, the fragility of traditional institutions and ideas widely recognised. 'The unconscious and largely innocent desire for ease and comfort which had followed the Seven Years' War was exhausted and had degenerated into slackness and sentimentality,' wrote Arndt in his Autobiography. 'In all directions, in social habits, art and science, theology and philosophy, there arose suddenly either new tendencies or the expectation of them. There was a new political as well as a new philosophical striving abroad, and it was felt with immense rapidity and liveliness in the tremblings and shakings which it brought from the cottage to the palace. Even in the narrow circle of our home, despite the conservative habits of my parents, this new epoch made its influence felt. Political interest grew from year to year. I, too, took my share, and for several years I had not only read the papers aloud, but also to myself.' If such was the case in backward Pomerania, far greater was the tension in the centres of thought and discussion. In Germany, as in France, prophetic voices gave warning of the wrath to come. 'Europe,' wrote Georg Forster, who had seen more of the world than any German of his time, 'is on the threshold of a terrible revolution. The mass is so corrupt that only the letting of blood can be effective.' 'Judging by every symptom,' pronounced Schubart in 1787, 'the political system of Europe is on the eve of a vast transformation.' 'I think it undesirable to marry,' wrote Johannes Müller to his brother in 1782, 'because, in the judgment of all great statesmen, Europe is preparing for revolutions; and on such occasions it is better only to have to look after oneself.' In Germany, as in France, men of insight required no instruments to inform them that the earth was trembling beneath their feet. For the former country, no less than the latter, the eighteenth century ended in 1789.

MIRABEAU'S *Secret Letters from Berlin*

I

MIRABEAU'S spectacular performances during the opening phases of the French Revolution have diverted attention from the fruitful decade of travel, study and authorship which went to the making of the ripe statesman of 1789. The scandals of his early years, his shameless immorality and measureless extravagance, the feuds with his parents and his wife, the long incarceration at Vincennes, had gained him an unenviable notoriety throughout Europe. Yet this dissolute aristocrat possessed some solid attractive qualities which made him a welcome guest wherever he went. A hard worker, an omnivorous reader, and a brilliant conversationalist, his boiling passions were strangely mated to a cool and critical mind, and the sincerity of his reforming zeal was never in doubt. With all his faults he was a better man than Talleyrand or de Retz. His heart was warmer, his spirit more generous, his political ambition more disinterested.

The elder Mirabeau, known and admired in many lands as *L'Ami des Hommes*, from the title of his most celebrated work, transmitted to his eldest son not only his dynamic temperament but his eager interest in public affairs. His mission in life, as he understood it, was to overthrow the prevailing heresy of Mercantilism with its doctrine of economic nationalism, and to establish the system of physiocracy formulated by Quesnay and himself, which proclaimed that a flourishing agriculture was the sole foundation of prosperity. In this field the precocious young man was to prove a loyal disciple, but, unlike his father, he also challenged the whole political structure of the *ancien régime*. His earliest treatise, *Essai sur le Despotisme*, published in Holland, the paradise of unlicensed printing, struck the note which was to echo through all the writings and speeches of his stormy life. 'A despotic state becomes a sort of menagerie of which the head is a fierce beast. The King is hired, and he who pays has the right to dismiss him who receives payment. If other Frenchmen have thought so before me, I am perhaps the first to say so in print.' He declined to be dazzled even by the rays of *Le Roi Soleil.* 'The long habit of command corrupted the prince, and the long habit of obedience corrupted the people.' What his country needed was a good constitution reconciling order with liberty. *Laissez l'homme libre!* was the core of his gospel. Even had he not been the outstanding figure of the Constituent Assembly he would have received honourable mention as one of the pioneers of constitutional government on the Continent.

Mirabeau's conviction that freedom in every sphere was the highest prize of man was strengthened by a visit to England in 1784, undertaken to escape a *lettre de cachet.* Through Gilbert Elliot, afterwards first Earl of Minto and Governor-General of India, who had been a school-fellow in Paris, he was introduced to the *élite* of Whig society. His closest contacts were with Lord Shelburne and the distinguished circle at Bowood and Lansdowne House. It says something for *Monsieur Ouragan* (Mr. Hurricane), as his father called him, that he won the respect of Romilly, a man of spotless character, and with Bentham the leading law reformer of his time. His hope of securing a footing in England at a time when he had made France too hot for him was disappointed, but his visit was not in vain. After eight busy months he recrossed the Channel confirmed in his belief that limited monarchy was the best type of government. 'Perfection is beyond our reach,' he wrote to Chamfort, 'but in England one finds much less that is bad than elsewhere.' Liberty, he believed, was more a tonic than a temptation. Adam Smith he found as much to his taste as the earlier writings of Burke, whom he visited at Beaconsfield. Political liberty, economic liberty, liberty of utterance, were the three main tests by which he assessed systems of government. From this lofty angle of vision he awarded high marks to England and Holland, low marks to France. What would he say to the Prussia of Frederick the Great, the classic land of the system which he loathed?

Mirabeau, like Voltaire, though for other reasons, had made himself impossible in France, and in January 1786, at the age of thirty-seven, he arrived in Berlin.[1] He was accompanied by what he called his *petite horde,* consisting of Mme de Nehra, the most reputable of his mistresses, his *'fils adoptif,'* Lucas de Montigny—his own son by an unknown mother—and his lttle dog. After his passion for Sophie Monnier had burned itself out he found rest and understanding in the

[1] The best accounts of Mirabeau's residence in Germany are in Loménie, *Les Mirabeau,* vol. iii, and Alfred Stern, *Das Leben Mirabeaus,* vol. i.

company of this patient and motherly Dutch lady. 'My poor Mirabeau,' she remarked, 'you have only one friend in the world and that is myself.' He recognised her worth and confessed that she was too good for him. To retain the affection of the most unstable of men for four years was something of a triumph. Crippled with debts and forced to earn his living, he had nothing but his pen and his boundless self-assurance to sustain him. His plan was to study the youngest of the Great Powers at close quarters, to watch the working of autocracy in a shape unknown in ill-governed France, to make the acquaintance of Frederick the Great, and if fortune smiled to enter his service. There was, moreover, just a chance that first-hand knowledge of Prussia at a time when the old king was visibly failing might be of use to the French Government and perhaps lead to the official or semi-official appointment which he craved. Rebel though he was on the moral and social plane, he longed to recover his footing and to play an active part in public life. 'Though the object of the journey is a secret,' reported the Austrian Ambassador to Kaunitz, 'it must soon be revealed.' There was no secret. Mirabeau felt that Berlin was safer than Paris and he had to earn his living. Though travelling as a private citizen he brought an introduction from Vergennes, the Foreign Minister, to Count d'Esterno, the colourless French Ambassador; but he had another string to his bow. Prince Henry of Prussia, he felt certain, would welcome him, for his acquaintance, the Marquis de Luchet, was attached to the little court at Rheinsberg.

How could he make a better start than by an interview with Frederick the Great, to whom he had paid homage in his *Essay on Despotism?* His name was a passport if not exactly a recommendation, and celebrities had never knocked at the door of the King in vain. Two days after his arrival he wrote to Potsdam. 'Sire, It is perhaps presumptuous to request an audience of Your Majesty when one has nothing to say of particular interest. But if you can pardon a Frenchman who from his birth has found the world filled with your name, the desire to see the greatest man of this and many other centuries at closer range than is usual with kings, you will deign to grant me the favour of paying my respects.' Frederick promptly replied that he would be glad to make his acquaintance, and gave him an appointment. The same day a parcel of books reached the palace and Count Görtz was instructed to thank him. 'I confess,' added the King, 'that I shall be very curious to know by what happy accident the traveller has found his way here and I shall be glad if you can tell me.' He also asked Formey, the Secretary of the Prussian Academy, to explore the motives of the journey. A few hours before the audience he wrote to his brother, Prince Henry: 'We have a M. de Mirabeau, whom I do not know. He is coming to me to-day. So far as I can judge, he is one of those effeminate satirists who write for and against everyone. It is said that this man is going to seek refuge in Russia where he will be able to launch his sarcasms against his country with impunity.' Though the King speaks of 'un M. de Mirabeau' he knew perfectly well who he was.

Frederick's obvious physical distress cut the conversation short, but the visitor was impressed by 'this extraordinary man, so superior even to his high station.' The meeting was followed up next day by a letter in which he came to the point. 'When Your Majesty asked me yesterday if I was going to St. Petersburg I replied: not yet. Two people were present and for personal reasons I do not want my movements to be noised abroad. Ill rewarded for my conspicuous services to France in the sphere of finance; compromised in my security and almost in my reputation by the present Minister [Calonne] because I would not mix myself up in his latest loan; obliged during my father's lifetime to earn my living; consumed by the desire to make myself regretted in France, I left it with the Sovereign's permission, but in the firm resolve only to return, so long as I was young and active, in order to inherit the considerable fortune my father will leave me. After satisfying the just curiosity which has led me to Berlin, where I shall probably await my brother who will ask leave to study the manoeuvres, I confess to you alone, Sire, my intention to seek employment in the country which most needs foreigners. So I shall make for Russia, though I should not choose that half-fledged nation and that savage country unless I thought that your government is too fully organised for me to flatter myself that I could be of use. To serve you, not to idle in the academies, would have been my chief ambition. But the storms of my early youth and the disappointments I have experienced in my country have too long diverted my thoughts from this fine plan, and I fear it is now too late. I owe you this confession, since Your Majesty showed some interest in my destination, but I beg you to keep it secret.' The reference to Russia was merely a rhetorical flourish, where Catherine the Great, in a letter to Grimm, declared that he deserved the esteem of Sodom and Gomorrah.

Frederick's reply to this offer of service was a courteous refusal, for what room was there for such a genius in a totalitarian state? 'You may rest assured that I shall keep your secret and that I shall always be interested in the fortunes of a man of your merit, wishing sincerely that they may realise your expectations. It is entirely for you to decide about staying in Berlin till the arrival of your brother, who desires my permission to be present at the manoeuvres. This plan is the more agreeable to me because I hope during this interval to have the pleasure of seeing you again.' No one with such blots on his scutcheon could have seriously expected employment from any foreign court, and the French Ambassador was in no way disposed to help him. Without the letter from Vergennes, wrote Count d'Esterno, he would not have presented the traveller: he had no apparent means of living and was certain to run into debt. He was accompanied by a woman whom he called Mme de Nehra and announced the arrival of a brother in the following spring. One Mirabeau was quite enough. 'I think he wishes to settle in Berlin in order to get his writings printed without interference. For that purpose he could not choose a better place, knowing that so long as no compliments are paid to the Court of Vienna, he can criticise with impunity God, the saints, and all the kings of the earth, including the King of Prussia.'

No assistance was needed to cross the threshold at Rheinsberg, where eminent Frenchmen were welcomed with open arms. It seemed particularly important to cultivate the man whom many people believed would play a leading part when the old King was gone. 'Prince Henry,' reported d'Esterno to his chief, 'began by being infatuated, but when he talked to me about him I took care not to sing his praises.' The Prince admitted that there was much to be said on both sides, but he was infinitely entertaining. 'He boasts to the Prince of the fifty-four *lettres de cachet* supposed to have been served on his family, and talks unceasingly of the horrible confusion in the finances of France; but it is easy to see that he will not find his feet at this court.' The King, he added, had received him very well, but had refused him a second audience, probably owing to unfavourable reports. Frederick indeed had remarked at table to one of his Ministers that he was very surprised at the reception accorded by Berlin to a man who had indulged in such criticisms. The Ambassador believed that publicity was desired for this observation and that the King had in mind an epigram on Prince Henry, who was beginning to tire of his visits to Rheinsberg, where Mirabeau, according to one witness, behaved as if he were a *habitué*.

The visitor had better luck in less exalted circles in Berlin. With the French Huguenots there was no difficulty. Dohm, a high official of the Foreign Office, describes in his memoirs the eagerness and open-mindedness of the distinguished Frenchman, his rapid progress in the language, his consummate skill in extracting information from men and books. While Dohm coached him in Prussian policy, Nicolai, editor of the *Allgemeine deutsche Bibliothek*, introduced him to the camp of the *Aufklärung*, of which Lessing and Moses Mendelssohn had been the brightest stars. Both were dead, but both received his homage. Kant he described as one of the greatest thinkers in Europe, though he often lost himself in abstruse speculations. With the young lions of the *Sturm und Drang* period he was as little in sympathy as the King. He was often to be seen in the crowded salon of Henriette Herz, who later declared that she had never heard such conversation. We are indebted to another Jewess, the incomparable Rahel, then a precocious girl of sixteen, for a vivid snapshot. 'He had dark, vivacious eyes, surmounted by thick eyebrows, and his face was pock-marked. He was squarely built but not stout. He made the impression of a man who had seen a great deal of life and mixed with many people. He was livelier than most of the aristocracy. Every movement indicated a man of energy who investigates everything for himself and wishes to get to the bottom of things. I knew nothing about him but I got a good impression, though he seemed elderly and was neither smart nor good-looking.' Even more vivid is the testimony of the woman who knew him best. 'When I first saw him,' writes Mme de Nehra, 'I started back with repulsion, but gradually I got used to his features and came to think them suited to his genius. His face was expressive, his mouth charming, his smile most attractive.' His father thought him as ugly as Satan, but the whole figure breathed dynamic energy, originality, and consciousness of power. There was no lack of invitations and he was frequently to be seen at Bellevue, the Berlin residence of Prince Ferdinand, youngest brother of the King. 'His reputation as a wit and his agreeable character,' writes his daughter Princess Louise, 'made everyone want him. My mother, however, was not fond of people who overawed her, and she indulged in bitter pleasantries at his expense which led to acrimonious discussions.' Yet study, not society, claimed most of his time. His scathing brochure on Cagliostro and Lavater, the charlatan and the enthusiast, was written and published at Berlin. It was designed as a warning to princes against the frauds and superstitions to which so many circles had succumbed. From these credulous rulers he excepts Frederick, 'who has rejected most of the playthings of human folly.'

After three crowded months in Berlin, where there was evidently no prospect of employment, Mirabeau decided to return to France. Explaining that his plans had changed owing to unforeseen circumstances and that his father was ill, he begged the King for a farewell audience. Frederick, though tormented by asthma and very near his end, consented. The conversation lasted an hour. The main topic was the position of the Jews, to whom the visitor was more favourably disposed than his host. He then passed to another theme. Why had not the Caesar of the Germans also been their Augustus? Why had he not associated himself with the glory of the literary revolution, fostering it with the flame of his genius and his power? That a literary revolution was taking place in Germany was news to the old man, who had recently revealed his ignorance in his little book *De la Littérature Allemande*. Mirabeau had wasted his time in Prussia as little as in England. His eloquent plea for a persecuted minority, *Moses Mendelssohn et la Réforme Politique des Juifs*, published in London in the following year, defended the gifted and unpopular race against its critics. If they had shown an excessive desire for money-making, they had very rarely sinned against the state. They should not be confined to commerce, but should be allowed to engage in agriculture and trade, and be treated with toleration, consideration and impartiality.

On his way home Mirabeau spent a few days in Brunswick. The celebrated Duke, whom he had hoped to see, was away, but he made the acquaintance of a man who was destined to be his collaborator in the chief literary enterprise of his life. Major Mauvillon, a friend of Dohm and the son of a French father, was an instructor in tactics, but he was far more than a soldier. As a student of economics, a champion of physiocracy, an opponent of standing armies, a believer in constitutional monarchy, freedom of utterance, and the friendly co-operation of nations, he instantly won the friendship and confidence of the brilliant French publicist, who found him a mine of information on Central Europe. How much they meant to each other during the following months is revealed in Mirabeau's *Lettres à Mauvillon*, published in 1792, the year after his death. The plan of a joint descriptive survey of the leading German states began to take shape before their eyes.

On reaching Paris in May 1786 the prodigal son went straight to Talleyrand, a man as ambitious and gifted as himself, no less immoral but more inclined to veil his sins. Condemned by his unloving father to an ecclesiastical instead of a military career on account of his lameness, *l'Abbé malgré lui*, as Sainte-Beuve calls him, resolved to exploit the rich possibilities of the Church. At the age of thirty-two he was the Abbé de Périgord and Agent-General of the Clergy, a post which brought him into contact with the Government; but he aspired to a bishopric and even dreamed of a cardinal's hat. His models were de Retz and Dubois, unprincipled adventurers who had used their orders as a stepping-stone to a political career, for the passions of his life were money and power. He had already introduced Mirabeau to Calonne, the Minister of Finance, for the calculating ecclesiastic believed that the partnership might yield useful results to them both. After hearing the traveller's impressions of Berlin he agreed that an observer, already intimate with Prince Henry and other high personages, might supply the French Government with information likely to prove valuable when the dying King closed his eyes. He had learned that Prince Henry desired a channel of communication to Paris. Could not the only person who possessed the necessary qualifications report to him, and could not he himself forward the despatches to the King and his Ministry with any necessary excisions and thus bring himself to their notice? There was also an unavowed motive which played a part in his advocacy of the mission. Talleyrand loved shady speculations, and a keen-sighted observer at Berlin might well give the greediest of men some useful hints. The Minister of Finance might be glad, for personal reasons, to muzzle a formidable critic who was also a financial expert; and perhaps he might find the money for the mission which he would persuade Vergennes, the Foreign Minister, to approve.

Before making his decision Calonne called for a report on the European situation, which was duly supplied and dated June 2, 1786. The King of Prussia, began Mirabeau, could not live another two months, and with him the keystone of European politics would collapse. Everything pointed to war. The turbulent megalomania of the Emperor Joseph portended trouble and discord. Frederick William, the heir to the Prussian throne, might be tempted to challenge him, for he had the best army in Europe and the best general (the Duke of Brunswick). The Prince distrusted France, and resented the attempt of the Dutch to diminish the authority of the Stadholder, the husband of his sister Wilhelmina. The English, encouraged by tales of France's financial embarrassment, were spoiling for a fight, for her weakness and misgovernment rendered her incapable either of keeping the peace or waging war. The cure should be sought in an alliance with England based on a commercial treaty, to which Prussia should accede, each power formally guaranteeing the possession of its partners. 'Is it not time,' he concluded, 'to restore our position abroad and to strengthen it at home?' It was a dark picture, but there was little exaggeration in the colouring and the memorandum produced the desired result. Calonne's consent was facilitated by Talleyrand's hint that in case of refusal a damaging attack on his financial administration might be launched: in Mirabeau's phrase, the Minister of Finance preferred to muzzle him. The expenses of the mission were defrayed, not by the Foreign Office, but by the Ministry of Finance. The reports, it was arranged, would pass through the hands of Talleyrand, who would edit them at his discretion.

Mirabeau left Paris on July 3, 1786, and stopped at Brunswick to see the Duke, at once a Francophil, one of the leading soldiers of Europe, and one of the model rulers in Germany, to whom Talleyrand had given him an introduction. The visitor counselled him to exert his influence at Berlin when the Prince of Prussia should ascend the throne, and the host's desire for an alliance between France, Prussia and England to guarantee their possessions evoked enthusiastic approval. Very different was his reception at the French Embassy at Berlin, where he was frigidly informed that the Ambassador was too busy to see him. A Hamburg paper had stated that he had been ordered out of France, but that was not the reason for the snub. Count d'Esterno, unaware that the mission was semi-official, resented the reappearance of a man whom he regarded as a shady adventurer. The King was now too ill to receive foreign visitors, but an invitation to Rheinsberg enabled the envoy to offer advice to Prince Henry. The only way to obtain influence over the future ruler, he argued, was to terminate his feud with Hertzberg, the Foreign Minister, whose position was too strong to challenge. Host and guest agreed that the future was unpromising. 'What do I anticipate?' wrote the latter to Talleyrand on August 15. 'Nothing but weakness and incoherence. It seems clear that little intrigues, the arts, the Illuminati will lead the new king. Has he a system? I do not think so. Intelligence? I doubt it. Character? I do not know enough to say.' On his return from Rheinsberg the envoy reported that even his host had no idea how his nephew would act. There would obviously be a struggle for power between Hertzberg, the champion of the English system, and Prince Henry, the ardent Francophil.

Mirabeau wrote nearly as well as he talked, and the letter on August 17, on the passing of the great King, contains a passage which has been quoted a hundred times. 'Tout est morne, rien n'est triste; tout est occupé, rien n'est affligé. Pas un visage qui n'annonce pas le délassement et l'espoir; pas un regret, pas un soupir, pas un éloge. Et c'est donc là qui s'aboutissait tant de batailles gagnées, tant de gloire, un règne de près d' un demi-siècle, rempli de tant de hauts faits! Tout le monde en désirait la fin, tout le monde s'en félicite.' Old General Möllendorf alone shed tears when he addressed the troops. 'We have lost the greatest of Kings, the first of heroes. I have lost my master and, if I may say so, my friend.' A subsequent letter added a few details of the last phase. 'His illness, which would have killed ten men, lasted eleven months without interruption and almost without respite. Nature only abandoned one of her finest creations after the total destruction of the organs worn out by age, the unceasing strife of mind and spirit for forty-six years, the fatigues and agitations of every kind.' The champion of limited monarchy found little to praise in the Prussian system, but for the unique personality of the last of the kings, as Carlyle describes him, he felt profound respect.

II

So long as Frederick the Great was on the throne, Mirabeau could only observe and report: now it seemed possible that he might have his chance. He had spent a good deal of time in composing a *Lettre à Frédéric Guillaume*, to be published on his accession. This blend of wisdom and phantasy is at once a scathing criticism of the

Frederician regime and a programme for the new ruler. Existing methods, declared the author, could not continue; the people was so dragooned that some alleviation was imperative; in the event of war the whole edifice would collapse; only drastic reforms could avert a catastrophe. The caste system should be scrapped, the peasant emancipated, the status of civil servants and officers equalised, the country schools improved. Foreign recruiting for the army should cease, and the term of service be shortened. A land tax should be substituted for monopolies, transit trade encouraged, hoarding of the precious metals cease, the censorship disappear. There were too many regulations and the individual should have more opportunity of following his tastes. The *Letter*, which has been described as the admonitions of a Physiocratic Posa, was a foretaste of the eight-volume treatise on the *Prussian Monarchy*, published two years later, and a partial anticipation of Wilhelm von Humboldt's celebrated treatise, *The Limits of State Action*. All three were denunciations of the *fureur de gouverner*. In the field of foreign affairs the ruler was adjured to make Prince Henry his adviser and to confine Hertzberg to the home front. The author sent a copy to the King, who discreetly replied that anything from his pen would always give him pleasure.

Frederick William II, the most unworthy of Hohenzollern rulers, who ascended the throne at the ripe age of forty-two, inherited something both of the charm and the futility of his father, August Wilhelm. Becoming heir to the throne at the age of fourteen, he seemed to make a good start, for he had nothing of the severity of his terrifying uncle, and liked to see happy faces round him. But the years of adolescence revealed his tragic insufficiency: his sensuality was a public scandal, his indolence notorious. Frederick thought with horror of the time when his unworthy nephew, surrounded by his favourites and mistresses, would in all probability tear down a large part of his work. No serious tasks were allotted to him, for he was incapable of fulfilling them. His congenital laziness increased as he became enormously fat. Except for his competent performances on the violoncello, he had no cultivated tastes. His first marriage was dissolved, and he soon parted company with his second wife. The earliest and greediest *maîtresse en titre*, Wilhelmine Encke, married to a minor functionary of the name of Rietz and in due course promoted Countess Lichtenau, retained her pernicious influence even when first the Voss and after her death the Dönhoff became the most favoured beauty. Such was the man whose failings were to be realistically described in Mirabeau's three score despatches during the first five months of his inglorious reign.[1]

After less than three weeks of the new order the envoy despatched an incisive analysis of the atmospheric change. 'Frederick II, whom nature had fashioned for command, who believed himself the universal soul of the world and only credited others with some sort of sensibility, a certain animal instinct, was never afraid of seeming to be led. He knew he was not, whereas the present king trembles at the thought and cannot escape his fate. While things run by themselves he will not seem to be led; nothing is easier in this country than to receive and to spend, for the machine is so arranged as to favour abuse. With some modifications in detail, some surveillance of the police, certain changes among subordinates, a few blandishments to the nation, it will go by itself. But at the first roar of the guns, indeed at the first storm, how it will collapse, all this petty scaffolding of mediocrity! How the lesser ministers will shrink in stature! How everyone, from the frightened convicts up to the distracted chief, will call for a pilot! And who will he be? The Duke of Brunswick? I think so; because *amour-propre* no longer avails in the hour of danger; because he does not care for outward appearances; because he will be the servant of the servants, the most polite, the most humble and certainly the most adroit of courtiers, while at the same time his iron hand will keep all the little views, all the intrigues, all the parties under control. There is my horoscope, the best I can make to-day.' Meanwhile, till an emergency arose, Hertzberg was the man to cultivate—a task beyond the French Ambassador, who had neglected him in the past. The notes struck in these early despatches were to be repeated again and again in the winter months. The Duke of Brunswick alone receives full marks. Prince Henry, despite his faults, might be useful if his services were requested, but such a prospect was remote. Hertzberg was the most formidable obstacle to a rapprochement with France, but he could not be overthrown by direct assault. It was not a pretty picture, but not even a flatterer could have made much of the Prussia of Frederick William II.

[1] The fullest surveys of the reign are by Heigel, *Deutsche Geschichte 1786–1815*, vol. i, and Philippson, *Geschichte des Preussischen Staatswesens*.

Without some official recognition Mirabeau could do little but report on the king's mistresses and comment on public affairs. His letters breathe a sense of exasperated frustration. 'This prince is very difficult to study with success,' he complained. 'He is a stickler for German etiquette. People think he will not see foreigners at present. I know what can be learned from the petty espionage of valets, courtiers, secretaries and the indiscretions of Prince Henry. But there are only two ways of gaining influence—giving or rather suggesting ideas either to the master or to his ministers. To the master? But how, if one cannot approach him? To the ministers? It is neither easy nor appropriate to talk politics with them when one is not accredited, and casual conversations are brief and vague. If I am deemed useful I should be accredited; otherwise I fear I shall cost more than I earn.' Voltaire had had the same experience in 1743, when Frederick declined to do business except with a recognised spokesman of the French Government. His appeal produced compliments, but nothing more. An appreciative letter from Talleyrand declared that Calonne and Vergennes were pleased with the letters and wished them to continue: no official instructions were needed, for an envoy knew best what was useful to see and report. He had performed his task extremely well so far and should remain strictly incognito. To watch the performance from the wings, however, could never satisfy a man of genius. 'I will try to follow things,' he rejoined, 'but so long as I have no status and am thought out of touch with France, I shall be more fitted to write about literature. If I am to start as a junior in the diplomatic service I might be just as useful in Hamburg; for, independently of its great commercial connections, of which we are ignorant and in which our share is too small, we need a good look-out.'

Mirabeau's realistic pictures of the Prussian Court are in no way overdrawn, for confusion reigned in the royal household. 'No master, no manager, no financial assignments; the servants and the functionaries are in control. It is impossible to exaggerate the turpitude, the disorder, the waste of time. The servants are afraid of his violence, but they are the first to mock his incapacity. Not a paper is in its place, not a memorandum annotated, not a letter personally opened; no power on earth can make him read forty consecutive lines. Only his illegitimate son stirs him from his lethargy. He adores the child, beams when he sees him, and spends a large part of the mornings with him. He is regular only in his pleasures. *Pauvre règne! Pauvre pays!* I have two convictions. The first is that he has planned to become a great man by making himself purely German and snapping his fingers at French models. The second is that he is inwardly resigned to leaving affairs to a principal minister, perhaps muttering under his breath: 'Well! I might do worse than summon the Duke of Brunswick or my uncle!' The first of these notions emanates from Hertzberg, who says: 'There is only one way for you to be somebody, and that is to give a lead to your nation, which should date a new kind of glory from your reign. This you can only do by placing yourself at its head. What could you ever be as a Frenchman? A feeble imitation of Frederick II. As a German you will be original, revered in Germany, adored by your people, extolled by men of letters, an object of consideration in Europe.' This line of argument seems to Hertzberg a short cut to becoming principal minister, but the situation demands or will soon demand someone else. This country, though servile, is not inclined to grovel before a minister; and Hertzberg, long subordinate, more astute than clever, more false than shrewd, more violent than peremptory, more vain than ambitious, old, infirm, and not counting on a long innings, could not break them in. They need this Wöllner, so much in favour to-day that no outsider knows the full range of his influence. What is required is a dominating personality. Such men are rare: I only see two of the necessary stature, Prince Henry and the Duke of Brunswick. In addition to the disadvantage of absence, the latter appears formidable to a prince who is not only weak and indolent, but vain and jealous. So Prince Henry's stock is rising despite his *faux pas*.'

It must have cost the proud Frenchman a pang to go on his knees to the cynical Talleyrand. 'Is it really worth while, *mon très cher maître*, to sacrifice to such a minor interest as curiosity my time, my tastes, my talents? You know I am not a charlatan; you know it is not my way to exaggerate my difficulties and labours. Well, I swear they are not few. I employ three men in copying my writings. I utilise the work and knowledge of several others; all my time and nearly all my thoughts are centred on it. If there is not more to show for it (and you cannot yet assess it because my largest works remain in my portfolio), it is the fault either of my insufficiency or my position or of both—perhaps only of the latter. Anyhow, I am immersed in it, and at nearly thirty-seven I ought not to wear myself out in trifles. For trifles they are if it leads to nothing for myself or others. If I am wrong, prove it. In my position I require some encouragement. Forgive me if I have gone too far. But to whom shall I confide my anxieties if not to you, my friend, my consoler, my guide, my support? To whom shall I say: What am I getting out of all this? Not even money, for it all goes to the cause, none to my personal satisfaction. I should want nothing more if my future were assured. You know that money will never be anything to me, at least when I have some. But where am I going, and where am I leading others? Have I made a good bargain to barter my life, stormy though it was, but not without its delights, for a sterile activity which deprives me of your society? You are for me more than a statesman; you for whose handshake I would give all the thrones in the world! Ah! I am much more fitted for friendship than for politics.' What he really thought of his cold-blooded correspondent we learn from a letter to another friend. 'My misfortunes have delivered me into his hands, and I must steer my course carefully with this vile, greedy, low intriguer who loves mud and money. For money he would sell his soul, and he would be right to do so, for he would be exchanging dung for gold.' Perhaps this celebrated outburst need not be taken too literally, for the writer was a man of moods.

On November 7 the envoy suggested a time limit for the task of which he was utterly weary. 'Do they think I cost too much? My dear master, they have only two alternatives—to recall me or to place me. I am quite ready for the first. As for the second, it is not my fault if it has not occurred to them that a man in the right place would save them the salary of a *fainéant* (Comte d'Esterno) and of a supervisor (himself) who does his work. If the Government is not inclined to decide my fate before the middle of December, I ask it to pay my debts here and to send money for my journey home. One must be something or nothing. Something—that is your affair: nothing—that is mine. What shall I do here on the present footing except run up debts which will close all doors, deprive me of all consideration, cause me the most cruel embarrassments? I beg you to show this letter. It cannot go on, I cannot and will not suffer. My past career was sown with pitfalls, but for that I think the Government can accuse my father and itself more than me. If I am considered useful, perhaps my reputation is my testimonial. What others request as a favour I claim as a right. In a word, I am better born than most of the King's ministers, and as to my capacity you can judge for yourself. I do not see that it should be difficult to find me a place. This is my last word.'

Meanwhile he continued his lively reports on the deepening confusion. 'Letters are not despatched, a room is filled with unopened packets, everything is in arrears, everything is slipping back.' Wöllner, who lacked neither ability nor knowledge, controlled home affairs; the chronic disorder of the accounts, plus the distrust of the financial officials, must have impelled the King to entrust himself to a man whose obscurity was a recommendation. 'I say the chronic disorder because Frederick William I, the founder of nearly all the domestic institutions, which his son scarcely changed, had of set purpose no general budget, since he alone knew everything and wished none of his ministers to guess that he made incomplete and inaccurate accounts. So Frederick II, who never understood finance, but was well aware that money was the foundation of power, confined himself to saving, and he was so sure of large surpluses that he contented himself with inadequate accounts. Anyhow, that version seems more probable than the imputation of having burned the tables of receipts and expenditure in order to embarrass his successor. The latter rightly wishes to get them straight, but it is like cleaning the stables of Augeas, and I cannot detect any Hercules in his entourage. *Pourriture avant maturité!* I fear that may be the motto of Prussia.'

Here is the most elaborate of the many sketches of Frederick William II to be found in this scintillating correspondence. 'You may say that three elements form his character: falsity, which he believes to be cleverness; an *amour-propre*, which bristles at the slightest incident; the love of money, which is not so much avarice as the passion to possess. The first of these vices makes him mistrustful, for systematic deceivers always believe they are being tricked. The second leads him to prefer mediocrities of low birth. The third tends to make him lead an obscure and solitary life. Violent in his domestic circle, impenetrable in public, fundamentally caring little for glory and seeking it mainly in not seeming to be governed, seldom occupied with foreign policy, a soldier by necessity, not by taste; leaning to the spiritualists, not from conviction but as a means to penetrate consciences and to sound hearts.' The money accumulated and reserved by the late king for military purposes was used to pay his successor's debts. 'People say that he has estranged the bourgeoisie since his return from his coronation at Königsberg; the army since the first day of his reign; the General Directory by ignoring it; his family by courtesy without confidence; the clergy by the project of a third marriage; the functionaries by the suppression of the tobacco *régie*; the court by the confusion of the accounts.' A scathing survey of ministers and courtiers completes the sombre picture of a country in galloping decline.

The final comments from Berlin are more pungent than ever. 'At first the public were astonished to see the King faithful to the comedy, to the concert, to his old mistress, to the new, finding time to look at prints, furniture, shops, to play the 'cello, to hear about the bickerings of the Court ladies, and snatching a few minutes to listen to ministers on affairs of state. To-day they are astonished if some new folly or some sinful habit has not filled the whole of the day.' His duties as a soldier bored him. 'He goes to Potsdam, witnesses the parade, gives the word of command, dines and is off again. And that is what happens in the same house where Frederick II, full of years and glory, used to spend two hours in the depth of winter, exercising, thundering, grumbling, praising, in a word, keeping harassed troops in perpetual activity but delighted to see 'the old man,' as they called him, at their head. With a thousand louis one could learn every secret of the Cabinet. The papers lying on the King's table could be read and copied by two clerks, four valets, six or eight lackeys, two pages, without counting the women. The Emperor gets a faithful record of all his doings, day by day, and would know of his plans if he had any. Never did a kingdom display more signs of speedy decadence. It is being sapped and mined from all sides. The revenue is falling; expenses are increasing; principles are ignored; the army is let down; the few competent men are discouraged; able foreigners are removed. The King surrounds himself with the *canaille* so as to seem to be sole ruler, and this fatal mania is the cause of all present and future troubles. If I remained here ten years I could report fresh details but no new result. The man is judged, so are his connections, so is the system. No change, no improvement is possible so long as there is no chief minister. When I say no change, that does not mean that individuals will not come and go. Sand will succeed to sand so long as piles are not dug to form a base.'

What could this brilliant special correspondent accomplish in such a benighted country? 'Nothing useful; only some paramount interest could induce me to tolerate this odious amphibious existence if further prolonged. Once again, what I deserve, what I am, what I am worth, should now be known to the King and his ministers. If I am worth nothing, I cost him too much; if I am worth something, nine months of most trying subordination, in which I have met thousands of obstacles and not a single helping hand, have gained me some knowledge of men, some insight, some wisdom, without counting the treasures in my portfolio. I owe it to myself to request and to obtain a place or to resume my trade as citizen of the world, which will be less fatiguing to body and mind and less sterile for my fame. So I declare plainly, or rather I repeat, that I cannot stay here, and I beg for formal permission for my return, whether or no there are plans for my services elsewhere. I shall not decline any kind of useful occupation. My heart is still young, and if my enthusiasm has waned it is not extinct. What I have experienced to-day I regard as one of the best days of my life—your news of the Convocation of the Notables, which will doubtless form the prologue to that of the National Assembly. I foresee a new order which may regenerate the Monarchy. I should deem myself really honoured to be the humblest secretary of this Assembly, the idea of which I have had the honour to supply, and which needs you as a member or rather as its soul. But to stay here, condemned to be a beast of burden, to sound and to stir the muddy depths of a Government which marks each day by a new exhibition of cowardice and blundering: that I can stand no longer because it has no purpose.' The last letter, written on January 19, 1787, the day of his departure, recorded the latest gifts showered on 'the favourite Sultana' by the infatuated King. No longer was the promise of paid employment by the French Government a condition of departure. The time had come when he must shake the dust of Berlin off his feet.

Returning to Paris at the end of January 1787, Mirabeau burned to play his part in the Assembly of Notables which met on February 22. When Calonne was forced by the financial situation to summon it, his disastrous official career was over. His former agent rejoiced at his downfall for personal as well as national reasons, for he deeply resented the ingratitude for his services at Berlin. His *Dénonciation de l'Agiotage* was admired by the King and read by all the reformers, but it was so outspoken that he was warned of the danger of arrest and advised to cross the frontier once again. In May he was back in Berlin, putting the finishing touches on *La Monarchie Prussienne,* and returned in September to Paris, where a double disappointment awaited him. His request for a diplomatic post was contemptuously ignored and permission to publish his comprehensive survey in France was refused. When the eight volumes appeared in London in 1788 they ruined the publisher Le Jay and brought no profit to the needy author. These experiences help to explain, if not to justify, a new attempt to turn his handiwork in Berlin to account.

The author of scores of sparkling despatches was aware that they were too good to be buried in the archives of the French Foreign Office and that their publication would help to fill his empty pockets. Accordingly, without asking permission to reveal confidential documents which he knew would be refused, he published his *Histoire Secrète de la Cour de Berlin* in two volumes at Alençon in January 1789. It was in vain that the sub-title pretended that it was the work of an anonymous writer who, according to the preface, had died in some remote German village in 1788. It was equally futile that he formally and repeatedly, publicly and privately, denied his authorship when he was charged with the offence. Everybody was aware that it could have been written by nobody else. That he had been an envoy of the French Government was a state secret, but that he had spent many months in Berlin was known to all the world. Four editions were exhausted in 1789 and a German translation appeared at Cologne. A sixth edition was published in 1793 and the *Letters* were included in his collected works in 1821. All these versions were incomplete and not till 1900 did they appear as they were written, admirably edited by Henri Welschinger under the title *La Mission Secrète de Mirabeau à Berlin 1786–1787.* There was something for all tastes in the dishes served up by the most brilliant political *chef* of the age—scandal in plenty, full-length portraits of celebrities, useful statistical information, thoughtful discussion of current international issues, and above all an ideology which appealed to a rapidly growing number of reforming Frenchmen of all classes. An attack on absolute monarchy—in a neighbouring country—at the opening of 1789 was excellently timed. Discerning readers realised that a treasure had been cast up on the shore. 'Tout Mirabeau et Mirabeau supérieur,' wrote Chateaubriand long afterwards on the eve of taking up the post of French Minister at Berlin, 'est dans cette correspondance diplomatique; l'avenir de l'Europe y est à chaque ligne.'

The French Government, gravely embarrassed by the publication of this scathing exposure of the ruler of a friendly state, conveyed its regrets to Berlin and ordered the book to be publicly burned. That the author was not molested was doubtless due to his growing popularity and to the fear of compromising revelations in a public trial. Never, explained the Foreign Minister to the Prussian Ambassador, had the King and his Council been so anxious to close the affair by a *lettre de cachet*, but in the existing ferment of opinion it was impossible. Moreover, though not free from exaggeration, it was in no real sense a libel, for Europe had long taken the measure of the successor of Frederick the Great. Finally, France had no cause to love Prussia, who had twice let her ally down in the first two Silesian conflicts and had been her enemy in the third.

The frowns of Paris were nothing to the storm aroused at Berlin. Though the King had almost forgotten how to blush, he was furious at the public washing of his dirty linen and exclaimed: 'That is how Frenchmen behave when they travel in my dominions.' It was still worse for Prince Henry. Whereas Mirabeau had only exchanged a few trivial words with Frederick William II, he had often enjoyed the hospitality of his uncle, who by an unfortunate coincidence was paying his second visit to Paris at the moment the book appeared. The Marquis de Luchet, his *homme de confiance*, timidly announced the publication of a work containing insolent references to his master. 'Why worry?' was the reply. 'If what he says of me is true, he only anticipates the historian and I have no right to grumble. If it is false, history will do me justice. Go and buy sixteen copies at once.' The copies were presented to friends with the injunction to decide if the portrait resembled the original. Whether Prince Henry, one of the vainest of men, was quite so philosophic we may doubt, and his explanation of the attack, if correctly reported to Thiébault, whom he had known during his long residence at Berlin, is unconvincing. 'I will tell you how I incurred his displeasure. You saw how my brother's health was failing, and I felt that his death might be followed by very dangerous intrigues, particularly at Berlin. I believed that France alone could help. But the worthy Count d'Esterno did not seem to me to possess the character or activity needed for the situation, and therefore, despite my liking and esteem for him, I wrote to some friends in France urging the despatch of someone of greater energy and resource. My letter was forwarded to M. de Calonne, who chose M. de Mirabeau, and instructed him to do nothing except in concert with myself. I knew his talents but I also knew his morality. I disapproved the selection and resolved to be careful. He came to me whenever he could and I received him politely. He told me his views in flattering letters, and I responded with compliments but without letters. He never obtained my signature nor a note in my hand. He was far too clever not to recognise that he did not possess my confidence; and I understood that he wanted above all to procure some letters or notes from me, though I do not know for what purpose. His failure to get them explains my ill-treatment at his hands.'

Next to the King and Prince Henry the chief victim was the Foreign Minister. 'As regards Mirabeau's *Secret Letters*,' wrote Hertzberg, 'I confess that I cannot ignore the fact that this ill-natured and ungrateful man, to whom I showed every respect and consideration, tries to blacken my character.' It was all the more painful, he complained, since his public and private character had always stood high, and no honest and impartial person had ever charged him with falsehood and deceit. 'What he says of me is all a scandalous invention, except that I am not a slave of France, that I wish to be not a French or English but solely a Prussian Minister, and that I have stoutly maintained the system I think the best for my country. I shall not treat the work with silent contempt, as most people advise, but shall expose its untruths in a short article.' Mirabeau, he declared, was even worse than Procopius or Aretino. That the book swarms with errors was pointed out by Baron Trenck, the ill-fated friend of Princess Amelia, in a *brochure* which denounces 'the Paris charlatan' and pleads for a milder verdict on the worst and weakest of Prussia's kings. Moreover the opening of the archives and the revelation of his eager interest in foreign affairs led Ranke to pronounce the picture of a *roi fainéant* a mere caricature. Yet even the faults of ignorance and credulity cannot wholly destroy its value both as a snapshot of the country in decline under Frederick William II, and as a sparkling revelation of the temperament and ideology of one of the greatest Frenchmen of his time.

MIRABEAU ON THE PRUSSIAN MONARCHY

IN the interval between Mirabeau's return from Berlin in January 1787 and the publication of the *Secret Letters* in January 1789 his main task was the compilation of his most ambitious work, *De la Monarchie Prussienne sous Frédéric le Grand*, published in London in 1788 simultaneously in four quarto and eight octavo volumes. The friendly association with Talleyrand was over and once again he had to live by his pen. 'My position, thanks to the infamous conduct of the Abbé de Périgord, has become intolerable,' he confided to a friend. What provoked this outburst we cannot tell. The revolution was soon to bring them together again, and the younger man visited the great tribune on his death-bed.

The plan, the structure and the ideology of the book belonged to Mirabeau, but the major part of the preparation and the composition was the work of Mauvillon. 'The germ is exclusively the child of his brain,' writes the latter in the modest preface to the collection of letters published by him after his employer's death; 'it is the pure fruit of his genius. He cast it into the soul of his friend who would never have thought of it and would never have accomplished such a task. The Count did more. After he had nourished, enlarged and given birth to the germ, he, like a true father, cared for its education, adjusted some healthy but dislocated limb, removed some wens and stains, and decked it out to appear to advantage in the world. Thus it is evident that he has large rights in the work although he did not make it, and that he has reason to claim the merit.' Mirabeau, he declared, had placed a pen in his hand, but his services were none the less warmly appreciated. 'You will be delighted to see *our work* again,' he wrote in May 1788, 'since you wish me to call it so, a little revised and touched up.'

The survey had been almost completed during three busy months at Brunswick in the summer of 1787, and only finishing touches were required. Both men were rapid workers, and Mirabeau was spurred on by the urgent need of money. 'Hasten more than ever the completion of your great work,' he wrote, 'which will secure either our fame or our fortune, for if it is printed it shall bear our names.' He described the partnership as a marriage of souls, and it is one of the many blots on his character that this promise was ignored. The good Brunswicker was far more than a mere journeyman, and indeed some sentences in the correspondence reveal that certain purple passages which give the book its main interest were drafted by his hand. The military sections were exclusively the work of the professional soldier, the elaborate statistical and technical surveys hardly less. Mirabeau's voice, on the other hand, is clearly audible in the Introduction, the equally comprehensive Conclusion, and the sections devoted to religion and the fiscal system. Mauvillon appears to have been quite content to play second fiddle to 'the most attractive of men, who can make one think, believe, say, and do exactly what he wishes.' Mirabeau was proud of his work. 'I should die unhappy,' he wrote to his colleague, 'if this monument were not placed on my tomb.' No one read it with greater satisfaction than his reconciled father, the old Marquis, then in his last year, who found little to disapprove except its denunciations of the influence of the Church.

The dedication to his father, dated August 19, 1788, explains that the author had not sought his permission, fearing that it might be refused. He had, however, no alternative but to pay homage to *L'Ami des Hommes*. 'I did not dare to offer you my early essays, and I waited till I could present a work illustrating all the truths associated with your name. There you will find their most complete and irrefutable demonstration. The further I advanced the more I felt that it was right to dedicate it to you; both to one of the most distinguished authors or rather to one of the founders of that noble science of political economy which should one day make the world happy, and also to compensate in some small measure by this honourable employment of my riper years for the trouble I caused you by my turbulent youth. You cannot be indifferent to the fact that I am becoming really useful.' He felt inordinately proud of himself, as he confessed to Mme de Nehra. 'When this work appears I shall only be thirty-eight. I venture to predict that it will make my name, and perhaps my country will regret that it has not employed an observer of such calibre or rewarded his labours.'

The Preface explains the practical and didactic nature of the massive treatise. A true history of Frederick II, which some people believed him to be writing, was impossible while nearly all the actors were still alive. What mattered was to understand his political and economic system, his army, his laws, and the situation in which he left his land. The value of 'this great work' was enhanced by the abilities of his collaborator Mauvillon, by the wealth of material, by oral discussions with eminent Prussians. His admiration for 'the most astonishing man who had ever worn a crown' would not influence his judgment, for the greatest of mortals are subject to ignorance and errors. If the reader complained that there were too many details the author would reply that these were essential to his purpose of studying a country in all its aspects, particularly in the case of a totalitarian state. Even though many officials were moved by the purest motives, their inquisitorial activity, their desire to 'trop gouverner,' was none the less a grave evil. 'When rulers learn wisdom they will only have two tasks—to preserve peace by a good system of national defence, and to maintain internal order by an impartial and inflexible system of justice. Everything else will be left to private enterprise, which in securing the maximum satisfaction for each citizen will infallibly produce the greatest measure of public happiness.'

How was the truth of this doctrine of *laissez-faire*, of leaving the maximum freedom to industry and reducing the functions of government to a minimum, to be proved, and how could the fallacies of the rival system be exposed? Only by a thorough examination of the state with the most absolute government, continually occupied with supervision and regimentation. In this way the book would serve as a guide to statesmen visiting any other land. If similar investigations should be made elsewhere, Europe would become a familiar subject within ten years; every country would become aware of its own maladies, advantages and resources, and good citizens would propose suitable remedies. Governments could find such inquirers if they wished, and their combined surveys would cost less than the production of a couple of new operas. A treatise on England would have been far easier, more colourful, and of wider appeal. Yet without renouncing this tempting project, he thought it best to begin with a task for which fewer Frenchmen were qualified in view of the prevailing ignorance of the German language and German affairs. It was a wise decision. Of French works on England there was no lack, while Germany remained to the ordinary Frenchman an unknown land.

The First Book, entitled *General Considerations on the Rise of the House of Brandenburg,* fills half a volume. Mirabeau, like Frederick in his history of the dynasty, only gets into his stride with the Great Elector, 'one of the greatest men who ever reigned,' and from whose career certain maxims of government could be learned. The first lesson of his life, suggested by his sojourn in Holland, is that the best way of educating a prince is to send him abroad, above all to a free country, under the supervision of a man of honour. If he makes good without such training, it is mere luck. It is asking too much to expect success from an heir educated at his own Court, where he cannot learn sound principles. Women, courtiers and flunkeys will corrupt him despite the utmost vigilance, and he will become an old man while still in his infancy. A second lesson of the reign is derived from the admission of the persecuted Huguenots, a decision as wise as it was humane. Not content with registering the utility of this particular decision, Mirabeau pleads for the general adoption of the open frontier. 'If it is disgraceful to prevent people leaving a country, it is unjust and cruel to close the door in their face. You men of influence, do not go out to look for them; let them all come along, give them moderate encouragement without injuring your old subjects, that is enough. But when religious fury compels part of the population of a neighbour state to flee, prudence suggests and humanity demands that you invite them. They are not vagabonds, prevented by illness and misconduct from earning their living at home; they are probably honest, industrious, loyal, decent folk. That is usually the case with persecuted sectaries, either because only an exemplary life brings credit to their sect, or because the more disorderly desert to the dominant party. Except, however, for religious or political persecution, you will only attract a large number of useful citizens by the spectacle of a government wiser and more prosperous than their own. Remove excessive and unwise taxes and prohibitions, spend money on useful undertakings such as canals, emancipate serfs, abolish forced labour, and you will soon obtain the population you desire both in numbers and quality.'

Returning from these wider generalisations to the Huguenot immigration of 1685, the author notes two further results, the one favourable, the other on balance the reverse. The first was the introduction of the French language and the cultural enrichment which it brought. The second was that the rapid increase of manufactures and revenue resulting from the skill of the immigrants dazzled the rulers and diverted their attention from the soil. 'They resembled people who, after a run of luck at the gaming table or in a lottery, exchange useful labour for the benefits of chance. The sudden increase of their resources from more active commerce and a wider range of manufactures led them to believe that they were the sole roads to fortune. Such success is derived, not from the natural order of things, but from a combination of very exceptional circumstances. For who could imagine that the neighbour of countries exhausted by a thirty years' war would have a sovereign crazy enough to force his industrious subjects to go and repair those calamities in order to escape from his tyranny? The German princes, so far from appreciating this truth, believed that their patronage could produce similar results. Henceforth agriculture was for them a secondary object, subordinated to the wizardry of manufactures and commerce.' Here Mirabeau is exaggerating, for in Prussia at any rate agriculture received just as much consideration as before the arrival of the Huguenots with their profitable ways. No one realised more fully than Frederick William I and his greater son the necessity of extracting the last ounce of produce from the ungrateful soil of their country. The Physiocrats, of whom the joint authors were the last in their respective states, were as narrow and one-sided as the Mercantilists whom they strove to dethrone.

After a perfunctory notice of the first two Prussian Kings, Mirabeau reaches Frederick II, whom he had visited in his closing days. The belief that he had no heart is flatly rejected. 'Never was such expression, such enchanting tones of voice, such lively imagination mated to an insensitive soul; the harshness attributed to this great man is perhaps one of the finest triumphs of his genius over his nature.' The rape of Silesia was as just as wars and conquests can ever be. The Seven Years' War was undertaken *malgré lui*; convinced, though perhaps mistakenly, that war was inevitable, he decided to strike the first blow. 'Never, it must be confessed, was there a juster war. His existence was at stake.' Equally lenient is the verdict on the Partition of Poland. 'We offer no philosophic judgment on this strange usurpation. It is impossible to justify these alliances, these partition treaties which bring to Europe the peace of servitude, and which can dispose of the liberty, the property and the lives of men at the whim of certain despots. But, to be fair to Frederick, we must remember that he would perhaps never have thought of this acquisition unless he had been dragged into it by the ambition of the two Imperial Courts. He preferred a share in the spoils (though his portion benefited, having nothing to lose) to a war with two formidable powers. Only ignorance of the human heart and perhaps of the duties of kings would too severely condemn him for not pursuing a more generous course.' The War of the Bavarian Succession is declared to need no apology, for Frederick merely decided to preserve the *status quo*, and the German sovereigns were grateful for his noble intervention on behalf of their liberties. If the Fürstenbund, which had the same object, could be left in being, perhaps they would be able to save their liberties, their independence, their existence once again from the undying ambition of the House of Austria. 'Perhaps this ancient and tottering edifice of the Germanic Constitution will survive amidst its ruins. Its preservation cannot appear unimportant for the tranquillity of Europe and even for the happiness of mankind except to those who do not know the country.' This attack on Vienna illustrates the fact that the Franco-Austrian alliance laboriously constructed in 1756 had ceased to count. In Mirabeau's eyes even the Holy Roman Empire seemed preferable to the heavy hand of the Hapsburgs.

Passing from foreign affairs the writer proceeds to discuss the leading features of the Frederician system. The great King had been admired, almost adored, by his contemporaries for his proficiency in the art of government; indeed he seemed to have become for the science of autocracy what Egypt had once been for seekers after wisdom. From its study it might be possible to conclude whether for instance the sole cause of the evil conditions in Turkey was the ineptitude of the ruler. The foundations of power, as Frederick realised, were the army and agriculture. The former he understood thoroughly, the latter only partially. His good intentions were largely frustrated by a mass of laws and proceedings, some inherited from previous rulers, some imposed by himself. The large-scale agriculture practised on the royal domains and the great estates was far less important than the labours of the peasant proprietor. Yet throughout Germany as in most parts of Prussia the peasant was the serf; even when legally free, his tenure was precarious. 'Frederick knew that property and liberty were essential to good agriculture. He could of course have compelled all the great landowners to emancipate their serfs, but he had no desire to upset the nobility on whom he depended for his officers. Nevertheless he strove to improve their lot in several ways and to extend their privileges as well as by furnishing practical aid in difficult times.'

If agriculture in Prussia was too little favoured, too much was done for industry. 'Frederick was obsessed by the financial fallacy, the source of so many evils, that articles must be manufactured in one's own country so far as possible—itself a branch of that other senseless system which desires that every nation should have a favourable balance of trade in order to increase or maintain its store of precious metals.' Of the true principles of commerce, namely the maximum exchange of goods, he was wholly ignorant, faithful to the fallacy of self-sufficiency practised by his predecessors from the Great Elector onwards. The best of his ventures was the establishment of the silk industry. The rivers and canals should have been more fully utilised for transit trade and the system of tolls suppressed. The worst feature was the excise, administered by French officials, so hated by the people and so meagre in its yield. On this latter topic the fiery apostle of Physiocracy lets himself go. 'Such is the excise, a devouring lion, insatiable. No truce with it! Either it or the state must perish. All ages, all countries, all climates have witnessed the same evils. They have always become judges in their own cause, open oppressors of humanity, destroyers of morality, professional robbers of the state.' Almost equally deporable was the King's passion for monopolistic commercial companies.

Reared on such flimsy economic foundations, argues Mirabeau, Prussia was not nearly so strong as she appeared, and the vast edifice of power constructed by Frederick might topple over at the first blast. Wiser counsels would permit of a larger and more stable population, since its existence would not depend on artificial and precarious factors. Agriculture, commerce, industry, revenue would increase. The state, strengthened by its own bulk, could sustain the torpor of a weak and indolent King, the profusion of a vain and ostentatious ruler, the blows of fortune which might sometimes occur. In a word the King of Prussia would not be the only rich man in his kingdom, and his ruin, or even his embarrassment, would not expose three quarters of his country to perish in misery. The failings of kings must be taken into account in estimating the stability of states. The Prussian Monarchy was so constituted that it could not confront a calamity, not even that of a blundering government. Even with all the arts of the late King this complicated machine could not endure. False fiscal measures undermined the state. In vain did Frederick administer cordials; the body politic wasted away and needed a radical cure. He saved a considerable sum every year, but that was not enough, for the economic system was wrong. On the other side of the ledger must be set his reform of the law, his religious toleration, his welcome to foreign scholars. What was the result? Berlin had become the refuge of many victims of persecution, the home of many truths. Thanks to liberty of thought no state possessed a larger number of educated men.

Though strong enough in herself Prussia was also in a dangerous situation from an international point of view. 'A jealous, hostile, infinitely formidable Power is watching her. Independently of all designs on the liberty of Germany, of which the King of Prussia is the natural guardian, the House of Austria cannot swallow the loss of Silesia nor overcome the desire to regain it at any price. She contrived to make a close alliance with Russia, which renders the situation of Prussia infinitely more dangerous. True, she has found useful support in the League of German Princes who possess the best troops, but they depend entirely on Prussian money. If it were dissipated or locked up in landed property, most of them would abandon Prussia and turn to the House of Austria.' Nothing in the book is more significant than the recurring statement that Austria is the black sheep in the European flock.

At the end of the *Considérations Générales* which fill the First Book of *La Monarchie Prussienne* Mirabeau chants a hymn of praise to the hero from whose territories 'floods of light have streamed out to illuminate the whole horizon. Great King! receive my homage; receive the thanks of all thinking men for this immortal service. May thy ashes rest in peace in reward for thy inestimable gift to mankind of toleration. If thou wast mistaken in the sphere of administration, that is a limited and transitory ill. From half Europe superstition, bigotry, ignorance, mental slavery were banished by thy command. Thou broughtest light to Germany, and it will not fail. Such was Frederick, for ever illustrious among the sons of men. Nature seemed to reserve for him this exceptional glory that the heir to the throne was also the first man of his nation and his century. Equally eminent by the boldness of his conceptions, his sagacity of mind, his combination of energy and prudence, the firmness of his character, one does not know whether most to admire the range of his talents, his profound judgment, or his greatness of soul. Endowed with every physical and moral quality, strong as will, beautiful as genius, a miracle of activity, he perfected all these gifts and owed as much to himself as to nature. Easy-going by temperament he learned to be severe. Absolute to impatience, he was wonderfully tolerant. Quick, ardent, impetuous, he schooled himself to be moderate, calm, deliberate. His destiny was such that events always turned to his advantage, often by his virtues, sometimes despite his faults. Everything, including his errors, bore the imprint of his greatness, his originality, his indomitable character. No man was ever so born to command, and he knew it. He seemed to consider himself the universal soul of the world, and only credited others with some sort of sentience, some more or less ingenious animal instinct. He despised them, yet he laboured unwearyingly for their happiness according to his lights. Thus his wonderful balance of mind did more to render him equitable and beneficent than the equivocal goodness of naturally tender hearts would have achieved. He knew only one passion—glory—yet he hated praise; one *penchant*—himself—yet he lived for others; one occupation—his noble trade of King. He practised it for forty-six years with inimitable perseverance without a break till the day before his death after eighteen months of suffering borne without complaint.'

'It will be the task of history,' continues Mirabeau, 'to paint his portrait; to note his great deeds, his marvellous resourcefulness, the grandeur of his reign, the simplicity of his life and death; to describe his efforts to raise his nation and enlighten the human race. Having seen and heard him, I shall retain till my dying day the sweet pride of having aroused his interest. I still quiver with anger at the spectacle of Berlin on the day of the hero's death. *Tout étoit morne, personne n'étoit triste; tout étoit occupé, personne n'étoit affligé; pas un regret, pas un soupir, pas un éloge. On étoit fatigué jusqu'à la haine.* The explanation is simple—he was not loved. Yes, but let us dare to say it, goodness alone in the highest place will never achieve anything really useful for a nation. To restore it, increase it, educate it, even to make it happy, it is more important to be obeyed than to be loved. Doubtless man hates to be oppressed, yet he desires to be ruled. He needs justice more than goodness, which in the highest spheres usually does him harm, and a prince greedy for popular acclamation will never receive the admiration of posterity.' Never has a distinguished Frenchman paid homage to a Prussian ruler in such glowing terms, all the more significant since in 1787 he had no longer an axe to grind.

After the majestic panorama in the First Book, the authors proceed to examine every aspect of the Prussian state in turn. Beginning with a survey of the land and the people they pass the provinces in review from East Prussia to the Rhine. West Prussia and Silesia, they declare, are much better off under Prussia than under their old Polish and Austrian rulers. The toleration extended to the Catholics in Silesia earns special praise, though as regards the Jesuits it was carried too far. The policy of state-aided settlement receives less praise than usual, and it is suggested that the population would have shown a larger increase *en laissant aller les choses*. The third Book, dealing with Agriculture, reiterates the gospel of *laissez-faire*. Since food is only exported from a free country when there is a surplus, there is nothing for a government to do: the cultivators of the soil know their own business best.

The Book devoted to Industry and Commerce explains that the authors neither despise nor ignore them, but wish to aid them by leaving them free. Their formula is of a disarming simplicity. If an undertaking is good, it can easily find the necessary capital; if it is bad and contrary to the nature of things, why establish it? Frederick never understood this principle and wasted money on unprofitable enterprises. What is true of industry is equally true of commerce. Governments are confronted by two major tasks sufficient to occupy the whole of their attention: the maintenance of order and the defence of their territory. Everything else should be left to private enterprise. 'When the Government intervenes, it spoils what it directs. The arm of Hercules, in striving to cultivate a tender plant, mutilates and destroys it.' The system of French philosophers (Quesnay and his father) would be the salvation of the world. A man of genius had made it known in England, and his classical work (*The Wealth of Nations*) was immortal. A philosopher too little recognised (Mauvillon) had preached the gospel in Germany, hitherto without much success. 'We shall be satisfied if we can help to spread their principles: no monopolies, no subsidies!'

The volume on finance is a further variation on the theme that totalitarian rulers waste most of their energies. The hoarding of the precious metals moves Mirabeau to exclaim that they are best employed in circulation. 'Let the King keep his treasure but let him cease to increase it. Let him use his economies to free his people from the various fetters which prevent them from growing rich; let serfdom, forced labour, prohibitions, tolls, indirect taxes be the foes he has to overcome! Let all the liberties flourish under the shadow of the Prussian throne!' The volume on the army finds little to blame except the employment of non-Prussian elements, and the survey closes with a resonant exhortation to France to copy the Prussian military model. In the larger part of the treatise Mirabeau is preaching to German readers; here he is writing with an eye on Paris and Versailles.

The most arresting portion of the detailed analysis of the Prussian state is Book VIII, which deals with Religion, Education, Legislation, and Government, for here Mirabeau himself is speaking. The first section concentrates on the Catholic minority and reiterates his familiar views on toleration which, like Frederick, he places high among the axioms of government. To love toleration, however, is to detest its foes, particularly the clergy, who persecute when they get the chance and oppose enlightenment in every sphere. 'Of all curses that is incontestably the most permanently harmful to the happiness of mankind. If the King relaxes his vigilance for an instant, you will see it display its fury. Catholicism is very powerful, and its priesthood labours unceasingly to recover what it has lost. The constant efforts of a very large number of rich and influential men, all directed to the same end, have always produced miraculous results. In Germany people are rightly alarmed at its progress in the last century, and in our opinion Frederick did not watch it closely enough.' Unlike Voltaire the author was not interested in theology, but as a publicist he had enlisted under the banner *Écrasez l'infâme*.

Mirabeau had pleaded for the complete emancipation of the Jews in his brochure on Moses Mendelssohn, and here he returns to the charge. There were rich Jews in Berlin, the only rich business men in Prussia, yet there were still Jewish disabilities such as the prohibition of agriculture as a career. How could there fail to be very grave moral corruption in a community to whom only professions are open most calculated to deprave morality? Drawing on his personal experience in 1786 he declares that there were many enlightened men in the Berlin colony, but they had had too short a time to transmit their principles to the people. 'The Jewish community, despite its laws and its sages, seems to have retained some very equivocal practices, but remove the necessity of being corrupted in order to live and they will improve. If you permit them to engage in agriculture and the arts, their industry and activity will become very productive and much more innocent. Since they extract money from stones, so to speak, they will turn the most arid soil to account if allowed to own it. Encourage them to form settlements on land newly reclaimed and their morality will quickly change. Think of the useful changes in Berlin due to Mendelssohn's example without the aid of legislation. The Jews of this town have already discarded every kind of prejudice. They love instruction, and study is the hobby of the well to do. There are clever doctors, mathematicians, scientists. Dr. Marcus Herz has long given a free course in experimental physics, where we have seen the *élite* of Berlin and even the King's sons.'

In the field of education Mirabeau also finds much to praise. Rousseau's *Émile*, 'perhaps the most perfect of books, which ranks the author among the leading benefactors of mankind,' had served in Germany as a torch. Basedow's school at Dessau was a useful experiment. Frederick had reared excellent schoolmasters and good text-books were in use. The Prussian Academy tended the lamp of learning, and Nicolai's journal spread liberty of thought. Kant, unfortunately, was almost unintelligible. The great King had neither helped nor hindered men of letters. For the Masons and other Secret Societies the author has nothing but contempt. 'Let us work to spread true principles, and the revolution we desire will come in the form we prefer, slowly, gently, surely, and without rascals taking a hand.' There was no short cut to wisdom. Frederick's reforms in the sphere of law with the support of Cocceji and Carmer are acclaimed as unique.

The Conclusion, which fills half the sixth volume, emphasises Mirabeau's didactic purpose. The object of the whole work, he explains, was to demonstrate important truths—by which he meant primarily the teaching of Quesnay and his father—by the sheer weight of evidence. 'Physiocracy, this simple scheme which finds the whole art of government in the liberty of men and things, is still a small school.' Frederick preferred to develope the towns, and the number of cultivators in the Mark had fallen. 'Agriculture only needs good legislation in order to flourish, and wise laws of this character are the sole means of making provinces rich, populous and productive.' The assertion that his settlement policy and his new industries had led to the growth of population was incorrect, for the provinces containing the most settlers and crown enterprises were least populous. The flax industry is regarded as a form of agriculture and therefore approved. The only large and flourishing concern was the cloth of Silesia and Westphalia, which he left alone. 'Wool flourishes; silk (which is not favoured by nature) languishes despite subsidies and monoplies.' Government aid ruined industry. The only way to encourage all manufactures suited to the country was to leave them entirely to themselves, *les laisser faire*.

The most striking feature of the Conclusion is a second eloquent tribute to the great King and his country. 'Amidst his errors his services hold a sublime place. Let us glance at his influence, not merely on his own people, but on Europe and on his century. No monarch ever showed so fully what ability and the resultant prestige can do. His glory inspired the Prussians with an enthusiasm which would have done honour to the English. All citizens co-operated, almost against their will, in the drive of a government inspired by a master spirit. His example stimulated other German princes, particularly in regard to intellectual freedom. To-day, except for a very few states ruled by imbecile despots, one can discuss, theoretically at any rate, every question of theology, philosophy, economics, politics. Books for which before the reign of the apostle of enlightenment would have been burned are now on sale. The desire to repress or punish liberty of thought is considered a disgrace.' Next comes the wise and generous toleration of the sects. 'The example of Holland and England did not suffice. The former being a republic and the latter a strictly limited monarchy, the Sovereigns of Europe did not feel bound to take them as a model. When, however, they saw that a monarch enjoying all their rights—indeed more absolute than themselves owing to his personal qualities—opened his country to a thousand sects without experiencing the slightest disadvantage, and that all these sects, with one possible exception (the Jesuits), vied in their attachment to him, even the most fanatical priests could no longer dazzle the eyes of sovereigns by harping on the dangers of this policy.'

A second important result of the royal example was to be seen in the life of the German Courts. Though Charles XII and Frederick William I preferred effective authority to luxury, their lead was not followed. 'But when people saw a King who, with powerful resources, knew how to augment them, to do great things, and to scorn empty splendour because these glittering trifles do not constitute real power, his example provoked imitation. The German princes, who in the Seven Years' War took his side, had an imposing *rôle*. The troops they mobilised and assimilated to those of Prussia won them consideration out of all proportion to their resources. These potentates began to understand that there were other joys than drinking, hunting, having mistresses or even an opera, and the spirit of order and economy took possession of most of them.' The fact that Frederick did not hunt and that many princes followed his example saved the tillers of the soil from infinite evils. 'Most German princes now do their duty and of only a few can it be said that their rule is intolerable. One reason is that they are not sufficiently powerful to be insensate, tyrannical or even stupid with impunity. They lower themselves if they enjoy no personal consideration. As a rule princes have the reputation they deserve. Thus Germany possesses a very fair number of men of merit and indeed some of eminence. Moreover they keep each other in order. The certainty that a bad prince will lose his subjects to a better one prevents him from yielding to his uncontrolled passions. These sovereigns are not absolute; they cannot commit flagrant injustices even against humble citizens without disagreeable consequences the prospect of which acts as a deterrent. Still less can they arbitrarily harass the whole community or a single class. They would be brought before the tribunals of the Empire, or there would be an appeal to more powerful rulers whose intervention they could not safely decline. Thus the spirit of equity, regularity, permanence is very marked in Germany. Officials are morally certain of keeping their posts unless they commit a grave offence, and the succession of a new ruler rarely threatens their security.'

Indirect oppressions, continues Mirabeau, are much more difficult in small than in large states. It is impossible for a sovereign however industrious to know even the principal affairs of two millions of his subjects, but if he only rules over a few hundred thousand the task is more manageable. The capital is never far from the frontier, and nothing is easier than to bring complaints to the sovereign, who is surrounded neither by bayonets nor by courtiers, which is even more important. 'Can you tell me if the father of the country is here?' he was asked by a peasant in the streets of Brunswick. Such sovereigns are and always will be rare, but in Germany the simple peasant can usually speak to his prince if he wishes. 'Frederick! that is one more of your services to humanity. Thanks to you it has become a disgrace to prevent the plaint of a subject from reaching his sovereign. Your example has proved that the noblest and holiest of his functions is to hearken to the humblest of man. You have popularised this fine example, particularly in Germany, and oppressions by the tools of authority have almost disappeared. May your mighty shadow terrify them after your death! May the infamous courtiers be cursed who, while your ashes were still warm, did not blush to say that it was beneath the dignity of a King to descend to such details, and urged your successor to drop it. May the fatal order which essayed to limit the number of private petitions and threatened punishment if they were ill-founded be wiped away by tears of repentance and forgotten.'

For many reasons Mirabeau preferred small to large states. A great monarchy involved a large capital, to which the rest of the country was usually sacrificed. 'In a great country divided into little states it is very different. Light shines in each one of them, and men of capacity are everywhere to be found. All princes need good doctors, surgeons, mathematicians, lawyers, stewards, in a word men versed in all branches of knowledge. If they are estranged a ride will take them over the frontier and everywhere they will be well received. In Germany outstanding men are put up to auction and good salaries are needed to keep them. This virtually amounts to a legal freedom of thought and writing. Of course a ruler can forbid anyone in his state to write on this or that subject, but he cannot prevent the same thing being written nor his actions being discussed just across the frontier. If men of letters had known how to use this weapon, abuses of authority and errors of policy would have gone down before their assault. Moderate energy added to ordinary courage would have sufficed for them to exercise such a great influence as to be the benefactors of their country and humanity.' Here Mirabeau is unjust to several valiant publicists in different states who were doing precisely what he asked. 'But no! Frivolous hopes, futile rewards, the exchange of mean flatteries, the little halo round one's head at being noticed for a moment by some grandee: there are the shoals on which most men are wrecked. Their dignity, their prestige, even their safety fails in face of such contemptible obstacles. Some have been molested, exiled, even illegally imprisoned, from one end of Germany to another; yet no protests have been raised, and the tyrant has not been brought before the tribunal of public opinion and posterity. But a better generation will arise.'

Small states should be federated, and only in such conditions could the human race grow to its full stature. 'If they are free, reason, good sense, useful culture permeate all classes; if not, the lower class remains ignorant and stupid. Illiterate peasants are much rarer in Germany, especially among Protestants, than in France; culture is infinitely more diffused, at any rate on the surface, than in a great monarchy. These advantages seem to us infinitely superior to the facilities for public works, communications, abolition of tolls, uniform weights and measures, even internal peace which is so highly prized. Peace is doubtless, after liberty, heaven's first gift; without peace man wears himself out in futile efforts and nothing can endure. But internal tranquillity in a big monarchy is too often only the rigidity of a corpse, and losses in war are less than those arising from an evil administration.' Would the system of small states endure? He hoped and believed it would. 'If Germany is not united to form a large monarchy she will never have a fine capital, a magnificent national theatre, excellent artists, actresses, dancers, nor perhaps courtesans rivalling those of Babylon, Rome and Paris.' He cared far more for the sciences than for the arts, and his restricted list of advantages deriving from a large state reveals where his sympathies lie. In his belief the ordinary German felt his happiness to be bound up with the maintenance of little states. 'As for the aristocracy one can hardly conceive that they would be cowardly enough to prefer the kind of fortune which the House of Austria might bring to their liberty and independence.'

There was also a military problem. France was too well fortified and defended to be invaded even if Austria and Prussia combined. But suppose Germany to be united under the one sceptre, the result of a conflict with France would be uncertain. The French were doubtless brave, but so were other nations. France had perhaps more *élan*, but she was not so military as the Germans. 'Better duellists, no doubt, worse soldiers, more active, more impetuous, more capable of achieving the impossible, but less capable of calm, obedience, order, discipline, which is almost everything in war: that is what we are. Besides we live in a better and more fertile country and thus shall always be in danger of attack. The possessor is tranquil; he who covets his possessions is animated by the desire for riches, the liveliest of passions. In such a situation the former is inevitably the worse off; that is the history of all the southern peoples attacked by the men of the north. How could France fail to dread this event? How could she neglect the means of defence? The hour of danger would depend entirely on the power of the House of Brandenburg. If it loses for a moment the artificial equilibrium gained by superior wisdom, or if it loses the first round with the Imperial House, it will forfeit confidence, authority, power, existence. The Emperor would then become the chief and soon the King of Germany, either by stages or at the moment of his choice. The House of Austria, taught by its mistakes and reverses, is far from being so inferior to its enemy in brains as hitherto, and in everything else it is infinitely superior. The House of Brandenburg has climbed high enough to serve as a bulwark against the Austrian torrent which threatens to inundate Germany. It has been swollen by resistance; if the dyke is pierced or overrun for a moment, it will pour in a destructive flood over the undefended countries which it has threatened so long. So let the dyke be kept in repair and its level raised! Let the House of Brandenburg mount still higher! Let the neighbours and princes of Germany who have some energy put their shoulder to the wheel!'

How could this be achieved? By additions to or exchanges of territory? 'Never shall our tongue or pen counsel such injustices—the policy of usurpation which counts expediency as everything, the peoples as nothing. Before wishing the great Bishoprics to consolidate Prussian power in order to defend the liberty of Germany against Austrian ambition, we must know if the peoples wish to pass under another government. What a strange manner of protecting German liberty it would be to begin by destroying it, by attempting conquests, by dismemberments in order to prevent others doing the same! No, no! As a citizen of the world and a Frenchman we revere the King of Prussia as the natural protector of the German constitution, but he would be odious if he thought of aggrandising himself from the débris of the Empire. The bartering of states without consulting the inhabitants is no less iniquitous than annexations, unworthy of our enlightened age when the rights of man are known at last. Happily the House of Brandenburg has no need of resorting to any of these detestable methods of resisting the efforts of the House of Austria. There is a gentler, finer, surer way. Let it adopt the measures indicated in this book to increase the population and wealth of its provinces; order, economy, favours, everything should be devoted to this sacred purpose. Let it introduce a truly wise and productive administration; let it liberate men and things; let serfdom disappear from the royal domains, following the fine example of the Emperor in Bohemia; divide up the Domains, abolish indirect taxes, destroy monopolies, give unfettered liberty to commerce. No doubt that involves a large outlay, just as a big landowner year after year enriches sandy soil with clay in the knowledge that in ten years he will be repaid a hundred fold.'

How long a period is needed for these improvements and how can one be sure of the future? 'Try to keep the peace long enough for the House of Brandenburg to lay the foundation. But keep it in the only way open to a wise and brave man by constant readiness for war and by rendering it terrible the moment a conflict becomes clearly inevitable. There is no need to know who begins it; when circumstances maturely considered appear to demand it, strike the heaviest blows at the earliest moment—that is the only way of reaching the goal. Nothing is more natural or sensible in the present European situation than the firmest and sincerest defensive alliance of all Germany's neighbours with the King of Prussia, in order to guarantee not merely his possessions but those of all the sovereign states of Germany, including those possessing no dynasty which seem at each vacancy a prey to the first comer. The Fürstenbund is a masterpiece, but if it is to count the members must be armed. To be merely the owner of a large territory without thinking of one's duty as a unit of a great federal republic is rank cowardice. A Prince of the Empire cannot indulge in dreams of conquest, and cannot even defend himself against the rest, but he can and should contribute to the general defence according to his means. To leave it all to Providence, which only helps the wise and industrious, or to the powerful princes is to lose his prestige, risk his existence and render himself unworthy of the name of sovereign. Where would the princes of Germany be to-day if their ancestors had entertained such ideas, if the Dukes of Saxony and Brunswick and the Margraves of Baden had not armed their subjects and led them bravely to battle in civil wars of which religion was the pretext but the real issue of which was the liberty or the enslavement of Germany? Thus, if the House of Austria infringes the least of their rights or the smallest scrap of the liberty of Germany, unite, attack, impose peace and teach ambitious men a lesson. That is the plan best suited to the interests of the German princes, all the more since it would be the worse for them if the Houses of Brandenburg and Austria combined to divide up the country.'

Such a sinister combination seemed to Mirabeau altogether improbable. 'For the present ruler of Prussia is known as a loyal and generous prince, proud to have helped in making the Fürstenbund when he was heir to the throne. Moreover the ambition of the House of Austria will probably not allow an Emperor to venture on such a plan. If ever he seems to favour it for a moment it would be a snare set for the King of Prussia. The House of Austria desires Germany for itself. To share it with another House rich in clever men and of which it is the implacable enemy would be fatal to the larger prospect. The struggle between the two Powers would become too equal, and the Imperial dignity, on which the conception of Austrian greatness rests, would be destroyed. Yet such a design cannot be altogether dismissed, and the German princes should stand ready to resist till the neighbouring Powers, to whose interest the unity or division of Germany is opposed, come to their aid. Given the sincere will to be the faithful protector of Germanic liberties a King of Prussia will not find himself alone. So let us not discourage those who do their part, and perhaps more than their part, for the defence of Germany. Tell the others: the first duty is to exist, the first benefit for Germany the preservation of their constitution. Very defective though it be, it provides numerous advantages essential to humanity which would be lost in the proposed alternative of a large monarchy.'

The treatise ends with a burst of praise to the German people and the Prussian dynasty which, coming from a Frenchman, almost takes the reader's breath away. 'If we were not convinced of this important truth; if the Prussian Monarchy were not the palladium of German liberties, to which we attach the most decisive influence on the welfare of Europe; if it were not for the example and steady advance of the human race in Germany, what would this country and its constitution be to us? If they are not to be useful to Europe and the world; if this vast and proud Empire is to be the estate of one despot or of two, the eternal arena of their bloody strife, our eyes would turn away with contempt and horror and we should beg America to deliver the human race from the crimes of its tyrants. Citizens of Germany, whatever your station, listen to a foreigner who reveres you because you form a great, wise, enlightened nation, less corrupted than most other peoples, as little inclined by your character as happily incapable by your constitution of subjugating or even of ravaging Europe. Regard the standard of the House of Brandenburg as the standard of your liberty; join its side, support it, smile on its equitable expansion, rejoice in its successes, try to save it from fatal mistakes since its only solid foundation is a wise policy. As an admirer of the great King to whom it chiefly owes its power, I should be deeply interested in this fine but too fragile edifice merely as the work of this extraordinary man. But if the happiness of Europe were not involved, I would not adjure you—you, my country, and all Europe—to sustain the Prussian Monarchy, to give it time to strengthen and broaden its foundations. It is above all in order to develope the means to this end that the long and arduous studies embodied in this book have been undertaken. These means are simply peace and liberty. The civil liberty of all subjects, of commerce, of religion, of thought, of the press; liberty of things and of man: that is the whole secret of governance, and there as in a fruitful germ resides the prosperity of Empires. The Prussian Monarchy is more suited than any other to reap such a bountiful harvest. May the tutelary genius of Europe and the human race watch over its destinies, save it from errors, sustain it in the dangers which threaten it, lead it to the summit of greatness and power to which it can only attain by justice and wisdom.' It needed no prophetic vision to foretell the ever growing importance of a state which had become a Great Power in a single reign; but how could a man of Mirabeau's wide knowledge and experience have expected Prussia to use the leadership to which he summoned her more wisely than the House of Austria whose ambitions he so hotly denounced?

The seventh and eighth volumes of *La Monarchie Prussienne*, dealing with Saxony, Austria and Bavaria, are described by Mirabeau as an Appendix, and they were not included in the German edition. Owing to lack of time and means, it is explained, the survey was less complete and authoritative, and his share in them was small. Yet Germany, it is stated in the Preface, was little known to the rest of Europe, interest in the countries under the sceptre of Joseph II was rapidly increasing, and it was part of the plan of the book to compare Prussia with Austria. The survey of Saxony, which Mirabeau had visited, paints a more sombre picture than we find in the *Secret Letters*. The darkest feature was the colossal debt incurred by

Augustus II and Augustus III, who for two generations had combined the Electorate with the glittering bauble of the Polish crown. When the expenses of the Seven Years' War were added to the extravagance of the rulers and their favourite Count Brühl, 'a rich Elector was turned into a poor King.' The taxes were like a vulture tearing at the entrails of the state. The brightest factor was the character of the reigning Elector, Frederick Augustus II, yet it would be necessary for him to reign for many years and for his successors to be equally wise if the wounds of the suffering country were to be healed. There were some good schools and the population was industrious, but the Saxon is described as having less character than any other German stock.

If Mirabeau discovers little to praise in Saxony he finds even less in Austria, where religious intolerance and aggressive ambition were rife. Himself a *libre penseur*, he shared Frederick's preference for Protestant countries since Protestantism, founded on liberty of thought, encouraged liberty. Catholicism, on the other hand, generated various political evils, above all the subjection of intellectual freedom to the pleasure of an individual who said: Thus far and no further! and was able to enforce his decision. Monks were superstitious drones. The Emperor Joseph had limited their power, but the essential reforms would be to let any monk leave the convent if he liked and to allow the clergy to marry and keep their revenues. 'The root of hierarchical power being thus cut, priests would become citizens and we should witness the gradual disintegration of this terrible edifice which weighs on most European countries.' The Emperor had gone as far as a Catholic ruler could go, but it was not enough and his Edict of Toleration was totally inadequate.

The clericalism and obscurantism prevailing in the territories of the Hapsburgs increased Mirabeau's repugnance to any extension of their rule. As a child of the *Aufklärung* he regarded the Catholic Church and the leading Catholic power in Central Europe as the most formidable foe of the free spirit of man. 'There are two parties in Germany. One looks to the enslavement of this vast country under a single monarch: we may call it the Austrian or Catholic party. The other may be described as the Protestant or Prussian party, consisting of all those who love civil, political and intellectual liberty and desire humanity to share all these benefits. They are Prussians because Prussia alone can stand up to the Austrian party; and so they will remain as long as that Power does not itself become predominant and able to menace Germanic liberty. This latter party watches with delight the errors of the Austrian ruler. For so long as he rejects true enlightenment, which liberty of thought alone can provide, he is much less formidable. All that the Protestant party has to fear is the secret, continual and infinitely subtle machinations of the priests, still more of the Orders, above all of the Jesuits. But if Austria adopted true enlightenment she would soon abandon this insatiable greed which in the long run cannot succeed; and her efforts, instead of tending to the subversion of her neighbours and the acquisition of thousands of slaves, would seek solely to develope her immense possessions, to civilise the many millions of her semi-barbarian subjects, and to induce them to work by the certainty of reward.'

After pronouncing judgment on the head of the House of Austria as a ruler in his own domains Mirabeau passes to his *rôle* as Emperor. Though the Imperial title carried with it not an inch of territory, and though the power of the Emperor was extremely limited, there was a dangerous magic in the name, the trappings, the symbols of ancient things. 'They generate a crazy ambition to make them realities, and in those who dress him up a marvellous aptitude for being dazzled which facilitates the designs of the office-holder, who is always consumed by the desire to restore the Roman Empire. In other hands the danger would be so remote, and so many steps would be needed before Germany could be enslaved, that no sensible person could be alarmed. If the Imperial office were really elective and passed from hand to hand, this peril would disappear since the insecurity of tenure, at the mercy of an illness, would allow no time for the execution of projects dependent upon continuity. But the House of Hapsburg had possessed the Imperial dignity during three centuries almost without interruption, for the election of the ruler of Bavaria in 1742 cannot be described as a real break. This House has worn the Imperial crown at a time when it possessed much more effective power than to-day. Only ancient forms remain when the scales are level; but if they incline even slightly towards the House of Austria, these forms quickly regain their significance, and the nominal head of the Empire would soon become the real leader and ultimately the sovereign.'

It was astonishing and alarming, continued Mirabeau, when one studied history, to see how often Europe had been close to deliverance from the legitimate terror aroused by this powerful and ambitious House. The last of its narrow escapes was at the battle of Kolin, where a Prussian victory would have lost it Bohemia, the most useful of its provinces. 'Fortune has been kind to it, and to-day it is stronger and more formidable than at any time since Charles V. If it secures Bavaria, now its principal and almost its sole aim, the balance in Germany would incline so decisively to its side that the Empire would infallibly become subject to its will. All the weak members would join it out of fear and would drag the strong ones in their train. Then the German Constitution, the Peace of Westphalia, the Capitulation signed by every Emperor on his accession would be a network which it would break at will despite the protests which it would not fear. It will devour one fief of the Empire and one province after the other till it becomes irresistible. Bavaria, wisely administered, would mean a great increase of strength and would render the House of Austria invulnerable. This situation is infinitely perilous and unfortunately it is difficult to find a remedy.' Any aggrandisement of this dangerous dynasty must be prevented and Europe must above all oppose the incorporation of Bavaria. The Imperial title should pass for a time to the Wittelsbachs, and the Hohenzollerns would retain the proud *rôle* of protector of Germanic liberties. The volume on Austria, at first sight an irrelevance in a treatise on Prussia, becomes an essential link in the chain of argument, for the significance of the latter could be fully grasped only if the alternative were taken into account. Mirabeau hated Austria more than he loved Prussia, but he was correct in his assumption that Berlin alone could prevent the domination of Vienna. That was as far as he desired the Hohenzollerns to go, for he had not the slightest wish to see them or any other dynasty transforming Germany into a centralised nation-state.

PRINCE HENRY OF PRUSSIA:
STATESMAN AND DIPLOMATIST

OF the three brothers of Frederick the Great Henry alone counts.[1] Voltaire saluted him as the Condé of the North, and Catherine the Great pronounced him one of the outstanding personalities of the century. His place in the first rank of Prussia's soldiers is secure, and his performances in the Seven Years' War earned the praise of Napoleon. Alone of the Royal Family he declined to admit the intellectual superiority of its head; indeed he regarded himself as the better general and diplomatist of the two. Proud of his abilities and recognised throughout Europe after the early death of his elder brother August Wilhelm as the second personage in the state, he fretted against his impotence in a community ruled by a superman. A morbid touchiness and chronic sense of frustration poisoned his relations with the King, and the tragedy of his life was his dread that he would figure in history merely as the brother of Frederick the Great. Fate, however, was not quite so unkind, and after his active military career was over he was privileged on more than one occasion to become a maker of history.

I

The main lesson for Prussia of the Seven Years' War was the necessity of co-operation with Russia. Since the robber of Silesia desired above all things to avert the renewal of the Three Power Coalition which had brought him to the edge of the abyss he had no alternative, for Austria was incurably hostile and France was her ally. England had withdrawn her subsidies when Pitt was displaced by Bute, and the memory of her desertion rankled in the Prussian capital. Only the death of the Empress Elizabeth at the opening of

---

[1] The best biography is by Chester V. Easum (1942). Krauel, *Prinz Heinrich von Preussen*, contains the more important political memoranda of his later years. A selection from his correspondence with Frederick is in *Œuvres de Frédéric le Grand*, vol. xxv., and in Frederick's *Politische Correspondenz*, passim.

1762 and the accession of the Prussophil Peter had saved the hunted monarch from final collapse. After the assassination of the young Emperor the paramount duty of the King of Prussia was to win and keep the favour of the formidable widow who seized the reins and held them firmly for thirty-four years. The first step was to approve her selection of the young Pole Stanislas Augustus, one of her early lovers, to fill the Polish throne on the death of Augustus III of Saxony in 1763. A few Russophil Poles thought of Henry, who would have welcomed a crown, but the matter was never officially discussed since Catherine's assent was known to be unobtainable. The second was to conclude an alliance in 1764 for eight years, each signatory promising to supply 12,000 men or the equivalent in subsidies in the event of war. Frederick detested the notion of Poland being completely dominated by Russia and of helping to finance her campaigns, but as Catherine's friendship was impossible on cheaper terms he was ready to pay her price. Silesia, he felt, was safe at last. When the partnership was formed Prussia's need was the greater, but a few years later the situation changed; for Catherine's expansionist ambitions at the expense of Turkey and Poland involved the antagonism of the Hapsburgs who pursued similar aims. The outbreak of hostilities between Russia and Turkey in 1768, and the simultaneous revolt of a section of the Polish nobility against Russia's tightening grip, played into Frederick's hands. In 1769 the alliance was renewed till 1780, for Prussian subsidies were highly acceptable during the Turkish war.

In his classical work *The Eastern Question in the Eighteenth Century* Sorel describes a number of projects for the partition of Poland from the sixteenth century onwards, and in the opening years of the reign of Stanislas the idea was in the air. In February 1769 Frederick flew a kite at St. Petersburg and discovered that Russia favoured a comprehensive deal with Prussia and Austria. The best solution from her point of view would have been the bloodless appropriation of the whole country; but neither of her ambitious neighbours could be expected to permit such a shift in the balance of power, and if they acted together they could bar the road. Frederick had always craved for West Prussia as a bridge between East Prussia and the core of his dominions, though he had no intention of fighting for it; Austria coveted Galicia, and Russia was out for as much of eastern and central Poland as she could get. By the summer of 1770 the stage was set and the actors were waiting in the wings.

At this moment Henry moves up to the front.[1] His first task was to visit his sister the Queen of Sweden, and to inform her that Frederick had been compelled to include in his treaty with Russia an obligation to preserve the Swedish Constitution of 1720 which crippled the royal prerogative. Any change, she was reminded, would upset the Tsarina, who might be tempted to retaliate just when it was particularly important for Prussia to keep her in good humour, for Stockholm was only the first stage of a journey towards a more distant goal. Henry and Catherine had known each other as children, and it was believed in some quarters that he might have become her husband had she not been selected for the heir to the Russian throne. Slightly alarmed at the meetings between Frederick and Joseph in 1769 and 1770, she seized the opportunity of his visit to Ulrike to suggest a call at St. Petersburg on the way home. She would have preferred a meeting with the King himself, but a hint to this effect evoked no response. 'Herewith a copy of the letter just received from the Empress of Russia,' wrote Frederick shortly after his brother's departure for Stockholm in August 1770. 'She is so anxious to have you that I do not think you can refuse. It may not greatly appeal to you, but you must make a virtue of necessity. If you need money I could put 8000 crowns at your disposal. You realise, my dear brother, how careful we must be with this woman. If you can reconcile her with my sister in Sweden I shall be delighted. In general you will have to consider all matters which concern our interests. Please convey my most flattering compliments to the Empress and tell her all you can of the universal admiration she excites. During your journey you will be able to collect a store of eulogies which you can produce at the fitting moment. I rely on your skill to seize occasions when they come. You will be fully repaid for the hardships of the journey by the sight of one of the greatest princesses in the world. You will find many things in St. Petersburg to admire, but what are mansions and a pompous Court in comparison with the princess who rules the country with so much glory? This is the only experience I envy you —to meet this powerful genius who almost surpasses Peter the Great. To congratulate the Empress on every triumph of her arms would become tedious to her, and so in sharing her victories in Bessarabia,

---

[1] See Krauel, *Briefwechsel zwischen Heinrich Prinz von Preussen und Katharina II von Russland*. The Tsarina's letters to Grimm (in French) fill vol. xxiii. of the publications of the Imperial Russian Historical Society.

on the Pruth and at Bender I admire in silence. The reigning Empress puts the coping stone on the labours of her predecessors.' Subsequent letters described her genius as far surpassing that of Peter the Great, and foretold that if all her grandiose projects were carried out Russia would be the first nation in the world. Such bouquets, needless to say, were intended for the lady's eyes.

Henry needed no pressing, for he had taken the initiative in the spring by a confidential message to St. Petersburg that he would welcome an invitation if his brother were not informed of his step. Whether Frederick himself had acted first we cannot be sure, but as early as January 1770 he informed Russia through his Minister of Henry's coming mission to Stockholm, where he would try to persuade his sister to adopt a wiser policy, in other words to show greater consideration for Russia. The message produced a grateful reply from Panin, the Prussophil Foreign Minister. Having received a favourable response from Potsdam, the Empress sent a formal invitation to the traveller. 'I could not see Your Royal Highness so near my dominions without desiring an interview with a prince I so highly esteem. I have requested and received the permission of the King. He encourages me to believe that you will not be disinclined, but I desire your own consent and earnestly beg you to honour the banks of the Neva with your presence. True, you will only find there what you find everywhere—unlimited veneration for your virtues, so universally known to fame.' Henry gallantly replied from Stockholm that nothing could flatter his ambition more than to admire her eminent qualities at close range. His journey, he added, had no other object but to display his gratitude and attachment and to merit her friendship and esteem.

Accompanied by a large suite Henry, now in his element, reached St. Petersburg via Finland on October 12, 1770. Though they had not met for twenty-six years his stiffness soon wore off. He was only outwardly cold, reported the hostess, and it soon became obvious that he was very clever and an accomplished conversationalist. After a few days they were on such cordial terms that he was invited to visit her in her leisure hours and to share her meals whenever he chose. Their talk ranged over many fields, for both were Intellectuals. 'This hero,' she wrote a week after his arrival, 'is at the height of his fame and is a man of the first rank quite apart from his birth.' After three months she declared that she had never seen anyone with whose ideas she so entirely agreed. 'Often we open our mouths at the same moment to say the same thing. Perhaps that explains why he likes my society. I confess that no princely visitor could be more welcome. Nothing escapes him and one must really admire him very much. He is always bright, his character is upright and humane, his mind lofty and noble; in a word he is a hero who has given me abundant friendship.' He was no less impressed by the versatility of his hostess and the splendour of her Court.

The best was still to come. The principal object of the journey, explained Frederick to Solms, his Minister in the Russian capital, was to render the ties between the Courts indissoluble: that was the sole advantage he sought. Henry, however, was eager to discuss the future of Poland if he saw his chance. Since the Russians had so far reaped all the benefits of the alliance, he wrote to the King, now was the time to use their influence with Stanislas Augustus to secure portions of Polish territory for Prussia and to make her lord of the Baltic coast. 'I give you an absolutely free hand while you are in St. Petersburg,' wrote Frederick, 'for you are on the spot and better able than I to see what is the best course.' This, however, was only true within limits. Henry could talk as frankly about attempting to end the conflict with Turkey and the civil war in Poland as about the friendly sentiments of his sister Ulrike, but he could hardly raise the delicate question of partition without instructions, which Frederick deemed it premature to supply. When on January 8, 1771, he reported to his brother that he expected to leave at the close of the month, it looked as if he would return with empty hands. On that very day, however, a postcript announced joyful tidings. 'Since writing this letter I have visited the Empress, who jokingly remarked that the Austrians had seized two starosties in Poland and set up the Imperial arms; why should we not follow suit? I replied that though you had drawn a cordon in Poland, you had not occupied any starosties.[1] "But why doesn't he?" rejoined Catherine with a smile. At this moment Count Czernichew came up and remarked: "Why not take the Bishopric of Varmia? After all everybody must get something." Though it was said in joking fashion, there was obviously something in it and I have no doubt you will be able to profit by the occasion.'

Three days later Henry reported a conversation with Panin, who

[1] Shortly before Henry left for Stockholm, Frederick had drawn a military cordon round certain Polish territories on the pretext of isolating cattle disease.

condemned Austria's action and made no reference to a Prussian occupation of the Bishopric of Varmia. There were two parties in the Russian capital, explained the visitor to his brother. 'The champions of aggrandisement wish everyone to get something in order that Russia may profit at the same time, whereas Count Panin inclines to tranquillity and peace. I shall find out more about this affair, and I feel that you run no risk in taking this Bishopric on some plausible pretext if it is true that the Austrians have definitely occupied two starosties to which they advance claims on documents in the Hungarian archives.' Frederick commented without enthusiasm on the reported conversations, for he failed to grasp the full significance of Catherine's admission that she could not secure all Poland for herself. 'I realise, my dear brother, that there are differences in the Council, but I can say positively that Count Panin's ideas about Austria are impracticable. The secret hatred felt in that country for the Russians passes all imagination, and, if I may say so, I am the only person who tries to prevent an explosion. As for the Duchy of Varmia I have abstained: such a trifle would not be worth the outcry it would arouse. Polish Prussia, on the other hand, is a prize, even without Danzig, for we should have the Vistula and free communication with East Prussia. That is worth paying for, even a large sum. Snatching at trifles suggests a character of insatiable greed, worse than that which I already bear in Europe. If anything were done let it be in the grand style and let the Balance of Power be preserved.'

On his return in February 1771 Henry spent a week at Potsdam. He brought a letter thanking the King for permitting the visit, and Frederick replied in the fulsome style which he adopted with the Tsarina alone. 'He has returned, Madam, overwhelmed by your kindness, more charmed with the happiness of meeting you than with all the astonishing things he has seen. His talk transports me in imagination to Russia. He tells us of the great things Your Imperial Majesty has accomplished in that vast empire, of your maternal care for your people, of your immense establishments, of your infinite concern for the morals and culture of a young race, of your legislation. Then he dilates on the details of your personal life, telling me that no ordinary person allows more freedom and liveliness than a great Empress when she deigns to leave the throne for a few minutes to seek diversion among her subjects from the burdens of rule.'

These flowery compliments were reinforced in the brisk exchange between Henry and Catherine which continued throughout 1771. 'My heart is filled with gratitude in recalling the friendship with which you have honoured me,' he wrote in thanking her for his reception. 'I am always thinking of the time which passed so rapidly and in which I received every day new proofs of your attention.' The Empress replied that her friendship was assured and that the memory of his visit would never fade. 'Birth is an advantage in the eyes of the world, but merit and mind surpass it and set it off. If all the kings in the world except your brother had come to me I should have been bored and should not have felt the satisfaction derived from your short visit. Your friendship is most precious, for among your fine qualities is that of sincerity.' All the letters were shown to the King, who encouraged Henry to cultivate the correspondence. The attempt to terminate the Russo-Turkish war, for which Frederick grudged the treaty subsidies, had failed, but the ground had been prepared for the bloodless acquisition of West Prussia. The Prussian Minister at St. Petersburg reported that the Prince had made himself generally beloved and that the Empress spoke of him in the most flattering terms. To Frederick she wrote as she had never written before and was never to write again. 'We are left only with the imperishable memory of a beautiful dream.'

The King realised that the time to act had come, and two days after the traveller's arrival at Potsdam the brothers collaborated in drafting instructions to the Prussian Minister at St. Petersburg. Prussia, he was informed, intended to advance her legitimate claims and to follow the Austrian example by occupying Polish territory in order to prevent a disturbance of the equilibrium between herself and Austria. Henry also helped to shape Frederick's reply to the note from the Empress which he had brought. Never before or after did his political advice receive so much consideration, though there was some disagreement about tactics. While Henry advised a deal with Austria which the two powers would press Russia to accept, Frederick preferred an agreement with Russia in the belief that Austria would have to come in, and his will naturally prevailed.

Since Catherine favoured partition and Panin ceased to object there was nothing to prevent the opening of formal negotiations. On July 21 the King wrote in high spirits to Henry that a Russian offer received that day was *fort honnête* and well worth his subsidies for the

Turkish war. Yet it was easier to agree on the principle than on the boundaries, and in the late summer of 1771 he began to despair of peace. 'I much fear that you and I will not enjoy sweet repose in our solitude next year,' he confided to Henry. 'The Russians want everything and the Austrians refuse all concessions. By December or January we should be better able to gauge the plans of the latter, and then we must get ready to enter on the campaign about the end of August next year. Do not be surprised if I keep worrying you with my politics and annoyances. My present situation is critical and alarming till the hour of decision arrives. It is certain that when they draw the sword I shall have to take part. If the Russians are beaten I lose an ally and place myself at the discretion of reconciled enemies in whom I could never feel confidence. If the Austrians are defeated the Russians, prouder and more arrogant than ever, will resent my peaceful disposition, and indeed I might be sacrificed to a rapprochement between those Powers after their fight is over.' Henry urged his brother to arrange in advance for a definite compensation in the event of Prussia being dragged into an Austro-Russian war, and to warn the Tsarina that refusal would be followed by a declaration of neutrality. Frederick kept him informed of the progress of the negotiations throughout the autumn and winter of 1771. 'I am trying to add Danzig to our portion,' he wrote on October 2. 'If we do not get it now we must give up the idea. The honour of coming events, my dearest brother, will be due to you in equal measure. For it is you who laid the foundation stone of this edifice, and without you I should never have felt able to form such designs, being unaware before your journey to St. Petersburg what attitude that Court adopted towards me.' At the opening of 1772 the goal was at length in sight. A secret treaty was signed at St. Petersburg between Russia and Prussia on February 17, and two days later Maria Theresa and Joseph signed a provisional act in Vienna accepting the plan of partition on condition that the three states should receive equal treatment. 'The larger portion of our work is achieved,' wrote Frederick in April. After further discussions the tripartite treaty of partition was signed on August 5, 1772.

Henry received the thanks he deserved from the two rulers who alone knew how much he had contributed behind the scenes. 'I have seen this Prussia,' wrote Frederick in June, 'which I receive in some degree from your hands. It is an excellent and most valuable acquisition both for its political situation and for our finances.' There were over six hundred thousand inhabitants, he added, and there would soon be more. After signing the February pact the Empress wrote to her old friend expressing her gratitude in connection with 'the great affair now terminated between the King and myself. Your Royal Highness has had so direct a part in it that I cannot refrain from expressing my entire satisfaction. Here there are many people who, thanks to your efforts, are about to enjoy a long period of sweet tranquillity.' 'Your letter,' replied Henry, 'breathes the kindness which goes straight to the heart. Happy are the peoples who are about to pass under Your Majesty's sway! If my feeble efforts, as you so flatteringly suggest, have contributed to the success of this great affair, I should be proud of the happiness which your new subjects will enjoy when they come to know the beneficence and enlightenment you spread throughout your vast domains. They will emerge from the brutishness in which they were kept by bad government, and my own country will bless your handiwork. It is for me to recognise how much your alliance means to us, what a favourable and happy thing it is. All I desire is that in my little corner I may find further occasions to let you know how these truths are engraved on my heart.'

Henry was always proud of his share in the partition, on the ground that it enlarged his country, that the Poles in the Prussian zone fared far better than under the old regime, and that the agreement had brought the King and Empress nearer together. So proud was he indeed that he begged the Prussian Minister to procure from Catherine a written testimonial to his services which, he declared, he would regard as the greatest memorial of his fame; and the coveted letter, dated September 24, 1772, was as warmly phrased as the vainest of men could desire. 'Après la prise de possession des gouvernements de la Russie blanche je n'ai rien de plus empressé à faire qu'à témoigner à Votre Altesse Royale combien je sens Lui être redevable pour tous les soins qu'elle a bien voulu donner à cette grande affaire de laquelle elle peut être regardée comme le premier moteur; ma reconnaissance sera à jamais ineffacable.' This feather in his cap gave him even keener pleasure than his triumphs in the field by its recognition of his capacity to deal with the highest affairs of state. The King's gratitude took the form of a substantial grant of money, particularly welcome to a man who always lived beyond his means. In his later years, in bold defiance of the truth, he went so far as to inform the Comte de Ségur that he had suggested the idea of partition to Catherine the Great.[1]

No sooner was the partition treaty signed than a storm blew up in the north. On August 19, 1772, a year after his feeble father's death, Frederick's gifted nephew Gustavus III restored the absolute authority of the Crown in Sweden by a bloodless *coup d'état*. The decision was attributed by Catherine to French and Russophobe influences, and for a moment she thought of war; but the young King had needed no prompting and foreign policy had played no part in his decision. Any ruler of spirit would have seized the first opportunity to strike off the fetters imposed by the aristocracy half a century earlier. For Frederick, on the other hand, it was unwelcome news, since it was certain to excite the wrath of the Tsarina. The only means of saving Sweden, he wrote to Henry on September 5, was for the King to accept a compromise, and he had written in that sense both to Stockholm and St. Petersburg. 'If that fails, we shall find ourselves engaged in a war against our nephew, which is a detestable idea.'

Here was a golden opportunity of turning to account the cordial relations established between the Empress and Henry during his recent visit. Writing on September 18, 1772, of course with the approval of Frederick, he forwarded to her a letter from his nephew to himself explaining the reasons for his high-handed conduct, and added a tactful appeal. 'With the interest I take in your glory, Madam, and with the sentiments inspired by the close union between you and the King my brother, I cannot conceal from you that I am anxious about my sister. I should like to find means of averting any eventualities, and should be happy if I could serve you in smoothing out anything opposed to your interests in the recent action of the King of Sweden, and in combining those interests with the tranquillity of the family to which I belong.'

Catherine's stinging rejoinder was obviously intended for the eyes both of Frederick and Gustavus. The excuses of the young King for 'his attack on liberty and the established constitution' are contemptuously brushed aside. 'This prince says he was about to be imprisoned or murdered. If such a criminal plot existed I know nothing of it, and nothing has transpired since its failure. It would be equally strange

[1] Ségur, *Mémoires*, ii. 145–153.

that, in order to parry such a plot and to punish the guilty, there should be no other means than the overthrow of the government. I am convinced that every member of the party which in defence of the law opposed his views, far from plotting against his life, would have been ready to shed his last drop of blood to defend it. As for this liberty which he pretends to have restored to his nation, the world knows that the new form of government gives him an authority almost as unlimited as that of any sovereign in Europe. What sort of liberty is it which is imposed by cannon stationed at the door of the Assembly, soldiers with fixed bayonets surrounding the hall, the Senate under arrest, anyone resisting or suspected of resisting kept under guard, all the inhabitants confined to their houses? Would servitude have worn a different garb? All this would be merely a domestic disturbance were it not unfortunately true that the revolution has other motives. French intrigues and French money were the cause, not danger to the King or the desire to restore liberty to his people. Knowing it is all the handiwork of the power most hostile to me, and that the prince so closely bound to me by ties of blood has been tricked by her, how must I feel as Empress of Russia? How can I fail to dread further action of the kind that has just overthrown the government of my nearest neighbours? How can I trust to words when oaths are ignored?'

Henry's response to this broadside, 'the most interesting letter I have ever received,' was a subtle blend of flattery and appeal. 'If I try to envisage the King of Sweden I see a young prince who has allowed himself to be led into a precipitate step which he cannot easily retrace. He is surrounded by people whose interests lie in urging him to continue his course, and who are perhaps in the pay of a power which delights to foment trouble in the north. To aid him it is necessary to show him the way, and the helping hand can only be yours.' The fire, he added, might become a conflagration. 'Such are my anxieties, Madam. But what reassures me is my conviction that in this labyrinth you will find means which will avert danger and secure your interests. If I could hope that my counsels would influence the King and that I could indicate some honourable way of escape from his embarrassment, I would certainly try. I have already spoken to him in all sincerity about his precipitancy, but I confess that I felt I was dealing with a sick man more in need of remedies for his malady than of precepts.'

Catherine's reply was a shade more conciliatory than her original broadside. 'I wish nothing better than to discover a middle course which might serve alike the interest of Russia, peace, the northern system, and the personal position of the King. The thick cloud which his overthrow of the old regime has spread over the whole affair is such that the best intentions are in vain. His military movements against Denmark and his stealthy intrigues in Norway suggest that he may wish to attempt the same acts of violence towards his neighbours as against his subjects. However, I do not despair of improvement and then I will tell you what my friendly disposition suggests.' A grateful rejoinder, explaining that his sister had no share in her son's escapades, ended a difficult chapter in the story of Henry's relations with the Russian autocrat. To Frederick he wrote that the Empress was *très vive*, but that it was possible to make her see the truth. The young King of Sweden was at the start of his fortunes, and his entourage hailed him as a new Gustavus Adolphus. If things were not rushed, harmony might be restored at a later date. Once again Henry had rendered timely service to his brother, to whom the notion of a conflict between his Russian ally and his headstrong nephew was a nightmare. A wistful letter written at this moment reveals the writer's unending regret that he was not an eldest son. 'I have always felt that occupation is the salt of life. I believe, my dear brother, that you must enjoy arranging the finances, distributing benefits, making people happy by appointments, holding the balance on the political stage, creating armies, and keeping the machinery of state running.'

A few months later, at the opening of 1773, Henry once again served his country by supporting Frederick's plan for the marriage of the Grand Duke Paul to a Princess of Hesse-Darmstadt, a relative of the Prussian house.[1] He was still in high favour at St. Petersburg, and early in 1774 an invitation to pay another visit was accepted with delight. 'Further visits cannot be as interesting as the first,' commented Frederick, 'and even if there were now some definite matter, which there is not, I would not urge you against your will. But the only reason I see is to keep this princess in her present good humour and to preserve your credit, which may prove very useful to our nephew after my death; because if she is in touch with you, in addition to the marriage of the Grand Duke, you will always be in a position by your letters to maintain good understanding between Russia and

[1] The best account of the heir is in Morane, *Paul I de Russie avant l'Avènement*.

Prussia and thereby to render our country the greatest service open to a prince of our House.' A prolonged residence of the Court in Moscow postponed the journey for two years, during which Henry despatched assurances of devotion at frequent intervals. 'I thought I was approaching a time of life when the sentiments of pleasure are no longer so keen,' he wrote in November 1775, 'but Your Majesty's letter has inspired such joy and satisfaction that I begin to believe I am still young. I cannot describe my satisfaction when I read that you have fixed the hour for my happiness.' Easter, 1776, he added, would suit him excellently. There was political purpose in all this gush, for so long as Austria dreamed of Silesia the good will of Russia was essential. Frederick's satisfaction was expressed in less flattering terms. 'She treats you as a friend and desires to see you again. To decline is to break with her, and you know the Indians say they must worship the devil to prevent him from harming them.' Henry was the only person to keep the friendship in repair, and the King described him at this period as 'my other self.'

The Empress apologised to her guest for the interruption of the usual festivities owing to the death of her daughter-in-law a fortnight after his arrival in St. Petersburg in April, 1776. 'Prince Henry, I think, is dying of boredom,' she wrote to Grimm, 'though he is too polite to confess it. We gossip occasionally but I do not feel quite up to entertaining him. He will tell you he is not bored here, but do not believe it. He loves *fêtes* and I could not give him any. Everything has been dull on account of mourning.' Though something of the glamour of 1770 had gone the visit was not without result, for the friendship of the heir to the throne, however powerless he might be during his mother's life-time, seemed worth winning and was effectively won. When the childless Grand Duchess died in giving birth to a dead son, Catherine immediately begged her visitor to support her request for the hand of a Württemberg princess, grand-daughter of the Margravine of Schwedt, the sister of Frederick and Henry, despite the fact that she was already engaged to the Hereditary Prince Ludwig of Hesse-Darmstadt, brother of the deceased Grand Duchess. To remove this obstacle Henry's services were requisitioned and the disagreeable task was discharged with zeal. He was writing, he explained, not only in his own name but in that of the Empress and the Grand Duke. 'I am charged to inform you that after the sad loss of your sister it is absolutely essential to think of another alliance for the

Grand Duke. Since the choice for so influential a prince, which also concerns a great monarchy, is most important; since no one except the Princess of Württemberg, my niece, is suitable; and since we count on your attachment to the Imperial house and on your grasp of the necessity of this step, it is hoped that you will lend yourself to the plan, not only by renouncing your engagement but by insisting that the Prince and Princess of Württemberg should carry out the intentions of the Empress and the Grand Duke. I may add that Your Highness may in this way not only efface the impressions which the Empress has formed of your conduct but also may hope for the continuance of her favour. If, however, you are unwilling to make your contribution to this most useful and necessary arrangement, you will incur the resentment of the Imperial Court. As an old friend of your respected mother I cannot give you better advice than to submit to the wishes of the Empress, since I cannot doubt that, now or later, you will reap the reward of a sacrifice which precisely because it is great is all the more noble to make.'

The censorious reference to his past is explained by the fact that during a period of voluntary service in the Russian army the conduct of the young Prince had earned the disfavour of the Empress, and that after returning to Germany he had spoken indiscreetly of conditions at the Russian Court. The combination of threats and promises produced the desired result. On receiving a written renunciation of his claim to the hand of the coveted princess, Catherine produced the anticipated reward. 'He has gone to feed his sheep with a pension of ten thousand roubles,' she wrote contemptuously to Grimm, 'but on condition that I do not see him again nor hear anything more of him.' Unlike his brother and the Empress, Frederick sympathised with the young prince who was so peremptorily summoned to surrender his prize and expressed his gratitude for the sacrifice. The interview, he confessed to Henry, had moved him to tears. In every letter Catherine assured Henry that her friendship and esteem would only cease with her life. At her request he had stood by her son at the death-bed of his wife and had won his affectionate regard. Since no time was allowed for mourning, the Prince accompanied the heir to Berlin where he made the acquaintance of his second wife. 'I am more grateful than I can say for all the care and attention you have been good enough to show the Grand Duke during his journey,' wrote his mother. 'He has described it in a letter full of gratitude, and you have increased my debt by informing me of the safe arrival of my young Télémaque under your aegis. The welcome by the King, the Royal Family, and the public has been all I could desire. You know that when my feelings are deepest words fail me. I anticipate the success of the project since the affair is in your hands.'

The new Grand Duchess, an attractive girl of seventeen, won all hearts and formed a fresh link between the two countries. 'My gratitude can never equal your services,' wrote the happy Paul on his return to St. Petersburg with his bride. 'I receive from your hands a person who makes and will surely continue to make the happiness of my life. You have given me advice about my conduct towards the Empress which I have followed and which has put me on a footing with her which can only contribute to my happiness, serve the tranquillity of the country, and affect every one else by the confidence and harmony between us. You have enabled me to make the acquaintance of the King, to visit a country eminent for its laws and good order, to see things with my own eyes and make comparisons, which is most essential for one in my position.' A second letter, written on the morrow of his marriage, was even more exuberant. 'It is your doing, my dear uncle,[1] and it is at this happy moment that I realise the full dimensions of the benefaction received at your hands. Your divine niece is the object of the affection of the Empress, of my love and friendship, of the good wishes and approval of everyone. She knows how to chase away all the dark shadows and restore the tone I had entirely lost in these three unhappy years.'

Catherine was genuinely delighted. 'I have got her at last, this charming princess, and we are all literally enchanted. I shall never forget all you have done to give her to me.' Never had the relations of the two Courts been more friendly. 'I regard this union,' she wrote to Frederick, 'as a strengthening of the ties between our two Houses. I cannot help mentioning how grateful I am to the Prince, your brother, who has shared all my feelings and shown me a thousand signs of friendship.' Frederick's gratitude was no less sincere. 'I note, my dear brother,' he wrote on May 18, 'that you contrive to achieve all your purposes and that everything goes according to plan. I admire your dexterity and the trouble you are good enough to take about our affairs. May heaven shed on you all the benedictions I desire for you, for this confidence which the Empress so justly places

[1] Uncle by marriage.

in you is the surest bond of union between Russians and Prussians. If anything were to occur as the result of some folly on the part of somebody I will not name,[1] you will always be able to put things straight.' In the following year the treaty of 1764, renewed in 1769, was secretly renewed once more for eight years.

Despite entire approval of her son's second marriage, the imperious ruler continued to exclude him from all share in power, and his letters to Henry are full of lamentations. He detested his unloving mother who kept him out of his rights. 'You will be glad to hear of the happiness of two persons who owe it solely to you,' he wrote in January 1777, 'who are attached to you so closely and for so many reasons. We possess each other's love, which makes us take more philosophically many things which are going on around us and which would worry me if I were the cause or if I could have applied a remedy.' A fortnight later he was more explicit. 'I live contentedly in my home, taking your counsels as my guide, turning them to account whenever possible and always with excellent effect. A spectator of many things but never an actor, I employ my time in reflections, reading, and trying to establish contacts in order to make myself known and to know myself. I often miss my old custom of unburdening myself to you and letting you see many things which look differently at a distance. From a certain angle one seems to be always in the wrong, from another always in the right. You will charge me with hypochondria, no doubt, but inaction is some excuse.' A letter from the Grand Duchess of the same date must have given even keener pleasure. 'My happiness grows from day to day, partly owing to the kindness of the Empress, partly to the friendship shown me by my adorable husband, to whom I am devotedly attached and for whom I would give a thousand lives if I had them. Et c'est à vous, mon bien chérissime oncle, à qui je dois tout mon bonheur.' Henry was too self-centred to be loveable, but such gratitude could hardly be inspired by a man with a frozen heart.

Since Frederick was haunted by the memory that his father and grandfather had died in middle age, and since his nephew and heir was a lazy voluptuary, his thoughts turned for a brief space to his brother, who had rendered such conspicuous service in peace and war. 'I shall not die happy about the state unless I see you in some manner its guardian,' wrote the King in 1776 at the age of sixty-four. 'I

[1] The heir to the throne.

regard you as the only person who can sustain the glory of our House and become the pillar of our fatherland. I can explain my ideas more fully in conversation.' The interview seems to have been satisfactory, for the lonely ruler despatched a grateful letter after the visit. 'I should make an unpardonable mistake if I did not arrange that a person of your wisdom should share in the government, so that your good advice may make up for the negligence, imbecility and weakness of a creature incapable of governing himself, much less others. Convinced of your friendship for me, I have opened my heart on this matter which has long occupied me, I thank you a thousand times for your willingness to do as I wish. If heaven could be moved by our prayers I should ask it to pour down on you its richest blessings.' Never before had he written in such terms, yet nothing more was heard of the plan of a virtual regency. For the heir was now thirty-two, and in Prussia as elsewhere the ruler's authority lapsed with his death.

The first overt step towards a partition of Poland had been taken by Austria, and Frederick had little expectation of a similar bloodless settlement when the young Emperor decided to throw the dice once more. That Maria Theresa was sick of bloodshed was well known in Berlin, but in foreign affairs she could no longer resist a united demand from Kaunitz and her restless son. 'People in Paris are beginning to talk of the Emperor's designs against us,' reported Frederick to Henry at the close of 1776. 'So you see, my dear brother, that I receive confirmation from all quarters concerning the gathering storm. Yet I am not afraid. All my arrangements are made in the provinces to accelerate the march and assembly of the army.' 'I know for certain,' he added in April 1777, 'that Prince Kaunitz has said: "The Imperial Court should never support the power of Prussia; to secure our domination we must destroy it." These solemn words should be engraved on the heart of every Prussian so that we do not go to sleep. Assuredly that House will long compel the sovereigns of this country to keep their muscles taut; otherwise we shall be lost.'

When the dangerous problem of the Bavarian Succession suddenly loomed up at the opening of 1778, on the death of the childless Elector, Joseph snatched at the tempting bait. Henry pleaded for caution. If a conflict, as he expected, proved unavoidable, he recommended an alliance with France and Saxony. In February Frederick explained that the utmost he could hope from the former, with her chaotic finances and her Austrian Queen, was neutrality. It was not a case of acquiring territory, but of setting bounds once for all to Austria's ambition, so that she did not obtain despotic power in the Reich, which would be very damaging for Prussia. 'Thus whatever acquisitive designs they put before me, I shall reject them, for I am firmly resolved not to sheathe the sword till they have restored all their usurpations.' Henry, like Maria Theresa, had had his fill of war and feared to endanger his own unbroken record of victories. In April, while the Austrian and Prussian armies were slowly moving into position, the King felt it necessary to administer a tonic. 'Please remember that in the last war you and I often had 26,000 men against 60,000, and yet we pulled through. Now, including the Saxons, you have 80,000, and I almost as many, so I see no reason for anxiety. If however this war goes against the grain, you have only to tell me like my brother Ferdinand and you are your own master. But I really do not see why you need worry.' His exhortations fell on deaf ears, and a further dose of encouragement was needed in June. 'I am grieved that you paint everything so black and anticipate a gloomy future, whereas I merely envisage the sort of uncertainties which precede all great events. There is no glory, my dear brother, except in surmounting great difficulties, and nobody thinks much of things which cost no trouble.'

Frederick never feared that Catherine would take the Austrian side, and perhaps she might be induced to help her ally by frowning on Joseph's plans. Accordingly Henry despatched several letters inviting her to use her influence for the preservation of peace, and a special envoy to St. Petersburg was coached at Rheinsberg before setting out. That he still counted for something was confirmed by the Prussian Minister's report from the Russian capital that, influenced by a letter (not preserved) from Prince Henry on the eve of hostilities, the ruler, if her diplomatic representations at Vienna failed, would openly declare for Prussia and furnish troops as by treaty bound. 'Your letter to the Empress,' wrote Frederick, 'has helped more than a battle. Rest assured that the memory of this will remain with me till death.' The King's enthusiasm was premature, for Catherine's reply, however flattering to the recipient, was studiously vague. 'The wishes of a large part of Europe accompany Your Royal Highness in the glorious career on which you are once more entering in defence of your country. Even the indifferent are interested in the actions of heroes, and friends follow every move in the game. I am glad you have long numbered me among the friends of yourself and your country, and that you realise my desire to witness the restoration of peace. My actions will never belie these sentiments.' A second letter, dated September 3, congratulated him on his strategy and added: 'You are irresistible.' On the outbreak of war the Grand Duke and his wife wrote to wish him success and to beg for news. 'Allow me to write to you as often as my heart needs consolation, particularly in the sad life I lead. Do not reply, I beg you. I implore you to allow my brothers-in-law, myself and my wife to send our letters through the Chancellery or the Secretaries. I am till death, my dearest uncle, Paul. My tears prevent me from writing more.' This warm attachment was no longer to the taste of the jealous autocrat who disliked the notion that her unhappy heir possessed direct approach to a foreign court. With the approaching transfer of her political sympathies from Berlin to Vienna her attitude to Henry became more reserved. The correspondence which had flowed so freely since 1770 ceased in 1780, and an attempt in 1781 to renew contact through Grimm with a present received a chilly acknowledgment through the same intermediary.

The war of the Bavarian Succession provided fresh opportunities for friction between the brothers regarding the conduct of the campaign. Though it was the only conflict in modern history between great powers without pitched battles and indeed there was scarcely any fighting, Henry's heart was never in the fight and his health was seriously impaired by the campaign. He wished to resign the command of the army in Saxony in October, and in December his release was urgently requested on the ground that he was physically unable to perform his task. Frederick replied rather coolly that an immediate change of leadership would be very embarrassing, but promised to appoint the Duke of Brunswick if the campaign were renewed in the spring of 1779. By that time negotiations resulting from Russian and French mediation were in full swing and the war ended with the treaty of Teschen. Henry was as dissatisfied with the settlement as he had been with the policy which led to the conflict; for, if he was more cautious than his brother in the military sphere, he was less inclined to compromise in the political field. At Teschen, as at Hubertusburg, he complained, nothing was demanded for Prussia. 'We secure the great advantage,' rejoined the King, 'that we shall be regarded in the Reich as a useful counterpoise against Austrian despotism.' Henry

5*

was now thoroughly disgruntled. 'I will never draw the sword for him again,' he confided to Ferdinand in March. In April he wrote sulkily to the King that his career was over and that he was nearing the goal which delivers us from human misery. He had experienced so much injustice in the last thirty-nine years[1] that he ought to have learned to bear it without indignation, but that he had failed to do. So long as Frederick lived it was clear that he could hope for nothing more than *otium cum dignitate*. The King was tired of his complaints, and during the closing years of the reign he almost ceased to count. In 1781, on the occasion of a journey to the Austrian Netherlands, the Emperor visited him at Spa, and reported to Kaunitz that he made no secret of his discontent. He hoped that the reign would not last much longer and that relations with Austria would improve under his successor, whom he believed he could influence in that direction. Joseph was not impressed, suspecting that these indiscretions might be intended to provoke him to follow suit. The suspicion was unfounded, for Henry talked in the same vein to everyone who was willing or compelled to listen to his complaints.

Complete exclusion from public affairs increased his restlessness. The celebrated soldier who had dreamed of the Polish crown, or at the very least of the family duchies of Ansbach-Bayreuth, had to console himself as best he could with literature and the arts. As a lover of French culture, who could hardly speak German correctly, and, like his brother, never read a German book, he had always longed to visit *la ville lumière*, to renew old acquaintances, to make new friends, perhaps even to dabble in politics once again. Paris beckoned to him as Rome to Winckelmann and Goethe.[2] When as a young man he had desired to travel his request had been declined on the ground that it might cause political complications. At last, in 1784, at fifty-eight it was granted: it could do no harm, thought Frederick, and perhaps it might even do some good. The prestige of France had been dimmed since the days of Fleury and Choiseul; but she remained a Great Power, the Austrian alliance was still in being, and Joseph II was a nightmare. If the life-long Francophil, whose friendly sentiments had been gratefully reported by successive French Ambassadors, could loosen still further the ties between Paris and Vienna and persuade the French Government of the goodwill of Berlin, the

---

[1] Since Frederick's accession.
[2] See Krauel, *Prinz Heinrich von Preussen in Paris*.

journey might be worth while. Frederick supplied no instructions, contenting himself with a warning to be on his guard. France's polite refusal of the plan of a defensive alliance in the previous year indicated that there was not much to be done.

Henry may well have hinted to d'Esterno, the French Minister in Berlin, that he would like an invitation, but in any case for such a *persona grata* a warm welcome was assured. On his way he met Goethe at Weimar, Necker at Geneva, and Gibbon at Lausanne. His old friend Grimm, Minister for Saxe-Gotha in Paris, opened all doors in society and the literary world. 'You cannot imagine what the French are like,' wrote the joyful traveller to Ferdinand. 'You know I always loved them, and now I would be ready to die for them. Everything here is delightful and lovely.' France, he exclaimed, was a land of the gods. No one, however, believed that the brother of Frederick the Great was bent solely on pleasure, and rumours of secret negotiations began to spread. Joseph felt sure that something was afoot, and ordered Mercy, his Minister in Paris, whom Frederick described as the Viceroy of France, to keep a sharp lookout. On August 16, the day before the Prince's arrival, Mercy reported that the visit greatly displeased the Queen, but he thought it would have no official result. Goltz, on the other hand, the Prussian Minister, dreaded interference in his domain and was worried at receiving no orders from Berlin. Though Henry asked him not to report since he was in direct correspondence with his brother, Goltz described the impressions of Vergennes and Mercy. Since the Foreign Minister was tepid about the Austrian alliance and therefore was not in favour at Court, he avoided anything so calculated to increase the suspicions of the Austrian party as close association with the Prince. The anti-Austrian party, on the other hand, welcomed the visit in the belief that it had a political aim.

At the outset Henry seemed to be bent on sight-seeing and social delights. On his first visit to Court 'Count Oels' was welcomed warmly by the King and frigidly by the Queen. 'They send the King out hunting,' commented Frederick, 'to shield him from your influence and out of deference for the Court of Vienna.' What Louis XVI thought of him we do not know, but the visitor told Ségur that he was impressed by the knowledge, the sense, and the goodness of the host. Friendly relations were also established with Artois, brother of the King, Condé and the Duke of Orleans. Courtesy visits were paid to the Ministers and he won the confidence of the influential Finance Minister Calonne. Every one was charmed, not least the ladies of high rank. He attracted Mme de Sabran who, with Boufflers, was later to find shelter at Rheinsberg from the revolutionary storm; the Duchesse de Polignac, friend of the Queen and Governess of the royal children; Mme Lebrun, the artist, and Princess de Lamballe, destined to a tragic end. In the literary world he met Condorcet and Beaumarchais, whose *Figaro* he enjoyed without sensing its revolutionary trend. Marmontel, secretary of the Academy, greeted him at a session. Ségur described him as 'a valiant warrior, a clever general, a profound politician, a friend of justice, science and art, a protector of the weak, a friend of the unfortunate.' He was the lion of the season, yet he wanted something more.

There is no mention of politics in the letters to his brother Ferdinand, doubtless for security reasons, and with Frederick he corresponded in cipher. When he reported that a large party was Prussophil, the King replied that France would not change her course despite fair words, though perhaps she might wish to show Vienna that she could if necessary look elsewhere. Henry refused to be daunted. 'It is incredible how eagerly the nation desires our alliance. Public opinion here is of great importance. Artois said: We must be friends, all my circle wish it.' Names were omitted owing to the danger of letters being opened by the French Government and the cipher read. It was a wise precaution, for we learn from Mercy's correspondence that the Prussian despatches from Paris had been tapped for years. Frederick approved his brother's caution, but his own letters were frank enough. 'I venture to hope that your stay will turn people in our direction and that France at last will see that it is necessary to change her system and to choose us as her *pis-aller*.'

Henry interpreted this sentence as an authorisation to go ahead, though he was aware of their divergent presuppositions. Frederick held that the Government would not seriously contemplate a breach with Austria and that France was too weak to be of much value as an ally. 'All we can do is to keep the Court in good humour but not rely on help. You will see only traces of the vanished greatness of the France of Louis XIV.' He had never forgotten the collapse at Rossbach, his first and last encounter with French troops. Yet Joseph was not without anxiety. 'You have Prince Henry in Paris,' he wrote to the Queen, 'I can imagine what he is at.' To Mercy he wrote in greater detail. 'I am very curious to learn what success he has had and what he is doing. Judging by what they say of me, he will only need half his perfidy and skill in putting over the most preposterous fabrications. But I think you will find he is not the man he was.' Mercy reported that he had not ventured on politics and had only seen Vergennes once, but perhaps he was working through third parties. Meanwhile the Prussian Minister felt extremely uncomfortable. Knowing nothing, he feared that things might be settled behind his back, and he was not quite sure whether the King had authorised his brother's activities. No one, however, was so perturbed as the Queen. 'Prince Henry leaves in two days,' she reported to the Emperor on November 5; 'all the better, as he has for some time been intriguing and making trouble.' Vergennes, who was censured by the Queen at Mercy's instigation, explained that the Prince had vainly attempted to converse with him about politics. He left Paris on November 2 for Rouen and Chantilly, and it was only now that serious business began. Though Vergennes avoided much direct contact in order to say that he had no political discussions, he kept in touch through third parties, above all through Calonne, who was deputed by the King to visit Henry while staying with the Duke of Orleans in the country.

On November 8 Henry despatched an important cipher letter to Frederick. 'During my stay in Paris I did my best for your interests. I was able to inspire confidence in the five Ministers, of which I have had clear proofs. When the Dutch incident became more critical I spoke to Vergennes, who is on intimate terms with Calonne, so that both of them might discuss the most secret matters with the King. Calonne was sent to me twice to give me news and to ask what I thought about the 60,000 men the Emperor is setting in motion. Yesterday he came here unexpectedly to give me a message from the King. He will inform the Emperor that he regrets the attack on Holland, and cannot allow her to be unjustly oppressed and thrown into the arms of England just when he is about to conclude an alliance with her. He will press the Emperor to accept his mediation, and if the latter insists on marching against her he will have to place a similar force on the French frontiers. This declaration will be communicated to the Courts of Europe. If it produces no results he is inclined to combine with the King of Prussia to oppose any threat to peace. You are requested, my dear brother, not to mention this to Goltz till I have spoken to you. You will then understand why I ask this and why I was silent in my cipher report. Calonne assures me that 60,000 men will be placed in Flanders within fifteen days.'

With this communication we may compare Calonne's less explicit report to Mercy. Prince Henry had come to him in Paris—on the pretext of seeing the art treasures in his office—to discuss the situation. He said he knew that his brother was gravely concerned by present happenings. True to his principle of prevention he would probably take sudden action one day which the French Court would not like— if it left him any longer in doubt as to its views. It would therefore be wise to write to Berlin. Calonne answered without committing himself: The Court would inform the King of Prussia of its decision as soon as the Emperor's plans became clearer. This was vague enough, but the French Minister at Vienna informed the Emperor that France might have to act; and at a Council the War and Navy Ministers strongly urged co-operation with Prussia, a course grudgingly approved by the King. Henry was proud to have been the first to receive this information, and was confirmed in his conviction that France would act with Prussia. This was too much to hope, but at any rate she took no action against Prussia in the following year when Frederick formed the Fürstenbund to resist Joseph's second attempt on Bavaria. Henry might flatter himself that his visit had not been in vain and that he had left the ties between Paris and Vienna even looser than he found them. The Baden Agent in Paris reported that he had had remarkable success. The Emperor sent no reply to the communication from the King of France, but he suspended the march of his troops and the crisis came to an end.

Having expected little from his brother's journey Frederick was mildly pleased with the result. 'There will be nothing doing,' he wrote, 'unless the Emperor breaks the windows or attacks the Turks or some ally of France, and the credit of the Queen will be strong enough to affect the nerves of Ministers even if one of them chanced to have the right ideas. So we must limit ourselves to keeping the Court in good humour with the Prussians; to count on them would be a mistake.' He always believed that Joseph would give way if France took a firm line. On the other hand Henry, who visited Potsdam on his return, could not persuade him that France seriously contemplated the termination of the alliance or that she would be a reliable partner in a European war. The Prince's gallomania, indeed, was too much for many of his countrymen. 'Prince Henry,' complained Karl Friedrich of Baden in 1786, 'is so Frenchified that it is really a spectacle.'

In addition to the delights of society and the lure of high politics the tourist's programme included some private business. He had always lived beyond his means, despite substantial rewards for his services, and he was now deeply in debt. The patience of the thrifty monarch was not inexhaustible, and he had finally forbidden Prussian bankers to assist either his brother or the Crown Prince. Under these circumstances the former had to look abroad, and a way was opened by the Duc de Cars, who visited Rheinsberg in 1784 after attending the Prussian military manoeuvres. The reception, he records in his Memoirs, though extremely polite, was chilly. Henry attacked the whole political system of the French Cabinet as subordinate to Austria and sharply complained of the influence of the Queen. De Cars noted the remarkable intelligence of his host and his perfect knowledge of the state of Europe; his judgments, however, were in no way impartial and the conversation became tiring as there was too much monologue. The visitor parried embarrassing queries with the formula that he was a soldier, not a diplomatist. The Prince talked freely of his financial worries and the acquaintance was soon renewed in Paris. De Cars arranged an interview with the banker La Borde, his father-in-law, who promised to find the 400,000 francs of which Henry stood in need, contemptuously remarking: 'Il faut faire quelque chose pour ce pauvre diable de prince Prussien.' La Borde informed his friend Mercy, but he quickly cooled off. Henry was too proud to ask him again, but an urgent letter written in January 1785 after his return to Berlin led De Cars to try elsewhere. This time he explained the situation to Vergennes himself, who informed the King and Calonne, and De Cars was instructed to take 400,000 francs to Rheinsberg. The loan was repaid in 1786 after the Prince came into possession of the little Hohenzollern principality of Schwedt. Such state aid to princes was not unusual, and in Henry's case it was considered a good investment, for Frederick's strength was waning and perhaps the borrower might soon have an opportunity of rendering service to France.

When Frederick formed the League of Princes to thwart Joseph's second attempt to seize Bavaria, Henry displayed his instinctive dislike of military risks. Though in 1778 the Tsarina had been the ally of Prussia she was now the ally of Austria and she favoured the Hapsburg scheme. Since Prussia was too weak to resist Austria and Russia in combination, he argued, it was vital to win over France, lukewarm though she was. 'She must be handled with consideration as a doctor handles a patient with weak nerves till suitable remedies have restored his strength.' He criticised the League of Princes on the ground that it was unnecessary, that it would be distasteful to France, and that a French alliance would be far more useful. There was also a more fundamental objection at the back of his mind. He hoped that sooner or later, perhaps on the basis of a deal with Austria, Prussia might possess not only the southern shore of the Baltic from the Elbe to the Vistula but the states through which the Elbe flowed; and for that reason he frowned on the idea of a permanent League of Princes including some whose possessions he earmarked for the Hohenzollerns. Such notions were far more ambitious than anything in either of Frederick's Political Testaments. The criticism of the League of Princes was ill-founded, for Frederick's creation achieved its limited purpose of preserving the *status quo* without the shedding of blood. It was indeed the most skilful and successful of all his diplomatic performances, raising the prestige of Prussia and placing no obstacle in the way of further advances.

In a letter of 1775 to his nephew the Crown Prince Henry had denounced the King as 'the author of our common miseries, the tyrant we must suffer till the hour of deliverance.' He shed no tears at the death of his brother, not only because he had never loved him, but because it left him, so far as prestige was concerned, the first man in the state. Having watched Frederick William II grow from an attractive lad into a corpulent, idle, sensual and superstitious man, he hoped that the new ruler might feel the need of the wisest counsellor he could find. Hertzberg, who remained at the Foreign Office, represented the Frederician tradition too faithfully to find favour at Rheinsberg; for though he was as anti-Austrian as his old master, he was friendly to England, not unfriendly to Russia, and above all lukewarm towards France.[1] Yet he was not the chief obstacle, for power passed into the unworthy hands of the King's adjutant, Bischoff-

---

[1] See Preuss, *Graf Hertzberg*, and Krauel, *Graf Hertzberg als Minister Friedrich Wilhelms II.* The best account of the reign of Frederick William II is in Heigel, *Deutsche Geschichte seit dem Tode Friedrichs des Grossen*, vol. i; Martin Philippson, *Geschichte des deutschen Staatswesens vom Tode Friedrichs des Grossen*, 2 vols., is also useful.

werder, a Rosicrucian adventurer from Saxony, and Wöllner, the sworn foe of the *Aufklärung* and its tolerant ways. Though Henry was only sixty and often complained of his health, he was still burning with ambition and more than ever convinced of the wisdom of his views. Little did he dream how correct would prove the forecast despatched by Hertzberg to the Prussian Minister at Paris a few days before the death of Frederick the Great: 'The influence of a certain prince will be as null in the future as it is to-day, despite the assertions here and in France to the contrary.' For the remainder of his life his main preoccupation was to drive the ship of state towards the alliance with France for which he had always yearned, from which he did not allow even the horrors of the Revolution to deflect his gaze.

II

ON the day after Frederick's death Henry had a long and friendly talk with his nephew, following it up three days later with the first of many memoranda on matters of high policy.[1] The new ruler was exhorted to write a personal letter to the King of France to propose closer relations on the ground that Prussia was afflicted with open frontiers and exposed to two powerful enemies, Austria and Russia, who might at any moment combine in arms as in the Seven Years' War. Austria, he assumed, was irreconcilable, and the Russian bear, with its insatiable appetite, was just getting into its stride. Without some such encouragement, he added, Vergennes and Calonne could do nothing for the good cause. Rejecting a draft submitted to him by his uncle, Frederick William contented himself with a colourless message through his Minister expressing his hope for the continuance of good relations. The first bid for political influence having failed, Henry spent most of the winter of 1786-7 in Berlin, since out of sight would be out of mind. It was all in vain. Though treating the distinguished veteran with respect, the King avoided serious discussion and when the Prince begged for a command he was refused. He was reminded that he had resigned in 1778 during the War of the Bavarian Succession on the ground of health, though every one knew that he had merely chosen a formula to cover his discontent. So incensed was he at this unexpected boycott that he informed foreign Courts that he

[1] This numerous memoranda presented to Frederick William II and Frederick William III are printed in the appendix to Krauel, *Prinz Heinrich als Politiker*.

had no responsibility for foreign affairs. Despite his endeavours Hertzberg, the High Priest of the anti-French school, remained at his post. It was a scanty consolation that in the spring of 1787 he was sounded by General von Steuben, the German hero of the War of Independence, on the possibility of his becoming Stadtholder of the United States, though who sent the invitation we cannot tell. He replied that he could only accept the position of a constitutional king like that of England, the most perfect of all constitutions, and then only in response to a unanimous demand.

We are indebted to Mirabeau for some snapshots of the old Prince immediately before and after his brother's death.[1] Welcomed to Rheinsberg as cordially as other distinguished Frenchmen, whatever their political opinions, he listened eagerly to the blazing indiscretions of his host and forwarded them to Paris. At the outset no praise was too high for the most Francophil of Prussians. The wind quickly shifted when the French Minister in Berlin cautioned Henry against the brilliant adventurer, and the offended visitor proceeded to dip his pen in gall. 'Prince Henry has already sealed his fate,' he wrote a fortnight after the change of ruler. 'The meanness of his character is shipwrecked on the rock of his immense vanity. Now as at other times he displayed a craving for power, a disgusting conceit and insufferable pedantry, while his whole life is only one low intrigue. He despises influential Ministers, while, with the exception of a Baron threatened with apoplexy, he has no one of consequence round him who is not a fool, a worm, or a knave. He no longer deceives himself about his position. Like all weak men passing from one extreme to the other he already bewails that the country is lost, that priests, idiots, concubines and the English will hurtle it into the abyss, his violent language destroying the last trace of regard the King might feel for him. If permitted he will leave this country where he has not a single friend, or die.' Such lurid colouring damages the portrait-painter more than his sitter, though the statement that Henry's naive gallomania harmed the French cause is true enough.

Now that *le vieux*, as Henry always called Frederick, was gone, there was nothing to prevent a second visit to the land of his dreams, and the new ruler made no difficulties. Though he sometimes talked of settling permanently in France, and Louis XVI sent a message that

[1] The best edition of the Letters from Berlin is in Welschinger, *La Mission Secrète de Mirabeau à Berlin, 1786–1787.*

he would be welcome, it was doubtless merely an expression of resentment at his unexpected exclusion from public affairs. Moreover the situation might change and he had no intention of burning his boats. 'Count Oels' reached Paris on December 1, 1788, and left on March 21, 1789. Ignorant of popular movements, he failed to realise that the *ancien régime* was tottering to its fall and that the Assembly of Notables was a symptom of weakness, not of strength. His letters to Ferdinand breathe the unreflecting optimism of the aristocractic circles in which he delighted to move. He resumed contact with Necker and made the acquaintance of his brilliant daughter, Mme de Stael. 'Prince Henry, whom I suspected of intrigue, has had a very tepid reception,' reported his old enemy Mercy, the Austrian Minister; 'he appears very seldom at Versailles, is hardly ever with the Ministers, and is quite outside things.' Montmorin, who had succeeded Vergennes at the Foreign Office, wrote to the French Minister at Berlin in March 1789 that the Prince was about to leave Paris. 'It is impossible to be more cautious than he has been throughout his stay. It is sad that he no longer counts in Berlin. The Prussian monarchy would be the gainer if he did.' Even Goltz, the Prussian Minister, now sang his praises. Despite its lack of political significance, Henry enjoyed his second visit no less than the first. 'One feels reborn, one breathes a different air, the mind becomes more cheerful.' Conscious of the settled hostility of the Queen he only appeared at Court on ceremonial occasions, but Society was once again at his feet. 'I feel more at home in Paris, live more in accordance with my taste, am better loved and better known, than in Berlin.' His reserve melted in the warm rays, and he was more than ever convinced that France and Prussia should be friends.

During his stay in Paris a bomb exploded at his feet, for Mirabeau's *Secret Letters from Berlin* appeared and were eagerly read. 'He is universally despised,' he reported, 'and I have learned that his pen is venal.' On January 26, 1789, he added that Mirabeau had left the capital three weeks ago. 'I do not receive him, though he inscribed his name three times. Shortly before he left, the *Letters* appeared in which everyone is shown up, beginning with the King. I fare no better—like the Emperor and the Tsarina. In a word, it is a heap of slanders. He speaks with the same impudence of his countrymen in Germany, beginning with Count d'Esterno. Only the Duke of Brunswick comes in for praise. The disgust of the Court and the public is impossible to describe, and the consideration paid to me has doubled. He would be lynched if he dared show his face in Paris now. The Court has forbidden the book, which is to be denounced to Parliament, and he will probably be treated as a criminal. I am happy at such a strong proof of the sympathy of the French nation. I have received tokens of friendship and respect which only an ungrateful man could forget. Even the villagers have expressed their disgust. Such reactions are indescribable and in Berlin they are unintelligible. But it is a fine spectacle to witness the contempt of the whole nation for such a scandalmonger.' He advised his brother Ferdinand not to read the book as Mirabeau cast doubts on the fidelity of his wife. Thiébault's story that Henry bought sixteen copies for his friends is improbable, for he writes that he possessed two copies and would not lend them. His satisfaction at the ostracism of Mirabeau was short-lived, for the offender remained unpunished and in a few weeks he was back again, the chief pilot in the revolutionary storm.

Anxious to learn his uncle's impressions of the convulsions in France the King paid a pleasant visit to Rheinsberg in September 1789. 'I wish with all my heart,' wrote the host to his brother Ferdinand, 'that this King, who is good and has such an excellent heart, was always surrounded by honourable people, for then this land would be the paradise of the world.' Yet no increase of political influence ensued. 'It is sad to see the edifice one has helped to construct falling to pieces,' he confided to Grimm; 'but if one has nothing to reproach oneself with and no way of preventing it, patience is the only course.' The two men wore different spectacles, the elder surveying events beyond the Rhine with hopeful expectation, the younger with distressful alarm. The *Émigration* widened the gulf, for Henry, while ready enough to help individuals in their distress, disliked their intransigence and opposed armed intervention on their behalf. He was no whole-hearted champion of autocracy anywhere, and after its collapse in France he would not lift a finger for its restoration. England he detested as the most formidable enemy of his beloved France. 'These famous islanders,' he wrote to Grimm in 1791, 'are the most treacherous allies in Europe, the greatest robbers when it is a question of seeking their own advantage and sacrificing thereto that of their so-called allies.' Yet, though the memory of Bute still rankled after thirty years, he admired the British Constitution and approved the attempts of Anglophiles in Paris to copy it. If England could work the system, why should not France, the first nation in the world?

The declaration of war by the Girondin Ministry in April 1792 was a shock. Henry had expected the catastrophe, if it came at all, to be started by champions of the old order at Vienna and Berlin. He described the fiery Brissot as horrible, turbulent, violent. 'I confess I loathe the Jacobin party and would give anything to see it destroyed. France is in a terrible situation. If I thought force would be useful I would support it, but I am convinced it would do more harm than good.' This shrewd forecast was repeated in August, when the angry scream of the Brunswick Manifesto doomed the discredited Monarchy and stirred Republican France to the depths. The invasion, he wrote prophetically to Mme de Sabran, would enthrone the Jacobins and involve the death of the King. That Prussia should have joined hands in a crusade with Austria, the arch enemy, made it still worse. Valmy was no great surprise to him, and the failure of the invasion provided him with a fresh argument for his thesis that war with France was a mistake. He spoke bitterly of the chauvinism of 'King' Bischoffwerder and of the obscurantism of 'King' Wöllner.

Henry was generally though erroneously regarded as a Jacobin, and the King suspected everybody who did not share his crusading zeal. 'As you are going to Karlsbad,' wrote Catherine to Grimm in June 1792, 'you will doubtless see Prince Henry, and you must tell me if it is true that he has become a fiery democrat.' Two months later she thanked her 'fag' for his report, adding that she knew the Prince had been threatened during the past winter with imprisonment for seditious language. This, of course, was malicious gossip, but his movements were closely watched. When war broke out he went to Karlsbad to escape shadowing, but Bischoffwerder warned the Austrian Government to keep a sharp eye on him. He foretold that the invasion would fail and that the French people would never welcome the troops. 'I have a very low opinion of the prospects of the campaign,' he wrote in the autumn of 1792. 'The Manifestos have spoiled everything.' The rulers of Prussia, he bitterly declared, could neither conduct war nor make peace.

On the last day of 1792 Henry felt it his duty once again to tender advice to the King. Two or three victories were possible and a few towns might be taken, but success on a large scale was highly improbable. 'I confess, my dear nephew, that I foresee nothing but the exhaustion of the finances and the destruction of a considerable part of the army, with your position greatly worsened. Do not covet laurels on your brow. I will not dwell on the methods employed to persuade you to embark on war, though I am well aware of them; but the intriguers who pulled the strings knew how strongly I disapproved. That is why I avoid all personal matters, while entertaining the profoundest contempt for my calumniators. Remember that I volunteered for service though aware how I was exposing myself. I saw that you were rushing to your doom, and I would have accepted a post far humbler than I used to fill in the hope of saving you from the misfortunes into which you have been drawn.' Plans for the coming campaign and the peace, he added, could best be discussed in conversation, and he offered to come to Frankfurt. The assumption that the King had not been the maker of Prussian policy was not very tactful, and the suggestion of a visit was ignored. Three weeks later, on January 21, 1793, a second letter was even more outspoken. 'A war is only of use when it serves the state interest: that is what constitutes your glory. The further you stray from this interest, the greater the risk of lifelong regrets. It is a recognised truth that this war cannot profit the state from any point of view, and that, once started, the sooner it ends the better.'

On the day that the second letter was written Louis XVI perished on the scaffold. Now that it had proved impossible to save either the Monarchy or the monarch the conflict seemed to Henry more futile than ever. Yet his appeals fell on deaf ears and the realisation of his impotence filled him with bitterness. 'I would rather live in a barn or in Siberia than in Berlin,' he lamented to Ferdinand; 'the political imbecility must lead to a disastrous conflagration, but I shall not fetch water to put it out.' Since Frederick William was still in crusading mood, the Francophil uncle could only grumble and bide his time. When the fall of Robespierre seemed to some observers the signal for a monarchical restoration, Henry saw in it merely the hatred of rule by a single person. The Republic, he believed, was safe for the present. He remarked that the republican spirit gave the mind wings, whereas in an autocracy the vanity of an individual stunted the capacity of the masses. Such heresies increased his unpopularity in Court circles, and even the liberal-minded Duke of Brunswick was horrified to hear them from the lips of a prince. The Duchess of York, a daughter of the King of Prussia, complained that Rheinsberg, from the guests to the lowest menial, was nothing but a Jacobin club, and she wondered how the King could tolerate such a coterie.

The counter-revolutionary fervour of the monarch wilted in face of military defeat, and the plunder of anaemic Poland appeared a more tempting bait. The part-author of the first amputation felt no satisfaction at the second and third: happy he could never be while France and Prussia were at war. 'Would to God the French made peace,' he wrote to his brother in September 1794, 'but I fear they will demand too many sacrifices. Prussia's rôle is ended—no men, no money, a ruined army, like the sick lion in the fable who is kicked by an ass.' The conversion which his memoranda had failed to achieve was accomplished by the progress of French arms and the exhaustion of Prussia's finances. When Malmesbury was despatched on a special mission to hold her to her obligations under the treaty of 1788, the King explained that his circumstances, though not his convictions, had changed, and that it was impossible to continue the war without large subsidies.[1] Even Hertzberg, now living in retirement and near his end, wanted peace. Henry's hour had come at last and he requested an audience of the King. In October 1794 he was received for the first time since the beginning of the war, and his niece, Princess Louise, found him radiant after his return from Sans Souci. For the next six months he was as happy as his self-centred and hypersensitive nature ever permitted him to be; once again, as at St. Petersburg in 1770, he felt that he was making history. Even if his nephew did not entirely trust him and showed no sign of selecting him as a plenipotentiary, he was at any rate more inclined to consider his advice. The original purpose of the war had lapsed, argued Henry in a memorandum of October 29, for the King and Queen of France were dead; now it was useless slaughter and financial ruin. Secret negotiations through Switzerland should be promptly initiated. No obligations to Austria or England need stand in the way, for they were out for themselves and Austria was quite capable of deserting her partner. Moreover their armies were now in a bad condition. Peace, he believed, could also be made with the Reich, perhaps even a general peace, based on the recognition of the French Republic, which he believed had come to stay, and the loss of the Left Bank of the Rhine. The memorandum had produced an excellent effect, he reported to Ferdinand, and he had learned that his advice would be followed to

[1] Malmesbury, Diaries and Correspondence, iii. 1–150.

the letter. His attitude was largely determined by considerations wider than the necessities of the hour. Regarding both Austria and Russia as fundamentally hostile to Prussia, he had no desire for the total overthrow of France even were it possible. Prussia's interest was to balance herself between the Powers, and neutrality seemed the lesser risk. The hatred of the Revolution in Court circles was undiminished, but Haugwitz and Bischoffwerder now agreed with their master that Prussia had no choice, though, unlike Henry, they regretted the necessity of leaving their allies in the lurch.

A second memorandum to the King, dated November 2, 1794, discussed some questions likely to be raised during the conference. For instance, the French might propose an alliance with Prussia which it would be equally dangerous to accept or decline. Too sudden a break with her recent partner would diminish the confidence felt by a new ally, and it would be wiser to postpone discussions while accepting the project in principle. Henry was informed that the King entirely approved the memorandum, and a third communication brought a grateful reply from Frederick William himself, concluding with regrets that there were so many obstacles to the best intentions. The old Prince, delighted to find himself taken seriously after so many years, replied that the making of peace undoubtedly involved many difficulties. 'But I beg you, my dearest nephew, to reflect that they would be infinitely increased by a further campaign. I start with the assumption that it is impossible for Your Majesty to continue the war without entirely ruining your subjects or without new subsidies from England.' The latter would in any case need to be supplemented. Peace was absolutely essential and every honourable means to that end must be sought. At the King's wish he now entered on conversations and correspondence with Haugwitz.

Returning to Rheinsberg Henry drafted a lengthy *Projet d'instruction pour celui qui doit traiter de la paix*,[1] advising the King first to conclude peace with France and then to mediate on behalf of the Reich and Holland, perhaps even of Austria and England. The treaty with France would have to include recognition of the Republic, restoration of occupied Prussian territory on the left bank of the Rhine, French non-interference in the Polish settlement, and tacit recognition of the Second Partition of 1793. The author was rewarded by a letter from the King informing him that Count Goltz,

[1] Printed in Ranke, *Hardenberg*, v. 56–72.

for many years Prussian Minister at Paris, had been selected as Prussian plenipotentiary and that he would visit Rheinsberg for consultation before leaving for Basle. There were some good things in the memorandum, commented Frederick William to Haugwitz, but also some impracticable suggestions, such as that of withdrawing the Prussian army during the negotiations.

Portions of Henry's elaborate *Projet* were incorporated in the official instructions to the Prussian plenipotentiary. 'General von Goltz was extremely pleased with his stay,' reported Struensee, the francophil Finance Minister, 'and has fully entered into the great scheme of Your Royal Highness.' Even more flattering was a letter from Bischoffwerder, the King's Favourite, on December 12. 'The first step towards the plan conceived and worked out by Your Royal Highness was taken to-day when Major-General Count von Goltz set out, furnished with instructions entirely conforming to your wise proposals.' His mission was generally attributed to Henry's initiative, though not in all quarters with satisfaction. Despite fair words from Berlin Vienna was alarmed, and the Duke of Brunswick, who disapproved the principle of separate negotiations with France, lamented to Lord Malmesbury that the Prince had been to Potsdam and was paying court to Haugwitz and Bischoffwerder. Prince Henry, he declared, was the most dangerous foe of any rapprochement with England.

Spending the winter of 1794–5 in Berlin as usual, Henry was in touch with the King and memoranda flowed from his busy pen. The French conquest of Holland weakened the bargaining power of Prussia, and the hope of retaining territory beyond the Rhine began to wane. If necessary Goltz could accept the sacrifice in return for a secret article providing for suitable compensation: France should obtain Swedish Pomerania and Rugen from Sweden and hand them over to Prussia. The Ministers were divided, England offered fresh subsidies, and the Duke of Brunswick preferred the risks of a further campaign to a humiliating peace, yet Henry felt confident of success. 'Peace with France is certain,' he remarked to Colonel Massenbach.[1] 'I started it and I am working at it here. This war was stupidly commenced and has been stupidly waged. It is against the interest of our country and it must end. We have other enemies than the French.' His vanity led him to exaggerate his influence, for, as Haugwitz

[1] *Memoiren*, ii. 91.

confided to foreign diplomatists, the King only gave his uncle half his confidence and merely appeared to follow his advice. The appointment of Hardenberg as Prussian plenipotentiary when Goltz died on February 5 further weakened his position, for the sympathies of the Hanoverian statesman were with England rather than with France. Henry's counsels were reinforced by financial exhaustion and the military inferiority of Prussia. On the day that the Treaty of Basle was signed, Bacher, Barthélemy's colleague in the French delegation, assured him that the French Republic would welcome the renewal of friendly ties under his auspices. Henry's reply expressing the wish that the peace would strengthen friendly relations between all peoples, especially between the French and the Prussians, had the honour of being published in the *Moniteur*. That the French negotiators were grateful for his steady support is clear from the fifth volume of the *Papiers de Barthélemy*.

'The King is at heart extremely vexed at the success of the negotiations,' reported the British Minister at Berlin. Though a disagreeable necessity he regarded it as both a national and a personal humiliation to desert his allies and to be the first to make peace with Republican France. Now that he had been compelled to swallow the bitter pill, he had no wish for further intimacy with the importunate uncle who had striven to force it down his throat. Henry, needless to say, congratulated him on the return of peace. The country, he declared, might now again enjoy happiness and prosperity; the frowns of other Powers merely proved the advantage of the settlement. Such effusive tributes evoked no response, and a draft declaration from Rheinsberg to be issued by the King explaining his reasons for leaving the coalition was ignored. 'Now the affair is over,' complained Henry to his brother, 'the good King believes he does not need me further. He cannot see that this declaration would have been most useful.' To Haugwitz he wrote bitterly that he had borne all rebuffs, slanders and intrigues, but that it was the last time he would present a memorandum. 'I let the curtain fall, for it suits neither my character, nor my age, nor my way of life to be merely a penman, though that I was from love of the fatherland and the general good.'

Some consolation was found in the knowledge that his part in the settlement was recognised and even exaggerated by friend and foe. 'Prussia consents to peace on the terms proposed by France,' wrote Lord Malmesbury in his diary on February 20, 1795, when the news reached Brunswick where he was arranging for the marriage of Princess Caroline to the Prince of Wales. 'Infamous and incredible. Prince Henry's doing.'[1] A few days later he wrote to Grenville, the Foreign Minister, in the same tone of exasperation and disgust. 'Prince Henry of Prussia prides himself upon having managed the whole of this disgraceful measure. How he acquired the ascendancy, and how he maintains it, I can neither conjecture nor learn. He is probably brought forward as the temporary instrument of that mass of corruption and treachery which surround the King of Prussia and will be sacrificed whenever their work is complete.' The reaction in St. Petersburg was even more violent than in Vienna and London. In a letter to Grimm Catherine spoke of 'this infamous, disgraceful, disastrous peace which a faithless King has signed with the regicide bandits and the scum of the human race.' Having formed the lowest opinion of the capacity of Frederick William during his visit in 1780, she believed that he was the tool of his Francophil uncle. 'So the great Henry has led his nephew into a course which flouts all his treaties with the Emperor, England and myself,' she wrote to Grimm. 'He heartily detests his nephew; for, if he had the least affection for him, he would never have urged him to actions as disgraceful to himself as detrimental to the rest of Europe and perhaps to the King of Prussia above all.'

Convinced that he had been impelled by purely personal motives, she suggested that 'le grand petit Henri' had worked for peace in the hope of becoming Regent for the Dauphin if the monarchy were restored and, in the event of his death, King of France. 'If so,' she wrote to Grimm, 'I wager that His Royal Highness will be guillotined within six months.' During the closing years of her reign she could hardly mention his name without anger and disgust. 'Everyone, even the Prussian Minister himself,' she wrote in October 1795, 'says that Prince Henry has completely adopted the system and conduct of Philip Égalité, of infamous memory.' The Prince was aware of her displeasure but bore it with composure, for his conscience was clear. 'To-morrow I put on mourning for the Empress,' he wrote to his brother on learning of her death, 'in memory of the marks of friendship she gave me and for the sake of her genius which is a loss for the whole world.' From a political standpoint, he added, it was welcome news.

[1] Malmesbury, *Diaries and Correspondence*, iii. 200–250.

The Treaty of Basle, signed on April 5, 1795, like the Treaty of Utrecht, has been praised and blamed by historians of many lands for a hundred and fifty years. It was naturally approved by the Prussian School, but Ranke, who was no Austrophobe, also gave it his blessing. Austrian scholars, equally naturally, agreed with Thugut's contemporary verdict that it was a peace of scandalous disloyalty. Later and cooler observers agree that Prussian statesmen were confronted by a choice of evils. There was no national policy either in Vienna or Berlin, declares the Bavarian Heigel, the leading German authority on the period. Neither Thugut, nor Haugwitz, nor Lucchesini was a German patriot, their whole purpose being the power and profit of Austria or Prussia. Yet though the Treaty was not treachery it was a political mistake. Without being defeated Prussia played a humiliating *rôle*, while she helped France, bleeding from a thousand wounds, to a preponderance in Europe which even Louis XIV had never possessed. The cowardly separation from the allies was unworthy of a great state, and the fulfilment of Prussia's German mission was thereby postponed for many years.

The withdrawal of Prussia from the war was only the first item in Henry's programme, which aimed at a general peace with France. When the King declined the suggestion of an interview he set forth his views in a lengthy memorandum dated November 27, 1795. The French Republic, he was convinced, would last for a considerable time, despite the assertions of the *Émigrés* that it was weak. He had sympathised with their troubles and gone beyond his means to help them, but most of them were ungrateful firebrands, selfishly lamenting the loss of their power and wealth. The treaty should be followed up by contributing towards a general settlement, thus increasing Prussian territory and winning the glory of making peace in Germany. No alliance with France was needed, merely a rapprochement, and compensation for Prussian losses on the Left Bank could be found at the expense of the Ecclesiastical Electorates and other small fry. The most modest expansion in Germany was more important for Prussia than anything in Poland. Austria, if thus isolated, could not prevent the conclusion of peace between France and the whole Reich. Moreover, since she would never be a friend, it was vital to be on good terms with France. That French ambitions might one day grow into a deadly danger to Prussia never entered his single-track mind.

When diplomatic relations between Paris and Berlin were renewed successive French Ministers testify to the moral support they found in the veteran Francophil.[1] Caillard met him for the first time when he came to Berlin for the baptism of the King's grandson, afterwards Frederick William IV. 'I found him just the same in Berlin as we saw him in Paris, gentle, affable, witty, urbane, always manifesting a most decided *penchant* for France and Frenchmen, in fact just what we desire; the revolution has not changed his feelings towards us in the slightest degree. He told me how deeply he had been distressed by this unfortunate war, how much he had desired its termination, how proud he was of contributing to the restoration of peace. He appears as eager for our success as ourselves, as I saw by his satisfaction at the capture of a British convoy and warships. An hour's talk made me regret that his residence in Rheinsberg destroys the hope of seeing him as often as I should like.'

Though peace had been made it was doubtful whether it would endure, for France had more foes than friends in high places at Berlin. Hardenberg and others, reported Caillard in January 1796, were striving for the renewal of the war. 'I have consulted among others Prince Henry, who on his arrival sent word secretly that he must see me. He expressed his indignation at the detestable intrigues designed to distract the King from his true interests and to put him once more in English and Russian chains. He confided to me that he had received a welcome so distinguished, so friendly, so unusual, that he had been surprised; at first he feared that these blandishments concealed some snare. He had been mistaken, for the King himself started political conversations; the British Minister, Lord Elgin, at his first audience had made proposals and offered fresh subsidies. He had resisted all efforts to upset his decision, being resolved on the strict application of the Treaty of Basle and on a good and sincere understanding with France. The King had asked his opinion on how to reach a general peace, and how to satisfy the princes whom the war had wholly or partially deprived of their possessions. He had replied that it could only be at the expense of the ecclesiastics, an expedient approved by the King. Prince Henry assured me that we need not worry; the King had taken his stand, and intrigue would have no effect.'

When Caillard had learned to know Berlin a little better he

[1] Their despatches are published in Bailleu, *Preussen und Frankreich, 1795–1807*, vol. i.

reluctantly realised that Henry's day was over. 'None would wish more than myself,' he reported in March 1797, 'to see the Prince count for much in the direction of affairs and directing Haugwitz and the Ministry; then I should have a powerful lever in my hand against which the eternal indecision of the Cabinet, its timid caution, its chimerical fears, would not long prevail. Unfortunately all you have been told about him is completely unfounded. His journey to Berlin is approved but in no way initiated by the King. The vanity of the uncle matches the vanity of the nephew. He is rightly incensed at not being consulted, and the King would be miserable if the people thought he needed him, since he fears above all that there should be talk of leading-strings. Add to this the jealousy of the Ministers, and judge whether under these circumstances Prince Henry could possibly secure solid and permanent credit at Court. The Crown Prince may esteem him highly, but that is no good for he counts for nothing in great affairs.'

Meetings with the French representatives gave pleasure to both parties. 'He talks very cleverly, with grace and facility,' reported Caillard in March 1797, 'and I noticed that he greatly enjoyed talking. In him we have a true friend, and I encouraged this sentiment by flattering his *amour-propre*, a chord which arouses a powerful response in his ear and heart. He had had several talks with the King about how to deal with Vienna. Fearing his advice might be discounted by the common reproach of his partiality for France, he cleverly changed his tactics. 'You see,' he told the King, 'that the France I loved is gone; the France of to-day is for me just a foreign Power where I know no one. She only interests me in relation to the general political scheme. I continue to favour her, not owing to any personal sentiments but solely because I see that it is in Prussia's interest.'

The King, declared Henry, seemed pleased with the conversation, but his course was nearly run and Haugwitz was at last permitted to initiate the Crown Prince into affairs of state. 'Prince Henry enjoys, or at least appears to enjoy, very great consideration with him,' reported Caillard in July, 1797. 'Greatly attached to his family, like his father he regards the Prince as its outstanding member, sees in him the comrade in arms and equal of the great Frederick, respects his talents, his intelligence, his experience, and shows much attachment to him and deference to his opinions.' 'The heir,' remarked Prince Henry to me, 'lacks grace and ease and knows little outside the military sphere. There is a touch of severity in his character which you might sometimes be tempted to take for rudeness. But in a man destined to rule over others the exterior is nothing when the inside is good, and with the Crown Prince it is excellent. In place of brilliance there is plenty of good sense. The appearance of severity is connected with a strong sense of justice, order and economy. Luckily he realises his lack of instruction. Yet do not imagine that he blindly follows the opinion of his entourage. He wishes to be informed and persuaded, and he only decides for good reasons and after considering all objections which occur to him. It is thus that I helped him to make up his mind, which oscillated between France and Russia and at first seemed to lean towards the latter. I had to conduct the attack in accordance with all the rules, balancing advantages and disadvantages, anticipating situations, indicating resources. Only after clear and convincing arguments did he say: "I see, my dear uncle, that you are absolutely right. I thank you for having enlightened me, and now I am convinced that nothing can be more advantageous for Prussia than an alliance with France." So you see it is important that he should have good influences. I hope he will continue to give me his confidence, and I am less afraid of Haugwitz now I see he has joined the French party. His wife is an angel. Rest assured that he is a very honourable man; if he does not quickly decide, at least one can count on him when he has made up his mind. Such was Prince Henry's account of his nephew. He believes that both Prussia and the Republic have much to gain from his accession.'

Henry was as distasteful to the Austrians as he was *persona gratissima* with the French. Prince Reuss, the Austrian Minister, who was striving to induce Prussia to rejoin the Coalition, wrote of him in June 1797 with contempt. 'Prince Henry, always active and never doing anything, always busy in asserting himself, and always condemned to be a cipher by the Sovereign and the Ministers whom he overwhelms with memoranda which no one reads, has come here evidently to discover the condition of the King and to try his credit with the Crown Prince, whose mentor he aspires to be. Unfortunately both of them, taking the same view of him, have displayed the same attitude, so that he will soon return with the conviction that his reign which he thought was approaching will never come.'

When it became obvious that Frederick William II, worn out by self-indulgence, was nearing his end, Henry turned hopefully for the second time towards the rising sun. 'You are the heir,' he had written in 1796, 'and it is right that you should be informed of everything.' On the eve of the King's death at the close of 1797 a lengthy memorandum addressed to the Crown Prince argued that Prussia could not stand alone, and that the only possible partners were Russia and France. 'I will not speak of Austria, for an ingrained national hatred, divergent interests, indeed everything, separates us and combines to veto a rapprochement.' An alliance with Russia was undesirable because it would increase her power, whereas Prussia's interest was to diminish it. He proceeds to grapple with the objections to an alliance with France. To the argument that no one could rely on a government so shaky and variable as the Directory he rejoins that French foreign policy did not change and that an alliance combined with a general peace would stabilise it. To those who feared that contact with a republic might endanger the institution of monarchy he rejoins that French political ideas were unlikely to cross the Rhine.

When Frederick William III at the age of twenty-seven succeeded his unworthy father the ambitious septuagenarian made yet another bid for influence. Like everyone else he respected the King's high character and admired the beautiful Queen; but he had never been intimate with his great-nephew, and his attempts to gain a footing through political memoranda had failed. The young monarch treated the old warrior with unfailing consideration and visited him at Rheinsberg, but he had no intention of accepting his lead. That Bischoffwerder and Wöllner were dismissed and the Countess Lichtenau, the favourite mistress, arrested, was an excellent beginning, but Haugwitz, of whom Henry had a poor opinion, remained at the helm. Yet perhaps after all Haugwitz, flabby as he was, might listen to advice. Three memoranda were accordingly presented calling for a change in methods of government no less than in the sphere of foreign affairs. Prussia, it was argued, was weak because her finances were in confusion, partly owing to the unnecessary war of 1792–5, partly on account of extravagance and corruption at home. 'It is painful to have to speak of the entourage, of both sexes, of the late King, who have received and spent large sums and, owing to his excessive indulgence, have controlled affairs of state.' Many others, profiting by the disorder, had obtained pensions or gifts, and an inquiry should be held. Realising that only a superman could carry the whole burden of government unaided, he advised joint sessions of the

Ministers and joint recommendations to the Crown. In other words a Ministry, instead of merely Ministers, was required, though it would in no way diminish the royal prerogative. In addition he urged the creation of a small Privy Council, including the Foreign Minister, two soldiers and perhaps a member of the Royal Family—the latter proposal a broad hint that he himself would be available. There should also be a Council of Commerce and a Council of War.

There was no response, for the timid ruler shrank from far-reaching changes in the administrative machinery, and, neither loving nor hating France, was satisfied with the policy of neutrality followed since the Treaty of Basle. He replied that he would maintain peace and neutrality until he was attacked. Henry rejoined that he hoped peace would continue, but in the event of war Prussia's geographical situation pointed to an alliance with France. His first impressions of the new ruler were excellent. 'I have seen Prince Henry several times,' reported Caillard a few days after the accession. 'He tells me he has talked with the King very often and was inexpressibly pleased; he found a degree of knowledge and even intelligence he had not expected; he worked very hard, but with order and method, without wanting to deal with a hundred things at a time like the Emperor of Russia. He had shown great confidence regarding many domestic matters, but when he tried to talk of foreign affairs he found him silent, reserved, and deliberately vague. Yet he knows from several sources that the King is entirely in the French system, and that his great probity, purity of life, love of justice, and lack of prejudice should make him infinitely more agreeable to us than his father.'

It was not long before Henry, like the *corps diplomatique*, realised that the change of ruler denoted neither a new course nor an increase of his influence. 'He is friendly to his great-uncles, Prince Henry and Prince Ferdinand,' reported Count Reuss, the Austrian Minister, 'but without allowing the former to interfere in politics, which he is always trying to do, and also making disparaging remarks about the Duke of Brunswick and praising the Republicans, for whom the King entertains the greatest distaste, and he has no inclination for the French nation.' Sieyès, who succeeded Caillard as French Minister at Berlin, reported on his isolation in July 1798, scarcely more than six months after the change of ruler. 'Ill though he was, he gave me an audience with which I was extremely satisfied. I admired the clarity of his thoughts at his great age and the purity of his language.

As regards his ideas I felt I was talking with a Frenchman; such a contrast to all I have seen. But, as you know, in public affairs he does not count.'

Henry remained so obsessed by the notion of his superior wisdom that in September 1798 he addressed a final lengthy memorandum to the King. He complained of personal attacks from champions of the policy of joining the new Coalition against France. 'My whole life proves my devotion to the state, yet I know of people who have traduced me. I beg you to read and re-read my memorandum.' Prussia's neutrality system, he insisted, would fail in the event of a European war, and a purely defensive attitude was unwise even if peace were preserved. Now that the Left Bank of the Rhine was lost she should strive for compensation in the negotiations between France and the Reich, thus becoming strong enough to maintain her position between Russia and Austria. It was dangerous to stand alone, for neutrals had no friends, whereas a French alliance would facilitate the territorial expansion urgently needed for national security. Even after Napoleon's dazzling victories in Italy and after he had become First Consul, Henry remained obstinately blind to the peril from France's ambitions and believed that she could always be relied on to study Prussia's interests. During the war of the Second Coalition, from which Prussia stood aloof, his sympathies were on the French side and the victory of Marengo was greeted as splendid news. For him Austria had always been the enemy.

It is not surprising that Haugwitz regarded Henry as a thorn in his side. After his return from a cure at Teplitz he wrote to his colleague Finckenstein in 1798. 'Having expressed a wish to see me, I went to him and met Sieyès coming out. I found him as French as Sieyès could desire. I must keep the details of a four hour conversation till we meet. I will only mention that he tried to pledge me to influence the King to abandon neutrality.' A year later, in April 1799, the Austrian Minister reported a talk with Haugwitz who had poured out his heart about the unfortunate counsellor. Haugwitz told him of the Prince's hatred and contempt for the Austrians and how the French and he, who thereby thought he would play a part, tried to induce the late King to join them in an attack. He (Haugwitz) had firmly replied that the King always regarded himself as the ally of the Emperor. He (Haugwitz) had had a sharp encounter with the Prince, who asked how he could have given such a foolish reply to the

French. 'For a decisive reason,' was the answer, 'which Your Royal Highness does not appear to understand—honour.' A report from General Beurnonville, the successor to Sieyès, in June 1800, suggests that even the French Legation no longer expected any help from the old champion of France. 'Prince Henry has been here for some days. This journey to Berlin is like an annual tribute which he pays to the remains of an ambition always frustrated but always alive. It would be in our interest if he could gain some influence and if his ideas were adopted. The two brothers of Frederick II expressed admiration for the First Consul and their desires for the triumph of the Republic. At their Courts we see only friends of the French nation. He had only come to tell the King his views, and to warn him that co-operation with Austria might lose Prussia her powerful and natural ally France. He advises a League of German princes under Prussian auspices to assure their independence against Austrian despotism. He also approached Haugwitz. He returns to Rheinsberg, and probably his visit will have brought no change in policy.'

At the opening of the nineteenth century even the Prince himself came to realise that his time was over, for his offers to discuss matters with the King were ignored. 'I am like an old pattern, no longer in fashion,' he wrote in 1801 at the age of seventy-five. His French attire amused Berlin society, and in his uncritical devotion to France he stood alone. Though Count Lavalette, arriving on a diplomatic errand in 1801, was surprised at the scanty respect with which his name was mentioned, the sole survivor from the heroic age remained an object of interest to visitors from abroad. Quincy Adams, the young diplomatist destined to become the sixth President of the United States, met him at the funeral of Frederick William II and records an interesting forecast in his voluminous diary.[1] 'He said that America was a rising and Europe a declining part of the world, and that in the course of two or three centuries the seat of arts, science and empire would be with us and Europe would lose them all. Their progress had been westward, beginning in Asia, and it was natural that America should have her turn.' Lord and Lady Holland visited Rheinsberg in 1800 and found a congenial topic in their common detestation of Pitt.[2] Louis Bonaparte, who followed in 1801, was shocked by the host's rabid depreciation of Frederick's military gifts.

[1] *Memoirs*, i, 210–211.
[2] Lord Holland, *Foreign Reminiscences*, 59–62.

The hostile annotations on his copy of his brother's *Histoire de la Guerre de Sept Ans*, posthumously published in 1788, were not intended for the public eye; but in 1791 he erected a War Memorial at Rheinsberg in honour of his brother August Wilhelm and other leaders in the three Silesian wars which told its own tale. For the name of the principal hero we look in vain, and that of Winterfeldt, Frederick's favourite General, is also conspicuous by its absence. 'I have recalled the names of those unmentioned by the great Frederick in his lying memoirs,' he explained. Time never softened his jealousy of the elder brother whose fame, as he was sorrowfully aware, far outshone his own.

The chief consolation of the closing years was the unchanging devotion of his brother Ferdinand and his children. It was a joyful excitement when his nephew, the dashing and romantic Prince Louis Ferdinand, with his handsome face and dynamic personality, broke into the stuffy atmosphere of Rheinsberg, finding a welcome and an understanding denied him by his exasperated father and ill-tempered mother in Berlin.[1] Here at last, despite his amours and his debts, was an authentic Hohenzollern hero, brave as a lion, who might perhaps revive the glories of the past. Equally welcome was his niece Princess Louise, whose Memoirs paint an attractive picture of the old recluse.[2] 'I saw Rheinsberg for the first time,' she writes of the year 1791. 'I was enchanted with my stay; the castle beside the lake, the magnificent trees of the park, the French play, my uncle's warm welcome. His Court was large. A number of ladies of mature years, but very agreeable, were of the household. But the charm was soon destroyed for me by fresh discussions between my mother and my uncle which revived their old animosity. Her attitude put my father in a cruelly difficult position. Respect for his brother forbade him to undertake even the smallest enterprise without consulting him, while on the other hand his deep attachment to my mother made him largely amenable to her influence. For the moment that of Prince Henry was in the ascendant; he admitted that he had advised my father to seek a divorce, but this my mother never knew.' Subsequent visits were more tranquil since Princess Ferdinand wisely stayed at home. 'My uncle loaded us with favours,' she writes of 1797. 'He loved to talk

[1] Life in his beloved country home is described in Krauel, 'Prinz Heinrich von Preussen in Rheinsberg,' in *Hohenzollern-Jahrbuch*, vol. vi.
[2] *Forty-five Years of My Life*, 17.

with Anton, Prince Radziwill,[1] about his country. He had always felt a great interest in Poland ever since he heard how two Poles had asked Frederick to let them have him for their King. He always disapproved the later partitions, and never ceased to extend his active protection to such Poles as happened to be detained there.' He desired to see a Prussian prince, perhaps Louis Ferdinand himself, on the throne of a reunited Poland. The old man was full of reminiscences reaching back to the almost legendary era of Frederick William I.

Henry's brother, nephew and niece were at Rheinsberg when the curtain fell in 1802. A kindly fate spared the old prince the shock of the Jena campaign four years later and the death of his adored nephew on the field of honour. If fortune had not granted him all he desired, either in his public or his private life, he had at any rate played a distinguished part on the European stage for half a century and had earned an honourable place among the military and political architects of the Prussian state.

[1] Her husband.

GOETHE'S POLITICAL BACKGROUND

THOUGH it is generally agreed that Goethe was an essentially unpolitical nature, his lot was cast in such an eventful time and he touched life at so many points that his relation to politics deserves more attention than it has received. Despite the overwhelming number of monographs on the greatest figure in German literature, there is still need for a detailed record of his contacts with public life and a comprehensive study of his opinions on government and society. Of the larger biographies that of Hume Brown alone is the work of a trained historian, but the distinguished Edinburgh Professor spoke with greater authority on Scottish than on German history. Seeley, the learned author of the *Life and Times of Stein* and a close student of Goethe, might have given us the book that we need, but he contented himself with a birdseye survey of the man and the writer in his little volume *Goethe after Sixty Years*. In the present address I can do no more than suggest the interest and importance of a comparatively neglected department of Goethe studies.

The notion of Gervinus that Goethe deliberately averted his gaze from the pageantry of events and buried himself in art, literature and science, is without foundation. No citizen of Frankfurt could fail to be vividly aware of the existence and significance of the system under which Central Europe had lived for a thousand years. The Holy Roman Empire, in regard to which Voltaire caustically inquired in what sense it was either holy, or Roman, or an empire, was a mere ghost of its former self. The revellers in Auerbach's Keller shouted in disrespectful mirth:

> Das Heilige Römische Reich,
> Wie hält es doch zusammen?

Yet its gigantic frame still sprawled across Germany, and its wheels, rusty though they were, continued to revolve. The Emperor, though nominally elective, had for centuries reigned at Vienna; the Diet with its three Colleges of Electors, Princes and Free Cities, sat at Regensburg; the Supreme Court was located at Wetzlar. Behind the façade of the central machinery were the Circles or larger administrative units, the ecclesiastical and secular principalities, the Free Cities, and finally the Imperial Knights, whose duodecimo possessions were sprinkled by hundreds over the map. It was, indeed, the consecration of anarchy and particularism. 'In my childhood,' wrote Wieland, 'I was told a great deal about duties; but there was so little about the duty of a German patriot that I cannot remember hearing the word German used with honour. There are Saxon, Bavarian, Frankfurt patriots; but German patriots, who love the Empire as their fatherland, where are they?' Well might Friedrich Karl Moser cry in the bitterness of his heart that the Germans were a great but despised people. Yet while publicists and pamphleteers lamented in chorus the creeping paralysis of an institution which had once filled Europe with its prowess and fame, none of them could suggest an effective remedy. The Empire had virtually ceased to exist but seemed unable to die.

Its mortal sickness never clouded the spirits of the youthful Goethe, who, like most of his fellow-citizens, saw rather the glamour than the hollowness of a picturesque survival. 'If we can find a place where we can rest with our belongings,' he wrote in 1773, 'a field to support us, a house to shelter us, have we not a fatherland? And do not thousands in every state possess it? Wherefore then the vain striving for a feeling which we cannot and indeed do not desire to entertain, which is the result of special circumstances in certain peoples at certain times?' The mighty past appeared to revive for a moment in the pageantry at Frankfurt, where the Arch-Chancellor, the Elector of Mainz, crowned the Emperor. The new ruler received the homage of the Estates on bended knee and the herald brandished his sword towards the four quarters of heaven in token that all Christendom was subject to his master's sway. It was a great event in the life of the Imperial city, fully described in *Dichtung und Wahrheit*, when on April 3, 1765, the high-souled Joseph II was acclaimed in the Römersaal. When in 1792 his nephew Francis was the central figure, the spectators were blissfully unaware that the last successor of Charlemagne had been crowned.

Goethe's brief residence at Wetzlar in 1772 was calculated to diminish the respect for the Empire which he had imbibed in his native city. The Court of Imperial Appeal, like Chancery in the time of Lord Eldon, had earned an unenviable reputation for procrastination, and its name was tarnished by suspicions of venality. Moreover, its prestige was impaired by the fact that important cases were reserved by the Emperor for the Aulic Council at Vienna. If a few petty tyrants were thwarted or punished by its decrees it was too weak to strike at powerful offenders. Young jurists spent a month or two in the sleepy little town to learn the routine of Imperial law; but Goethe's heart was never in his profession, and Wetzlar, alike to Goethe and to the world, stands for Werther and Lotte, not for the musty memories of the Reichskammergericht.

Goethe was wholly free from the contempt for the Empire which was felt by so many of his contemporaries, but he combined benevolent neutrality towards the system under which he lived with an ardent admiration for Frederick the Great. In a well-known passage in the autobiography he records how his victories awoke Germany from her slumbers, supplied the poets with an inspiration which they had hitherto lacked, and aroused respect for German prowess throughout the West and South scarcely less than in the Protestant north. It was, however, a personal as well as a transitory sentiment for a daemonic personality. 'He was Prussian,' he writes, 'or, to be more accurate, Fritzian (fritzisch); for what was Prussia to us? It was the personality of the great king which appealed to every one.' It was to the Seven Years' War that the poet also owed his first experience of a French occupation, in which a French officer was quartered in his father's house.

An essential part of the Imperial system was the petty principality whose fortunes depended on the virtues or vices, the smiles or the frowns of its autocrat. While Goethe was growing to manhood Germany could boast of some of the best and some of the worst rulers of the age. On the one hand, men like Charles William Ferdinand, Duke of Brunswick, and Karl Friedrich, Duke of Baden, were fathers of their people; on the other, the Landgrave of Hesse-Cassel sold his subjects to George III as mercenaries for the American War, and the Duke of Württemberg's tyranny aroused the attention of Europe. The abominations of selfish autocracy are enshrined for ever in the fiery pages of *Emilia Galotti* and *Kabale und Liebe*.

Goethe's autobiography records his debt to the writings of Karl Friedrich Moser, who denounced the soulless autocrat and preached the gospel of service, but of the darker features of princely rule the poet had no personal experience. While Schiller chafed under the yoke of an extravagant despot, Goethe was privileged from the age of twenty-six to co-operate with one of the most enlightened rulers of his time. The Young Karl August inherited a principality with only 100,000 inhabitants and an infertile soil, but after sowing their wild oats the prince and the poet resolved to make the Duchy of Weimar a model principality. At this task Goethe laboured with unflagging zeal for a decade and his master for half a century. On the birth of an heir in 1783, the Duke gave expression to his gratitude. 'Here is a hook on which I can hang my pictures,' he wrote to Merck. 'With the help of Goethe and good fortune I will paint them in such a way that posterity will perhaps say *Anch' egli fu pittore*.' The poet's admiration for the ruler is enshrined in the beautiful lines in the *Venetian Epigrams*, written after he had laid down the more exacting burdens of public life:

> Klein ist unter Germaniens Fürsten freilich der meine;
> Kurz und schmal ist sein Land, mässig nur was er vermag.
> Aber so wende nach innen, so wende nach aussen die Kräfte
> Jeder; da wär's ein Fest Deutscher mit Deutschen zu sein.

His gratitude to the man was no less sincere than his respect for the prince:

> Denn mir hat er gegeben, was Grosse selten gewähren,
> Neigung, Musse, Vertraun, Felder und Garten und Haus.
> Niemals frug ein Kaiser nach mir, es hat sich kein König
> Um mich bekümmert, und Er war mir August und Mäcen.

Elected Councillor of Legation in 1776, Privy Councillor in 1779, President of the Council in 1782, Goethe threw himself heart and soul into the tasks of government.[1] To Herder he was 'the Weimarfactotum,' to Knebel 'the backbone of affairs.' He promoted the development of agriculture, industry and mines, the reform of education and finance, the amelioration of the lot of the poor. He was in fact a capable, energetic and conscientious official. Though he returned to literature after ten years of ministerial activity, his experiences of public life left deep traces on his life and thought. All that he had done and all that he had wished to do had been or could be accomplished by the will of a benevolent autocrat. The elements of any political structure in Weimar other than paternal government were absent. The people had a right, not indeed to govern themselves,

---

[1] See the essay 'Goethe als Staatsmann' in Schöll, *Goethe*.

but to be well governed. He stood mid-way between the legitimists, to whom princely power was sacrosanct, and the democrats, to whom the voice of the people was the voice of God. He was a conservative reformer, convinced that reforms must come from above, that changes must be gradual, and that order was heaven's first law.

Goethe's love of order and economy, combined with his humane feelings, aroused in him a lifelong detestation of war. The extravagance of Karl August was a sore trial to his minister, and he was haunted by the fear that the blood and treasure of the little duchy might be poured out in quarrels not its own. As a boy he had been dazzled by the flashing sword of Frederick the Great, but as a man he had no desire to see Weimar tied to his chariot-wheels. Karl August, like other rulers of little states who are born for action, fretted at his impotence, and sought an outlet for his energies by revolving round a larger sun. The later years of Frederick were troubled by the restless ambitions of Joseph II, and in 1778, when yet another struggle between Prussia and Austria seemed inevitable, Goethe accompanied his master to Berlin to make arrangements. Happily the War of the Bavarian Succession was a small affair, in which no pitched battle was fought. In 1785 the Fürstenbund, the last achievement of the great King, was formed to hold Joseph in check. The demonstration sufficed and again Bavaria was saved; but in 1790 Frederick William II, alarmed by Austrian operations against Turkey, led Prussian troops into Silesia. Karl August hurried to the front and ordered Goethe to join him at Breslau, but for a third time a conflict was avoided. Goethe throughout disapproved the policy of adventure which appealed so strongly to his master. The duty of rulers was to provide good government for their subjects, to ignore the siren calls of ambition, and to conduct their business on the principle of limited liability.

The impressions and convictions formed during his years of active service at Weimar provided the compass by which Goethe steered his course through the tempests of the revolutionary era.[1] Being well aware that misgovernment brought its nemesis, he was not one of those whom the French Revolution caught unprepared. 'As early as 1785,' he wrote long after in the *Annals*, 'the history of the Diamond Necklace had made an indelible impression on me. Out of the bottomless abyss of the immorality in city, court and state there

---

[1] See Gooch, *Germany and the French Revolution*, ch. 7.

emerged, spectre-like, the most horrible apparitions. These so affected my behaviour that the friends with whom I was living when the news arrived have confessed to me that I appeared like one demented.' The figure of Cagliostro haunted him, and on his visit to Palermo in 1787 he sought out the family of the impostor.

'Hardly had I settled afresh into the life of Weimar,' we read in the *Annals*, 'than the French Revolution attracted the attention of the world, and I followed the development of the drama with close attention.' We cannot expect to find in Goethe the enthusiasm which the birth pangs of a new world inspired in Kant and Klopstock, Wieland and Herder, Forster and Johannes Müller. He was the subject, friend and counsellor of a model prince. His administrative experience had convinced him of the practicability and the value of reforms carried out from above. The phase of *Sturm und Drang* was over, and he believed that the ship of state should be steered by the brain, not by the emotions. His contempt for the political capacity of the masses was revealed in *Egmont*. Though recognising the justice of the punishment that fell on the monarchy and the privileged classes in France, he never expected any benefit to arise from the violent methods of the reformers; and the Declaration of the Rights of Man, which was music to the ears of some of his Weimar friends, was to him as meaningless as to Bentham and Burke.

The first literary expression of his views on the French Revolution is to be found in the *Venetian Epigrams*, written during his second visit to Italy in the spring of 1790:

> Alle Freiheitsapostel, sie waren mir immer zuwider,
>   Willkür suchte doch nur jeder am Ende für sich.
> Willst Du viele befreien, so wag es vielen zu dienen.
>   Wie gefährlich das sei, willst Du es wissen? Versuchs!
>
> Könige wollen das Gute, die Demagogen desgleichen,
>   Sagt man; doch irren sie sich: Menschen, ach, sind sie wie wir.
>
> Nie gelingt es der Menge, für sich zu wollen, wir wissens.
>   Doch wer verstehet für uns alle zu wollen, er zeigs.
>
> Frankreichs traurig Geschick, die Grossen mögens bedenken;
>   Aber bedenken fürwahr sollen es Kleine noch mehr.
> Grossen gingen zu Grunde, doch wer beschütze die Menge
>   Gegen die Menge? Da war Menge der Menge Tyrann.

These are the strong, simple outlines of his unchanging political faith. Since the masses cannot save themselves, it is the duty and the privilege of their rulers to save them. To princes and people alike the Revolution brought a solemn warning: for the prince to do too little and the people to attempt too much was to invite disaster.

Goethe made several attempts to embody the Revolution in dramatic form, but without complete satisfaction to his readers or himself. *Der Grosseophta* is a satirical study of a corrupt and credulous society. Cagliostro, the hero, is an impostor in the grand style, and the history of the Diamond Necklace lays bare one of the festering sores of the *Ancien Régime*. Though not a directly political play, its analysis of social and moral decay embodies the conviction that monarchical France was sick and in need of a physician. Goethe thought better of the work than did his friends. 'It was a good subject,' he remarked to Eckermann, 'for it was not merely of moral but of historical significance. The Queen, through being implicated in the unlucky story of the Necklace, was no longer respected. Hate injures no one; it is contempt that drags men down.' Whatever we may think of the literary merits of this sinister drama, no reader can regard its author as an apologist of the *Ancien Régime*.

In the spring of 1792 the Girondins compelled Louis XVI to declare war against feudal Europe, and the poet accompanied his master to the front. 'Goethe with the army!' wrote Heyne; 'what profanation!' The invitation was unexpected and not wholly welcome, for he was deep in the study of optics. Yet he promised himself an interesting experience, and it was expected that the Coalition army would reach Paris without delay. 'After home and bed and kitchen and cellar,' he wrote to Jacobi from Frankfurt, 'life in a tent will indeed be a change, all the more since the death of both aristocratic and democratic sinners leaves me cold.' At Mainz he made his first acquaintance with the Émigrés, and passing through Trier and Luxemburg he reached the Duke of Brunswick's camp at Longwy on August 27.

With the aid of his letters and diary we can follow his movements almost day by day; and in the *Campaign in France,* worked up in 1820 from his own materials and from the Memoirs of Dumouriez and other protagonists, he has told the story of one of the most memorable episodes in his life. The surrender of Longwy, the first French town, seemed to confirm the assurance of the Émigrés that the invaders would be welcomed with open arms; and on the capitulation of Verdun after a brief bombardment he wrote to Christiane that he would soon be with her again and would bring her something from Paris. A week later he wrote in a more chastened mood. 'It is very interesting to be here. To see the ways of war under so great a general, and to learn to know the French nation, affords even an idle spectator plenty of entertainment. What is to happen next? We are all wondering. The business is lengthening out. It is a stupendous enterprise, even with all our resources.' The September massacres, the rejoinder of Danton to the Brunswick Manifesto, seemed to him likely to facilitate the invasion, but the blood-bath in the prisons proved the beginning not of anarchy but of organised resistance. A week later the battle of Valmy, in which he received his baptism of fire, turned the tide. In the most celebrated passage of the book he described the Allied camp on the evening after the brief conflict. 'People avoided each other's glances. We could not even light a fire. After a time some one asked me what I thought, as I had often amused the circle with oracular utterances. On this occasion I remarked, "Here and to-day commences a new epoch of world-history, and you can boast that you were present at its birth!" ' It was a bold prophecy, but a century dominated by the forces of nationality and democracy was to prove its truth.

The retreat began under conditions which prompted the witticism that Jupiter Pluvius had turned Jacobin. 'I hasten back to my fleshpots,' he wrote to Herder, 'there to awaken from a bad dream.' Though he kept his spirits and his health, his letters and diary are filled with lamentations. 'In six weeks we have borne and seen more misery and danger than in the rest of our lives. No pen and no tongue can describe the plight of the army. This campaign will cut a sorry figure in history.' Yet despite its failure and its horrors, he was glad to have taken part. 'In these four weeks,' he wrote to Knebel a few days after Valmy, 'I have learned much. I am happy to have seen everything with my own eyes, and I can say of this historic epoch, "Quorum pars minima fui." '

Ranke has complained that the *Campaign in France* makes no real contribution to history, since the author was never in the confidence of Brunswick, the King of Prussia, or the other leaders of the ill-starred enterprise. Other historians have expressed a higher view of its value, and the reader can see for himself with what power and skill the atmosphere is reproduced. It is, however, less as a footnote to history than as a revelation of mind and character that the book retains its place. To his courage and serenity Goethe added a clearness of vision to which few if any of his companions could lay claim. There is not a word of hatred or recrimination in the *Campaign* or in the letters on which it is based. Aristocrats and democrats, he feels, have sinned alike, and the French people is the victim of its rulers, old and new. Though temperamentally unfitted to scale the heights and plumb the depths of the Revolution, he never shared the delusion that it was merely the outpouring of human wickedness or that it could be suppressed by the sword alone. His heart is filled with compassion for the victims of war, the civilian sufferers no less than the combatants. His pages breathe a genuine humanity, and the sufferings of the humble never fail to strike a responsive chord. He returned home with a shuddering horror of war, more convinced than ever that revolutions were not worth their price and that the highest duty of rulers was to render them unnecessary.

The repulse of the invaders was followed by the execution of Louis XVI. 'Who was there who had not from childhood shuddered at the execution of Charles I,' wrote Goethe, 'and comforted himself with the hope that such scenes would never recur? Imagine the feelings of those who had marched forth to rescue the King and now were impotent to intervene in the trial or to prevent the execution of the sentence! The world appeared to me bloodier and more bloodthirsty than before; and if the death of a King in battle counts like a thousand, it is of far greater significance in a constitutional struggle.' The unfinished fragment of a philosophic tale, written at this moment, *The Sons of Megaprazon*, which only saw the light a century later, describes the terrific experiences of the volcanic island of Monarchomany (France) and the devastating effects of the eruptions on the dwellers in neighbouring lands. It is a sombre little study of confusion and delusion; but the author's emphasis on the fact that an ancient law forbade the tillers of the soil ever to satisfy their hunger reveals his unchanged conviction that the revolution was not without a cause.

After recovering from the distracting experiences of the campaign, the poet threw off the sparkling little one-act play *Der Bürger-General* in three days. The French were now on the Rhine, and incendiarism, it was feared, might set the whole countryside ablaze. George and Rose, a newly-married couple, are happy and contented in their little holding, the landlord of which is a kindly nobleman. Old Martin, however, Rose's father, has caught the Jacobin fever, and is egged on by Schnaps, the villain of the piece, who proceeds to illustrate French principles by removing some eatables from the cupboard. He is arrested, and the judge proceeds to unravel the threads of what he believes to be a formidable conspiracy. At this moment the landlord appears, and proclaims the Weimar gospel of the duties of man. 'My children,' he says to Rose and George, 'love each other and look after the land and your household.' Old Martin is advised to let foreign countries settle their own affairs. 'Let every one begin with himself and he will find plenty to do. Let him honourably seek the advantage of himself and those dependent on him, and he will thus contribute to the general welfare.' The judge breaks in with a plea for punishment, only to receive an admonition in his turn. 'Not too fast! Vindictive penalties only breed trouble. In a land where the prince is accessible to all, where all classes live in harmony, where no one is hindered in his activity, where useful knowledge is universal, there will be no parties. The drama of the world will attract attention but seditious opinions will find no entry. Let us be thankful to have the blue sky over our heads when too many fields are ravaged by hailstones. It means something that we can laugh at the cockade and the cap and the uniform which have brought so much evil on the world.' Beneath the sunlit ripples of this little satire—the most successful of his efforts to portray the Revolution on the stage—lies the major part of the poet's political creed.

Shortly after completing *Der Bürger-General*, Goethe once more emerged from his sheltered home at the bidding of the Duke to witness the wild surge of war. Custine had seized Mainz when Brunswick was thrown out of France and had held it throughout the winter, but his forces were small and at length the French garrison found itself besieged. The expulsion of the invader appealed to the poet's sympathies much more than the Brunswick Manifesto. Once again we can follow his adventures and emotions both in his letters and in the finished narrative *Die Belagerung von Mainz* which he compiled in later years. The horrors of war, though on a smaller scale than in the previous year, awoke the old compassion for the combatants on both sides, and for the civilians whose sufferings were often scarcely less poignant. 'My friends can be thankful,' he wrote, 'not to witness the misery in unhappy Mainz.' He displayed the same bravery as before.

'Every moment one was filled with anxiety for the Duke and one's dearest friends, and one forgot to think of one's own safety. As if enchanted by the confusion, one rushed to the danger-points and let the cannon-balls fly over one's head and burst by one's side.' Once again there is no bitterness against the French, whom he watched march out of the city singing the *Marseillaise*. 'It was a poignant spectacle as the cavalry rode past. Individually they looked like Don Quixote, but in the mass extremely impressive.' His rebukes are reserved for the Clubists, or German Jacobins, who co-operated with the invaders, yet he witnessed with shame and indignation the sack of their houses and the pillaging of shops. Though he told Jacobi that the closing days of the strife and the capitulation were among the most interesting of his life, his second and last campaign intensified the loathing of war which was one of the master-passions of his life.

On his return home Goethe began a new play on the Revolution, with the revealing title *Die Aufgeregten*. The subject was once again the effect of propaganda on the ignorant masses; but while *Der Bürger-General* skated lightly over thin ice, its successor dealt more comprehensively with the causes and the results of agitation. The scene is laid in a village, the inhabitants of which have been grievously wronged by a deceased landlord and a fraudulent steward. The grandfather of the youthful Count had remitted some feudal burdens; but the charter of emancipation had disappeared, the son of the benefactor had exacted the old dues, and his widow, fearing to compromise the rights of her son, made no change, though her kindly heart yearned for restitution. At this point the French Revolution brings to a head the discontent of the villagers, who plot to obtain restoration of their rights. The second act opens with the return of the Countess from Paris, where her experiences have made her more, not less, inclined to concessions. Thus at the very moment that the villagers are preparing to secure their rights by force, the Countess is about to do justice by her own free will. From this point we only possess the outlines of the play, with a few scenes worked out in detail. The revolt begins, but tragedy is averted by the masculine daughter who at the point of her gun compels the villain to produce the lost charter from its hiding-place. Thus the play ends harmoniously. The rustics are depicted as usual with good hearts and no brains, and the Countess embodies the spirit of liberal conservatism which severed

Goethe as much from the Émigrés as from the Jacobins. 'With the words I have put into her mouth,' observed Goethe to Eckermann, 'I have expressed how the nobility ought to think. She has convinced herself that the people may be ruled but not oppressed, and that the revolutionary outbreaks of the lower classes are the consequence of the injustice of the upper classes.' The moral of the play is that abuses should be corrected without waiting for the explosion.

Of a second unfinished revolutionary drama *Das Mädchen von Oberkirch*, a tragedy in five acts, only two scenes were composed, and we have no clue as to the probable development of a story which opens with the Jacobin dictatorship in Strassburg. Goethe was indeed in no mood for sustained literary composition. 'To have been an eye-witness of revolutions threatening the peace of the world,' he writes in the *Annals* for 1794, 'and to have seen with one's own eyes the greatest misfortunes that can befall citizens, peasants and soldiers, clouded my mind with sadness. Robespierre's deeds had terrified the world, and all sense of happiness had been so utterly extinguished that no one presumed to rejoice over his destruction, least of all while the horrors of war were in full blast. French revolutionary songs floated about in secret. News of fugitives flowed in from all quarters. There was not a family, not a circle of friends, which had not suffered. Several times I offered my mother a quiet residence with me, but she had no fear at Frankfurt, finding comforting passages in the Psalms and Prophets.'

His disgust with the times led Goethe to refashion the old beast-epic *Reinecke Fuchs*, whose fierce onslaught on the follies and baseness of mankind was in tune with his own sombre feelings. 'As I had hitherto occupied myself *ad nauseam* with the revolts of the mob, it was a real pleasure to hold up the mirror to Courts and rulers.' Though it tells its tale and points its moral without ambiguity, Goethe could not resist the temptation of interpolating a few lines of his own.

> Doch das Schlimmste find ich den Dünkel des irrigen Wahnes,
> Der die Menschen ergreift: es könne jeder im Taumel
> Seines heftigen Wollens die Welt beherrschen und richten.
> Hielte doch jeder sein Weib und seine Kinder in Ordnung,
> Wüsste sein trotzig Gesinde zu bändigen, könnte sich stille,
> Wenn die Thoren verschwenden, in mässigen Leben erfreuen.
> Aber wie sollte die Welt sich verbessern? Es lässt sich ein jeder
> Alles zu und will mit Gewalt die anderen bezwingen.
> Und so sinken wir tiefer und immer tiefer ins Arge.

The Revolution obsessed Goethe to such an extent that he seemed unable to write without direct or indirect reference to its problems. In the winter of 1794 he amused himself with a new Decameron, the French armies playing the disruptive part which in the distant days of Boccaccio had been taken by the plague. The stories in the *Unterhaltungen* are flimsy enough, but some of the contrasted types are of interest, and their heated discussions reflect the distressing scenes which the author knew only too well. The siege of Mainz provokes a passionate altercation on the Clubists and other German champions of France. 'They will fall into the hands of the Allies,' cries one, 'and I hope to see them all hanged.' 'And I hope,' snaps another, 'that the guillotine will reap a rich harvest in Germany and that no guilty head will be spared.'

At a time when Goethe complained that some of his old friends were behaving in a way that bordered on insanity, the new friendship with Schiller proved particularly welcome. Schiller had outgrown the romantic radicalism of his youth, had tired of politics, and had embraced the classical tradition; and though one of the friends had known autocracy at its best and the other at its worst, they were now in close agreement on political theory and practice. The first-fruits of their co-operation was the *Xenien*, which the authors compared to foxes sent into the land of the Philistines with burning tails to destroy the harvest. It was their wish that the winged words of the German Dunciad should be regarded as their joint work, but we catch the authentic accents of Goethe in the couplets which reiterate the familiar message of Weimar.

> Majestät der Menschennatur! Dich soll ich beim Haufen
>   Suchen? Bei wenigen nur hast Du von jeher gewohnt.
> Willst Du frei sein, mein Sohn, so lerne was rechtes, und halte
>   Dich genügsam, und sieh niemals nach oben herauf.
> Wisst ihr auch wie der kleine was ist? er mache das Kleine
>   Recht. Der Grosse begehrt just so das Grosse zu thun.
> Freiheit ist ein herrlicher Schmuck, der schönste von allen,
>   Und doch steht er, wir sehn's, wahrlich nicht jeglichem an.
> Das Verfassung sich überall bilde, wie sehr ist's zu wünschen,
>   Aber ihr Schwätzer verhelft uns zu Verfassungen nicht.
> Zur Nation euch zu bilden, ihr hoffet es, Deutsche, vergebens.
>   Bildet, ihr könnt es, dafür freier zu Menschen euch aus.
> Was das Luthertum war ist jetzt das Franztum in diesen
>   Letzten Tagen, es drängt ruhige Bildung zurück.

Yet Goethe is as ready as ever to dissociate himself from the sterility of legitimism.

> Wer ist wirklich ein Fürst? Ich hab es immer gesehen,
>   Der nur ist wirklicher Fürst, der es vermochte zu sein.
> Was ist das würdigste Glied der Regierung? Ein würdiger Bürger,
>   Und im despotischen Land ist er der Pfeiler des Staats.

The progress of French arms and the extension of the war to Italy filled Goethe with apprehension and sorrow. 'Into what misery has that beautiful land fallen!' he wrote to a friend in 1796. He was anxious about his mother and thankful that Weimar at least was at a distance from the storm. Prussia and the North had withdrawn from the fray in 1795; and though Frederick William II was denounced for leaving his allies in the lurch, no one more whole-heartedly approved the Treaty of Basel than Goethe. 'We have all cause to be thankful,' he wrote to Karl August, 'for there is no question that the French could and would ravage us as they ravaged the districts of the Rhine and the Main, or even worse.'

'For me it was a new spring,' wrote Goethe in thankfully recording his friendship with Schiller, 'in which everything secreted in my nature burst into joyous life.' Having recovered his poetic inspiration he turned from the controversial fireworks of the *Xenien* to the idyll of *Hermann und Dorothea*. 'I have tried to smelt the life of a German village in the epic furnace,' he explained to a friend, 'and to reflect the great movements and changes of the world arena in a modest mirror.' The poem is saturated with politics and familiar axioms are proclaimed anew. The bonds of the world are unloosed; who will rejoin them? States fall to pieces when the restraints of law are removed. To build and maintain one happy home serves mankind better than all the talk about the rights of man. Goethe's own experiences gave poignancy to his picture of the sufferings of the refugees flying before the armies of Republican France, and it is against the dark background of war and confusion that the shining angels of Love and Hope stand out in sharp relief.

Hermann und Dorothea is a sermon on war, but it is the monster itself that is denounced rather than the warriors. And once again Goethe recognises the gold as well as the dross in the revolutionary ore.

Denn wer leugnet es wohl dass hoch sich das Herz ihm erhoben,
Ihm die freiere Brust mit reineren Pulsen geschlagen,
Als sich der erste Glanz der neuen Sonne heranhob,
Als man hörte vom Rechte der Menschen, das allen gemein sei,
Von der begeisternden Freiheit und von der löblichen Gleichheit?
Damals hoffte jeder sich selbst zu leben; es schien sich
Aufzulösen das Band das viele Länder umstrickte,
Das der Müssigang und der Eigennutz in der Hand hielt.
Schauten nicht die Götter in jenen drängenden Tagen
Nach der Haupstadt der Welt, die es schon so lange gewesen
Und jetzt mehr als je den herrlichen Namen verdiente?
Waren nicht jene Männer die ersten Verkünder der Botschaft,
Namen den höchsten gleich, die unter die Sterne gesetzt sind?
Wuchs nicht jeglichem Menschen der Mut und der Geist und die
   Sprache?

In the summer of 1797 Goethe paid one of his rare visits to Frankfurt. 'It is very interesting to be here just now,' he wrote to a friend; 'intercourse with people who have known almost all the important actors in this war-drama is most instructive. One sees the French Revolution and its effects much more directly, because it has had such great consequences for the city and because here one is in such manifold relations with that nation. What a curious people they are! The Frenchman is never still for a moment; he walks, chats, jumps, whistles, sings, and makes such a noise that one expects to see a larger number of them than there is. If one does not understand them, they grow irritable; but if one can talk with them they are at once *bons enfants*. In the armies of this kind one sees a peculiar energy and power at work. Such a nation must be terrible in more than one sense.' He had no desire to see Germany under the yoke of the Republic, but no word of hatred ever escapes this cool observer who stands above the battle.

Ten years after the meeting of the States-General at Versailles Goethe made a final attempt to embody the cataclysm in dramatic form. The plan of *Die natürliche Töchter* was suggested by the Memoirs of Stephanie Louise de Bourbon-Conti, published in 1798. 'Into this work, as into a vessel, I desired to pour reflections of many years on the French Revolution.' The story was to be unfolded in three full-length dramas, the first of which appeared in 1803. Eugenie, the Natural Daughter, ranks high among Goethe's heroines. She is born for great deeds and great sacrifices in the crisis which is drawing near in the French monarchy. We are acutely conscious of the approach of tragic issues and the ferment of revolutionary ideas. The finely moulded drama deserved and received the approval of the poet's friends, but the coldness of the public discouraged the author and the later parts of the trilogy remained unwritten.

Of all Goethe's attempts to embody the French Revolution in literary form, *Hermann und Dorothea* alone can be pronounced a complete success, and that glittering jewel is the least directly concerned with politics. That so many were unfinished testifies not only to his dissatisfaction with his efforts but to the irresistible fascination of the theme. His nature, yearning for harmony in life as in art, was thrown out of gear by the storm and the earthquake. Moreover, his incapacity to love or to hate the doctrines for which men fought and died cut him off from the deepest springs of inspiration. The Revolution, in his mature judgment, was a lesson alike to rulers and ruled. 'I could be no friend to the Revolution,' he remarked to Eckermann in 1824, 'but I was as little a friend to arbitrary rule. Indeed, I was perfectly convinced that a great revolution is never the fault of the people. Revolutions are utterly impossible so long as Governments are just and vigilant. If there exists an actual necessity for a great reform, God is with it and it prospers.' Eckermann describes his master as a mild aristocrat, but Goethe preferred another title. 'Dumont is a moderate Liberal, as all rational people are and ought to be, and as I am myself.' Whatever political label we may ultimately affix to his name, he cannot at any rate be placed in the camp either of indifference or reaction.

The stupendous figure of Napoleon claims as large a space in the life and thought of Goethe as the French Revolution, but his opinions of the Emperor are to be found rather in his conversations and correspondence than in his literary works.[1] He had followed with breathless interest the lightning ascent of the young General, welcomed Brumaire as the end of the Revolution, and accepted the proclamation of the Empire as the reward of incomparable services. It was not, however, till 1806 that the greatest of historic men won an abiding place in the foreground of his consciousness and claimed an allegiance which never waned or wavered till death.

Prussia had retired from the conflict with France in 1795 and re-entered it in 1806, and in both cases Weimar followed her lead. To join Russia and Austria in 1805 might have been wise, but to plunge

[1] See A. Fischer, *Goethe und Napoleon*.

after Austerlitz was madness. In July 1806 the Rheinbund was formed by sixteen Princes under the presidency of Napoleon, and in August the Emperor Francis proclaimed the dissolution of the Holy Roman Empire. The announcement, declared Goethe, disturbed him less than a quarrel between his servant and his coachman on the box seat, nor did he in any way deplore the creation of the Rheinbund. He had had enough of war and dissensions, and was ready to accept any system, national or anti-national, which seemed likely to promise a quiet life. He had always disapproved his master's close association with Prussia, and the quartering of the Duke's Prussian cavalry in Weimar had provoked complaints of the officers' arrogance. The army of Frederick the Great had not yet encountered Napoleon, and he never shared the delusion that it would prove invincible. There was no talk this time of his joining Karl August in the field, but since the Duchy lay right athwart the track of the French advance, he could not escape the gathering flood of war by staying at home. Alone of the Ducal family the valiant Duchess Luise remained in the capital, where she and the poet anxiously awaited the march of events.

October 14, 1806, was the most terrible day of his life. The thunder of the cannon at Jena reverberated through the little town, and bullets whistled over the roofs. Prussian soldiers in headlong flight soon told the citizens who had won, and the pursuers proceeded to exact the usual price of defeat. Some Alsatian Hussars who entered Goethe's house behaved tolerably well, and an officer soon arrived to report that Augereau would establish his headquarters there. The Marshal only arrived next day, and during the night two soldiers broke in, forced their way to the poet's bedroom, and threatened his life. The bravery of Christiane at this moment was rewarded three days later by marriage. On the following morning Ney appeared and left a guard, and Augereau spent two days under Goethe's roof. The soldiers drank twelve casks of wine, and the owner estimated his losses at 2,000 thalers.

Goethe cared as much for the Duchy of Weimar as he cared for Germany; and the political framework of the state was saved by the Duchess, whose courage and personality made a deep impression on Napoleon. Karl August was to leave the Prussian army, pay an indemnity, and enter the Rheinbund, the presence of French troops guaranteeing the fulfilment of the terms. The settlement was better than Goethe had dared to hope, and when peace was restored at

Tilsit, it seemed as if Germany might live quietly under the aegis of the Emperor whom he resolutely declined to regard as an enemy or a barbarian. He had never loved Prussia and he shed no tears over her overthrow. Moreover, the fascination of a daemonic figure, impersonal as fire or water and irresistible as fate, blinded him to everything but the splendour of creative genius.

At the Erfurt Congress in 1808 Napoleon was the central figure of a dazzling throng, which included not only the Tsar but more than forty kings, princes and dukes. He had brought Talma and his troupe from Paris, and it was his wish to appear as the ruler of the most civilised no less than of the most powerful country in the world. Karl August summoned the most distinguished of his subjects to the rendezvous, and on October 2 the two greatest men in the world met face to face. When the poet entered the room, Napoleon—as a rule the least impressionable of men—exclaimed: 'Vous êtes un homme!' The conversation turned on drama and on *Werther*, which the Emperor took with him on his campaigns and knew almost by heart, and ended with questions on his personal affairs and his relations to the Ducal family. Goethe was treated throughout as an equal, and on his leaving the room the Emperor ejaculated: 'Voilà un homme!' It was the most memorable day in his life, and every detail of the audience combined to heighten its effect. The value of the Emperor's admiration for *Werther* was enhanced by his criticisms, which struck the author as both penetrating and just. 'I gladly confess,' he wrote to Cotta, 'that nothing higher or more gratifying could occur in my life than thus to stand before the Emperor. Of the great ones of the earth I can truly say that no one had received me in such a manner— I mean on terms of such confidential equality.'

Four days later Napoleon visited Weimar, and again conversed with Goethe at the ball which followed the performance of Voltaire's *La Mort de César*. The poet was exhorted to write a tragedy on the same theme which would prove that the murder of Caesar was a blunder. Tacitus was condemned for his partisanship and Shakespeare for mixing comedy with tragedy. Goethe was invited to Paris, where he was assured that he would widen his outlook and find rich material for his craft. The Emperor also conferred the Cross of the newly-founded Legion of Honour on him and Wieland. The Man of Destiny was in a gracious mood, for fortune had smiled on him. Having decided to spare the dynasty, he proceeded to win its goodwill by exempting the Duchy from providing troops for Spain and by indemnifying the town of Jena for the damage wrought by the battle.

The Emperor's pressing invitation—'je l'exige de vous'—to settle in Paris occupied Goethe's thoughts for a time, and led to inquiries as to the practical questions involved in such a step. His worship of Napoleon strengthened his lifelong desire to see 'das ungeheure Paris,' and the provincialism of Weimar lay heavy on him. The project was dropped, though not from any doubt as to the permanence of his favour. Indeed fidelity to his hero survived all the vicissitudes of fortune, and he defiantly continued to wear the Legion of Honour after the French yoke had been broken. He never pretended to approve all the Emperor's actions and he sympathised with his brother Louis, King of Holland, whom he met at Karlsbad and whose 'goodness' he warmly admired; yet he never lost the conviction that Napoleon was such a unique and almost supernatural genius that he could not be weighed in the scales of ordinary humanity.

Though he constantly talked and wrote of him and enjoyed the society of the French Minister, Baron de St. Aignan, it was not till 1812 that he rendered poetical homage to the lord of the world. The presence of Marie Louise in Karlsbad during her annual sojourn inspired the poem: *An Ihro der Kaiserin von Frankreich Majestät*. The structure was suggested by the firmament, where Jupiter and Venus were close together in May. The Emperor is Jupiter, the Empress Venus, and the French Revolution night. Jupiter-Napoleon terminates the confusion, banishes the darkness and rules by power and wisdom:

> Worüber trüb Jahrhunderte gesonnen,
> Er übersieht's in hellstem Geisteslicht;
> Das Kleiniche ist alles weggeronnen,
> Nur Meer und Erde haben hier Gewicht.
> Ist jenem erst das Ufer abgewonnen,
> Dass sich daran die stolze Woge bricht,
> So tritt durch weisen Schluss, durch Machtgefechte
> Das feste Land in alle seine Rechte.

The dynasty, he adds, is established by the birth of an heir, and the poem ends with the hope that the Emperor, 'der alles wollen kann,' may will peace.

The French yoke in the Duchy was light and in Goethe's view it was neither necessary nor possible to overthrow it, but the *débâcle* in Russia gave patriots their chance. The poet stubbornly declined to believe that the end was near, and cynically observed that the burning of Moscow was nothing to him. As the Emperor passed through Weimar on his way home, he inquired about Goethe and sent a greeting from Erfurt. The French garrison surrendered to a body of Russians and Prussians a few days after the poet had left his home, taking some valuables with him and burying others. On his way to Teplitz, where he hoped to escape from the blinding storm of war, he broke the journey at Dresden, where he witnessed the entry of Frederick William III and the Tsar. There Arndt found him 'much depressed, with neither joy nor hope in the changed condition of affairs.' When the elder Körner and his greater son gave vent to their enthusiasm, he uttered his second famous prophecy: 'The man is too great for you; you may shake your chains, but you will not break them.'

On his return home three months later Dresden was French again, and Napoleon's birthday was celebrated by illuminations and processions. No wonder that at this moment he bet a gold ducat that the French would not be driven beyond the Rhine. The bet was lost, for in October the slaughter of Leipzig made Germany free. French troops had marched through Weimar to the battlefield, and after the titanic conflict the little capital once again witnessed a flight from the striken field. In 1806 the Germans were pursued by the victorious French; in 1813 the French were chased by the triumphant Allies. Once again the town was filled with wounded men, and once again officers were billeted in Goethe's house; but his inconveniences were minimised by the friendly intervention of Metternich. 'It is uplifting,' he wrote, 'to obtain an insight into the views of such men as he who directs the stupendous whole, by the smallest fraction of which the rest of us feel oppressed and indeed overwhelmed.'

Goethe watched the march of events with heavy heart. If the French triumphed their revenge would be terrible; if they were beaten, arrogant Prussia and savage Russia would be supreme. He, at any rate, would not lift a finger to aid the national cause. When Karl August, emerging from his forced neutrality, appealed for volunteers, August Goethe desired to serve; but the father interposed on the ground that his son was acting as his secretary and could not be spared. During these weeks of national exaltation he found himself a lonely man wherever he went, and when Fouqué recited some patriotic verses at the house of Johanna Schopenhauer he refrained from joining in the applause. Yet when the Allies had entered Paris in the spring of 1814 and Napoleon was caged in Elba, Iffland invited him to contribute to the festivities which were to welcome the allied sovereigns to Berlin. He replied that he was busy with another theatrical piece, and that a month was too short; but a day or two later he wrote that an idea had occurred to him, and he thanked the Director of the Berlin Theatre for enabling him to tell the German people how he had sympathised with its joys and sorrows. His heart, however, was not in his work, and *Des Epimenides Erwachen*, like Gerhart Hauptmann's *Festspiel* in 1913, was deemed unworthy both of the occasion and the author. Of the tumultuous emotions of the War of Liberation there was not a trace, and indeed no one could tell who Epimenides was intended to be. The concluding chorus, however, was clear enough, and embodied the poet's longing that now at last his countrymen would find peace:

> So rissen wir uns rings herum
> Von fremden Banden los.
> Nun sind wir Deutsche wiederum,
> Nun sind wir wieder gross.

Six years later Goethe paid his last homage to the hero by translating Manzoni's fine ode *Il Cinque Maggio*.

When the long peace of the Restoration descended on tired Europe, Goethe's thoughts constantly turned to Napoleon. On one occasion Eckermann observed that he had been reproached for not taking up arms at that great time. 'How could I take up arms without hatred?' rejoined the old man. 'And how could I hate without youth? I have never shammed. I have never given utterance to what I have not experienced. I have only composed love-songs when I have loved. How could I write songs of hate without hatred? And between ourselves I did not hate the French, though I thanked God when we were free of them. How could I, to whom culture and barbarism are alone of importance, hate a nation which is among the most cultivated on earth and to which I owe so great a part of my own possessions? There is a stage where national hatred vanishes altogether, and where one stands to a certain extent above the nations, and feels the weal or woe of a neighbouring people as if it were one's own.' It is the voice of the last and greatest of the cosmopolitans of the eighteenth century. In his own way he too was a patriot, but patriotism was to him the lifelong endeavour to enrich German culture and to set it in the forefront of the march of civilisation.

The last chapter in the story of Goethe's political contacts is a time of relative tranquillity. Europe desired and required to recover breath after the exhausting struggle; revolutionary doctrines were discredited, and a period of quiet growth, such as the poet loved, seemed at hand. Moreover, Weimar had emerged from the fiery ordeal not only unscathed but enlarged. The Duchy had doubled its territory, Karl August had become a Grand Duke, and his prestige stood higher than ever. The poet might well have looked forward to a tranquil eventide, untroubled by wars, invasions and revolts.

On the disappearance of the Holy Roman Empire and the collapse of the short-lived Rheinbund, a new political framework was provided by the Deutscher Bund, a loose federation of forty states with its Diet in permanent session at Frankfurt. It was a decided improvement on the decrepit Holy Roman Empire, but it lacked power and prestige, and control remained in the hands of its component units. Generous hopes had been aroused and encouraged during the exaltations and agonies of the War of Liberation; but when victory was achieved the two strongest members, the King of Prussia and the Emperor of Austria, determined to continue the system of autocracy in which they had been bred, and Goethe was the last man to blame them.

The 'ideas of 1789' had been temporarily discredited by the Terror and the revolutionary wars; but the doctrine of political self-determination had been scotched, not killed, and article XIII of the Constitution of the Bund provided that every member should introduce a constitution with assemblies of Estates. The South German rulers proceeded to grant constitutions, Karl August himself leading the way in 1816 by reviving and expanding the provisions of the Constitution which he had granted in 1809. The Privy Council was succeeded by a Ministry of which Goethe became the head. Yet the rise in his worldly fortunes, combined with an increase in his salary, brought him no joy; for he disapproved his master's concessions, which included election by ballot of representatives to all Estates, and liberty of the Press. His apprehensions of the latter were quickly confirmed by the journals which sprang up like mushrooms throughout the Duchy, and to which both the teachers and students of Jena made outspoken contributions. It was his wish to suppress the more radical organs, but the Grand Duke loyally upheld the privileges which he had granted. It was a painful duty for the Prime Minister to stand at the right hand of his master in 1816 when the dignitaries paid homage for the Constitution. Still more distressing was the discovery that as President of the Commission for Art and Science he was obliged to report to the Landtag. He flatly declined to make a statement on his expenditure, and it required the tactful intervention of the Grand Duchess to induce the Landtag in this instance to waive its rights.

The Wartburg festival intensified his conviction that his master had embarked on the wrong course. Young Germany had combined in the Burschenschaften to work for unity and self-government, and on October 18, 1817, the German Burschen met at the Wartburg at the invitation of the Jena branch to commemorate the tercentenary of the Reformation and the fourth anniversary of the battle of Leipzig. The festival was organised with the approval of the Government, and the speeches were harmless enough, but the proceedings ended with a bonfire of reactionary writings, among them those of Kotzebue. Two years later, when the dramatist, who had become an agent of Russia, was murdered at Mannheim by the student Sand, Metternich exploited the panic to issue the Karlsbad Decrees, which muzzled not only the Press but the Universities. The arch-reactionary, who throttled the political life of Germany for a generation, held Karl August in large measure responsible for the dangerous spirit of the German youth, and Goethe, who visited him at Karlsbad, shared his opinion. For the remaining thirteen years of his life he lived in a country which possessed scarcely more freedom than it had enjoyed in his youth.

Goethe grew up in the eighteenth century when the ruling conceptions were benevolent autocracy and cultured individualism, and he remained to the end a child of his age. He was a stranger in the nineteenth, whose ideals of democracy and nationality were to change the face of the world. Democracy meant to him the enthronement of inexperienced mediocrity, the cult of incompetence, to use Émile Faguet's uncomplimentary phrase. He lacked the belief in the instinctive wisdom of the people which is the kernel of the democratic faith. Nationality recalled to him visions of the French on the Rhine and the Wars of Liberation with their tumultuous emotions which he never shared. Throughout life he looked down on the struggling masses as from the housetops, wishing them well with all his heart, but utterly unconvinced of their capacity to work out their own salvation. The world swings rapidly forward, and few of us can keep pace with all its moods and tenses. Goethe's services to his countrymen and to mankind were manifold enough to dispense with the title of political prophet and pioneer.

GERMANY'S DEBT TO THE FRENCH REVOLUTION

DURING the years preceding the French Revolution Germany presented a pathetic spectacle of political decrepitude. The Holy Roman Empire was dying and only waited for an order of demolition. No less urgent was the need of change in the majority of the units which composed it. While Germany could show rulers of conscience and capacity such as Karl August of Weimar and Karl Friedrich of Baden, the Duke of Brunswick and the Duke of Gotha, nowhere in Europe was absolutism more repulsive than in the little Courts where Frederick's doctrine of service had never penetrated, where mistresses ruled supreme, where venality placed the unfittest in office, where reckless ostentation stood out in glaring contrast to the poverty of the people. 'The peasant,' wrote a satirist grimly, 'is like a sack of meal. When emptied there is still some dust in it; it only needs to be beaten.' For the most part the victims suffered in silence, but discontent found powerful interpreters in Moser and Schlözer, Schubart and Weckhrlin. The revolt of the American Colonies and the establishment of a democratic republic free from courts and armies, feudalism and poverty, was at once a warning to rulers that there was a limit to tyranny and an inspiration to downtrodden peoples all over the world. At the same time the intellectual revival which had given birth to the *Aufklärung* began to produce its effect on the political plane. During the generation of peace which followed the Seven Years' War Germany learned to read, to think, and to ask questions. The critical spirit, once aroused, spread rapidly, finding nourishment in the rank evils which overspread the land. 'In my youth,' wrote Goethe in 1790, 'it hardly occurred to anybody to envy the privileged class or to grudge them their privileges; but knights, robbers, an honest Tiers État and an infamous nobility—such are the ingredients of our novels and plays during the last ten years.' He was thinking above all of Schiller, whose passionate denunciations of tyranny moved his audiences to frenzied enthusiasm.

Thus the lethargy which had weighed on Germany in the first half of the eighteenth century was passing rapidly away. The personality and victories of Frederick the Great, the object-lesson of the American War, the leaven of Voltaire, Rousseau and Montesquieu, the challenge of the *Aufklärung*, the radicalism of the dramatists, the barbed arrows of the journalists—these crowding and converging influences and experiences set the mind of the nation in a ferment. To borrow the words of Kant in 1784, it was not an enlightened age but an age in process of enlightenment. Change was in the air and the fragility of traditional institutions was widely recognised. In Germany as in France prophetic voices gave warning of the wrath to come, and sensitive observers felt the earth trembling beneath their feet. On the eve of the Revolution the mass of the population was poor, ignorant, ill governed, discontented and helpless; and when the Rights of Man were proclaimed from the banks of the Seine the German people, fast bound in the fetters of feudalism and autocracy, was ready to welcome the gospel of deliverance.

The opening scenes of the French Revolution were watched with delight by most leaders of German opinion. The Declaration of the Rights of Man put into words the muffled aspirations of the masses all over Europe, and gave to the humble and disinherited a new sense of human dignity. When France in trumpet tones decreed the downfall of feudalism, proclaimed the equality of burdens, and declared every man possessed of certain inalienable rights, generous hearts in Germany, no less than in England, were thrilled by the warmth and glory of the sunrise. Johannes Müller, the historian of Switzerland's struggles for freedom, pronounced the destruction of the Bastille the happiest event since the birth of Christ. Many a Sultan in the Empire, he hoped, would tremble and many an oligarchy would learn that there were limits to human endurance. Klopstock, the Nestor of German literature, regretted that he had not a hundred voices to celebrate the birth of liberty. It is glorious, cried Georg Forster, to see what philosophy has ripened in the brain and realised in the State. Herder proclaimed the Revolution the most important movement in the life of mankind since the Reformation, and welcomed it as a no less decisive step towards human freedom. 'The spirit of the time is strong within me,' exclaimed Gentz, the most brilliant of Prussian publicists. 'I am young, and the universal striving for freedom arouses my warmest sympathy. I should regard the shipwreck of this movement as one of the greatest disasters that ever befell mankind. It would be felt that men were happy only as slaves, and every tyrant, great and small, would revenge himself for the fright the French nation had given him.' 'You cannot be more convinced than I,' wrote Wieland in an Open Letter to the French reformers, 'that your nation was wrong to bear such misgovernment so long; that every people has an indefeasible right to as much liberty as can co-exist with order; that the person and property of every citizen must be secured against the caprices of power, and that each must be taxed in proportion to his wealth.'

In the salons of Henriette Herz and Rahel Levin the intellectual *élite* of the Prussian capital applauded the moving drama on the Seine. Cosmopolitan Hamburg and tolerant Brunswick welcomed the dawning age of reason with enthusiasm, and in distant Königsberg the greatest of German thinkers made no secret of his joy. Opinion was more critical in Hanover, where Brandes and Rehberg asserted the superior virtues of the British Constitution and placed Burke above Rousseau; while in Weimar Goethe and Schiller, though in no way blind to the sins of the *Ancien Régime*, lamented that the work of reform had fallen into the hands of the multitude and that the frail bark of culture was in danger of shipwreck in the revolutionary rapids. A more balanced view was advanced by Humboldt, who, while foretelling a short life for the new Constitution, maintained that the benefits of the great upheaval would be felt beyond the frontiers of France rather than in the land of its birth. Many of the most vociferous of its admirers, led by Klopstock and Gentz, changed their note when the reform movement degenerated into murder and anarchy; but others, like Kant and Herder, refused to allow even the Terror to blind them to the enduring value of its work for humanity.

The favourable impression made by 'French ideas' at the outset was enhanced by the appearance of the first batches of refugees on the Rhine. 'One must distinguish between the voluntary and compulsory emigrations,' wrote Madame de Stael; 'after the fall of the monarchy we all emigrated.' This distinction between 'the emigration of pride' and 'the emigration of necessity' was fully appreciated in the frontier lands in which the newcomers sought temporary shelter from the storm. Though they were kindly welcomed by the Ecclesiastical Electors, the citizens of Coblenz and Mainz watched their arrogance, extravagance and immoralities with indignation. Each haughty aristocrat seemed a fresh argument for the necessity of the Revolution, and even those who cared nothing for the Rights of Man sympathised with a nation which had been subject to such unworthy masters. A brief experience of their character and methods aroused no less anger and contempt in the breasts of the Emperor Leopold and Kaunitz than among the easy-going bourgeois of the Rhineland. The detestation they provoked was intensified by the cruel and disparaging tone in which many of their leaders referred to the sovereigns whom they had deserted. 'Till his death,' writes Ernest Daudet, the historian of the *Émigration*, 'Louis XVI had no worse enemies than the Émigrés, who were the principal authors of his troubles. The Princes were disobedient to their brother and disloyal to their country.' The result of their intransigence was clearly foretold by Mirabeau. 'By threatening us with the return of despotism,' he cried bitterly in 1790, 'they will drag us willy-nilly to a republic.'

In his dispassionate volume on the causes of the war of 1792 Ranke argued that a conflict between the new France and the old Europe was virtually inevitable; to which Sybel replied that its outbreak was solely due to the chauvinism of Brissot and his fellow Girondins, who believed that war would strengthen the position of their party. If the former explanation was too vague, the latter was too narrow. The antagonism between the doctrinaire radicalism of the French reformers and the traditionalism of the Great Powers rendered a conflict probable enough, but hostilities need not have broken out but for the two concrete problems of the abolition of feudal rights in Alsace and the gathering of armed Émigrés in the Rhineland. In the first case the German Princes had a legitimate grievance, in the second the French Government; and there were plenty of men in Paris, Berlin and Vienna who were eager to fan the smouldering embers into a flame. The first shot was fired by France, and after a decade of desperate struggle the victorious Republic pushed its frontier to the Rhine and established itself as the most formidable military power in Europe. 'I observe that minds are fermenting in that Germany of yours,' wrote Mirabeau to Mauvillon at the end of 1789. 'If the spark falls on combustible material, it will be a fire of charcoal not straw. Though perhaps more advanced in education, you are not so mature as we, because your emotions are rooted in the head; and since your brains are petrified with slavery the explosion will come with you much later than with us.' The great tribune's prophecy proved correct, for the main effects of the Revolution were manifested in Germany some years after the acute crisis in France was past.

The combined influence of the ideas of 1789 and of the Great War which followed their proclamation produced concrete results in Germany of incalculable importance. The first was the destruction of the political framework of the country. The patent weakness of the Empire in the war, the withdrawal of Prussia at the height of the struggle, and the collapse of the Ecclesiastical Electorates, left no attentive observer in doubt that the old firm was in liquidation. No ambitious and aggressive State could have wished for a neighbour less fitted to parry its thrust. Well might Napoleon write to the Directory from Rastadt, 'If the Germanic Body did not exist we should have to create it expressly for our own convenience.'

When the left bank of the Rhine was annexed to the French Republic, Görres wrote his celebrated obituary. 'On December 30, 1797, at three in the afternoon, the Holy Roman Empire, supported by the Sacraments, passed away peacefully at Regensburg at the age of 955, in consequence of senile debility and an apoplectic stroke. The deceased was born at Verdun in the year 842, and educated at the court of Charles the Simple and his successors. The young prince was taught piety by the Popes, who canonised him in his lifetime. But his tendency to a sedentary life, combined with zeal for religion, undermined his health. His head became visibly weaker till at last he went mad in the Crusades. Frequent bleedings and careful diet restored him; but, reduced to a shadow, the invalid tottered through the centuries till violent hemorrhage occurred in the Thirty Years' War. Hardly had he recovered when the French arrived and a stroke put an end to his sufferings. He kept himself unstained by the *Aufklärung* and bequeathed the left bank of the Rhine to the French Republic.' Görres was right. The Empire was not buried till 1806, but it was slain by the Revolution. It perished unwept, unhonoured and unsung, and its ghost had to be laid before Germany could be reborn.

Secularisation was in the air before 1789, and, when the Republican armies reached the Rhine, the princes whose interests were affected sought compensation on the right bank. When rude hands were laid on the ark of the covenant they quickly found imitators. By the Recess of 1803 the Ecclesiastical Electorates and principalities were swept away; the Free Cities, with the exception of Hamburg, Bremen, Lubeck, Frankfurt, Nürnberg and Augsburg, disappeared;

and the old organisation of the Circles was broken in pieces. In the College of Princes, where the Protestants obtained a majority, power passed from south to north, from the Austrian to the Prussian camp. The Hapsburg ascendancy was overthrown by the eviction of the ecclesiastics and by the aggrandisement of Bavaria, Baden, Württemberg and Hesse. 'Few among the great transformations of modern history,' declares Treitschke with truth, 'seem so detestable, so base and so mean as this Princes' Revolution. Not a glimmer of a bold idea, not a spark of noble passion, illuminated the colossal breach of public law. And yet the overthrow was a great necessity. All that was buried was already dead. The ancient forms of the State vanished in an instant as if they had been swallowed up in the earth.'

The Princes' Revolution left the historic structure little more than a ruin, and it was clear that its respite would be brief. A year later, when the First Consul crowned himself in Notre Dame, the Hapsburg monarch assumed the title of Emperor of Austria. In 1805 the cannon of Austerlitz battered down what remained of the crumbling walls and towers of the Holy Roman Empire, and in the following summer the curtain was rung down on a thousand years of German history. The Holy Roman Empire, with the Emperor, the Electors, the Diet, the Court of Appeal, the Ecclesiastical Princes, the Imperial Knights and Free Cities, collapsed like a house of cards at the touch of Napoleon's spear. When the Bund emerged from the Congress of Vienna, there were only two score states in place of the motley multitude which had composed the Empire. The transformation of Germany was accomplished without the savagery and sufferings which disgraced the French experiment of 1789. On the other hand the simplification of political geography brought gain rather to the princes than to the nation, for Germany as a whole secured neither unity, liberty nor strength.

The second momentous result of the Revolution was the renaissance of Prussia, but it was not till the *débâcle* of 1806 that her slow-witted ruler began to realise that he must take a lesson from his terrible neighbour. 'The Prussian Monarchy,' declared Mirabeau, 'is so constituted that it could not cope with any calamity'; and the calamity had now arrived. The work of Stein and Hardenberg was rendered possible by Napoleon's thunderbolts, but the ideas to which they gave practical shape were in large measure those of 1789. The counsellors of Frederick William II and his successor were men like Mencken, Lombard and Beyme, who desired the application of French principles in diluted form; and young Custine pronounced Struensee, the Minister of Finance, as much a partisan of the French Revolution as a Prussian Minister could be. But they were not statesmen of the first rank, and they lacked the resolution to carry out the changes which they knew to be necessary. The Prussian Code of 1794, the work of Carmer and Suarez, is almost wholly Frederician in spirit. The hour of reform arrived when the logic of the stricken field had revealed the need of building from the depths, and when men of ability and determination were permitted to carry out some of the most essential tasks.

Republican and Imperial France had shown how to develop and apply the latent strength and capacity of a nation, and the grandeur of her achievement impressed even those who suffered from her blows. The regenerators of Prussia, whether Prussians or not, shared the conviction that the need of the time was to revive the courage and mobilise the resources of the nation by inviting it to share in the privileges and responsibilities of government. 'The military as well as the political chiefs,' writes the French historian Cavaignac with patriotic pride, 'were penetrated by the example of the Revolution, imbued with its spirit, convinced that Prussia and Germany could only find salvation by following the paths it had opened.' This was recognised as frankly by Stein and Niebuhr, Scharnhorst and Gneisenau, who hated it, as by the eclectic Hardenberg and by Schön, the radical *doctrinaire*.

The Revolution had been saddled and bridled before Stein was called, in middle life, to play a commanding part on the Prussian stage, but its influence on his ideas and achievements is indubitable. After his appointment as Minister, shortly before the battle of Jena, he drew up a memorandum comparing Prussia to a machine which only functions properly when controlled by a superman, and demanding a limited monarchy. The memorandum was seen by the Queen but was considered too outspoken for the eyes of the King. Of greater importance was the 'Nassau Programme' written in Stein's ancestral home on the eve of his appointment as First Minister. 'If the nation is to be uplifted,' he declared, 'the submerged part must be given liberty, independence, property and the protection of the laws.' He agrees with the French reformers with regard to the emancipation of the peasants, the liberation of industry, the equalisation of taxes, and the abolition of patrimonial jurisdiction. 'Here is no catalogue of the Rights of Man,' comments his admiring biographer Lehmann; 'but the emphatic demand for the right of a nation to administer itself rules out the patriarchal system of old Prussia and implicitly contains the whole charter of citizenship.' Stein's historic Ministry was cut short before he had time to carry out more than a fraction of the Nassau Programme, but the emancipation of the peasants and the grant of municipal self-government stand out as monuments of his brief rule. Emancipation owed as much to Schön, who had drunk deeply at French springs, as self-government to Frey, who had diligently studied the French decree of 1789 on municipalities.

'What was it,' asks Lehmann, 'that attracted these thoroughly German minds in Königsberg to the revolutionary legislation of France, which they only approved with large reservations? The answer is that they desired to attain for their country the position of power which those laws had secured for France.' Reform in the direction of equality was in the air, and Stein and his colleagues were merely the agents of a change rendered inevitable by the ferment of the Revolution. As the abstract ideas of 1789 appealed to the writers and thinkers of Germany in the decade of revolution, their concrete results converted conservative German statesmen in search of a policy in the opening years of the nineteenth century. The sensational returns secured in France by the approximation towards equality and by the release of individual aptitudes were writ large on the map of Europe; and every statesmanlike brain in Prussia grasped the fact that if the nation was to live and grow it must learn from its conquerors.

The new spirit of reforming zeal was furiously denounced by Marwitz, the spokesman of the impenitent Junkers who looked back to the autocracy and feudalism of the Frederician system as to the golden age. 'Stein,' he complains, 'brought the Revolution into our country. He collected a gang of ideologues, drones and chatterers about him, and began revolutionising the Fatherland, inaugurating the war of the landless against property, of industry against agriculture, of crass materialism against the divine order. He inaugurated the so-called regeneration of the Prussian State with laws based on the principles of Rousseau and Montesquieu. The ideologues, from the Garonne to the Niemen, hailed the Emancipation Edict with a hymn of praise.' The impeachment has been adopted with patriotic pride by French historians. 'It needed half a century to establish throughout Germany the social principles born of the French Revolution,' writes Doniol in his work on the Revolution and Feudalism. 'Finally they took possession even of the most recalcitrant of the states. There was no longer room in people's minds for other laws than those fitted to endow both the people and the land with the independence which the French Revolution had made the indispensable condition of social vitality.' Prussia led the way. Stein's Edict of 1807 was the Prussian Fourth of August.' 'France did more than conquer Europe,' echoes Sorel; 'she converted her. The French won over to their ideas the very nations which revolted against their domination. The princes most eagerly bent on penning-in the Revolution saw it, on returning from their crusade, sprouting in the soil of their own estates which had been fertilised by the blood of French soldiers.' Cavaignac's *La Formation de la Prusse Contemporaine* is one long plea for the recognition of French influences on the modernisation of the Hohenzollern State. Stein's debt to France has been contested in Ernst von Meier's elaborate treatise on Prussia and the French Revolution; but Lehmann, whose biography called forth the protest of the Hanoverian jurist, never suggested that France was more than one source of his hero's inspiration or that he made uncritical use of foreign models. 'He never surrendered himself to the ideas of 1789,' declares Lehmann. 'His desire was to modify them and to combine them with the inherited conditions of Prussian and Protestant ideals.'

The political derivation of Hardenberg gives rise to no such controversy. 'While Stein swam against the stream of the time,' writes Meier, 'Hardenberg allowed himself to be borne along with it. He was an adherent of the French Revolution and desired to imitate it.' An enemy alike of autocracy and democracy, he greeted it and many of its early measures as making for the limited monarchy of his dreams. France travelled too far and too fast for a liberal conservative who abhorred violence, but he never doubted that a new era had dawned and that the task of statesmanship was to apply the lessons of the cataclysm. In an elaborate Memorandum written in 1807 at the King's request, he declared that the dominant principle of government should be the application of the ideas of the French Revolution to Prussia, for such was their power that any state which rejected them would either collapse or be forced to accept them. There must be a revolution in the good sense, a revolution from above. The form most suited to the spirit of the age would be a combination of democratic principles with monarchical rule. A government must work in harmony with the scheme of Providence, and should not shrink from the principal demand of the age, namely the utmost possible liberty and equality. He prescribed the same medicine when he assumed power in 1810. 'Your Majesty, we must do from above what the French have done from below.'

He was as good as his word. He completed the creation of a free peasantry begun by Stein, and carried forward the reform of the central and local administration; and it was not his fault that Prussia had to wait for a constitution till 1848. Like Stein he was denounced by Marwitz and the Junkers as a leveller; from their narrow standpoint they were right, for he had grasped the force latent in the conception of social equality. Throughout Europe a truceless conflict was in progress between the *Ancien Régime* and the ideas of 1789, and when a statesman decided to break with feudalism, he was compelled to study and to some extent to adopt French methods. 'Hardenberg's work,' testifies Cavaignac, 'is the most indubitable testimony to the action of the French Revolution on European society.' A mind so receptive to new influences and yet so firmly anchored in historic realities was of infinite value in the critical period following the battle of Jena; and Ranke, who edited his papers half a century after his death, declared that no statesman had engraved his name more deeply on the brazen tablets of Prussian history.

The lessons of the French Revolution were taken to heart by the reforming soldiers of Prussia no less than by the reforming civilians. The powerful intellect of Scharnhorst focussed on national strength, and he complained that the Declaration of the Rights of Man dealt only with the rights of individuals, not with those of the State; but he recognised that the upper classes were as a rule too selfish and too stupid to make concessions, and he declared that things could not go on as they were. In a pregnant dissertation on the French War, written in 1797, he argued that the evil fortune of the Allies was due not to accidents or details but to deeper causes. The first was ignorance of the strength of the foe, due to the false reports of the Émigrés, who led the Powers to believe that the Revolution was the work of a small minority. The second was the lack of stomach for the fight. 'When the French Revolution began, a large number of the noblest minds were fired by the ideal of a more perfect and beneficent government, especially among young men of lively imagination with a generous feeling for right and for the sufferings of the less fortunate class. France employed all her material and moral resources, while the Allies only utilised a portion of their strength and were sadly lacking in *moral*.' The main reasons for the loss of the first round of the match between revolutionary France and feudal Europe were thus to be sought on the moral rather than on the material plane. Every citizen of the Republic had been prepared for any sacrifice to defend his territory and his independence, and necessity generated a marvellous energy in the Government, the army and the nation. If the Powers were to triumph, they would have to penetrate the secret of national determination which had carried France through unprecedented trials and dangers.

The bracing challenge of the Revolution in the more intelligent military circles is further illustrated in the voluminous Memoirs of Boyen, the favourite disciple of Scharnhorst and co-founder of compulsory service in Prussia. 'The opening scenes made no great impression among a people which had given little thought to France except in regard to fashion. The Prussians despised her evil government and the immorality of the *noblesse* and higher clergy, and opinion did not blame the French for seeking to remove all these abuses as we felt we were much better off. On the whole Germans were comfortable and nearly all regarded the happenings merely as objects of curiosity, but the success of the American Revolution and the failure of the Dutch revolt against the Statthalter led to other views. In general the bourgeoisie and many of the Intellectuals were favourable. They looked forward to the abolition of burdensome feudal privileges, class distinctions, and waste. There were plenty of landowners, especially in East Prussia, who approved the abolition of serfdom and feudal services. The nobility and the officers, on the other hand, especially the older members, were utterly opposed to any action which threatened their position. On myself the abolition of many foolish privileges of the nobility and the emancipation of the peasant from his crushing burdens made a favourable impression. In the Declaration of the Rights of Man I saw an ideal of legislation never before reached, and my inexperience caused me to overlook the imperfections and unpractical character of this famous manifesto which should have mentioned duties as well as rights.' The efforts of the selfish Émigrés to win support for an ideological war against France filled him with angry disgust, and the military disasters caused him no surprise. Germany lacked leaders but he realised that there were also deeper causes at work. 'The Revolution in France had generated a mass of material and spiritual weapons which made her onslaught almost irresistible, since her foes omitted to take similar measures and were content to defend themselves as best they could with the old mechanical forms.'

Though Gneisenau, like Scharnhorst, cared more for order than liberty and more for obedience than self-realisation, he drew the same lesson from the crowning event of his time. 'One cause above all has raised France to this pinnacle of greatness,' he wrote after Jena. 'The Revolution awakened all her powers and gave to every individual a suitable field for his activity. What infinite aptitudes slumber in the bosom of a nation! In the breast of thousands resides real genius. Why do not the Courts take steps to open up a career to it wherever it is found, to encourage talents and virtues whatever the rank? Why did they not seize this opportunity to multiply their powers a thousandfold, to open to the simple bourgeois the Arc de Triomphe through which only the noble can now pass? The new era requires more than old names, titles and parchments. The Revolution has set the whole strength of a nation in motion, and by the equalisation of the different classes and the equal taxation of property converted the living strength of men and the dead strength of resources into a productive capital, and thereby upset the old relations of States and the old equilibrium. If other States desire to restore this equilibrium, they must employ the same instruments. They must appropriate the results of the Revolution. Then they will reap the double advantage of being able to mobilise their whole national strength against another Power, and of escaping the danger of an upheaval which threatens them so long as they refuse to obviate violent change by voluntary transformation.' Here are the same ideas and almost the same phrases as those of Stein and Hardenberg. Though their programme was never carried out in its entirety, the partial application of 'French ideas' produced the desired result in the Wars of Liberation, and enabled Prussia to cast off the yoke of the tyrant with the resolute passion of a united people.

While Prussia suffered more grievously at the hands of France than any other German State and looked back with loathing on the mighty Emperor, the west and south received a far more permanent impress from the ideas and institutions imported by the Revolution.

7*

The three Ecclesiastical Electorates collapsed at the first assault, and what was known as the Pfaffengasse (Parsons' Lane) was ruled by France for twenty years. The Republic of Mainz, established by Custine in the autumn of 1792, only lived till the recapture of the city in the following summer; but the experiment created extraordinary interest, and the fate of Georg Forster and Adam Lux, its deputies to Paris, threw round it something of the halo of romance. When the French armies again reached the Rhine in 1794, the Left Bank entered on a period of rapid change. Yet the invaders were never popular, for instead of liberty and fraternity they brought crushing burdens and military rule, administrative corruption and anti-clerical intolerance. Their watchword 'War on the palaces, peace to the cottages' was a parrot's cry and was dropped when it had done its work. The only disinterested friend of German liberty among the soldiers and statesmen of the era of the Directory was Hoche, whose premature death left the Rhineland a prey to the vultures.

In burning words Görres denounced 'the heartless and mindless men who are sent to govern us, adventurers who are the scum of France. Many of us believed that the French had been transformed by the Revolution into angels, but the arrogance of the conquerors waxed day by day, and there was no end to their extortions and exactions. Everything combined to create a universal detestation of the French. The cause was soon identified with its representatives, and hatred was felt not only for republicans but for republicanism and liberty. In my belief the century for the introduction of democracy has not yet dawned and will not dawn in a hurry. We say with Vergniaud: We have deceived ourselves not in liberty but in the hour. We believed we were in Rome, but we found ourselves in Paris.' A mission to the capital shortly before Brumaire convinced him that the agents of the Republic were no worse than those who had sent them. He bitterly compared the Revolution to a balloon which had soared majestically into the air and then exploded and sunk to the earth in flames.

The anger of Görres was shared by his fellow-victims on the Left Bank. Conscription was the first and the most detested of the penalties of conquest. The importation of English goods was prohibited, and the loss of the German market was but partially balanced by the commercial current directed towards France. The army of occupation lived on the country, and the burden of taxes and requisitions was increased by the dishonesty of unpaid and rapacious officials. The shock to religious sentiment was particularly resented. The clergy lost their endowments without receiving an indemnity from the State. Pilgrimages and processions were forbidden, while the republican calendar, with its three Decades a month, virtually suppressed Sunday. Under the fanatical Commissioner Lakanal the yoke became almost intolerable. Churches were closed, houses were searched, and incautious critics found themselves in prison.

Though the decade of republican rule inflicted grievous hardships on the Rhineland, there were nevertheless substantial entries on the credit side. On the outbreak of war the Left Bank had been ruled by nine Archbishops and Bishops, two religious Orders, seventy-six Princes and Counts, four Free Cities, and a host of Imperial Knights. Every one of these rulers and systems had been swept away by the broom of the war-god, and the nobility with few exceptions had fled across the Rhine. Feudal dues and tithes, privileges and exemption from taxation, were abolished. The sequestration of the lands of the dispossessed pointed to their sale in the near future. Liberty of industry was secured by the suppression of the gilds with their harassing rules, while French weights and measures and the decimal system gave a further impetus to trade. An efficient police guaranteed tolerable public security; a uniform legal procedure took the place of the innumerable tribunals of spiritual and temporal lords; and the mild criminal code of 1795 was applied. The gates of the ghetto at Bonn were thrown open, and the Protestants of Aachen and Cologne built their first churches.

A brighter day dawned in 1802 after the definite cession of the Left Bank by the Treaty of Lunéville, for the country was henceforward governed as an integral part of France. The local assemblies and muncipal councils were mere shadows, and there was as little liberty in the Rhineland as in the rest of Napoleon's dominions; but the reconciliation with the Church was welcomed and material progress was rapid. The property of the secular and ecclesiastical princes, the Émigrés, the Corporations and the Communes was now open to purchase by the peasants and burghers, who in working for their own profit rendered the soil more productive. The last traces of serfdom disappeared, education was fostered, and the navigation of the Rhine was improved. The Code substituted uniform procedure and modern ideas for a chaos of outworn practices. Roads were constructed, fruit-trees planted, agriculture and stock-breeding encouraged. Under prefects such as Jean Bon Saint-André and Lezay-Marnésia the Left Bank experienced a period of tranquil advance after a decade of war, billetings, exploitations and assignats.

'In the relatively short period of twenty years,' writes Sagnac, the latest French historian of the Rhineland, in a passage of eloquent pride, 'the French accomplished an immense work of which the Germans would never have dared to dream. The country was divided up into ninety-seven little States, jealous of one another and incapable of self-defence. It had remained feudal, and, being dominated by the petty interests of caste, was incapable of any comprehensive activity. It was called, not immediately but little by little and at the request of a large part of the inhabitants, to enter into a modern and centralised State, rich and powerful, and vitalised by economic liberty. To these weak and disunited peoples France gave what they needed most— protection and security. Having gone to war to liberate the peoples, not to enslave them, she brought all the free institutions which she had won in ten years of terrible strife. She abolished feudalism, liberated the soil, and transformed the peasant serfs into free proprietors. She sold to the burghers and the peasants the possessions of the late rulers and the lands of the Church and even a portion of the communal property, in order to multiply small freeholders and provide a competence. She established civil liberty and equality. In these Germanic lands, so unfamiliar with equality of rights and with liberty, so respectful of ecclesiastical and noble castes, it was a veritable revolution. No more distinction between citizens, no more religious intolerance! Protestants and Jews found themselves on the same footing as the Catholics who for centuries had governed the country in their own interest. The unity of laws was established. The Civil Code facilitated transactions from end to end of the Rhineland, and gave to the Rhinelanders the profound sentiment of the unity of their country and of their intimate union with France, who brought law and liberty in the folds of the tricolour.'

History thus seen through the invaders' spectacles overlooks not only the burdens imposed by an Emperor perpetually at war but the healthy dislike of civilised Europeans for alien rule. The dominant feeling of the Rhineland was in favour of a return in due course to German rule, combined with the retention of reforms introduced by the conquerors. No one ever dreamed of the restoration of the sway of the crozier and of the feudal order which had been swept into the dustbin by the revolutionary blast; but absolutism had been unknown in the Ecclesiastical Electorates, and the *Ancien Régime* had left no such bitter memories of oppression and humiliation as in France. Moreover, attachment to the Church had been strengthened by the attacks upon its practices and beliefs. The Rhineland as a whole was neither Jacobin nor reactionary, neither nationalist nor anti-national, and for this reason, though not immune from war, it was spared the horrors of revolution and counter-revolution. When peace returned to the world in 1815, the Left Bank reverted to German allegiance without regret and without enthusiasm. The reforms which had been introduced into the mushroom principalities of Westphalia, Berg and Frankfurt were for the most part swept away on the fall of their creator; but in the Rhineland, divided though it was between Prussia, Hesse-Darmstadt and Bavaria, twenty years of French occupation and assimilation left abiding traces. Friendly memories of the tricolour and legends of the Petit Caporal lingered on till they were swallowed up in the pride and glory of the German Empire; and the Civil Code remained as a link with the past till it was superseded by the Imperial Code at the close of the nineteenth century.

While the western fringe of the Empire was linked to France before the Revolution by many ties, Bavaria had deliberately cut herself off from contact with the world outside her frontiers. The country defined by Frederick the Great as an earthly Paradise inhabited by animals had sunk into a material and spiritual decadence without parallel among the larger states of central Europe. When the French Revolution burst upon the world the realm of the Wittelsbachs was rotten to the core. The Illuminati had been suppressed; reaction and superstition reigned supreme; and the later years of Karl Theodor, surrounded by his bastards, are among the darkest in Bavarian history. The Government's method of confronting the perils of the time was to tighten the censorship, to forbid the circulation of French newspapers, to bring education under stricter control, and to compel candidates for office to swear that they belonged to no secret association. The spiritless and ignorant people had sunk so low that for a few years longer these miserable expedients availed to stave off the inevitable change; but, on the death of its degenerate ruler in 1799 and the accession of his cousin Max Joseph of Zweibrücken, 'French ideas' flowed into the country like a torrent and carried away the ancient landmarks of Church and State.

Max Joseph, the last Elector and first King of Bavaria, had been a Colonel in the French army and lived with his regiment in Strassburg till the outbreak of the Revolution, when he migrated to Mannheim. To his easy-going nature rancorous hate was impossible, and he never lost his old affection for France. 'I was born there,' he remarked to the French *chargé d'affaires* on his accession, 'and I beg you to regard me as a Frenchman. Please inform the Directory that it has no truer friend than myself.' The British Minister in Munich reported the atmospheric change at Court and drew an unflattering portrait of the new ruler. 'The character of the present Elector is such, I fear, as offers little prospect of happiness to his subjects, the more so as he is surrounded by persons supposed to be devoted to the French Government, particularly a certain M. de Montgelas, who governs him. Fomenters of revolution remain unmolested here at a moment when many respectable but unfortunate Émigrés are persecuted and ill-treated. I have seen with pain the hordes of Jacobins with which this place swarms and have in secret condemned the system by which they are tolerated.' These conversations naturally reached the ears of the Elector, who showed himself decidedly chilling in the only audience that he granted and revenged himself by asking for another Minister.

Montgelas, the chief of the 'Jacobins,' possessed the drive and ability which his weak and benevolent master lacked. The creator of modern Bavaria was the grandson of a Savoy official, whose son emigrated to Bavaria and married a German wife. The future statesman entered the service of the State at the age of twenty, but like many other clever young men he listened to the siren voices of Illuminati. On the dissolution of the Order he lost the favour of the Elector and resolved to seek his fortunes at Zweibrücken, where he won the friendship and confidence of Max Joseph. When the Bavarian throne fell to his master, he returned to Munich and became the real ruler of the country for eighteen years. He looked like a French noble and wrote and spoke French in preference to German. His aim was to accomplish peacefully for Bavaria what France had achieved at the cost of anarchy and bloodshed. He approached his task with the critical detachment of a foreigner, and made no secret of his contempt for 'cette nation bornée.' He determined to remove all institutions which were likely to thwart his will, beginning with the

Estates and the Communes. Serfdom was abolished, the monasteries were thinned, and the material regeneration of the country taken energetically in hand. Protestants received equal rights from a prince who had married a Protestant and a Minister who felt equal contempt for every variety of religious belief. His most successful reforms were in the sphere of education. To root out Jesuit influence, the University of Ingoldstadt was abolished and a new seat of learning established at Landshut. The Academy of Sciences was revived and scholars were imported from the Protestant north. Elementary education was freed from clerical control and rendered compulsory. In a few crowded years the accumulated rubbish of centuries was swept away, and Bavaria was transformed from the most backward into one of the most advanced of German States. 'We are in the middle of a complete but bloodless revolution,' cried Anselm Feuerbach, the author of the new criminal code. The Minister was as little of a democrat as Frederick the Great; but his lucid and logical mind was offended by the absurdities of the traditional system, and like Hardenberg he had learned from France that revolutions could only be avoided by reform.

The work of destruction and reconstruction accomplished by Stein and Hardenberg in Prussia and by Montgelas in Bavaria was carried out with even more uncompromising determination by the last Duke and the first King of Württemberg. When Frederick succeeded to the throne in 1797 he found the duchy small and poor and the power of the ruler circumscribed, at any rate in theory, by constitutional rights granted as far back as the Reformation. The liquidation of the Empire and the distribution of the smaller units among the larger States gave the ambitious autocrat the opportunity he sought. With the new Catholic territories falling to his share he could do as he pleased, but he refused to rule over a country in a portion of which his will was fettered by traditional rights and claims. He therefore made a clean sweep of 'the good old law' and introduced a uniform system of administration. 'The *coup d'état*,' comments Treitschke, 'was the outcome not simply of a tyrant's overweening love of power but also af an undeniable political necessity. Over the united old and new Württemberg all the terrors of despotism now raged, but the autocracy endowed the country with indispensable institutions of the modern State. The edict of religions, King Frederick's best work, overthrew the dominion of the Lutheran

Church and gave equal rights to both creeds. By the secularisation of Church property and the abolition of the treasury of the Estates the unity of national economy was established and the duty of paying regular taxes was carried into effect. The defenceless country once more acquired a little army fit for war. With revolutionary impetuosity the enemy of the Revolution established modern legal equality in his own state.' The debauched and extravagant monarch was detested by his subjects, but the firm outlines of his work remained. Without the example of France to warn, to inspire and to guide, neither Montgelas nor Frederick could have overthrown the entrenched forces of tradition nor carried out the revolution from above of which Germany stood in need.

In the third leading southern state the transition from the old world to the new was more gradual, for Karl Friedrich, the father of modern Baden, had not waited for the storm to break before setting his house in order. As a lifelong friend of France and a correspondent of Voltaire and the elder Mirabeau, the Duke regarded her efforts for liberty with considerable sympathy; neither the Terror nor the horrors of invasion shook his belief in the wisdom of unhasting and unresting change. When he died in 1811, after a reign of seventy years, he had increased his territory tenfold and left behind him one of the freest, best educated and most prosperous states in Germany.

The French Revolution left an abiding mark on the rulers and peoples, the institutions and ideas of the south as well as the west of Germany, and men of a later generation looked back on it with gratitude as the inauguration of a better age. 'My birth and childhood,' wrote Welcker, the leader of Baden liberalism in the middle decades of the nineteenth century, 'synchronised with the Revolution, before which nobody thought of a Constitution.' While Prussia remained in tutelage till 1848, the South German States were furnished with Parliaments within a few years of the conclusion of peace. For a generation after Waterloo Liberals of the south and west looked to Paris for their inspiration as Liberals of the north looked to England. In the celebrated controversy between Thibaut and Savigny on the project of a Code for Germany, the Baden jurist appealed to reason, the Berlin Professor to tradition. The two most popular historical works of the Restoration era were the world-histories of Schlosser and Rotteck, which stretched priests and kings on the rack and shed tears over the oppressed masses. The central doctrine of the French Revolution—that the destinies of a country should be controlled by the people as a whole and in the interest of the common man—found far fuller acceptance in the south than in Prussia, and has coloured its thought and practice ever since.

The wish was expressed by Georg Forster that his country should warm itself at the flame that had been kindled in France without being burned. The aspiration was destined in large measure to be fulfilled. While in England the reform movement was thrown back forty years by the earthquake and tempest, in Germany it was strengthened and accelerated. If Saxony and Mecklenburg remained unaffected, and the old governments of Hanover, Brunswick and Hesse-Cassel on their return restored most of the old abuses, Prussia, the Rhineland and the south learned in a generation of conflict and suffering at least some of the secrets of enduring advance. Even Treitschke is compelled to admit that the constitutional ideas of the Revolution everywhere struck root in German soil, and without the Revolution the famous Article 13 of the Vienna Act creating the German Federation would never have seen the light. The political unification of the nation was deferred for a couple of generations, but the signal for its deliverance from the thraldom of medieval institutions and antiquated ideas was sounded by the tocsin which rang out in 1789.

RANKE'S INTERPRETATION OF GERMAN HISTORY

I

THE name of the greatest of German historians echoed round the world when his fourth and most artistically satisfying work, the *History of the Popes*, was published in 1835-6; and in later years he presented French and English readers with masterpieces on their respective countries which at once took rank among the classics of modern scholarship.[1] Yet his writings on his own country surpass them all in importance, not only because their bulk is greater and the research on which they rest is of wider range, but also because historians, like other people, speak with special authority on the land of their birth. As early as 1827 he confided to Varnhagen his belief that he was born for German, not foreign, history, which he could not understand so well. Though he was the least nationalist of eminent German scholars by temperament and conviction and may fairly be described as a good European, he loved his fatherland as well as any of them, followed its fortunes no less eagerly, and during his middle years was consulted by its rulers on high matters of state. Germany was the subject of two out of the five major works composed in his prime and also of substantial monographs dating from his ripe old age. Taken together they cover the whole field of German history from the close of the Middle Ages to the foundation of the Hohenzollern Empire. To readers of a later generation it is interesting to see how the main events and outstanding personalities of the last four centuries of the life of his people appear to the master who knew more of the political history of modern Europe than any man who ever lived. That he is less inclined to stand 'above the battle' than in dealing with Italy and Spain, France, England and Serbia is natural, for, like lesser mortals, he was a man of flesh and blood.

[1] See Ranke, *Zur eigenen Lebensgeschichte*; Guglia, *Rankes Leben und Werke*; Diether, *Ranke als Politiker*; Dove's article in the *Allgemeine Deutsche Biographie*, reproduced in his *Ausgewählte Schriftchen*; Oncken, *Aus Rankes Frühzeit*; Gooch, *History and Historians in the Nineteenth Century*.

Born in 1795 in that portion of northern Saxony which was assigned to Prussia twenty years later by the Congress of Vienna, Ranke was educated at Schulpforta, the most famous of Saxon schools, and at Leipzig, the oldest of German Universities. Most of his time was devoted to the classics, and the first historical work to grip his imagination was Niebuhr's *History of Rome*. Yet as the subject of a state whose ruler accepted the royal title at the hands of Napoleon and whose army served under his banner till the battle of Leipzig, he never broke his heart about the French occupation and the disasters of Prussia. Throughout life, indeed, he was incapable of hot anger. Nature had created a cool-headed observer of the human scene, not a would-be actor on the stage. Yet so far he had not decided to become its recorder. When Stenzel, destined like himself to become a historian of Prussia, inquired whether he proposed to devote himself to history, he replied in the negative.

The tercentenary celebrations in 1817 of Luther's protest against the sale of Indulgences moved Ranke to study his writings and to compose the remarkable Luther Fragment first published in 1926 as an appendix to the Academy edition of his *German History in the Reformation Era*. Though the work never advanced beyond the stage of notes, characterisations and reflections, there is enough to reveal the ideology and personality of the ardent young scholar who had just come of age. Never again did he let himself go to the same extent either about the Reformation or anything else. Twenty years later, when he came to deal with the subject in detail, he found little to criticise in the record of his illustrious fellow-Saxon, but in this youthful fragment there is only boundless admiration. Luther appears neither as rebel nor politician, but as renovator and liberator, impelled to action by the deepest experiences of his spiritual life. The responsibility for the break up of the unity of Western Christendom is attributed, not to the monk of Wittenberg, but to the Popes and officials who resisted overdue reforms. His watchword 'Scripture above the Church and the Church above the Pope,' declares Ranke, upset the whole edifice of traditional teaching, and in his opinion the Roman Church deserved its fate.

Luther, he explains, did not wish to establish a 'Lutheranism' embodying and preserving his particular dogma: he strove for religion itself, for the free life of the spirit as it burned within him, took shape and embodied the divine element. Hence the effect of his teaching was not confined to the narrow sphere of dogma. As Christianity shaped and permeated the world, so that we are bound to it by the innermost fibres of our being, so did his life and teaching transform all Europe, not only that part which bears his name. No land, no state had been able to evade the irresistible influence of the awakened spirit. How did it come about? Why did not for instance Spinoza or Descartes or Frederick the Great achieve what this peasant accomplished? Simply because he possessed a glowing heart which fashioned everything he wrote and strove to do, so that his living message was able to kindle the spirit which abides in us all and which must be struck in order that it may send forth sparks and shoot up like the divine flame. 'So, thou holy shadow, be not wrath that I speak of thee. To-day everyone girds on his armour who only knows thee from afar and celebrates thy immortal deeds. Shall I keep silence, I who have so often approached thee and besought thee, and persevered till I believed I had found the secret meaning of thy life? What is it that appeals to the spirit everywhere? It is the intimate and essential in us. Thence proceeds everything that is great and good; the legislators and poets of the old world felt it, the choicest spirits of the new world have held to it. Among the few heroes who have fully seized it and fully expressed it in word and deed is Luther.'

In his struggle for the restoration to the individual soul of its right to direct approach to God Luther was confronted by a decadent and largely mechanised Church which had strayed far from the simplicity of Scripture and primitive times. 'The Church itself was a sinner; it had forgotten and abandoned the fundamental religious life. The Pope was supposed to be God, for he who forgives all sins, he whom no one can ask: What art thou doing? even if he leads ten thousand souls straight to hell, he is God. All power in heaven and earth was his; no one dared say him nay. Then in the tortured breast of the mendicant monk, lying sick in his cell, glowed the thought of the forgiveness of sins by Grace. The idea saved his life, suffused his whole being; henceforth he lived in it. Only when the Papacy condemned this belief did he go into opposition. Forgiveness of sins was offered for money and the people sprang forward to buy, to the disgrace and deception of body and soul. Then he could bear the misery no longer; he stood forth and nailed the ninety-five theses to the door of the Castle Church at Wittenberg on the eve of All Souls day, 1517. To-day it is 300 years. How folly and wickedness combined against him! How timid were the good! There he stood alone and unafraid, like a rock in the sea against which the angry waves beat in vain. Nothing could have sustained him except the power of his inner life. What he said and did welled up from the deepest springs, and he could only have given up the struggle with his life. His words went straight to receptive hearts and took root, for they were founded on the divine element in man. Thus a revolution spread throughout Europe. Day by day he became bolder, clearer, greater, till finally he realised that the Papacy contradicted true Christianity, that it was the anti-Christ announced by Prophets and Apostles. He who can flee from it let him escape!' That the movement, so entirely against the feelings of its earliest leaders, became involved in politics was due to his summons to the Diet of Worms, which transformed a religious issue into a problem of the Reich. Though the overcharged emotion suffusing the Luther Fragment quickly evaporated, Ranke never abandoned his conviction that the Reformation was the most beneficent event in German history.

A year after the Wittenberg celebrations the young Saxon was appointed teacher of classics and history at Frankfurt on Oder. Though in entering the Prussian service he became a loyal subject and passed the rest of his life in Prussia, he remained a German first, approaching the study of his country's fortunes from the standpoint of the Reich as a whole. His main task during the tranquil years in the little town was the exploration of Western and Southern Europe on the eve of the Reformation which bore fruit in his *Histories of the Latin and Germanic Peoples 1494–1515*, published in 1824. The book received praise from leading scholars, among them Heeren and Niebuhr, Raumer and Stenzel, and also from Stein, the greatest of amateurs. Its appearance is generally reckoned as the starting-point of the critical study of history, owing to the devastating analysis which accompanied it of Guicciardini and other celebrated chroniclers. The technique of philology fashioned by Wolf was adapted to the needs of historians and became their daily bread. The book is also of interest in proclaiming the underlying unity of the Latin and Germanic peoples which was to echo through all his subsequent works. He saw Western Europe as a differentiated whole. The era selected for treatment, he declared, was one of the most significant. The invasion of Italy by Charles VIII of France inaugurated a closer relationship between north and south, while at the same time demonstrating that political unity was impossible, mainly owing to the emergence of the Austro-French antagonism which in various forms had dominated European history ever since. North and South had had many contacts and common experiences such as the *Völkerwanderung*, the Crusades, overseas colonisation, but they were not quite enough.

For the limited purposes of this essay we may confine ourselves to Maximilian, the founder of the greatness of the House of Hapsburg, and to the condition of the Reich on the threshold of the modern world. 'We have several portraits of the Emperor, but they disagree, for he had no dominating trait. He is all movement, all delight in things and plans. There is hardly anything he cannot do. In his mines he is expert with his pick; in his armoury he is the best moulder; the best shot gives orders in seven languages; he cooks his own food and mixes his medicines. The note of his public life is the sense of the future greatness of his House, inherited from his father, and the ceaseless striving towards that aim, inherited from the House of Burgundy. That was his policy, that the goal of all his plans—not the Empire, for whose true needs he showed little care, nor the welfare of his hereditary possessions. He is like a hunter who desires to climb a very steep mountain, now here, now there; gradually he ascends, his only anxiety to hide his tracks.' He was an impressive knightly figure at his first Diet at Worms, and Germany was full of armed men. 'Had he united his whole force under his command, neither Europe nor Asia could have resisted him. But by God's will they were employed rather for freedom than for imposing a yoke.' Yet there were as grave disadvantages to the German people in the weakness of the Reich as there would have been in its overmastering strength. 'What sort of Empire was it which, possessing such power, allowed its Emperor to be driven out of his hereditary dominions and was in no hurry to restore him? Remembering the Constitution, with its independence of the various Estates, the penury of the Imperial office, the election of the chief who then enforced certain rights over the Electors, one asks not why it ultimately fell but how it held together. The chief factors in its preservation were the rights of individuals, the formation of associations within the whole, the hierarchical structure. Those rights and privileges which defended the citizen, his gild and his town against stronger neighbours, and safeguarded the property of the greatest and the least, guaranteed its existence, a legacy from one generation to another. The Emperor's sacred prestige in the nation rested above all on the dignity of his office, the highest in Christendom, the coping-stone of the structure, on his trusteeship of traditional rights, his position as the fount of honour and privileges. But there were also great faults in the Reich. Liberties were often granted in a spirit of favouritism, law-suits were often held up for lack of money, dynastic matters were often treated as the business of the Reich. The Princes complained that the Emperor consulted his counsellors, not themselves. No wonder the Estates demanded reform.'

Princes and Peoples of Southern Europe in the Sixteenth and Seventeenth Centuries, published three years later, and mainly devoted to Spain, only touches briefly and indirectly on Germany in the portrait of Charles V. Ranke had spoken of him with respect in the Luther Fragment, and he now filled in the outlines with the aid of the invaluable Venetian despatches which he found at Berlin. The young ruler who became King of Spain at sixteen and Emperor at nineteen developed slowly, but he was never dominated by a Minister. Neither passionate nor headstrong, often jotting down on paper the pros and cons of an argument, he reflected long before reaching a decision, but then he never changed. He was the busiest ruler in Europe and he insisted on knowing the details of every issue. When he punished it was never in haste; when he rewarded it was after delay. 'Such a man, with his serenity and moderation, seemed well fitted to reign over several nations, though he had more success with Spain, Italy and the Netherlands than with Germany. His nature was incapable of the expansiveness which our nation loves and respects. Though he copied the ways of past Emperors with princes and lords, and in Germany wore his beard in German fashion, he always seemed to Germans a stranger in their land.' At forty he was already past his prime, lacking confidence in himself and his luck: racked by gout, he became increasingly melancholy and lonely. It is the picture of a man who narrowly missed greatness, conscientious but unloving and unloved, almost crushed by a burden too heavy even for a superman to bear. When the historical artist came to the intensive study of his subject in *The Reformation Era* he found that few of these colours had to be changed.

Returning to his chair in Berlin in 1831 after three fruitful years in the archives of Austria and Italy, Ranke accepted an invitation to edit the *Historisch-Politische Zeitschrift*, founded by Perthes, the influential publisher of the *Monumenta Germaniae Historica*, who desired a highbrow Conservative counterpart to the flood of democratic and anti-Prussian journalism generated in southern Germany by the French Revolution of 1830, of which Heine's letters from Paris to the Munich *Allgemeine Zeitung* were the most scintillating specimen. The Editor counted a few Liberals among his friends, above all Varnhagen and his brilliant wife Rahel; but he felt no enthusiasm for the twin causes of nationalism and constitutionalism which had challenged the Holy Alliance, and were now in revolt against the static system inaugurated by Metternich and extolled by Gentz with whom he had had many conversations in Vienna. Fifty numbers appeared between 1832 and 1836, when the enterprise collapsed, and of the thousand pages two-thirds were from the Editor's pen. In answer to those who sought salvation in French models he argued that Germany had much to be thankful for and that there was no need for fundamental changes. 'However faulty the old Reich, it provided that national unity which all German hearts desire.' Its successor, the Deutscher Bund, was more closely knit, above all through the Zollverein. Living in a country where constitutions were unknown, a citizen of a state with a strong monarchical tradition and repelled by the object-lesson of revolutionary France, he proclaimed the virtues of slow organic growth in the spirits of Savigny and Burke. 'My attitude,' he explained fifty years later, 'was neither revolution nor reaction. I had the bold idea of a middle course, resting on the past but hospitable to the new ideas. It proved beyond my strength, and how mistaken I was in thinking that everyone would agree with me! My earlier friends, like Varnhagen and Alexander von Humboldt, who saw the world's salvation in the progress of the revolution, were estranged, while my other friends Radowitz and Gerlach only tolerated me because I did not admire the revolution. Happily Eichhorn, Savigny and Schleiermacher gave me every support.'

Among the historical dissertations contributed by the Editor the broad survey of the evolution of the European system entitled *The Great Powers* holds pride of place. This essay, still highly prized by German students, is a paean to the Balance of Power. Beginning with France under Louis XIV, it shows how her hegemony was challenged and checked by the simultaneous emergence of three other Great Powers—England under William III, Austria after the expulsion of the Turks from Hungary, and Russia after the defeat of Charles XII of Sweden. A little later Prussia joined their ranks, fighting for her place in the sun but never desiring the destruction of any other Great Power, not even Austria at the height of the struggle for Silesia since her collapse would have left France irresistible. Frederick's aim was merely to be strong enough to manoeuvre between larger rivals. If it is a condition of a Great Power to be able to hold its own against others even in combination, he had promoted Prussia into this class. For the first time there was a state in North Germany needing no help. The great event of the century before the French Revolution was the defence of the independence of Europe against France, and the cataclysm was partly due to her loss of prestige in the field of foreign affairs. Once again Europe had to be defended against French domination, and after the downfall of Napoleon the equilibrium which seemed to Ranke the ideal distribution of power had been restored. Indeed he promoted the working formula of a Balance of Power to the dignity of a natural law. 'In great perils one can confidently trust to the genius which always saved Europe from the rule of unilateral tyranny and meets pressure from one side with resistance from the other. A combination of the whole, growing closer from decade to decade, has happily rescued the cause of liberty. Since France's preponderance rested on her internal strength, it could only be met by the advance of other states towards internal unity, independent power, and general significance. World history looks at first sight like a fortuitous concourse of events, states and peoples. Yet there are also spiritual, creative forces, moral energies, which we can perceive though not define.'

In the *History of the Popes*, which appeared in 1835–6, Germany occupies a subordinate place, for the Reformation appears merely as the background of the Counter-Reformation which forms its main theme. Ranke dwells lovingly on the efforts at reunion, above all of Contarini, the Papal Legate at the Diet of Regensburg in 1541. Even though the gulf proved too wide to bridge, the Peace of Augsburg, a triumph of common sense statesmanship, inaugurated the phase of German history in which Catholic and Protestant states and princes lived in tolerable harmony for two generations. There is more to say about Germany in the second half of the sixteenth century, when Protestantism won the largest part of the country and when the Jesuits succeeded in stemming the flowing tide. The whole story of the Papacy since the end of the Middle Ages is told with a cool detachment which aroused admiration throughout the world but which led many readers to conclude that neither the religious convictions nor the patriotic emotions of the author were very deep. They were soon to be undeceived.

'Of the *History of the Popes*,' declared the author in his ninetieth year, 'no one could say if it was written more for or against the Papacy: it was simply the result of thorough and impartial studies and as such it was received. Yet I felt that the Protestant element had had less than full justice. The book on the Reformation era has been described even by friends as far inferior. That was also my view, for it was impossible to make a readable story out of Reichstag proceedings and theological debates. But the material decided the form and my aim was quite different. I felt I must compose a comprehensive treatise on the fundamental event of modern times. I was not thinking of the general reader but of the satisfaction of German scholarship and religious convictions.' More than any of his other writings the *German History in the Reformation Era* was both a labour of love and a confession of faith.[1] The most controversial of his many books was his own favourite and it remains the historical classic of Protestant Germany. 'I am blamed for lack of philosophical and religious seriousness,' he wrote to a friend. 'That I lack interest in philosophy and religion is ridiculous, for it is that and nothing else which drove me to history.' Believing in what he sometimes describes as spiritual forces at work in human affairs and sometimes as the will of God, he never doubted that the Reformation fitted into the divine plan.

The inner urge to grapple with the Reformation era became a fixed resolve when on a visit to Frankfurt in 1835 Ranke found a superb collection of the proceedings of the Diets of the Holy Roman Empire in 96 volumes, from 1414 to 1613. For the earlier years they were very incomplete, but with the election of Maximilian the stream broadens, Imperial rescripts and reports from the members being added to the formal record of proceedings. When he had mastered the material down to the end of the reign of Charles V he felt firm ground under his feet. The personal and doctrinal struggles of the period were broadly familiar, but here was the key to the institutional history of the time, to the movements and policy of the Imperial

---

[1] The book should be read in the Academy Edition of the complete works, which contains a valuable Introduction. Its merits are also assessed in Gustav Wolf, *Quellenkunde der Deutschen Reformationsgeschichte*, vol. i, and Franz Schnabel, *Deutschlands Geschichtliche Quellen und Darstellungen in der Neuzeit*, vol. i.

Court. His first plan was to start with a monograph on the Diets, and in 1837 he composed an elaborate preliminary survey published a century later in the sixth volume of the Academy edition of *The Reformation Era*. In early Germany as elsewhere, he wrote, national development was bound up with the personality and activities of the princes. In the great days of the Empire everything depended on the Emperor. Later, as the states became more independent, the situation was not very different from the nineteenth century. The Reichstag was useful, but the great affairs of state were settled elsewhere.

Everything rested on the relations of the Courts. 'The essential developments of our history took place in the bosom of the separate principalities. Between these two periods—from the middle of the fifteenth century to the Thirty Years' War—Imperial power was no longer decisive, yet territorial rule was dominated by the idea of the Reich. Even Frederick III and Rudolf II, for instance, having no vital connection with events and busy with their own Hapsburg territories, were still rallying-points. This was the period of the greater Diets when the Emperor appeared in state and everything was discussed before important decisions were reached. The history of the Diets is the history of the government of Germany, the history of our unity and our divisions. Despite all misunderstandings it embodied an idea in which Germany lives, and which, so long as a Germany exists, will never disappear—the idea of a higher community which towers above all the activities of the smaller states, furnishes their direction, their significance, and indeed the higher laws by which the abuses of power should become impossible, in a word the idea of the fatherland and of law. Therein lies the difference of the German Reich from all other states and Empires. Elsewhere the idea of law is connected with force. In Germany there was always something above the separate state authorities which was not force, but which, resting on the laws of the Empire and on tradition, embodied the idea of a legal and juridically assured system. In the times we describe as the Era of the Diets such institutions were vital and operative, and for all practical conditions of paramount importance.'

The so-called Frankfurt Manuscript was laid aside, though most of it was utilised in the comprehensive work as it grew under his hands. Since only the framework was provided by the proceedings of the Diets, the personalities and policies of the Princes had also to be understood, and the historian found the clue in the archives of Dresden, Weimar and Berlin. Even now he was not satisfied, for he sought to understand the springs and changes of Hapsburg policy. Once again his discoveries surpassed expectations. 'I cannot describe my delight in Brussels,' he declared in the brief autobiography dictated in his ninetieth year, 'when I handled the well arranged volumes of the papers of the House of Austria in the Netherlands, especially those of Charles V. Even more of a joyful surprise were the unsorted documents of his latest years which were just what I needed to complete my work.' The *History of the Popes* had to be written without access to the treasures of the Vatican library, for Protestant scholars knocked at its portals in vain. In northern Europe, on the other hand, all doors were opened and the light streamed in.

The Preface to the first two volumes of *The Reformation Era*, published in 1839, prepares the reader for the broad scope of the work. The Constitution and public life of Germany, it was explained, rested on the Diets and their decrees. 'The time of Imperial domination was long over, that of the Princes had not yet come. The Diets decided on war and peace, legislation and finance. The cities, the minor nobles and the princes were represented, and the Diet alone embodied the unity of the nation. Everything could be and was discussed, everything had to be sanctioned. Let no one pity the man who occupies himself with these seemingly arid studies. True, they are dead paper, but they are survivals of a life which gradually takes shape. When I wrote the first part of the *History of the Popes* I purposely dealt with the Reformation as briefly as possible, hoping to investigate more deeply the most important event in the life of our fatherland. One cannot approach a theme of such intensive spiritual content and such world-wide significance without being obsessed by it. I foresee the time when modern history will rest no longer on reports even of contemporary historians but on the testimony of eye witnesses and the original documents.' That the prophecy has been fulfilled is mainly due to Ranke himself.

A long Introduction carries the reader rapidly over the seven centuries from Charlemagne to the Reformation era, during which the struggle between Church and State was a constant and dominating theme. 'In school-books and in literature we can separate ecclesiastical and political history; in the life of mankind they are intertwined.

A great nation is inconceivable whose political life has not been stimulated by religious ideas and which is not continually striving to develop and express them. A certain antagonism is inevitable, for the nation has geographical limits, while religions aim at universality and threaten the independence of the state. Neither of them can nor should dominate the other, at any rate in the west. The life of Western Christianity rests on the unceasing interaction of Church and State, whence proceeds the ever freer, wider, deeper movement of the spirit. Neither ecclesiastical nor political history is intelligible without the other, especially in Germany, the country which has most occupied itself with religious affairs. With such powerful forces in chronic conflict, order and progress were impossible. The Reich fell into anarchy and lost prestige abroad. By the fifteenth century the situation had become disgraceful and intolerable for a great nation, in sharpest contrast to the noble idea of law and religion on which the Reich was based. Everyone thought of himself and his immediate surroundings, no one of the whole. No great enterprises were possible, and the frontiers were incapable of defence. The life of the nation would have perished had it not taken steps to introduce order at home and to restore power abroad. This, however, was impossible without transforming ecclesiastical as well as secular conditions.'

After this suggestive prologue the curtain rises on the attempts to give the Reich a better Constitution at the close of the fifteenth century. Similar efforts were being made in France, England and Spain where strong monarchies arose and asserted their authority over the feudal lords. In Germany this was impossible, for the Empire was a shadow, the Emperor Frederick III almost a beggar. Yet the institutional machinery was there—the Diet, the Electors, the Princes, the Cities, the Imperial Knights, the Court, the levy for defence. All that was needed was to restore the ancient institutions to life. The key was the Diet, regular meetings of which were essential if results were to be achieved. Little could be done under Frederick III, weak, indolent, indifferent, more interested in astrology than in politics. With the election of his son Maximilian in 1493 and his first Diet at Worms in 1495 the sky seemed likely to clear. But the new Emperor, ambitious, bellicose and extravagant, was a disappointment. It was not entirely his fault that the effort to reform the Reich failed, for a strong central authority was desired neither by the Princes nor the other Estates who had learned to go their own way.

Turning to the even graver problem of the reform of the Church, the historian paints a dark picture of the prevailing abuses, such as the sale of Indulgences, the trade in relics, the immorality of priests, the substitution of arid scholasticism for the living waters of Scripture. 'I wonder if any sensible cool-headed person could seriously wish this system to have continued indefinitely and unchanged, if anyone can persuade himself that the truth-seeking mind could grow in it, if virile and intelligent religion could have flourished in it. And could anyone expect the salvation of the world from the spread of such a specifically western pattern to the far places of the earth?' It was well known that a main ground for the dislike of the Greek Church to reunion lay in the multitude of regulations among the Latins, in the crushing autocracy which the Roman See had arrogated to itself. Indeed was not the Gospel itself overlaid in the Latin Church? In those times when scholastic dogma had taken root the Bible was forbidden to the laity in the mother tongue, even to priests. The kernel of religion had to be brought out to the light of day from behind the veil with a thousand folds. If the Gospel were to be preached to all the world, it had firstly to re-emerge in its purity. It is one of the major coincidences of world history that at the moment when the system of the Roman-Germanic peoples opened a new chance for the Latin Church on other Continents, a religious revolution aimed at restoring the purity of Revelation. This great task was undertaken by the German nation.

It was not merely the conscience of individuals which was in revolt: the secular authorities were also critical of the *Imperium in Imperio* which diverted money from the state. The popular distaste for the greed and worldliness of the Church found vent in Brandt's *Ship of Fools*, the *Epistolae Obscurorum Virorum*, a scathing satire on a gross and ignorant priest, and above all in the masterpiece of Erasmus, *The Praise of Folly*. Rejecting the common temptation to exalt either Erasmus or Luther at the expense of the other, Ranke pays unstinted homage to both. 'The most famous man in Europe, turning from the Scholastics to the Fathers and the New Testament, helped to strengthen the spirit of the century in the anti-clericalism of which the Lutheran movement was only one embodiment. The national spirit became self-conscious. In the depths of the nation common sense emerges, prosaic, bourgeois, vulgar, but utterly true in its realistic judgment.'

After this review of the universal demand for radical reform of the teaching and morals of the Church, we are introduced to Luther, whose hard youth and spiritual struggles are lovingly portrayed as the story of a soul in search of God. Brushing aside the Scholastics, as Erasmus had done, he studied St. Paul, Augustine on free will, and the sermons of Tauler. The priests, he complained, did not preach the pure word of God. 'Works' such as prayers and fasting were useless in God's eyes, for everything depended on the spirit in which they were done. What mattered most was to restore belief in justification by faith. Religion was only the deepest inwardness. The historian shares to the full Luther's wrath at the sale of Indulgences and his conviction that Leo X had dragged the Papacy down to the dust; and he gratefully salutes Frederick the Wise, Elector of Saxony, the most attractive of the secular actors in the Reformation drama. 'He had never seen Luther and had no communication with him, but he understood and approved the challenge to Tetzel. He did not promise help, did not encourage, merely let it all happen. But that was enough. The starting-point of the great world event is the synchronisation of Frederick and Luther in opposition, one for secular, the other for spiritual reasons. The mighty blow awoke Germany. That a man arose who had the courage to enter on the dangerous struggle was a relief to the public conscience. The most vital interests were at stake: the deeper piety *versus* forgiveness of sins in its most superficial form; literature *versus* the heresy-hunters to whom Tetzel belonged; a rejuvenating theology *versus* scholastic dogma; the secular power *versus* ecclesiastics whose encroachments it endeavoured to resist; finally the nation *versus* the financial demands of Rome. There was no thought of secession, but from all the depths of the national life arose opposition and ill-will to ecclesiastical power in Germany. An opposition had begun which looked insignificant, but which found powerful backing in the sentiment of the nation and a powerful prince.' The anti-Papal movement in fact, was the work of the nation, and Luther was merely its most dynamic and courageous spokesman.

Ranke, like Luther and Melanchthon, would have preferred a thorough house-cleaning to an open breach. When Cardinal Cajetan, the Papal Legate, vainly summoned the troublesome monk to recant and unsuccessfully urged Frederick to expel him from Saxony, the Pope sent Miltitz, the Elector's agent in Rome, as Nuntius to try the method of persuasion. He found Luther most conciliatory, with no thought of leaving the Church; but the gentle tones of Miltitz were soon drowned by the strident voice of Eck in the public disputation at Leipzig, when Luther was pushed far beyond his original position. He had begun with an attack on Indulgences and Scholasticism; now, pressed by Eck, he rejected not only the authority of the Church but of Councils, the latter on account of the atrocious treatment of Hus. The only authority he would recognise was that of Scripture. There was no longer need for an official head of the Christian Church, of which the Orthodox Communities were also members. The Greek Church knew nothing of Purgatory, and as there was no scriptural authority for it he rejected the belief. After studying the writings of the martyred Hus he exclaimed: 'We are all Hussites without knowing it, and so were Paul and Augustine.' His anger waxed hotter when he read Lorenzo Valla's exposure of the Donation of Constantine. Scripture and the Church, he had come to believe, were irreconcilable antagonists, and indeed the Pope was anti-Christ. Melanchthon, too, of whom Ranke speaks with affectionate admiration and whom he salutes as the co-founder of Protestant principles, had also advanced. The Fathers, he taught, must be tested by Scripture, and nobody was bound to believe anything which was not there.

The contemplation of this partnership moves Ranke to exclaim: 'Providence brought these men together at this great moment.' Even in Hutten he finds much to admire, for, if not a distinguished scholar, his ideas were above all national. Germany for the Germans! No more tyranny of Rome! was his watchword. Thus the reform movement passed beyond theology and was joined by the elements of the opposition in the nation, in literature and in politics. Its national character was shown in Luther's first great tract *To the Christian Nobility of the German Nation*, published in 1520. The Pope might remain, not as overlord of the Empire nor the possessor of all spiritual power, but with limited prerogatives. Twelve Cardinals were enough; regional churches should enjoy the maximum independence; there should be a Primate in Germany to whom the appeals of Bishops could go. There should be fewer monasteries, and the lower clergy might marry. Nationalise the clergy according to the universal wish, and make them more independent of the daily interference of Rome.

Communion should be given in both kinds. Confession was unnecessary; men could confess straight to God, for all Christians were priests. This Declaration of Independence was symbolised by burning the Papal Bull.

In *The Reformation Era* Charles V advances to the centre of the stage at the Diet of Worms in 1521. A powerful Emperor would have resumed the old attitude of opposition to the Papacy and would have been backed by the nation. Maximilian was too weak, but he had advised the Elector Frederick of Saxony to 'take good care of the monk—he might be useful some day.' Spain, however, not Germany was always in the forefront of the thoughts of the young ruler. 'He understood neither our language nor our thoughts. A strange fate that the nation in the moment of its greatest experience had summoned a head who was foreign to its character, in whose policy, which embraced a far wider sphere, the needs and endeavours of the Germans played a secondary part! Not that he was indifferent to religious movements: he was greatly interested because they concerned and threatened the Pope, whom he wished to have on his side.' His wish was to destroy, not to lead, the reform movement, though Ranke admits that Luther had not made the latter alternative easy for him to adopt. 'If he had confined himself to attacking the abuses of the Papacy he would have had all the Estates with him, and perhaps the Emperor too, whom his confessor threatened with the wrath of heaven if he did not reform the Church. One could almost wish that Luther had stopped there. It would have strengthened the nation in its unity if it had waged a common war against the secular domination of Rome under his leadership. On the other hand his spiritual power would have been broken if he had been fettered by any but purely religious considerations.'

After describing his condemnation at the Diet of Worms, the historian pauses to ask whether separation from Rome could occur without peril to culture and the state. Such a dynamic movement, he admits, involved danger, as no one knew better than Luther himself. Carlstadt, his colleague at the University of Wittenberg, plunged forward, and the Zwickau Baptists raised their antinomian heads. The Elector Frederick, the most peaceable of rulers in a quarrelsome age, never took up arms, and it was against his advice that the Reformer left his sanctuary in the Wartburg to counterwork the extremists. The turning-point in his psychological evolution had come. Henceforth he desired merely to retain what had been won and condemned only what was contrary to Scripture. Caution was in the air, revealing itself in the *Loci Communes* of Melanchthon, the leader of the Moderates. When Sickingen came forward as the champion of the small towns and the small man against the power of the Princes, Luther wisely rejected the aid of that powerful Condottiere. But though the radical phase of the Reformation was over, we are reminded that the nation claimed more decidedly than ever full autonomy in religious matters. No one was ashamed of what had been achieved. The complaint that the Reformation split the Church is rejected on the ground that the need of drastic reform of the Church was universally admitted, and that the movement had sprung from the spirit of Christianity rooted in the depths of the German soul.

Ranke praises Luther as highly in his later conservative phase as in the old, and he describes his much criticised attitude towards the Peasants' Revolt without a word of blame. The revolt, he admits, was the result of increasing oppression and of the suppression of Protestant teaching, which stirred the common man to action more than any intellectual factor before or since. If it had confined itself to refusing unconstitutional demands and to claiming liberty of preaching, it might have made an assured advance: indeed in many places agreements were reached by which the lords removed the most onerous burdens. 'But it is human nature not to be content with a limited gain, and the victorious multitude never knows when to stop. The peasant thought it should go on till there were only peasant houses in Germany. And parallel with this fury went the fanaticism of the preaching which justified destruction and bloodshed, and the Reign of the Saints. Had it succeeded, all orderly evolution would have disappeared. Happily it could not succeed, and the strongest opposition came from the reforming movement itself. Luther had declined the suggestion of Sickingen and the Knights to engage in political enterprises, and the Peasants equally failed to win his aid. At first, as it seemed innocent, he advised peace, reminding princes and lords of their misrule, but at the same time condemning revolt as contrary to divine and evangelical law and threatening the collapse of the German nation in both secular and ecclesiastical spheres. But as this danger rapidly developed and his old opponents the Murder Prophets took the lead, and as he realised that the peasants might win—which would be the end of all things—his anger broke loose. With his immeasurable prestige what would have been the consequences had he joined them? He held firmly to the separation of the ecclesiastical and the secular—one of the fundamentals of his creed—believing that the gospel liberates the soul, not the body or material possessions. A pious Christian, he declared, should suffer death a hundred times rather than enlist in the peasants' cause. Authority should have no mercy. The time of wrath and the sword had come. It should strike: that was its divine duty. Whoever died in this service was a martyr of Christ. Münzer was executed. So the great movement was suppressed which threatened to turn German society upside down. No more was heard of the creation of a new Reich from below nor of the transformation of the world under the lead of a fanatical prophet.' The narrative of the Munster Anabaptists is even more severe. Ranke detested violence, and the story of John of Leyden with his harem and his executioner's sword in his hand excites utter disgust. 'The most revolting feature of this immense error is the blend of piety, self-indulgence and bloodthirstiness.' The only redeeming feature of the squalid intermezzo was that it cured the Baptists for ever of fanaticism.

The third volume of *The Reformation Era*, published in 1840, begins by recapitulating the conclusions of the first two. In a struggle of centuries the Church had defeated the State, but at the price to Germany of anarchy and waning prestige. The Conciliar movement failed, and the more recent attempt to strengthen the state by the partnership of the Imperial power and the Estates was equally fruitless. The spirit of violence and self-seeking lived on, angry resentment at abuses grew apace. As secular conditions were no better the national spirit turned to ecclesiastical affairs. When things were at their worst the pure idea of Christianity revived, resulting from the new study of the Bible in the original. 'In the resulting conflict Luther rallied the other elements of opposition with a coherence, a depth, and an understanding which gathered the whole nation round him. Never has any man had such a following.'

Ranke's approval of the caution in Luther's later phase is emphasised by severity towards Zwingli. Since he was not such a deep nature the separation from the old Church was less of a wrench. While Luther wished to retain everything not contradicted by Scripture, the Swiss reformer desired to abolish everything which it did not prescribe. The one remained on the *terrain* of the Latin Church while purifying its doctrine; the other attempted to restore the conditions of the primitive Church. Luther, for instance, allowed pictures to remain in the churches; Zwingli, thinking them idolatrous, had them whitewashed or removed. Both rejected transubstantiation, an innovation of the twelfth century; but while the one merely restored the reception of the wine and omitted the words about sacrifice, the other reconstructed the supper, each communicant breaking off a piece of bread for himself from a wooden plate. 'Luther left the Roman Church, or rather he was expelled from it and damaged it more than any other man. He is the organ through which the Latin Church system was transformed into a freer, less hierarchical, more primitive Christianity. He was treated by the Church with the greatest severity, Zwingli, though far more antagonistic to the traditional system, very gently. With all his zeal against the Pope and the secular rule of the Hierarchy, Luther was as conservative and historically minded as possible.

Ranke approved the Augsburg Confession, for it was the hour of moderate men. Melanchthon's gentle hand was at work, and Luther backed him up in keeping as near as possible to tradition, for instance regarding free will, condemning heresies condemned by Rome, and respecting secular authority. 'You cannot call us heretics.' The Augsburg doctrine, declares Ranke, was a product of the living spirit of the Latin Church and kept within it tenets. Of course it included Luther's idea of justification by faith, of which he was not the inventor, and the Fathers were freely used as authorities. The Reformers felt that they still rested on the old foundations as established by Augustine. They had tried to break down the particularism whose fetters the Latin Church had placed on itself in recent centuries, and they returned to Scripture alone. A large portion of the original Latin Church's interpretation of Scripture was retained. The Confession was the purest manifestation of Protestantism and was nearest to the purest source. It was not intended as a norm for ever. Part 2 of the Confession listed the abuses to be removed, clerical celibacy, Communion in one kind, vows, compulsion to fasting and confession, Melanchthon arguing how new and dangerous were such things and how they conflicted with old canonical rules. On the divine right of the Pope the authors of the Confession were silent. They were out not to convert but to defend. The Protestants, adds Ranke, had been wise not to confine themselves to the defensive but to appeal to all the strong reforming sympathies of the time. This, however, was now impossible since they had refused alliance with the Zwinglians. They found themselves almost outpaced and overshadowed by the popularity of the Swiss reformer's teaching, and most people in Augsburg accepted it. Philip of Hesse preferred Zwingli, and a direct appeal from Luther was needed to obtain his signature to the Augsburg Confession. They wanted nothing but peace and toleration; they believed they had shown that their doctrine was not heretical and was wrongly condemned. Luther explained this to his old foe the Bishop of Mainz, and Melanchthon in the name of the Princes begged the Legate Campeggi to avoid intransigence since any new movement would bring confusion to the Church. 'In this spirit of rapprochement, this feeling that the separation was not complete, the wish to bring out the close relationship, it was planned and drafted.'

The conciliatory spirit manifested in the Confession, though blamed by Zwingli, evoked no response from the Catholic majority at Augsburg, though there were moderates in their ranks. After the conclusion of the Diet Melanchthon, Eck, and others explored the chances of reconciliation. Dogma was not the trouble, but the construction and practices of the Church. The Protestants went very far in conciliation, but differences of standpoint were deeper than they admitted. The Catholics regarded the regulations of the Church authorities as the rule from which only the rarest departures could be allowed. The Protestants, on the other hand, saw the rule of faith and life solely in Scripture and could only sanction Roman practices as a rare exception. Catholics regarded Church institutions as of divine right, Protestants as revocable expedients. To Protestants the Papacy was a human institution, to the Emperor it was divine. The new Church rested on the independence of the lesser clergy and on connection with the regional government. The formation of the Schmalkald League registered the fear of certain Protestant princes that they might have to fight for the defence of their faith.

The Introduction to the fourth volume pays renewed tribute to the standard-bearers of the Reformation. The rejection of the hierarchical powers was bound to produce an immense transformation in ideas and practice, involving the danger of disturbance and excess. It was essential that the foundations of traditional culture should remain unimpaired, that the values created by past generations should be transmitted from century to century. The Reformers kept as close to tradition and doctrine as seemed to them compatible with Scripture. Thus Luther directed his weapons against both sides—the Papacy which was trying to reconquer lost ground, and the Sects which threatened Church and State. In a celebrated sentence which enshrines the message of the whole work, Ranke pronounces him one of the greatest Conservatives who ever lived. He had no wish to overthrow the Empire nor to disrupt the Reich, and no Protestant Prince coveted the Imperial Crown. The Reformers were content to safeguard their reforms and to loosen the tie between Emperor and Pope. The ambition to change the whole world, observes the historian, to hasten from success to success, is more interesting to watch but rarely leaves permanent results. They thoroughly understood that the new ecclesiastical pattern, based exclusively on the Gospel, was only secure if it found recognition and protection in the great partnership of the Reich; and this was only possible with tranquillity, self-control and moderation.

Despite the failure of the Diet of Augsburg to bridge the gulf there were men in both camps who cared more for peace than for victory. The idea of a representative Church Council, on the lines of the great Councils of the early fifteenth century where the differences could be fully debated, was in the air. In 1535, five years after the drafting of the Augsburg Confession, Luther was consulted by the Nuntius Vergerio in a frank exchange at Wittenberg.

Luther. We desire a free Christian Council, not for ourselves who already possess the wholesome doctrine derived from God's word, but for others still chained to your tyranny.

Vergerio. Take care what you say; you are a man and can err.

Luther. Then summon a Council if you like. I will come, even if you burn me.

Vergerio. Where?

Luther. Wherever you like—Padua, Florence, Mantua.

Vergerio. Would you come to a Papal city like Bologna?

Luther. Good God, has the Pope seized that place too?

Vergerio. He would come to you in Wittenberg.

Luther. We shall be glad to see him.

Vergerio. How? alone or with an army?

Luther. As he prefers; we shall be prepared for both.

The tendency towards a rapprochement reappeared at the Diet

of Regensburg in 1541. The Emperor, who was present, wished to end the split. Contarini, the Papal Legate and the chief of the Catholic moderates, accepted the idea of justification by faith and wished to break with the rigid Dominican system. Bucer, who now ranked with Melanchthon as doctrinal expert of the Protestants, was equally inclined towards compromise. Charles and Contarini were willing to allow clerical marriage and communion in both kinds in Germany, and some Protestant Princes were ready to recognise the primacy of the Pope as the supervisor, not the autocrat of the Church. It was the high-water mark of the reconciliation tide, but the failure to agree on transubstantiation ruined the talks.

At this moment Philip of Hesse moves to the centre of the stage. Next to Charles V and Frederick the Wise, the Landgrave is the most carefully painted portrait in the gallery of rulers. He was a bundle of contradictions, immoral but sufficiently aware of sin to abstain from the sacrament. When his favourite declined his advances, he proposed to marry her despite the fact that he had a wife. He only felt at peace with his conscience after obtaining the reluctant consent of Luther and Melanchthon, which he regarded as the equivalent of the Pope's dispensing power. The two Protestant leaders were horrified at the situation and realised the damage to their work. 'But so pressing were the demands of the Landgrave, such were his assurances of the inevitability of his action, that finally, not as before the world but before God and only on condition of the strictest secrecy, they summarised their objections but finally consented.' The marriage was celebrated privately but soon became known. Melanchthon fell ill with the strain. Joachim II, the first Protestant Elector of Brandenburg, was horrified. Ferdinand, brother of Charles V, had long been inclined to Protestantism, but this, he said, was too much. Here for the first time Ranke reveals disapproval of the record of the two Protestant chiefs.

At this moment Luther passed away and the historian fires a parting salvo over his grave. He had not grown milder. His last writing against the Pope was the fullest of invective. It was too soon for him to apply historical justice. The power he was fighting was then exerting its full strength to destroy the doctrine which he had brought to light. Yet while seeing the growing danger he looked quietly ahead, and his message to his followers was to pray without ceasing. Luther, confesses Ranke, had his faults, but his closest friend was not the man to stress them. 'Melanchthon's correspondence evokes loving reverence, but I wish he had never written the letter of 1548, soon made public, complaining of Luther's obstinacy and love of controversy. It was partly true, and there would have been no harm if confided to an intimate friend. One sees now a noble soul can fall when carried away by momentary influences. In him more than any other man resided the unity of the Protestant Church.'

Charles V now found himself without a rival on the German stage. His star rose higher than ever when he crushed the Schmalkald League at the battle of Mühlberg in 1547, but it was only a fleeting triumph. Not all the Protestant Princes had joined it, and when the slippery opportunist Maurice of Saxony changed sides in 1552 it was the Emperor's turn to collapse. Moreover, though he was an ally of the Pope in the struggle against Protestantism, neither wished the other to become too strong. It was the Pope's will which prevailed at the Council of Trent, where the Emperor would have liked to see a far wider representation. 'In a Council intended for Germans there was hardly a German.' The open rivalry strengthened the hands of the Protestant Princes who agreed with Charles, at any rate to the extent of desiring to limit Papal power in the Reich. He dreamed of restoring the power of the Bishops and of pacifying the Protestants without the Pope's aid. Moreover, his hope that his son Philip might succeed him as Emperor could only be fulfilled with the votes of the Protestant Electors. He was a good Catholic but never an ultramontane. Ranke never forgets the better qualities of a man who was a moderate at heart, and his portrait of Charles is truer to life than that of Luther. Though not a genius, he was wiser than his ministers. He was double-dealing, calculating, avaricious, unscrupulous, yet he possessed a lofty tranquillity, imagination, and strength of soul. His ideas had a certain brilliance, a historical magnificence about them. Like the old Emperors, he regarded himself not only as head of the Empire but as the secular head of Christendom.

After these years of turmoil the story ends on the note of compromise which appealed to Ranke's harmonious temperament. The Emperor's ideal of the unity of Western Christendom had proved impracticable, for other rulers, Catholic as well as Protestant, were too powerful to accept the preponderance of the Empire: political and religious independence was the order of the day. The only solution—to live and let live—was reached at the Diet of Augsburg in 1555.

The formula *cujus regio ejus religio* registered the obvious fact that neither side was strong enough to destroy the other. That the Princes were no longer subject to any external authority in ecclesiastical matters was a triumph for the Protestants, who were satisfied with the permission to develop on their own lines. 'It was not special opinions which were tolerated; it was a whole system of doctrine and life. What Luther had claimed in 1519 at Leipzig—independence of the doctrinal decisions of Pope and Councils—was now achieved. Henceforth no German prince could be persecuted for heresy: there could be no more talk of heresy in regard to the adherents of the Augsburg Confession who now had full equality of status with those of the old Church.'

The farewell to Charles is a masterpiece. He made the bold and magnificent attempt to realise his conception of a Roman Catholic Empire. What was power to him when it could no longer help to carry out his ideas? When he saw he had not explicitly to confirm unconditional peace in Germany, which he would never have done, but merely to accept it, he informed his brother that he transferred the Imperial dignity which had value for him only if his own conceptions were carried out. His retirement to Yuste was a fitting close to a life dedicated to high ideals, and he died in the thought of the unity of the Church. 'But for a Church of politico-religious unity there was no more place in Europe. Never again did the idea enter so vitally into a human soul. The southern nations resisted the Protestant movement, but the return of the north could not be expected. But does the unity of Christendom really rest so exclusively on confessional unity? If we look round, it has preserved itself amid the antagonisms which cannot deny their common foundations. The progress of European culture and power has supplanted ecclesiastical unity. How far the Divine will outweighs human thoughts and plans!' Luther had partially triumphed and Charles V had not wholly failed. Of the two great antagonists neither achieved all he sought. The Empire lost prestige now that it was no longer combined with vast dominions. The Estates, glad to be rid of such a master, prized their autonomy. 'The Emperor was honoured as the source of law, the expression and embodiment of the dignity of the Empire, but power was henceforth to reside in the union of the Estates. The claim of the Papacy to exert authority was only a matter of words; in reality it was powerless. A limit was set to the influence of the

Roman See which previously, even in secular things, was a real power in the Reich.'

The closing reflections of the whole work indicate the historian's sober satisfaction. 'Does anyone nowadays regret that Papal Legates no longer inaugurate German Diets, that the Imperial Court is no longer called on to control tolls or law-suits, that contributions are no longer exacted in the shape of Indulgences? The ideas of the fourteenth century, as expressed in the earliest meetings of the Electors, and the efforts of the fifteenth as against the claims of the distant Imperial and Papal Courts which were quite unable to repress disturbances, were now achieved. The original plan of a system of Estates was embodied in comprehensive conciliatory constitutions. Of this Protestantism was the main cause, but it was opposed to the Empire only because the latter combined with the ecclesiastical power. For the first time under their influence internal peace, the Court of Appeal, the duties of the Circles assume permanent shape. With the religious peace they form a coherent and protective system. Protestantism was henceforth under the protection of the Reich, which pledged itself not to allow any condemnation of it by a Council to take effect.' Though what Ranke calls 'the great institution of the Reich, in which the nation had lived for so many centuries,' lost some of its attributes, it still had a part to play in the life of the German people.

The Reformation Era had an enthusiastic reception throughout the Protestant world, and critics who had detected a lack of warmth in the *History of the Popes* were delighted at the resonant tones of its successor. The one was written for mankind, the other for the Fatherland. 'In reading the earlier works,' declares Sybel, 'my enjoyment is exactly the same as in visiting a gallery of excellent pictures and statuary. Utterly different is my feeling when I open *The Reformation Era* which breathes the enthusiasm of a German patriot for the greatest act of the German spirit.' Treitschke pronounces it the author's masterpiece, its style warmed by the love of country. Moriz Ritter, one of his greatest admirers, asserts that he never reached the same level again. Such a paean to the Lutheran movement, however, both as a religious advance and a national liberation, invited attack from militant Catholics. The first counterblow was struck in Döllinger's three massive volumes on the Reformation, which collected all the evidence he could gather of evil and confusion and attributed it to the Lutheran movement, above all to the Reformer's attack on 'good works.'

More readable, more comprehensive, and far more formidable were the eight volumes of Janssen's *History of the German People from the Close of the Middle Ages*, the Catholic equivalent of Ranke's masterpiece. None of Ranke's leading theses escapes challenge. Like his master Böhmer, Janssen revived the old romantic idea of the Reich; unlike Ranke, he made the people the hero, not the nation as embodied in its leaders. To Ranke the Reformation was the glorious era in which the nation became conscious of its institutional and spiritual independence, swept away glaring ecclesiastical abuses, and purified its faith. To Janssen it was the evil moment when, led astray by false guides, it broke with the past, plunged into heresy and moral anarchy, and initiated a century of religious war. Though the book was defiantly propagandist and often uncritical in the treatment of sources, it proved by a cloud of witnesses that Ranke's picture of Germany on the eve of the Reformation was too dark, that its impact on social life was more disintegrating than he had allowed, and that he had seen some of the Reformers in too rosy a light. Ranke dismissed this onslaught as easy to answer, but, though he revised his narrative more than once, he never modified his view of the Reformation as a blessing to Germany and the world. Still more violent attacks on Luther from the Catholic camp were launched after his death. However little we may be inclined to accept the fierce invective of Grisar and Denifle, no twentieth-century student can be content with Ranke's portrait which ignores the coarser side of the Protestant leader.

The story of sixteenth-century Germany is continued on a smaller scale in two substantial monographs published together in 1869 in a volume entitled *Zur deutschen Geschichte 1555–1619*. The first, *The Times of Ferdinand I and Maximilian II*, was based mainly on the reports of Italian diplomatists which Ranke had studied during his sojourn in Austria and Italy, and appeared in the *Historisch-Politische Zeitschrift* in 1832. Its reappearance without change so many years later indicate that it may be regarded as embodying his ripe judgment on the German aspect of the Counter-Reformation. Why, he asks, did the Reich, once the head of Europe, lose its unity and strength? The usual reply, he admits, is the Reformation; Germans were proud of their share in the necessary task of Church reform, but they also regretted the division, the wars, the decline. 'But if the Reformation, as both sides admit, was inevitable, was this result also inevitable? Was that which elevated and liberated us inescapably linked with what drove us into disunion? Or was it due to accidental circumstances and avoidable mistakes? Was unity impossible after the split?' Certainly not, is his reply, for the reigns of Ferdinand I and Maximilian II show it was possible to reconcile competing interests. Ferdinand was less able and less powerful than his brother, but he was largely responsible for thirty years of peace. The Diets passed unanimous decisions and the Circles functioned normally. 'It was a blessing for the Reich that the wish of Charles to be succeeded by his son as Emperor was unfulfilled, owing to the combination of Ferdinand and the Protestants who hated to be ruled by Spaniards.'

Ferdinand cared little whether a prince was Catholic or Protestant, for he knew they needed one another. Next to Frederick the Wise of Saxony, no monarch receives such high praise as the man who on the death of his grandfather Maximilian in 1519 found himself the ruler of Austria, to which the battle of Mohacz seven years later brought the addition of Bohemia and Hungary. Though he was on good terms with the Emperor, the brothers differed both in temperament and policy. The younger was lively, friendly, conciliatory, and, though born and brought up in Spain, grew to like Germany and won the confidence of the German people. He employed Lutherans in his household and only asked for good character in his entourage. 'Such was our Emperor after the abdication of Charles V in 1555, and such were other rulers of our Fatherland. It was an admirable generation of princes. Most of them gave the constitutions which lasted almost to our own time. The movements of the Reformation, the combination of secular and ecclesiastical business, stimulated their mental energies; a magnificent activity had ripened them. Changes of fortune and experience had taught them to moderate their views and efforts. They were strong and determined, sensible and peaceable, united by the great interest of the Fatherland.

The union of princes was paralleled by a *détente* in the people. The reformed teaching had won a decided superiority and made considerable progress even in Bavaria, Austria and the Rhineland. The prestige of Rome had fallen among Catholic rulers, and there was nothing of the fierce hatred of later times. Many Protestant officials were employed by the Ecclesiastical Princes. Mixed marriages were frequent, toleration was general. In the field of literature Hans Sachs and Fischart were at work. The towns and the mines were flourishing. 'We see the nation busy, powerful and flourishing, held together by its princes in harmony and jealous of foreign influence.' Rarely does Ranke express such enthusiasm. Maximilian II carried on the good work of his father. Highly cultured and pleasant, he loved Germany, was strongly attracted to Protestantism, studied the writings of Luther and Melanchthon, and was often critical of the Pope. He was in fact a Protestant at heart, though he did not wish to break with the Catholic world. This happy intermezzo ended with the Lutheran-Calvinist struggle and the Catholic revival symbolised in the rise of the Jesuits and the Council of Trent.

The second essay, written many years later, *Zur Reichsgeschichte 1575–1619*, continues the story of peaceful collaboration. 'There was never a serious attempt to Protestantise the Empire, nor could there be without a revolution. For it was a European and ecclesiastical as well as a national institution.' Charles V in distant Yuste continued to proclaim that no realm could exist without religious conformity; but the Reformation disproved his thesis, for dislike of foreign rule was a stronger sentiment than the tradition of religious unity. Maximilian II was a great figure in German history because he induced his father to end the subordination to the elder line and to make terms with the Protestants on the basis of Germany for the Germans. His sons Rudolf and Matthias carried on the policy of peace, though with less conviction and success. Rudolf's interest was in science and art, not religion or politics, and it was he who invited Tycho Brahe to Prague. In his later years he became increasingly reserved, suspicious, depressed, weak, moody, and the old bachelor was annoyed by talk of his successor, his brother Matthias. The latter was utterly different in taste and temperament, being sociable and extravagant. The brothers were inferior to their father and grandfather, but they were loyal to the statesmanlike policy of parity and peace. When the fourth of these tolerant Emperors passed away, the stage was set for the horrors of the Thirty Years' War. The record of these rulers embodies the historian's profound conviction that the Reformation was not incompatible with the unity of the German nation, and that it was the Catholic extremists, spurred on by the Jesuits, who shattered the long and fruitful truce.

The survey of German fortunes is pursued without a break in the

History of Wallenstein, published in 1869. Ranke was attracted to the subject not merely by its importance but because no agreement as to the character and policy of the most reserved and elusive of supermen was in sight. Utilising new material in the Vienna archives he pronounces that he cared nothing for religion, and that power and wealth were his principal aims. On the other hand he was more than a mere adventurer, and he would have preferred the continuation of the confessional equilibrium. His early experience led him to take a detached view of religious differences, for he was the child of Lutheran parents and was sent by an uncle to a Jesuit college after their death. Like Rudolf, he was more interested in astrology than theology. To achieve his purpose the restoration of the power of the Empire seemed to him indispensable. 'For only with the aid of the highest authority could he create an army and treat opponents as rebels. Though brought into being by his personal exertions and private resources, it was recruited in the name of the Emperor.' The thought of religion, which played a leading part in the suppression of the Bohemian rebellion, receded into the background when his star began to shine, and he announced that he could build his army of Protestants as well as Catholics. Sons of Protestant princes served under him, and regiments commanded by Protestants were often quartered in Protestant districts. How could the chief of such a motley throng make the revival and extension of Catholicism his principal aim?

The idea of military authority filled Wallenstein's mind. He opposed the League, and the Catholic princes never trusted him, ignoring his appeal for help to take Stralsund. He honestly tried to prevent excesses, but from mercenaries that was asking too much. Such an army under such a leader constituted the gravest challenge to the Constitution of the Empire. Always an enemy of the Electors, he wished to subject everyone to the Emperor. The Estates, he argued, were no longer needed. The Empire, like the monarchy of France and Spain, should be hereditary. Convinced that he aimed at the destruction of their traditional privileges and the subordination of the Estates, the Catholic Electors tried to prevent such a catastrophe by suggesting a union of arms with the two Protestant Electors in a common army opposed to the Imperial forces under Wallenstein, informing the Emperor of their fears of the overthrow of the old Constitution.

Wallenstein's system postulated a weak and moderate Emperor, but Ferdinand II was neither moderate nor weak. The Restitution Edict of 1628 was a bombshell, reclaiming the ecclesiastical endowments ceded to Protestant administrators after the Peace of Augsburg. The deadly thrust united the Protestants and brought Gustavus Adolphus on to the German stage. 'Contemporaries and later generations have found in Ferdinand II the ideal of a Catholic prince, but that is going much too far. He liked music and the chase, keeping a list of his trophies; he was a great eater, like Charles V. His extravagance piled up unpaid debts and he enjoyed life. His clericalism always coincided with the interests of his family and his House. Protestantism he regarded as a heresy to be destroyed by every means. The Edict of Restitution laid the axe at the roots of the Reformation. The declaration of war on the whole of north German thought and life combined secular confiscation and ecclesiastical restitution. The Imperial authority unfolded all its claims at the same moment and in all directions. The aim was not a well armed and highly intelligent Germany but an obedient and essentially Catholic nation.'

The Edict of Restitution displeased moderate Catholics, among them Wallenstein, who favoured Catholic preponderance under the Emperor's authority but opposed all persecution. The Catholic Electors and princes desired Maximilian of Bavaria, if not the Emperor himself, to command, and wanted the actual authority in the Reich to reside in the Electoral College with its Catholic majority. Their programme was the 'restitution' of ecclesiastical property and the removal of Wallenstein as one means of preventing the Emperor being too strong. His enforced resignation in 1630 left him a lonely man. Ferdinand, unlike his predecessors, worked closely with Spain for Hapsburg interests, but he had to give way to the Electors as he needed their support for the election of his son as King of the Romans. Wallenstein was recalled in 1631 when Gustavus Adolphus triumphed at Breitenfeld, but since his dismissal he had lost all sense of obligation to the Emperor and secretly negotiated with the Swedes. Ferdinand had never wished to dismiss the only man who could save him from the domination of the princes. Yet Wallenstein and the Swedish king pursued widely differing aims, the former wishing to preserve the forms of the old Reich with maximum consideration for Protestants, the latter to break the forms and ensure the survival of Protestantism.

By this time no one trusted Wallenstein, and even the victory at Lützen and the death of the Protestant champion failed to regain the confidence of the Catholic world. The intervention of Gustavus had ended the danger of Catholic preponderance threatened since 1620, and Wallenstein was not dissatisfied with the result of the war. He had never wanted to destroy Protestantism, and he dreaded the preponderance of the League, his implacable enemy. His wish was to live in splendour on his vast estates after restoring peace in friendly negotiations with the Protestants. If the Emperor would not make peace he would compel him to do so, and he would expel every Jesuit from the Reich. He started secret negotiations with the Protestants on the basis of the integrity of the Reich and the withdrawal of the Edict of Restitution. Since that programme was too moderate for the Emperor, the League and the Pope, he resolved to make peace with the Protestants and felt strong enough to do so, even dreaming of the Crown of Bohemia and of becoming Elector Palatine. Negotiations with Oxenstierna failed since Sweden was the ally of France, with whom Wallenstein would have nothing to do, and his programme included the withdrawal from the Reich of foreign troops, including the Swedes. He was now at the height of his power. An able financier and master of an army of many nationalities, while the League had only Catholics, and Gustavus only Protestants, Wallenstein never inquired about a soldier's religion. No Jesuit was allowed in the army, freedom of conscience, as he explained, being the privilege of the Germans. At that moment (1633) it might seem to him as if the future of the world was in his hands. Though no admirer of his cold and selfish character Ranke approved his aims: to end the war, to restore religious peace, to maintain the integrity of the Reich, to combine the independence of the Electors with the power of the Emperor, to expel the Swedes. The French and the Protestants sought contact with him not as a subordinate but as a virtually independent potentate.

The narrative of the closing phase is the most dramatic in the book. 'If the Emperor no longer recognises me as his General,' declared Wallenstein, 'I will no longer recognise him as my lord. I could easily join another prince, but I want no master. I want to be lord and I am strong enough to do it.' To be Elector Palatine or King of Bohemia under the authority of Vienna would no longer suffice. He coveted a place among the sovereigns of the world, if not with the Emperor's consent, then in opposition to the House of Austria, for all opponents of Hapsburg predominance would join him. He had at last become drunk with power and the end was near. The Scottish and Irish mercenaries who butchered him at Eger had received no orders, but, like the murderers of Becket, they knew what would please the highest quarters.

During the closing years of his life Wallenstein had been a rebel at heart. The League was his chief foe, but it would have been satisfied with his retirement into private life, whereas Spain desired his death. His few friends were tepid and far away, his foes close at hand. In the simple words of Oxenstierna he had undertaken more than he could carry out. The House of Austria, reinforced by Spain, proved too strong for him, and his fall was a misfortune for the Protestant cause. But now the war with France which he had always wished to avoid flared up and led to French hegemony and the devitalisation of the Reich. For a time he had been the main instrument in reviving the power and prestige of the Hapsburgs; but the suspicions he aroused prevented the full unification of the forces of the Counter-Reformation which might possibly have dealt German Protestantism a knock-out blow.

II

RANKE's writings on Germany fall into two groups. The first, dealing with the Reich, carries the story from Maximilian I to Wallenstein. The second is mainly concerned with Prussia, describing the growth of the state which rose into prominence when the Holy Roman Empire was on the wane. Though no item in the latter category is so moving or so personal in tone as *The Reformation Era*, he finds little to blame in the story of the Hohenzollerns in peace and war. During a visit to Paris in 1843 he consulted the despatches of Labori, the French Ambassador at Berlin during the early years of Frederick the Great, then crossed the Channel for the first time in order to understand the British angle, and finally delved deep into the Prussian archives hitherto closed to inspection. His first plan was to combine a detailed analysis of Frederick's achievement with an Introduction explaining the administrative and military foundations on which he built. The *Nine Books of Prussian History*, the third of his major works, which appeared in 1847–1848, briefly sketched the first three centuries of Hohenzollern rule, broadened its scope in the reign of Frederick William I, and closed on the eve of the Seven Years' War. Twenty years later in revising it for the Collected Works, he became dissatisfied with its structure, expanding the First Book into four and changing the title from Nine to Twelve Books. If the earlier effort is artistically inferior to the *Popes* and *The Reformation Era*, the final version ranks among the classics of German historiography and has never been superseded.[1]

Though the author expresses his desire to be as objective as possible, the Preface prepares us for a favourable verdict. At the opening of the eighteenth century, he reminds us, there were four Great Powers in Europe—England, France, Austria, Russia. In the North there was a vacuum which Prussia alone could fill. Her rise was due not so much to deliberate ambition as to the duty of self-preservation, for which an independent position was essential; and the condition of independence is strength. Beginning with the colonisation and conversion of the Mark of Brandenburg and East Prussia, he passes to the coming of the Hohenzollerns in 1415. They succeeded, he declares, not through violence, but because their advantage corresponded to the general interests of religious and political life. Frederick, the first Elector, is described as a political genius, as rich in ideas as he was full of talent to carry them out, a good soldier, cultivated and conciliatory, with a lofty conception of his duties though not an altogether trustworthy friend. To the next outstanding figure, Joachim II, the first Protestant Elector, the historian had paid homage in a previous work. 'The Reformation was an act of the whole community, and nowhere was the change effected with less friction. His conciliatory temperament and dislike of extremes prevented him from playing a leading part on the German stage, but he gave his subjects peace. Keeping aloof both from the Schmalkald League and the subsequent rally against Charles V, he welcomed the peace of Augsburg as a triumph of common sense. Though in no way a great man or indeed an able administrator and temperamentally disposed to play for safety, he was one of the founders of the fortunes of Brandenburg. With the establishment of Protestantism in the Mark at the wish of the Estates, the dynasty became fully identified with the lands over which it ruled.' His friendly relation to the

[1] It should be studied in the three volumes of the Academy Edition, which contains an excellent Introduction.

Estates earns no less applause, for Ranke, like the Elector, disliked the rigid centralisation associated with the so-called Reception of Roman law. The following decades are once again presented in a rosy light as the era of confessional equilibrium which lasted till the Austrian and Spanish branches of the House of Hapsburg combined in the attempt to recover the leadership of Europe. Even George William, the feeblest of the Hohenzollerns, is treated with consideration, for it was Ranke's instinct to see the best in everybody. 'His misfortunes came from the differences and distances of his provinces, the disagreements of his advisers, above all from the weakness of his own position. Though he rescued the dynasty and his territories, he left the Protestants in the utmost danger. In such a condition Brandenburg had little value for the world. Like a little boat in a stormy sea, it had to run before the wind.'

With the accession of the Great Elector, son of George William, in 1640, the prospect widens and a dynamic figure comes to life. The nephew of the Winter King and of Gustavus Adolphus, he had Protestantism in his blood. Educated in Holland, he was shocked when his father joined Austria by the Peace of Prague. On his return he was treated with suspicion and believed his life to be in danger from the omnipotent Schwarzenberg. The first task on coming to the throne was to create a strong executive by training a small standing army and breaking the power of the Estates. The termination of Polish suzerainty over East Prussia and the victory of Fehrbellin raised the prestige of Brandenburg, and he planned to seize Silesia if the Hapsburgs died out. The Great Elector, who is described as 'hard metal,' was the right man for the needs of a state which he transformed from a third into a second-class power by a combination of genius and luck. What less indulgent judges than Ranke have denounced as opportunism is charitably interpreted as a willingness to learn from experience. On the fundamental issue of preserving his little state as a bulwark of Protestantism he never compromised. Like other princes of his time, at home and abroad, he desired to enlarge his heritage, but he is described as unaggressive.

The portrait of the ablest Hohenzollern except Frederick the Great is one of the finest in the crowded gallery. 'Frederick William ranks with the greatest spirits of the religious and political struggles of the seventeenth century. Gustavus Adolphus and Richelieu were of incomparably greater importance in shaping world events, Wallenstein was bolder, Cromwell deeper and more original, Charles X of Sweden more impulsive. We shall never forget Mazarin, the skilful founder of the diplomatic hegemony of France, or the cautious Republican John de Witt, the inventor of the Balance of Power. Frederick William was not in a position to exert such a far-ranging influence, but his achievement is no less considerable. He did not live exclusively in the conflicts of the hour; his work was for all time.' The man of action had his softer side. He loved singing birds in his rooms, displayed taste in art, respected erudition, and was always eager to learn. His system was patriarchal, and after listening patiently to members of the Council he reserved his decision. His regime was neither easy nor popular, and there was general complaint of the burdens which grew heavier with advancing years. His outbursts of wrath were a trial, but he quickly regained his self-control. There was something wide-ranging in his mind, indeed almost too wide, but his imagination was combined with practical sense. He created a small navy, planned colonisation in West Africa, and invited the Huguenots to settle in his dominions. His supreme achievement was to breathe the idea of a state into the life of his people.

Though no one has ever made a hero of Frederick, the first King, Ranke treats him with unusual respect, and even his extravagance receives only a gentle rebuke. Starting with the handicap of his father's wills, which allotted portions of the national heritage to the second family, he restored the unity of the state by generous settlements. His principal achievement, the acquisition of the royal title, was like a national coming of age and was far more than an act of vanity. Prussia's task was to become an independent, Protestant, North German Great Power, and her emergence benefited Germany even though it weakened the Empire. By nature she was inclined to peace, legality and toleration, but she could not be peaceful while she was weak and insecure. The problem of the royal title was raised by questions of precedence at congresses, and at Ryswick in 1697 the Elector felt his status to be disproportionate to his power. Memoranda were drawn up for him pointing out the difficulties of the project. Would other rulers accept it, and would the Estates approve? To avoid such complications he decided to base his claim on the Duchy of Prussia which formed no part of the Reich. Vienna disliked the notion of strengthening a Protestant ruler, fearing that he might one day stand for election as Emperor. When, however, he hinted that he would go ahead if necessary without obtaining consent and that others would recognise him, Leopold gave way, for the aid of the petitioner in the coming War of the Spanish Succession might be useful. The treaty was signed in 1700 and the Elector was crowned at Königsberg in 1701. Though he left the finances in chaos and the army in decline, he made a notable contribution to the power of the state.

If the first Hohenzollern King is rehabilitated in Ranke's pages, his son Frederick William I may be said to have come to life. The dazzling figure of the Great Elector needed no pedestal, but the unattractive grandson at last received his due. The Memoirs of Wilhelmina and the quarrel with his eldest son had focussed attention on his boorish and brutal ways and diverted it from his services to the state to which Ranke was the first to do full justice. In the first edition he regretted that paternal severity destroyed elements of value in his son; in the second this verdict is omitted, and it is claimed that harsh methods made the heir a man and a soldier while leaving his resilience intact. While longing for an independent position for his little state, he realised that internal strength had to be built up before risks could be run. Here was the key to all his reforms. Though not a great statesman and though his regime was too absolute and oppressive, he was the greatest administrator in Prussian history. His legacy was the bureaucratic-military state, the *rocher de bronze* of which he proudly spoke, with the busy ruler in effective control.

In the *Nine Books* Frederick the Great completely dominates the stage, for his father's reign is presented merely as the background of his early years. In the *Twelve Books* he occupies only half the work, and his achievement emerges as the completion of a long historical process of diplomacy and organisation. Though there is little warmth in the narrative and no trace of enmity to the Hapsburgs, the victory of Prussia is pronounced beneficial to Germany on the ground that she contained at any rate one state which could determine its own course. The Empire had sunk to a territorial principality like the rest. 'Only in Prussia was there a great German, European, independent power which revived the full sentiment of independence for the first time for centuries.' Frederick's aims were at once limited and legitimate. He desired parity with Austria, nothing more. Reconciliation, though impossible in his lifetime, was easily effected during the Revolution and Napoleonic wars. Writing in the tranquil era of the Restoration when Prussia and Austria sat together at the round table of the *Deutscher Bund*, the historian might well feel that Frederick's goal—co-operation on the basis of equality—had been reached, and that the Austro-Prussian problem had been finally solved. The rise of Prussia, in other words, had proved a stabilising element in the life of Europe, and as a good European Ranke rejoiced in the equilibrium.

The seizure of Silesia, the key to the whole reign, is justified on the ground that Austria had broken faith. 'No one will maintain that a Power is tied to a treaty when the other party for any reason abandons it.' Frederick William I accepted the Pragmatic Sanction on condition that Vienna would help him to the Duchy of Berg, a condition which was not fulfilled. 'There was no trace of hatred or personal revenge, but father and son were full of ambition and determined not to be ignored or despised. Since the old friendship had ceased there was nothing to prevent the revival of ancient claims. The House of Brandenburg acted in good faith and had a good case. Convinced that a large part of Silesia ought to be his, Frederick felt it an obligation of honour to assert his rights. Picture the prince, a young man thirsting for action, resentful of recent errors, and with latent but all the stronger consciousness of ancient rights of which his house was deprived, and the feeling that the enterprise would make him a really powerful king.' Even had there been no Prussia and no Frederick, the end of the male Hapsburg line would have provoked a war of succession. France would have resumed the old struggle and the Wittelsbachs would have pressed their claims. 'It was fortunate that there was at any rate one state which fought for its own cause and acted without seeking foreign counsel. Prussia desired neither the Imperial title nor separation from the Reich, but she did not wish to see the supreme authority in hostile hands, and for this reason she supported the candidature of the Elector of Bavaria as Emperor.'

The twelfth and last book of the *Prussian History*, entitled Years of Peace, depicts Frederick as a ruler no less eminent in peace than in war. It is unjust, declares Ranke, to compare him with Charles XII, who confessed that in deciding to make peace he was thinking of the next war since he could not live quietly at home. Frederick, on the contrary, made a conquest which he believed to be necessary for the safety and dignity of Prussia: henceforth he drew the sword only to preserve it. This interpretation of the Austro-Prussian conflict naturally appeals more to the winners than to the losers or to the lookers on. Frederick, he suggests, never wished to destroy or endanger Austria's position as a Great Power, for the transfer of Silesia meant as little to her in terms of national strength as it meant everything to Prussia in her rightful quest for parity. That the two countries needed one another as a central bastion against attacks from west and east, and that they were able to co-operate in the defence of their common interests, was proved during the Napoleonic era, in the earlier phases of the Deutscher Bund, and finally after the foundation of the Hohenzollern Empire.

The *Nine Books of Prussian History* received far less applause than the *Popes* and *The Reformation Era*. The coolness of tone strikes every reader, and there is little excitement in the story till Frederick the Great takes the helm. Frederick William IV was dissatisfied with the first two volumes, though he approved the third. Strauss sighed for the brush of a Rembrandt. 'I am not surprised at Ranke's failure,' wrote Carlyle to Varnhagen; 'if I were a Prussian or even a German I should protest against his Frederick the Great.' Its importance as the first narrative based on the state archives was recognised by scholars at home and abroad, but the lay reader found it uninspiring.

The most formidable attack came from the founder of the Prussian School of historians. While some critics complained that the book was too courtier-like, Droysen found the temperature far too chilly for his taste. Except that the books cover the same period, his *History of Prussian Policy* differs in almost every respect. While the elder scholar reviews internal as fully as external problems, the younger confines himself almost entirely to foreign affairs. Equally divergent is the interpretation of the rise of Prussia. While Ranke calmly narrates and approves the sequence of events, Droysen exults in the fulfilment of a national mission. While the one never lost the conception of a Reich in which or in connection with which Austria should play an honoured part, the other regarded her, not France, as the chief enemy of a German nation-state. While Ranke, a son of the Restoration era, craved for a quiet life after the storms of the Napoleonic era, Droysen clamoured for a constitutional Prussia and a Prussianised Empire. Conservative and Liberal Prussia faced one another in the lecture-rooms and libraries of Berlin.

Differences of approach meet us at every stage of the journey.

Ranke accepted particularism, for he regarded the Princes as embodying the freedom of Germany; Droysen dismissed them, with the significant exception of Prussia, as playing for their own hand. Ranke has friendly words for the Hapsburgs except during the fanatical interlude of the Thirty Years' War; in Droysen's eyes their clericalism and dynastic selfishness made them a continual threat to Germany. Though both rejoiced in the Reformation, Ranke approved the state Churches as a bulwark against Catholic resurgence while Droysen denounced their fierce theological strife. Ranke's hero, the Elector Joachim II, is blamed by Droysen for not supporting the Schmalkald League against Charles V, just as George William is censured for failing to support Gustavus Adolphus. Ranke admires the Great Elector as a splendid opportunist bent mainly on self-preservation, Droysen as a crusader for the national idea. The harsh methods of Frederick William I appeal to Droysen more than to Ranke, and the portrait of his greater son is painted in more glowing colours.

Deeper than any difference of historical interpretation was the difference in temperament, and neither did justice to the merits of each other's books. When the *Nine Books* began to appear in 1847, Droysen was busy with his life of York and was quivering with the patriotic emotions of the War of Liberation. 'If I were Prussian Historiographer,' he wrote to a friend, 'I should want to do something better than write a perfumed book on the Great Elector and Frederick William I and to get more out of the archives than this dignified trifling in which there is nothing new. But one must have a heart for history.' A year later, when the second volume of the *Nine Books* appeared, he returned to the charge. 'Our best historians actually water down and perfume the heroic life of Frederick II.' He admitted that Ranke was the head of his profession, but complained that he lacked a big German heart and therefore could not assist the national cause. His tread was far too light and he saw everything in cheerful sunshine, as though there was no grief or pangs in human life, no guilt or passion. 'The good God,' confessed Droysen, 'has endowed me with too little serenity of soul.' To such a fiery spirit panting for action it would naturally appear that Ranke had too little red blood in his veins. Though the author was grieved at the cool reception of the book, his withers were unwrung.

The story of Frederick the Great was summarised and the main verdicts repeated in the comprehensive article contributed to the

Dictionary of German Biography in 1878. 'A heroic life, inspired by great ideas, filled with feats of arms, exertions and fateful events, immortalised by the raising of the Prussian State to the rank of a Power, inestimable in its legacy to the German nation and the world!' There is not a word of blame for the seizure of Silesia. 'Imagine a young Prince, able and ambitious, coming into the rights which his ancestors were unable to vindicate and also into the power to do so. Was it not inevitable that he should desire to act? He did not challenge the succession of Maria Theresa, but he held that the Silesian principalities had never been her father's property. He vindicated for his House an inalienable right to them which the time had now come to assert. Never was any acquisition more opportune and important for a state. No one can doubt that the enterprise could be undertaken with a good conscience. Resistance was inevitable: both attack and defence were legitimate. Prussia had accepted the Pragmatic Sanction, but Austria had broken the conditions of the recognition of Maria Theresa's claims. It was not hatred, but the House of Brandenburg felt itself freed from its obligations, and in the general confusion Frederick consulted his own interest.' The chief interest of the sketch is that it pronounces judgment on the later phases of the reign to which the *Twelve Books* did not extend. The First Partition of Poland is approved on the double ground that West Prussia was essential to the stability of the state, and that a deal with Russia and Austria was needed to avert a general conflagration. Resistance to Hapsburg ambitions in Bavaria in 1778 would have involved a major war if France had supported her Austrian ally, but the memory of Rossbach was still fresh and Catherine the Great lent moral support to her Prussian ally. That Frederick in his old age emerged as the champion of the Reich, and was gratefully recognised as such, confirms the historian's thesis that the rise of Prussia helped to stabilise Europe. In reviewing Frederick's domestic policy he emphasises the ruler's conviction that manpower was the foundation of strength and praises his efforts at internal colonisation. Serfdom he disliked, but he felt that its abolition would estrange the nobility on whom he depended for his officers. 'One sees that he left something to do in 1807.'

Zur Geschichte von Oesterreich und Preussen 1748–1763, published in 1875, containing a massive dissertation on *The Origin of the Seven Years' War* and a brief sketch of the course of the struggle, may be regarded as a supplement to the *Twelve Books*. Since Droysen's monumental enterprise was interrupted by death before he reached the opening of the Seven Years' War, Ranke's study remains the most authoritative presentation of the argument that both Prussia and Austria felt the conflict to be inevitable.

The German Powers and the League of Princes 1780–1790, published in 1871, portrays Frederick's closing years and the opening phase of his degenerate successor. The whole story, based on the archives of Berlin and Vienna, Brunswick, Weimar and the Hague, is dominated by the struggle between Prussia and Austria which had already led to four wars during a single reign and which seemed likely at any moment to unleash a fifth. While Frederick's guiding principle was to secure his hold on Silesia by counterworking the preponderance of Austria in the Reich, the policy of Joseph and Kaunitz was to establish such a commanding position in central Europe that neither Prussia nor any other German state could frustrate their aims. The ambitious young Emperor had gained only a fraction of his demands in the Treaty of Teschen which concluded the War of the Bavarian Succession, and it was natural that he should try again, as Frederick was convinced that he would. Help from France he no longer expected, though the alliance of 1756 remained nominally intact; but now Russia, bent like himself on the spoliation of Turkey, was on his side. Since, however, Catherine had no desire either to render Austria ominously strong by making Prussia dangerously weak, everything turned on the attitude of the Princes of the Reich. Prussia, so recently the challenger of the *status quo*, was now its bulwark; Austria, its champion till 1778, was now its most formidable foe. Through all the diplomatic tangle Ranke moves forward with his usual serenity. Frederick's final phase appeals to the conservative historian as much as the later phase of Luther.

The portrait of Joseph II, whose reign of ten years supplies the chronological framework of these volumes, is one of the historian's masterpieces. His merits are as fully recognised as his faults, for Ranke was never an Austrophobe. 'He was a born bureaucrat, meticulous in small things, but always with a view to the whole.' His dream was to transform his ramshackle Empire into a centralised, obedient, efficiently administered state. He, like Frederick, aspired to be the father of his people and to do everything himself. Years of hard work were needed before he could once again play for high stakes, and internal obstacles to the autocratic system which was his rule of life would have to be overcome. Directly Maria Theresa was gone, he fulfilled his old desire for religious toleration and the thinning out of the wealthy monasteries. When Pius VI invited himself to Vienna in 1782, in the hope of modifying the Josephan variety of Gallicanism, he found a courteous welcome but an unbending host. Kaunitz fully supported his master's resolve to assert the authority of the state in every sphere. He refused to call on the distinguished visitor, and when the Pope visited him the reception was chilly and the conversation was confined to matters of art. The recent suppression of the Jesuits by Clement XIII had cooled the ecclesiastical temperature and facilitated the task of a ruler who, though himself a believer, was also a child of the *Aufklärung*.

In addition to strengthening his hold on his subjects, Joseph prepared for the coming struggle in the Reich by visiting Catherine the Great and restoring the friendly relations which had existed under the Empress Elizabeth. Austria, it was understood, would favour Russian ambitions in the Black Sea region, and Russia would afford moral support in the next round of the Bavarian boxing match. Ranke's picture of the Reich on the eve of the French Revolution exhibits the balance of forces in that venerable but decrepit institution which, he assures us, still counted for something. Since the Reformation the Hapsburgs had always reckoned on the three Ecclesiastical Electors of Cologne, Trier and Mainz, but Joseph's covetous glances at Bavaria introduced a new factor. The minor members of the Reich could no longer hold up their heads if Austrian influence became irresistible, and Catholic rulers now joined the Protestants in defending their independence. 'Every member of the Reich wanted to be something and indeed was something.' There was no thought of reforms; all that was necessary was for it to use its powers. 'It survived in its traditional forms, though sundered by religious cleavage and above all by the growth of the great autonomous states. They stood facing each other, and their antagonism affected its constitution and led to efforts to rejuvenate it.'

When Joseph's plan, accepted by Karl Theodor, to exchange the Austrian Netherlands for Bavaria became known in January 1785, Frederick, old and broken in health though he was, bestirred himself once again. 'My God,' he exclaimed, 'we are surrounded by cowardice and venality. Shall we alone be able to maintain the constitution of the Reich?' Only a League of Princes could bar the Emperor's path to the domination of Germany, as a similar combination led by Maurice of Saxony had stood up to Charles V in 1552. The adhesion of Hanover carried with it that of Brunswick, Hesse and Mecklenburg, the latter ruled by the brother of Queen Charlotte. When Saxony joined up success was assured, The Duke of Zweibrücken, heir to the childless Elector of Bavaria, promised never to surrender his prospective territories, and the membership of the Elector of Mainz, the Arch-Chancellor of the Empire, put the finishing touch to the enterprise. Joseph was checkmated for the second time, not by war as in 1778 but by political strategy. The Fürstenbund, the last of Frederick's achievements, moves the old historian to admiration. There was the King of Prussia, surrounded by German princes in voluntary union—an anticipation of the Hohenzollern Empire which Bismarck was creating while he was finishing his book. It was something more than a barrier to Austrian ambitions, for it pointed the way towards unity. 'Let us remember that the national idea grew vigorously in those years. The plan was to make arrangements by which all the petty quarrels and party differences could be transcended. With a federation of princes based on right and law the German became aware that he possessed a fatherland. For the German nation this consciousness of solidarity was an inestimable prize.'

Ranke takes leave of Frederick in a passage of unusual warmth. 'From his little country-house, where he lived like a monk, he surveyed the European scene. His vision was not weakened by age, his mind worked efficiently and correctly. His political genius is almost without parallel in the modern world. By his moderation and circumspection he succeeded in holding back the hostile elements arrayed against each other. The attention of Europe was always fixed on Sans Souci, not only on what was done or planned there, but almost more on the problem how long the mind which everyone honoured or feared would endure. For the last few years there was talk of his expected end. The Emperor said that death seemed to respect the hero's grey hairs. A great life, unique in history, was finished.' Despite such unstinted homage the book failed to please the pundits of the Prussian School. 'I am more anxious than ever for your picture of the Frederician epoch,' wrote Treitschke to Droysen. 'Ranke's history does not fill the void. This soft-pedalling which says nothing of the most important things is horrible. He should stick to England and Italy, where one can admire his greatness without reserve. For Prussian history he lacks the essential factor—character.'

The most lenient of judges is kinder to Frederick William II than most historians, and he dismisses Mirabeau's *Secret Letters from Berlin* as malevolent gossip. He recalls the Crown Prince's vigorous support of the Fürstenbund at the time of its formation, and approves the new King's military co-operation with England for the restoration of the rights of the Prince of Orange, son of an English princess and husband of his sister Wilhelmina. The defensive alliance to which it led is acclaimed as a bulwark against French influence in Holland and against the Emperor's preponderance in north-west Europe, where the possession of the Austrian Netherlands rendered him a dangerous neighbour. The curtain falls on the death-bed of the reforming but tactless Emperor, whose reckless schemes had kept Europe's nerves on edge. His brother Leopold, a wiser ruler though not a better man, only reigned for two years, but in that brief period the whole landscape had been changed by events in France. The dissolution of the Holy Roman Empire was in sight, yet not everything was to pass away. 'The forms of the Reich were utterly destroyed, but not the idea nor the spirit of a national union which was nourished by great memories. When the time came it arose in full power and opened new paths to a nation.'

The Origin and Outbreak of the Wars of the Revolution 1791–2, published in 1875, carries on the story of German policy with the aid of fresh material from the Vienna archives, including the despatches of the Austrian Minister in Berlin. The work, confessed the author, was imperfect, but he hoped it was above party and would therefore contribute to an agreed interpretation. Prussia had to think of Austria as much as of France, and her obvious course was to carry on the Frederician tradition by securing the Reich against Hapsburg ambition. The German system, with Prussia at its head, was conservative in character, based as it was on the authority of the leading princes. Security throughout Europe rested on the equilibrium among the Great Powers, and the prospects of Austro-Prussian co-operation were improved by the disappearance of Frederick the Great and Joseph II.

Freeing himself from the tutelage of Kaunitz, Leopold drew nearer to Berlin and Frederick William was not unfriendly to Vienna.

The two monarchs liked each other, and it is characteristic of the mildest of historians that he speaks with respect even of the worst of Prussia's kings. The need for co-operation in view of the danger from the French volcano was so clear that Kaunitz himself was converted, though neither partner wished the other to wax too powerful. Ranke believes that a conflict between the new France and the old Europe was inevitable, but he explains that the Revolution was not the only cause, since France in any case desired to recover her lost hegemony. To threaten vengeance before victory was madness, and the Brunswick Manifesto doomed the French monarchy. The invasion of France was merely the opening phase of the long struggle for hegemony which, in the historian's mistaken belief, was finally settled in 1870. Ranke, like Metternich, regarded the Revolutionary and Napoleonic era, not as the dawn of a new world, but as a regrettable break in the orderly development of Europe. Throughout modern history, indeed, France, as he saw it, had been the main disturber of the peace, wheras the task of Prussia, slowly climbing up the ladder from small beginnings, was to preserve or restore the equilibrium so often threatened or temporarily destroyed by her neighbour beyond the Rhine. Self-preservation, not unbridled aggression, had been the policy of her rulers, and after becoming strong enough to defend her possessions she had become a stabilising influence.

This thesis was soon to be worked out in the most important enterprise of the historian's closing years. When Hardenberg's papers were released half a century after his death in 1822 in accordance with his will, Bismarck summoned the Historiographer of Prussia to witness the breaking of the seals and invited him to act as editor. The material covered the critical years 1793–1813 when the old Prussia was struck down by Napoleon and under inspiring leadership rapidly rose again. While Stein and Humboldt have found admiring biographers, Hardenberg, the third of the illustrious triumvirate, has never tempted scholars and to this day no satisfactory biography exists. No attempt could be made till his papers became available, and Ranke's imposing memorial seems to have frightened lesser men away. Of the five stout volumes entitled *Denkwürdigkeiten des Staatskanzlers Fürsten von Hardenberg*, published in 1877, two contain the narrative of the Editor. The letter accompanying the presentation copy to Bismarck declared: 'Your Excellency will recognise him as in more than one respect your predecessor.' The whole complicated story of Prussian policy is built up around the personality of the statesman whose main decisions are fully approved. Ranke's contribution, without the documentary material but utilising the papers of Haugwitz and other sources, fills three volumes in the Collected Works entitled *Hardenberg and the History of the Prussian State, 1793–1813*.

The first volume opens with a sketch of the zealous official who learned his trade in Hanover and Brunswick, administered the Hohenzollern Duchies of Anspach and Bayreuth after the abdication of the childless Margrave, and entered the Prussian service in time to negotiate the Treaty of Basle in 1795. He had never approved the Austro-Prussian combination against France, preferring neutrality between revolutionary France and feudal Europe. By 1794, after two years of war without victory, Prussia had had enough of it. The only objection to quitting the coalition was that England and Austria wanted to go on. But what else could she do, exhausted as she was and on bad terms with Vienna which she believed to be playing for its own hand? Like his Ministers Frederick William II was torn between his craving for peace and his honourable dislike of abandoning his allies. What they all desired was a general settlement, but this was not to be had. In Ranke's opinion Austria should have made peace at the same time as Prussia, in which case better terms might have been secured.

Of the wisdom and necessity of Prussia's retirement from the conflict he is fully convinced. It was not really a dissolution of the partnership, he explains, for it had virtually ceased to exist. Moreover it was not in Prussia's interest to see the total overthrow of France, even if it were possible. There was no absolute antagonism between Paris and Berlin, and Prussia's task was to survive intact by preserving her neutrality between the opposing forces. Frederick William II, at first the most zealous of anti-revolutionary crusaders, found it painful to admit failure, but the cessation of British subsidies forced his hand. Other German rulers, among them Karl August of Weimar, also wished to withdraw, for nothing had been gained. To avoid turning allies into enemies required skilful steering, and it was the first of Hardenberg's major achievements to bring the ship safely through the shoals. At no period of Prussian history, declares Ranke categorically, was peace more necessary, and Hardenberg was the best man to negotiate. That Prince Henry of Prussia was also working for the same purpose was less help than hindrance, for the King hated the notion that he was guided by his uncle's advice. Ranke quotes with satisfaction the dying confession of the King to Haugwitz: 'I should never have undertaken the war against France. If you had only been at my side at that time! Happily we got off with a black eye.' His successor approved and continued the policy of neutrality. Though it is not strictly relevant to his argument, the historian reminds his readers that the decade of neutrality was the most fruitful in the whole course of German literature. In taking leave of Frederick William II he emphasises the personal element in his policy. For instance he was at first sympathetic to the Poles, but turned against them when he felt that he was not appreciated. 'He lived in great impulses which spurred him on to hasty and sometimes unco-ordinated decisions.'

The most important part of the work opens with the disastrous Jena campaign, for which Hardenberg had no responsibility. Haugwitz, the chief adviser of the Prussian kings during the decade of peace, was not the pilot to weather the storm. Captains of larger intelligence and stouter heart were needed, and after the Treaty of Tilsit Hardenberg was supreme with Stein for a brief period at his side. The facile formula that everything was rotten in the system is rejected. Prussia required a firm hand at the helm, drastic military reform, and the removal of the Cabinet Councillors Lombard and Beyme who were widely believed to have too much power. Hardenberg's Memorandum of September 1807 on the reorganisation of the Prussian state, drawn up by order of the King and filling a hundred printed pages, is by far the most important of the documents revealed in 1877; for it outlined the programme of reform from above which was to be carried out in the following years and which was succinctly described by a Minister as democratic principles in a monarchical regime.

Though the octogenarian scholar cannot compete with Treitschke's brilliant pageantry, his restrained narrative of the national effort is not unimpressive and his admiration for the architects of victory is unconcealed. Stein, recalled to office by Hardenberg's advice, had been attracted to the service of Prussia by the prestige of Frederick the Great. In character the two men were very different. Napoleon is believed to have chosen him as Hardenberg's successor, unaware of the similarity of their principles, though Hardenberg was always more concerned with foreign affairs while Stein stressed the urgency of internal reform. Hardenberg was by no means correct in his private life, while Stein held firmly to the faith and morals of his forebears. 'The culture of the century made little appeal to him. He was in a class by himself, deeply rooted in the past; his old-fashioned German style was rugged and noble. He was master of his work. Thoroughly practical, he always showed himself a man of ideas. Hardenberg also never lost sight of Germany as a whole, but Stein possessed an even more German heart.'

The tribute to Scharnhorst, 'a man of moral nobility and infinite talent,' is equally warm. Coming from humble circumstances and learning the soldier's trade in the Hanoverian army, he realised that republican France had much to teach his country. The Duke of Brunswick, who liked and admired him, brought him into the service of Prussia. 'More than anyone he combined theory and practice. Externals meant as little to him as traditional systems or the charlatanries of the hour. His desire was to teach, not to shine. Though his hope of an independent command was unfulfilled, he was in full agreement with the King, himself a soldier by profession. While Napoleon trusted in his luck, Frederick William III feared that he was born under an unlucky star; yet his spirit was never crushed and he was always filled with a proud bitterness. He never doubted that, in the course of the war or after the return of peace, Prussia would regain the military power on which alone the independence of the state could rest.' The monarch is rather a shadowy person in the company of his paladins and his adorable wife, but the publication of the Hardenberg papers and the comments of the editor enhanced his reputation.

When the story reaches the turning-point of the campaign Ranke salutes the Tsar with a cheer. To Alexander as to Metternich Napoleon had always meant much more than the latest exponent of French Imperialism; he was also, as the saying went, the Revolution on horseback. Compromise with such a man in 1814 or 1815 was impossible, and Prussia under the general direction of Hardenberg took the only course. His grateful master gave him the title of Prince, adding that his true reward was found in the events he had helped to shape. Ringing down the curtain to the sound of victory bells the historian returns to the illustrious partners who created the new Prussia. 'In Stein lived the impulse of original ideas and sentiments;

Hardenberg was more accessible to the general tendencies of the time, which in large measure corresponded to his temperament, his studies and his experiences. They agreed in their condemnation of the outworn machinery of the state. The first idea of a national representation undoubtedly came from Stein, but Hardenberg seized the moment at which it became a possibility and worked for it in face of violent resistance. They were equally eager to create a basis of national defence. Amid a welter of opinion Stein drew up the plans which Hardenberg later carried out.'

In regard to the new legislation no one can decide who had the greatest share. 'Hardenberg's programme of 1807 laid the foundations of everything, but in some of the most important transformations Stein had his part, and the first two decisive edicts were his work. He was a pious believer; Hardenberg's religiosity was more philosophic. Stein wished to support the Church; Hardenberg was more interested in the University. Stein's sympathies were more aristocratic, Hardenberg's more democratic; neither overlooked the welfare of the whole or the royal will. The most powerful impetus to a popular rising against Napoleon came from Stein. Hardenberg was not opposed to it, but he tried to moderate it in order to avoid a premature break with France and to disarm Napoleon's prejudice against him. It is relatively unimportant that he encouraged the Tsar to resistance, for no such encouragement was needed. Stein had undoubtedly suggested the idea of continuing his struggle with the help of the German nation. He had done more than any man to bring the Germans into the league, and he planned the first connection of a German population with the activities of Alexander. Hence arose logically the resolve to destroy the French Empire and the Emperor. A more magnificent enterprise could hardly be conceived, but without Hardenberg it would not have succeeded. The skill of a trained diplomat was needed to procure space for its realisation without incurring the hostility of the formidable antagonist till the hour arrived. Hardenberg only threw off the mask when the whole nation declared for the new system.

If posterity saw in Stein the greater of the two, that was because he kept less strictly to the usual ways and possessed a moral fervour which aroused reverence. There was something in him which marks the great man. That we cannot say of Hardenberg, yet he possessed the fervour of political ideas and all the toughness to realise them.

His greatest achievement was that at the fitting moment he revived and executed his old plan of a coalition against Napoleon. That was the condition of Prussia's recovery. From the point of view of the Prussian state his services are beyond praise. After the great struggle he devoted his whole energy to strengthen the unity of the reorganised state, embracing in his vision foreign and domestic, material and ideal interests. The chief work of his later years was the introduction of a uniform system of taxation. No statesman had ever engraved his name more deeply on the bronze tables of Prussian history.' In this lofty tribute Hardenberg at last received his due. If the historian's feeling for Prussia had been a little tepid in his early years, he made up for it in his old age. Only Treitschke was still dissatisfied. 'All so nicely polished and touched up and so thoroughly untrue!' he acidly remarked. Complete approval from the Prussian School could not be expected nor indeed desired.

Ranke's attitude towards events in nineteenth-century Germany is revealed in his contributions to the *Historisch-Politische Zeitschrift* which he edited 1832–6, in the political memoranda drawn up at the wish of Frederick William IV during the middle years of the reign, and in his edition of that romantic monarch's correspondence with Bunsen. The articles approved both the Balance of Power, established after Waterloo, and the *Rechtsstaat* then prevailing in Prussia, but they exerted no influence on events. With the accession of Frederick William IV in 1840 his position changed, for the two men, born in the same year, were old friends. The new ruler admired his books, and the ideal of 'the Christo-Germanic state' was cherished by both. Soon after his accession he asked Ranke's advice on the reform of the Estates and invited him to enter his service. The offer was declined, but the historian remained a member of the royal circle. For the first time in his life he came close to the heart of affairs, and during the Year of Revolution the King leaned heavily on him.

Both men realised that the old system of autocracy must go, and that the only choice was between constitutional government and the sovereignty of the people. Ranke advised the maximum retention of monarchical rule combined with concessions in outward form, in other words a Constitution and a Parliament, since people had come to think in constitutional terms and the South German states were used to limited monarchy. That Prussia had been efficiently ruled without a constitution was true enough, but he recognised the need to bring her into harmony with German opinion. Constitutionalism, he declared, must be regarded without love or hate, 'as a form of government in which men of to-day desire to live.' Prussia, however, should avoid foreign models, above all the principle of the sovereignty of the people, for monarchy was primordial. A middle course should be steered between autocracy and democracy. Universal suffrage was undesirable, 'for happily the masses have no real political interest, desiring as they do above all to improve and secure their position.' To the Frankfurt Parliament Ranke was mildly sympathetic. He had grown to realise the insufficiency of the Bund and the need for closer union, but he rejected the doctrine of popular sovereignty and the plan of a merely suspensive veto. He welcomed the idea of an Empire with a Prussian head as 'falling like a ray of light into the chaos,' and proposed the title of 'Emperor in the German Confederation.' As an old friend of Austria he envisaged a perpetual political and military union with the Bund in which she would no longer possess overriding authority.

All such paper schemes broke down on Austria's refusal to relax her grip, and the Bund lived on with diminished prestige. Her intransigence was too much even for Ranke, who wished Prussia to take the lead in a North German union. The Bund might continue if Austria did not attempt to dominate it; if she did, Prussia would have to fight. Soon after these resolute words were written she bowed to Austria's will at Olmütz. Ranke's final memorandum, drawn up while Prussia stood neutral in the Crimean war, deplored her position and expressed a doubt whether it could be improved with Austrian consent. Nothing, it was generally recognised, could be done while Frederick William IV was on the throne; but the crowding events of 1848–50 had shaken the historian out of the static mood of the Restoration era. Like so many of his countrymen he was being driven towards the Bismarckian solution.

In 1873, twelve years after the death of Frederick William IV, Ranke published his correspondence with Bunsen covering the years from 1830 to 1857, when the brain of the highly-strung monarch began to give way. The book is much more than a selection of letters, for the Editor's chapters amount to something like an outline of the reign. More than any of his later writings it was a labour of love, based on thirty years of affectionate intercourse. The widowed Queen Elizabeth, distressed by certain features of the biography of

Bunsen published in 1868, desired to exhibit her husband in a more favourable light and appealed for Ranke's help. Permission to publish selections from his brother's letters was obtained from the Emperor William, and after examination by the Foreign Office the work was authorised by Bismarck. Though it was too early for critical history, explained the Editor, few collections were so revealing and the King was an admirable letter-writer. 'I am happy to make the Fatherland and the world a present of high value.' Ranke was slightly less of a Conservative than the King and a good deal less of a Liberal than Bunsen, a friend of equally long standing. The book is an apologia for a monarch whose sterling qualities and essential wisdom had received too little recognition, but it is also a confession of the historian's faith. In championing the King's policy he is defending his own lifelong conviction that direction should always come from above.

The core of the book is the revolution of 1848. The King's idea was a federation, independent of but not hostile to Austria. 'The moment and its dangers seemed to whet his ambition. He was told that the whole history of Prussia pointed to leadership—he might see the ruling of Providence. He had a heart which beat for Germany, for he was his mother's son. He feared that Germany, wedged in between revolutionary France and autocratic Russia, would incur grave danger if she were divided and therefore unable to maintain her central European position. Moreover his soul was filled with the most vivid pictures of the glorious past. He thought it possible, not only to reshape Germany, but to restore the dignity of the Holy Roman Empire in the House of Austria which, thereby satisfied, would no longer interfere in purely German affairs. In this conception memories of the past blended with the desire to meet the needs of the moment. His ambition was to stand as German King at the side of the Emperor. It would have pleased him to be chosen in the traditional manner in the Church of St. Bartholomew by the Kings as Electors, and by the Princes with the approval of the Roman Emperor, with the acclamation of the people and crowned by the Archbishop of Magdeburg as Primate of Germany. He wished to revive the old Diet and the Colleges—Kings, Grand Dukes, Dukes, Princes (including the mediatised). The Cities were to be transformed into a Lower House, strengthened by Imperial Knights, representatives of the nobility and the villages. He resembled an architect who plans to restore a ruined castle but at the same time to make it habitable.' The executive, he believed, should be limited by a responsible Ministry, though a free hand was to be left to the King. Austria, he felt, could not be completely excluded, but Prussia should not feed out of her hand. The King should be hereditary commander of all military forces except those of Austria. 'In his soul the Prusso-German idea always prevailed over the predominance of Austria.' But his ideas were not understood and Prussians thought that he was letting the country down. When Bunsen, who was not Austrophil, urged him to become Emperor, he replied that he desired both to resist the revolution and to satisfy the nation. Since his idea of revolution included the acceptance of a crown from a Parliament which in his view had no right to offer it, nothing could be done. 'In his soul lodged all the sentiments for the creation of Germany which filled his contemporaries since 1806, but he felt that Austria had a right to the first place.' At the moment the question was academic, for in 1850 the Prussian army was incapable of imposing its will. But the humiliation of Olmütz rankled, and henceforth even Frederick William realised that Prussia could not be content with the second place in Germany. The main reason for his ineffectiveness was his attempt to combine incompatible ideals.

The concluding chapter is at once an eloquent tribute to a friend and a confession of the author's faith. 'He visualised the community of Christendom from a freer standpoint than the Pope, and regarded the Latin, Greek and Protestant Churches as equal members thereof. Himself deeply religious, he preferred the Evangelical Church as the purest embodiment of the might of the Creator. He warmly respected Quakers and felt no hatred for any Church, but he disliked the recent manifestations of Ultramontanism, particularly the cult of the Virgin. His political sentiment was rooted in the struggle against Napoleon, not merely as a person but as the embodiment of the revolutionary principle which, in destroying all historic institutions, opened the door to usurpation and violence. Legitimacy provided the rallying point for opposition. He felt it necessary to hold to the old institutions dating from the rise of the western states and capable of further development, above all the Reich, in which he believed even in its decline. His ideal was a united and armed Germany, with Prussia playing almost the leading part. He wished to retain the territorial *status quo* of 1815 and to preserve the Bund in agreement with the allied Powers and often in opposition to the revolutionary forces. Hardly had Napoleon gone when the tendencies he represented reappeared, fostered as they were by the faults of the Restoration. He strove to develop the old institutions in a way suitable to the demands of the time.'

Frederick William IV, in Ranke's opinion, could perhaps have made terms with the liberal ideas which entered Prussia in the Stein-Hardenberg reforms; but in their train came another movement—the radicalism and socialism which threatened to destroy the foundations of society and which rejected not only revelation but belief in God. 'To oppose this he regarded as his first duty, as Prince, Christian and man. He rejected the Liberal system because he could not discover any clear demarcation between the fundamental conception of the Liberal and the Radicals, in whose partnership he scented danger to the world of culture. While engaged in erecting a bulwark against these elements, he was surprised by them and was compelled to yield. March 18, 1848, was a dividing line of the reign, but he himself was unchanged; otherwise he would have copied the Belgian Constitution and accepted the ideas of the Frankfurt Parliament. That he did not follow this course can be regarded as the noblest or at any rate the most decisive action of his life. In both directions he upheld the individuality of the Prussian state. In the Constitution he preserved the nerve of the monarchical principle. In regard to the Reich he controlled his ambition and did not allow the secret wish of his heart to lead him astray by abandoning the principle he had inscribed on his banner. This required a man of ideals but also of austere character, flexible in detail, firm on the larger issues, steeped in the institutions and the life of the past. A conviction of such tenacity and depth was necessary to prevent the conservative principle, a legacy of a great past, from being destroyed.'

After this glowing tribute the historian gently indicates that it was not always easy to work with the crowned idealist. 'A gulf yawned between his ideas and their application in the radically changed situation, and his mind, striving in many directions, created new difficulty for the Government. He could never get on with the useful bureaucracy as he always wished to steer in a direction which was not theirs. This gave his reign a character of uncertainty. He inherited a system patriarchal indeed but rather anaemic and unduly authoriarian. Everything then changed and became charged with life and energy though not without deep inner conflicts. Yet the balance-sheet is decisively in his favour. The letters partially contradict the impression of feebleness and vacillation produced by the consideration of special events and prove his constancy of purpose. The existing situation (the Bismarckian system) was largely his creation. It was of immense importance that he combined the absolute monarchy which he inherited with the Estates and deliberative institutions. He could not fully realise his aim, for liberal and democratic ideas prevailed. His chief aim was to rescue the essential conditions of monarchy in the Constitution by making the financial existence of the state independent of the fluctuations of parties and preserving the royal authority over the army.' Four years later the historian paid a final tribute to his beloved King in the *Dictionary of German Biography*.[1] The lengthy article contained new material on his education and on his plans for constitutional reform before 1848. 'It was his strange fortune that his actions produced long range results without bringing him satisfaction. He was a man of wide vision. He combined remarkable flexibility in details with unyielding tenacity in essentials. Perhaps these qualities were needed to confront the revolutionary storms of his time without sacrificing the monarchy. Perhaps he had too much temperament for his position. His ideals clashed with reality, and there was something in his ways which provoked opposition.'

The personal devotion enshrined in the book commanded respect, but the portrait was generally considered too flattering. Treitschke pronounced Ranke too much of a courtier to tell the whole truth about great people. 'It is good that we have overcome Schlosser's didactic moralizing,' he wrote to Droysen, 'but with the latest fashion of so-called complete objectivity the real meaning of history and even its facts are lost. Ranke's unfortunate book on Frederick William IV shows clearly to what untruthfulness this objectivity leads.' He added that he had himself read many of the King's letters in the original and therefore could measure the extent of the omissions in the outpourings of 'this royal chatterbox.' The charges, so far as the Editor was confined, were unfounded. Ranke, unlike his critic, knew the king intimately and wrote, not as a courtier, but as a friend. Moreover he was not solely responsible for the omissions, for a work which was commissioned had to be approved. The two men belonged to different generations and approached the study of the past in a

[1] The article, combined with that on Frederick the Great, appeared as a small volume in 1878.

completely different spirit. 'I shudder when I see Ranke approach the most recent periods and now actually Prussia itself,' wrote Treitschke to Baumgarten in 1872. 'How bad is his book on 1780–1790, a dim, courtier-like whitewashing for which my dear Prussia is really too good. But of course my admiration for his masterly works on more distant epochs and foreign peoples is unaffected.'

Ranke, like Frederick William IV, was satisfied with the Bund before 1848 but not afterwards, when the rough hand of Schwarzenberg shattered the delicate system of parity. He supported Bismarck in his conflict with the Prussian Parliament over army reform, regarded the war with Austria as a regrettable necessity, welcomed the North German Confederation, applauded the annexation of Alsace-Lorraine, and approved the reconciliation with Austria in 1879. 'We agreed in our political views,' declared the Iron Chancellor after his death. This was saying too much, for Bismarck's ruthless methods repelled him, and he disapproved the annexation of Hanover and other states in 1866. Surgical operations were distasteful to the champion of continuity. Yet his attitude was widely different from that of Droysen and Treitschke, fiery trumpeters of a Prussian nation-state. With his usual habit of surveying events against a European background, he welcomed the Hohenzollern Empire above all as a bulwark against foreign foes, a duty which the Holy Roman Empire had been unable to discharge. 'Why is the Empire necessary?' he asked in a note written in 1872. 'It was formed in the struggle against France without our doing and it must be preserved. If South Germany had taken the French side, our position, since Austria and Italy were against us, would have been very difficult, perhaps impossible. A similar danger in future must be averted. People tell me that France is no longer to be feared and will be torn to pieces by civil war. I do not believe it, for beyond all their quarrels is the wish, the passion, for revenge, to which everything will give place. They are arming, and with the enemy in sight we cannot be too strong.' Though never a Francophobe, the long record of French aggression was always in his mind. The new German Empire was precisely what he had desired—neither military nor democratic, but federal, Protestant, tolerant, with the princely power and the army intact.

Another reason for his satisfaction emerges in the closing chapter of the final edition of the *History of the Popes*, published in 1878. Ranke, like Bismarck, had regarded the Vatican Council of 1870 and the Infallibility decree with profound misgiving, and a French victory, in his view, would have made things worse. 'Who can measure the result if the luck of arms had been with the Catholic nation or to what new preponderance of the Papacy it might have led? It turned out otherwise. A power (Prussia) which had developed in antagonism to the exclusive rule of the Papacy and now championed the German cause thereby secured an important share in the politico-religious movement of the world. A convinced Protestant would like to say that it was the divine decision against the Pope's claim to be the sole interpreter of faith.'

The ideas of the octogenarian had undergone little change since the far off days of the Luther Fragment and the *Reformation Era*. Gazing back over the course of German history, he found not 'Black Record' but grounds for gratitude and pride. Hurrah-Patriotism, as the phrase goes, repelled him. Yet none of his contemporaries had a deeper belief in the qualities and destiny of the German nation; few citizens of the modern age served it so faithfully and so well. His supreme achievement was to raise the whole standard of scholarship and to make the German school of history the first in the world. Impartial in the strict sense he never claimed to be, but he came nearer to Bacon's ideal of dry light than any historical writer of the first rank. 'It would be impossible to have no opinion in all the decisive struggles of power and ideas,' he wrote in his seventy-fifth year, 'yet the essence of impartiality can be preserved. For this simply means that one recognises the operative forces and keeps their relations in view. One sees them emerge, confront each other, and collide. In this antagonism events and tendencies work themselves out.' To this task of lucid and fair-minded interpretation the Goethe of history dedicated his matchless qualities for two generations. 'In early years,' wrote Treitschke to Erich Marcks in 1893, 'I detested his cold, anaemic way, and only later did I learn to admire his wisdom. I should be ashamed to have thought otherwise as a young man, and even to-day I learn gratefully from him without imitating him. If you compare my *German History* with my *Essays*, you cannot deny that I have drawn nearer to him.' Three years later the last and greatest of the Prussian School passed away, and the cry of Back to Ranke! resounded through the land. The Academy edition of his complete works commenced during the era of the Weimar Republic is the finest and fittest tribute to his incomparable achievement. He remains the master of us all, for the Prussian School is dead.

TREITSCHKE IN HIS CORRESPONDENCE

I

THOUGH Treitschke's *German History in the Nineteenth Century* is familiar to all serious students of the growth of modern Europe and has been admirably translated into English, one of the most striking personalities of his time is little known outside his country and his voluminous correspondence is scarcely known at all. No full-length biography has appeared. Schiemann's substantial monograph only comes down to 1866, when the historian was thirty-two, and Hausrath's little book is hardly more than a vivid sketch by a colleague of his Heidelberg days. Not till the appearance of the three stout volumes of his letters edited by Max Cornicelius (1912–20)[1] was it possible to know the whole man and to reconstruct the evolution of his political ideas. 'The Bismarck of the Chair' was a maker as well as a recorder of history, thirsting for action and only prevented from following his father into the army by the almost total deafness resulting from neglected measles at the age of twelve. Despite this cruel affliction he fought incessantly with pen and tongue—as historian, professor, journalist, editor, poet, Member of Parliament—for the cause which was dearer to him than life. Though his elder contemporaries Droysen and Sybel also combined politics with learning, the youngest and greatest member of the Prussian School exerted a far wider influence than any other academic figure of the Bismarckian age and was indeed the outstanding German publicist of his time. His statue at the entrance to the University of Berlin symbolises his unique contribution to the making of a nation-state.

Unlike General von Treitschke, who was fully content with the Deutscher Bund created in 1815 and unfailingly loyal to the royal family of his native Saxony, Heinrich rebelled against the political impotence of his countrymen as soon as he began to think for himself.

[1] Supplemented by *Briefe Heinrich von Treitschkes an Historiker und Politiker vom Oberrhein*, edited by W. Andreas, 1934. The best of many tributes is by Erich Marcks, *Heinrich von Treitschke, Ein Gedenkblatt*, 1900.

Why should there be an England, a France, a Spain, a Russia, but no Germany? That was the question asked by 'the Professors' Parliament' at Frankfurt in 1848. The resistance of Austria and the reluctance of Frederick William IV of Prussia, a believer in divine right, to accept the Imperial Crown from a popular assembly shattered the fair project of combining the closer unification of the German states with the introduction of constitutional government. When the Frankfurt Parliament assembled Treitschke was still at school, but he was old enough to know what was at stake and to regret the failure of the most promising effort of German liberalism. Though he was soon to drift far away from his early moorings, his formative years were passed under the banner of the Patriots of the *Paulskirche*.

The two strongest influences of his life were Dahlmann and Bismarck, though when he entered the Prussian University of Bonn in 1851 at the age of seventeen Prussia's superman was still waiting for his call. The veteran historian could look back on a long series of services to his countrymen in the academic and political field. He was one of the 'Göttingen Seven' dismissed from the University in 1837 for their protest against the overthrow of the Hanoverian constitution by the new king, Ernest Augustus, uncle of Queen Victoria. He had played a prominent part in the deliberations at Frankfurt and had sung the praises of limited monarchy in his book on the English Civil War. The man, however, was greater than any of his writings, and his personality left an abiding mark on the young student. 'His serious and rugged character,' reported Heinrich to his father, 'made the greatest impression on me. He has had many bitter experiences —hence his unsmiling way. And then his treatment of history: his clarity and power of speech; his total absence of empty phrases and pompous rhetoric; his talk flowing clear and unadorned, with now and again a striking passage which one can think about for hours! Old Arndt is the exact opposite, a friendly talkative veteran, lively and cheerful. When I entered he took my hand, did not at first ask my name, but at once began to talk about a thousand things with incredible rapidity. Yet his whole personality breathes such simplicity, such sincerity and such deep piety that it does one good to attend his lectures, not to learn anything, but to enjoy his youthful energy.'

Treitschke was already looking beyond the lecture room to the wider issues of European politics. 'Among us students there is no sign of radicalism,' he reported to his father. 'In the whole Rhineland there is not a radical paper. The French sympathies of which the *Kreuzzeitung* is always speaking are a pure invention. True, the Government has few supporters. The *Kölnische Zeitung* is read everywhere and most of our professors agree with it, though they never mention politics in their lectures. Only old Arndt cannot leave them alone. Recently he said: "The Hapsburgs wish to mix their dirty Slav mess with our clean German water. That is pure selfishness, for they don't care a fig for Germany." ' At this stage Treitschke himself cared much more for Germany than for Prussia, which since her capitulation at Olmütz in 1850 was little more than a satellite of Austria. He found relief in reading Pertz' gigantic *Life of Stein*, then in process of publication. 'I cannot say how the study of this strong man delights and elevates me,' he wrote to his father in 1852; 'I find in all great men of action the same noble modesty, the same striving after duty alone, without the least suggestion that they are doing anything unusual.'

Treitschke's budding patriotism and the urge to write found their earliest expression in poems collected in two small volumes in 1856 and 1858. ' I have shown them to a few friends, who liked them,' he reported. 'I wrote only because my heart was full and I could no longer contain myself. Professor Simrock says there was still much exuberance in them, but also much talent.' The author appreciated good poetry too much to exaggerate the merits of his own. 'I have found a publisher,' he reported in February 1856. 'The poems were composed at various times, some in Bonn, and only worked up into a whole in the summer. They are intended as a poetical expression of the sentiments which crowd on a good German in our present unspeakable circumstances, especially when he seeks comfort in our history. Of ten "patriotic" poets nine do not count. Kleist stands out —his *Hermannsschlacht* is the most magnificent glorification of patriotic hatred; even Schiller has not written better in freedom's cause. I am not satisfied with my performance, but it is good to begin my literary career with these patriotic verses. Every word that reminds us of our disgrace is blessed. If they find a welcome among the readers for whom they are chiefly designed, namely the young men, I will gladly accept every merited criticism.' In presenting a copy of the *Vaterländische Gedichte* to his father he explains their purpose. 'You know most of them already and their tendency. But I fear, when you see the whole collection, much will surprise you and clash with your views. Germany is powerless and is the contempt of foreigners. Almost everywhere reigns a terrifying silence about the holiest affairs of our people.' The author was a poet with a purpose, hardly a poet in his own right, and before he was twenty-five he realised that prose was his best medium.

The historian always looked back to the years at Bonn as the happiest period of his life. Never again was he so carefree, for with every succeeding month he became increasingly obsessed by his country's plight. Prussia alone, he felt, could help, yet under the nerveless sway of Frederick William IV and his reactionary advisers she seemed unconscious of her mission. 'Whether it will be possible for the fate of our Fatherland to be changed by legal methods,' he wrote from Göttingen in January 1856, 'becomes ever more problematical. When I reflect that present German conditions cannot last because they are in ludicrous contrast to the needs of our people, and when I also reflect that the measure of illegalities is now practically full and can only be surpassed by bloodshed, who can be so blind as to believe in a peaceful solution? Perhaps I regard these questions more seriously than other people. The difference from my father in political matters, and the grief it causes, makes me take them very seriously indeed. My conviction that we are living in a period of transition remains, but it is an effort not to quarrel with fate that I have to live in such a time. So far as my historical knowledge extends, I find no example of lying and wrong so shamelessly enthroned. Injustices doubtless occur under every government; that they are not excused or disowned by authority but rather praised as statecraft is a sacrilege which the Manteuffel Ministry has invented. And Prussia has lost her place among the Great Powers. Under these circumstances will she ever regain it? I have a lofty conception of her vitality, but it is not the first time that a healthy stock would have been destroyed by the consistent madness of its pilots. The element on which the restoration of a decrepit state must always be based, the *morale* of the people, is being successfully undermined. That the state will never absorb all the forces of the people is guaranteed by our whole history; the opposite danger is much greater. We have come to regard the state as a burden, even as an immorality; no honourable man willingly and without conscientious scruples enters its service.' The sentiment of frustration and exasperation generated in these impressionable years left abiding traces on Treitschke's political teaching and coloured his verdict of Frederick William IV nearly forty years later in the fifth volume of his *German History*. Though he still regarded himself as a liberal of the Dahlmann school, he had become a Bismarckian before Bismarck. Weakness, he felt, was the unpardonable political sin, for without a strong hand at the helm no people could call its soul its own.

A new era dawned when the mentally afflicted King of Prussia handed over the reins in 1858 to his brother, Prince William, who functioned as Regent till the death of the royal sufferer in 1861. Here was the first ray of sunshine in a dark sky, for the new ruler was a soldier, not a *dilettante*, a realist, not a dreamer. But would he take the lead which was required if Germany was to become a nation-state? Would he have strength and courage to stand up to Austria and to put the minor German rulers in their place? After studying at various universities, and after earning his doctorate with a work on *Society and the State*, Treitschke started his academic career as *Privat Dozent* at Leipzig in 1859. Returning to Saxony as a man of twenty-five, he made no attempt to conceal his contempt for the little states, including his own, which, no less than Austria, seemed to block the road to a healthy national life. His attitude nearly broke his father's heart, though each recognised and respected the other's sincerity.

'I believe that no state ever pursued a more loyal or less selfish policy than Prussia under the Regent,' he wrote in July 1859 to a friend, 'but never was the danger greater that, as the old saying goes, the man of honour has the worst of it. But now the moment has come to show that the government is German. A reform of the Federal Constitution must be proposed by Prussia at Frankfurt; if it fails, as is probable, there must be an appeal to the German people, a German Parliament. The strong will of the noble man in Berlin, to whom millions of Germans like myself look with confidence, may struggle against it, but without this revolutionary course—which is not really revolutionary, for it rests on the unforgotten claim of the Prussian crown—Prussia is lost. The decisive step must be taken this summer before the despots in the south and west (Austria and France), and perhaps also in the East, have time to turn their crushing superiority against us. And then? Well, Germany will again, like two centuries ago, bleed for the liberty of the whole continent, though with a strong

Prussia at the head we shall make a better settlement than the unhappy Peace of Westphalia. Believe me, I know a good deal about the sentiments of influential circles in Austria's vassal states; the downfall of Prussia was never so firmly resolved as now. I cannot act as a publicist in this matter; I do not know enough. I beg you to write a pamphlet entitled *A German Parliament*. Gloss over nothing; speak out on the disgust and anger at Germany's misery which is breaking our hearts.' In the words of Erich Marcks there was something of the fire of a Hussite preacher in this descendant of the Protestant family which had left Bohemia after the Battle of the White Mountain.

What Germans needed above all was political education and administrative experience, such as Englishmen had long possessed. 'I do not advise you to read the thousand pages of Gneist on English self-government,' he wrote to a friend in 1860, 'but I believe that a lasting improvement of the German state will not be reached till the political ideas of this book become common property. The daily discharge of serious political duties in county and parish seems to me the only thing which binds our educated classes to the state, the only thing which can in some degree make up for the civic instinct of the classical world. The difficult book is after my own heart. The systematic alienation of our best brains from political activity always seemed to me unnatural, and I could never understand why an independent political judgment is only attributed to people who take no practical part in the state.' Yet in the English nation he missed as much as he found. 'You seem to think,' he wrote to his father in February 1860, 'that I share the fashionable Anglophobia. I am sorry. I feel that England is faced by a terribly grave crisis, yet when we think of our own future we have very little reason to look down on her. I should be destitute of all sense of human greatness if I did not admire this powerful nation. But I feel that a large sphere of culture is for ever closed to them; Plato and Kant have always been mere names. If you read Macaulay's essay on Bacon you will understand my meaning. The heroism of thought (not of will) is only understood by the Greeks and the Germans. This lack in English culture strikes me particularly in their recent literature.' Treitschke never seriously studied English history. His admiration was always reluctant and waned rapidly with advancing years.

While Prussia seemed to be marking time he found consolation in reflecting on the solid qualities of his countrymen and combated disparaging comparisons with other lands. 'You do our people an injustice if you put us below the Italians,' he wrote from Leipzig in February 1860. 'Our moral standard, our popular education, our sound economy—all that stands high above every other European people. If there is a God in heaven, this precious material will find some powerful political embodiment. The detachment from genuine political education is not so great as you think. Remember one undeniable fact: eighteen million Germans, old and young, democrats and conservatives, live in the conviction that their state—Prussia—is destined to become Germany. Except for a few thousand Ultramontanes and even fewer extreme Junkers, her calling is no longer a subject of dispute in Prussia. Not that the Prussian stock is better than ours, but a living political consciousness only develops in a real state. And outside Prussia? Think how Italy suffered under foreign rule and how political life had to take refuge in secret societies. We have in our small states a thoroughly immoral regime, but there is no foreign yoke. Our self-government in the parishes, limited though it be, gives the city-dwellers and the peasants the opportunity to share in public life. I hope to see the day when Kaiser Wilhelm I takes over here. It is a lofty goal, and even a generation of hard struggles would not be too high a price to pay.'

That Treitschke's class-room was fuller than that of any other *Privat Dozent* at Leipzig was a satisfaction to one of the most brilliant lecturers of his time, but his heart was in politics and all his writings had a practical aim. In the newly founded *Preussische Jahrbücher* he found an organ eager for his articles, and his reputation as a publicist was quickly made. It was during the Leipzig years that he planned the pattern of his life. Beginning with historical essays and articles on current affairs, he would devote his mature powers to describing the life of modern Germany, teaching his readers to share his devotion to what he regarded as the noblest community in the world. It was a consolation that his greatest friend at Leipzig, Gustav Freytag, novelist, dramatist, historian and journalist, shared his belief in Prussia and his fervent admiration for the German race.

To a man of Treitschke's ideology the atmosphere of Saxony was stifling and academic promotion was barred. 'You ask about my prospects of a chair,' he wrote to Haym in April 1860. 'Here I shall get neither a chair (for which I am much too young and unlearned) nor any lower post. A course on Prussian history is regarded as something like treason. If you knew our position you would have to listen day by day to the most shameless lies about Prussia from official pens. You would understand that here every honourable German is utterly devoted to Prussia and looks anxiously at the clouds which for the moment veil her star. My hopes rest entirely on the good conscience of the German people, which, in the event of a real danger for Prussia and Germany, would, I hope, nay I am sure, prove stronger than respect for the dynasties and the serried ranks of the bureaucracy of the little states.'

In Treitschke's eyes the trouble came from rulers and officials. 'We poor middle-staters feel the German misery much more directly than you,' he wrote in April 1861. 'We know so well how measureless is the hatred and fear of Prussia in the small courts. That is why we demand an iron policy; the overthrow of the illegitimate Diet is in my eyes Prussia's chief task.' A visit to Munich in 1861 strengthened his conviction that the common man in South Germany was sound at heart. 'In all my German wanderings my deepest thought has always been what monstrous *fables convenues* and hateful lies estrange the German stocks or whatever one calls them. I see for Germany only one solution: a single indivisible monarchy. All the talk of a federation of monarchies strikes me as a contradiction in terms, and any idea of a republic is folly. Prussia has no choice; she must conquer with the aid of the German people. The crisis in Prussia must eventually come to a wholesome outbreak. I hope the people will do its duty and choose as democratic a Chamber as possible. The time is ripe for a decisive break with Junkerism. Here is the Achilles' heel of the north, as is Ultramontanism of the south. Such a bold stroke would take us halfway along the road to the German crown, for the feeling of our disgrace is too universal. Only one thing prevents the majority saying: We wish to be merged in Prussia—the knowledge that as regards the aristocracy and the military caste spirit Prussia is worse than most other German states. Here in Bavaria, of course, there are stronger obstacles to a national policy. Not only do the parsons rage and foolish prejudices against Berlin are rampant; here for the first time I find a naïve particularism which no longer exists in Swabia. Yet I think this corner of German soil will not oppose the course of events if the bullets begin to fly. I am sure this development will occur, perhaps sooner than we expect.'

The young publicist never ceased to proclaim that, if his head was Prussian, his heart was beating for the whole Fatherland. 'You must at last cease to regard me as pure North German,' he wrote in March 1862. 'In these Saxon-Bohemian mountains never since my childhood have I known whether I belong to north or south. I am just German, especially when I sharply rebuke the low Bavarian particularism. For that reason I am a radical unitarian. If the Prussian people in the next elections courageously exercises its rights, that would help more than anything to dissipate the prejudice of the south.' Prussia's unpopularity, he believed, was due above all to the fact that she lacked liberal institutions. 'Anyone who, like me, has witnessed the stateless existence of the five middle states all these years must envy you Prussians that you have a state. I never thought unity would come to us through Parliament; no, only by Prussia's sword. Yet there is no simpler method of smoothing out the childish tribal prejudices than co-operation in Parliament. I love my fair native land and the inexhaustible vitality of its much misunderstood stock, but for the rotten state I have nothing but honest hatred.'

Bismarck's appointment in 1862 seemed to Treitschke a step backwards, since he embodied the tradition of the detested Junker caste. 'You know how passionately I love Prussia, but when I hear such a shallow Junker as this Bismarck boast of the "Blood and Iron" with which he will subdue Germany, the vulgarity is only exceeded by its absurdity. That the astonishing determination of the Prussian people will and must obtain victory in a few years I do not doubt. Yet unhappily a few years of delay may have the gravest consequences in this fast-moving time, especially as Germany's most dangerous enemy to-day, that crafty Schmerling, is laying his mines. We are supposed to rejoice that the Germans become conscious of their unity in personal contacts and congresses, but so long as an integrated Reich does not confront the Austrians such comradeship with that cunning race is very dangerous. The verbal dust which the Austrian so cleverly raises intoxicates the easy-going German, and people think that the national task is accomplished with a few high-sounding speeches.' Yet now, as so often before and after, he, like Droysen, found consolation in the thought of Prussia's manifest destiny. 'I do not think her position is quite hopeless, however disgusting the utter frivolity at the steering-wheel. People begin to feel that she is the first German state, not only for her power but for her people; and I foresee the time when

Prussians will look back with pride on this twenty years' struggle which no other German stock has attempted.'

In default of a call to some Prussian university Treitschke welcomed an invitation to Freiburg, not least because it would ease the friction with his father. Baden, like Saxony, was *in partibus infidelium*, but 'the enmity of the Ultramontanes in Freiburg is no worse than the vulgarity of the Saxons in Leipzig.' Moreover, there was a significant difference between the two states. In Saxony Beust, the leading Minister, was as Austrophil as King John himself. In Baden the Grand Duke Frederick, son-in-law of King William of Prussia, was on the throne, and among his Ministers were avowed Prussophils such as Roggenbach and Mathy. The next three years were to be a testing time, but Treitschke had a freer hand on the Upper Rhine than on his native heath. Meanwhile his reputation as lecturer and publicist was growing rapidly, and his arresting personality compelled the Badeners to ponder the grave problems which filled his ardent mind. His happy marriage to Emma von Bodmann forged a new link with the south, though without weakening his conviction that the unity of Germany under Prussian leadership should and would be achieved by the sword.

II

THE death of Frederick VII of Denmark in 1863 opened up far-ranging possibilities, at first only visible to Bismarck's piercing eyes. Treitschke had not yet taken the measure of the new Minister and he continued to groan over the impotence of the Bund. 'Only a fool can expect anything except disgrace for Germany. So long as Austria rules over us we shall do our duty and write and speak till we are tired, but at present without hope. One day we shall cast off this drowsy laziness, but perhaps not for a generation.' At the opening of 1864 he saw little prospect of improvement. 'At a time when only two of the thirty minor States are deserving of honour, I feel as if I am the only sane person in a crowd of lunatics. You know my arch Prussianism, and in Freiburg it grows daily, as I find that in all the denunciation of Bismarck there is nothing but the lowest Prussophobia. It is good that the world sees that the Prussians have the best army in Germany; but, blind as is my love for Prussia, I do not wear rose-coloured spectacles. Would to God that Schleswig-Holstein were to become

Prussian, as the Philistines here are bleating. I see little such prospect, and even if it occurs it would be bought by suicidal concessions to Austria, from which heaven preserve us. But perhaps it is good for the easy-going Germans that the importance of might in politics is for once mercilessly displayed. The day is coming when the two natural allies, the Prussian State and the German people, will find each other.'

With the outbreak of war in the spring of 1864 and the storming of the Danish defences at Düppel a new chapter in European history dawned. 'At last, at last,' he wrote to Hirzel, his publisher, 'something real and decent in this immense whirling of the winds! I rejoiced like a child. Every foot of earth that has been won for Germany in the last two hundred years has been conquered by Prussia. The history of such a State cannot end in vile nonsense. I shall be happy if I see a Prussian Germany when my hair is grey, but that a happier generation will reach this goal I am convinced.' It was an unequal struggle and the fight was soon over. 'The two lands (Schleswig and Holstein) are German again,' he wrote in high spirits to his father; 'that is the greatest success of our foreign policy for fifty years. We have every reason to rejoice; all other questions are secondary.' Though Denmark had been defeated by the combined forces of Austria and Prussia, the latter had made the larger contribution to victory. The ultimate fate of the provinces was still obscure, but Treitschke's confidence in Bismarck was growing. Perhaps after all he might not have to wait for a united Germany till his hair was grey.

It was at this moment, in his thirtieth year, that the first volume of his essays appeared. The time was well chosen, for the Prussophil Saxon felt that he was no longer a voice crying in the wilderness. The presentation copy to his father was accompanied by a letter which does honour to both. 'Herewith the book, with some trepidation. You are the only person whose opposition really pains me. You know my views and I cannot thank you enough for your unvarying kindness in spite of them. These I could not change, for a man of honour naturally proclaims his opinion. But I realise that a book is different from a letter, and I fear it will hurt you, especially the essays on Wangenheim and the Bundesstaat. I can only beg you to believe that in all human relations you will find in me an obedient son. In matters of conviction other duties apply. Anyhow you will discover that I have reasons, many of them, and carefully considered, for my view.

I do not covet the reputation of being called impartial by opponents —that is asking the impossible. A historian in unsettled times is only called impartial after his death. That anaemic objectivity which does not say on which side the narrator stands is the exact opposite of the true historical sense. All great historians have openly revealed their attitude. Thucydides is Athenian, Tacitus an aristocrat. The historian should present his material as completely as possible, but the author, like the reader, is free to pass judgment. That I have done so far as my knowledge allows. German historiography is marked by a high standard of truthfulness, and I thank the gods that something of that spirit has passed into my blood. The French hardly know what it means, and the English are more partisan than we. Macaulay surveys history as a Whig, Hume as a Tory. Real falsification is recently found only in the Austrian camp; when Onno Klopp praises the Walloon Tilly as a German patriot and a friend of religious liberty, that is the limit. Like his *confrères* Hurter and Gfrörer, he quite logically became a Catholic. For myself I intend to remain a German and a Protestant, and I will never praise the un-German Catholic despotism of the House of Austria.' Every essay was a confession of faith, a trumpet call, an act. 'Love of the Fatherland is not just a fine word but a holy passion, the only thing which enriches and ennobles life. We Germans are a great people, and we are honestly striving to cast off the errors which the misfortunes of centuries have taught us. It will be long before more pride, more fiery passion, flows in our veins, but our sons will witness the respect of Germany by other nations.'

After the Schleswig-Holstein war Treitschke's denunciation of the Bund rose to a scream. 'The more I think of it, the more intolerable does the world of *fables convenues* of the theory and practice of our federal constitution become,' he wrote to Mohl in November 1864. 'I resolved for once to fight without gloves. Liberal particularism will be the leading party in the immediate future. I regard it as the most dangerous foe of the Fatherland, so I decided to oppose it with all my strength and to come out clearly for the unitary idea. I am not so unwise as to prophesy about these infinitely difficult matters; a federation of monarchies is not absolutely impossible. But I believe that our nation in its striving for unity will obtain nothing till it decides to stake everything. You will not think me foolish enough to believe that these questions can be solved in two years. I am well aware that we shall need to exert our best energies for years to organise the States satisfactorily. My patriotism is perhaps rather warmer than is usual in our climate.'

Treitschke never flinched from the grim arbitrament of the sword. 'My father sees in Prussia simply the deadly enemy, and millions of South Germans share his view. These things are sad beyond words. Whoever knows the South despairs of a peaceful solution of the German problem. The eagles of Hohenfriedberg and Leuthen must fly again, and I shall thank heaven if I live to see this inescapable civil war. Meanwhile it is a relief to have given vent to my convictions in a book.' None of the smaller States aroused such indignation and contempt as his own. 'You know from experience,' he wrote to Mommsen, 'that Saxon air fills everyone who is not a weakling with disgust. Anyone who like myself could observe the sentiments of the Saxon Court at close quarters must become a unionist. You in the North have no notion of the feeling in the South. Even sensible people here talk about Prussia like the Confederates about the Yankee. Only under discipline of a real State will these excellent stocks become Germans in the full sense of the word.' He was doubtful if the history of Germany, unlike Switzerland and America, pointed to federation. 'If we ever have a federal constitution, it will not last long.' So obsessed was he with the impotence of the structure created in 1815 that he anticipated a certain weakness even from a federation such as Bismarck was soon to create. Power, he was convinced, must be concentrated, not diffused.

He seized the occasion of the Schleswig-Holstein war to elaborate his ideas in the treatise entitled *Bundesstaat und Einheitsstaat* (*Federation or Unitary State*) which fills 160 closely printed pages in the second volume of his *Historical and Political Essays*—the first of the two large-scale expositions of his deepest thoughts. Germany under the Bund, he lamented, was merely a geographical expression, a federation of princes, not of peoples; purely dynastic unions were always weak, and the sovereignty of the princes must go. Tinkering with the constitution was useless; Germany needed a complete break with the past. The novelty of his message was that, while many Germans desired to see the federal system tightened up, he had no use for it in any form. He would, of course, prefer a *Bundesstaat* to a *Staatenbund*, but an *Einheitsstaat* would be better still. Federations could not work unless their units were closely bound by common memories, common sympathies, common interests. Between the members of the Bund such cohesion had never existed and could not exist. Austria, an un-German State pursuing an un-German policy, had no conception of German needs and was an irreconcilable enemy. The German princes were little better, for they blocked the road to a healthy national life. Even if Austria were to be eliminated a federation would be unworkable, for the successful functioning of such a system postulated something like equality of size or strength among the members. Moreover federations, through the stress of practical needs, tended to grow into unitary States. There was only one solution—the hegemony of Prussia, 'the greatest political achievement of our people.' She alone of German States could maintain and defend herself: authority and responsibility should go with power. Moreover, only a united Germany could deal with such undesirable elements as the Junkers and the Ultramontanes. And just think what Prussia had done for the German race! As Frederick William III had remarked, 'What Prussia had obtained is won for Germany.' Written and published before Bismarck had shown his hand, this eloquent manifesto enrols the young historian among the founders of the German Empire.

At the opening of 1865, when the Danish duchies had been divided between Austria and Prussia, Treitschke defined his changing attitude towards Bismarck in a letter to Freytag. 'If I have to choose I shall side with Bismarck, since he fights for Prussia's power, for our rightful position in the North Sea and the Baltic. An admirer I am not and shall not become, though I rate him higher than you seem to do. I feel it a duty to support his foreign policy; it operates partly with discreditable means, but if it fails we are in for a second Olmütz, a triumph for all the foes of the Fatherland. Alas! I cannot share your hope that a liberal Prussian regime can unify Germany in ten years. I have lived six years in the South and reached the melancholy conclusion that, even if a Cabinet of Steins and Humboldts held office in Berlin, the hatred and envy of the southern States would not wane.'

In the same month an article on Schleswig-Holstein in the *Preussische Jahrbücher* raised the Prussian banner aloft. 'The most important advance towards German unity in the last two centuries is the growth of Prussia to the status of a Great Power, and she has grafted decrepit States on to her strong body. To increase the power of this State is in my view the first duty of a German patriot.' Writing in the autumn of the same year he explained that his attitude was unchanged. In 1860 he had described himself as a democrat, and in 1862 he spoke of 'we liberals.' He was still enough of a liberal to dislike the raising of taxes without the consent of the Prussian Parliament, all the more because he was unaware of the Minister's plan for a trial of strength with Austria. 'A fine letter from Freytag has stirred me deeply. My poor friend, with his noble highly strung temperament, cannot reconcile himself to Bismarck's vindictive policy. I confess I am of coarser material. I agree with all he says about the dishonesty of Prussian policy. But compared with the intrigues of the Dresden and Munich courts, the unscrupulous demagogues who in the service of the Augustenburg prince destroy a fine people, and the mindless talk of the Nationalverein, his policy seems to be not only rational but ethical. It aims at what we lack and is a step forward towards the lofty goal of German unity; anyone who is a man should help. To misuse the great words Right and Self-determination is an old trick of evildoers. Even if they denounce us as unscrupulous and foolish, the good cause will triumph, the heirs of Frederick the Great will rule in Schleswig-Holstein, and the nation will soon feel ashamed of its present folly. I need all my self-control not to despair of this people. What a spectacle we present to the world! What disputation, hatred, envy and frothy rhetoric are festering in Germany!' The patriot in him, he confessed, was a thousand times stronger than the professor.

While he was learning to trust Bismarck's foreign policy, little though he guessed his far-reaching aims, the Minister had begun to value approval from the *Preussische Jahrbücher*. The guns of Sadowa were to bring the National Liberal professors trooping into the Government camp; but at this early stage support from the academic world was scanty, and the fact that Treitschke was a Saxon and passed as a Liberal enhanced his significance. The first contact occurred when the Prussian Minister in Baden informed the young publicist that Bismarck was delighted with his Schleswig-Holstein heresies. Among them was the demand that the Augustenburg claimant, whom Bismarck appeared to champion, should be dropped, and that both duchies should be annexed by Prussia. That was precisely the Minister's programme, though the time to proclaim it had not arrived. Moreover, public opinion, to say nothing of the King, had to be trained to the notion of a conflict with Austria, and for this purpose the pen of an independent scholar was a weapon not to be despised.

Treitschke's first letter to the man whom he had described three years earlier as 'that shallow Junker' was dated December 10, 1865. The appeal for facilities in compiling his *German History* combined a personal request with a confession of faith. Roggenbach, he began, had allowed him to use the Baden archives at Carlsruhe, which, in the main, reflected Austrian views. 'It is my duty as a historian to hear the other side and to learn about Prussia's policy from the best sources. The archives of the small courts are doubtless closed to me. The only governments of which I have any hopes are Berlin and Florence. Professor Pauli tells me of your ready permission to him to use the English material, and this emboldens me to ask for an even greater privilege. I am Liberal and my book will naturally bear this stamp. But I believe I have given proof of my endeavour to free myself from the prejudices of my party, and the Prussian State and its right of self-preservation is for me above party interest. My request presupposes a high degree of confidence. An applicant whom you do not know has no claim to this. I can only promise that I will tell the truth as I find it, and will not misuse the Berlin documents to Prussia's disadvantage. But this assurance, I hope, is unnecessary; for after the visit of Count von Flemming last spring I must assume that Your Excellency has heard of my writings and does not regard me as an enemy of Prussia. I believe she has less cause to conceal her policy in the Bund than any other German Government; for, whatever the sins of Berlin, all real and lasting results of our national policy in the last fifty years are her work. Almost every Prussian document which I discovered in Carlsruhe has strengthened my conviction that the usual verdicts on the Bund policy of the last two Prussian Kings are false. They were formed in the days of the supremacy of Rotteck and Welcker, when Liberalism and Prussophobia were synonymous. The series[1] is widely read. So I think it is not without importance if the volumes on the Bund rest on authentic material and thus contribute to dispel a mass of traditional prejudices. Your support of a work which has occupied and will occupy me for years will be most gratefully received.'

Bismarck replied in a letter in his own hand dated December 16, 1865, that Treitschke might use the archives of the Prussian Foreign

[1] In which the *German History* was to appear.

Office subject to the usual condition that his excerpts must be approved. 'But this does not mean that you need fear you will be deprived of the fruit of your labours. For if you find our old linen not so clean as I should like, I do not believe you would have to withdraw the assertion that Prussia of all States has the least reason to conceal her policy in the Bund. In any case I have no faith in the importance of documentary secrets of a period anterior to that of the present rulers, and I am sure that even the failings of our earlier policy as presented by your impartial pen will not appear worse than the average of German officialdom. You are quite right in saying that only acquaintance with the documents enables one to understand how much friction has to be overcome with us before enough power is available for practical use.'

Treitschke was delighted. 'Bismarck's answer,' he reported to his father, 'is not only clever and friendly, but also removes my anxiety. I feared the people in Berlin would try to secure me for the ministerial party, and this, since I could not have agreed, would have put me in an awkward position.' The exchange was followed by a meeting in Berlin in March 1866, described in a letter to Hirzel. 'Personally Bismarck made a very agreeable impression on me; politically all the worse. He talked much of his plans for federal reform, so that I could hardly control myself in astonishment at these fantastic follies. Yet I do not for that reason despair about the Schleswig-Holstein affair, tactician as he is. On the subject of war he spoke very moderately and sensibly; he does not want it, but he believes he can carry it through in case of need and quite realises that after all that has happened annexation is a matter of honour. Berlin pleases me more than ever; at every step one senses a great future. If one could only live a hundred years and see the Prussia of the future!'

That the visitor made a favourable impression was shown by an invitation a few weeks later when the Prussian Minister in Karlsruhe sounded him about moving to Berlin. He can hardly have been surprised and he was ready with his reply. 'The great majority of Germans are liberal first and national second. Therefore without a different system in internal affairs the best Prussian plans for the reform of the Bund will lack the necessary backing in the nation. If it comes to war and a German policy in the grand style, these objections of course fade into the background. Then the first duty would be to maintain Prussia's just cause with sword and pen against Austria and the small fry. I should feel happy to take a modest part in this work; but I beg Your Excellency to remember that my independence is my most precious possession and that I cannot sacrifice it.'

To Bismarck himself he explained his difficulties at greater length. 'Your Excellency did me the honour to ask if I could come to Berlin. I feel I must add a few lines to the hasty answer I gave Count von Flemming, and I beg Your Excellency to pardon a few remarks on the political scene. The formal objections to a visit to Berlin are not irremovable. If I thought that my presence would not be quite useless, I should feel it my duty to resign my post as professor. But there is an objection of substance. The Government's course till now has not led me to hope that I could serve it, and I cannot at present feel sure of the success of federal reform. How I view the situation, and whether my views can be in some degree reconciled with those of the Government, Your Excellency will see from an article in the *Preussische Jahrbücher*. Its object was to win over some Liberals who are not hopelessly blinded; so I had to weigh my words about the *Fortschrittspartei* and to hide my utter contempt for these fanatics. I consider the unconditional recognition of the rights of the Deputies in regard to the Budget an absolute necessity: no scheming will ever create a Prussian Diet which surrenders this right. Forgive me for saying that this question of law and liberty can easily become absolutely vital for Prussia. The Berlin Cabinet is aware of the unworthy sentiments of several South German courts. What hinders them from marching with flying colours into the Austrian camp is only the instinctive timidity of minor States and the uncertainty as to the feeling of their own people, who waver between Prussophobia and a vague craving for a Parliament. If we lose the first battle—which I do not expect but cannot exclude—and if at that time the conflict in Prussia is not settled, the malice of the little courts, the radicalism, and the powerful Austrian party in South Germany, would probably outweigh all counter-efforts of well-intentioned patriots and the South would unite with Austria. It is horrible that the greatest Foreign Minister Prussia has had for decades is also the best-hated man in Germany. It is even sadder that the best federal reform ideas which a Prussian Government has ever suggested have been received in the nation with such disgraceful indifference. But this fanatical liberalism exists and cannot be ignored. Even after a victory of our arms, if the internal conflict is not settled, the ineradicable mistrust of the Liberals will cause the greatest difficulty in the plans of federal reform. Your Excellency has been almost miraculously preserved for our land.[1] May you contrive to restore the internal peace which is essential for the success of your great national plans. So long as I live outside Prussia my task as a publicist is easy. Directly I connect myself with the Prussian Government I should have to assume responsibility for its internal policy, which is impossible till legality is restored. Accept my heartiest wishes at the opening of the coming struggle.'

A letter to Freytag added a few details. 'I have had some difficult days. Bismarck wanted to have me at his headquarters; I was to write war manifestos, to work for the German policy of the Government, and so on. A Chair at Berlin, my old ambition, was assured. A proclamation against Austria in favour of a German Parliament I could write with an easy conscience. In short the temptation was very great, all the more because Freiburg has become almost intolerable. Yet I had to decline; I could not pledge myself to a policy whose goal is known to one man alone and whose sins I have no power to prevent. According to my code of political morality one should sacrifice one's reputation for the Fatherland, but only for the Fatherland, that is, only when one has power and can hope really to help the State by measures which seem harsh to the crowd. The moment I forfeit the reputation of an independent, my pen loses its force.'

A second letter to Bismarck dated June 14 declined a less exacting request and frankly reiterated his dislike of constitutional improprieties. 'Your plan for federal reform seems to me a masterpiece. It is so moderate that one hopes after two victories for the votes of the German courts, yet it cuts deep into the worst faults of the German system. If carried it opens the road to a better future. Yet it pains me deeply that I cannot write a manifesto in its support. Clearly a Baden official cannot draft a State document for the Prussian Cabinet. Even if I wished to ignore this scruple there is another impossibility: a manifesto cannot contain personal ideas. Even the first draft must emanate from a man who knows the detailed plans, that is from a member of the Government. It is most desirable that it should be in warm and forceful terms, but its contents are far more important. And if Your Excellency asks me what should be said I can only repeat: the suspicion of the nation against the Prussian Government is unfortunately unlimited, and the only way to diminish it is the

[1] After an attempt at assassination.

restoration of the Diet's constitutional rights. If that is impossible (and I know only too well that the blindness of the *Fortschrittspartei* makes reconciliation extremely difficult) even a fine bold manifesto will arouse no echo. The number of politicians who can rise above party is almost infinitesimal. In such a situation words are useless; we can only look to victories to convert the nation. For myself there is only one task: personally and through my friends to support in the Press the Prussian reform plans with the warmth and full approval they deserve. As to the result I have no illusions. Pamphlets at such times fall flat, so there is only the Press. The *Weser Zeitung*, the *Preussische Jahrbücher*, some Hessian and Thuringian journals, will do their duty, but those in South Germany are terrorised by the Austrian party and are usually too cowardly to shake off the yoke. I am deeply grieved that for the moment I can do so little for the good cause. But perhaps the time will come when, as an absolutely independent man who has never tied his hands, I can support Prussia's German policy more effectively than I could to-day by direct action.'

That moment was closer than he had dared to hope.

III

TREITSCHKE had long expected and desired a trial of strength between Prussia and Austria, but when it came it was a shock to learn that Baden sided with Vienna. 'I write under the first impression of the ghastly news from Frankfurt. Comments are superfluous. Why must this unfortunate nation at such a moment be ruled by such animals? Tell me at once: how was it possible for Baden to vote with the majority? What will Mathy do? Might Roggenbach return to office? From this decision to a declaration of war against us it is a long way; it is clear that this madness invites foreign intervention. Yet henceforth nothing will surprise me. Every hour strengthens the conviction that I can stay here no longer. If Baden fights against Prussia I could not remain a Baden official another moment; yet even if the worst is avoided my position is becoming intolerable. For weeks I have realised increasingly that I ought to go to Berlin, for that is where I belong. With my Prussian patriotism I am so deadly in earnest that now of all times I cannot separate my fortunes from those of that State.'

On the eve of leaving Baden Treitschke poured out his heart to

Mathy, his closest friend in southern Germany, and the most Prussophil of the Grand Duke's Ministers. 'The last two days I have realised that I cannot stay here. To-day there can be no thought of academic leisure. I am impelled by all that is good in me in this great crisis to do my best for the State to which our future belongs. If our excellent Grand Duke is forced by the wickedness of his neighbours to march against Prussia it would be morally impossible for me to remain his official. Moreover the barrier between north and south makes it physically impossible for me to do anything for the good cause. I see only two possible results of this war. Either, which heaven forbid, we are beaten, in which case Prussia begins a period of internal convalescence as after 1807; or we win, in which case the new Germany receives a new parliament and a useful publicistic activity becomes possible. For the moment words can do nothing—the guns must speak. In the last four weeks, to my great surprise, Bismarck has twice tried to get me for his headquarters. Both times I declined. Perhaps in a few weeks or months the reconciliation of parties in Prussia will be possible. If he then invites me again I could not refuse. But for that I must be in Berlin and no longer a Baden official.'

1866, not 1870, was Treitschke's *annus mirabilis*. He arrived in Berlin without waiting for an official post, just in time to receive the joyful tidings of Königgrätz. His younger brother, fighting in the Saxon army on the Austrian side, was gravely wounded in the battle, but personal matters were trifles in comparison with the fortunes of 'our state.' 'I have come into indescribable jubilation,' he wrote on July 4; '101 cannon salvos have just been fired. Our army is glorious. It is a joy to rub shoulders with people, so brave and confident, yet so modest in their talk. Thank God the inferiority complex of 1806 is expelled. Bloody work remains, but as to the issue I am not in doubt. The change of attitude in the people is complete; it justifies my often expressed view of the small value of so-called public opinion. How gloriously the inexhaustible efficiency of our state is displayed! I do not boast, but I am sure that with the frightful battles in Bohemia a better era dawns for our fatherland.'

The Seven Weeks' War, ending with the expulsion of Austria from the Bund, was one of the shortest and most decisive on record. At last Prussia could do as she liked, but what use would she make of her victory? Treitschke's answer was that she should annex every other German state, beginning with her North German antagonists in the struggle, Saxony, Hesse-Cassel and Hanover. The two latter were duly annexed, but Bismarck wisely decided to leave Saxony intact. The historian's shrill demands for the annihilation of his native state nearly broke the heart of his father who publicly denounced him in the local Press: he had read the attacks on 'this dear Royal Family,' in the article on *The Future of the Middle States*, with indignation and profound grief. The young Hotspur was too attached to the old General not to wince, but he realised how differently German problems appeared to an older generation which had lived contentedly under the Bund for half a century. 'My father knows only one Fatherland—Saxony,' he wrote; 'it is the old era going to the grave.' In the following spring General von Treitschke, described by his son as 'the splendid man,' passed away, consoled in some degree by the knowledge that his beloved Saxony was allowed to survive.

Treitschke would have liked a Chair in Berlin, but he was only thirty-two and, apart from poetry and some articles in the *Preussische Jahrbücher*, had only published a volume of essays. He accepted a stop-gap appointment at Kiel, which lasted only six months. He found the place provincial and dreaded the prospect of bringing his South German *fiancée*, whom he was to marry in March 1867, to the chilly north. At this moment the death of Häusser created a vacancy at Heidelberg, and he joyfully returned to the land which he had left in haste the previous summer. Since Baden's belligerence had only been half-hearted, since the Grand Duke Frederick was Prussophil, and since it was widely expected that Baden would before long join the North German Federation, there seemed no reason why he should not return as a *persona grata*. Saxony, 'my God-forsaken land,' would have been impossible.

Baden, he declared, was a little better than before, especially the students, but there was still plenty of Prussophobia. 'Even the national Press in the South,' he wrote a year after his appointment, 'is reverting to the old folly of patronising Prussia, as if she had to sue for the favour of the South instead of the other way round. People here have learned practically nothing from the great year 1866. Even the nationalists dream the old nonsense, as if they were the free and happy ones who have something to give to the North. In addition there is an absolute apathy, stirred only by Prussophobia and the everlasting confessional strife. When one looks at the fearful rottenness in Swabia and Bavaria and the universal indifference in Baden, one cannot help asking what the old liberalism was worth which produced such conditions. I think we are waiting till the North is fully consolidated and then to clean up with the sword or—what is improbable—with moral pressure.'

Though Treitschke trusted Prussia's pilot implicitly in foreign affairs, he was never a blind admirer of his domestic policy. In the 'Conflict Era' he had sharply condemned the unconstitutional treatment of the Diet: now he complained that the Constitution of the North German Confederation contained a serious flaw. So rapidly had he shed his early liberal skin that he found the Bismarck of 1867 too advanced for his taste. 'You know I have always enjoyed saying something very unpopular but needing to be said,' he wrote to his *fiancée* early in 1867. 'The absurdity of universal suffrage for our people, which happily does not at present copy the French fanatical equalitarianism, was always clear to me. Our people's strongest point was always its idealism, so it is thoroughly un-German that stupidity and ignorance should decide.' He described it as 'a crude and frivolous experiment, of all Bismarck's doings the most disastrous. We are a cultivated people and not inclined to bow down to the sovereign folly. It will provide him for the moment with an obedient majority, but it will mean endless confusion in the future.'

Before the echoes of 1866 had died away Treitschke was expecting, though not desiring, another war. 'My dearest wish,' he wrote to Freytag in May 1868, 'is that our state may be granted a quiet interval to carry out the administrative reforms needed for even greater tasks. Will it be granted? I hardly dare to hope so. France's armaments may stampede her government, and it seems almost a necessary consequence of our old history that our independence cannot be secured without a struggle with France. These people (in Baden) are not men of steel. The same folk who to-day complain of provincialism would accept a new Confederation of the Rhine without much opposition. Here in the South nothing helps except conquest; here is a tremendous task before us, but I hope Prussia will solve it some day.' While the best type of nationalist respects the nationalism of other races, Treitschke cast covetous eyes at Germany's neighbours. 'I have been one of the few Germans who regard the recovery of the Rhine as one of our greatest tasks,' he wrote a month later; 'but since I have seen the country and the people my hopes have sunk. They have developed such independence and self-sufficiency in state and economics, language and literature. The Dutch are also so proud that I can no longer believe in peaceful amalgamation: even a federal connection is unthinkable. They will always remain unpleasant and narrow-hearted neighbours—if they do not (as is very possible) compel us by their crazy hostility to conquer them. Then we should have a German Poland, a festering wound in our body which would never heal. In Belgium I enjoyed the arts, but I am deeply grateful that I do not have to live in this model constitutional state. If our doctrinaires could only see these wretched conditions, the unlimited power of a stupid and fanatical clergy, the suppression of the Flemish majority by the Walloon minority, they would perhaps ask themselves if the privilege of a few constitutional paragraphs is not purchased at too high a price.' Russia pleased him no better. 'She will be great in extent, regrettable though it is, but they will never be a truly civilised people. What separates us is not serfdom, which we also possessed, but a fundamental difference of spirit. They are Asiatics in religion, and the thin layer of Gallicised *demi-monde* does not make them Europeans.' England, France and Austria had never attracted him, and of the New World he knew nothing. Thus by the process of exclusion only Germany was left. No great historian had a narrower range of sympathies.

The war of 1870 was no surprise to Treitschke, who welcomed the chance of completing German unity and felt little anxiety about the issue. 'The coming weeks will bring us hard and terrible things,' he wrote to his sister on July 18 from Heidelberg, 'but no one doubts of victory and a third entry into Paris. Here everyone is full of courage and life. I feel as if everyone is growing better, as if petty and common things fall away.' Bismarck promised to call him if he thought his pen could be of use, but no summons came, and the historian was only happy when he was absolutely his own master. 'My dear sister, in these days man must become pious: a higher hand is over us Germans and compels us to become one people. My first regret is that our dear father did not live to see it. He would have judged me more mildly. With what prospects would Germany have begun this frightful war if the old Diet and the thirty-four small armies had remained? God be praised for sending us the hard year 1866. Do not worry about me. The French would only arrive after two victories, and in that improbable event I should have time to think of my safety. We are prepared for everything, but we hope after heavy sacrifices for a great victory which will wipe out the sins of three centuries and restore Strassburg to the Germans.' Among the sacrifices was his brother who died of a wound received at Sedan. Once again he felt his soldier's blood throbbing in his veins. 'I pity you that you cannot spend these wonderful days in Germany,' he wrote to a friend abroad. 'You will have to learn to think more idealistically of war. The comradeship in arms in this great and righteous struggle creates a bond of union for which there is no substitute.' That the South had at length begun to see the error of its ways rejoiced his heart. 'I have never lived through finer days,' he wrote on August 4. 'The South is by no means fully converted, and after the war we shall still see sharp party conflicts. But it is an immense success that the majority can now feel German again, and the treacherous minority has to be silent or sham. Such blessed transformations only a war can bring; there are certain moral forces which peace can never release.'

While waiting for victory Treitschke wrote *The Black Eagle*, the most popular of his ballads, and argued in the *Preussische Jahrbücher* that Prussia must have her reward. Four days after Sedan he begged Bismarck to read the end of his article *Was fordern wir von Frankreich?* 'I want to make Prussian readers realise a fact too little understood in the North—that all sensible men in the South wish to see Alsace in Prussian hands. It is a gross error if the North thinks the South must be rewarded by territory and population. If Prussia does what is needed and takes the enemy territory which only a great state can retain, all patriots in the South would agree. I wrote at the urgent request of South German friends, and I only venture to trouble you because my article echoes educated opinion in the South. The South wishes it to be a Prussian province, wedged in between France and Baden. If the Prussian Government works for this it can reckon on the support of all true Germans in Bavaria, Baden and Württemberg.' Unconvinced by the appeal, Bismarck's cooler brain decided that the Rhine Provinces should go neither to Prussia nor the South, but should become a Reichsland with a Statthalter controlled by Berlin.

Treitschke's contempt for the institutions and ideology of the South outlived the common effort and the joint victory. 'You judge the minor states much too favourably,' he wrote to the historian Baumgarten on November 9. 'To me it seems clear that the whole conception of political liberty as invented in France and developed in the small states is worthless. Among the blessed results of this war is the recognition of the emptiness of our small-state liberalism. That you are entirely free from it I am aware, but you speak too mildly of the utterly perjured Jesuitical little Courts which have adopted this system.' With the Southern states safely and voluntarily inside the Reich, Bismarck wisely determined to leave them full internal autonomy, and Treitschke complained that they still had too much power. The Iron Chancellor could be ruthless enough in case of need, but he could also be conciliatory, mindful of his axiom that politics are the art of the possible. To the hot-blooded historian, a patriot but never a statesman, compromise was anathema.

Despite their different approach, Bismarck knew his worth, and when the Heidelberg Professor consulted him about his plan to stand for the Reichstag the answer was that it would be extremely desirable. Though he could not hear a word and could take no part in the cut and thrust of debate, he sat for thirteen years, and his speeches, later collected in a volume, always commanded attention. He sat with the National Liberals till 1879, when Bismarck introduced Protection; thenceforth, till his retirement in 1884, as a Conservative, zealously supporting the Chancellor in his conflicts with the Roman Hierarchy, the Social Democrats, and the Free Traders. The least judicial of men could never understand the appeal of political, economic or religious ideas different from his own. What the urban worker found to attract him in Socialism was even more a mystery to him than to Bismarck, who at any rate sympathised with the craving for social security and in his measures of national insurance was the first European statesman to meet it. 'Why does this wholly un-German nonsense of sensuality and slavery spread so quickly?' he exclaimed to Freytag in 1877, shortly before the anti-Socialist law was introduced in 1878. Lack of imagination, inability to enter into the feelings of other men and other nations, was his greatest weakness both as historian and publicist.

Liberalism at home and abroad was the bugbear of Treitschke's later years, as particularism had been of his early manhood. Government by shifting Parliamentary majorities seemed to him utter folly, and British foreign policy was equally detestable. 'As my studies advance,' he wrote in July 1876, when the Eastern question was looming up again, 'I understand ever more fully England's invariably hostile policy towards Germany. That we should pull the East Indian chestnuts out of the fire for these Beefs! Bismarck would never do such a thing. I hope to visit London in September. It is really a flaw in my education that I was never there. I look forward to seeing the greatest miracle of material civilisation and shall get my impressions impartially, however contemptible the political *rôle* of present-day England seems to me.' 'This country becomes ever more unintelligible to me,' he confessed to another friend; 'I must see it for myself.' It was not however till the summer of 1895, the last summer of his life, that he crossed the Channel. 'Oxford and Cambridge pleased me most,' he reported to his wife. 'Such a collection of academic palaces is only possible in a land united for a thousand years and secure from invasion. Edinburgh is almost as fine as London is ugly. The Scots are much nearer to us than the English, more natural, more cheerful, more human; they please me greatly in their rough way.' Unable to speak English, he could learn little of a country which he had never seriously attempted to understand. A celebrated passage in one of his latest articles declared that, after Austria and France had been dealt with, 'the great reckoning' with England remained. Even if this does not mean the clash of arms, as the context suggests, it indicates a resentful hostility which grew with advancing years. The French were far more to his taste. 'They are a pleasant and intelligent people,' he reported after a visit in 1890, 'human like ourselves, so different from the disgusting English hypocrites. I deeply regret that their attachment to Alsace has separated them from us, their natural allies.'

After the proclamation of the Empire in 1871 the main theme of the correspondence is the composition of the *German History in the Nineteenth Century*. The work had grown under his hands, and it was not till 1879 that the introductory volume appeared, tracing the decline of the Reich, the rise of Prussia, and the War of Liberation. Everyone realised the need of such an enterprise and it was generally known that he was at work on it. His collected historical essays and the steady flow of his contributions to the *Preussische Jahrbücher* left no doubt as to the character of the book for which the world was waiting. 'I write for Germans,' he announced in the preface, and he was the last man to hide his feelings of admiration or contempt. He regarded Droysen as his master, though he never sat at his feet. 'I have long wished to thank you warmly for your manifold teaching,' he wrote in 1863. 'My essay on the Teutonic Knights will have shown you how much I owe to your *Prussian Policy*.' Fifteen years later, on Droysen's seventieth birthday, he renewed his homage. 'How much you are my teacher and how great is my debt to your example you will have seen in my writings.' Though both were ardent Prussophils and specialists in Prussian history, there was no personal competition. Droysen's vast work began with Frederick of Hohenzollern at the opening of the fifteenth century, and had only reached the eve of the Seven Years' War in the fourteenth volume when he died in 1886 at the age of seventy-eight. A second difference was that he confined himself almost exclusively to foreign affairs, whereas Treitschke strove to picture the whole life of the nation. 'Unlike Sybel, who only gives extracts from the archives,' he explained, 'I try to write history.' A third was that Droysen, though an impressive lecturer, lacked the gift of style, and in consequence was only read by students. Treitschke's aim was to clothe the bones of history with flesh and blood, to fill his readers with pride in the great statesmen, soldiers and writers of their race. Ranke's *Reformation Era* was the first extensive work on German history which combined erudition with popular appeal; the *German History*, well described by Marcks as the Victory Hymn for 1866 and 1870, was the second, and there has been no third. Neither could be expected to please all readers. Both, however, claim an enduring place among the historical classics of the modern world, and they have been described as books of devotion for the German people.

The first volume took Germany by storm and aroused little criticism. Artistically it was the most satisfying of the five, for great events were described with a dynamic energy and a Venetian colouring approached among the author's German contemporaries by Mommsen's *Roman History* alone. His real difficulties began when in the second volume he reached the Restoration, and it is a tribute to his genius that he was able to interest his countrymen in the stagnant decades between the downfall of Napoleon and the Year of Revolution. From the angle of the historical student this and the succeeding volumes are the most valuable, for they contain a mass of new material from the archives not merely of Prussia but of some of the minor states. Treitschke was fully justified in claiming that he was the first to illumine the dark corners of a period which, just because it was so recent, had never tempted a scholar of the first class. Yet his path was bordered by precipices, for the creation of a nation-state had softened but in no manner obliterated the traditional antagonism of North and South. He never expected to please Austrian, French or British readers, and indeed he welcomed attacks from hostile camps. On the appearance of the second volume, however, which covered the years 1815–20, he received a wound from an old friend and comrade which never healed, for the *German History* was written with his heart's blood.

Hermann Baumgarten was one of the distinguished academic publicists who had co-operated with the staff of the *Preussische Jahrbücher* in working for the unification of Germany under Prussian leadership, and Treitschke's numerous letters to him breathe unstinted confidence and respect. His massive works on Spanish history had won him an honourable place in German scholarship, and his assault on the *Deutsche Geschichte* was the harder to bear because it was a bolt from the blue. Treitschke, he complained, had one pair of scales for Prussia, another for the South. Droysen and Sybel, his fellow-members of the Prussian School, rallied to his defence, and the latter procured him the coveted Verdun prize for the first two volumes. Less expected but no less welcome was a message from Dove, one of the most faithful of Ranke's disciples, that the great scholar was 'filled with joy in living to see this novel and thoroughly original blossoming.' In thanking Sybel for his moral support 'in such unpleasant days,' he added: 'I am long used to Press attacks, but I had not expected that this book, which I really believed would please the Germans, would be pelted with dirt. Happily the Press is not the nation. You are quite right in your criticisms. My blood is unfortunately too hot for a historian; yet the tone in the second volume is quieter than in the first, and I intend to work on myself, to read industriously in Thucydides, and gradually to adapt myself more to the historical style.'

His attitude to the South was explained in a letter to Heigel, one of Bavaria's leading historians. 'Only politically am I a Prussian. As a man I feel more at home in the South and the Middle States than in the North. Nearly all my dearest memories lie in the South. My wife comes from Lake Constance; my daughters, born in the Palatinate, are regarded here (in Berlin) as Southerners. I hope they will not let Baumgarten's malevolence affect their judgment. It was my duty to show that the old Prussian absolutism, even after 1815, accomplished great and good things, and that South German life had to go through hard years of apprenticeship before it saw the light. If these irrefragable facts are unwelcome to the liberal party of to-day that is no reason for me to conceal them. Whatever you may think, I hope North German prejudices will not be found in my book. In my view it was rather Baumgarten who embodied the most detestable fault of the North Germans, bitter fault-finding. It seems to me almost a joke that he has come out as the advocate of the South Germans at a time when I am receiving appreciative reports from that quarter.' A letter to his publishers, while he was at work on the third volume, covering 1820-30, reveals the persisting smart. 'Let us hope it will have better luck than the second, though I do not expect it. The Austrians attacked the first, the Liberals the second; some party will be embittered by succeeding volumes.' Happily the sky was not so dark after all. Apart from Baumgarten's attack he had no reason to complain of the reception of the whole work. He was appointed Historiographer of Prussia in succession to Ranke in 1886, and in 1887 he received the highest honour of all, *Pour le Mérite*, the order founded by Frederick the Great. That his old and valued friend Gustav Freytag received it at the same time increased his satisfaction. Most precious of all was the approval of Bismarck, who pronounced the book masterly in its range of knowledge, literary skill, and characterisations.

Treitschke's admiration for the Iron Chancellor grew with the years. His only son, whose death at the age of ten broke a father's heart, was named after him, and the dismissal of the founder of the German Empire was the most poignant public grief of his life. 'Both sides were right,' he wrote to his wife. 'The blow was not unexpected; there is a tragic necessity therein, yet we are all stunned. Everything depends on whether the Emperor is able in some measure to be his own Chancellor. God give him strength. Not for a moment must we doubt of our Reich, which is stronger than any mortal.' Six months later he was still brooding over the catastrophe. 'His fate shakes me to the depths. Such ingratitude is unknown since Themistocles.' It was some comfort at any rate that the Emperor Frederick had not reigned long enough to change the political system under the malign influence of 'the Englishwoman.'

First impressions of the new ruler were favourable. 'Our young Emperor steadily improves,' he declared. 'We must have a little patience with him,' he wrote six months after the fall of Bismarck;

'his tribute to Moltke shows once again that there is a noble core in him. It is a curse for him that no one tells him the truth: everyone grovels.' The worst feature of the new regime was the lack of a strong government. A year later, in September 1891, the Emperor's speech in the London Guildhall was a new cause of offence to the inveterate Anglophobe. 'Public affairs grow ever worse. Why must we in so undignified a manner throw ourselves on Grandmama's neck, since in England every infant is out to trick us? We all know it except the Emperor, Caprivi and Marschall. The Roumanians have left the Triple Alliance, for which I cannot blame them, since the Tsar offers them Transylvania and we nothing. Step by step the diplomatic situation worsens, unfortunately through our own fault. Of course I am far from despair, but it is very sad that abroad they are ceasing to fear us.'

Treitschke was never a courtier. He was profoundly grateful to the Hohenzollerns for their services, and the chapter on Frederick the Great in his first volume is a full-throated hymn of praise; but he judged each one of them on his merits. His researches in the archives led him to revise his attitude to Frederick William III. 'The old King, with all his failings, appears in a more favourable light than with the older generation.' Frederick William IV, on the other hand, the central figure in the fifth and last volume, did not improve on acquaintance. 'I have discovered several attractive traits in him,' he wrote to his wife, 'but for greatness you need strength of soul. Lacking it he is only a *dilettante* on a large scale.' Fortunately the historian was spared the grief of witnessing the consequences of the abandonment of the Bismarckian policy of limited liability by the last Hohenzollern ruler.

The fifteen hundred pages of Treitschke's letters leave the impression of a powerful brain, a dynamic temperament, and an excellent heart. 'One had to love him or hate him,' declares Marcks, and those who knew him had no choice. The relationship of father and son, strained almost to breaking-point by political differences, reflects credit on them both. The refusal of tempting offers from Bismarck at a time when the young teacher had his career to make reveals a sturdiness rare in German academic circles. His delight in poetry and nature softens the harsh outlines of a career of storm and stress. The letters to his wife, in later years a chronic invalid, breathe a touching tenderness. It was a dedicated life, devoted to the service of what appeared to him to be the highest ideals. That he was constitutionally unable to do justice to different ideologies was a failing he shared with Macaulay and other celebrated historians. He read history backwards while Ranke took it as it came. Regarding himself as a man with a mission, he dealt lusty blows at individuals and parties, institutions and countries, which seemed to block the way to his longed-for goal. He had no patience with the particularism of the minor German states, with the doctrinaire liberalism which declined to put first things first, with the Roman clericalism which he regarded as obscurantist and unpatriotic. It was the natural outcome of his fiery temperament that he came to glorify force more and more and valued the liberty of the individual less and less.

Growing up at a time when the star of nationalism was in the ascendant, Treitschke was blind to its radical insufficiency. That it involved perpetual struggles did not alarm him, for he believed that a unified and Prussianised Germany could take care of herself. Ranke's conception of Central and Western Europe as a community bound by a thousand visible and invisible ties meant as little to him as to Bismarck. The most eloquent German teacher of his generation except Nietzsche, his scorn of minorities and constitutional obstacles prepared the way for Hitler's totalitarian state. His annual course on political science, published in two volumes after his death, drew crowded audiences, in which officials and members of the public mingled in the cheering throng.

Friendships he formed in plenty, but he founded no school. Throughout his voluminous correspondence we hear little of academic themes and of the pupils who are the pride of teachers absorbed in their work. Yet it was largely this concentration of interest and purpose that gave him his hold on the generation which grew to manhood during and immediately after the wars of unification. In a world crying out for co-operation and conciliation his strident tones proclaimed that the final decision lies with the sword. If we seek to understand the atmosphere of Bismarckian and post-Bismarckian Germany we cannot ignore the writings of the most popular of German historians and publicists. In the *German History* he had constructed an imperishable monument for which students of every race can be grateful; yet he was also a destroyer, sharing with Nietzsche and the Iron Chancellor the grave responsibilty of uprooting what little liberalism survived the Frankfurt Parliament. No one would class him among 'good Europeans,' and indeed such a title to fame he would have rejected with scorn. No leading figure on the nineteenth-century stage had less sense of the fundamental unity of Western civilisation, less craving for an organised and interdependent world. And no German historian was so heartily admired by the Nazis as this fiery nationalist, the standard-bearer of the academic anti-Semites, the ardent gospeller of war, who never ceased to proclaim the challenging message that 'the state is power, not an academy of arts.'

THE STUDY OF BISMARCK

THE student of recent European history exclaims about Bismarck, as Victor Hugo exclaimed of Napoleon, *Toujours lui, lui partout*.[1] Next to the great Emperor he fills the largest space on the nineteenth century stage, and the two figures stand together and alone in the first class of men of action of the modern world. Frederick the Great and Cavour are not far behind, for there is no more consummate achievement of brain and will than the making of a nation. The Iron Chancellor seems to assume almost superhuman proportions in comparison with his bungling successors. The two World Wars have focussed attention on the principal author of the international system which perished in their flames, and scores of German historians have worked the rich Bismarckian seam. Some find in him an oracle the neglect of whose maxims led to the catastrophe; others challenge the whole philosophy of force of which he was the supreme embodiment. Hero-worshippers and critics are at one in their recognition of his towering stature and in the zeal with which they explore every aspect of an unique career.

I

To begin with the biographies, the English reader who commands no tongue but his own is better off than the citizen of any other foreign country. The first serious survey was attempted in 1885 in the volumes of Charles Lowe, *Times* Correspondent in Berlin, revised in 1892, which are still worth reading as the work of a contemporary and in some cases an eye-witness. A shorter narrative was published soon after the Chancellor's death by J. W. Headlam, afterwards Sir James Headlam-Morley, the first and last Historical Advisor to the Foreign Office. While Lowe was merely a competent journalist, Headlam wrote as a trained scholar who could set his subject in the framework

---

[1] There are useful surveys by Maximilian von Hagen, *Das Bismarckbild in der Literatur der Gegenwart* (1929), and Lawrence D. Steefel, 'Bismarck,' in the *Journal of Modern History*, March, 1930. The best bibliography is in Dahlmann-Waitz, *Quellenkunde der deutschen Geschichte*, ed. 1931.

of German history. On the other hand the proportions of his book are faulty, for the stream shrinks to a trickle after the foundation of the Empire, and the reader never really learns to know the legislator and the man of peace. The most interesting of his verdicts approves the annexation of Alsace though not of Lorraine. A third English biography, by Sir Charles Grant Robertson, published in 1919, devotes adequate attention to the later decades which interested our fathers so much less than the earlier years. Though the work appeared before the opening of the German archives, it remains the best guide for English readers, as Paul Matter's three-volume biography (in its second edition) is the obvious approach for the French.

Among single-volume presentations by German historians the first and still one of the most important is Lenz's *Geschichte Bismarcks*, which appeared in its original form in the *Allgemeine Deutsche Biographie*. It is a careful chronicle of events by a scholar of the first rank who lived through the whole era, and was scarcely less interested in military than in political affairs; but the twenty years of peace are merely a sketch. Smaller in size but superior in proportion and even greater in authority is *Otto von Bismarck: Ein Lebensbild*, by Erich Marcks, like Lenz a Professor at Berlin and a no less ardent admirer. Writing for the centenary during the first winter of the First World War, he presents a hero 'the contemplation of whom is strength and comfort and courage and hope and faith.' The most original feature of the best popular survey ever written is the discussion of the *Kulturkampf*, which is exhibited as a virtually inevitable clash between national and super-national concepts. Even smaller in scale but hardly less authoritative and equally laudatory is A. O. Meyer's richly illustrated *Bismarck* in the well-known series *Velhagen und Klasings Volksbücher*. The centenary, synchronising with the early intoxications of the First World War, inspired two co-operative enterprises of enduring value. The more substantial, *Erinnerungen an Bismarck*, edited by Brauer, Marcks and K. A. von Müller, contains contributions from friends and associates, among them Schweninger, the formidable doctor, who always found him simple and natural, and Dryander, the Court theologian, who describes him as a pious evangelical. The second collection, *Das Bismarckjahr*, edited by Lenz and Marcks, contains brief articles, in addition to those by the editors, by Brandenburg, Hintze, Meinecke, Oncken, Rachfahl, and a dozen other specialists.

The task of telling the whole story in two thousand pages in the light of the vast mass of new material has been undertaken by Dr. Erich Eyck, a Berlin lawyer who migrated to England after Hitler's accession and is now a British subject. His biography of Gladstone revealed his liberal leanings, and the approach to his hero's greatest contemporary is highly critical. It is easier for his generation to pronounce judgment than for such scholars as Sybel and Treitschke, Lenz and Marcks, who had known the superman and grown up in a Germany reverberating with his fame. Though Eyck recognises his almost superhuman greatness, of hero-worship there is no trace, for his spiritual home is the Frankfurt Parliament. The second volume, devoted to the making of the Empire, emphasises the utter ruthlessness of the man of blood and iron. That Germans had as much right as Italians to make a nation-state is admitted, and no one has explained how it could have been done in either case without an appeal to arms; yet the methods described in these pages are repulsive enough. It is no wonder that the men with whom he had to deal at home and abroad dreaded his deep-laid stratagems, his double-crossing, his lightning strokes. The old King was clay in his hands and the Crown Prince had no stomach for a fight. High marks are given to the Parliamentary Liberals, such as Twesten and Forckenbeck, who compelled him to seek an amnesty for his unconstitutional procedure in the years before 1866 and inserted some valuable provisions in his Constitution. Some readers, indeed, may be surprised to learn how much genuine liberalism once existed in Prussia; but Bennigsen, Lasker and Eugen Richter left no successors and the liberal flame burned down. In engineering the Hohenzollern candidature for the Spanish throne Bismarck, in Eyck's opinion, was in truth the author of the war of 1870. 'A trap for Napoleon!' observed Lothar Bucher, who knew all his master's secrets. The biographer's belief that the union of the South German states with the North German Confederation, the ostensible object of his machinations, could have been secured without a war can be neither proved nor disproved.

The third volume reviews the triumphs abroad and the failures at home during the two closing decades of peace. Surveying his achievements as a whole, Eyck finds far more to blame than to praise, for even when he pursued the right course his methods were often needlessly harsh. He bullied friends and enemies, parties and Churches, and wrecked his son's happiness by forbidding him on political grounds to marry the woman of his choice. The chapters on the Kulturkampf and the anti-socialist campaign reveal an impatient, unimaginative, short-sighted man infuriated by opposition and convinced that force was the only remedy. Only the system of social insurance moves the author to applaud, but even here it is suggested that he may have been chiefly concerned with party tactics. He grew ever more despotic, and no Hohenzollern except the modest old Emperor would have consented to reign on such terms. By 1890 he had become intolerable and William II was right to dismiss him. Perhaps his greatest error was that he failed to prepare his countrymen to govern themselves when he was gone. Here is the final verdict. 'He could be supple as a courtier, polite and accomplished as a marquis of the old school, contemptuous and satirical as Heine, sensitive as a poet, but also hard and brutal as a Renaissance despot, sly as a fox, bold as a lion. Rarely has nature dealt more lavishly with any human being. Yet she denied him the sense of right and justice. Thus he stands among the giants, a figure not to love and still less to imitate, but to study and, despite his limitations, to admire.'

When the student has familiarised himself with the personality of the principal actor in the best biographies, he should seek a closer acquaintance with the stage. English readers are fortunate in posessing two authoritative guides, Sir Adolphus Ward and W. H. Dawson, who combined erudition with lifelong knowledge of the country and its people. Though written when he was approaching his eightieth year, the former's survey of German history during the nineteenth century betrayed no sign of failing powers. The first volume, covering the years from 1815 to 1852, provides the best account of the revolution of 1848–9 in our language. The second, bringing the story to 1871, narrates the process of unification with sovereign impartiality. To a mind wearied and confused by the partisanship of Sybel and Friedjung, Ollivier and La Gorce, it is an emancipation to follow the unravelling of Prussian, Austrian and French diplomacy by a scholar who knew all there was to be known of the rival attitudes and kept his head. In his youth he had spent several years in Germany, and his account of the Schleswig-Holstein question utilised the papers of his father, William Ward, who was accredited to the Hanse cities during the critical decade 1860–70. The third volume, which carries the story to the fall of Bismarck and briefly sketches the reign of William II down to 1907, is smaller in bulk and of inferior importance.

If the Master of Peterhouse knew more of the history of Germany from 1815 to 1871 than any man born beyond her frontiers, Dawson possessed a many-sided acquaintance with the Germany created by Bismarck which no English scholar could approach. Though written during the First World War, like Ward's volumes, his work is no less honourably free from the passions of that distracted period. It is a striking testimony to the general fair-mindedness of modern British scholarship that these two works should reach approximately the same conclusions. Yet though their attitude of discriminating sympathy is almost identical, the differences in treatment are so great as to render them complementary to one another. Ward, the professional historian, wrote for students of history, while Dawson, the Civil Servant, catered for the needs of the general reader. Though his book bears the title *The German Empire 1867–1914 and the Unity Movement*, the larger part of the two volumes is devoted to Bismarck, whom he visited at Friedrichsruh while pursuing his studies in Berlin.

However suggestive foreign interpretations may be, the history of a country can never be fully understood without the aid of its sons, who alone can tell us how they think and feel. *Der Aufstieg des Reiches*, published in 1936, the last and most important work of Erich Marcks, the oracle of Bismarckian studies, is of such outstanding merit that we can forgive the author for leaving the large-scale biography of his hero a torso. 'It was designed as a thank-offering to the man who willed everything, accomplished everything, embodied everything. It has become a work of personal devotion and personal experience by one of the last surviving scholars of the classic Bismarckian era. I wish to write it as a mark of piety and delight. Fragmentation was only to be overcome, national unification in any permanent sense was only possible, through limitation, through struggle and loss. I am still convinced of the necessity of the actual course of events, the inevitability of civil war and separation as a stage of German evolution which, one hopes, will lead to an all-German system. The narrative reveals the tragic inevitability of 1866 as the sole means at that time of German salvation, of a Germany strong within and without, of the right to live. It is the author's hope that the book will keep alive the memory of the heroic past which quickened the pulse of his own generation and filled it with warmth and light.'

Our verdict on Bismarck's hammer blows depends in large measure on our attitude to the Bund which he destroyed, and here Marcks speaks with no uncertain voice. 'It refused Germans the German state, the political nation, unity, outward power, inward freedom. It was an alliance of princes imposed from above—not a Reich, not a Federation (*Bundesstaat*), only a Confederation (*Staatenbund*). It had no head, no representative assembly. Yet it did offer something. It expressed the connection of the German states, safeguarded them against internal war, kept the peace among them for half a century—a peace of inactivity, of national innocuousness. It was *Grossdeutsch*: that was its virtue, but for that very reason the structure had to be loose. It contained the old Reich in a less ambitious but more realistic form, and was infinitely better than what that had become, less romantic but more defined. It preserved, under Austria, the mid-European position of the Reich, keeping open its advantages and possibilities. It was thought that flesh would grow on the impoverished skeleton, but was such growth possible? The Reich had to lean either on Austria or on Prussia in order to become a state —to the detriment of the other. Nobody was satisfied, though Austria was the least dissatisfied. Here was no Emperor, no strength, no vitality; between the two large states stood the German people in shameful impotence. Here was no German state, only the sum of the separate states of 1803 and 1806. Everything vital in Germany had developed in opposition to the Bund. It remained an empty shell— that is the historic truth. A German state in 1815 was impossible; Europe, Dualism, the immaturity of all conditions, all sentiments, all plans, barred the way. The most vital national force since 1807 and since 1813 had been Prussia. That pointed to the future; the present did not belong to her, and she was not ripe and did not claim it. Yet the collapse of all hopes was shattering. After glowing love and sacrifice a state emerged, cold and soulless, commanding neither affection nor respect. The highest embodiment of the state for this great people was empty, hostile, indifferent. The German people were not in it, only in its component parts.' We might be listening to the voice of Treitschke himself.

The situation inherited by Bismarck becomes more intelligible, explains Marcks, when we realise that the Frankfurt Parliament never had a chance. Frederick William IV, it was said, was all nerves, no muscle. He and his contemporaries spoke different languages and never understood each other. His refusal of the Imperial crown was right and inevitable, for with such an irresolute pilot at the helm success would have been impossible. The events of 1848-9 showed both the need of change and the impossibility of effecting it by peaceful means, for after Olmütz Austria's position in the Bund was stronger than ever. Bismarck was not the first North-German to feel that Prussia could only escape from her position of inferiority by an appeal to the sword. Yet Marcks is entirely free from the old contemptuous bitterness of the Prussian School. 'Austria, Bavaria, Saxony and Prussia could not have acted differently. The Bund condemned them all to unfruitful conflict, itself suffering under the conflict and still more under the impossibility of changing the situation, under the paralysis of all political life. Prussia was the chief object of attack since her demand for clarification barred every proposal. Yet she had to demand it if she did not wish to abdicate as a Power—to abdicate for herself and also for the future which 1848 had announced. Not till William succeeded his brother was it possible to advance, and not till a superman was called to office was action possible in the grand style.' The first volume ends with the summons to Bismarck in 1862, despite the disapproval of the Queen and the Crown Prince.

The second volume opens with an elaborate portrait of the hero who evolved at Frankfurt from a party leader into a statesman. Henceforth he was both a lion and a fox. Though he called himself God's soldier and, according to Marcks, honestly believed in his divine mission, he realised that the Sermon on the Mount was inapplicable to the rough game of politics: without force and deceit it was impossible to win. 'His hands itched for the reins of power for which he was born.' Nothing could have been achieved without the unwavering support of his noble master who, when asked about his health, pointed to Bismarck with the words: 'There stands my doctor!' As he passes the milestones on the road to the Reich the historian finds nothing to condemn. Wiser than his old Conservative comrades, the superman made peace with the Prussian Chamber by requesting an indemnity for overriding the constitution; wiser than the Liberals, he rejected demands which threatened the authority of the state. The major responsibility for the conflicts of 1866 and 1870 is attributed to the rivals who refused to recognise Germany's right to become a nation-state under the only possible leader. Both wars were as nearly inevitable as collisions can ever be. The Hohenzollern candidature, he admits, though not without danger, was not necessarily an act of war. What right had Napoleon III to veto Spain's choice of a king? The villain of the piece was neither Bismarck nor the feeble Emperor but Gramont, his Foreign Minister, who forced Prussia to choose between humiliation and an appeal to arms. The Ems despatch is defended as taking up a challenge which ought never to have been made.

The full-length narrative ends with the foundation of the Empire, but an epilogue enthusiastically surveys its opening phase. Prussia necessarily remained predominant, as she had been in the North German Confederation, but the Reich was much more than its leading member. It was warmed by the love and the hopes of the nation, and its creator was the friend, not the enemy, of the minor states. 'He struggled with the old Prussianism of his ministerial colleagues who so often looked askance at the wider conceptions of the new time. A Great Prussia which thwarted unity and displeased the federal units was not in his scheme: supported by Prussia, the new Reich had to tower above it. He studied their interests and fitted them increasingly into the new structure.' His main decisions in home affairs are sympathetically explained even when not entirely approved. His much criticised refusal to admit Bennigsen and his National Liberal supporters into the Ministry is defended on the unconvincing ground that the Chancellor, who bore the ultimate responsibility, could not risk being thwarted or overruled. The failure of the *Kulturkampf*, in which he underestimated the strength of his opponents, is admitted, but he felt himself on the defensive against a Church with Austrian sympathies and no love for a Protestant Power. His strongest ally was the bourgeoisie, the most powerful political and social force in Germany though itself incapable of leadership. Together they created the Reich, and they stood together against 'the party of denial' with its strident challenge to society, the throne and the Church. Though he failed to arrest the growth of Socialism he was not without a feeling for the common man, and his conception of national insurance was a model for the world. Indeed the many-sidedness of the creative work of this gigantic genius was almost inconceivable. Though no foreign reader of the most authoritative book ever written on the foundation of the Hohenzollern Empire is likely to accept all these judgments, its place among German historical classics is secure, not merely for its ripe learning but because it enshrines the convictions and emotions of a great people at a crisis of its fate.

The other histories of a later generation have described the building of the Empire with such power and mastery of materials that they cannot be ignored. Brandenburg's *Die Reichsgründung* is more convincing because more detached than the inspired advocacy of Sybel, and is one of the most satisfying interpretations ever attempted. Bismarck's whole policy, he declares, was shaped by the determination to maintain the authority of the state. 'At home he was resolved to preserve the independence of the Crown against a parliamentary regime by every means, in case of need even by a temporary dictatorship, but he had not the slightest desire to revert to absolutism. For Prussia as for Germany he held the co-operation of a representative assembly to be essential, provided it kept within the limits which seemed necessary for the state to hold its own in the international sphere. This was always the deciding consideration. He never approached matters of internal policy from any other standpoint; in every case the decision turned on whether it would strengthen or weaken the power of the state. There was nothing of the romantic or the *doctrinaire* in him. It was one of his greatest qualities to see things as they really were and to assess the results of his measures with astonishing accuracy. It never occurred to him to promote any ideology; his task was to represent the interest of his state. He never judged political theories and convictions according to their truth or falsity; he simply inquired as to the measure of their support, and therefore how far they had to be reckoned with in order to secure certain ends. Yet he was no chilly calculator or pure intellectual like Richelieu; his fiery temperament often drove him to utterances which in calmer moments he would have repressed. Potent passions and strong feelings always stirred within him; his wife, his family, his homeland, his state, the dynasty, called forth deep love and devotion. But towards humanity as a whole, or individuals lacking such ties, he felt no such obligation and was always ready to sacrifice them to those he loved. For this reason he was often charged with contempt for mankind, though he had no more and no less of it than every great statesman or commander who must always be prepared to sacrifice life for the attainment of great ends. That he was ruthless in his choice of means, a master of the arts of intrigue and of trickery, is generally agreed. But when could a statesman, the world being what it is, have dispensed with such methods?'

That this ruthlessness denoted lack of conscience Bismarck always denied. Whoever blamed him as a politician without a conscience did him injustice, he declared, and should test his own conscience in the political arena. 'Yet it must be admitted that there was more elasticity in his public than in his private morals. Impelled by his passionate and challenging temperament he desired to beat down all opposition with force, and regarded every method of deceit as legitimate in dealing with a stronger foe. Worse still, he did not disdain similar dealings with friends and associates if they rejected his lead. Even with his royal master he economised truth if that seemed the only way of securing assent to decisions he deemed necessary in the interests of the state. His greatest political quality was his readiness to assume responsibility, and he never considered the personal consequences of failure. He strove for power with all his might and all his wits. He trembled with excitement when internal obstacles to his will emerged, but personal power was never an end in itself. It was only worth having as a means to secure his aims and to strengthen his state as the necessary basis of political achievement. He cared little for the pomps and vanities which power confers. At any moment he would have been ready to exchange his glittering position with that of an independent and carefree country nobleman had he not known that as Minister he could do something for his fatherland which others could not, and that it was his peculiar destiny to perform these acts. He knew he would stand before the world and his own people and King as an unscrupulous charlatan, indeed as a traitor, if his policy failed, particularly if Prussia were to be vanquished in the great struggle with Austria on which he was bent. He would certainly not have outlived a Prussian defeat. He chained his fortune to that of his state, and only some higher power—his King or death—could have wrenched the helm from his hand.'

Bismarck, asserts Brandenburg, was no lover of war or adventure, but in 1866 he saw no other way. Prussia attacked, yet in a large sense war was forced on her. 'For a powerful, growing, dynamic organism is compelled by the interest of self-preservation to break the chains which hinder its growth as soon as it can. Moreover Austria also violated the spirit of the Federal Constitution by transforming her honorary predominance into an hegemony over Germany to which she had no rightful claim.' A somewhat similar judgment is pronounced on the war of 1870. He engineered the Hohenzollern candidature, but was it really a deliberate snare for Napoleon III, as Lothar Bucher maintained? 'No, but he wished to thwart Napoleon's efforts to secure allies in the event of a future war. He knew it involved the danger of war, but he regarded this struggle as ultimately inevitable and saw that Napoleon was also preparing for it. Should he simply wait till the Emperor felt strong enough to strike? Should Prussia neglect a desirable strengthening of her political position because France might object and appeal to arms?' Though his action was the occasion of the war, the ultimate cause was the wrath of France at the unification of Germany and her wish to prevent it.

Oncken's last and greatest work, *Das Deutsche Reich und die Vorgeschichte des Weltkrieges*, published in 1933, is above all a paean to Bismarck for whom his admiration knows no bounds. His main theme is foreign policy, and he shares the conviction of Marcks that the right thing was done in the only possible way. 'Never for a moment did he forget that a very steep and narrow path led through the surrounding obstacles, German and European. The strongest will was combined with the greatest elasticity, the soberest realism with creative imagination.' He knew that Austria, whose membership of the Bund blocked the road to a nation-state, would only go if she were expelled. The Blood and Iron declaration was perhaps too frank, but Italy had pursued a similar course. The three wars were not a unified programme, for only that of 1866 was willed by Berlin. That he alone, in the generation of Louis Napoleon and Gortchakoff, Victor Emmanuel and Cavour, Palmerston and Disraeli, Francis Joseph and Beust, wore armour under his diplomatist's coat is nonsense.

His responsibility for the war of 1866, the climax of his life, is admitted and defended, but that for the war of 1870 is stoutly denied. The editor of *Die Rheinlandpolitik Napoleons III* emphasises the territorial appetite of France and the consequential necessity of a bulwark against the flowing tide of aggression. It would have been intolerable if the new Germany were too weak to undertake the *Wacht am Rhein*, and the fulfilment of the task justified the means. His patience was as remarkable as his sense of timing. 'That German unity at this moment is not ripe is obvious,' he wrote in 1869. 'We can put our clocks forward, but time does not go quicker if we do, and the capacity to wait till the situation develops is an axiom of practical policy.' The encouragement of the Hohenzollern candidature for the Spanish throne was far less of a provocation than the efforts of the Emperor to form a Triple Alliance with Austria and Italy. France, indeed, was crazy for the Rhine and spoiling for a fight. 'Seldom does a great conflict begin with such open and deliberate will to war on the one side.' The Hohenzollern candidature was merely a pretext, for the maxim of preventing German unity had dominated French policy since 1866. The incident of the Ems telegram merely accelerated the declaration of war already decided on by the Emperor and Gramont.

Bismarck is portrayed throughout by Oncken as a statesman with legitimate and limited aims. After creating the nation-state he became the main pillar of European peace. Certain French activities in 1875 provided some cause for anxiety, but the danger was exaggerated by the General Staff. Moltke advocated a preventive war, but neither Bismarck nor his master ever dreamed of it. The alliance with Austria in 1879 is hailed as a triumph of statesmanship which healed the wound of 1866 by the creation of the new and better Bund. The final triumph was to prevent Russia and Austria from flying at each other's throats.

II

Our next task is to study the writings and correspondence, the conversations and the speeches. When the most powerful personage in the world found himself at seventy-five in the ranks of the unemployed, he set himself, like fallen demigods before and after, to fight his battles over again. Accepting an offer from Cotta to publish his Memoirs for 100,000 marks per volume, he secured an ideal assistant in his old associate of the Foreign Office, Lothar Bucher, who knew more of his master's secrets than anyone else and who, unlike Holstein, remained loyal when the shadows began to fall. Encouraged not only by his collaborator, who resided for long periods at Friedrichsruh and Varzin and pored over the materials, but also by his son Herbert, the old statesman dictated fragmentary reminiscences and reflections, which the 'pearl,' as Bismarck described him, sorted out into chapters. It was uphill work, for the chief kept irregular hours and wasted a great deal of time in reading the newspapers. The method of dictation gave a certain conversational ease, but since he trusted entirely to his memory and Friedrichsruh possessed few works of reference, the first text was bound to swarm with errors which it was Bucher's task to correct from the libraries of Berlin. When 'Buchlein,' as the faithful old scribe was called by Princess Bismarck, passed away in 1892 the foundations had been well and truly laid. In the following year the first version was set up in type and served as a basis for the extension and revision which continued to the end. The circumstances of its composition are reflected in the character of the work. It bears little resemblance in form to the large-scale apologias of Clarendon, Guizot and Bülow, who told their story with documentary materials and in orderly sequence from beginning to end. Yet despite its omissions, factual errors and misstatements, it is the greatest of its class, not only on account of the stature of its author, but owing to its wealth of reflection on politics and diplomacy. The original title *Erinnerungen und Gedanken* was restored in the critical edition published in 1937 as volume XV of the *Gesammelte Werke*, edited by Gerhard Ritter.

The first two volumes, which were published directly after his death under the editorial direction of Horst Kohl and close with the reign of the Emperor Frederick, are of infinitely greater importance than the scolding supplement which could not appear till the Hohenzollern Empire was gone. The narrative of his fall, which forms its exclusive theme, was dictated in 1891 when the smart of the wound was fresh and damages its author more than the young ruler whom he despised. Though his picture of William I, on the other hand, is painted with affectionate gratitude and is essentially true to life, his comments on rivals and enemies, among them the Empress Augusta and Count Arnim, are vitiated by the gnawing bitterness of Prometheus chained to his rock. But the faults of temperament which diminish the significance of the work as a contribution to history, and compel us to check every statement by contemporary evidence, enhance its value as a revelation of personality. Here is the whole authentic man of blood and iron, fighting with the gloves off as he had always done, and hating to the last. The student should re-read the book at intervals as his knowledge of the period grows, keeping at his elbow the critical commentary *Fürst Bismarcks Gedanken und Erinnerungen* by Erich Marcks.

The next step is to study some of the principal speeches in the fourteen volumes edited by Horst Kohl, or in the less complete edition in volumes X–XIII of the *Gesammelte Werke* edited by Schüssler. Bismarck was never an orator, occasionally hesitated for the right word, and had a weak and unimpressive voice; but though he had less difficulty in finding expression for his thoughts than Cromwell, his utterances sometimes recall the great Protector in their sudden flashes and rugged strength. Of the declarations on domestic policy none exceed in interest those of his first storm-tossed years as Prussian Premier, collected in the second volume of Horst Kohl, when he bluntly declared that Germany's problems would be solved not by speeches and resolutions but by blood and iron. In the field of foreign affairs the two comprehensive surveys of the European situation delivered in 1887 and 1888, and printed in the twelfth volume, stand out as imperishable statements of the maxims by which he steered his course. Though less witty and polished than those of Bülow, his utterances impress us by the sincerity and range of vision which his successor conspicuously lacked.

While the apologia and the speeches were addressed to the world, the early despatches were written for his official superiors, and, when he had succeeded to the command of the ship, for his subordinates. Nothing is more instructive in the literature of diplomacy, except perhaps Talleyrand's communications during the Congress of Vienna, than his elaborate reports from Frankfurt in the fifties. Appointed to the most difficult post in the Prussian service without any technical training, he quickly transformed the situation. Instead of being the mouthpiece of his Government he worked out a policy of his own, explained it to his superiors in Berlin, and proceeded to apply it unflinchingly. While Prussia was still ruled by Frederick William IV, who accepted the primacy of Austria without question, Bismarck was forming the resolution that Prussia should take the lead. That the situation in central Europe was entering a new phase was sensed by Austria's harassed representatives at the Diet before it was proclaimed to the world at the cannon's mouth in 1866. The Frankfurt despatches were published in the early eighties by Poschinger in four volumes under the title *Preussen im Bundestag*, with the omission of passages deemed offensive to the susceptibilities of Austria, no longer a rival but a trusted ally. Twenty years after Bismarck's death the despatches from St. Petersburg and Paris during 1859–1862 were published by Raschdau, the last survivor of the Bismarckian Foreign

Office. Though they do not compare in importance with the dramatic story of the prolonged duel at Frankfurt, they are of interest for their glimpses of Gortschakoff and Napoleon III on the eve of the Ambassador's promotion to the highest office in the state.

The despatches from Frankfurt were republished forty years later without omissions, when both Hapsburgs and Hohenzollerns had passed away, as a portion of the grandiose monument raised by a defeated nation to its greatest son. The first and most important section of *Bismarck: die gesammelten Werke*, the nineteen magnificent quartos published between 1921 and 1935, contains the Political Writings. Three volumes, edited by Petersdorff, cover the period down to his appointment as Premier and Minister of Foreign Affairs in 1862, and reproduce from the originals the larger part of the material discreetly edited by Poschinger and Raschdau. Neither of these two collections, however, can be set aside, since the new edition for reasons of space makes no pretence to completeness. On the other hand it contains some new letters and reports, and includes the private correspondence with Schleinitz the Foreign Minister.

The second section of the *Politische Schriften*, edited with valuable prefaces by Thimme, covers the Prussian Premiership and the creation of the Empire in six volumes in which more than three-quarters of the documents are new. The main interest of this fresh material lies in the modification of our traditional reading of Bismarck's attitude to Austria as set forth in his own apologia and the semi-official narrative of Sybel. The notion of an implacable Prussian sharpening his knife for Austria's throat over a long period of years fades away, and we discover a political Conservative welcoming Austro-Prussian collaboration as a bulwark against the democratic flood. The annexation of the Elbe Duchies turns out to have been no part of his original plan to free them from the unpopular Danish yoke, and even after the campaign of 1864 a conflict with Austria was rather a possibility than a postulate. Austrian approval was to be sought for a North German Confederation under Prussia and a South German Confederation under Austria, co-operating on equal terms against radicalism and foreign foes. Only when the plan miscarried did he press on to a *Kleindeutsch* and warlike solution, though Thimme believes that the strife of 1866 was due to the intransigence of Vienna rather than to the policy of Berlin, where compromise was favoured till the eleventh hour. The strongest impression derived from the *Political Writings*, comments the enthusiastic editor, is that the founder of the Empire strove for unification by peaceful means.

The same conclusion, he assures us, results from a study of the new material on the war with France. Never did he seek a conflict in order to hasten the union on which his heart was set. Why should he gamble for high stakes when he knew that after the defeat of Austria the willing adhesion of the three South German states was merely a matter of time? Baden, indeed, was already knocking at the door. Napoleon III, on the other hand, had a compelling reason to act. He had lost prestige in 1866 when Prussia passed him in the race, and he longed to strengthen his throne by blocking her further growth. The war of 1870, in fact, was a long meditated aggression against a country which had as much right to national unity as France herself. The two most damaging items in the case against Bismarck, the secret encouragement of the Hohenzollern candidature in Spain and the manipulation of the Ems telegram, are brushed aside: to the end, we are assured, he preferred a bloodless solution. Moreover, in the hour of victory, he proved as moderate as he had shown himself in 1866, for he abandoned the claim to Belfort and was prepared to leave unfortified Metz in French hands. Whether or not we are converted by the advocacy of the learned editor, the new evidence added to that published by Oncken from the Austrian archives demands patient study. The final volume of the *Politische Schriften*, edited by Frauendienst, covering the years 1871–1890, is almost wholly confined to domestic issues, since the material relating to foreign affairs had appeared in *Die Grosse Politik*, the first six volumes of which reveal his efforts to safeguard his conquests by the permanent isolation of France.

The private letters, if less historically significant than the official papers, are essential to our understanding of Bismarck's temperament and outlook. The most important item is the correspondence with William I, which was published immediately after his death by his express desire, as he considered that it would best reveal the nature of a unique relationship. Beginning in 1852 and ending in the winter of 1887, it exhibits the two men at their best, the monarch abounding in gratitude for incomparable services, the Chancellor fully conscious of the value of unfaltering support. A second volume contains correspondence with colleagues and other public men selected by Bismarck himself. The two volumes, which appeared in an English translation in 1903,[1] were designed to authenticate and supplement his autobiography and should be regarded as an elaborate appendix.

Next in importance are the letters to his wife, published at the wish of Herbert Bismarck in 1900.[2] Beginning with the request to Herr von Puttkamer for the hand of his daughter in 1846, and ending in 1892, they reveal 'Ottochen's' softer side. Husband and wife were seldom parted for long after 1866, but for the first two decades of his public life, which began at the time of his marriage, the stream is steady and copious. The letters written during the French campaign, which were not at first to be found, were published later in a little volume of a hundred pages and subsequently added to the larger work. Johanna provided the loving care that he needed, and her limited capacity saved her from the temptation to have a political will of her own. The letters to his sister Malwine von Arnim and her husband, covering an even longer period, were edited by Horst Kohl in 1915, and the shorter series to his younger son Bill was published by his daughter-in-law in 1922. Those of the fifties to General Leopold von Gerlach were published in 1896 by the indefatigable Horst Kohl, who also sponsored the smaller budget to Kleist-Retzow, leader of the Conservatives in the Prussian Upper House. The correspondence with Schleinitz, covering the years 1858 to 1861, appeared in 1905. The two volumes of *Private Letters* in the *Gesammelte Werke*, edited by Windelband and Frauendienst, provide a good deal of fresh material. Other letters and memoranda, addresses and articles, are to be found in the six volumes of the *Bismarck-Jahrbuch*, 1894-9, edited by Horst Kohl, and the *Bismarck-Portefeuille*, edited by Poschinger. A handy selection from the writings and speeches is available in *Otto von Bismarck: Deutscher Staat*, edited with a thoughtful introduction by Rothfels, in the series entitled *Der deutsche Staatsgedanke*.

The greatness of Bismarck was so unmistakable from the moment of his appointment as Premier in 1862 that notes of his conversation were made by large numbers of friends and colleagues, agents and visitors. The *Gespräche* in volumes VII–IX of the *Gesammelte Werke* take their place with the table-talk of Luther and Goethe. The most

---

[1] *The Correspondence of William I and Bismarck, with other Letters.*
[2] English translation, *The Love Letters of Prince Bismarck*, 2 vols.

celebrated reporter was Moritz Busch, whose *Bismarck und seine Leute während des Krieges mit Frankreich*, published in 1878, made him a creature of flesh and blood to his countrymen. The diary, continued till his fall in 1890, was published in 1898 directly after his death, the English edition in three volumes, entitled *Bismarck: Secret Passages from his Life*, containing a few passages omitted in the German original. The garrulous journalist must be checked by other witnesses, but his vivid volumes will always attract as a picture of the superman at work. Less entertaining and less important is Poschinger's *Fürst Bismarck und die Parlamentarier: Die Tischgespräche des Reichskanzlers*, containing copious records of the varied conversation at the *Bierabende* and *Frühschoppen* to which Members of Parliament were invited. The three large volumes have been abridged by Charles Lowe in an English version entitled *Bismarck's Table-Talk*.

Next to Busch no diarist gathered such a harvest as Lucius von Ballhausen, a leading Conservative member of the Reichstag and Minister of Agriculture from 1879 to 1890, whose *Bismarck Erinnerungen*, published in 1921, cover the last two decades of the dictatorship. While Busch was a mere reporter, Ballhausen was a colleague of independent position and a valued friend. His accounts of the Ministerial councils reveal the working of the machine, and the record of the final crisis is impressive in its simplicity. The much slighter testimony of another Ministerial colleague, the *Erlebnisse und Gespräche mit Bismarck* of Adolf von Scholz, Minister of Finance, illustrates the domestic policy of the later years of the Chief, whom he continued to revere in the days of eclipse and whom he depicts in an attractive light. The superman is seen from another angle in the two little volumes *Erinnerungen an Bismarck* by Mittnacht, the Prime Minister of Württemberg, who shared the responsibilities of Versailles and paid the Chancellor frequent visits in Berlin and elsewhere. In his *Persönliche Erinnerungen an Bismarck* Hans Blum, the admiring biographer, describes his contacts from the first meeting in 1867 till the end. Christoph von Tiedemann's *Sechs Jahre Chef der Reichskanzlei*, which forms the second volume of his Memoirs, covers the years 1875–81. Though he spent weeks at a time at Varzin and kept a diary, the book, which is almost entirely concerned with domestic politics, makes rather dull reading.

The memoirs of agents and diplomatists provide a rich feast.

Keudell's *Fürst und Fürstin Bismarck*, the work of an intimate friend of them both as well as a trusted political associate, covers the early years 1846–72, before his appointment as Minister to Constantinople. Of far greater historical importance, though lacking personal intimacy, are the two volumes of the diaries (*Denkwürdigkeiten*) of General von Schweinitz, who represented his country in Vienna and St. Petersburg during the whole of the Bismarckian era. The diaries of Prince Hohenlohe, the greatest political figure on the German stage after Bismarck himself, supply a mass of information on the latter's mind and moods. The two men were never intimate, but they respected each other and worked together for decades in the cause of German unity. Of equal value are the first two volumes of the *Denkwürdigkeiten* of Count Waldersee. Moltke's right-hand man and successor as Chief of the Staff was as much a politician as a soldier, and in his later years he was credited with the ambition to succeed Bismarck as Chancellor. The two men had no love for each other, but they preserved appearances and their paths constantly crossed till the end. The *Aufzeichnungen und Erinnerungen* of Radowitz, son of the friend and Minister of Frederick William IV, are useful for the whole period, especially for the seventies when he worked in the Foreign Office, during the Berlin Congress, of which he was one of the Secretaries, and for the crisis of 1890. The fourth volume of Bülow's Memoirs contains pleasant snapshots over a period of forty years. None of these witnesses has drawn such a vivid picture of the ageing statesman in his family circle, in sunshine and in storm, as Prince Eulenburg in his fascinating recollections *Aus 50 Jahren*. Otto Baumgarten's *Bismarcks Religion* traces the intellectual and spiritual evolution of a Prussian Protestant to whom church-going and dogma made no appeal, but who believed in Providence and felt himself responsible for his actions to a higher Power. 'He experienced God as a reality before which he seemed himself small.' The same conclusion is reached in A. O. Meyer's *Bismarcks Glaube*, based on the study of his well-thumbed volumes of devotion.

III

For intensive study we must set sail on the vast ocean of monographs. Forty years ago Erich Marcks set out to produce a biography which enjoyed the approval of the family. His unrivalled knowledge of the period and his literary skill rendered him an ideal biographer; but the *magnum opus* began and ended with the masterly first volume published in 1909, which only brings the story down to 1848 and therefore falls into the category of monographs. The first half of a second volume, written in 1910 and covering the years 1848–1851, was edited after his death in 1938 by his son-in-law Willy Andreas. Despite this valuable fragment, which discusses the marriage, religion and political ideas of his hero, with special reference to the influence of Stahl, the stormy years from the United Landtag to the appointment as Prussia's representative at the Diet are the least known and the least documented of his public career. At this stage he approved Prussia's surrender to Schwarzenberg at Olmütz and scorned the Frankfurt Parliament which strove for a constitutional and united Germany. In attempting to reconstruct the stage on which he made his *début*, and to understand the ideas which inspired the various groups in the middle of the century, we should supplement Marcks by Meinecke's classical treatise *Weltbürgertum und Nationalstaat* and Veit Valentin's massive volumes *Geschichte der deutschen Revolution* 1848–9, of which an abridged translation has appeared.

On the Frankfurt period we are fortunate to possess one of the best monographs in the field of modern German history. The Prussian envoy's reports, already mentioned, only presented one side of the struggle between the two leading members of the Bund, and no satisfactory reconstruction was possible till the Austrian version became available. It is the merit of Arnold Oskar Meyer's *Bismarcks Kampf mit Oesterreich am Bundestag zu Frankfurt 1851 bis 1859* to have provided the first full account from the Prussian and Austrian archives, combining a fervent admiration of his hero with vivid sketches of the Hapsburg representatives. The fateful rivalry was analysed from another angle in the second volume of Srbik's masterpiece, *Deutsche Einheit*. Frankfurt, explains Austria's greatest living historian, was Germany's mirror, and Austria regarded Prussia as an impertinent claimant to the place of the eldest son. Bismarck was in no sense an Austrophobe at the date of his appointment, and his instructions from Berlin were to co-operate with Austria against the revolution. His price, however, was full equality for Prussia in the formulation and application of federal decisions: if it were refused he would 'bring home Austria's scalp.' From the first he distrusted the Diet, which he regarded as an obstacle to Prussia's needs, and he found that Vienna was in no mood for parity. At the outset there was no thought of a breach, for a working partnership still seemed possible. Yet he regarded himself as entrusted with a mission like Frederick the Great to work for Prussia, and he came to wish for 'a good war, like the Seven Years' War.'

This struggle, complains Srbik, was waged not only with loyal but often with unchivalrous weapons: stubborn obstinacy, hair-splitting, craving for prestige, disputes about rank as in the old Empire, lies and misrepresentations. Bismarck caricatured his opponents and always depicted himself in his reports as on the defensive, whereas he constantly launched his attacks. He concealed a good deal from Manteuffel, the Prussian Premier, and cleverly employed every method of warfare, menaces, intrigues and pinpricks. He combined astonishing publicity with diplomatic untruth. There was always a deep reason for these tactics, but how fearful, how incomparably hard was this struggle. He had no consideration for Austria's principle of the solidarity of the Conservative Powers. He demanded the realistic exploitation of her European embarrassments, ruthlessly diminished the dignity of the Bund, paralysed it as only he could do, and was largely responsible for the denigration which has lasted till our own day. 'With the Prussian horse pulling in front and the Austrian horse behind,' he wrote in 1853, 'the federal cart must soon collapse.' He spoke openly of 'the good war against Austria to drive her out of Germany,' if necessary with France's help; and he displayed bitter enmity to her representatives at Frankfurt.

The Kleindeutsch picture of the restored Bund painted by Bismarck, declares the Austrian historian, is no longer acceptable. The Diet was not a group of mediocre, lazy folk fettered by the instructions of their governments, neither adapted nor inclined to serious activities. There was plenty of knowledge, plenty of serious work by men of brains and experience. For many Austrians—and others—it was a common possession of the whole German fatherland. Yet Srbik is no unreserved admirer of his country's policy, and her *rôle* in the Crimean war under Buol's guidance was her undoing. Prussia declined to follow her lead, and Prussian neutrality saved Russia from an overwhelming coalition. 'Austria had now lost the game both in Berlin and in Frankfurt. The Bund refused to help when she went beyond the limits of German interests, and Prussia had taken her place as leader. It had again displayed its unsuitability for large-scale European policy; its inner fragility and its dependence on the unity or disunion of the two Great Powers became clear to all. The old idea of the co-operation of the Conservative monarchies remained: in Francis Joseph, obsessed by dread of the social revolution, in Frederick William IV in the longing for the union of legitimist princes favouring Christian principles, in the German dynasties of the middle and smaller states whose existence was threatened by the fear of mediatisation and the sovereignty of the people. Yet how deep were the rifts in this Germanic world, how infinitely more difficult was Austria's German position, since she could not and would not grant full equality to Prussia, and since her conduct confirmed the conviction that some day there must be a struggle for leadership on German soil.' No one saw this more clearly than Bismarck. 'As a result of the Vienna policy,' he reported, 'Germany is too small for us both. So long as there is no honourable arrangement about our respective positions we are ploughing the same contested field, and Austria remains the only state which could bring us loss or gain.' 'At intervals during a thousand years,' and since Charles V in every century,' he wrote in 1857, 'German dualism has regulated relations by a major war. And in this century too no other means will set the clock at the right hour. I must express my conviction that we shall soon have to fight Austria and that it is not in our power to prevent it, since the course of things in Germany indicates no other way.' Srbik's little book *Oesterreich in der deutschen Geschichte* summarises the conclusions of the four volumes. *Eine gesamtdeutsche Volkseinheit*—not to be confounded with the wild dreams of Pan-Germanism—is his ideal, for only in such a family relationship are ancient rivalries resolved. Schwarzenberg claimed too much power for Austria, and in consequence Bismarck demanded too much for Prussia. The conflict of 1866 was a tragedy for both sides; yet there is no need for moralising since irresistible forces were at work. Stronger than Bismarck, King William or Francis Joseph was fate—the defeat of the universalist tradition by nationalism in its flowing tide.

While the Prussian envoy at Frankfurt was planning to liberate the Bund from the Austrian yoke, Frederick William IV surrounded himself with members of the Christo-Germanic school, inspired by Stahl and led by the Gerlach brothers. Bismarck agreed with the ruler and his friends in detesting Liberalism, but he was equally hostile to the flabby romanticism of his master, whom he despised both for his subservience to Austria and his weakness of will. The two men met from time to time, and the King was aware of the volcanic fires which burned in his envoy. The note written against his name—'only to be employed in a crisis'—was a sentence of exclusion from high office during the reign of a gifted dreamer who had had enough political excitement in 1848 to last him the rest of his life. Bismarck's personal relations with the ruling clique are mirrored in his correspondence with Leopold von Gerlach, and are analysed by Augst in *Bismarck und Leopold von Gerlach*, which presents the younger man as the friend but never as the disciple of the old General.

Our knowledge of the three years in Russia, hitherto derived from the official despatches and the private letters to Schleinitz, received a welcome enrichment with the publication in 1921 of Kurt von Schlözer's *Petersburger Briefe 1857–1862*. 'My new chief,' complained the exasperated First Secretary of the Prussian Legation after a brief acquaintance, 'is a man without consideration, a man of might who aspires to *coups de théâtre*, who desires to shine, who knows everything without having seen it, and is omniscient though there is much that he does not know. He has been used in Frankfurt to young Attachés who trembled at his approach.' A year later he reported that they were getting on splendidly, though he added: 'A devil of a fellow! Where is he making for?' The greatness of the man conquered him, and he remained a friend up to and after 1890. The years in Russia are reviewed in Nolde's *Die Petersburger Mission Bismarcks 1859–1862*.

The first full and authoritative record of the diplomacy of the eight years which followed the summons to Berlin in 1862 was attempted by Sybel, who, after sharply attacking the new Premier's unconstitutional proceedings in Parliament, was converted by the victory of Sadowa into a member of his academic bodyguard. The suggestion that the famous historian should devote his closing years to describing the founding of the German Empire came from the Chancellor himself, who promised him the use of the archives. The first five volumes, published in 1889, brought the story to the end of 1866; but William II considered that his adored grandfather had not received his due, and meanly excluded him from the archives after the quarrel with his patron in the following year. Thus the last two volumes, which reach the outbreak of war with France, lack the full documentary value of their predecessors, though the fallen statesman gave what help he could. Whatever else we read on the most eventful years of his life, Sybel's narrative must be read too. When asked his opinion of the book by Justizrat Philipp, Bismarck replied that the historian had written with discretion, but that, despite the necessary omissions, the work was thoroughly reliable in all essentials. Thus we are listening to the story in the shape that the chief actor desired it to be told. Rössler wittily remarked that the title *The Founding of the German Empire by William I* contained a misprint, and that it should have been 'despite' instead of 'by.'[1] This, however, is not the criticism that we should make to-day. Sybel's chief weakness is his Prussian partiality and his failure to paint the hero with his warts. A critic complained with humorous exaggeration that he had transformed the tiger into a tame cat. The German Empire was not founded by a Sunday school teacher, and the Bismarck of the sixties was more like Vulcan in his forge than Sybel cared to admit.

The dynastic vanity of William II was partially soothed by Ottokar Lorenz in *Kaiser Wilhelm I und die Gründung des Reiches 1866–1871*, published in 1902. Utilising materials supplied by Ernst, Duke of Coburg, the rulers of Baden and Weimar, and various South German statesmen, he presented a picture strikingly different from that of Sybel and hailed the old Emperor as the master-builder. But the pendulum had now swung too far in the other direction, and Lorenz was pulled up by his brother specialists. He vigorously defended himself in a little book entitled *Bismarcks Verkleinerer*, but his writings have failed in their main purpose. The personal and political relations between the old Emperor and his Minister are most fairly depicted in Marcks' classical biography *Kaiser Wilhelm I*. For a later and more judicial version of the making of the Reich we may turn to the eighth, ninth and tenth volumes of Alfred Stern's *Geschichte Europas 1815–1871*, written in the temperate zone of neutral Switzerland. For French views of the sixties we naturally turn to the *Histoire du Second Empire* of La Gorce, to Ollivier's prolix apologia, and to the vast official publication *Les Origines Diplomatiques de la Guerre de 1870–1*, which opens in 1862; for the Austrian version to the entertaining Memoirs of Beust, to Friedjung's famous book *Der Kampf um die Vorherrschaft in Deutschland*, which may be read in an abridged English version, and to the still more authoritative record in Srbik's *Deutsche Einheit*.

[1] *Trotz* for *durch*.

The most important individual addition since Sybel to our knowledge of the diplomatic game in the sixties is contained in Oncken's three volumes of documents *Die Rheinpolitik Kaiser Napoleon III von 1863 bis 1870*, which reveal the innermost thoughts of the Imperial adventurer. The astonishing story of ambition and intrigue unfolded in the reports of Metternich, the Austrian Ambassador at Paris, is summarised in the vigorous and polemical Introduction, which has appeared separately in English as *Napoleon and the Rhine*. It is a fascinating if not elevating occupation to watch the two chess-players, Napoleon itching for the Rhineland, Bismarck bent on the unification of Germany under Prussian leadership, the one plunging wildly, the other exploiting his mistakes. *Grossherzog Friedrich I von Baden und die deutsche Politik von 1845 bis 1871*, edited by the same distinguished scholar, covers part of the same ground. The correspondence, memoranda, and diaries of the son-in-law of the Emperor William are of equal value for the relations between North and South Germany and for the external conflicts from which the Empire emerged. A luminous Introduction furnishes the key to the two bulky volumes, and enables us to visualise the wisest and most influential of Bismarck's princely collaborators. When the immense enterprise entitled *Die auswärtige Politik Preussens 1858–1871* is completed a fresh survey of Bismarck's early activities will be needed.

Since the whole of Europe was involved in the birth-pangs of the German Empire, it is not surprising that monographs on the sixties follow each other in unending succession. Steefel's *The Slesvig-Holstein Question* utilises the little known Danish material on the diplomatic campaign which Bismarck always regarded as his masterpiece. The intricate story of the promise in Article V of the Treaty of Prague of a plebiscite in North Schleswig, and of its cancellation in 1878, has been told in *Bismarck und die Nordschleswigsche Frage 1864–1879*, published in 1925 by order of the German Foreign Office. In his Introduction to the documents Platzhoff challenges the traditional belief that Bismarck never intended to fulfil the pledge, and points out that he was ready to surrender the frontier districts on condition that the transferred German minority should be protected and the honour of Germany maintained. That all attempts at a peaceful understanding failed, concludes the Editor, was due not to Bismarck but to the obstinacy of the Danes, who demanded a plebiscite in the whole of Schleswig.

Zechlin's *Bismarck und die Grundlegung der deutschen Grossmacht* grew out of a plan to describe the making of the Constitution, but the interaction of foreign and domestic politics proved to be so close that the work developed into a panoramic survey of policy in the sixties. So great, however, was the mass of fresh material that this volume of 600 pages, after an introductory survey of the European situation and of Bismarck's political ideas, only covers 'the new era' during 1862 and 1863. In Chester Clark's massive work *Franz Joseph and Bismarck*, based largely on the Vienna archives, the latter appears more of an opportunist feeling his way than as the crusader depicted in his apologia. The end of the same decade has been illuminated, with the aid of fresh material from the Prussian Foreign Office, by Horst Michael's *Bismarck, England und Europa, 1866–1870*, in which special emphasis is laid on the importance of the problems of the Near East, and we are warned not to dwell too exclusively in the west in visualising the foundation of the German Empire. The essential condition of a victorious struggle with France, which Bismarck anticipated rather than desired, was the neutralisation of Austria; and in these pages it is the angry Beust, who was summoned from Dresden to the Ballplatz after the *débâcle* of 1866, who claims our attention rather than Napoleon III.

The latest important contribution to our understanding of the sixties is provided from a foreign angle in Wertheimer's *Bismarck im politischen Kampf*, based on the archives of Vienna and Berlin. The official biographer of Andrassy, though a patriotic Hungarian, assures his readers that he writes as a lifelong friend of Germany and that his book is a sign of his special reverence for the greatest statesman of German blood. After a survey of the apprenticeship at Frankfurt, St. Petersburg and Paris, he deals with the background of the war of 1866, Bismarck's relations to Hungary, the visit of the monarchs to the Paris exhibition of 1867, and the relations with Prince Jerome Napoleon. The longest chapter describes the domestic and other obstacles which had to be overcome before the King of Prussia could assume the Imperial title. A final chapter on Bismarck's relations to Taaffe brings us to the period of peace. A curious addition to our knowledge of the struggle with Austria has been made in Hermann Wendel's *Bismarck und Serbien in Jahre 1866*, which reveals the plan of stirring up Serbia as well as Hungary against the Hapsburg foe.

The internal history of the founding of the Empire has received less attention than the diplomatic side. Bismarck's work was facilitated—it may almost be said rendered possible—by the *Nationalverein* founded in 1859 by Rudolf von Bennigsen. The Hanoverian statesman, who owed his influence as much to his high character as to his ability, has found a sympathetic biographer in Oncken, whose enormous volumes, stuffed with political correspondence, are indispensable for the whole era. A full-length portrait of his eloquent collaborator Miquel, who found his way from Marx to Bismarck and ended as Finance Minister to William II, was undertaken by Wilhelm Mommsen, whose first volume reaches 1866. The Dictator's relations with Lassalle received fresh illumination when in 1927 a forgotten chest in the Foreign Office collapsed from old age and disclosed the lost correspondence, which Gustav Mayer has published with an admirable Introduction as *Bismarck und Lassalle: Ihr Briefwechsel und ihre Gespräche*. For his conflict with the Liberals we have the collection of letters published with the title *Deutscher Liberalismus im Zeitalter Bismarcks: eine Politsche Briefsammlung*, edited by Geritzcke and Heyderhoff. His dealings with the Conservatives are related in detail in Siegfried von Kardorff's biography of his father Wilhelm, leader of the faithful little group of Free Conservatives; in Gerhard Ritter's *Die Preussischen Konservativen und Bismarcks Deutsche Politik, 1858–1871*; and in the *Denkwürdigkeiten* of Roon, a man of singularly inelastic mind.

When the Deutscher Bund perished on the battlefield of Sadowa Bismarck set to work to construct a constitution for the newly founded North German Confederation, which, in the fullness of time, could be enlarged to embrace the South German states. The classical presentation of the new constitutional structure is in Laband's monumental *Deutsches Staatsrecht*, but those who shirk the German Anson will find an excellent substitute in B. E. Howard's *The German Empire*. That united Germany might have come earlier into the world if the attitude of Hesse-Darmstadt had been more forthcoming is the argument of Schüssler's learned monograph *Bismarcks Kampf um Süddeutschland 1867*. The constitutional relations of the Empire to its largest unit are traced with a wealth of new material in Hans Goldschmidt's *Das Reich und Preussen im Kampf um die Führung: von Bismarck bis 1918*.

On the immediate causes of the last of Bismarck's three wars we possess *The Origin of the War of 1870* by the Harvard historian, R. H. Lord, who prefaces a translation of the most important Prussian documents with a critical discussion of his policy. There is a vivid account of the historic scene at Ems in the life of Abeken, the Wilhelmstrasse representative in attendance on King William, translated under the title *Bismarck's Pen*. Fester has collected the relevant material on the last days of peace in *Briefe, Aktenstücke und Regesten zur Geschichte der Hohenzollernschen Thronkandidatur in Spanien*, a topic on which light is thrown in the ninth volume of Bernhardi's Memoirs. The *War Diary* of Crown Prince Frederick, 1870–1871, from which Geffcken published a few sensational extracts in 1888, appeared in 1926, and the diary of the Grand Duke Frederick of Baden concludes the second volume of his papers to which attention was called above. The important *rôle* of the Bavarian Government and dynasty in the creation of the Empire is described from a Bavarian standpoint in Döberl's *Bayern und die Bismarcksche Reichsgründung*, which pays fitting tribute to the statesmanship of Bray. Johannes Haller's suggestive little book *Bismarcks Friedenschlüsse* compares and discusses the contrasted settlements of 1864, 1866 and 1871. Nikolsburg, he contends, was a perfect peace, while Frankfurt was in some degree vitiated by the failure to acquire Belfort. What British statesmen thought of it all may be studied in Veit Valentin's *Bismarcks Reichsgründung im Urteil Englischer Diplomaten, 1848–1871*, enriched by new material from the Record Office.

IV

WITH the return from Versailles we enter on the second and less eventful chapter of the twenty-eight years of personal rule. Till then Bismarck had lived the feverish life of a gambler ever playing for the highest stakes. He had won every round in the game owing to an unparalleled combination of skill and luck, but the ground was never firm beneath his feet till German unity under Prussian leadership had been attained. A French triumph in 1870, like an Austrian victory in Bohemia in 1866, would have flung him headlong into the abyss. The great adventure was now at an end. No one was tempted to attack the strongest state on the Continent, which had struck down two formidable rivals within a space of five years. Henceforth his position was unassailable. He had enemies but no rivals. The laurels were thick on his brow, and he enjoyed the unchanging confidence of the old ruler whom he had raised to the pinnacle of earthly fame.

The sources for a study of his diplomacy in the nineteen years following his crowning victory accumulate from year to year. The first six volumes of the *Grosse Politik* provide the solid groundwork for an interpretation, and there is much to learn from the first seven volumes of the *Documents Diplomatiques Français*, which, like the *Grosse Politik*, begin in 1871. The first two fill in the outline drawn in the poignant Memoirs of the sorely-tried French Ambassador Gontaut-Biron and in the slighter volumes, *La Mission du Comte de St. Vallier*, compiled by Ernest Daudet from the papers of his happier successor. From the Austrian side we derive precious assistance from the third volume of Wertheimer's biography of Andrassy and from Pribram's edition of the *Secret Treaties of Austria-Hungary*, prefaced by an illuminating sketch of the formation and evolution of the Triple Alliance. From the British side useful material has become available in the official biographies of Disraeli and Salisbury, the second and third series of Queen Victoria's correspondence, and the temperamental *Letters of the Empress Frederick*, edited by Sir Frederick Ponsonby. The Congress of Berlin should be studied in the work of Medlicott and in Sumner's *Russia and the Balkans, 1870–1880*.

No detailed study of Bismarck's later diplomacy has been attempted on the scale of Sybel. Rachfahl's *Deutschland und die Weltpolitik*, consisting of his University lectures, lacks notes and references. We owe the best bird's-eye view to Japikse, whose work has appeared in German as *Europa und Bismarcks Friedenspolitik*. Standing as he does outside the rivalries of the Great Powers, the verdict of the distinguished Dutch historian is of peculiar weight when he asserts that from the defeat of France till the day of his dismissal the governing principle of his policy was the maintenance of peace. The same conviction inspires A. O. Meyer's brochure *Bismarcks Friedenspolitik*, which contains fresh material supplied by the family.

This favourable reading of twenty years of Bismarckian diplomacy, though generally accepted by historians, has been challenged within and beyond the frontiers of the Fatherland. The severest critic is the American scholar Joseph Fuller, who launched a preliminary attack in an essay on the war scare of 1875 in the *American*

Historical Review, January 1919. Rejecting the Chancellor's contention in his apologia that he was the innocent victim of designing soldiers, Fuller argues that the crisis was his own work. Herzfeld responded to the challenge in his brochure *Die deutschfranzösische Kriegsgefahr von 1875*. The most damaging item in the indictment is the report by Gontaut-Biron of an after-dinner talk with Radowitz, a high official of the Foreign Office enjoying the full confidence of Bismarck, in which he was stated to have spoken openly of a preventive war. The publication in *Die Grosse Politik* of Radowitz' very different account of the conversation sets the problem in a new light, though it is highly improbable that the Ambassador invented the incident which caused him and his countrymen so much alarm. Holborn has cleared up the mystery of Radowitz' visit to St. Petersburg in his documented monograph *Bismarcks Europäische Politik zu Beginn der 70er Jahre und die Mission Radowitz*, in which the vain old Gortchakoff appears as the villain of the piece. The latest and best discussion of the war scare is in the biography of Lord Odo Russell by Dr. Winifred Taffs, which utilises the correspondence of the British Ambassador and fresh material from the archives of Berlin. She concludes that Bismarck was neither as white as he painted himself nor as black as the Quai d'Orsay believed, for he was genuinely alarmed at the rapid military recovery of France: he rattled the sword but had no desire to draw it. Moreover, the rally of Russia and Great Britain to the side of France showed him, as it showed the world, that he had made a mistake, and taught him to be more cautious. Selections from the private correspondence of two British Ambassadors at Berlin with the Foreign Secretary, Lord Granville, 1871–4 and 1880–5, were edited by Professor Knaplund for the American Historical Association in 1942. That Bismarck liked Lord Odo Russell in no way blunted his critical faculty. His successor, Sir Edward Malet, never became *persona grata* and therefore failed to gain similar insight into his character.

A more sustained attack by Fuller on Bismarck's reputation as a man of peace after 1871 was delivered in his learned volume *Bismarck's Diplomacy at its Zenith*, a study of the European crisis inaugurated by the revolutionary unification of Bulgaria in 1885. Unlike most historians, who see in him the giant whose mighty arm kept Austria and Russia from flying at one another's throats, he presents an angry bungler whose duplicity and brutality left Germany at the end of the crisis between two potential foes about to join hands across her frontiers. Hardly less severe is the criticism of the handling of the same incident in *Bismarcks Friedenspolitik und das Problem des deutschen Machtverfalls* by Ulrich Noack, though the indictment is of an opposite character. While the American scholar accuses him of playing with fire, the German historian condemns him for his moderation. Bismarck, he declares, lost an opportunity which could never recur of ending by a fourth victorious war the growing Slav danger. He should have joined with Austria against Russia, and after the victory should have satisfied the autonomous aspirations of the various Slav races, from the Baltic to the Aegean, within the orbit of Austro-German hegemony. The task of remodelling Eastern Europe shirked by the Man of Destiny in his distaste for preventive wars was taken up and solved thirty years later by the victorious allies at the expense of the Central Empires after the First World War. Very different in tone and conclusions is Otto Becker's treatment of the same group of problems in *Bismarcks Bündnispolitik*, the first volume of a work which passes beyond the later phases of the master's diplomacy to the tragic blunders of his successors, and vindicates the secret treaty of reinsurance concluded with Russia in 1887 as serving the interests of each of the three Empires.

Less controversial than the writings of Fuller and Noack is Rothfels' *Bismarcks Englische Bündnispolitik*, which discusses our relations to the New Empire down to the offer of an alliance in 1889. While Germany remained purely a Continental power there was nothing to quarrel about, but the decision in 1884 to follow the fashion by cutting a few slices off the African joint led to temporary friction. A comprehensive survey of the creation of a colonial Empire is provided in Maximilian Hagen's *Bismarcks Kolonialpolitik*, which English readers should compare with the account in Lord Fitzmaurice's biography of Granville. How Bismarck mended the wire to St. Petersburg in 1881 after the dangerous tension of 1879 we learn from the *Memoirs* of Saburow, the Russian Ambassador at Berlin, edited with an Introduction by J. Y. Simpson. The European chessboard during the final years in the Wilhelmstrasse and on the morrow of his fall is reconstituted in the opening chapters of William Langer's *The Franco-Russian Alliance 1890–1894* and in Brandenburg's masterpiece *From Bismarck to the World War*.

In his domestic policy Bismarck was as fallible as lesser mortals.

At a time when it was desirable to rally all the forces of national life round the new Imperial structure, he engaged in a struggle with the Roman Church which stirred millions of loyal subjects to anger and from which he emerged bruised and saddled with a powerful *Centrumspartei* under the formidable Windthorst. His conflict with the Catholics is described from the Government side in Erich Förster's fully documented life of Falk, the Minister whom he used as his tool in the days of his wrath and who, when he recognised the futility of the struggle, was thrown aside. The Catholic side can be studied in Kissling's *Geschichte des Kulturkampfes im Deutschen Reiche,* the first volume of which traces Prussian policy towards Catholics down to 1870. The settlement with the Papacy is vividly described in the *Letze Römische Briefe 1882–1894* of Kurd von Schlözer, Prussian Minister to the Vatican. A suggestive sketch of the long quarrel is provided in the closing lecture in Siegfried von Kardorff's *Bismarck,* which describes the mission of peace of Prince Hatzfeldt Trachenberg in 1886 from material furnished by the envoy.

The battle with the Socialists was equally unsuccessful, though in this case Bismarck is not open to the charge of provoking a conflict. Socialism was a world-wide problem, the child of modern industrialism, and he can hardly be blamed for not knowing how to deal with it. But his repressive legislation was a complete failure, and the working-class movement developed in bitter hostility to the State. The Socialist version may be read in the fourth volume of Mehring's *Geschichte der deutschen Sozialdemokratie* and in Bebel's autobiography, the latter available in an English translation. The Government's constructive policy of state-aided insurance and pensions, which followed the passing of the anti-socialist law of 1878, is sympathetically outlined in Dawson's *Bismarck and State Socialism.* The struggle with the Liberals is illustrated in the life of Georg von Bunsen by his gifted daughter Marie.

The sharpest condemnation of the authoritarian spirit of Bismarck's domestic policy has been passed by Ziekursch in the first two volumes of his spirited *Politische Geschichte des neuen deutschen Kaiserreiches.* The Dictator, he complains, gave the dynasty such power that a Frederick the Great or a Bismarck on the steps of the throne was required to avert disaster. The edifice was top-heavy, for it rested on a quasi-autocratic government which was bound to become increasingly out of touch with the spirit of the age. The unpardonable error was the omission to train the nation for self-determination. Though the *bourgeoisie* had no keen desire for larger responsibilities, a statesman of clearer vision would have realised that an educated and prosperous community could not forever be kept in leading-strings. The lack of contact between the government and the people, as he points out, was to prove one of the contributory causes of the revolution of 1918. A far more flattering verdict on his domestic statesmanship is pronounced in Wahl's *Deutsche Geschichte 1871–1914*, the first two volumes of which carry us to 1890. While the Liberal Ziekursch lectures him on his blindness to the merits of democracy, the Conservative Wahl salutes him as the author of an admirable constitution capable of resisting the assaults of radicalism and socialism. No recent work has emphasised so strongly his services to Conservatism in the broadest sense of the term. On the other hand the *Kulturkampf*, which he treats in great detail, was admittedly a failure.

The accession of William II in 1888 was the beginning of the end, though the crisis took two years to develop. The parties to the quarrel have presented their case to the world, one in the spiteful third volume of his apologia, the other through the medium of Nowak's *Kaiser and Chancellor*, published in 1930 as the first volume of a survey of his reign utilising written and oral matter from Doorn. Nowak has made out a better case for the fallen ruler than he made for himself in his self-righteous Memoirs. The Chancellor is depicted as drunk with power and past his prime. An appendix reprints the letter to Francis Joseph dictated by the Emperor on April 3, 1890, describing the events of the critical days in vivid detail, which was first published in an Austrian journal in 1919. The valuable memoranda of Bötticher, Minister of the Interior, and Rottenburg, Secretary of the Chancellery, were published in Epstein's *Bismarcks Entlassung*, which establishes Bötticher's loyalty both to the Kaiser and the Chancellor. The first critical summary of the evidence was provided in Schüssler's *Bismarcks Sturz*, for which the Austrian and Bavarian archives were explored, while Wilhelm Mommsen's *Bismarcks Sturz und die Parteien* analyses the Parliamentary and press reactions of the catastrophe. The work of Gradenwitz, *Bismarcks letzter Kampf 1888–1898*, which despite its title is almost wholly concerned with his resignation, utilises the reports of Baden's Minister at Berlin. In *Bismarcks Entlassung* Gagliardi, the Swiss historian, who sides with the Emperor, adds new light from Swiss and Austrian archives and from reports of the envoys of minor German states at Berlin. The impression after studying the whole evidence is that the breach was inevitable, resulting from a clash not only of temperaments and policies but of generations. The dropping of the pilot was clearly a danger to the navigation of the ship, yet the young Emperor was right in rejecting advice to adopt violent courses against strikers and Parliamentary opponents. The surprising story of the old statesman's unconstitutional projects, which was hinted at in Delbrück's little book *Bismarcks Erbe* published in 1915, was repeated in the pages of Nowak and is worked out in detail by Zechlin in *Die Staatsstreichpläne Bismarcks und Wilhelms II*.

The last eight years must be reconstructed from the material collected in Penzler's seven volumes, *Bismarck nach der Entlassung*; in the two volumes entitled *Fürst Bismarck 1890–1898*, edited by Hofmann, editor of the *Hamburger Fremdenblatt*, which contains the articles inspired by the old *frondeur*; in the third volume of the *Gespräche* in the *Gesammelte Werke*; and in Julius von Eckhardt's *Aus den Tagen von Bismarcks Kampf gegen Caprivi*. The conflict between Potsdam and Friedrichsruh reached its climax when the fallen statesman, on his visit to Vienna for the wedding of his eldest son, was publicly boycotted by order of the German Government. His retaliation in a memorable series of speeches at Jena and elsewhere as he returned home through Germany is described in Gradenwitz' *Akten über Bismarcks Grossdeutsche Rundfahrt vom Jahre 1892*. Among the many pilgrims to Friedrichsruh in the years of eclipse none possessed a quicker mind or a sharper pen than Maximilian Harden, who defended the Bismarckian tradition against the new regime in his weekly *Die Zukunft*, and whose memories were embodied in the essay on Bismarck published in the first volume of his *Köpfe*. The sympathetic study of Johanna Bismarck in the same volume brings the rather colourless companion of his stormy life vividly before our eyes.

V

THE era in which the permanence of Bismarck's work was taken for granted ended with the collapse in 1918, when the Hohenzollern Empire, hitherto regarded at home and abroad as the consummation of German history, was recognised to be merely a parenthesis. In a challenging little brochure *Bismarcks Schatten*, published in 1921, Professor Hermann Kantorowicz argued that the path of deliverance was over the ruins of his cult, and foretold that in another generation he would be recognised as the great seducer who had led his country astray. A similar repudiation came in the same year from F. W. Förster, Germany's leading pacifist, who revived the arguments of Constantin Frantz and sharply condemned the *Kleindeutsch* or Prussian solution of the problem of unity. Most recent surveys of German history by younger scholars reflect the atmospheric change. Gazing ruefully at the fallen pillars, they ask themselves if the temple might not have been constructed on some other plan.

Let us, however, first take Johannes Haller, a fervent and eloquent representative of the Old Guard. The pages which conclude his well-known Tübingen lectures, *Epochs of German History*, accept as an axiom the declaration of Clausewitz that there was only one way for Germany to attain political unity, namely by the sword, and that one of its states must bring all the others into subjection. 'Bismarck was no conjuror, no miracle-worker, but his mind was a magic mirror which reflected things as they were. He realised that German unity was only attainable if the duel begun in 1740 was fought to a finish. He was the right man in the right place, equipped with every qualification: an experienced Parliamentarian, a professional diplomatist, conservative without prejudices, German and Prussian combined, strong and subtle, bold and shrewd, a man to be trusted. And every possible obstacle was placed in his way. He was opposed, hated, despised, vilified; only a merciful fate spared him from falling to an assassin's bullet at the most critical moment. The nation did not recognise her saviour, and would indeed have crucified him or burned him alive. He had to save his country, as he once saved a groom from drowning, by gripping it by the throat. When he had won and the work was practically over, they cheered and lauded him to the skies. But what was the value of such belated converts? From the vast majority of the nation there never came a spark of understanding for the statesman who gave them what they wanted but could not obtain for themselves. As for learning from his wisdom, they obstinately refused to do anything of the sort. I confess I cannot utter the name of Bismarck without a sense of shame. The celebrations constantly being held nowadays strike me as almost blasphemy. What right have the men of this generation to celebrate his glory when they have done worse than kill him, have abandoned his structure to decay and ruin?' Such full-throated paeans were rare in the Weimar years and even during the Nazi era, and for the last three decades the tide has been flowing the other way.

The Bismarck chapter in Veit Valentin's last work, *The German People: Their History and Civilisation from the Holy Roman Empire to the Third Reich*, is singularly cool. As a Frankfurter of Huguenot descent, a Liberal, and one of the few German academic champions of the League of Nations, he stands completely outside the Prussian tradition without seeking refuge in the Austrian camp. Vienna's *rôle* in 1866, he declares, was by no means that of the innocent lamb attacked by the wolf of Berlin. 'While Bismarck was preparing to shatter the imperial state of Austria from within, Francis Joseph was planning to degrade Prussia to a secondary state such as it had been before the time of Frederick the Great. In those critical weeks before the war broke out both the great German Powers were repeatedly guilty of violating federal law, though it was Prussia that was regarded as the law-breaker and war-monger by Germany and the world.' Of the victor he speaks without enthusiasm. 'Prussia wanted to make use of modern constitutionalism only so far as it would not affect the basic conditions of Prussian life, which were anti-democratic and so remained.' In his later years Bismarck became a tyrant, branding his critics as enemies of the Reich. His domestic policy was largely a failure and his fall was hailed in many quarters with relief. Only when the blunders of the New Course led to isolation did the tragic significance of his loss become fully apparent.

The handling in Prince Hubertus Loewenstein's *Germans in History* is more lenient than we might expect from a Bavarian Catholic Democrat to whom the idea of the unity of western civilisation once embodied in the Holy Roman Empire is the essence of political wisdom. That Europe meant nothing to the greatest German statesman of his century is regretfully admitted; but 'his tragic guilt is the guilt of an age. The universal idea was in abeyance and he was not the man to summon it back to life.' In the game of power politics he was no more and no less moral than the other players. In one respect he was wiser than most, for he kept the army chiefs in their place by insisting on civilian control of policy. 'Here speaks the true Bismarck, cynical indeed but civilian, a civic statesman through and through, not the fabulous Bismarck in the boots of a grenadier who lives in the mind of German nationalists, National Socialists, anti-German propagandists, and some German *émigrés*.' Prince Hubertus asserts that he disliked wars and tried to avoid them. That of 1864 was the fault of Denmark, that of 1866 as nearly inevitable as any conflict in history. On the evening after Königgrätz he remarked: 'The issue is decided, and now we must regain the old friendship with Austria.' The war of 1870 was unleashed in Paris, and public opinion in England took the German side. The editing of the Ems telegram merely called the Emperor's bluff, and the victor's terms were infinitely milder than Gramont's plans of spoliation had the iron dice fallen the other way. His moderation helped to procure for Europe one of the longest periods of peace that it ever enjoyed. As a man he had great personal charm; he was a perfect gentleman, a perfect host, a loyal husband and father. The compliments cease when we come to domestic policy, where the Man of Destiny bungled the struggles with the Socialists and the Vatican.

Dr. Steinberg, another South German Liberal, describes his *Short History of Germany* as a history of Germany, not of Brandenburg-Prussia's expansion into Greater Prussia. He regards the Bund, not indeed as an ideal creation, but as something more than a temporary makeshift. 'It was not Germany in which Prussia and the lesser states were merged; it was Prussia which absorbed the rest of Germany. The German Empire of 1871 was not the consummation of the longing for national unity. While he deliberately excluded the Germans of Austria, he did not hesitate to incorporate several millions of Poles, Frenchmen and Danes, not on a federal basis with which these foreign nationals might have agreed, but as subject races under a foreign yoke. Not German nationalism but Prussian militarism was the foundation-stone of the Bismarck empire.' The dissolution of the Bund meant the virtual end of Germany as the word had been understood for a thousand years: Greater Prussia had taken its place. The liberalism of the South prevented the integral application of the Prussian system which rested on the absolutism of the Crown and the predominance of the army. Yet the Bundesrat was a shadow and the Reichstag little more than a *façade*, for the Chancellor was responsible to the Emperor alone. The bourgeoisie paid the piper but Junkers and officers continued to call the tune. Unconditional surrender of mind, body and soul for the state was required. The death of the old Emperor at an earlier date might have become a turning point of history, but the hope of a liberal evolution was buried in the grave of his afflicted son. That the Bismarckian structure was not a final solution was evident before its collapse in 1918. Prussia scorned the idea of a free federal union of the German tribes, and did not rest till she had forced on Germany that unity which was the reverse of a thousand years of German history. The German tribes were far from wishing to obstruct a reasonable federal union. What they resented was the imposition of a centralised rule which would have stifled their national growth. Dr. Steinberg speaks of Prussia as critically as if she were a foreign Power. 'Uniformity was and is contrary to the racial, cultural and political divergence of the Germanic tribes; the complete independence of each part would have been and will be contrary to the economic, cultural and political interests of those parts.' The synthesis has still to be found.

Two English works written during the Second World War swell the chorus of criticism. In *The Course of German History Since 1815* Mr. Taylor denounces Bismarck as a selfish Junker. 'He had no rigidly defined programme when he became Prime Minister in 1862 beyond preserving the Junker social order. Sentimentally, as a matter of private taste, he would have preferred a return to the days of Metternich—Austria and Prussia co-operating to resist liberalism within Germany, and Austria, Prussia and Russia co-operating to resist liberalism in Europe. But this Holy Alliance had broken down. One aim he never pursued: that of uniting all Germans in a single national state.' Greater Germany would involve the end of Junker Prussia, a Roman Catholic majority, and a conflict with Russia. 'Cooperation between Russia and Prussia was vital for the subjugation of Poland and so for the security of the Junker estates. Ultimately Greater Germany, with its programme of central Europe united under German authority, implied conflict not only with Russia but with all the world, a conflict which Bismarck knew the Junkers were not powerful enough to sustain. He was ceaselessly active and his mind endlessly fertile in expedients, but in the last resort his policy was, like Metternich's, negative: to bar the way to Greater Germany. Both despaired of the old order for which alone they cared. Metternich defended it without hoping for success, Bismarck went with the new forces in order to draw their sting. He conjured up the phantom of unification in order to avoid reality.' Prussia's refusal to attend the meeting of princes invited to Frankfurt by Francis Joseph in 1863 laid the ghost of the Holy Roman Empire, the ghost of a civilised stable Germany, the ghost of the Free Cities and of German Liberalism. For Mr. Taylor the greatest of political Germans was for Germany the greatest of disasters.

Professor Barraclough's interpretation in *Factors in German History* is much the same. Though the failure of the Frankfurt Parliament prepared the way for him, Bismarck was rather its enemy than its heir. Its gospel was the combination of national unity and constitutional government: his the employment of nationalism to promote Prussian aggrandisement and resist the challenge to the social order for which he stood. Thus he defeated the forces of 1848 by a policy of *divide et impera*. His achievement, which served only the purposes of the Junkers, was to make nationalism an end in itself and to wean it from its liberal past. 'He offered the German people unity but at the expense of the radical reform which alone made unity worth while.' His task was eased by the industrial activity of the fifties and sixties which side-tracked the movement of radical reform. 'The establishment of German unity, implicit in the sweeping revolutionary movement of 1848 and thereafter overpoweringly fostered by rapid economic change, was inevitable. Bismarck determined the form and the moment. The Prussian solution of the German problem was anything but inevitable; without Bismarck the unification might well have been accomplished against both the Prussian monarchy and the Prussian aristocracy.' How this was to be achieved and what part the Prussian army would have played in the process is not explained. The constitution of the new Reich finds as little favour in the author's eyes as the methods by which it was made. It was only a federation in name, for the minor states possessed no power. Liebknecht's description of the Reichstag as the fig-leaf of absolutism was correct. 'Beneath this monarchical exterior, decked out with the trappings of representative democracy and federal balance, was the hard reality of the Junker class.' Heavy industry was admitted into the citadel of privilege by the tariff of 1879; but the Chancellor never dreamed of allowing his countrymen to govern themselves, and when the Socialist vote steadily increased he wished to destroy his own handiwork.

After such extremes of eulogy and censure it is a relief to turn to the wisest and ripest book produced by a German historian since the fall of the Nazi regime. At the age of eighty-four Meinecke confessed in *Die deutsche Katastrophe* that he had come to regard Bismarck's achievement in a more critical light. 'Prussianism and militarism lay like a heavy hand on his work and were transmitted to his hybrid successors. But there was also something in his own achievement in the borderland between the sound and the unsound and which in its further development was to incline increasingly to the latter. That is a difficult admission for those who grew up in an era of creation and enjoyed its blessings to the full. How free and proud we felt ourselves, in contrast to the whole German past, in this mighty emergent Reich which gave every one of us a feeling of having room to live! Yet the terrifying course of the First World War and still more of the Second compels us to ask whether the seeds of disaster were not there from the start. It is the question which courageous and mature historical thinking must ask about every great and beneficent movement which degenerates at a later stage. To-day one recalls with deep emotion the apprehensions of major disaster of such significant figures as Burckhardt and Constantin Frantz. Bismarck's doings, they say, destroyed certain foundations of western civilisation and constituted a profound revolution, with other revolutions and wars to follow, registered the triumph of Machiavellism over ethical and juridical principles in the intercourse of nations, and allowed the finer and more intellectual standards to perish in the struggle for power and enjoyment. Let us be frank: however one-sided these charges may be, there is a kernel of truth in them. Yet we must remember that Europe witnessed other examples of Machiavellian policy in the same period and that after 1871 he rendered service to the West European community of nations.' 'I cannot love Bismarck,' remarked a Danish historian to Meinecke during the Third Reich, 'but now I must admit that he belonged to *our* world.'

The last word on the Iron Chancellor will never be spoken, not merely because historians will always wear spectacles of different tints, but because with the passing years it becomes ever more difficult to disentangle the consequences of his actions from the impact of his successors and the swirling tide of events. There is of course among competent students a good deal of common ground:—that he was better qualified to deal with foreign than with domestic affairs; that as a Junker he despised democracy and never learned the alphabet of liberalism; that he did too little to prepare his countrymen for an effective share in political responsibility; that after creating a nation-state at the cost of three wars he knew when to stop and helped to preserve peace in Europe for a generation. All this, however, does not take us very far towards 'the verdict of history' of which amateurs dream. Wholesale condemnation is as much out of place as idolatry, for the rules of public morality have never been codified. A generation which drifted into two World Wars and is only now beginning to sense the deadly perils of unbridled nationalism has little right to throw stones at the supreme embodiment of the spirit of his age. Such elemental occurrences as the fashioning of Germany and Italy appear to many observers to be in Nietzsche's phrase 'beyond good and evil.' Neither country could call its soul its own till Austria was excluded, and as she declined to go ardent nationalists never doubted their right to drive her out. The conditions which enabled England and France to become strong homogeneous nations by leisurely process were lacking in Central Europe. If the work were to be done at all it had to be achieved in a few brief years of passionate endeavour. To make omelettes, as the French say, you have to break eggs.

To admit that the Prussianisation of Germany was within the rules of the game as played by statesmen and peoples in the nineteenth century in no way pledges us to approve every step which led to the goal or to admire the use that was made of spectacular victories. The annexation of a portion of Lorraine, however natural a penalty for aggression and defeat, was an error of the first magnitude; for although Alsace might conceivably have been disarmed by tact and kindness, Lorraine was French in blood, speech and sentiment. Metz could only be held by the bayonet, and the endeavour to hold it transformed Europe into an armed camp. Moreover, although it was easy enough to keep France in quarantine while she was weak, it was impossible to perpetuate her isolation when she recovered her breath. The choice of Austria in preference to Russia in 1879 was inevitable under the circumstances, but henceforth a Franco-Russian rapprochement was in the logic of events. Though no irrevocable step was taken while Bismarck was at the helm, the process had begun in 1875 and was in full swing before his fall. 'We Germans fear God and nothing else in the world,' declared the Dictator in 1888. It was not strictly true, for he confessed that he was haunted by 'the spectre of coalitions.' For such a regrouping of the Powers he paved the way by the annexation of Lorraine, which rendered a high-spirited nation an irreconcilable foe, biding her hour till the international situation brought the ball to her feet. Force alone could not guarantee a settlement resented by millions of civilised human beings any more than it could break the strength of Catholic claims or Socialist ideals.

The weakness of the 'realists'—and Bismarck was the greatest of the tribe—is that they tend to think more of immediate than of ultimate returns. Vast and splendid as was his intellect, the vision of an international order resting on a partnership of contented self-governing national units was beyond his ken. The main task of the twentieth century as it emerges from the shattering ordeal of two great wars is the organisation of a rapidly shrinking world. To the shaping of the human spirit for that supreme adventure Bismarck contributed nothing. He was content to work for his country alone—first for Prussia and later for a Prussianised Germany—and he was satisfied with its applause.

BISMARCK'S TABLE TALK

I

THREE of the eighteen enormous quartos entitled *Bismarck's Collected Works*[1] are allotted to conversations with the Man of Destiny who in the space of eight years changed the face of Europe and made the Hohenzollern Empire the strongest military power in the world. During the gloomy decade following the collapse of 1918 many Germans found comfort in the cry: Back to Bismarck! Back to the Master-Builder who knew not only how to strike but when to stop! What more patriotic service could be rendered to a disillusioned nation than to collect his letters and speeches, his despatches, his autobiography, and his conversations within the compass of a single gigantic enterprise, reverently edited by some of the leading scholars of the time?

The selection of the recorded conversations from the mass of published and unpublished material was entrusted to Professor Willy Andreas of Heidelberg, who has added to each item information as to its circumstances and its source. Few readers of these sixteen hundred pages will challenge the Editor's assertion that they rank with the table-talk of Luther and Goethe among the most precious possessions of the German people, and that his many-sided genius often emerges more vividly than in his formal declarations. 'Here is the man, the statesman, the history of a whole epoch which is called by his name, a dialogue of the hero with his age.' His personality was so arresting that almost everyone who had occasion to meet him—friends and foes, officials and visitors—instinctively recorded his impressions. Busch is merely the most copious and the most famous—some would say the most notorious—of the army of witnesses whose combined testimony carries us through half a century of unparalleled achievement. Though some of the items are of little interest, and though there is inevitably a good deal of repetition, taken together they bring the greatest figure of his age, warts and all, vividly before

[1] Bismarck, *Die Gesammelten Werke*, vols. 7–9.

our eyes, and constitute a precious addition to our understanding of the latter half of the nineteenth century. They are best described as a colossal supplement to his *Recollections and Reflections*.

The first volume, which extends to the foundation of the Reich in 1871, opens with a few brief records of the Junker's political *début* in the Year of Revolutions, the enthusiasms and aspirations of which left him cold. 'What has kept us going,' he remarked to the Editor of the newly founded Conservative organ *Die Kreuzzeitung*, 'has been the specifically Prussian elements, the old Prussian virtues of honour, loyalty, obedience, courage, which inspire the army, this best representative of the people, from the backbone of the officers' corps to the youngest recruit.[1] Prussians we are and Prussians we shall remain when this bit of paper is forgotten like a withered leaf. We shall not allow the Prussian monarchy to lose its character in the idle ferment of South German complacency.' Throughout these early years nothing mattered to him except Prussia. 'What are the little states to me?' he exclaimed to Keudell in 1849.[2] 'My whole aim is the consolidation and increase of Prussian power.' To him, as to Metternich, Germany at this time was scarcely more than a geographical expression.

Bismarck's appointment to Frankfurt in 1851 as Prussia's representative at the Diet brought him face to face with Austria's hegemony, and transformed him from a champion of the dictated Olmütz settlement into a fiery advocate of equal status. As Count Thun, the Austrian representative, frankly confessed, Prince Schwarzenberg, whom Francis Joseph in old age described as the ablest of his many Ministers, desired to keep Prussia in the second place.[3] 'There is nothing to be done with the Bund,' explained the new Prussian envoy to General Leopold von Gerlach, the head of the King's reactionary Camarilla; it was in Austria's hands and if Prussia took her own line she would hardly carry four votes. After two years of humiliation he poured out his heart to the faithful Keudell, who remarked that a North German Union was in the logic of events, though it would involve war; the adhesion of South Germany might follow a generation later.[4] 'That is just about what I expect,' commented Bismarck. 'So long as Metternich's principle of the unbroken partnership of the two Great Powers in the Bund prevailed it was able to work. But the

[1] I. 13, June 9, 1848.   [2] I. 18.
[3] I. 25.   [4] I. 27, November 4, 1853.

present system—the enforced subjection of Prussia—is in the long run unendurable. How many years will pass before arms decide, and under what circumstances the quarrel will occur, no one can foretell. But it will come to that if Vienna remains unreasonable.'

Bismarck's mounting Austrophobia distressed and alarmed his timid master in Berlin. For Frederick William IV the predominance of the Hapsburgs in the Bund was as much part of the established order as the divine right of kings and the Christian creeds. The envoy was well aware of the situation.[1] 'Nowadays I have little influence in Berlin,' he confided to Keudell in 1857. 'For the last two years the King has not shown me the same confidence. If he were to make me a Minister, as he occasionally thought of doing, he would not bear me for a week.' After his latest visit Keudell wrote to a friend that Bismarck had grown in stature and was no longer a party man. 'After being with him I have felt myself becoming wiser and better every day. His many confidences, however interesting, were not the main thing. His independent survey of the situation at home and abroad, his bold designs, his manly character, brought stimulus and refreshment of spirit.' He had taken up his post as a hard-shelled Junker and a tyro in foreign affairs. He laid it down on his appointment to St. Petersburg at the opening of 1859, a fully-fledged statesman, emancipated from party ties and with a coherent policy for Central Europe in his mind.

We catch a glimpse of him on the way to his new post in a conversation in a Berlin hotel in the spring of 1859, where a visitor found him reading an article in the *Neue Preussische Zeitung*.[2] Throwing it down he exclaimed that the paper had no spark of Prussian patriotism, since it urged the support of Austria against France and Italy in the war. To support Austria, he explained, would be suicide, for she was only awaiting her opportunity to ruin Prussia. Had not Prince Schwarzenberg said: *Il faut avilir la Prusse et puis la démolir*? Many people, interjected the visitor, feared that when Austria was defeated by France it would be Prussia's turn. Bismarck rejoined that history never repeated itself in that manner. Prussia would not attack France: if she were attacked and unable to defend herself she was unworthy to be a nation. A far greater danger would be a defeat by Austria. If Prussia were unable to expel her from Germany proper the Kings of Prussia would become Electors and vassals once again.

[1] I. 33–4.   [2] I. 37–8.

Thus if Prussia's aim was to exclude her rival from the Bund, it was desirable that she should be weakened by France.

The summons to the helm in September 1862 was quickly followed by the new Premier's declaration in the Budget Commission of the Chamber that the questions under discussion would be settled, not by votes and speeches, but by blood and iron. Though the ominous aphorism echoed round the world, he explained to a visitor that he had been entirely misunderstood.[1] The King, he was arguing on that occasion, needed blood and iron, that is a powerful army, not Parliamentary speeches on which he could not build, in order to deal with the German question. He had in no sense threatened the use of force against other German states, though he admitted that his words might have been ill-chosen. That the phrase 'other German states' was intended to cover Austria is improbable, for a month later he spoke in the plainest terms to a Hungarian *émigré* who pleaded for his country's independence.[2] 'I have made it my aim to revenge the disgrace of Olmütz, to overthrow this Austria who treats us in the most unworthy way and would like to make us her vassal. I want to raise up Prussia, to win for her the status in Germany to which she is entitled as a purely German state. I recognise the value that Hungary might be to us, and I know that Hungarians are not revolutionaries in the ordinary sense. Moreover Frederick the Great discussed an alliance with malcontent Hungarian magnates. If we win, Hungary will be free: you can rely on it.'

An important conversation took place at the close of 1862 with the Austrian Minister Count Karolyi.[3] Relations between the two states, began Bismarck, were impaired by press attacks, and their continuance would lead ultimately to war. Why did they get on before 1848? 'We gladly followed your lead in the great European questions because we were able to utilise our position in Germany without Austrian rivalry. Thus arose the Zollverein, for instance. For us it is vital to have complete freedom of movement in our natural sphere of influence, North Germany. Hanover and Electoral Hesse must be open exclusively to Prussian influence, yet your antagonism has been increasingly felt in these two states. I have told Platen that his policy involves that, when the first shot is fired in Germany, Hanover will promptly be occupied by Prussia—and of course Electoral Hesse too. If you wish to act somewhat on the lines

---

[1] I. 62.   [2] I. 66.   [3] I. 69–72, December 4.

of Metternich you will find us ready for a close alliance. I can tell you that you will not easily get another Prussian statesman so little affected by public opinion as myself. When I went to Frankfurt I hoped for co-operation with Austria, but I found it was impossible. Resentment is growing. I, who am regarded by public opinion as the arch opponent of Austria's influence in Germany, am now left far behind and have become a moderating element.' In painting so gloomy a picture of their relations, commented Karolyi, the Prussian Premier doubtless hoped to convince Vienna that improvement was impossible without acceptance of Prussian hegemony in the North.

The death of the King of Denmark in 1863 and the reopening of the question of the Duchies of Schleswig and Holstein necessitated temporary co-operation between the rivals without in any way diminishing their fundamental antagonism. Accompanying the King to the front Bismarck, as we learn from Keudell, his travelling companion, speculated on Austria's motives in joining in the fray.[1] 'It is hard to understand why they have accompanied us here where they cannot remain. In the diplomatic field they have been concerned with Denmark for years, and they have several times specifically demanded the fulfilment of the Treaty of London; but they could have left the task of military coercion to us. Perhaps the Emperor was quite glad to give his troops the chance of displaying their prowess in a winter campaign. But the chief reason is doubtless the anxiety lest we should become too powerful in Germany if we alone handled the Danish question. Our position in relation to the other Powers would certainly have been embarrassing if we were waging the campaign alone, and as a means of avoiding attempts at intervention it was of great value that Austrian troops marched at our side. Yet it was not easy to get them into Jutland, and similar difficulties may recur at every step. Hitherto we have dragged our allies along with us on a slender string, but some day it may break.'

When the brief Danish campaign was over, Austria and Prussia divided the spoils. Such a settlement could hardly be expected to last, for since the loss of the Low Countries in the Napoleonic Wars Austria coveted no territory in Northern Europe; on the other hand, the latest acquisition tended to increase her weight in the Diet. Bismarck's programme was already framed in his mind: both Duchies

[1] I. 85, April 22, 1864.

should fall to Prussia, since she could tolerate no challenge to her domination in the North. Moreover the conviction of Austria's hostility which he had reluctantly formed at Frankfurt had grown with the passing years. As a political novice Prussia had filled his horizon. Now, as he remarked again and again: 'My highest ambition is to make the Germans a nation.'

Two years after the Danish war it was clear that the rivals were girding their loins for a decisive struggle. The surviving intimates of Frederick William IV were horrified at the prospect of what in their eyes would be civil war. In May 1866 Ludwig von Gerlach, a veteran Austrophil and a member of the *Kreuzzeitung* group, appealed to Roon, the Minister of War, to avert a catastrophe, but received the chilling reply that no one could avert coming events. His interview with Bismarck was even more discouraging.[1] 'He was harsh, pale, passionately worked up. I warned him against the deeply disastrous war, described Olmütz as partially his work, and begged him to continue our personal friendship, an appeal of which he took no notice. There was an air of restless desperation about him. He also spoke of God, of prayer: the matter was one between himself and God, not for friends or party comrades.' Gerlach sorrowfully realised that the Austrophil policy of Frederick William IV had been buried in his grave.

A month later, on June 4, the Berlin Correspondent of *Le Siècle* secured an interview with the man in whose hands lay the issues of peace and war.[2] 'I was reared in admiration, I might almost say the cult, of Austrian policy,' declared Bismarck, 'but it did not take long to shed my youthful illusions and I became her declared antagonist. The humiliation of my state, the sacrifice of Germany to foreign interests, was not at all to my taste. I did not know I should be summoned to play a part, but from that time I conceived the idea, which I am to-day striving to carry out, of freeing Germany from Austrian pressure, at any rate that portion which is connected with Prussia's destinies by mind, religion, habits and interests, I mean the North. There is no thought of overturning thrones or seizing petty principalities: even if there were, the King would forbid it. To reach my goal—North Germany under Prussian leadership—I would face anything, exile, even the scaffold. I have told the Crown Prince, who by education and instinct favours a parliamentary regime, "No matter if

[1] I. 117–18. [2] I. 119–22.

I am hanged so long as the rope binds your throne tightly to this new Germany."'

The broad highway to a North German Confederation under Prussian leadership was opened at Königgrätz, the conflict which in a few hours decided whether the Prussian Premier should commit suicide or dominate the Continent. His satisfaction was enhanced by his affectionate admiration for his master. 'I know all the Sovereigns of Europe,' he remarked to a friend of his student days soon after the campaign, 'and for many of them I have the highest respect.[1] But you will not take it as a mere phrase if I assure you that there is none whom I so profoundly honour as our King. Yet I should not like to see him an absolute monarch, for I consider absolutism the worst of all political systems. You cannot imagine what a part is often played in an absolutist regime by a designing lackey.' The ideal system, as he often explained, was neither Parliamentary democracy, where continuity and rapid decisions were difficult to secure, nor autocracy, where unofficial influences had free play, but a strong constitutional monarchy guided by an experienced Minister responsible to his master and his conscience alone. The constitution of the North German Confederation, shortly to be extended over a wider area, embodied his political creed. To a Saxon Minister who came to Berlin for the constitutional discussions he explained that many powerful enemies were trying to overthrow him, and that he had no hesitation in using similar methods in self-defence. For instance, since King William was not much of a newspaper reader, he only saw extracts approved by the Minister himself.[2]

After Austria had been expelled, Bismarck's main preoccupation was France. The earliest reference to an armed conflict is found in a report by the Hungarian General Türr who visited Berlin in February 1867.[3] During the conversation, which began with a glance at the recent struggle, the visitor suddenly and intuitively felt that his host was meditating another war. 'I must tell you,' he boldly remarked, 'that if you ever go for France I must oppose you. My personal enmity is of no importance for you, but I hope that the whole (Hungarian) Liberal Party, which was on your side in 1866, would do the same.' Bismarck's eyes blazed when he found that the visitor had guessed his thoughts, but he controlled himself and replied: 'Not for a moment do I desire war with France.' Yet the impression left by the

[1] I. 172, December 20, 1866. [2] I. 173–7, January, 1867. [3] I. 181–3.

angry glance was not dispelled by friendly words, and the visitor's apprehensions were confirmed the same day by a remark of a member of the Prussian General Staff. 'We require four years to reorganise the troops of the annexed territories and to fit our South German partners into the Prussian system. Then we are ready and can march on Paris.'

A month later, in March 1867, the Free Conservative group in the Prussian chamber which supported the Government sent one of its members to learn the Chancellor's wishes.[1]

Count Bethusy-Huc. Do you think that a war with France is inevitable within the next five years?

Bismarck. I regret to say I do.

Bethusy. Do you agree that within this period the present moment is the most favourable for our forces?

Bismarck. Without doubt.

Bethusy. Could you launch a war in the next 24 hours?

Bismarck. Certainly the Government can. But I can anticipate your fourth question: Why then do you not advise the King to make war? Yes, unhappily I believe in a war with France before very long; her vanity, injured by our victories, will drive her in that direction. Yet I cannot regard it as absolutely certain, because I know of no French or German interest requiring an appeal to arms. Only for a country's honour—not to be confused with so-called prestige—only for its most vital interests may one resort to war. No statesman has the right to begin it simply because he deems it inevitable within a given period. If Foreign Ministers had always followed their sovereigns to the front history would tell of fewer wars. I have seen on our battlefield—and what is far worse, in the hospitals—the flower of our youth carried off by wounds and disease; from this window I see in the Wilhelmstrasse many a cripple who looks up and thinks that if that man had not made that wicked war he would be strong and well. With such memories and such spectacles I should not have a moment's peace if I had to reproach myself for making war from vanity or for fame. Yes, I made the war of 1866 in painful fulfilment of an imperative duty, because otherwise Prussian history would have stood still, because without it the nation would have fallen into political stagnation and soon become the prey of greedy neighbours. If we stood to-day where we did then I would do it again. But I will never

[1] I. 186–7.

advise His Majesty to wage war except for the most vital interests of the fatherland.

The emergence of the Luxemburg problem seemed to bring a conflict within sight, and in April 1867 Bismarck confided to Bennigsen that he expected it during the current year.[1] On returning to Berlin in June, after four years in Paris as Military Attaché, Colonel von Loe received the Chancellor's congratulations on his despatches, which emphasised that France was incapable of waging war against Prussia. 'I know what you want to say,' he added. 'You are wondering why the Minister who was not squeamish in 1866 does not seize his chance now he is sure of victory. Squeamish I never am if I find it necessary for my fatherland to wage war as in 1866, when there was no other possibility of solving the secular conflict with Austria. After that peace was equally essential. I cannot advise a war merely because France is weak. I will never issue a challenge because we are the stronger party and in order to avert a future war. I am responsible to the fatherland and God for the heavy sacrifices which every war involves.'

The Luxemburg crisis was settled at the London Conference, and the rivals met at the Paris Exhibition in June on friendly terms, though there was still thunder in the air. A number of conversations with his legal adviser Wilmowski reflect Bismarck's mood during the years between the Austrian and French wars.[2] Of the King he constantly spoke with reverence and affection, asserting that he would remain in office only so long as the old ruler was on the throne. 'The political creed of the Crown Prince is not mine. As we know, he always wishes to rule with the consent of the majority. In my view that is not always right, and it assumes a surrender of character and conviction of which I am incapable.' Of the heir's personal friendliness, on the other hand, he spoke in the warmest terms. The distaste for soft characters extended to peoples and races. The Germans, he declared to George Bancroft, the American Ambassador and historian, in August 1867, were a masculine race, the strongest and best fitted for mental labour.[3] Celts and Slavs were feminine. Unmixed races were not the most capable. Much of Germany had been overrun in the great migrations. The Swabians in the south, being sheltered by their position, were unfitted to govern, possessing neither judgment nor energy. The pure Russian lacked perseverance and

[1] I. 191. [2] I. 206–16. [3] I. 222–4.

could only do mental work for three or four hours. Recently they tried to remove all Germans from the Administration, but they soon had to take them back.

The fullest and frankest account of the Chancellor's attitude to France at this period is to be found in a conversation with Carl Schurz on January 28, 1868.[1] The famous German exile, who had risen to the rank of General on the Northern side in the American Civil War, was amazed at the lack of reserve in dealing with questions of *haute politique*. 'War with France will come, but do not think I love war. I know it well enough to detest it. Memories of the terrible things I have seen will never leave me. I shall never agree to a conflict which can be avoided, still less shall I bring it about. But this war with France will come, the Emperor will force us into it. That I recognise clearly.' The position of an adventurer on the throne was utterly different from a legitimate ruler such as the King of Prussia. 'I know you do not believe in divine right, but many do, especially in Prussia, perhaps not so many as before 1848 but more than you imagine. The people are traditionally loyal. A King of Prussia can make mistakes, can suffer misfortune and even humiliation, but the old loyalty remains. The adventurer on the throne possesses no such heritage of confidence. He must always produce an effect. His safety depends on his personal prestige, and to enhance it sensations must follow each other in rapid succession in order to satisfy the ambition, the pride, or the vanity of the people, particularly of a people like the French. He has recently lost more prestige than he can afford, and this diminution, unless quickly repaired, can endanger the Empire. Directly he feels his army is in good order and ready for war he will strive to recover the prestige that is vital to him, and for that purpose he will start a dispute with us on some pretext or other. I do not believe he personally wishes this war, indeed I think he would prefer to avoid it, but his insecurity will drive him on. I expect the crisis in about two years. Of course we must be prepared, and so we are. We shall win, and the result will be the reverse of what he is seeking, namely the complete unification of Germany without Austria and probably his own overthrow.' A real Atlas! comments Carl Schurz, for he bore the fortunes of a whole people on his shoulders.

Though the coming struggle was continually in his mind,

[1] I. 231-40.

Bismarck felt no apprehension. 'The fear of France,' he remarked to Bluntschli, the well-known Baden scholar and Liberal, 'does not tie my hands in the German problem. I am not afraid of her. We are far stronger. I am not boasting; that is not my way. We have weighed the matter with care. All our Generals agree. Of course a rapid thrust might bring the French to Mainz and Coblenz—but no further. They have not more than 300,000 men available for attack, and we can confront them with a larger force at every vital point. In the last war we had 640,000 men under arms, and others were in reserve. Against the French everyone up to thirty-six will march in case of need: fighting for one's hearth is different from invading a foreign country. The French might possibly push forward in the south. But I do not expect it, for the 50,000 men required for such an enterprise would be missed at the point where the decision takes place. In that case I give you this advice: Let them take what they can, but give them nothing. Do not negotiate, make no concessions. At the worst a few places and individuals may suffer, but the whole struggle will end in victory and your losses will be fully repaired. I estimate the individual Frenchman no higher than the German, and there are more of us. If God favours us, we shall beat off the attack and then march on Paris. Napoleon knows how strong we are, and that is why we have peace. I have full confidence. The German people, militarily united, is the greatest Power in the world and has nothing to fear.'

Passing to Germany's other neighbours the Chancellor found no less ground for satisfaction. 'Austria will remain neutral under all circumstances. Even apart from her finances she cannot wage war, and all her interests forbid her. The German Austrians know that an Austrian victory would rob them of their gains. The Hungarians know that a victorious Austrian army would overthrow their constitution. The Austrian Slavs are subject to Russian influences. In case of need we and Russia would hold Austria in check. They will not dare to draw the sword. A few Archdukes, of course, would always be ready to do so, but what interest has she to risk her existence? Even if France won Austria would be lost, for she would be at the mercy of the French victor and would have to do what she was told. We should not need to give the Russians anything for an alliance in a war with France. Their weak spot is Poland. With England we are on excellent terms. In old days the English leaned on Austria because they regarded her as a security against France and thought her the leading Power in Germany. But since 1866, like practical people, they have played the other card: they have no objection to our unification. So you see we are sure of ourselves and we shall continue to work peacefully at the development of Germany.'

On February 24, 1870, an event occurred of scarcely less significance than the first meeting of Boswell with Johnson and of Eckermann with Goethe. Though the Chancellor had never neglected the papers, they were henceforth to play a far more important part in the exposition of his policy. Busch requested and was allowed to be independent of the so-called Literary Bureau which was part of the Ministry of the Interior. Since the Foreign Office possessed no such instrument Lothar Bucher had often written for official and unofficial papers, but Busch was expected to devote his whole time to the press. Having merely seen the Chancellor from the Press Gallery he now stood before him 'as if at the altar.'[1]

Bismarck. What have you been doing till now?

Busch. I have edited the *Grenzboten*, a more or less National Liberal organ, which I left over the Schleswig-Holstein question. Then I had a post in Hanover where I worked for Prussian interests in the press. Recently at the wish of the Foreign Office I have written for various organs, including the *Preussische Jahrbücher*.

Bismarck. So you know our policy, particularly in the German question. My idea is that you should write articles and correspondence for the papers and arrange for others to do the same according to my directions, since I cannot write leaders myself. We will have a trial period. I must have somebody entirely for that purpose, not merely now and again as at present when I am not properly supported by the Literary Bureau. The German question is going well, but I need time, perhaps a year or five or ten. I cannot hurry it.

'So now I was one of his staff,' records Busch in happy pride. 'The next evening I was summoned to him twice to receive instructions for articles, later even oftener, also in the morning, sometimes four or fives times a day, on one occasion eight. I had to keep my ears open and not mix up the information. But I soon got used to this new and tiring work, as he usually presented his views and instructions in a form easy to retain and recapitulated the chief points in different words. I gradually succeeded in memorising long sentences, even

[1] I. 304.

whole monologues, and I could always go to him in important matters or to get his approval.' Since Busch's memory satisfied his exacting chief, we may assume general reliability in the unofficial entries in his voluminous diary.

Six months after his appointment the long expected war with France broke out and Busch was ordered to the front. His vivid war diary, published in 1878 after revision by Bismarck, records his sayings and doings, reminiscences and grumblings, his numberless visitors and his gargantuan repasts. Most of the entries naturally relate to the fortunes of war, but at times the conversation assumed a deeper tone, for instance at Ferrières on September 28, a week before German headquarters moved to Versailles.[1] The feeling that it was good to die obscurely for the fatherland and honour, observed the chief, was permeating the people, particularly since it was dyed in blood. The N.C.O. had the same sense of duty as the officer. The French could easily be rallied into a herd which then became very powerful. 'With us every one has his own views, but when large numbers share the same opinion you could do a good deal with the Germans. The sense of duty which allows one to be shot at dawn alone and in the dark is lacking in the French. It comes from the remains of faith in our people, from the feeling that there is someone who sees us when the Lieutenant is not looking.' 'Do you believe, Excellency,' asked one of the guests, 'that they think about such things?' 'No, it is a feeling, a mood, an instinct. How an orderly community can exist without belief in a revealed religion, in a God who desires the good, in a higher judge and a future life, I do not understand. If I were not a Christian I would not serve the King another hour. If I did not reckon with my God I would snap my fingers at earthly rulers. If I did not believe in a divine order which has destined the German nation to something good and great I would abandon the trade of diplomacy or would never have taken it up. Orders and titles do not appeal to me.'

Without challenging the sincerity of such confessions, the Chancellor's innumerable enemies and victims at home and abroad may well have concluded that he kept his theology and his politics in watertight compartments. On January 10, 1871, in commenting on the bombardment of Paris, he referred to Franco-Prussian conflicts as a familiar historical experience, and expressed satisfaction that his

[1] I. 360–2.

younger son had seen war at the age of eighteen.[1] 'I should have been born in 1795 in order to be there in 1813. For generations there was not one of my ancestors who did not draw his sword against France, my father and three of his brothers against the first Napoleon, my grandfather at Rossbach, their ancestors against Louis XIV. Several of us fought in the Thirty Years' War on the side of the Emperor, others with the Swedes.' History was above all the story of blood and iron. He differed from contemporary statesmen not in his readiness to employ war as an instrument of national policy, for that was common to them all, but in the frankness with which he admitted the fact. He often spoke of the scenes of a battlefield but never with horror of the institution of war. Like other statesmen he preferred to reach his goal without bloodshed, but that war was the normal method of realising national ambitions was an axiom. It was the traditional instrument of Prussia, and not of Prussia alone.

Though all the world saw in Bismarck the Master-Builder whose will was law, he had often to fight for his way. A heated conversation with the Crown Prince on November 16, 1870, reveals the two men in a somewhat unexpected relationship, the heir urging drastic measures in dealing with the South, the Chancellor arguing for moderation. Did the Crown Prince desire to use threats? 'Yes,' was the reply, 'there is no danger. If we take a firm line you will see I was right in maintaining that you are not sufficiently aware of your strength.' Bismarck retorted that menaces at this stage would drive the South German states into the arms of Austria. On taking office, he continued, he was fully resolved on war with Austria, but he was careful not to tell the King till he felt the right moment had come. In the same way they must give the German question time to mature. The Crown Prince replied that, as representing the future, he could not be indifferent to such procrastination. It was unnecessary to use force, and they could wait calmly and see whether Bavaria or Württemberg would dare to join Austria. Nothing was easier than to have the Emperor proclaimed by the majority of the assembled princes, and also to create a constitution satisfying the legitimate demands of the German people: such pressure the King could not resist. Bismarck rejoined that in this view the Crown Prince stood alone: it would be better for the initiative to come from the Reichstag. When the Crown Prince was reproached for expressing such views, he tartly retorted

[1] I. 468.

that it was his duty to leave no doubt about his opinion, and that the King alone had a right to decide what subjects he might or might not discuss. He would gladly make way for another Chancellor whom the Crown Prince held to be more suitable, replied Bismarck, but till then he must stand by his principles. When all the obstacles to the proclamation of the King of Prussia as German Emperor were overcome and the Hohenzollern Emperor was proclaimed in the Galerie des Glaces, it was the Crown Prince who joyfully acclaimed the new title and his father who resented the summons to set out on uncharted ways.

On the return of peace Bismarck inaugurated evening receptions for members of the Reichstag. On one such occasion in the second half of April 1870, he commented freely on the peace settlement.[1] 'I have been attacked for treating France with too much severity. On the contrary I was far too mild. We shall have to wage a final war with the French and after our victory we must make quite different terms. Our victory in that final war is probable, for in the history of the peoples the Germans play the part rather of a man, the Romance peoples that of a woman. A man often falls, but he can always pick himself up; a woman, once fallen, cannot recover. In dealing with a revengeful woman—for such is France—we require quite other arrangements than those we are now obtaining in order to secure lasting peace. Then France must be broken up. Spain's old territory north of the Pyrenees as far as the Garonne must be restored to her. Italy will recover her former territories, Savoy, Nizza and Provence. England will resume her old possessions in the North. Germany will require a frontier zone at least twenty (German) miles wide from which the French population must be removed and in which German colonists must be settled.' When the reporter laughed at such absurdities the host stared at him and replied: 'Your own brother-in-law sent me a map to Paris showing Germany's earlier frontiers and expressing a wish for their restoration. He was quite right, and, as I said, our peace has been far too mild. Another great war is inevitable and next time these plans will be carried out.' These extravagances were merely a paradoxical improvisation, and his expectation of yet another round in the boxing match in no way indicated such a desire, for he had secured everything he had set out to obtain. In a conversation on May 12 with Waldersee, who was about to return to Paris

[1] I. 511.

as Chargé d'Affaires, he spoke more like the statesman he was.[1] The peace settlement, he declared, should be judged as a whole. Desiring its rapid conclusion, he could not trouble too much about individual interests. For him the only criterion could be whether this or that arrangement would be blamed in fifty years.

II

THE second volume, containing five hundred items and filling seven hundred pages, covers the two decades of peace. The leading *rôle* played in the earlier period first by Keudell and later by Busch is now in some measure assumed by Lucius von Ballhausen, a prominent figure among the Free Conservatives who followed their old chief when Roon and the main body of the party frowned on some of his doings. Elected to parliament in 1870 and appointed Prussian Minister of Agriculture in 1879, he became a frequent and ever welcome guest in the Chancellor's home. Copious selections from his diary were published in 1920 in a volume entitled *Bismarckerinnerungen*. While the pages of Busch resemble a gramophone record, the attitude of Lucius is that of an equal and at times a critic. Their first interview, arising out of an interpellation as to delays in the field post at the end of the French war, was a complete success. 'In the lively and at the same time confidential manner in which he treated me like an old friend he made a most winning and indeed fascinating impression.'[2] Among the other principal recorders during these years may be mentioned Thiedemann, the trusted head of the Chancellery for six years, Cohen, his Hamburg doctor, Hohenlohe and Waldersee. The transfer of the control of the Press Department of the Foreign Office to Aegidi, a Bonn professor, at the close of the war of 1870, was resented by Busch, who attributed it to unfriendly influences. The Chancellor, however, was not wholly satisfied with his activities and saw him less and less. Two years later, in 1873, he resigned and returned to independent journalism, receiving a pension in return for which he gave general support. The parting was friendly, and it was agreed that Busch should receive information through Lothar Bucher, who was fully trusted by both sides. The friendly association was renewed in 1878. 'You know I worship you,' exclaimed Busch in 1883; 'I would let myself be cut in a thousand

[1] I. 512.   [2] II. 72-5.

pieces for you.' 'Not quite so many,' rejoined the chief; 'that is not necessary.'

The picture of the Iron Chancellor at the height of his power emerges with extraordinary vividness from the testimony of many witnesses. In 1873 he told Busch that he had never had so much influence,[1] and the change was noted by Hohenlohe in his diary directly after the war.[2] 'He handles everything with a certain arrogance. That is nothing new, but now there are his great triumphs, so that he is the terror of all diplomatists.' Yet he was full of complaints of overwork, ill health, and hostile influences at Court. His work, he lamented to Lucius in May 1871, really needed three men—one for the Court, a second for the Reichstag, a third for foreign affairs.[3] The first would have the hardest task. 'The old gentleman' became increasingly difficult, wanting to know and do everything himself, while the Crown Prince also liked to have his say. A year later it was the same story.[4] 'One would think that in the course of so many years our association and indeed each interview would become ever easier. It is just the contrary, and the difficulty increases with the weakness of age. Yesterday I was utterly worn out. A thorny question, it is true, had to be discussed, but his inability to reach decisions was growing ever more intolerable.' The Chancellor seemed unaware that he himself was much more difficult to work with than the modest old ruler. 'Unfortunately he is often pathologically irritable,' noted Lucius on February 4, 1873; 'and if he has frequently to suffer from the laziness and inefficiency of his colleagues and Court intrigues, working with him is hard enough. How much he could do if he were less irritable! But it is his temperament, and he as well as other people have to suffer.' When on one occasion the name of a leading Conservative politician was mentioned, his glance reminded the visitor of an angry lion.[5]

The Chancellor's sharpest arrows were reserved for the Empress, whom he always regarded, not only as his most dangerous foe, but as the friend of all his political enemies—French Royalists, German Ultramontanes, envious rivals. When she visited Queen Victoria in 1872 he exclaimed excitedly to the British Ambassador: 'I wish you would keep her in England and never let her come back to Berlin, for she is interfering in public affairs in a manner that will kill my old King who needs rest and quiet.' The Empress, he added, was govern-

[1] II. 73.   [2] II. 4–5.   [3] II. 6.   [4] II. 37.   [5] II. 66.

ing her husband's country.[1] On a visit to Friedrichsruh in 1877 Lucius found his host raving against her intrigues.[2] The only way to get equal with her, he explained, was through the Press, as she dreaded public criticism; but the parties and papers friendly to him failed to render him proper support. Just to spite him she extracted all sorts of concessions from her husband, not only as regards individuals but in the field of foreign affairs. She wrote autograph letters to foreign sovereigns, nominally at her husband's wish, in opposition to the official policy. She often conferred with Gontaut-Biron, the French Ambassador, and with Windthorst, the leader of the Catholics in the Reichstag, and followed their advice. To her it was due that the Alsace garrisons were so weak and that the Coblenz military railway made such slow progress. Her intrigues indeed were not far from treason. With her limited intelligence she always sided with the opponents of her husband as well as himself. At the moment her chief instrument was her daughter, the Grand Duchess of Baden. The Emperor was afraid of his wife and was easier to influence through the daughter of whose love he was assured. The Chancellor never hesitated to speak his mind about the Empress, and never enjoined secrecy on his visitors, knowing that she was fully aware of his sentiments. For over a quarter of a century the Prussian Junker and the Weimar princess fought with the gloves off, the former always getting his way in the major decisions, the latter often scoring in matters of minor significance.

If he detested the Empress for the antagonism of the hour, he dreaded her successor when the old Emperor should have passed away. 'The freedom of Bismarck's language about everything makes it often difficult to report him officially,' wrote Lord Odo Russell to Lord Granville in September 1872.[3] 'He is a powerful hater and makes no secret of it. Much as he hates the Empress, he hates the Crown Princess even more, I regret to say. I never allude to her in his presence, so as to avoid a quarrel. With the Crown Prince he has made up all his differences since the war. From all I hear and observe I fear that the Crown Princess on ascending the throne of Germany will meet with a more difficult task than is generally known. I hope I may be mistaken.'

[1] *Letters from the Berlin Embassy*, edited by Paul Knaplund, 58, 67.
[2] II. 209.
[3] *Letters from the Berlin Embassy*, 66.

Bismarck's political animosities were on the same colossal scale as his appetite. In a conversation suggested by a picture of Hartmann, the philosopher, he spoke approvingly of the pessimism which Schopenhauer had brought into vogue.[1] 'How can we believe that we are born for happiness? Goethe said that if he added together every second in which he had been really happy, it would hardly amount to half an hour. And yet he clung to life like ordinary mortals. And Goethe was so much loved, so little hated. Yet hatred is just as much a spur to life as love. Two things preserve and adorn my life— my wife and Windthorst. The one is there for me to love, the other to hate.' While his devotion to Johanna never changed, the objects of his wrath, with the exception of the Empress, varied with the times. For a brief space he had hated and feared Arnim more than he was ever to hate and fear Windthorst, and the day was to come when the Catholic leader was to be welcomed at the Chancellor's palace.

Bismarck's visitors were impressed above all by three things— his almost superhuman personality, his frankness of utterance, and his fabulous appetite. His craving for food, drink and tobacco was insatiable. If he was to found the German Empire, he explained, he must be well fed. After his marriage no one ever saw him drunk, but the overworked digestion revenged itself till in old age the rough-tongued Schweninger took him firmly in hand. Here is a typical extract from the diary of Lucius, February 20, 1878.[2] 'A delightful evening. Doing the carving himself, he ate half a turkey, drank between a quarter and half a bottle of cognac and two or three bottles of Apollinaris. In daytime, he said, he could not enjoy anything, neither beer nor champagne; cognac and water suited him better. He compelled me to drink with him so that he did not notice how much he consumed. One felt anxious lest such errors in dietetics might result in a stroke.' Yet he lived till the age of eighty-three.

Against such stories of irritability, invective and gluttony we may set the charming portrait painted by Motley, the celebrated American historian and diplomatist, a friend from the far off Göttingen days.[3] Writing to his wife from Varzin in 1872, he describes him as very little changed since their last meeting in 1864. Host and hostess were as kind and friendly to his daughter, afterwards the wife of Sir William

[1] II. 138, January 25, 1875.   [2] II. 247.   [3] II. 60, July 25, 1872.

Harcourt, as if she had known them all her life. Marie von Bismarck was a pretty girl, simple, natural, and, like her parents, full of humour. They lived entirely without ceremony. 'During a long walk in the woods he talked in the most natural, humorous and arresting manner about all sorts of happenings in the great years, but exactly as ordinary people discuss ordinary things. He shows himself so simple that one had formally to remind oneself: That is the great Bismarck, the most important man alive and one of the greatest personalities of all time. I know no one who poses less than he.' 'Really to know and understand him,' wrote Radowitz, a high official of the Foreign Office from Varzin in 1873, 'one must see him in his element as a country nobleman and landowner.[1] I have found a measure of personal confidence and good-will which is infinitely precious to me. Here, to a degree unknown when he is in the capital, he shows the attractive and human side of his character without forfeiting a shred of his intellectual stature.'

When the victor informed the world that Germany had enough (*wir sind satt*) he was speaking the literal truth. On taking leave in 1872 of the faithful Keudell, the newly appointed Ambassador to Turkey, he remarked that with God's will Germany had secured her needs.[2] But new dangers would arise, and he would do his best to deal with them, though he could not always be sure of success. 'I often long for rest, but for me there can be no rest.' His primary aim was the preservation of the *status quo*; he coveted nothing and therefore would not make trouble. The man of war had become the chief pillar of European peace. Germany, he told Motley, could commit no greater folly than to attack other lands.[3] If Russia were to offer the Baltic provinces as a gift he would not decline. As regards Holland it would be sheer madness to endanger her independence by occupation or invasion, and no one had ever dreamed of such a thing. As regards Belgium France would gladly have paid any price for his permission to annex.

A far-ranging unofficial conversation with the British Ambassador in February 1873 filled in the outlines of the picture.[4] The Queen of Holland, he began, a bitter enemy of Prussia and of German unity, had told friends in England that Prussia sought to annex the Netherlands with a view to acquiring colonies and a fleet. No German

[1] II. 91–2.   [2] II. 43, October 7.   [3] II. 41.
[4] *Letters from the Berlin Embassy*, 87–9, February 11.

Government could ever desire nor public opinion consent to such a thing. He craved neither colonies nor fleets. Colonies would only be a source of weakness, for they could only be defended by a powerful fleet, and with Germany's geographical position there was no need to be a first-class maritime power. She merely required a fleet which could cope with that of Austria, Egypt, Holland, perhaps Italy, scarcely Russia; and so long as she had no colonies it could scarcely be her intention to compete with maritime powers like England, America or France. Many had been offered him, but he wished only for coaling stations acquired by treaty. Germany was now large enough and strong enough, and even the Emperor's insatiable desire for more territory had not led him to covet the Netherlands. After the Danish war his master had not spoken to him for a week for not having annexed a larger portion of Denmark, but Germany had already too many Danish and Polish subjects. The Swiss were a German-speaking nation, but Switzerland was of greater value as an independent friendly neighbour than as a province of the Reich. Here was the pure milk of the gospel of limited liability which in his later years won for the Chancellor the growing confidence of Europe and helped him to keep the peace between the Great Powers for a generation.

The key to the preservation of peace was to keep France in quarantine. Since she could do nothing alone, even when she had recovered her breath, his task was to prevent her finding an ally. This could only be accomplished if no other Great Power needed her help in attaining its ambitions. Germany therefore should refrain from challenging England's supremacy at sea and thwarting Russia's ambitions in the Near East. Austria had learned the bitter lesson of 1866 and Italy did not count. France, he was well aware, would never forget the lost provinces, but time would soften the smart, all the sooner if the young Republic were treated with consideration. He had confidence in the statesmanship of Thiers and did what he could to keep him at the helm. Peaceful assurances were exchanged when the first French Ambassador to the Reich presented his credentials on January 5, 1872, but the two men never took to each other. That Viscount Gontaut-Biron was *persona grata* with the Empress was bad enough: that he belonged to the Clerical-Royalist party in France was even worse. In Bismarck's eyes a Republic was less likely to find allies in monarchical Europe than a king. Though he would have tolerated a Bonapartist restoration, he had no wish to see the Comte de Chambord or the Comte de Paris on the throne.

The *rôle* of the French Ambassador in Berlin was naturally much less important than that of the French Ambassador in Paris. No one contested the abilities of Count Harry Arnim, but his selection for the most difficult of diplomatic posts was a grievous mistake, for his sympathies were with the Royalists, on whom his chief had always frowned. By the spring of 1873 the relations of the two governments began to show signs of strain. On April 21 Gontaut-Biron, just back from a visit to Paris, confessed to Bismarck that at a dinner given by Thiers he had noticed a certain chilliness on the part of the German Ambassador: the Chancellor replied that he was dissatisfied with him, but entered into no detail.[1] A month later Thiers had to make way in the Presidency for Marshal Macmahon, whose Royalist sympathies were unconcealed, and now for the first time since the Treaty of Frankfurt was there mention of war.[2] 'If the French force us into war again,' observed Bismarck to the Bavarian Military Attaché, 'we shall not be so lenient as in 1870, and I hope that all Europe will then see that these Redskins in pumps are and will remain the incorrigible disturbers of the peace.' Count Arnim's sympathies, he added, rendered any sensible policy in France impossible. 'And I, who am held responsible for the peace of Europe, must rub along with this man for years.'

Hohenlohe, his destined successor at Paris and an exceptionally unprejudiced observer, shared the Chancellor's distrust. 'Bismarck talked pretty bitterly about Arnim,' he noted in his diary on February 17, 1874.[3] 'Apparently he has shown himself what I have always thought him, vain, selfish, false, but extremely clever.' That relations with France had deteriorated was held by the Chancellor to be partly his fault. 'We want to maintain peace,' he declared, 'but if the French rearm in such a way that they are resolved to hit out in five years we shall start in three.' He had told them so frankly. He reproached Arnim for overthrowing Thiers, or at any rate for not keeping him at his post.

The offending Ambassador was transferred from Paris to Constantinople, but before he had time to take up his new post it was discovered that he had removed official documents from the Embassy

[1] II. 78. [2] II. 86–7. [3] II. 103.

archives, and the sensational Arnim trial began. A conversation on January 6, 1875, recorded by Lucius, was prompted by Arnim's remark during the trial that this conflict was the grave of an old friendship of the early years.[1] He had never been his friend, commented Bismarck. Quite early he had seen through him as an intriguing and unscrupulous *arriviste* who approached him when he sought some personal advantage. He had inherited a large income but lived far beyond it. He had always thought him an able man who wrote good reports, and had appointed him to Cassel, Munich, and finally Rome. There he wrote despatches the political colour of which varied as one side or the other paid him court. While on leave in Berlin he had intrigued in the attempt to become an Under Secretary or Minister, and he had had to order him back to his post. In Paris he had disobeyed instructions. Money placed at his disposal had been employed in manipulating German papers, and he had therefore been deprived of the control of this fund. He had also speculated on the Bourse. In 1872, after he had been only a year in Paris, Bismarck had told the Emperor: 'He or I.' 'Then he must go,' was the reply. The Chancellor, however, suggested postponing action for three months in the expectation that the indiscreet Ambassador would compromise himself, and this occurred when he removed 140 documents from the Embassy archives. At their final interview, for which Arnim had asked, he was in tears when he entered. Bismarck was silent, let the visitor cry himself out, and at first listened in stony silence.

Bismarck. You have plenty of words and tears at your disposal, but they have no effect on me.

Arnim. So you think me a hypocrite and actor? Won't you shake hands?

Bismarck. In my own house I cannot refuse, but elsewhere I would.

Every reference in the conversations to the war scare of 1875 displays Bismarck in an attitude of injured innocence. Gortchakoff was the chief author of the legend that the Chancellor, annoyed and alarmed by the rapid military recovery of France, was contemplating a preventive war. The Tsar, in Bismarck's opinion, had nothing to do with this libel. To Aegidi, head of the Press Department, he described how Alexander II, on arriving in Berlin with his Foreign

[1] II. 130–2.

Minister, appeared unannounced and said: 'Let me speak first, so that I may anticipate any assurance from you. I do not believe in the rumour that either Germany or you desires war, and I come here with confidence in your policy of peace.'[1] Shortly after this unsolicited testimonial Gortchakoff issued the famous *communiqué* stating that the Tsar had found at Berlin a serious danger of war but that, owing to his intervention, peace was now assured. Aegidi hurried to his chief with a newspaper in his hand. The Chancellor read it without turning a hair, and to the query whether a denial should be issued, he replied with a smile: 'I desire no refutation. Let Gortchakoff enjoy himself.'

Bismarck's equanimity on this occasion was a pose, for he never forgave either the Russian statesman or his supposed accomplices, with the Empress at their head. Visiting him at Varzin in the following September, Hohenlohe found him incensed not only against individuals but against England.[2] Gontaut, he complained, had never asked for an interview, which suggested that he had a guilty conscience. He would be glad of a man with whom he could talk on easy terms. Not till the end of the year 1875 did the angry Chancellor receive the Ambassador.[3]

Gontaut. I am glad to see that the relations between our countries are calming down and that the Press is quieter, as has always been my aim since I came to Berlin.

Bismarck (slowly and gravely). I am pleased you have this information. But a few months ago people in France believed in war. They were convinced that we wished to attack. I ask you, who could spread these false reports? Can you enlighten me? I know there is a group of speculators on the Bourse who everywhere, especially in Germany, circulate such news from time to time. There is also the correspondence of women of high rank. The good Queen Victoria wrote a lamentable letter about the dangers of war. Where could the rumours have originated except in Paris? They were sent on to London and Vienna, but in Vienna no one believed them. So I was everywhere believed to desire war and to be ready at any moment to let loose this scourge on the whole of Europe; however much I spoke of my peaceful intentions I was not believed. So it is useless to repeat them. But it is very annoying for me, and these rumours have produced grave disturbance which will long be remembered. You were

[1] II. 144–5.   [2] II. 151, September 8, 1875.   [3] II. 161–4.

in Russia last year and are supposed to have said that you believed we intended to attack France.

Gontaut. I was there two years ago, not last year. I do not recall my exact words, but I may have expressed my apprehension. That is only natural in view of the recent conflicts and the language of your press.

Bismarck. Perhaps the public may be influenced by such newspaper articles, but Governments should not be.

Gontaut. Pardon me. In certain circumstances a Government can be strongly influenced by indications which seem to you hardly worth notice. What was it which so upset the Versailles Cabinet? An article in the *Post.*

Bismarck. That was of no significance.

Gontaut. Perhaps, but that does not apply to the article in the *Norddeutsche Zeitung,* which repudiated such intentions towards Austria and Italy, but not as regards France. That is why we were alarmed. If we exaggerated these symptoms, it shows at any rate that we were far from preparing for a war of revenge and that we dreaded war. Your words show that you too did not desire it. And that is the main point.

The Chancellor's principal domestic anxiety during the first decade of peace was the attitude of the Catholic minority. The proclamation of Papal Infallibility at the Vatican Council of 1870 aroused his fears of political encroachment, and the spectre of an Ultramontane International working against the new Protestant Reich haunted his dreams. When Professor von Schulte, the eminent Canonist, visited him on January 12, 1873, to request recognition and help for the Old Catholics, he was received with open arms. Previously, declared Bismarck, he had troubled about Church matters 'only when an immediate issue arose.'[1] He had expected the majority of the German episcopate to stand firm, but they had disappointed him. Now he had no longer to deal with individual bishops but with the Pope: the Archbishop of Cologne was simply his shadow. If the state were not to perish he must do everything possible to break the power of these hostile elements. He now realised how the ground had been undermined. The Empress had fostered Ultramontanism for years and had worked on the Emperor in that sense. In Russian Poland the power of the clergy had grown beyond all bounds: re-

[1] II. 46–51.

actionary and Ultramontane elements had combined. When Schulte asked whether the Government would recognise a bishop, the Chancellor replied that he regarded Old Catholics as the only Catholics, to whom everything by right belonged. This principle could not be applied, but on reading the memorandum sent in by Schultz he had said to himself: Choose a bishop and then ask me for recognition. He would consult his colleagues and propose a grant. 'Rest assured that I will stand by you, that I have the greatest personal confidence in you, that I will never draw back, and will do everything to forward a cause which, I am convinced, is in the interest of society and the state.'

A year later, on January 13, 1874, the Chancellor invited the French Ambassador, whom he increasingly distrusted and now rarely met, to discuss the *Kulturkampf*; for the Ultramontane danger, as he saw it, now extended far beyond the frontiers of the Reich.[1]

Bismarck. In France and everywhere else nowadays the clerical party is striving to seize control over the state. Here we are open enemies. The Pope, whose infallibility has gone to his head, has declared war on the rights of the state. We are confronted by an obstinate resistance. We cannot silently hand over the German Catholics to the yoke of a foreign power. The attacks of the Belgian, English and Austrian Bishops who receive their orders from Rome cannot leave us unaffected and we must defend ourselves. Our news from France is particularly grave, for there the attacks are based on brooding resentment and foster opposition which we cannot ignore. If the Bishops are ordered from Rome to whip up our subjects to rebellion, and if continual attacks on German policy are launched from France, then we feel ourselves menaced. Your Ministers are no clericals, but I fear they may be too weak to repel the Ultramontane attack. Do you realise that the whole position of the Catholic Church has changed since the Vatican Council? The Bishops, no longer independent, are only tools of the Pope. A word from Pius IX suffers to throw the whole Catholic world into confusion. In my conflict with the Catholic Church I am determined to win. It is a struggle for the freedom of the state like that of the Empire against the Papacy in the Middle Ages. Take care that the masses are not wrought up by the slogan of the persecuted Catholic religion, and that in consequence a Clerical Government does not seize power and then make all Roman questions its own; for that would inevitably lead to a

[1] II. 93–9.

clash. In such a situation we could not let you strike the first blow; we should not wait till you are ready. I do not wish to interfere in your affairs, for I know it must not seem as if in any measures against the French Bishops you are yielding to our pressure. But cannot you act against the Bishops who have attacked us?

Gontaut. I admit that the Pastoral Letter of the Bishop of Nîmes is offensive for the Emperor William, but I feel it would be best to avoid the excitement of a public trial. As you have been informed, my Government has issued a circular directing the cessation of episcopal attacks.

Bismarck. Yes, that was a small step along the right road, but do you think it is enough?

Gontaut. I do. Yet I quite understand that you wish to end these excitements which may have been caused by the violent language of our Bishops.

Bismarck. I don't think I have made my meaning quite clear: this incident concerns my domestic policy as well. The Government of a great country cannot ignore attacks by such prominent personages as Bishops. The Pastoral Letters made a deep impression on Protestants and Catholics alike. I must prove to the nation that I have tried to obtain satisfaction for these attacks on our ruler. I cannot expose myself to the charge of weakness in dealing with the Clericals and their friends.

Gontaut. You overestimate the influence of the Clerical party. The Bishops are greatly esteemed, but neither they nor the clergy have real political influence. Since the eighteenth century and the French Revolution practically the whole people is instinctively against it.

Bismarck (smiling). I would sacrifice a province if, as you say, the clergy are not dangerous. We have no thought of war. What advantage would it be? The peace of 1871 affords us security.

The long interview ended with a renewed appeal for some action against the Bishop of Nîmes, the worst of the offenders. There was no response from Paris, and the hostility of the French Bishops counted scarcely less than the military recovery of France in preparing the soil for the war scare of 1875.

The Tsar's benevolent neutrality in 1870, which held hostile elements at Vienna in check, was a vital factor in German calculations. Russia gave no trouble in the early years of peace, and in 1873 the Chancellor accompanied his master to St. Petersburg. A long conversation with a Russian official whom he had known during his residence as Ambassador reveals his anxiety to keep the friendship in repair.[1] Keudell, the new Ambassador at Constantinople, had been instructed to make no difficulties for Russia in the Near East. 'We have no political interests there—merely to look after our subjects and develope our trade. Any credit we enjoy must be at the disposal of the Power with whom we require and desire good relations. Political considerations, not sentiment, tell us that this power is Russia, who alone is really of use to us and whose friendship is indispensable.' Knowing that the conversation would be reported to Gortchakoff, he added: 'I have high respect for your illustrious chief and I admire his character, particularly one quality: he is truly good-tempered (gutmütig). This quality is a priceless possession for a statesman. Unfortunately it is lacking in me. Resentment plays too great a part and torments me and, what is worse, it sometimes obscures my judgment.'

The War Scare of 1875 shattered the Chancellor's illusions about Gortchakoff but left his confidence in Alexander II intact. In conversation at Varzin in August 1875 with Mittnacht, a leading Württemberg statesman, he observed that there was no danger of the Tsar dropping his friendship for Germany.[2] The two states had no conflicting interests. Neither coveted the territory of the other, and Russia needed a solid and powerful ally. That might not be Gortchakoff's view, but the Tsar exerted great influence on him. Germany's rôle in the Turkish troubles was to foster agreement between Austria and Russia. If they agreed, Germany would approve. If they quarrelled, he would find it very difficult to choose sides, for neutrality in such cases was always dangerous. On the one hand there was the strong traditional dynastic tie, no conflicting interest and the advantage of great stability, while in Austria the system was constantly changing. On the other hand there were the racial ties and many close associations in the cultural sphere. To join Austria would be to turn Russia into an irreconcilable enemy of Germany and drive her into the arms of France; to join Russia would make her dangerously strong.

The choice he hoped to avoid was forced on him at the Congress of Berlin, which had to decide whether, as Austria and England

[1] II. 79–84. [2] II. 146–50.

desired, the Treaty of San Stefano should be cancelled. He agreed that the 'Big Bulgaria' which it created would enable Russia to dominate the whole of the Near East and therefore to threaten the security of Austria. In discussing the results of the Conference with Mittnacht on August 11 he expressed considerable satisfaction.[1] Peace was assured, so far as one could say. He did not think the Bosnian troubles would lead to war between Austria and Turkey. The former ought to have occupied the province earlier, as he had always urged. The occupation was only of importance for Austria in shielding it from Russian intrigues. For a time it seemed as if Russia might turn, not against Turkey, but against Austria, and he was glad when the first shot fell in the former. In 1876 the Tsar had asked the Emperor William through his military representative whether he could rely on his neutrality in the event of a war with Austria. Acting on his Chancellor's advice the Emperor had replied that the question could only be answered if it were put in official form; and this had not occurred. Austria's mistrust of him had been completely dispelled in the course of the Congress. On the other hand there was now bad feeling and suspicion in Russia. Gortchakoff had tried to persuade his master to believe in a European conspiracy under Bismarck's leadership. He was a Germanophobe, and his policy during the last five years had been crazy. First the coquetting with France, then the peace comedy in Berlin in 1875 when he pretended to have held Bismarck back from war, whereas nothing had occurred except a journalistic row started by the provocations of the French Press. Gortchakoff was now finished, but he did not wish to quit his post without making a final splash. As the friend of both Russia and Austria he could not have acted in any other way.

Though Bismarck modestly described his *rôle* at the Berlin Congress as that of an honest broker, his attitude rankled in the heart of the Tsar. On the one hand he had supported Austria's plan to occupy Bosnia and Herzegovina; on the other he had scrapped the Treaty of San Stefano. Such was the gratitude of Berlin for benevolent neutrality in 1870! Feeling the chill blast from St. Petersburg the Chancellor turned towards Vienna, where, in resisting his master's desire for trophies of victory in 1866, he had kept the door open till the old rivals were ready to co-operate again. At last the hour had struck. Inviting the Austrian Minister to Friedrichsruh in January 1879, he

[1] II. 266–7.

explained both his difficulties and his hopes.[1] 'You can scarcely imagine my difficulties with the Emperor directly I suggest a rather firmer tone towards Russia. Just when I feel I am making way, one of those private letters from the Tsar arrives and I find myself up against a barrier which it requires all my diplomatic skill to circumvent. We have nothing to ask from Russia and Russia nothing to ask from us. It is a tried friendship of almost a hundred years. But we also wish Austria to be our friend, and in our own interest we should like to see her strong and flourishing. The Triple Entente is a fine thing, but only so long as it is a real entente, for a majority vote leads nowhere. I have told St. Petersburg frankly that in an Austro-Russian war we could only remain neutral so long as one of the two Powers does not cripple the other. If Austria were to win and to start resurrecting Poland, she would find us in her path. But equally we could not tolerate a Russian victory which opened the way to the heart of the monarchy, perhaps even to Vienna itself. This annoys Russia, who complains that our friendship is platonic, but as a German I must think entirely of German interests. The Emperor Alexander is a sincere friend and he was always nice to me, but the older he grows the more exacting his friendship becomes. He is always harping on Russia's services in 1866 and 1870. But we had also given her a free hand in 1828 and in the Crimean war; what they did in 1870 was only a return. This too we have made clear to him. Yet directly I begin to argue that it is Russia's interest to carry out the Treaty of Berlin, hostile influences come into play. Unfortunately the Emperor Alexander is very vacillating.'

By the summer of 1879 the Chancellor had convinced himself, though not his master, of the necessity of an Austrian alliance as a bulwark against Russian ambitions; and at Gastein, where he negotiated with Andrassy the Austrian Foreign Minister in August, he confided his apprehensions to Mittnacht, the Württemberg statesman.[2] Since the crisis in the Near East Russia had been arming rapidly despite her financial difficulties. She had created twenty-four new divisions and Poland was full of troops. She had sounded France about an alliance without success, for France did not want war at present and she distrusted England. Italy had also been sounded with a similar result. Germany's only friend in Russia was the Tsar, and even he had become unreliable. He was under the

[1] II. 293–5.   [2] II. 323–7.

influence of the Generals, especially Milutin, the War Minister, and also of the Pan-Slav movement. For some time he had used threatening language to the German Ambassador; an autograph letter to the Emperor William had stated that things could not remain as they were, and that Germany's co-operation with Austria might lead to the most disastrous consequences. Thus compelled to choose between Russia and Austria he would vote for the latter, a constitutional and peace-loving state, her territory commanded by German guns, whereas they could not get at Russia. A glance at the map showed that a hostile Austria was a threat to South Germany. Hungary favoured Germany, and England would be friendly. If the two great neighbours, who could place two million men in the field, stood together, they need fear no one. The moment had arrived to make an alliance with Austria in place of the old Bund, otherwise she would gravitate towards Russia or France. If his master vetoed an Austrian alliance, he would feel compelled to resign. Though the old Emperor, who detested the idea of a breach with his nephew, also talked seriously of resignation, he finally gave way: the conflict had been even more painful than when in 1866 he reluctantly consented to lenient terms for the foe. Happily the smart of surrender was soon diminished by the creation of the Three Emperors' League in 1881, and, when Austro-Russian rivalry made its renewal impossible, by the secret Treaty of Reinsurance with Russia in 1887.

Alexander III, the husband of a Prussophobe Danish princess, was less Germanophil than his father, who was assassinated in 1881. Never for a moment did Bismarck regret the momentous decision of 1879. Austria proved a loyal ally, though her racial stresses were sapping her strength. When Francis Joseph sent his son the Archduke Rudolf to the celebrations of the silver wedding of the Crown Prince Frederick in 1883 he received a warm welcome at Berlin. The Chancellor expressed his pleasure that the alliance was becoming ever firmer, resting as it did on the convictions not only of the rulers and statesmen but of the peoples themselves.[1] The peace and future of both states were founded on the alliance, which provided the only guarantee of effective resistance to foreign foes and to the republican tide now rising in every land. 'I am glad we have renewed the treaty. I am an old man and I desire to see this work placed beyond challenge and doubt. The future of Europe depends on it. It must be preserved

[1] II. 468–71.

for all time from follies and incidents. For the moment the tie is strong enough, but the future, I believe, will make it even closer.' It might well receive the force of law, so that its termination would require the assent of both monarchs and both Parliaments. An intimate commercial partnership was equally essential.

The Emperor, added Bismarck, mindful of old ties, wished the alliance to be of wider scope so that Russia should not be regarded as the sole potential antagonist. Though he had earnestly but vainly endeavoured during the negotiations of 1879 to induce Austria to include France, he now informed the Archduke Rudolf that the matter seemed to him unimportant. 'You are strong enough to deal with Italy and we with France; moreover if we are engaged in the west you would have enough to do to defend yourselves and us in the east. If, however, we are attacked from all sides, we should be forced into a more defensive *rôle*; on our western frontier we are fully prepared for a defensive war. Though our allied armies are excellent, the difficulties of our situation must not be minimised. England would have to be friendly, and I try to win her by courtesy and compliments, for at the critical moment a vote in Parliament, not reason, decides.' Italy's friendly assurances were of little value, for even if there were goodwill she lacked the power to implement it. Moreover her King might be forced to choose between taking the lead in a popular movement for a brief period and loyal observance of his obligations to his allies. The Italian flank could never be left uncovered, but they must try to strengthen the ties with Rome. As the Archduke took his leave the Chancellor observed: 'One thing is certain—our alliance remains firm. That is to me the greatest satisfaction and I shall always work for its continuance.' These words were the literal truth. The Austrian alliance was not only his outstanding achievement after the foundation of the Reich, but the corner-stone of German policy for forty years.

Relations with Russia improved when the Germanophil Giers succeeded the disgruntled Gortchakoff in 1882, and so anxious was Bismarck to keep the wire to St. Petersburg in working order that in 1884 he vetoed the marriage of Prince Alexander of Bulgaria to a daughter of the Crown Prince. 'Germany has no interest in Bulgaria,' he remarked to the unhappy Prince; 'our interest is peace with Russia.[1] For this purpose Russia must be convinced that we are

[1] II. 509–11, May 12, 1884.

pursuing no aims in the Near East. On the day that a Prussian princess becomes Princess of Bulgaria, Russia would grow mistrustful and no longer believe our assertion. Moreover the marriage would upset my plans. I have assured the Emperor so long as I remain Chancellor it will not take place, and I added no successor would allow it. I should advise you to marry an Orthodox heiress. That would strengthen your position in Bulgaria; for in the East to reign means to bribe, and that needs money. With morality one gets nowhere.'

When the harmony of the three Empires was rudely disturbed by events in Bulgaria, it was Bismarck's earnest endeavour to prevent Austria and Russia flying at each other's throats. For him, at any rate, the Eastern Question was not worth the bones of a Pomeranian grenadier, and at this moment he had to watch Boulanger in the west. His attitude was explained to Crown Prince Rudolf, who arrived in Berlin in March 1887 for the celebration of the ninetieth birthday of the Emperor William.[1] He desired peace, and he resented the newspaper talk of a military party in Germany pressing for war: there was no such thing. On the other hand he regretted that the whole army was always talking of war, and that high officers such as Moltke and Waldersee used incautious words. 'They wish to force me into war, and I want peace. To unleash a war would be frivolous; we are not a robber state which makes war simply for its own convenience. Germany will attack nobody, and if Russia and France do not start it will be a year of peace. If Boulanger were to gain power there would be war.' In that case Germany would need far more troops in the west than in 1870, for victory was now less certain. In view of a possible war on two fronts a firm coalition was needed. Austria must make a treaty with England and Italy so that she could stand up to Russia without much German help. What Russia would do in the event of a Franco-German war he could not tell; if France was getting the worst of it the Tsar's hand might be forced by the Pan-Slavs. She might also attack Austria or, more probably, occupy Bulgaria and march on Constantinople. In the latter case his advice to Austria was to hold her hand, since England would doubtless intervene. He thought little of the Russian army, and an unsuccessful war might bring down the dynasty. He was not expecting war in 1887, one reason being the age of the Emperor, yet danger was ever present.

[1] II. 557-60.

Despite this reassuring language Rudolf found the Chancellor in a grave mood, restless and excitable, lacking the quiet confidence he had displayed at previous meetings. To Crispi, the Italian Premier, who visited Friedrichsruh in the following autumn, he declared that he had tried everything to make friends with Russia but without success.[1] Alexander III had no desire for war, but there were revolutionary elements in his army.

The Chancellor was always wondering how long his old master would live and what might happen when he was gone. Would he be invited to remain and, if so, ought he to consent? Office without unchallenged authority, at any rate in the field of foreign affairs, was unthinkable, but could he really expect a free hand from any other ruler? 'It seems that the Crown Prince wishes to keep me,' he observed to the faithful Busch in 1885, 'but I shall have to consider whether I remain.[2] There is much to be said on both sides, but at the moment I am more inclined to go. I might think like Götz von Berlichingen when he joined the Peasants: that it might not be too bad, that I might prevent certain things or water them down. But think if I were denied a free hand, if I had colleagues like Forckenbeck or Georg Bunsen and continual friction with them, whereas the old gentleman let me do what I thought best, even to the extent of choosing and changing the Ministers! And then the Crown Princess, who has him under her thumb! Yet what would happen if I leave them to themselves? The whole position of the Reich rests on the confidence I have established abroad, for instance with the French, whose attitude is determined by their trust in me. The King of the Belgians told me recently that a signed contract meant less to him than my word. It is the same with Russia, where the Emperor builds entirely on me. And the Empress, the Danish Princess, told me that they absolutely trusted me because they knew I should keep my promises. Of course I could withdraw and see how it went without me; perhaps they would call me back, if things had gone wrong. He would only make experiments because he holds me in reserve.' The Crown Prince, he added, with his *penchant* for England, would be thinking of Queen Victoria; he knew little about affairs of state, took little interest in them, and lacked courage.

As things turned out, the difficult choice had never to be made. The 'Hundred Days' of the Emperor Frederick were too few for the

[1] II. 571–9, October 1–3, 1887. [2] II. 524–6, May 31, 1885.

long expected trial of strength between the old world and the new. They wished him to remain, 'she too,' he reported to Busch on April 7, and 'wrapped him in cotton wool.'[1] The sufferer, declared Bergmann, might live three weeks or three months, but whatever the interval between William I and William II the Chancellor would only stay if his will prevailed. 'If I can only postpone and not wholly prevent these English influences on our policy, if they no longer listen to my voice, why should I slave any longer? I decline to be a mere whipping-boy for the follies of other people. This Englishwoman shall not use me for her whims, for foreign interests, to the danger and detriment of our country. The new Empress has always been an Englishwoman, a channel for English influences, a tool for their purposes, and now in her present position more than ever. In England they will not tolerate any foreign influence. You know how Palmerston and others resented and opposed the influence of the Prince Consort, but we are to bear it and to regard it as a matter of course. We are an inferior race fated to serve them! So thinks the Queen, and her daughter no less. I suggest that you deal fully with this theme—how England has tried again and again to use us for her purposes, often contrary to our interests, for their security, for the extension of their power, recently through the daughter and female friends of Queen Victoria.' The angry Chancellor then proceeded to denounce British policy during the last two centuries. 'The aim was always the same—to sow or to continue discord among the Continental Powers, to play them off against one another, so that they should be weakened and injured to England's advantage.' Despite the fierce antagonism of thirty years the speechless Emperor on his death-bed placed the Chancellor's hand in that of his broken-hearted wife, gently pressing them as if entrusting her to his care. Little did he guess that the Man of Destiny whom he would never have dared and perhaps scarcely have wished to dismiss would in less than two years become as powerless as the widowed Empress herself.

III

THE Chancellor's first impressions of William II were favourable, for the heir to the throne had always expressed unbounded admiration for the founder of the Reich. He was very satisfied, confessed the

[1] II. 604–9.

latter to Waldersee, and for that reason he looked to the future with confidence.[1] As late as the end of 1889 the verdict was still relatively favourable.[2] 'He could not be more amiable to me,' he remarked to an old friend at Friedrichsruh, 'and so far he has never ventured to oppose my views. Even when he took a strong line and I contradicted him energetically he ended by yielding, shrugging his shoulders as though surprised at himself. If he sulks a little it is soon over. He respects in me the statesman, the councillor of his father, the old hand; but my successor will have a difficult time. He has plenty of political judgment and quickly understands what is explained to him. The trouble is that he does just what comes into his head, that he sends his *aides de camp* with orders, letters and questions, and in this way harm often occurs in a flash. If I were younger and could be with him all day as I was with the old Emperor, I could turn him round my little finger, but he lets himself be influenced by adjutants and above all by the soldiers. Before his visit to the East the Empress begged me to prevent it; she thought it was not good for his reputation and his continual journeyings were beginning to worry her. She displayed more intelligence and judgment than I expected. I replied that some months earlier I might have opposed it on political grounds, but now it was too late. In any case I felt that he might have his liberty this year since he had been in leading-strings all his life.' When the visitor inquired about Waldersee's influence, the host explained that the new Chief of Staff flattered him, anticipated all his wishes and caprices, compared him to Frederick the Great, and thus made him more and more Olympian. The worst of it was that Waldersee did not possess the confidence of the army, and therein lay a great danger. 'He thinks he has to fill the void left by the old Moltke, and he prattles like a magpie.'

Though such mischief-makers played a part in the coming catastrophe, and the Chancellor's prolonged absences from Berlin gave them their chance, honest differences of opinion were the proximate cause of the final breach. He had shown his practical sympathy with the working class by his system of National Insurance, but the steady growth of the Social Democratic party filled him with anger and he was in no mood to bestow fresh favours on the working man such as the Emperor had in mind. Returning from Friedrichsruh on January 24, 1890, after an absence of over three months, he discovered in a

[1] II. 615, July 10, 1888.   [2] II. 672–3, December 5, 1888.

Crown Council that the ruler was resolved to go his own way. Next day he informed Rottenburg, chief of the Imperial Chancery, that his continuance in office was impossible, since the Emperor was entirely alienated from him and listened to other people. The Crown Council had shown that his colleagues had deserted him. Tears were in his eyes as he spoke, and Rottenburg sensed that a compromise was impossible.

On January 30 the wrathful veteran explained the situation to the Saxon Minister at Berlin.[1] If the labour legislation were accepted he would resign. The Emperor had listened to unauthorised counsellors, beginning with his old tutor. 'If it goes on like that, Hinzpeter will soon be Chancellor. At seventy-five, and with my not wholly unsuccessful record, I cannot consent to my master receiving advice from unauthorised quarters. Finally he asks some officers how he ought to solve the social question, and then he will try to force his opinion down my throat unless I protest in good time against transacting business in such a way.' The Social Democrats, he added, must not be led to believe that the Governments were weak. The social question was not to be solved with rose water; blood and iron were needed. He deeply regretted the Emperor's view that certain concessions to revolutionary tendencies were necessary, but his master had announced that he would accept the scheme and so it must be. For years his wife and doctor had implored him to retire, and he longed to escape from his oar in the galley. He had therefore decided to reduce his activities, to surrender the Prussian premiership, and to confine himself to foreign affairs. If, however, the new project of social legislation were accepted it would provide the desired opportunity to resign all his posts. That would be good for him and his family, but it might not serve the public interest if the only member of the Prussian Ministry who exerted a certain authority over the Emperor were to withdraw. Moreover as regards the preservation of European peace his contribution was recognised even by his enemies: it was mainly the result of his personal influence in St. Petersburg and London, Vienna and Rome, an asset he could not bequeath to his successors. On the same day he repeated the story to the Bavarian Minister and sourly complained that the Emperor wished to satisfy everybody at once.[2] Such enthusiasms, he thought, were dangerous to the Crown. He had long felt that the ruler found

[1] II. 679–61.   [2] II. 681–3.

him in the way as a mentor who always said No. He avoided seeing him, thought he could do everything himself, and would breathe a sigh of relief when he was gone. An hour's talk left the impression on Count Lerchenfeld that for once the old gladiator had not made up his mind what to do.

The drama moved rapidly to its predestined close. Though on February 3 the Chancellor warned the Emperor that he would resign if the decrees were issued contrary to his advice and without his signature, they were announced on the following day. The deeper grounds of his opposition were explained to Count Lerchenfeld on February 10.[1] The ideas enshrined in the decrees were utopian; their aim was to win popularity with the lowest classes; the Emperor would live to regret it, since they would acquire the power lost by the throne. His policy had always been to strengthen the monarchy, whereas popularity-hunting would lead to Parliamentarism. The Emperor was sapping the prestige and power bequeathed by his grandfather; if he continued he would exhaust the capital. That is what grieved and surprised him. Retirement would be painful, but the chronic friction was unbearable. To remain would involve a speedy and irreparable breach and this he desired to avoid. He would be willing to direct foreign policy as Chancellor, difficult though the situation would be. This, however, was only a passing fancy, for supermen are not made to run in double harness.

When 'Büschlein' was summoned on March 16 he found his old chief amid piles of documents.[2] 'Now I shall write my memoirs and you must help me. As you see, I am packing up. I must send off my papers at once or they may be seized. The sooner I go the better— perhaps in three days, perhaps three weeks. It has grown intolerable. When I am at Friedrichsruh you must come to me and we will work together.' Yet despite all that had occurred the announcement on March 20 that the request to resign had been accepted was almost as much a surprise to himself as to the world. When the Austrian Ambassador brought him an autograph letter from Francis Joseph, the old man bitterly remarked: 'If only my Emperor had half the feeling for me expressed in this letter, I could still be what I was.[3] No, no, I have not gone willingly. It was not I who thought the time had arrived; it was the Emperor who turned me out. They say my health was broken and my powers in decline. Never was I better and I feel

[1] II. 684–7.   [2] II. 692–4.   [3] II. 701–2.

quite up to my task. It is not further work that would injure my health but unaccustomed idleness and the fact that I have been deeply wronged.' To Radowitz he complained that the Emperor had no heart.[1] He was already looking back to the Ninety-nine Days as a golden age in which his power had been more unchallenged than ever before; he felt sure he could have got on not only with the Emperor Frederick but with the Empress. Every caller was assured that he felt better than at any time in the last ten years and that he had been dismissed. 'The saddest feature,' reported Lerchenfeld after a farewell visit, 'is his pessimism about the future.'[2] Of course it is not unnatural that the long years of absolute power have made him identify his creation with himself. Though he thinks very highly of his successor, he does not believe that he will influence the Emperor. He has lost every trace of confidence in the latter and regards him as the destined destroyer of the Reich.'

'I cannot lie down like a hibernating bear,' cried the fallen statesman in the bitterness of his heart. Visitors to Friedrichsruh in the following weeks were astonished at his vitality. A good deal of time was spent in looking through the vast mass of material covering forty years. Not only Busch but Poschinger hoped to be selected as his chief assistant; but the final choice fell on Lothar Bucher, who knew more of his old master's secrets than either of them and indeed more than anyone except Holstein, now despised as a snake in the grass. Though it was not till several months had elapsed that he settled down to the task of composition, rapid progress was made in 1891, for the past was continually in his thoughts. That he had old scores to settle as well as tributes to pay was a powerful stimulus.

The third volume of the *Gespräche* differs from its predecessors in two main respects. In the first place the superman is no longer on the stage but in the stalls. Secondly, whereas hitherto he had neither leisure nor inclination to receive everyone who wished to meet him, he now welcomed visitors of all kinds who were prepared to listen to his monologues. Everyone was struck by his physical and mental vigour, and by the fact that, while resenting his dismissal, he was not depressed. Though often complaining that he had nothing to do, he was never lacking in occupation. His rides and drives in his extensive woods were an unceasing delight; hours were spent over newspapers, and he re-read Schiller's dramas in chronological sequence. The

[1] II. 704–5. [2] II. 705–6.

stream of German and foreign journalists which flowed into the house proved that he was not forgotten. A deeper comfort was derived from the conviction that his work would stand, that the Reich was safe, and that the German people felt grateful. Life at Friedrichsruh was sweetened by the devotion of his adoring wife, his children and the grandchildren who shared his home. He coquetted with the notion that he might enter the Reichstag, but an easier method of conveying advice was available through the friendly medium of the *Hamburger Nachrichten*.

The European situation was excellent, he declared to Ernest Judet, Editor of the *Matin*, one of the earliest foreign journalists in search of copy.[1] 'Everywhere peaceful prospects, no cloud, no shadow: that is my doing. The German people knew very well that I was resolved to preserve peace; that is why they trusted me and thought me a good Chancellor. Modern nations can no longer be dragged into war against their will, and its horrors are so great that no one will begin it. Germany will never attack France. Compulsory service is the best guarantee of peace. Mighty armaments would be a burden, not a bulwark, unless the heart of the people was in the fight. So one should not complain too much of the military budget. As long as the dislike of armaments is weaker than other sentiments and interests, disarmament will be impossible. We want nothing more, neither Dutch, nor Poles, nor Baltic provinces, nor anything else. We have plenty of foreigners already who retain their national sympathies; more we could not digest.' The strongest bulwark of peace, he proudly explained to a correspondent of the *Daily Telegraph*, was the Triple Alliance.[2] Broadly based on mutual confidence and common interests, it would continue because it benefited everyone and represented common sense. Relations with Russia were satisfactory, as good as with France. 'We wish Russia well, and she will certainly not attack us. She has no quarrel with us and we shall not make the slightest trouble for her. I am honoured by the confidence of the Tsar, a friendly and well-meaning sovereign. He loves his home and family, is well disposed to Germany, and is opposed to war.' War with England was unthinkable, and even a serious disagreement was extremely improbable.

The fullest discussion of the breach with the Emperor took place with a Bavarian editor who visited the ex-Chancellor at Kissingen in

[1] III. 31–5.   [2] III. 38–47, June 8, 1890.

August 1890.[1] After thanking the journalist for his articles, which had declared that a Bavarian farmer would not have dismissed a faithful old farm hand with so little ceremony, the host advised him to deal a little more gently with the Emperor. 'Otherwise people will think me a grumpy old bear who craved for honey but tumbled off his branch and was badly stung by the bees. That is not the case. Only the drones sting me and they do not penetrate the skin. Thus I am perfectly tranquil, *veteranus meritus procul negotiis*. It is harder for my wife to get over the change. Women are like that: they resent injustice to their husbands more than their menfolk themselves. My dismissal was not a thing of yesterday. I had long seen it coming. The Emperor wished to be his own Chancellor, with no one intervening between his Ministers and himself. He possesses the best intentions, talent, ambition and energy. But he is influenced by irresponsible people, makes up his mind too quickly, and then forges ahead. His flatterers applaud, though behind his back they criticise without mercy. I am not angry with him, far from it, but with these gentlemen you can use a thick stick. Sooner or later he will learn from experience, and you must not make it more difficult by insults to do so. Tell him the truth: he will take it better from the press than he ever could from me. There were disagreements at the beginning of his reign, though on the major issues of European policy we are at one. But then there came a change and other influences were at work. He had ideas, both in domestic and foreign policy, which I could not approve. And our characters did not harmonise. The old Emperor asked my opinion about everything of importance and told me his own. The young one consulted other people and wished to decide for himself. He wanted to be rid of me. I, too, wanted to go, though not just at the moment when he despatched two messengers to hurry me up. Matters of importance for the Reich were in progress, and I did not wish to see my achievements of a quarter of a century scattered like chaff before the wind. Yet I am not angry with him, nor perhaps he with me. Broadly speaking my successor is carrying on my policy; for the moment he has no choice. Yet I fear it may not last, for he cannot stand up to the doctrinaire influences of the Emperor's entourage.'

On a visit to Friedrichsruh in January 1891 the faithful Poschinger found him mellow and resigned.[2] 'Never have I seen him at

[1] III. 76-99, August 16, 1890.   [2] III. 109-113.

once so gentle and so bright. He is often sarcastic but I did not hear a bitter word, even about the Emperor. He seems almost to have overcome the smart.' This attitude of philosophic resignation was also noted at the first visit of Maximilian Harden, the most incisive and independent German journalist of the age, and the chief literary champion of the fallen statesman.[1] Another new and frequent and ever welcome guest was the British journalist Sidney Whitman, whose records stress the charm and refinement, the courtesy, mellowness and simplicity of his host. In the words of Harden, the dross of thirty years of strife had fallen away. With the final volume of the *Gespräche* it becomes possible for the reader to feel a certain affection for the maker of the Reich.

The Indian Summer seemed almost too good to last, and with the marriage of Herbert Bismarck to Countess Hoyos in the spring of 1892 the smouldering embers shot into flame. Shortly before starting for the festivities at Vienna he told a friendly editor that he harboured no deep resentment against the Emperor or anyone else.[2] 'Apart from my aches and pains I feel happier and more contented since my dismissal than ever in office. The chuckers-out deserve my gratitude.' His tone changed when the visitor mentioned rumours that the fallen statesman desired to make it up with the Emperor before the ceremony. 'These statements emanate from the Government and are designed to saddle me with a wish for reconciliation because I feel I have something to make good. The phrase "reconciliation with the Emperor" is nonsense, since the presupposition does not exist, at any rate on my side. My criticism is directed solely against the false political course of my successor and his colleagues which fills me with anxiety for the Empire. Seldom, perhaps never, have I been so mistaken as about Caprivi, and there can be no worse apprenticeship for the Foreign Office than a lawyer's career. The King is beyond the sphere of criticism. I say no word against him, and I beg you, like all my visitors who champion my political views, to spare his name. But the insinuations that I am stretching out my hand and that I ought to make the first approach, as if I wanted something from him! Whether I possess his favour or not I cannot say. Since I have done nothing to forfeit it, I can do nothing to regain it. Now and then some visitor tells me he desires a rapprochement. Such utterances are apocryphal and ridiculous. I am

[1] III. 109–13.   [2] III. 203–9, May 31.

convinced he desires no other relationship than that which he has made.'

The assumption that William II had as little desire for a reconciliation as himself was confirmed a few days later by the instructions of Caprivi to the German Ambassador in Vienna and the letter of the Emperor to Francis Joseph requesting them to ignore the ex-Chancellor on his visit to the Austrian capital. While his request for an audience of the Emperor had therefore to be declined and he was boycotted by the official world, the cordial welcome by the people showed what they thought of the thunderbolt from Berlin. On the day of his departure he requested Dr. Benedikt, the influential editor of the *Neue Freie Presse*, to publish a message of thanks.[1] 'I have been very happy in Vienna,' he began. 'I am particularly glad that Austria has a better recollection of my co-operation than of my enmity. Naturally I acted in the interest of my country, and then the alliance was concluded which served the interests of both.' A further service, he continued, had been the maintenance of good relations between Germany and Russia, which resulted in lessening the friction between Vienna and St. Petersburg. Since his fall, Russo-German relations had gravely deteriorated, for the Tsar's friendly attitude had been largely determined by confidence in himself.

At this point Benedikt inquired whether he did not feel the need to return to the helm. 'Impossible. I was quite well enough to go on, but now I do not know if I should meet with the same confidence as of old in Russia or even here in Austria, though as to the latter I am not afraid. I have kept away from the Reichstag because I should have to attack the Government as a sort of leader of the Opposition, which would involve me in many controversies. Of course I owe no consideration to the present personages or to my successor. The bridges are broken down. There has been talk of making me President of the Council of State. And why not General-Adjutant? Then I could support the Ministers against the Emperor or *vice versa*, and there would be a Camarilla. That is not my line; for that sort of thing I lack the necessary Christian humility.' The latter phrase was accompanied by a hearty laugh. 'Have you abandoned the idea of entering the Reichstag?' 'Certainly not; it depends on circumstances.' Benedikt detected no sign of embitterment. Well aware that the Emperor and Caprivi had damaged themselves far more than him-

[1] III. 214–19.

self, Bismarck bore the affront with remarkable self-control. When Sidney Whitman a few days later at Kissingen quoted a newspaper which deprecated attacks on him on the ground that they would only intensify his anger, he quietly replied: 'They need not be alarmed. I shall keep calm.'[1] The rapturous homage paid to him at various stages of his journey home was balm to his wounds.

A French journalist who visited Varzin in the autumn of 1892 found him resigned to his fate.[2] 'The rest of my days are dedicated to ruling over my trees instead of over men: that I have given up for ever. If I had not been deprived of power, I could still be carrying on. I cannot abandon my interest in politics which have been my whole life. Yet I look at things as a philosophic observer, not desiring to take a hand again even if—which I consider impossible—I were invited back. For then I should have to refashion the machine which I constructed with difficulty and which has been transformed by other hands. For that I have neither courage nor strength; at my age one cannot start again. I have done duty to my country and wish to die in peace.' He was still very popular with the German people, interjected his visitor. 'When I paid my first visit to Germany shortly after your retirement one seemed to note a sigh of relief; to-day it is quite different.' 'Yes, I understand that sigh,' rejoined the host; 'my rule lasted a long time and for many it was a burden. If I am now remembered with regret it is less among politicians and the revolutionary masses than among the best workers. Whatever happens, I have given my Fatherland all I had.' Would he not take his seat in the Reichstag? 'I hardly think so, or, rather, certainly not. I have no house in Berlin, and I hate hotels and hotel beds. I am only happy at home, among my own people and belongings. In Berlin I could not cross the street without causing scenes. That I discovered this year on my way back from Vienna; it is a great and needless effort. Moreover if I went to the Reichstag my every word would be commented on, exploited, and contradicted: the authority which office confers is no longer mine. I should only be a soldier in the ranks, perhaps even a hindrance. No, no. I shall remain in my own home.' Age seemed at last to be cooling the fires, and in March 1893 an old friend found him not only quieter than two years before but more indifferent.[3]

This was hardly the impression of a little group of National

[1] III. 225–7. [2] III. 292–9. [3] III. 326, March 20, 1893.

Liberal Professors who visited Friedrichsruh a month later.[1] Once again the host emphatically dismissed press rumours as nonsense. 'I have lost favour, and whether I shall ever regain it I do not know. Reconciliation would merely mean resuming my duty to appear at Court; otherwise nothing would be changed. He would listen to my advice as little as during the last three years and would do exactly as he liked. He has his own plans, and I should count merely as a silent assistant and be held responsible for everything. I could not fail to disapprove this or that measure, and it would be falsely attributed to personal embitterment. Nor can I enter the Reichstag. I could have no dealings with the Centrum, the Radicals, and the Socialists, so there would only be my own old party friends, the National Liberals and the Conservatives. But my name would suffice to discredit anything and I should be a voice crying in the wilderness. My part is that of the onlooker, and no one shall deprive me of my right to criticise. The task of the hour is to strengthen the Reichstag, which can only be done by the election of independent men. The electoral system is not the deciding factor, for I see the same dear faces returned by universal suffrage as by the three-class system. No system is perfect. Now that the Bund has gone the Reichstag must stand up to the Government and form its own opinions, for governments cannot do everything and sometimes they make mistakes. If it allows itself to be degraded into a chamber of Yes-men, absolutism would be preferable. For in a constitutional state the Government can always excuse its errors by saying to a Parliament: It was your wish. Absolutism, on the other hand, as in Prussia, has more sense of responsibility. But how is it with the Reichstag? No, criticism can be too severe. It has got off the track, owing chiefly to its own fault. The decline is owing to the fact that it turns itself into a ministerial department and is gradually becoming a royalist chamber. That is because certain parties are seeking for office; it is just a grovelling-match. While I was there that practically ceased, but afterwards everyone thought he had a chance.'

The impressions carried away by the Professors were sorrowful. 'He was pessimistic and excited. His whole soul is still bent on politics and it is a great grief to have to stand aside. Anything done contrary to his intentions he regards as meddling with his work. He does not speak of Caprivi, but he feels deeply wounded by his lack of

[1] III. 344–52, May 27.

consideration. He finds nothing to approve, only to blame.' His listeners could not help reflecting that much that he censured was the same as he himself had done or would have done—for instance the treatment of the Reichstag. In his view things went right so long as he was there, since he was strong and wise enough to dispense with Reichstag supervision. His present liberal views sprang from his feeling: 'I could manage so long as I was at the helm, but now a powerful Reichstag is needed.' 'The impression was of youthful fire, clarity of thought, retentive memory, incomparable powers of expression. I found no difference between the man of 70 and 78. As we came away we were all filled with grief that this marvellous and unexhausted capacity, which could still accomplish so much for the welfare of the Fatherland, must lie unused. God knows how we need it.'

That his 'liberalism' was merely skin-deep was revealed in conversation with George Smalley, the well-known American journalist.[1] The old fear and detestation of the Socialists were undiminished, and he still felt that the policy of the anti-socialist law of 1878 was right. 'That the Government treated them as a party, as a force in the country which must be reckoned with instead of as robbers and thieves who ought to be suppressed, greatly enhanced their power and prestige. I would never have allowed it. They are rats and should be exterminated.' They were anti-Imperialists and were dominated by their class interest. 'They wish to turn pretty well everything in Germany upside down, above all the army and compulsory service, even the army estimates, not caring if the Reich is left without defence.' The Radicals were little better. Universal suffrage had been granted because he had no choice, but he had little belief in democracy. Governments must govern. 'There is now an idea that the world can be ruled from below. That is impossible.' Certain people and certain parties, he regretted to say, desired to introduce English Parliamentarism.

The outward rapprochement with the Emperor, so ardently desired by millions of his countrymen, occurred at the opening of 1894, when an exchange of visits was arranged. Though he knew that the wound was too deep to heal, William II had come to believe that in the national interest it should at any rate be plastered over, and he carried out his part with dignity and skill. The reception in Berlin, declared Bismarck, was something of a surprise.[2] 'I told my wife

[1] III. 352–60, Summer, 1893.   [2] III. 383–8.

that we should have to look round for a hotel, instead of which we were met by the Emperor's carriages and lodged in the palace. The whole episode may have produced a favourable impression on outside observers who do not look below the surface. That was not the case with me. I alone had made a sacrifice, for the relationship created by the unfriendly attitude of the Emperor and his advisers was quite to my taste. This action necessitated a courteous response, but that does not debar me from having my say, as some folk in Berlin seemed to expect. For this reason, and because I do not mince my words, and because I continue to make use of the press, people in the other camp are disappointed and annoyed.' A further gesture was made when Hohenlohe, who succeeded Caprivi as Chancellor later in the same year, called at his master's suggestion and was cordially received.[1]

On March 26, 1895, William II journeyed to Friedrichsruh for the eightieth birthday of the founder of the Reich. The meeting was outwardly friendly, but when the distinguished guest had departed Waldersee had a long talk and learned how little it all meant. 'I can state with the greatest certainty that the coolness on both sides remains. Playing a game with each other, they use the friendliest language and the Emperor overwhelms him with attentions. To the uninitiated it looks most satisfactory, and yet it is all pretence. The Emperor avoids state affairs and harbours old resentments due to Caprivi, while Bismarck always feels he has not received the reparation which is his due. And thus it will remain.' The forecast was correct. On the Emperor's rare subsequent visits a certain embarrassment was noted beneath a veneer of courtesy, and all attempts by the host to introduce politics into the conversation were ignored by the self-invited guest.

The conversations between the three years between the eightieth birthday and the fall of the curtain in 1898 diminish in number and interest. The veteran statesman felt the burden of years, the faithful Johanna was gone, and the chronic facial neuralgia often disinclined him to talk. He preferred the experienced Hohenlohe to the amateur Caprivi in the Chancellor's palace and the younger Bülow to Marschall at the Foreign Office, but he found little in their policy to praise. Though he respected the Boers as a healthy farming community, condemned the Jameson Raid, and dismissed Rhodes as a financial

[1] III. 405-8.

speculator, he deplored the Kruger telegram. Had he been in office, he remarked to Sidney Whitman, he would never have allowed his personal sentiments to influence his attitude in such a distant field, nor have encouraged the Boers to risk a conflict which they could not possibly win. Even were it in Germany's power to help them it would not have been in her interest to make trouble with England. Nothing should be allowed to lead to a conflict, and it would be a misfortune for Germany if England's position in the world were to be seriously threatened.

Holding such views Bismarck disapproved the policy of a naval challenge in the North Sea. On his appointment as Minister of Marine in 1897 Tirpitz visited the hermit of Friedrichsruh and craved his blessing on the naval programme.[1] In the early years of the Empire, he argued, the army sufficed, but a navy was now needed to underpin the Reich, for instance in the event of the anticipated Anglo-Russian war. The response was chilly. The host thought little of capital ships and preferred a number of 'hornets' which could move freely about the world. There was no need to worry about the Anglo-Russian conflict, for in such a case Germany should be neutral. Perhaps a new Pitt, interjected Tirpitz, might prefer belligerence to neutrality: there were other possibilities, and only a fleet could procure allies. The possibility of an English attack provoked nothing but derision. The English were worthy of respect as individuals, but in politics they were commercially minded. If they set foot on German soil the Landwehr would deal with them. That a strict blockade might wear down German strength the Admiral could not persuade him to believe. 'The old Prince was obviously thinking of the agrarian Germany of 1870 and of the political England of 1864, and he failed to grasp the commanding position of the British Empire in 1897. Living in the past, he did not trouble to listen to new ideas.' Despite this lack of mental elasticity, however, he delighted his visitor with the words: 'You do not need to convince me that we need more ships.' How many more were needed and of what character they should be—the twin problems on which the wisdom or unwisdom of the *Flottenpolitik* turned—was not further discussed. With his policy of limited liability it is safe to assume that he would have condemned the alienation of the friendly Mistress of the Seas.

The last distinguished visitor was Li Hung Chang, who repre-

[1] III. 477–9.

sented his country at the coronation of Nicholas II.[1] The veteran Chinese statesman observed that he had looked forward to their conversation particularly because he wished for advice.

B. What about?

Li. How can we reform China?

B. I cannot judge so far away.

Li. How can I succeed when everyone at home—the Government and the country—tries to prevent me?

B. One cannot oppose the Court. A Minister can only carry things out or give advice.

Li. But if the monarch is always subjected to other influences? It is the daily difficulties at Court which paralyse the Ministers.

B. The same as here. I had plenty of it, including feminine influences.

Li (with a smile). But you have a temperament which gets its way. Did it always go peacefully?

B. With ladies, always.

Li. But how is one to start carrying out the ruler's will?

B. Only with an army. It can be quite small, perhaps 50,000, but it must be good.

Li. We have the men but not the training. I have seen the German army, the best in the world. We must reorganise on the Prussian model and with the aid of Prussian officers.

B. There is no point in having troops all over the country. All you need is a force ready at any moment and facilities for sending them where they are required.

Li. I have achieved nothing and can accomplish little more in face of the obstacles which confront me.

B. You underestimate yourself.

Li. You have scored the greatest successes and will look back on your life with satisfaction.

B. Here, as in China, the old Greek adage remains true; all is in flux; in the end everything passes away.

Had the aged statesman perchance a prophetic vision that the stately edifice he had constructed and preserved for thirty years with matchless skill might perhaps one day be hurled into the abyss by some madman who forgot that politics are the art of the possible and that 'tempted fate will leave the loftiest star'?

[1] III. 465–9, June 25, 1896.

HOLSTEIN: ORACLE OF THE WILHELMSTRASSE

I

FRIEDRICH von Holstein, a member of an old Mecklenburg family, was born at Schwedt on the Oder in 1837. The precocious boy, the only child of a retired officer and an elderly mother, was privileged to travel abroad almost every year and learned French, English and Italian without effort. His favourite playmate was his cousin Ida von Stülpnagel, *née* von Holtzendorff, whom in his early years he was expected in family circles to marry and with whom he maintained regular correspondence to the end of his life. After leaving the University of Berlin where he studied law under Gneist, Stahl and other celebrities, he spent four years as an official in the City Court of the capital. The young lawyer was introduced into society by his friend Schlieffen, later Chief of the Prussian General Staff. His youth was darkened by the tragic death of his father in a fire on the family estate.

In 1860, at the age of twenty-three, he decided to enter the diplomatic service. He was attached on probation to the Prussian Embassy at St. Petersburg, where Bismarck, to whom he was already known, had been stationed for more than a year. 'A fortnight ago,' wrote Kurd von Schlözer on January 16, 1861, 'Baron Holstein came to us as Attaché, twenty-three years old, speaks French and English fluently, a good lad, many prejudices, very young and unobservant, will have to unlearn a good deal, but is zealous and not stupid.'[1] Two months later Bismarck wrote to his sister that he was very satisfied with his work, and was trying to train him for social life. Thus began an intimate association of thirty years with the founder of the German Empire, who presented him to Nesselrode with the words 'A future diplomat!' In June of the same year the Ambassador wrote to the Under Secretary for Foreign Affairs that he had the makings of a very good and industrious worker.[2] In 1862 he reported favourably on the young Attaché to Bernstorff, the Prussian Minister of Foreign

---

[1] Kurd von Schlözer, *Petersbürger Briefe*, 187–8.
[2] Bismarck, *Politische Schriften*, iii. 256.

Affairs.[1] 'In addition to very good natural gifts he has shown himself an earnest and indefatigable worker, and in a short time he has made himself so fully acquainted with his professional duties that he has been of real service in the transaction of business. His academic training is complete, and he is equally master of French, English and Italian. At first he lacked *savoir faire*. But here too he revealed the same capacity to learn as he had displayed in his official tasks, and he ended by winning a recognised place in all the circles he frequented. I therefore recommend to Your Excellency a young man who promises to be extremely useful in the diplomatic service.' For some years he was regarded almost as a son in the Bismarck family, and there were even rumours of a match with Marie, who later became Countess Rantzau. A less flattering comment on his sojourn in St. Petersburg is the caustic observation of a Russian diplomatist quoted twenty years later by Lothar Bucher to Busch: 'Ce jeune homme sait une foule de choses, mais il n'est pas capable de faire une seule.'[2]

After returning to Berlin for his final examination in 1863, Holstein was posted to Rio de Janeiro and seized the opportunity of exploring the interior of Brazil. There was so little to do in the Legation that his old chief, now the undisputed master of Prussia, inquired if he had had enough of South America, and on receiving an affirmative reply summoned him home. A more congenial task was to accompany Field Marshal Wrangel, Commander-in-Chief of the Allied forces during the campaign against Denmark in 1864, as assistant to the diplomatic representative of the Foreign Office. He drew up reports for Berlin, but this was not enough to satisfy his craving for new experiences. He begged a General to take him to the front and they rode out together to reconnoitre. At the storming of the Düppel lines he worked as a volunteer among the wounded, exposing himself to danger and receiving a slight wound on the foot. 'I cannot refrain from honourable mention of Legation Secretary Baron von Holstein,' reported his chief to Bismarck. 'He has helped me zealously in everything, and through his daily presence at the front and his friendly relations with the Prussian officers has managed to bring me reliable news of the operations.'

The next post was London, where he spent a year without much

[1] Sass, *Preussiche Jahrbücher*, March, 1930, 232–4.
[2] May 12, 1882. Busch, *Some Secret Pages of his History*, iii. 49.

minority in the Landtag and indeed find it difficult to get seats.' Parliament was only a passing fancy, for no one was less temperamentally suited for such a career.

After nearly two years in America Holstein was recalled in the summer of 1867 to Berlin and never left Europe again. His first post was Copenhagen, where, as in London and for an even stronger reason, Prussia was detested and social life was confined to the narrow little world of the *corps diplomatique*. 'I have seen and shall see nothing of Danish society,' he reported to his cousin.[1] 'That they do not mix with us Prussians is intelligible, but they also keep the other diplomats at arm's length. Danish fanaticism is also revealed in the schools. Instead of German they are now teaching Icelandic, the original Scandinavian tongue, but a dead language, for the Icelanders of to-day speak Danish. The poor children!' After a dull winter he was granted leave of absence from the diplomatic service for a year and settled in Brussels, where he joined some Belgian acquaintances in founding a company for a new method of transport on the Rhine. That such a promising member of the diplomatic service who was also *persona gratissima* with Bismarck went into business, and that his leave of absence was extended for a second year, suggests some official purpose the nature of which has not been discovered.

He returned to the diplomatic fold in July 1870 on the eve of the Franco-German war, and found himself plunged into the political whirlpool. A certain Angelo de Angeli, in the name of a Committee to organise an Italian Legion of 3,000 in the service of Prussia, wrote to Bismarck on July 15, and Holstein was promptly despatched to establish contact.[2] 'Italian soldiers,' commented Bismarck, 'are impracticable, and we have enough men; but Freicorps annoying the French from Italy would be very valuable.' Despite the Prussian brotherhood in arms in 1866, which drove the Austrians out of Venetia, Victor Emmanuel and his Ministers were Francophil. Public opinion, on the other hand, was sharply divided. Meeting Mazzini in Florence, Holstein argued that a victorious France would never allow the occupation of Rome, and Mazzini promised to find a way of keeping Visconti-Venosta, one of Cavour's disciples, from indiscretions. Staying in the house of a Garibaldian he negotiated with

[1] *Lebensbekenntnis*, 68.
[2] Bismarck, *Politische Schriften*, vi. b., 421, 430-2.

Crispi and General de Fabrizi, leaders of the Francophobe Opposition, who undertook to organise a revolutionary rising in the event of an alliance with France and to send an emissary for further discussions to Berlin. He brought Cucchi, a Garibaldian Deputy, to the Prussian capital and thence to Headquarters, but no definite results were achieved.

For some months he watched the victorious campaign from his quiet room in the Wilhelmstrasse and longed for the front. 'It will soon be over,' he wrote to his cousin late in September 1870. 'The French have had quite enough. The bravado of the Paris press is mere nonsense. They would like to stop, and the talk of war to the bitter end and burying themselves under the ruins is silly. They do not dream of it. Large numbers of the Landwehr are being sent to France to advertise our strength. When we secure all the places we wish to retain peace will not be far off; the problem of whom to negotiate with is easily solved as soon as the will to negotiate is there.' In two letters to the *Times* signed 'A German' he challenged a Frenchman's contention in that organ that French policy had for centuries been benevolent towards Germany.[1] France, he rejoined, had always coveted not only the Rhine frontier but territory on the right bank as well: in view of her record since the Congress of Vienna it was astonishing to hear it said that Germany should now win her by magnanimity as in 1815. Whether or not Alsace were recovered, 'the French will always hate us; for even if we leave their frontiers intact, we cannot restore their self-respect, and they will await their opportunity to attack us directly they can.' This conviction of France's incurable hostility remained with him and coloured his policy throughout life.

Bismarck's attention was called to these letters by Thile, whom he left in charge of the Foreign Office, and in January 1871 Holstein appeared in Versailles. He had received no summons, and the Chancellor's entourage expressed doubts about the reception, for the superman was poorly and extremely difficult. Their anxieties were unfounded, for he was very well received. In October 1870 he was introduced to young Bernhard von Bülow, son of the Foreign Minister, by Herbert Bismarck with the words 'Our truest friend.' He had welcomed Herbert and Bill in London during 1865 and was liked by the whole family: now he was to have his chance. 'He lay on the sofa in his dressing-gown,' he reported to his cousin, 'and reminded me of the

[1] *Lebensbekenntnis*, 94–6.

engraving of Richelieu lying ill on his boat with de Thou in tow.[1] He talked to me at length about all the snubs he received. He could not leave his post in the face of the enemy, but after the war, simultaneously with the presentation of the Imperial Crown, he would send in his card with p.p.c.' The Chancellor was glad of a sympathetic listener, for he had to let off steam. 'How long I shall be here is uncertain,' reported Holstein, 'not on account of Bismarck, but because Headquarters is always grumbling at his numerous entourage. That he will send me back without necessity I hardly believe. My presence seems to cheer him up, yet the favour of tyrants is changeable.' Henceforth he belonged to the diplomatic staff with Abeken, Bucher, Hatzfeldt and Busch.

At this period Holstein appears to have found no difficulty in working with people. 'The bureau has been reinforced by two officials,' noted Busch in his diary on January 6, 1871; 'one of them was Holstein.'[2] Three days later he adds that he has turned out to be 'exceedingly amiable, hardworking and helpful.' The German Boswell records conversations at the Chancellor's table in which he took a minor part, but there is no suggestion of such unquestioning discipleship as that which secured for Lothar Bucher and Busch a privileged position for life. It was a political education to be at the heart of events, but he found the Man of Destiny not exactly *facile à vivre*. Hatzfeldt confided to his wife that he was terribly overworked, and that without Holstein he did not know what would become of him. The latter's capacity for clear and cogent statement in impeccable French was of value in drafting the memoranda and correspondence which preceded and followed the surrender of the beleaguered city, and also the French text of the preliminary peace signed by Thiers and Jules Favre on February 26. The young official retained as a memento the inkpot and pen used on that historic occasion.

When the struggle was over and the Chancellor returned home, Holstein was attached to General von Fabrice, Governor-General of the occupied zone, with his headquarters at Rouen and acting as Ambassador pending the resumption of official relations. The chief task was to carry out the preliminaries of peace, to draft the communications of his chief to Thiers and Favre, and to report to the Chancellor. Paris was now in the hands of the Commune, and General Cluseret promptly approached the German authorities.

[1] *Lebensbekenntnis*, 97.   [2] Busch, i.

Bismarck instructed Fabrice to reply that he would listen to any overtures and would forward them to Berlin. Holstein received a visit from Cluseret, who proposed an arrangement with the Commune, to be followed by German mediation between it and the French Government at Versailles. Fabrice reported the proposals to Berlin, but the Chancellor made no response and the Communists were quickly suppressed by Galliffet's iron hand. Holstein was not sentimental and he had no love for France, but he respected and pitied Jules Favre. 'I am sorry for the poor old fellow confined to his capital.[1] It is not only the misfortune of defeat and the complete fiasco of republican principles for which he has struggled for over thirty years. He says he thought France ripe for liberty and less ignorant, but it was all illusion. The depression of an honourable man has always something saddening, and I do my utmost in my communications to consider his feelings. Fabrice, who despite his hot temper and his pessimism has decent instincts, shares my view and also tries to soften things in Berlin.'

Bismarck's close association with Holstein at Versailles had confirmed his favourable opinion, and he attached him to the German Embassy at Paris. Count Waldersee, who had been Military Attaché in 1870, returned in June 1871 as Chargé d'Affaires for three months and took him over as Second Secretary. 'He was a very restless spirit, very vain and lacking in thoroughness,' reported the General on nearer acquaintance.[2] 'Despite his immense zeal and his desire to do everything, he really accomplished nothing. But he wrote and spoke French admirably, and therefore was very useful to me and was often employed in tasks outside the Embassy.' The soldier and the civil servant, equally greedy for power, were destined both to co-operation and conflict during the decades that lay ahead.

The position of the first Ambassador of the German Empire in Paris was bound to be difficult, and the Chancellor displayed less than his usual acumen in transferring Count Harry Arnim from Rome. His ability was beyond question, but his views as to the policy to be pursued towards France differed radically from those of his chief. A few weeks after his appointment an entry in Busch's diary suggests that the Wilhelmstrasse was already dissatisfied. 'Bucher tells me that Arnim has shown great want of skill in negotiating the agreement

[1] *Lebensbekenntnis*, 103.
[2] *Waldersee in seinem militärischen Wirken*, i. 386, June 15, 1871.

relating to the Customs of Alsace-Lorraine. He is incapable, and so are his subordinates. Holstein is otherwise quite an able man, but he has no real knowledge of state affairs.'[1] The Chancellor, however, was soon to find the latter's services of inestimable value. While the official policy was to uphold the Republic on the ground that it was unlikely to find allies in a monarchical Europe, the Ambassador openly favoured the Royalists, and it was useful to learn from a man on the spot what game he was playing. The feud was embittered by Bismarck's suspicion that Arnim, who had powerful friends at Court, was intriguing to succeed him as Chancellor.

Holstein had met Arnim in Brussels in 1869 when the latter was Chargé d'Affaires during the absence of the Minister, and the close association now began which ended three years later in a crash. A letter of his aunt to her daughter Ida expresses her fear that the appointment might lead to Fritz's resignation, since they disliked each other, and she declared her intention of urging him to be careful. After a few weeks of partnership, however, Holstein reported that their official relations were very good. 'He is a silent and nervy man but we get on excellently. Till the treaties were finished I had hard work and was employed for all purposes. The French notes were my job, and he rarely made changes. He dictated to me the German reports, partly, he said, in order that I might call attention to errors of style. Strictly speaking it is below me, but I was glad to do it as I was compensated in another way. I wrote certain reports, some of them signed by him, some by myself. I have also to collect information, and have had several very interesting discussions with Thiers. Arnim's wife and family arrive to-morrow. She has been here once and is very nice. I look after the political side under Arnim, and the First Secretary does the non-political work. So I would rather remain here as Second Secretary than be First Secretary in some other post where there is nothing to do. I believe that no Mission is better informed than ours.'[2] The sun seemed to be shining brightly and in the summer of 1872 he spent part of his holiday with Bismarck at Varzin.

The first sign of trouble appears in a letter of March 1873. 'Arnim and Bismarck have been snarling at each other, and so it will go on. Needless to say the conflict of the big people brings nothing but unpleasant consequences for myself.'[3] He added that he was not

[1] Busch, ii. 117, September 22, 1871. [2] *Lebensbekenntnis*, 114–15.
[3] *Ibid.*, 119.

expecting and did not desire to be moved. A month later he was in Berlin. 'He came, I tell you in confidence,' wrote his aunt to her daughter, 'to arrange for his continuance in Paris as Second Secretary, and he believes Bismarck will consent. I should have liked to see him First Secretary, as he would have been in London or Vienna. The Bismarcks were all very nice to him, the sons rejoicing at his arrival.' Next day she supplied a little more information. 'Fritz wishes either to remain in Paris or to come to Berlin and has taken discreet soundings. He seems to have noticed that the officials do not want him here, fearing his intimacy with the Bismarcks, and for the same reason Arnim is afraid of him in Paris. I wonder how it will end. Anyhow the young Bismarcks are keen on getting him here, and perhaps that will help.' A fortnight later, on May 9, 1873, she wrote: 'Yesterday's paper with the hint of trouble between Bismarck and Arnim makes me anxious. If only it does Fritz no harm!'

In 1874 the difficult Ambassador was transferred from Paris to Constantinople. His successor, Prince Hohenlohe, received instructions in which reference was made to earlier communications from the Wilhelmstrasse. Search was made in vain for the documents, and Bismarck asked Arnim if he had removed them by mistake. The latter coolly replied that he had taken them with him because they dealt with ecclesiastical questions, and concerned, *inter alia*, Cardinal Hohenlohe, adding that he wished his successor not to see the documents relating to his brother. When the Chancellor peremptorily ordered their restoration to the Paris Embassy, Arnim defiantly retorted that he regarded them as his personal property. Bismarck hereupon summoned him before a Court on the charge of removing documents belonging to the State. The offender was condemned to imprisonment, fled to Switzerland, and died in exile, a broken man.

In this *cause célèbre*, in which the Chancellor was less interested in vindicating the authority of the State than in striking down a possible rival, Holstein was the principal witness.[1] Arnim's lawyer informed the Court that he did not accuse Holstein of spying, but that the Second Secretary had sent reports to the Wilhelmstrasse, without the knowledge of his Chief, which envenomed the conflict. Holstein replied that he had never addressed, nor been invited to

[1] The documents are printed in *Der Arnim'sche Process*. Arnim's apologia, *Pro Nihilo*, charges Holstein with reporting confidential conversations, 12–14 (English translation). An authoritative work on Arnim is needed.

address, reports to the Chancellor or his entourage. At first, he added, he and all the members of the Paris Embassy had greatly admired their chief. Indeed when he was at Berlin in the spring of 1872, at a moment when the Chancellor was credited with the intention of resigning, he had observed that there could not be a better successor than Arnim. After returning to Paris in the autumn of 1872 from a visit to Varzin, he had found that the opinions of the Ambassador differed widely from those of the Chancellor, who had promised Thiers his support to any Government which made and carried out the peace. Thiers had done his part, yet Arnim desired a change of regime. 'I opposed his view, but I soon realised that it was his fixed idea. His proceedings raised the question which of the two men was to rule the Empire. For fourteen years I had been in close relations with the Chancellor. I wrote my impressions to several friends. Later I spoke to Arnim and told him that I wished to change my post. He saw no reason for such a step, but the interview made me feel that he had not behaved very well. This impression was confirmed when I learned that his relations with the Chancellor were very strained. He has accused me of being the cause of all the trouble. That charge is answered by the documents themselves. From January 1873 my social relations with him ceased completely. In the autumn of 1873 I learned at Berlin that there was open war. Everybody talked of it. My position between the two was impossible. I wished for a change, but friends agreed that I should seem to be shirking a difficult task.'

Holstein's conduct was variously judged at the time. The trial aroused keen interest in France, and in his Introduction to a French translation of the evidence, Valfrey defends him against the charge of dishonourable conduct on the ground that he showed himself an open adversary.[1] In his own country, on the other hand, his attitude was generally condemned. 'I remember the scene in Court when Holstein gave evidence against Arnim,' writes Baron von Eckardstein, 'and I recall the excitement when it appeared that at Bismarck's orders he had systematically spied on his Chief.'[2] His action, echoes Prince Alexander Hohenlohe, always remained a blot on his character, and made him an embittered recluse.[3] Henceforth he was the Judas of German politics. He was cut by old friends and turned out of his

---

[1] *Le Procès d'Arnim.*   [2] *Erinnerungen,* i. 22–3.
[3] *Aus meinem Leben,* ch. 12.

club on the Pariserplatz. 'Many took Arnim's side and blamed Holstein,' writes Count Hutten-Czapski, a member of the same select club. 'I told them, though at that time I did not know him, that I disagreed, since an official must sometimes report if another official or even his chief commits treachery.' Holstein heard of this unsolicited championship and showed his gratitude in after years.[1] For the rest of his life he suffered from persecution mania. The man who had enjoyed society and good living became a hermit in an unfashionable quarter of Berlin, taking solitary holidays, and seeking consolation in the favour of the Chancellor. 'The Bismarcks have branded me on the forehead like a galley slave,' he complained to a friend, 'and therewith they hold me fast.'[2] In his fiftieth year he sadly confessed to his cousin that he was like an old monk and could only peep into family life.

The Arnim incident remains the most obscure episode in Holstein's life. That he enjoyed the Chancellor's entire confidence is clear. Some years later Count Wesdehlen, formerly First Secretary at Paris, told Count Monts that his colleague, the Second Secretary, had occupied an unusual position; that he possessed the right to see all papers; that he had no relations with the Ambassador; and that he (Wesdehlen) was instructed by the Chancellor to keep in close touch with him.[3] Monts, who was never his enemy, expresses the view that Holstein's denial of spying does not exclude the possibility that he sent information which reached the Chancellor through third parties. Shortly before his death Bülow told Rosen a curious tale of a conversation between his wife and Holstein many years earlier during an evening walk in the Thiergarten.[4] The Bismarck family, he bitterly complained, had ruthlessly exploited him and made him a galley-slave. 'Yes, they made me the unhappiest of men. They branded my forehead with the letters T.F. (Travaux Forcés). First they made me correspond secretly about Arnim, my chief. The letters were addressed to the governess of Marie Bismarck. In this way I supplied materials for the trial of Arnim in which again I had to do a slave's work. I had to hide myself and could never play a public rôle or obtain high office. Instead I had to work like a galley-slave, also

---

[1] Hutten-Czapski, *Sechzig Jahre Politik und Gesellschaft*, i, 51–2.
[2] Theodor Wolff, *Das Vorspiel*, 77.
[3] Monts, *Erinnerungen und Gedanken*, 187–93.
[4] Rosen, *Aus einem diplomatischen Wanderleben*, i. 92–3.

under Herbert, who was tactless enough to let me feel his power. But I bitterly revenged myself on the Bismarcks when the moment arrived.' Since Bülow was eighty at the time of this conversation, and since a considerable portion of it was concerned with the failings of the man whom he had been glad to have as his principal adviser in the days of his power, we must make allowance for his usual embroidery.

Holstein remained at Paris for two years after the eviction of Arnim, and his conduct during the reign of the second Ambassador to the Republic confirmed in some measure the unfavourable impression produced by his record under the first. Princess Hohenlohe, records her son Alexander who was then a boy, used to complain that when she and her daughters walked out they were often followed by him. They received friendly warnings from French officials against the practices of the Second Secretary, who, whatever he may have done under Arnim, now corresponded direct with the Chancellor. Prince Alexander adds that, though his mother retained her profound distrust and antipathy to the end of her life, Holstein won the confidence of his father, in whose diary he occasionally appears. 'I met a Prussian Legationsrat Holstein,' he noted on December 8, 1870, 'who told me a great deal about his sport on the American prairies.'[1] On succeeding to the Paris Embassy in 1874 Hohenlohe records dinners and visits to the theatre with his subordinate; and on December 18, 1875, while on a visit to Bismarck, he notes the decision that he was to be First Secretary.[2] Twenty years later the two men were to renew their association in even more responsible positions.

II

In 1876 Holstein was recalled to the Wilhelmstrasse where he was to labour without ceasing for thirty eventful years. 'The faithful Fritz,' as he was called in the Bismarck household, had proved himself an ardent disciple of the Chancellor and shared many of his secrets. 'The old gentleman is very friendly with me,' he reported to Ida.[3] 'Of society there is nothing to tell. Recently I accepted an invitation from an English Secretary of Legation because I could not refuse, but I realised more closely than ever that intercourse between officials of the Foreign Office and foreign diplomatists is impossible. People

[1] *Denkwürdigkeiten*, i. 33. [2] *Ibid.*, i. 177. [3] *Lebensbekenntnis*, 123–4.

always ask indiscreet questions and one has to lie in order to give nothing away. And in the society of Germans intercourse is disagreeable because conversation on party questions is unavoidable. The young Bismarcks have dropped most of their contacts. For me it is a welcome pretext since I hate sociability, especially now I am getting on in years. That was one of the reasons I liked Paris. In many ways life was more agreeable there, though here it is more interesting.' According to Monts, who entered the Foreign Office in 1878, he played a relatively minor *rôle* at this time. 'He was friendly to newcomers, doubtless in order to test them. Occasionally he invited us to excellent lunches at Borchardt's, which always began with oysters—whence the nickname *Austernfreund* in the subsequent attack in *Kladderadatsch*.'[1]

Even in his early years at the Wilhelmstrasse he exerted an authority hardly to be explained by his official status alone. In 1876 the elder Bülow informed his son Bernhard that he had intended to send him to the Embassy in Paris, but that the plan had been frustrated by Holstein.[2] 'Who is Holstein?' asked the young diplomat; 'I hardly know him.' 'Who is Holstein?' repeated the Foreign Minister. 'That is not so easy to answer. He came as a raw Attaché to Bismarck in St. Petersburg. Since then he has been to our great man what Père Joseph was to Richelieu.' He added that he made him feel uncomfortable and that he had warned Bismarck. The Prince replied that he must have someone whom he could thoroughly trust. When Bülow rejoined that the Chancellor could trust him too, he received the flattering reply: 'Yes, but only for the good things. Sometimes I must do evil things in this evil world. *À corsaire corsaire et demi.* Holstein is a corsair, ready for anything. Besides his capacity for dirty business he is an outstanding political brain. He has doubtless opposed your appointment to Paris because you might have learned more of his intrigues against Arnim than he would like.' The *ipsissima verba* cannot be guaranteed after so many years, particularly with such an unreliable witness as Prince Bülow; but the conversation as served up in the Memoirs of the ex-Chancellor may well have represented the attitude of his father and Bismarck at the time. In October 1877 Busch records a visit to Varzin when Holstein was the only other guest.[3] On the latter's return after a sojourn of five weeks with the

---

[1] Monts, *Erinnerungen*, 42.   [2] Bülow, *Denkwürdigkeiten*, iv. 386–7.
[3] Busch, ii. 317, 319.

Chancellor, he reported his chief's views and plans to Lucius von Ballhausen.[1] Though only a minor official of the Foreign Office, it is clear from this conversation that Bismarck discussed internal questions with his trusted subordinate as well as foreign affairs.

As one of the Secretaries of the Berlin Congress in 1878 Holstein appears in the large official picture painted by Anton von Werner. His mastery of English and French made him a useful satellite, and he had the pleasure of introducing to the Chancellor the incomparable Blowitz whom he had learned to know at Paris. He was rewarded by the French Government with one of the lower grades of the Legion of Honour, but the drudgery of the Secretariat was by no means to the taste of a man who had seen so much of the world. He proved himself useless, complains his colleague Radowitz in his Memoirs.[2] 'In the first meetings for drawing up the protocols he made himself so objectionable by his uncalled-for observations and contributed so little to the work that we at once saw that it was impossible to get through our heavy task, for which every minute was of importance, if he were to remain. Henceforth he devoted himself to the foreign journalists, which was his *métier*. Steady, thorough work bored him. During the Congress he did as good as nothing, but he tried to have his finger in every pie. He never forgave me for evicting him and began his embittered campaign against me, which, when he became so powerful, had a fatal influence on my career.' Radowitz is a hostile witness, but he was one of the best brains in the service and his testimony cannot be wholly ignored.

The removal of Holstein from the Congress Secretariat was, however, a Pyrrhic victory.[3] Soon afterwards he tried to poison the younger Bülow against Radowitz and through him to influence the Foreign Minister.[4] In the winter of 1879 Bismarck was led to believe that Radowitz had intrigued against him during his latest illness and aspired to the post of Foreign Minister under a new Chancellor.[5] In February 1880 the Dictator called for a report on his activities, but the official selected for this duty happened to be a friend of Radowitz

---

[1] Lucius von Ballhausen, *Erinnerungen*, 114–5.
[2] *Aufzeichnungen und Erinnerungen*, ii. 23.
[3] *Ibid.*, ii. 42.
[4] Bülow, *Denkwürdigkeiten*, iv. 452–5. According to Bülow the quarrel arose because Radowitz received a higher Order than Holstein, but Radowitz is here a better witness.
[5] Radowitz, ii. 117–9.

and told him what was in the wind. It seemed obvious that the preposterous story had reached the Chancellor through Holstein, who had been with him in Varzin during the autumn and winter. Holstein, adds Radowitz, possessed not only the ear of the Prince, who believed in his utter devotion, but the confidence of the Princess, whose influence in personal matters was not to be despised. No proof of Radowitz's disloyalty was forthcoming, but a difficult situation was ended by keeping him abroad for the rest of his life.

Holstein stood close to his chief during the critical weeks of August and September 1879 when a decision was taken which affected European history for forty years. While Bismarck was wrestling with the unwillingness of the Emperor to approve an Austro-German defensive alliance against the Russian menace, Holstein, whom the Chancellor had taken with him to Gastein, suggested that Hohenlohe's mediation should be invoked. The Ambassador, then on leave, was summoned by telegraph and was met by Holstein, who explained the situation. Hohenlohe was quickly converted to the need for an alliance and was despatched to convert the harassed ruler.[1] No sooner was the Dual Alliance signed and ratified than Bülow, the Foreign Minister, died. On October 28, 1879, Hohenlohe's diary records a discussion at the Wilhelmstrasse in which he was pressed from several quarters to shoulder the burden.[2] Next day he journeyed to Varzin, where he found Holstein, who strongly urged him to accept the post if he received the offer. When Bismarck proposed his appointment, Hohenlohe explained that the salary was too low for his needs, but volunteered temporary service for the following summer while the Chancellor was away. The zeal with which Holstein urged the nomination was an additional cause of resentment to Princess Hohenlohe, who feared that the work would be too much for her husband's strength. Her apprehensions were fulfilled; and Count Hatzfeldt, whom Bismarck described as the best horse in Germany's diplomatic stable and who was a *persona grata* with Holstein, became Minister for Foreign Affairs.

Bismarck and Holstein needed one another, but there was no real affection on either side and neither of them was made to be loved. 'This is my tenth week here, that is three weeks in October and again since November 29,' reported the latter to his cousin on January 15,

[1] Hohenlohe, *Denkwürdigkeiten*, ii. 274.
[2] *Ibid.*, ii. 278–80.

1880.[1] 'It was not always pleasant, for the Prince was very poorly during the first half of December. He is well again and next week we go to Berlin.' The friction involved in the making of the Austrian alliance had upset him very much. 'He is exceptionally fretful. A doctor was summoned twice in the night. Once he said to him: "And when I think how many pig-dogs (schweinehunde) in the world are in good health, while I lie here like a dog just because I have done my duty!" The Chief and I have got used to each other. I take no notice of his rough ways. With his nature he soon gets over everything if he has no worry. But he is like all highly charged machines—there is always danger of an explosion.'

In 1880 Holstein, hitherto a Legationsrat, was appointed a Vortragender Rat (Assistant Under-Secretary) and held the post for the next twenty-six years. Bülow declares that he never exercised a greater influence than in the second half of the Bismarck era.[2] 'His power at that time in regard to questions of *personnel* was very far-reaching, his position almost impregnable owing to the absolute confidence reposed in him by the great Chancellor and to his intimate friendship with Herbert. Especially since the death in 1879 of my father, who by his old and trustful relations to Prince Bismarck and his tranquil clarity was a useful counterweight, Holstein came more and more into the foreground. My father did not love him; they were utterly different natures.' Nobody would now assert that his influence reached high-water mark at this period; yet none of his colleagues enjoyed so much of the confidence of Hatzfeldt, who appointed him *interim* Under-Secretary in the summer of 1882, to the disgust of Lothar Bucher and the disturbance of the harmony hitherto prevailing in the Political Department.[3] The work of the Foreign Office was complicated by the fact that the Chief was often away for months at a time, and even the faithful Lothar Bucher was tempted to grumble. 'Bucher complains that he occupies himself too much with the press,' wrote Busch in his diary, October 25, 1881.[4] 'Instructions arrive from Varzin almost daily. No one in the office understands them—neither the sons, nor Holstein, who is a mere bungler.' Bucher returned to his theme a fortnight later.[5] The press campaign had been very foolishly conducted. 'We have no less than four

[1] *Lebensbekenntnis*, 126–8.
[2] *Denkwürdigkeiten*, ii. 112–3.
[3] Poschinger, *Stunden bei Bismarck*, 72.
[4] Busch, iii. 9.
[5] *Ibid.*, iii. 13.

Secretaries—(Klemens) Busch, the real one, who is good; Herbert at Varzin; Rantzau and Holstein here. These know nothing and can do nothing properly. None of them reads the papers or knows what is going on, and if the Chief gives violent instructions they are carried out with still greater violence.' Bucher's growing dislike of Holstein is reflected in an entry in Busch's diary two years later.[1] 'He has recently developed, owing to his ambition, into a very dangerous intriguer. He tells Hatzfeldt everything he hears.' In the following year Bucher again complained of the shocking way in which business was conducted in the Foreign Office by Hatzfeldt and Holstein, with the latter of whom he had ceased to exchange salutations.[2] Neither under nor after Bismarck does the Wilhelmstrasse appear to have been a happy place.

Despite the undiminished favour which he enjoyed, Holstein's letters to his cousin during the last decade of Bismarck's dictatorship reveal growing dissatisfaction. On September 23, 1882, the anniversary of the latter's call to the Premiership in 1862, he told her that he would not write to Varzin about it.[2] 'With a man who has shed most human feelings one is exposed to the imputation of false motives.' Nearly three years later, in 1885, he reported that, to pay off the mortgage on Schönhausen, Mendelssohn had given him 200,000 marks, Bleichröder 100,000, and Schwabach 50,000. 'Yes, the man has great faults of character, but where shall we be when he is gone? It will be a wretched business.' It was too early to think of his successor, but the tie between master and disciple was wearing thin.

In 1885 an important change occurred in the Wilhelmstrasse. The Chancellor was dissatisfied with Münster's handling of the colonial negotiations with England, complaining that his representations to Lord Granville had been lacking in vigour. He was therefore transferred to Paris and was succeeded in London by Hatzfeldt, while Herbert Bismarck became Foreign Minister. Herbert, observed Lothar Bucher to Busch, had selected Holstein as Under-Secretary, and would probably get his way, though the Chancellor had another candidate in view. Herbert had made up the differences between his mother and Holstein.[3] If the latter were appointed, added Bucher, he would retire. The new Foreign Minister failed to carry his point, for Berchem was chosen; but he worked in full harmony with Holstein, who had known him since childhood. 'He is extremely useful,' re-

[1] Busch, iii. 118.   [2] *Lebensbekenntnis*, 135.   [3] Busch, iii. 146.

marked Herbert to Count Lerchenfeld, the Bavarian Minister in Berlin, 'but one must never let him go alone.'[1] Herbert assigned him the room next to his own, a strategic position retained till his retirement twenty years later. He was still *persona gratissima* to the Chancellor, and Dryander records that he was specially skilled in persuading his Chief to talk about the dramatic incidents of his life.[2]

The appointment of Herbert was a sign that the dictatorship was entering its last phase, for his father spent less and less time in Berlin. 'It is sad to see how the Bismarck regime is ending without honour,' wrote Holstein in November 1885.[3] 'Bismarck has lost his old energy,' he added in April 1886. 'He gives way too much to the passionate and incautious Herbert whose dislike of Austria, I fear, may lead to too close intimacy with Russia.' Holstein's letters to his cousin now become definitely hostile, though so long as the old Emperor was alive it was useless to speculate on a change. 'I regard the Bismarck regime, present and future, as a great danger,' he wrote in May 1886. 'Ordinary men without megalomania would be better. The Chancellor meddles in everything but does not study the materials and carries nothing through. The way he has stumbled out of the questions of the Carolines and the *Kulturkampf* turns them into defeats, and in foreign policy he talks differently almost every day. In his weaker moments he confesses it to his sons, but he will hold on for pecuniary reasons since his estates bring him nothing and his forests little.' His method of work was growing more and more *dilettante* and inconsequent, added Holstein in October. 'He thinks he can rule the world in half an hour at breakfast; the rest of the day he idles or dictates articles all of which would be better unwritten.'

Waldersee, now Quartermaster-General, records in his diary that he was in constant touch with the Foreign Office, chiefly through Holstein; and he now began to realise both the lofty position to which his old subordinate had climbed and the curious twist in his mind.[4] It was easy to work with Hatzfeldt and Berchem. 'It was otherwise with Holstein. One always had to reckon with his suspicious and swift resentments. But I was well acquainted with the eccentric from 1871, and enjoyed what was for him a very high degree of his confidence. I must say too that till Bismarck's departure he was always the

---

[1] Lerchenfeld, *Erinnerungen u. Denkwürdigkeiten*, 385–392.
[2] Dryander, *Erinnerungen*, 165.   [3] *Lebensbekenntnis*, 137–142.
[4] *Waldersee in seinem militärischen Wirken*, ii. 31–3.

same and took an interest in me, apparently, like Berchem, regarding me as a candidate for the Chancellorship. I very often went to him and he occasionally visited me. He was at that time very communicative and gave me everything to read that could interest me, so that I obtained a considerable insight into the diplomatic situation.' The confidence of the Chancellor was still unshaken. In 1885 Klemens Busch, the Under-Secretary, asked for a post abroad. 'You cannot get on with my son?' inquired Bismarck. Busch replied that he could not get on with Holstein. 'There I cannot help you,' was the rejoinder; 'I must have somebody on whom I can absolutely rely.'[1]

In 1886, when William I was in his ninetieth year, Waldersee records audacious Bismarckian attempts to obtain control of his heir. 'To monopolise the future Emperor,' he wrote on April 2, 'everyone is to be removed who might possess or attain power and discreditable means are employed. One of the worst of the agents turns out to be Holstein. He is clever enough to keep out of the limelight so that many people scarcely know of his existence.'[2] In November 1886 he records a fresh attempt to remove someone from the entourage of the Crown Prince. 'The driving force behind Radolinski is again Holstein, this evil spirit of last winter. He has such a bad conscience that he avoids me since the spring. I have discovered that it was he who talked scandal to the Crown Prince and Princess about me; and he actually painted me as an evil counsellor of Prince William, the same prince before whom he cringes and whom he always tells how much he reveres him. With the Crown Prince he pretends to be a champion of the Battenberg marriage, though he knows quite well that Bismarck will never consent.'[3] Though Waldersee had taken the measure of Holstein, he preferred even an uncertain association to a perilous enmity. 'To-day I was in the Foreign Office,' he wrote on May 31, 1887, 'and established friendly relations with Holstein. Third parties seemed to have an interest in this reconciliation and maintain that there were misunderstandings. That is quite possible. So I came forward gladly and had the impression that he was immensely relieved.'[4] In the following March he records a dinner with Holstein, 'with whom I am quite on the old footing. I hear from

---

[1] Bülow, iv. 623.

[2] Waldersee, i. 286. Eulenburg asserts on the authority of the Bismarcks that Holstein urged the Chancellor to have the Crown Prince poisoned, but this was doubtless nothing more than a grim joke. Haller, *Eulenburg*, 383.

[3] Waldersee, i. 304.   [4] *Ibid.*, i. 327.

several quarters that he is really exerting himself in my interest.'[1] For the next year or two Waldersee was in high favour, and his correspondence contains lengthy letters from his political mentor.

Numerous portraits of Holstein have been painted by friends and foes, but all agree in regard to his range of knowledge, his brain power, and his morbid temperament. He was the first of the higher officials to arrive and the last to leave. No one could now complain that he shirked drudgery. He read every document and report, could explain the history of any negotiation, and possessed an uncanny acquaintance with the private affairs of the *personnel* of the diplomatic service. Yet the greatest worker in the Wilhelmstrasse was regarded in some quarters as more of a liability than an asset. Schweinitz, the veteran German Ambassador in St. Petersburg, records a visit to Berlin in the autumn of 1887.[2] 'This eccentric, who compelled my respect when in 1864 before Düppel he assisted the wounded in the front ranks and who still does much good in secret, has a spiteful character, allows himself to be influenced by personal dislikes, and secretly makes mischief by his odious press methods. He has a remarkable brain but the spirit and character of a hunchback. He perfectly understands the great dangers into which we have fallen through our over-subtle and yet often brutal policy. He explained so clearly and coolly all that may happen that I left with an uncomfortable feeling.' If Raschdau is to be believed, Holstein talked better than he wrote, for his drafts required the most careful revision.[3] It was about this time that Prince William was allowed to work in the Wilhelmstrasse, of which the Chancellor, for his guidance, described the *personnel*. 'When he came to Holstein,' relates the fallen ruler in his Memoirs, 'it seemed to me that a warning sounded through his words. As I became more intimate in the Bismarck circle, Holstein was discussed with greater frankness. He was very clever, very industrious, immensely vain, full of mistrust, dominated by fancies, a good hater and therefore a dangerous man. Bismarck called him the man with the hyaena eyes, whom I should be wise to avoid. The sharp criticism of later years was already ripening.'[4]

[1] Waldersee, i. 365.
[2] Schweinitz, *Denkwürdigkeiten*, ii. 349.
[3] Brauer, Marcks and Müller, *Erinnerungen an Bismarck*, 30.
[4] *Ereignisse und Gestalten*, 6. The reference to the hyaena eyes is not so bad as it sounds, for Holstein had almost lost the use of one eye in a shooting accident, and he was sometimes called Polyphemus.

Holstein was now in fact, though not in rank, second in importance to the Foreign Minister, and he took an active part in discussions of high policy. The renewal of the Triple Alliance in 1887 involved a good deal of friction owing to Italy's demands and Austria's unwillingness to concede them. No such repugnance was felt by Bismarck, whose fear of simultaneous attack by the France of Boulanger and the Russia of Katkoff disposed him to accept almost any proposals from Rome and to urge their acceptance at Vienna. When Prince Reuss reported his unsatisfactory conversations with Kalnoky, Holstein expressed to the Austrian Ambassador, Count Szechenyi, his concern at the 'not easily comprehensible decision' of his chief.[1] What would become of Austria, he asked, if she failed to settle the Bulgarian question with Russia and at the same time lost her Italian ally? To the rejoinder that no reliance could be placed on the Italians he replied that it was a question, not of a permanent alliance, but of acquiring a paid corps of auxiliaries like the mercenaries of the Middle Ages. To dispel Kalnoky's fears that Italy might demand southern Tirol in return for support in an Austro-Russian war, he consulted the Italian Ambassador, who authorised him to declare that Italy had no such idea. On the other hand, added Holstein, it might be impossible to prevent Italy establishing herself in Albania. A few days later he referred angrily to Italy's demand for *pourboire*, but once again urged the necessity of concessions. Not, however, till Bismarck threw his whole weight into the scale of surrender did the stubborn Kalnoky purchase the continuation of Italy's support at her own high price. On the other hand Holstein considered the Chancellor too subservient in regard to Russia, and disapproved the Russophil policy in the case of the Battenberg marriage.[2] It was the first overt sign of an ominous independence.

III

THE accession of William II in 1888 changed nothing for the moment, and indeed the death of the liberal Emperor Frederick removed a potential menace for the Chancellor and his friends. 'One feels a

---

[1] Pribram, *The Secret Treaties of Austria-Hungary*, ii. 69–75.
[2] Waldersee, *Denkwürdigkeiten*, i. 340, December 12, 1887, and Bülow, iv. 607. Bülow believes that his hostility to Russia was due to his lack of social success in St. Petersburg as a young man, but this is surely fanciful.

ruler is there, not only a Chancellor,' wrote Holstein to Ida in July 1888. 'The latter takes the greatest pains with the young gentleman and stands well with him, but Herbert is in a bad mood.' Yet shrewd observers began to ask whether the old pilot was as invulnerable as he believed. 'At the Emperor's accession,' noted Waldersee in his diary in July 1889, 'I prophesied to Holstein and others that he would not for long put up with Bismarck, but no one believed me. In the late summer they began to see it, and henceforward the rats gradually left the ship. One of the first to go was Holstein; Eulenburg and Kiderlen soon followed.'[1] We cannot tell when Holstein began to regard the fall of the Chancellor as a probability, and it is not certain that he worked for a change before the catastrophe was in sight: in so exposed a position it was dangerous to play for high stakes. Bismarck's second son, Bill, had never trusted him,[2] Herbert no longer treated him with the old consideration, and the Chancellor had long ceased to be his oracle. 'He is an egoist to the finger-tips,' complained Holstein. Yet it was not his habit to burn his boats till the necessity arose, for his perch in the Wilhelmstrasse was all that he had in the world. Moreover, like most Germans, he desired the Chancellor and the ruler to co-operate.

'As a Bismarckian,' he wrote to Waldersee in August 1889, 'I ought to desire an unfavourable result to the elections, for the more difficult the internal situation becomes, the more indispensable is the Chancellor.'[3] The young Emperor clearly needed guidance, yet he seemed to be making a good start. 'I am very satisfied with what I see,' he wrote in November, 1889.[4] 'Firstly, with friendly manners, he has the quality—desirable in a sovereign —of heartlessness. There is therefore no fear of the rule of favourites. He dislikes official papers but reads extracts from the press by the hour. Military and foreign matters interest him; other things less, except the social question. There he wishes improvement of the lot of the workers, while the Chancellor after long wobbling has come down stiffly on the side of the employers. I myself understand nothing of this question, but I see that the Chancellor in this issue stands alone. Of course no Minister or official dares oppose him.' A remarkable letter to Bötticher, dated January 7, 1890, advising him on a forthcoming visit to Friedrichsruh to dissuade the Prince from his

[1] Waldersee, *Denkwürdigkeiten*, ii. 56, July 7.   [2] Bülow, iv. 453-4.
[3] Waldersee, *Briefwechsel*, i. 317.   [4] *Lebensbekenntnis*, 152.

projected declaration against the ruler's plans on social reform, points in the same direction.[1] Otherwise, he argued, the Chancellor would lose the election, find himself more isolated than at any time since 1866, and provide the Emperor with an opportunity of getting rid of him. It would therefore be the best for himself and the nation if he were to compromise or at any rate not to be directly antagonistic. 'Holstein,' testifies Maximilian Harden, a friend of both in later years, 'declared a hundred times that he had neither worked nor wished for Bismarck's overthrow.' When he saw the sapping and mining he urged Herbert to hurry his father to Berlin in order to avert the explosion, but the old Prince came too late. When the young ruler complained of the Chancellor's 'lectures' in the presence of others, Holstein wrote to Herbert from a sick-bed to say that the Prince could tell the Emperor anything he liked in private but not before the Ministers.[2]

There is evidence that Holstein was not so loyal as these quotations might suggest. In the winter of 1887-8 he told a friend of the Emperor that Bismarck was losing his memory and getting too old for work.[3] He had disapproved the secret Reinsurance Treaty with Russia in 1887 on the ground that it was dangerous for Austria and that Russia could not be trusted; and in the autumn of 1889 Bülow found him sharply critical of the Russophil policy of his Chief.[4] Having quarrelled with Rantzau, he no longer visited his wife or her mother, Princess Bismarck. 'Your brother Adolf, the Adjutant and friend of the young Emperor,' asked Holstein as they parted, 'is for Bismarck?' 'Certainly,' replied Bülow, 'and he would regard his retirement as a grave misfortune.' Holstein's face assumed an almost diabolical expression, and he turned away without a word. It was clear to Bülow that he had already broken with the old statesman. Yet he concealed the change from the family so cleverly that on the following day Herbert exclaimed at a lunch party: 'He is true as gold: whoever attacks him will have to reckon with me.' No wonder he was often called the mole, for he worked in the dark.

Holstein was a dangerous foe because he possessed so much compromising knowledge. 'Bismarck only shows the Emperor despatches which reflect his policy,' wrote Waldersee in his diary on January 2, 1890, 'and his agents hardly dare to send in anything which has not been ordered. Nothing from foreign papers respecting

---

[1] Eppstein, *Bismarcks Entlassung*, 35–6.   [2] Harden, *Köpfe*, i. 101.
[3] Sidney Whitman, *German Memories*, 230–1.   [4] Bülow, iv. 627.

the real opinion in Russia may be shown.'[1] The diarist adds that he learned this from Holstein, who had often invited him to transmit news to the monarch. Holstein himself told Lucanus, the Emperor's Political Secretary, that the Chancellor withheld certain documents; and Bülow assures us that the alarming reports from the German Consul, which Bismarck had kept from the Kaiser and which were brought to his notice by Waldersee, were supplied by Holstein.[2] It was obvious that a breach was at hand, and he was too ambitious not to join the winning side in good time, for if Bismarck were to leave the stage he might control the Wilhelmstrasse. It was true that the Iron Chancellor had made his career, but had he not also partially ruined his happiness? As a young man with his way to make in the world he had obeyed his master's orders: now he had to think of himself. Harden tells us that he tried to persuade Herbert to retain the Foreign Office, as the Emperor desired, when the Prince left office;[3] but this may mean very little, for Herbert's honourable resolve to stand and fall with his father was generally known. After the Ides of March Holstein had no further dealings with the Bismarckian *Fronde* and openly linked his fortunes to the new regime. 'When Herbert gave a farewell dinner to the officials of the Foreign Office,' wrote Lothar Bucher to Busch on July 10, 'Holstein, Lindau, Kayser and Raschdau declined the invitation. All four owed everything to the Prince.'[4]

The Chancellor could hardly expect all his old staff to resign in sympathy, but his heart was filled with angry suspicions. In some cases he saw conspirators where clearer eyes saw only grieving friends, such as the blameless Bötticher, who is held up to obloquy in the third volume of his apologia. His condemnation of Holstein had much more justification. When Princess Bismarck observed that he had for some time avoided their house, her husband bitterly rejoined: 'Yes, he always had a good *flair*.' 'He was rather Arnim's disciple than mine,' he observed later to Harden; 'he is only useful for work below ground and has spots on the inner iris.'[5] On another occasion he added: 'Extremely useful in the second and third position, but dangerous in command.'[6]

Sharp condemnation of his conduct at the time of the Chancellor

---

[1] Waldersee, ii. 85.   [2] Bülow, iv. 637.   [3] Harden, *Köpfe*, i. 101–2.
[4] Busch, iii. 341   [5] Harden, *Köpfe*, i. 127.
[6] Nowak, *Das dritte deutsche Kaiserreich*, i. 149.

crisis comes from his old enemy Radowitz, who happened to be in Berlin and visited the Wilhelmstrasse on April 2. 'Berchem does not seem likely to stay long,' he wrote.[1] 'How should he? The real political control will be in Holstein's hands, as he is long and intimately acquainted with Caprivi. At any rate he has been in touch with him for some time, since he noticed that the Bismarck regime was nearing its end. The change occurred just at the right time for him. His personal position in the Office had deteriorated so much in the last months that there would probably have been a crash. He had quarrelled with Rantzau, the son-in-law of Bismarck, and ceased to speak to him, and he was at enmity with Lothar Bucher. Quicker than anyone in the Foreign Office he has deserted and repudiated the Bismarckian banner. Young Attachés who worked under him are astonished at the satisfaction with which he speaks of the change and at the lack of respect with which he criticises the Prince. That is the man in whom the Bismarck family believed as "the truest of the true," and by whom they allowed themselves to be influenced against everyone who stood in his path. I hear to-day that he is the only official to whom the Prince did not say goodbye on leaving the office. Indeed he kept out of the way. Now he remains as the *Spiritus Rector* for the new men. Caprivi told me he had the fullest confidence in him and would have to trust to his great experience, and Marschall will be clever enough to enter into partnership. Kiderlen is already, I could see, quite his amanuensis. During my present visit I have not seen him. Berchem warned me against him and described him as semi-irresponsible when personal antipathies arise such as exist in my case.'

Eulenburg's verdict is no less severe. Holstein, he declares, till now a house-dog on Bismarck's chain, had played a sort of whist with a dummy hand against Bismarck and his son.[2] 'Who was the dummy? The Emperor. If the Bismarcks lost, the Emperor was his partner. If the Bismarcks won, then it was only a game. In any case he knew that Bismarck passionately opposed the idea of a Congress. His opposition to Herbert was known to me before; now he secretly turned against the Chancellor. For he thought he could play his part in the Foreign Office better without Bismarck—if his enemy Waldersee were not his successor—and he succeeded in eliminating him. I

---

[1] *Aufzeichnungen und Erinnerungen*, ii. 326–7.
[2] Eulenburg, *Aus 50 Jahren*, 244–5.

believe that Machiavelli himself could have taken lessons from his crafty dealings at that time. He always assumed the airs of an old Prussian official, but he was at heart a democrat. In this connection he often betrayed himself to me. A nature like his could only be revolutionary.' His clever manoeuvres extorted Eulenburg's reluctant admiration.[1] 'That Holstein, the inseparable companion of the Bismarcks and the confidant of Bötticher in the burning issues between Kaiser and Chancellor, was not included in the list of the arch "traitors" shows his extraordinary skill. I cannot explain his secret thoughts in the days of the catastrophe. But I cannot help thinking that he had perhaps a larger share in Bismarck's suspicions of Bötticher than is generally known, in other words, that he sacrificed his friend Bötticher to save himself. For it is always a riddle to me that Holstein, who had such a large part in the quarrel between Bismarck and William II, was not more hated by the former.' Herbert, on the other hand, was filled with anger, and Bülow roundly accuses Holstein of stabbing the Prince in the back.[2] Against these charges may be set his reiterated declaration that he had no share in the overthrow of his old chief.

IV

WILLIAM II had selected Caprivi as his second Chancellor before he parted with the first, but the choice of a Foreign Minister to succeed Herbert proved more difficult. Though he was widely expected to receive the appointment, Holstein shirked the post because he felt unequal to its Parliamentary and social duties and preferred the reality to the show of power.[3] On the other hand he was largely responsible for the selection which was made. According to Julius von Eckhardt he vetoed the appointment of two diplomats on the ground that he could not work with them.[4] 'Holstein and Berchem,' wrote Hohenlohe in his diary on March 27, 1890, 'have proposed Marschall von Bieberstein, after Alvensleben declined.'[5] Marschall represented Baden in the Bundesrath, and the Grand Duke Frederick recommended him as a good speaker and an economic expert. He

[1] Eulenburg, *Aus 50 Jahren*, 253.   [2] *Denkwürdigkeiten*, i. 498.
[3] Waldersee, *Briefwechsel*, i. 351, and H. von Rath, 'Erinnerungen an Holstein,' *Deutsche Revue*, October, 1909.
[4] *Aus den Tagen Bismarcks Kampf gegen Caprivi*, 1–9.
[5] *Denkwürdigkeiten*, ii. 466.

was certainly a competent lawyer, but Bismarck contemptuously described him as the *Ministre étranger aux affaires*.

No sooner had the Bismarcks left office than a momentous decision was taken which deeply angered them against the man whom they regarded as its principal author. Holstein had approved almost every important move of Bismarck on the European chessboard down to 1887, but the Reinsurance Treaty with Russia in that year made him feel that the master-builder was losing his sureness of touch. Austria and Russia were on such bad terms in consequence of the prolonged Bulgarian crisis that a second renewal of the *Dreikaiserbund* of 1881 was out of the question, and Bismarck determined to save what he could from the wreck. His desire to inform Francis Joseph of what he had done was frustrated by the Tsar, and in Holstein's eyes the dangers involved in a precarious secrecy outweighed the value of Russia's promise of neutrality in the event of a French attack. 'Nothing tangible is to be expected from it,' he observed, ' and if it leaks out we are blamed as false fellows.' Shortly before Bismarck fell the consent of the Emperor had been obtained to the renewal of the treaty for another three years when it expired on June 13; and so anxious was its author that his handiwork should endure that his son's continuance in office for a day or two longer was attributed by Holstein to his desire to renew it, perhaps in a revised form, before handing over the reins. But the power of the Bismarck dynasty was at an end.

The day after his father's fall Herbert asked for the papers and was told they were in Holstein's room; for the latter, without the knowledge of his official chief, had laid them before Caprivi, Marschall and Schweinitz, the Ambassador in St. Petersburg, who happened to be in Berlin. Herbert turned his steps thither and an angry scene ensued. The opinion of Berchem the Under-Secretary and the Assistant-Secretaries who discussed the question with Caprivi was unanimous against renewing the treaty; and Schweinitz, who had supported its conclusion in 1887, was converted by a sight of the treaty with Roumania signed in 1883 of which he had been unaware. 'As it contradicts other treaties,' argued Holstein in a letter to a friend on March 27, 'our good name would depend on Russia's discretion. But Russia's interest is to be indiscreet, for directly it became known our other friends would leave us. Then we should be compelled to look to Russia alone and she would make her own conditions as to our further relations.'[1] Caprivi accordingly advised the Kaiser to let it drop, explaining in his simple way that the relationship was 'too complicated'; Bismarck could juggle with five glass balls at a time while he could only manage two.

Alexander III took the news calmly, but Giers, his Foreign Minister, pleaded for its continuance even if in an attenuated form. The Assistant-Secretaries in the Foreign Office were now asked to record their opinion. Holstein's Memorandum, dated May 20,[2] maintains that the modifications proposed by Giers were useless since the objections to the pact were fundamental. 'The mere fact that a secret treaty exists between us and Russia would have a devastating effect on our relations with Austria, Roumania and Italy. Italy, in particular, in accordance with the text of the German-Italian treaty, has the right to be informed by us of our arrangements and those of other Powers in all questions relating to the Aegean and the Ottoman coasts and islands. Everything that can arouse suspicion against Germany's policy would operate with special force at the present moment, since many of Prince Bismarck's recent utterances are calculated to unsettle our allies. Only a public agreement with Russia could be considered so that our allies might convince themselves that neither we nor Russia intended to abridge treaty rights.' The Austrophil Marschall expressed his entire agreement with the Memorandum; Kiderlen and Raschdau, the other Assistant-Secretaries, drew up statements on similar lines, and Prince Reuss, the German Ambassador in Vienna, volunteered his opinion that the slightest suspicion of German sincerity would lead to the permanent alienation of Austria. Schweinitz, on the other hand, desired to meet Giers half-way. Thus in face of the almost unanimous opinion of the official authorities the secret treaty was regretfully allowed by the Kaiser to lapse.[3]

Holstein divided the responsibility for this momentous decision with his colleagues and official superiors, but his advice weighed

[1] Eckardstein, *Erinnerungen*, iii. 18-9.
[2] *Die Grosse Politik*, vii. 22-3. See a subsequent Memorandum written in 1904, *ibid.*, 48-9
[3] The documents are collected in *Die Grosse Politik*, vii, ch. 44. For careful discussions of the incident and of Holstein's share in it see Otto Becker, *Das Französich-Russische Bündnis*, ch. 1, and Appendix IX; and Frankenberg, *Die Nichterneuerung des deutschrussichen Rückversicherungsvertrages*, 33-9. Holstein remarked later to Hammann that it would have been dangerous to leave the secret in Bismarck's keeping; Hammann, *Der neue Kurs*, 33.

heavily in the scales, and the larger part of the condemnation now usually meted out to its authors is visited on his head. Russia, it is true, had already begun to gravitate towards France, but nothing irrevocable had occurred, and the Germanophil Giers was almost pathetically anxious to avert the cutting of the wires. The argument that the treaty was incompatible with loyalty to Austria was repudiated by its author, who was so little ashamed of his handiwork that he revealed the secret in 1896. Its termination, as Bülow sorrowfully declares, led automatically to the Franco-Russian alliance, and when Russia was tied to France it proved impossible to restore full contact with St. Petersburg. Had German policy under 'the new course' been conducted with greater skill, and had the goodwill of England been retained, as Holstein assumed, the danger inherent in the decision of 1890 would have been minimised; but the *Flottenpolitik* and the surrender of control over Balkan policy to Vienna led straight to the entanglement of Germany in the Austro-Russian quarrel which it had been Bismarck's aim and achievement to avert.

Bismarck held Holstein chiefly responsible, for Caprivi and Marschall were novices and the Emperor a reluctant convert. 'The men in Berlin possess no experience or knowledge of statecraft,' he complained; 'I am afraid the Privy Councillors have it all their own way.'[1] The new position held by Holstein and the animosity with which his old patron had come to regard him are reflected in a letter from Lothar Bucher to Busch from Varzin on October 14, 1890, six months after the catastrophe.[2] 'Holstein, whom for ten years nobody took seriously, now does everything. He not only slanders the Prince, which he did twelve months ago, but also abuses Herbert, who, with inconceivable blindness, had supported him to the last.' If it was not strictly true that Holstein now did everything, 'the great Geheimrat,' as he was called, was at any rate the oracle of the Wilhelmstrasse, where nobody approached him in knowledge of the *Arcana Imperii* and where he discharged the duties of Under-Secretary when that official was on holiday. 'The figure of Holstein,' reported a member of the Austrian Embassy in September, 'comes more and more into the foreground. There is only one opinion in the Foreign Office—that he is its life and soul. No important political decision is taken till his opinion has been asked by His Majesty or the Chancellor.'[3] 'Caprivi

[1] *Süddeutsche Monatshefte*, 1931, 379.   [2] Busch, iii. 343.
[3] Otto Becker, *Das Französisch-Russische Bündnis*, 307.

and Marschall,' declares Bülow with the contempt of the professional for the amateur, 'who had no conception of the international chessboard or the technique of diplomacy and not even the necessary knowledge of languages, clung to him like drowning men to a safety belt.'[1] Berchem, the Under-Secretary, remained for a time under the new regime, but when he found that Holstein was usurping his position as chief adviser to the Foreign Secretary he made way for the more pliable Rotenhan. 'Berchem thinks Holstein has got rid of him,' wrote Waldersee in his diary on May 30, 1890, 'in order to rule without a rival. Certainly Marschall is a friend of Holstein and depends greatly on his advice.'[2]

'There will be trouble with Holstein,' remarked Herbert Bismarck to Monts in the early nineties; 'though useful in the second or third place, he is impossible in the first owing to his misanthropy and his nerves.' He now began to practise the methods which were to tarnish the later years of his official life. When Eckardstein entered the Foreign Office in 1891 he discovered to his amazement that he withheld copies of important despatches from diplomatic representatives abroad whom he disliked. 'Behind cool and reserved forms,' wrote Julius von Eckhardt at this period,[3] 'there was a hidden passion. The veil of melancholy gave a special charm, and he was a good talker when he was in the mood, but he was thought dangerous because he was believed to be implacable. For fourteen months he cut me owing to an unfounded accusation. Then it was explained and he was friendly again.' He adds that Caprivi feared both Holstein and Kiderlen, who stood next to him in influence, but that he felt them both to be indispensable. Hohenlohe, indeed, described Holstein as 'the diplomatic chart of the Foreign Office.'

We owe a vivid picture of the Mystery Man at this period to Otto Hammann, who was appointed by Caprivi to direct the Press Department of the Foreign Office. 'I was a complete stranger to the Great Unknown. On crossing the threshold of this uncanny master of the deepest secrets I felt like the pupil in *Faust*. Like all who approached him, I knew I was in the presence of a man of outstanding gifts. His masterly manner of conducting the conversation and of clothing his thought in striking language commanded respect for his capacities. A powerful will and a warning Take care! seemed written on his face,

---

[1] Bülow, *Denkwürdigkeiten*, ii. 112. [2] Waldersee, *Denkwürdigkeiten*, ii. 129.
[3] *Aus den Tagen Bismarcks Kampf gegen Caprivi*, 1–9.

with its Roman nose and darkly glittering deep-set eyes. Despite the friendliness with which he welcomed the novice I carried away the feeling—perhaps in consequence of what I had already heard about him—that there was something abnormal and morbid about the man.'[1] One of his colleagues remarked that if he wanted to reach Madrid from Berlin he would go round by Jerusalem. He was never photographed, belonged to no club, and only visited in a few houses where he was sure that he would meet no strangers. When Sir Rennell Rodd, then on the staff of the British Embassy, rallied him on his unsociable ways, he replied that the service of the State had spoiled him as a human being.[2] It was typical of his misanthropy that he carried a loaded revolver. His best quality was his sturdy independence. 'The better I came to know the political world of Berlin,' writes Chirol, the *Times* Correspondent, 'the more I respected him for the possession of sterling qualities which grew exceedingly rare during William II's reign.'[3] Monts noted that he was on terms of perfect equality with his superiors. 'No one was less of a courtier in word or deed, and on two occasions he declined the title of Excellency.' Since the fall of Bismarck, he confided to his cousin in 1895, his resolve against promotion was stronger than ever. Not till 1898, when he was over sixty, did he accept the title of Wirklicher Geheimrat and Excellenz.

Like an oriental despot he had favourites whose rise was as rapid as their fall. He had inherited a modest fortune which was used up in secret kindly actions and which petty speculations on the Bourse failed to replenish.[4] A privileged young diplomat or Secretary would receive what he called *le droit de la porte*, the right to enter his room unannounced. This concession, however, might at any moment be withdrawn, for no one was so ready to take offence. Two servants who stood before the door would break the news to the astonished visitor that the Baron was unable to receive him, and no explanation was given. In one case a daily and confidential intercourse of two

---

[1] *Der neue Kurs*, 57–8.

[2] 'Der Staatsdienst hat mich als Mensch verdorben.' Rodd, *Social and Diplomatic Memories*, i. 135.

[3] *Fifty Years*, p. 269.

[4] See *Berliner Tageblatt*, December 16, 17, 24, 1925. His admiring friend Trotha, nephew of Frau von Lebbin, believes on internal evidence that the letters were fakes, while Thimme finds a decisive verdict impossible. Trotha, *Fritz von Holstein*, with an Introduction by Thimme.

years was suddenly ended because 'the monster' discovered that his *protégé* had lunched with Herbert Bismarck twice in a single week, and he never spoke to him again. Another victim, young Count Pourtalès, who also possessed *le droit de la porte*, found the way barred one day by the lackeys, and the Baron cut him ever afterwards.[1] 'Even from my prentice years,' testifies Bernstorff, 'I regarded him as an abnormal eccentric.' 'One of the most complicated persons I ever knew,' comments Lerchenfeld, the Bavarian Minister at Berlin; 'Marschall told me that he espied somebody behind every bush. One evening I forgot a dinner engagement and he cut me for nine months. He loved to sit in a dark corner, like a spider.'[2]

Holstein determined to gather all the threads of foreign policy into his hands. 'A conflict with Caprivi is approaching,' noted Waldersee, now Moltke's successor as Chief of the Staff, in his diary in August, 1890.[3] 'I have long tried to raise the position of the Military Attachés. The Emperor agrees to make them independent of the Minister. Caprivi gives orders to the contrary, and instructs them never to discuss politics in their reports, though they are cleverer than almost all the diplomats. There is only one opinion—that Caprivi had been egged on by Holstein and that the whole *coup* is directed against myself. I have often defended Holstein and given him my confidence: if this is really his doing it would be an infamy. It would be not only evil but frivolous, for he has delivered himself into my hands owing to my knowledge of his double game with the Bismarcks.' Holstein, added Waldersee in a note of a later date, had in 1889 and 1890 often asked him to procure direct and purely political reports to show to the Emperor, not only in regard to Russia but in reference to a dispute with Switzerland. 'He asked me to tell the Emperor that Bismarck's policy was mistaken, and supplied me with the necessary material. Thus he intrigued against his direct superior and betrayed him, and yet he had the face to say I carried on a forbidden correspondence with the Military Attachés.' Waldersee complained to Marschall, who replied that the whole affair was due to the rancour of Holstein against Major Engelbrecht, whom he could not bear, though the point was directed against the Chief of the Staff.[4] Waldersee

[1] Nowak, *Das dritte deutsche Kaiserreich*, i. 155-7.
[2] Lerchenfeld, *Erinnerungen u. Denkwürdigkeiten*, 385-92.
[3] Waldersee, *Denkwürdigkeiten*, ii. 136.
[4] *Ibid.*, ii. 139, August 13.

next appealed to Caprivi, who complained of secret correspondence behind his back but added that he needed his services for the present. The dispute dragged on throughout the autumn. 'Holstein is ill because he cannot get Engelbrecht moved from Rome,' wrote Waldersee at the end of the year.[1] 'I said I did not like the *rôle* he made us play—he pulls the strings and we had to dance.' A month later the Chief of the General Staff had lost his post. Holstein had begun to avoid him in the summer of 1890 and now confided his satisfaction to a friend. 'Well, that *was* a job to get rid of him, as he was so in with the Kaiser.'[2]

Waldersee had warned the Emperor that Holstein was intriguing against the Chancellor; but Eulenburg stood up for his friend, and neither the ruler nor Caprivi took any notice of the baseless charge. 'Caprivi is fairly safe so long as Bismarck looms on the horizon,' he reported to his cousin in June, 1891.[3] 'Apart from that I do not feel sure of the constancy of the Emperor. Let us hope that without being too severely tried he will ripen a bit. Anyhow, if we do not want a republic, we must take the princes as Providence sends them.' The consequences of dropping the Reinsurance Treaty were now appearing in the Franco-Russian rapprochement. 'The meeting at Kronstadt,' wrote Holstein in August 1891, 'has made the situation graver, since the self-confidence of the war party both in France and Russia is increased. Peace, like some one with a weak heart, may be preserved for years, but a small complication can suddenly end it. We are militarily as prepared as we can be, and politically too. If the conflict comes within a year, while Salisbury is at the helm, it would be an advantage. Just for that reason I incline to think that our opponents will wait till the present English Ministry is gone. Our chief difficulty will be the Emperor, who may be inclined to assert himself in military affairs. The danger can only be met if the Chancellor and the Chief of the Staff stand together. Yesterday I had an intimate talk with Caprivi about it.'

Holstein. In our army circles many think we shall be unlucky in the next war. Not that they are doubtful about the army; on the contrary, it is expected—right up to the commanding Generals—to do everything imaginable. It is only the supreme direction which inspires mistrust; the Emperor, it is believed, will wish to command.

---

[1] Waldersee, *Dunkwürdigkeiten*, ii. 170, December 22.
[2] *Ibid.*, ii. 195.   [3] *Lebensbekenntnis*, 154–7.

I hear that Schlieffen is intellectually outstanding, but his quiet way would not impress the Emperor. Your Excellency is also expected to take a hand. It would be asking too much of a General who was considered a possible successor to Moltke to sit back and say nothing. The army fears that this divergence of views may breed disaster.

Caprivi. Something would have to go wrong before I took a hand.

Holstein. I think it would be better if you reached agreement on the chief questions by talking it over with Count Schlieffen. Despite your politeness you are very often sharp with your pen, whereas in conversation, as I know from experience, you can say disagreeable things without creating offence. So I suggest that you deal directly with him weekly or once or twice a month instead of writing through the War Office. If you two agree, no third party, hardly even the Emperor, can oppose you.

Caprivi promised to summon Schlieffen. 'I shall say to him,' continued Holstein's report to his cousin, 'you must reach agreement with Caprivi, now and later, in regard to every military action. I assume you know more of the military machine than he. But even an inferior plan agreed on with Caprivi and supported by both of you will be infinitely better than anything the Emperor suggests. Caprivi and Schlieffen are hard-headed but honourable men and fine patriots. I attach the greatest importance to the success of their first talk, otherwise Caprivi will not pursue the matter and they will drift further apart. Why am I so anxious to form a group? Because His Majesty is unpredictable. Caprivi sent in his resignation at the end of June as the Emperor proposed financial demands which no Reichstag would approve. He dreams of an ideal Reichstag which would grant unlimited sums for army, navy and sumptuous buildings. Unfortunately Prince Bismarck in his last phase ruled from hand to mouth: *après moi le déluge.* He suggested a conflict with the Reichstag and Caprivi has to suffer from it. A conflict with the Reichstag is impossible. The other Princes would stand aloof, and if the Emperor applies force Russia and France would intervene as often before. From this you will see that my time is more fully than agreeably filled. On the whole I still hope the Emperor will realise the impracticability of his plans.' The more Holstein learned of the impulsive young ruler, the more essential it appeared to clip his wings.

The Chancellor was well aware of Holstein's peculiarities. 'I criticised the way the business of the Foreign Office was transacted,' wrote Schweinitz after a talk with Caprivi in 1892; 'a personage not quite right in the head had too much influence.[1] Caprivi replies that he knows very well Holstein has the grave fault of being swayed by personal prejudices, but it was impossible to do without him. The Chancellor in his great modesty realises that he does not possess the technique of diplomacy, and neither he nor Marschall nor Rotenhan has the power or will to replace these people by more capable men. Thus the real direction of our policy falls into the hands of the only official who combines the tradition of the office and the knowledge of the machine; for he served thirty years under Bismarck and was honoured for a time with his confidence, and he was also used for secret and not always quite savoury affairs, especially in regard to the press. He never wished to shine, asked nothing for himself, neither high posts nor decorations, and has many excellent qualities; but he has personal rancours—not only against me—and allows them too much influence in his actions.'

Among his victims was the Bismarckian Schlözer, who lost his post as Ambassador at Rome in 1892.[2] Waldersee noted in his diary in August 1892 that Holstein wished to keep Caprivi at all costs as a guarantee of the continuance of his power, but he felt no obligation of loyalty to his inexperienced Chief. Bismarck had withheld despatches from the three Emperors or presented them in garbled form, and Holstein copied the evil precedent. For instance he instructed Eulenburg, the Prussian Minister in Munich, to communicate the report of a conversation between the Chancellor and the Bavarian Minister in an altered form, and actually ordered him in advance how to reply.[3] This was too much for Eulenburg. 'Directly a situation boils up Holstein goes absolutely mad. The suggestion that I should report what Crailsheim ought to have said is grotesque. The letter can be kept as a curiosity.' In 1894 he suggested that Eulenburg should limit the scope of his official despatches and communicate everything of importance in private letters to himself. 'So the Chancellor is to be eliminated!' noted Eulenburg in disgust. 'If poor Caprivi saw this note Holstein's days would be numbered. But as—I had almost said unfortunately—we cannot do without him, I shall take no notice of the hint and shall not show the note to the good Caprivi. My God,

---

[1] Schweinitz, *Denkwürdigkeiten*, ii. 443.
[2] Kurd von Schlözer, *Letzte Römische Briefe*, 175, 179, 183–4.
[3] Haller, *Eulenburg*, 166.

what a comedy!'[1] On the other hand Holstein was shrewd enough to know with whom he could or could not afford to quarrel. 'He rules in the Foreign Office,' noted Waldersee in his diary in the summer of 1892, 'and he has divided up business with Kiderlen, with whom he has to reckon on account of his relations with the Emperor.'[2] The Swabian Bismarck, as Naumann called him, was still in high favour at court, and he was a man who, if attacked, was certain to hit back.

Though Holstein was supreme in the Foreign Office he was haunted by the possibility of a reconciliation between Bismarck and the Emperor which the German people ardently desired. 'Caprivi and Holstein and perhaps some of the small fry of the Foreign Office alone oppose it,' wrote Waldersee in his diary in June 1892.[3] The journey of the Prince to Vienna to attend the marriage of his son Herbert enabled the Chancellor to break down the frail bridge which many good patriots were endeavouring to build. Francis Joseph was requested not to receive him, and the German Embassy was forbidden to take part in the ceremony, a deplorable error of taste and policy. The counter-attacks of the Bismarckian press on Caprivi and his henchmen were unceasing, and the former Chancellor indulged in bitter comments on his old *protégé*. 'Holstein,' he remarked to Poschinger in October 1892, 'is now one-eyed, but among the blind men of the Foreign Office the one-eyed man is king.'[4] He had displayed exceptional elasticity at the time that the officials were changing over from the Bismarckian to the new regime. 'He was useful in drafting French documents; but as man and character—well, you know him as well as I do. I hear that he has quarrelled with all his colleagues and that Raschdau declines to take orders from him. He has only one friend—Radolin.'

To his horror Holstein found himself one day in the limelight for the first time since the Arnim trial. At the end of 1893, *Kladderadatsch*, a comic journal of Bismarckian sympathies, launched a campaign against the trio, Geheimrat von Austernfreund, Geheimrat von Spätzle, and Graf Troubadour.[5] The former was described as a sly old fox who preferred the backstairs and never mentioned the Arnim

---

[1] Haller, *Eulenburg*, 166.
[2] *Denkwürdigkeiten*, ii. 245, June 12.
[3] *Ibid.*, ii. 247, June 26.
[4] Bismarck, *Gespräche*, iii. 254, 257.
[5] Hammann, *Der neue Kurs*, 58–66. (The Oyster-lover, the Sparrow, and Count Troubadour.)

trial. The allusions were obvious: the names stood for Holstein, Kiderlen and Eulenburg. 'I believe they do not wholly trust one another,' commented Waldersee in his diary, 'but they stick together because it pays them.'[1] For weeks the trio figured prominently in the paper, the theme of satirical verses and caricatures. After this careful preparation readers were presented with an apologue, entitled 'Three Men in a Fiery Oven.' 'There was once a King, who had many faithful servants. But three of them, whose names were Insinuans, Intrigans and Calumnians, were deceitful, and accused several of his most faithful servants, so that they were turned out of the palace. Then a plain man arose and had the three evildoers cast into a fiery oven.' Holstein, who hated the publicity as much as the attack, brooded over the problem 'Who is behind it? ' and Hammann heard that he had sent his seconds to Herbert Bismarck. Emissaries from the Foreign Office were despatched to the editor and the publisher of the paper, but in vain. The *Zukunft* reminded its readers that Holstein had betrayed Arnim and discredited himself in the eyes of the world. 'But will the Emperor open his eyes? No, because that would be to confess his own shortsightedness.' The scandal was now the talk of the town. Kiderlen challenged and wounded a member of the editorial staff. Holstein, who was a good shot and had fought a duel in Washington, challenged Count Henckel von Donnersmarck, 'since the attitude of the *Berliner Neueste Nachrichten* suggests that he is privy to the attacks.' The Count declined to fight as there was no ground for the suspicion, and the angry man accepted his assurances.

'It is useless to speculate whence the attacks come,' he wrote to his cousin in May 1894.[2] 'In Germany there is no legal defence against slander. A lawsuit takes ages, stirs up all sorts of dirt, and ends with acquittal or a fine of 100 to 500 marks. Attack advertises the paper, as in the case of the recent lawsuits about insults to the Emperor or Chancellor. So the Foreign Minister, the Chancellor and the Emperor are against a lawsuit. I have never striven for anything. Twice I could have been Foreign Minister. But I am in the way of all sorts of people and I am hated. In addition, for many years, and now for reasons of health, I lead a lonely life. Of a hundred people who hear me attacked perhaps only one knows me and he may not like me. So if history mentions my name, I shall probably figure as an intriguer, though I have done my duty according to my lights.' The

[1] *Denkwürdigkeiten*, ii. 300.   [2] *Lebensbekenntnis*, 167.

prime mover in the campaign was von Bothmer, an official of the Legal Department of the Foreign Office, but the secret was only revealed thirty years later.[1]

Marschall, like Caprivi, started as an amateur in foreign affairs, and there was a widespread belief that neither of them would retain his place for any length of time. On January 13, 1893, Hohenlohe noted in his diary a conversation with Eulenburg, who declared that Holstein and Kiderlen desired him to become Foreign Minister if Bötticher were to resign the Home Office, to which, they believed, Marschall would be gladly transferred.[2] Eulenburg, however, had no desire for the post, and felt unequal to it; he asked Hohenlohe to discuss with Holstein the succession to Marschall and to convert him from the plan of proposing himself. Hohenlohe promised to try but did not think Holstein would change his view.

Hohenlohe had exchanged the Paris Embassy in 1884 for the office of Statthalter of Alsace-Lorraine, but he continued his practice of discussing the political situation with his old subordinate whenever he visited Berlin. 'I talked with Holstein,' he records on December 14, 1893, 'about the attacks of the Bismarckian press on the New Course and its foreign policy.[3] He replied by enlarging on Bismarck's mistakes—the Berlin Congress, the prevention of a conflict between England and Russia in Afghanistan, and his whole policy towards Russia. His last plan to leave Austria in the lurch would have made us so contemptible that we should have been isolated and become dependent on Russia.' Passing to another subject, Holstein informed his visitor that the Chancellor and the Foreign Office were disturbed by the activities of Crispi whose actions were beyond prediction. It was therefore necessary to send a clever Ambassador to watch the situation in Rome, and Bülow was proposed for the task.

At the opening of 1894 Caprivi's position had become insecure, for his commercial treaties angered the Agrarians who hated the lower duties on Russian cereals. Moreover the outward reconciliation of Potsdam and Friedrichsruh increased the *malaise*. 'Bismarck will come and thank the Kaiser for his present of wine and the congratulations on his recovery,' wrote Hohenlohe in his diary on January 22, 1894.[4] 'My friends in the Foreign Office are afraid he may suggest a new Chancellor. Holstein thinks I ought to advise the

---

[1] Jäckh, *Kiderlen-Wächter*, i. 98.
[2] Hohenlohe, *Denkwürdigkeiten*, ii. 497.
[3] *Ibid.*, ii. 507.
[4] *Ibid.*, ii. 509.

Kaiser to summon me too if he receives Bismarck. That I should not do, but, if opportunity offered, I would advise him to have a witness. If a Bismarck regime returned, I should have to make room for one of his friends at Strassburg.' Bismarck's visit to Berlin on January 26, which roused Holstein to fury, delighted the German people; but politics were avoided, and the incident did nothing either to solve or to complicate the problems of succession which were agitating the Wilhelmstrasse. A letter from General von Stosch to Bennigsen, dated July 3, 1894, proves that William II had already resolved to change his principal adviser.[1] 'The Emperor has told a friend, "Caprivi is useful to me but not sympathetic. He lacks imagination and does not understand me when I tell him of my wider thoughts. I shall choose as his successor a younger man who is nearer to me, and he shall be exclusively my man." ' Stosch added that the monarch was believed to be thinking of Eulenburg, and, if he refused the post, of Bülow.

V

CAPRIVI left office in the autumn of 1894 unregretted and without regret. He had never coveted the post, and he had lost the confidence of his master and the Conservatives. He had long mistrusted Holstein, whose room he described as 'that poison shop,' and Holstein was ready for a change.[2] Hohenlohe, who had wished for the office in 1890, accepted it without enthusiasm in 1894 when he was seventy-five. Holstein, on the other hand, was eager to have his old Paris chief installed in the Wilhelmstrasse, not only because they were on intimate terms but because a weary Titan could scarcely challenge his authority. 'My mother,' writes Prince Alexander Hohenlohe, 'tried to prevent my father becoming Chancellor, as he was too old; but Holstein, seeing that the days of Caprivi were numbered, worked for his fall, and wished for a Chancellor who would allow him to continue his *rôle*.[3] He believed that my father would do so and worked hard to secure him. One day my father received a telegram from the Emperor: "Come to Potsdam; important Imperial interests concerned"; and it was only during his journey that he learned from a

[1] Oncken, *Bennigsen*, ii. 591–2.
[2] Holstein's tortuous course is discussed in Zechlin, *Staatsstreichpläne Bismarcks und Wilhelm II*, Part II, *Die Entlassung Caprivis*.
[3] *Aus meinem Leben*, ch. 12.

newspaper of the fall of Caprivi. He intended to refuse the offer, but Holstein travelled to meet him at Leipzig and persuaded him to accept. My mother wired the Empress to help him to escape the burden on the grounds of health; but the Empress replied "The Prince sacrifices himself for Kaiser and Reich."'

Holstein's initial approach was a masterpiece of congratulation and strategy.[1] 'Your Excellency faces a great patriotic task. I know no one else who can avert the present dangers. Your name and record inspire more confidence than any German statesman except Bismarck. Success will entirely depend on choosing the right people as your agents, and therefore I beg Your Excellency not to settle anything before we discuss it. Marschall I consider to be indispensable. His knowledge of internal affairs and particularly of questions of constitutional law makes him the corner-stone of your regime. He is also admirable in debate. I mention all this because I know he has enemies at Court. When I discovered it I wrote a week ago to Philip Eulenburg, hoping he would pass it on, that if Marschall goes I shall go too. For Your Excellency it is vital that he should enter the Prussian Ministry as a make-weight against Miquel. Your Excellency will also have to fill a number of higher posts. More when we meet. Needless to say that, if I remain, I have no desire to change my position.' The letter, which proposed some names for promotion, reveals the ambition to become the mentor of the new Chancellor not only in foreign policy but in the field of appointments and in domestic affairs which, as he confessed to Trotha, he did not understand and which in any case lay entirely outside his sphere. 'We stand nearest to the old gentleman,' he remarked to Hutten-Czapski, 'and he will seek our advice in great matters.[2] It would be undesirable if we were to differ and thereby caused complications. I suggest that we always try to agree in preliminary talks; if we fail, we will go to him together, each having his say, and then loyally accept his decision.' Hutten-Czapski agreed, the Chancellor approved, the pact was observed, and the younger man was permitted to read portions of the private correspondence with the Ambassadors. Co-operation was rendered possible by the fact that the Polish nobleman usually confined himself to Polish and ecclesiastical affairs. A partnership of equals was

---

[1] Hohenlohe, *Denkwürdigkeiten aus der Reichskanzlerzeit*, 1931, 1–2, October 26, 1894.
[2] *Sechzig Jahre*, i. 237.

never to Holstein's taste, and the consuming thirst for domination waxed with advancing years.

'At the end of the Caprivi era,' writes William II in his Memoirs, 'Holstein, the *soi-disant* representative of the Bismarck tradition, began to become powerful, and showed reluctance to work with me. The Foreign Office thought it must carry on Bismarck's policy alone.'[1] No steps, however, were taken to diminish his influence, and the change of Chancellor brought no excessive jubilation in Bismarckian circles. 'It is good Caprivi is gone,' wrote the faithful Conservative Kardorff to Herbert on November 21, 1894; 'but if Hohenlohe is only chosen to keep the place warm for Eulenburg, and if Marschall and Holstein continue to direct foreign policy, and Bötticher and Berlepsch to protect the Socialists, there is still much to be done before things improve.'[2] Shortly after his appointment Hohenlohe, to the horror of Holstein, paid a visit of courtesy to Friedrichsruh at the suggestion of the Emperor, and was amicably received by his host who proceeded to give him some advice. 'If you do not at once get rid of Bötticher, Marschall and Holstein, they will intrigue you out of office as they did me.' The forecast was not fulfilled, for Hohenlohe was on his guard. He treated Holstein with invariable courtesy, but he never shared the blind confidence which the first Chancellor had entertained for twenty years. While fully realising his usefulness he was not in the least afraid of him. On one occasion, reports Hutten-Czapski, the draft of a circular despatch sent to the Chancellor to sign was returned with the alteration of an important sentence. 'I was present when it came back. He was very excited and talked of resignation. Never had a draft of his been corrected! I told Hohenlohe, who remarked with a smile: "He will calm down and then he will see that one can only sign what one is prepared to defend."'

Holstein had learned from his old chief the value of carefully timed threats of resignation, and three months after the change of Chancellor he proceeded to play the familiar card. 'It is clear,' he wrote on February 1, 1895, 'that my presence in the Foreign Office complicates the Emperor's attempted reconciliation with Bismarck, and I feel it my duty to remove it. Moreover my eyesight would in any case have caused me to resign before long. In these circumstances I beg Your Excellency to put through my resignation. I may

[1] *Ereignisse und Gestalten*, 51.
[2] Thimme, 'Bismarck und Kardorff,' *Deutsche Revue*, May 1917.

add that this request expresses a firm resolve. As my eyes have suffered in the service of the State I can claim the usual pension.' The Chancellor sent Hutten-Czapski to say that he could not manage without him, and his written reply was precisely what was desired. 'You urged me to accept office. I did so on your advice, counting on your help. It was a contract which you would now break if you desert me. My visit to Bismarck has made you suspicious.'[1] In securing this emphatic testimonial Holstein had gained his point, but his suspicions of the Emperor were undiminished.

Holstein's comments on the Imperial utterances to the British Military Attaché about British policy are contained in an excited letter to Eulenburg on December 21, 1895. 'I am quite crushed by yesterday's conversation of His Majesty with Swaine. He said things which might create great danger of war for us: the English should have freed the Dardanelles and he would have arranged that Austria and Italy had joined England. What if Salisbury, deeply hurt by His Majesty, informs Petersburg? The Russians would know that the Emperor is an *agent provocateur* to provoke Europe against Russia. Lobanoff would doubtless tell the Tsar: "Your Majesty in conjunction with France must first settle accounts with Germany; the other questions would then be easy." The danger is all the greater because it is not an open but a stealthy advance. Turn it over in your mind whether you will give His Majesty advice, or if Hohenlohe should take a hand. Emperor and Empire are nearing the precipice. If I had seen Hohenlohe I should have advised him to wake up. About a year ago I wrote you forecasting what is now taking place. To-day I warn you again. Take care that history does not portray you as the black horseman at the side of the Imperial wanderer when he took the wrong path. I do not mean that you have to do everything alone. Take counsel with Hohenlohe. And Bülow will surely be ready, when he has recognised the danger, to counterwork it by suitable despatches. Hohenlohe's great subservience involves the immense danger of confirming the Emperor in his autocratic ways. He should not have accepted this encroachment on his office, the conversation with Swaine: that he does so encourages the Emperor to go further. That must lead to a crash. It would be better that Hohenlohe, Marschall and I should all resign at once. It would be a lesson for him

---

[1] Hohenlohe, *Denkwürdigkeiten aus der Reichskanzlerzeit*, 175-7; and Hutten-Czapski, *Sechzig Jahre*, i. 263.

for such a yielding Chancellor he will not find again, not even if it is Schweinitz, with Monts or Raschdau as Foreign Minister. If you discuss it with Hohenlohe you must advise him on certain occasions to play the Chancellor. The old gentleman now behaves as if he were Second Chamberlain. Or say: Who is to advise the Emperor at this very grave time? Adjutants? Or do you think one must let him decide everything alone? Domestic policy makes more noise, but foreign policy is much more dangerous. His intervention may lead to results at which you and he would be surprised. So I am more discouraged to-day than in my worst experience. Remember Providence has assigned to you a sphere of personal influence where it is not enough to say at the close of life, *optima voluisse sat est*. More is expected from you. Mobilise your friends and followers. You will easily grasp what is needed when you abandon the fallacy that the king can do no wrong. This maxim, remember, was invented in a land where he is powerless. Power and responsibility go together.' With an unpredictable ruler and a yielding Chancellor Holstein had moments of deep depression. 'I was next on the list to be Wirklicher Geheimer Rat,' he confided to his cousin in August 1896; 'but I have asked for my name to be removed because I am not in the mood to say Thank you. Moreover it has no value for me, lonely old creature that I am.'

The two outstanding events of Hohenlohe's Chancellorship were the ill-judged interventions in the Far East and in South Africa. He was rightly anxious to restore the intimacy with Russia which had been impaired by the lapse of the secret treaty of 1887, and he believed that support of her ambitions in the Far East was the best approach. Moreover the arrangement which allowed her to swallow Port Arthur at her own convenience was accompanied by the Tsar's assent in advance to a German raid on Kiao-Chau. The belief, however, that Russia could be won back without far greater concessions was unfounded, and the failure to estimate the strength or to foresee the resentment of Japan was a glaring failure of statesmanship. 'We shall remember,' observed a Japanese statesman as he bowed to necessity in 1895, and his countrymen were to prove in 1914 that they had not forgotten. Holstein supported the policy, as he explained in a letter to Chirol,[1] on the ground that it was desirable to prevent the consecration of the Franco-Russian Alliance by joint salvos of artil-

[1] Chirol, *Fifty Years*, 191.

lery; for while Japan might possibly resist a summons from Russia and France, she would obey a command backed by Germany as well. His second motive was to encourage Russia to expand in the Far East and thus weaken Pan-Slav ambitions in Europe. The treaty for the lease of Tsing-tau in its final form was drawn up by Holstein and Tirpitz.[1] Though plausible arguments were thus adduced for intervention, the alienation of Japan was scarcely less a blunder than the snub to Russia in 1890.

The fullest story of the Kruger telegram was supplied long afterwards in an article by Thimme based on the diaries of Marschall and Admiral von Senden and other new material.[2] That Holstein played no decisive part was already known, but the extent to which he was involved had remained a mystery. A memorandum drawn up at the time, explaining his objections and his refusal to initial the document, was seen by an official of the Foreign Office in 1908, but has not been found or at any rate published. According to Eckardstein, he wrote to Hatzfeldt in March 1896: 'It was unfortunately impossible for me to prevent the Kruger telegram. The Secretary of State, spurred on by the Colonial enthusiasts, was set on it, and I could not alter it.'[3] No such letter, however, has been found among Hatzfeldt's papers.

We learn from Marschall's diary that on January 3, 1896, after hearing the Emperor's crazy suggestion of a Protectorate over the Transvaal and the despatch of troops, the Foreign Secretary proposed a telegram of congratulation to the President. The widow of Kayser, the Director of the Colonial Department, on the other hand, asserts that it was her husband, called in when agreement proved impossible, who proposed a telegram, and on the acceptance of the idea made the first draft, which was sharpened and promptly despatched. According to von dem Bussche Holstein was asked by Marschall during an interval in the discussion to come and take part, but declined, not so much because he disapproved his attitude but because he wished to avoid meeting the Emperor. It appears that he then returned from the Chancellor's palace, where the discussion was held, to the Foreign Office. According to Mumm von Schwar-

---

[1] Tirpitz, *Memoirs*, i. 76.
[2] 'Die Krüger-Depesche,' in *Europäische Gespräche*, May 1924. Cp. Meinecke, *Geschichte des deutsch-englischen Bündnisproblems*, ch. 5.
[3] Eckardstein, *Erinnerungen*, i. 277.

zenstein, an eye-witness, he was horrified when Marschall entered his room shortly afterwards with the fateful telegram in his hands, and implored him not to send it. The Foreign Minister explained that this was the price of holding back the Emperor from something worse. If Holstein flatly declined to take part in the discussion he had no right to blame the decision reached in his absence, and he deserves Meinecke's censure of 'the cowardly policy of the ante-chamber.' For it was not the telegram in itself but its sharp wording which aroused in equal measure the enthusiasm of the German people and the resentment of the British Empire. Bismarck immediately noted the mistake in phraseology. The monarch's attempt in his Memoirs to shelter himself behind 'the insistence of Hohenlohe, the powerful personality of Marschall, and the siren voice of Holstein,' can deceive nobody;[1] for his letter to the Tsar, written within a few hours of the despatch of the telegram, breathes a similar spirit of angry excitement. The impulsive ruler was held back, not spurred on, by his official advisers. Eckardstein's suggestion that Holstein had a finger in the pie is worth nothing, for he gives no evidence and was not in Berlin at the time. On the other hand, must we assume that he was a mere onlooker? That the Chancellor and Marschall did not seek his advice in a matter of first-class importance seems to Johannes Haller so improbable that he boldly suggests that the master of stratagems allowed the error to be committed in order to diminish the prestige and therefore the power of William II.[2]

Though Holstein was not directly responsible for the manufacture of the high explosive, he was in agreement with the general policy of German self-assertion by which it was inspired and must therefore shoulder some portion of the blame. At the close of 1894 Chirol, the *Times* Correspondent in Berlin, described him as 'a consistent advocate of close relations between the two countries,' though he found plenty to blame in British policy.[3] Chirol had never seen him so worked up against Great Britain as in the autumn of 1895, and he was full of mysterious hints as to the danger of incurring Germany's enmity.[4] The object of Marschall and Holstein was to frighten her by the spectre of a coalition into climbing down in the Transvaal and to force her into the orbit of the Triple Alliance. The idea of a Continental league appears for the first time in official Germany in a

---

[1] *Ereignisse und Gestalten*, 68–9.   [2] Haller, *Eulenburg*, 190–1.
[3] *History of the Times*, iii. 154, 268.   [4] Chirol, *Fifty Years*, 278–9.

Memorandum of Holstein, dated December 30, 1895.[1] He desired to use Italy's dislike of British policy in Abyssinia to enable Germany and Italy jointly to co-operate with the Franco-Russian group, thus preventing Italy from leaving the Triple Alliance and bringing the advantages of closer relations with it sharply before the statesmen in Downing Street. His exclusion of the Egyptian question from the discussion shows that his idea of a league was a means not an end. Thus his policy at the height of the Transvaal crisis was to hold the Triplice together, to make Great Britain more friendly to it, and, if that proved impossible, to combine against her with the Franco-Russian group. After discussing the price and terms of an agreement with France and Russia, he concludes that England will see the necessity of a rapprochement with the Triplice when she realises that it is not at her beck and call. On January 1, 1896, in a letter to Hatzfeldt, he spoke of the desirability of giving her a lesson—the very phrase used by Marschall a few days later to Chirol, the Berlin Correspondent of the *Times*, in reference to the Kruger telegram.

Holstein was in no apologetic mood during a conversation with Chirol on January 8 which he reported to Hatzfeldt.[2] He earnestly hoped that the direct negotiations between the Transvaal and England would succeed: if not, the matter would go much further. Germany could not accept a *diminutio capitis*. Russia had hinted that she would seize the opportunity to play off Germany against England. France would also have to come in, despite Alsace-Lorraine, because otherwise Germany would supplant her at St. Petersburg, and the German-Russian partnership would constitute a standing threat to France against which the British fleet would be of no avail. For these reasons he anticipated a satisfactory solution. The suspicion of a German seizure of Lorenzo Marquez was absurd, for it would drive France to the English side on account of its proximity to Madagascar, but whether the Transvaal episode would suffice to open English eyes to the need of a continental attachment was very doubtful. The Transvaal would probably suggest a discussion by the Powers if direct negotiations broke down. It was important for peace that England should not go so far with her naval demonstrations as to enable the German Admiralty to stage a partial mobilisation.

At this critical period Chirol visited Holstein every day and was struck by the gravity of his language. 'It would be wise for England

[1] *Die Grosse Politik*, xi. 67–9.   [2] *Ibid.*, xi. 41–2.

to avoid complications by coming to terms with Kruger,' he declared on January 7.[1] 'I can assure you, whether you believe me or not, that if you compel him to appeal to us, we shall not be isolated. There are things which I cannot discuss with you at present because I should have to disclose secrets, and you may think that because I make no answer to you at present I have none to make. But I assure you again and again that England is incurring the gravest danger.' Never perhaps since 1810, he added, had she been in such a dangerous position. Such warnings were almost indistinguishable from threats, but it was firing with blank cartridge, for the Continental bloc at which he hinted was impracticable. On the other hand the revelation of German hostility to England was a disagreeable surprise, the memory of which rankled when the German Government quickly realised that it had gone too far and began to use the soft pedal. Chirol himself was so distressed that he gave up his post in Berlin.

'We agree in thinking that the destruction of England's position as a Great Power would be a doubtful blessing for Germany,' telegraphed Holstein to Hatzfeldt on January 10.[2] 'So let us be glad if the matter ends, as seems likely, with a little diplomatic success for Germany and a little political lesson for England.' Holstein misunderstood the British nation in believing that it could be coerced into the orbit of the Triple Alliance by threats, but he certainly had no desire to push things to extremes. Hammann records a conversation in which he spoke of the dangers of estrangement from Great Britain and declared that South Africa was not worth a war. His attitude was well understood in the British Embassy, where the new Ambassador Sir Frank Lascelles was at once friendly to Germany and temperamentally inclined to take things quietly. 'He certainly did not like it,' reported Spring Rice on January 11 in reference to Holstein's part in the Kruger telegram; but he added in April that 'the underground inspirer of the Foreign Office is using all his influence against us.'[3] In six short years he had indeed done as much as any of his countrymen to alienate the goodwill of Russia, Japan and the British Empire.

The Kruger telegram increased the dread of interference from the highest quarters. 'Holstein tells me he cannot go on,' reported the

---

[1] Chirol to Wallace, Foreign Editor of the *Times*, quoted in *History of the Times*, iii. 262.
[2] *Die Grosse Politik*, xi. 48–9.
[3] Gwynn, *Letters and Friendships of Cecil Spring Rice*, i. 185, 204.

Chancellor to his son on January 18, 1896.[1] 'He and Marschall were very bitter against the Emperor, who in their view was encroaching on the authority of the Foreign Office.' Hohenlohe, however, rejected a draft protest on the ground that it was too categorical, and explained that he had always realised that William II would not be to him what William I had been to Bismarck. 'Otherwise I should have had to refuse the post and I must take him as he is.' This soft answer produced no effect. 'Holstein came to-day,' noted the Chancellor on June 15, 1896, 'and said I must stand up to the Emperor, who thinks he can do anything and does not show me proper respect. But the questions of the moment are not worth a row.'

A striking portrait of Holstein in the middle nineties has been drawn by Prince Alexander Hohenlohe, who acted as Private Secretary to his father.[2] 'He was one of the greatest personages in the Empire, before whom many an Ambassador grown grey in the service of the state trembled, and on whose whim depended the fate of many officials, not only in the diplomatic service but in the internal administration, and by whose decisions the course of the whole foreign policy of Germany was determined. He possessed diabolical skill in discovering the weaknesses or the private secrets of people and employing his knowledge to make them his tools. He was incredibly autocratic. When he went for his month's holiday he did not as a rule leave his address. On one occasion the Foreign Minister asked for an important document, and received the reply: "The Baron has locked it up and you cannot have it." The Minister did not dare to remonstrate with his subordinate. When German diplomatists were in Berlin he would often let them wait for days and some he never received at all. I know some Ambassadors who for years were never admitted to his presence owing to some personal pique. As my father's secretary it was often necessary for me to see him. Once, without giving any reason, he refused to see me for several days. My father, much inconvenienced thereby, inquired as to the reason. "Because he said, 'I should advise you,'" was the reply, which seemed to him disrespectful. My father persuaded him to see me again.' He could be charming when he liked, testifies Monts, and he was an admirable talker; but friendship with him was subject to sudden storms.

Despite his suspicious nature Prince Alexander enjoyed his talks with the man who held all the threads in his hand. 'From twelve to

[1] Hohenlohe, 161, 235. [2] *Aus meinem Leben*, ch. 12.

one daily a little gathering was held in his room. The Berlin Correspondents of the *Frankfurter* and *Kölnische Zeitung* were often there, with Kiderlen-Wächter, Hammann, Pourtalès, or Marschall. Foreign and domestic questions were discussed, and he often gave directions to the journalists. His morbid fear of personal attacks in the press made him decline office, though my father repeatedly offered it. He only accepted the title Excellenz reluctantly at the end of the nineties, long after it was due. He had a passion for power and a horror of its appearance. He was like a spider, sitting in a dark corner and watching its victims. He had learned from his great master to hate implacably. Yet I have rarely noticed such fascination in a glance, and I have had to defend myself against his magnetic power.' He was almost invisible. 'I worked for decades by his side,' testifies Wermuth, the Minister of Finance; 'only once did I see him and I never spoke to him.'[1] When the Crown Prince asked Richthofen to introduce him to Holstein, the Foreign Secretary replied: 'Your Royal Highness asks the impossible. If we enter his room by one door, he will escape by the other.' 'It is his nature to see intrigues everywhere,' complained Raschdau, 'and to imagine that others take the same pleasure in subterranean activities as himself.' In 1897 he described himself as a hermit.

In the ceaseless struggle for power Holstein, like Bismarck, regarded no obstacle as insurmountable. When Engelbrecht, the Military Attaché in Rome, who was honoured by his special hatred, complained of him to the Emperor at the opening of 1894, he received the reply: 'I know him well; he is a good honourable fellow.'[2] In reality William II hardly knew him at all. He met him for the first time in 1894, liked him, and gave him his portrait,[3] but he was then unaware of his vast and sinister influence. The publication by Johannes Haller of Eulenburg's fascinating correspondence revealed that Holstein, already almost undisputed master of the Foreign Office, flew at still higher game.[4] That the Emperor was impulsive and unbalanced was known to every German; but it was rather his power than his policy which prompted the spider to attempt to draw him also into his all-devouring web.

[1] Wermuth, *Ein Beamtenleben*, 192–3.
[2] Waldersee, *Denkwürdigkeiten*, ii. 303, January 5, 1894.
[3] Otto Becker, *Das Französisch-Russische Bündnis*, 43.
[3] Haller, *Eulenburg*, 164–222.

For a few years Holstein loved Eulenburg as much as his withered heart could love anybody. There was no warmer admirer of his poetical gifts, and Eulenburg's children talked of 'the good uncle' who provided them with sweets.[1] Moreover the assistance of the Emperor's most intimate friend might be of service in the highest circles. Yet Holstein was a jealous lover, and when he broke with anyone he expected his friends to follow suit. He was angry that Eulenburg had not attempted to prevent Bismarck's visit to Berlin and indeed approved it. That the Emperor, like Eulenburg, had a mind and will of his own infuriated him. When Count Henckel declined the challenge in the *Kladderadatsch* affair Holstein begged his friend to urge the Emperor to press the Count to risk his life. 'This time, my dear friend, I am really counting on your friendship. If His Majesty does nothing against Henckel, he will thereby join the side of my enemies.' To this insane proposal Eulenburg replied by advising him not to threaten any one else lest people should think him a fool, but he was alarmed at the prospect that the ruler might be added to the list of his foes. 'The danger has arisen that he will hate His Majesty if he does not come out against Henckel, and such a hatred would create a very serious situation.' That he was prevented from fighting an innocent man was an offence for which he could forgive neither the Emperor nor Eulenburg. He had never admired the young ruler, and his letters to Eulenburg had been sharply critical. When Hohenlohe became Chancellor Eulenburg felt it his duty to warn him that Holstein was working through the press for the removal of Lucanus, August Eulenburg and other high functionaries who had incurred his displeasure. Moreover the feud with Friedrichsruh was as fierce as ever. 'The attitude towards Bismarck, in which I support Hohenlohe, infuriates Holstein,' reported Eulenburg to Bülow. 'He can only love or hate. There is no middle course for our friend.' Eulenburg was soon to find terrible confirmation of this judgment in his own tragic fortunes.

Hohenlohe, who had spent his life in high politics, was less dependent on his officials than the amateur Caprivi, and Holstein feared that the Kaiser and his new Chancellor might occasionally go their own way. His tortured spirit now began to cavil at the system

[1] Muschler, *Eulenburg*, 388. In his obituary notice in the *Times*, May 10, 1909, Chirol describes him as the most kindly and generous of men, though prone to take offence where none was meant.

of personal government which he compared to *opera bouffe*. On December 2, 1894, Eulenburg, while confessing his own opinion that the time was ripe for a Parliamentary ruler, remonstrated with him for resenting the exercise of the Emperor's constitutional privileges. His correspondent rejoined that he did not grudge the prerogatives, but that behind the *façade* of personal rule he espied the spectre of Bismarck. Thus William II was put on the black list because the public feud with Bismarck had closed, and Eulenburg was trounced for going over to the 'Court-Conservatives' because he remained a friend of the monarch. His own days at the Foreign Office, remarked Holstein plaintively, were numbered, and Hohenlohe would not last long. The Emperor's private correspondence with the new Tsar was an added grievance, for he resented any move which he was unable to control. The growing hostility of the virtual head of the Foreign Office to the monarch filled Eulenburg with apprehension. 'Holstein is beside himself,' he wrote to Bülow in November 1895. 'He is no longer omnipotent. In our present difficult situation we cannot possibly do without his genius, but the Emperor's impulsive ways may easily lead to incidents.' That William II was a potential danger they agreed; but while the one sought salvation in the influence of wise and unselfish councillors, the other attempted to put spokes in his wheel. Holstein endeavoured to separate Hohenlohe from his master, not in order to overthrow him, but in the belief that the Chancellor should assert his authority, while remaining subject in foreign affairs to the ultimate control of his nominal subordinate.

At the end of 1895 Bülow wrote to Eulenburg: 'I not only admire the energy and genius of Holstein, but he has become very dear to me. Many people would not understand it, but you can. I love his tragic nature. I would never turn my back on him. I wish to help him. But it makes it very difficult for us that he loses all self-control if his system is or seems to be threatened. You fear that his dealings may lead to the break-up of the Hohenlohe-Marschall regime which you desire to maintain. You could perhaps give Hohenlohe a hint. But do not forget that the latter has been in the closest intimacy for twenty-two years, regards him as his surest support, and inclines rather to his view of a Parliamentary bureaucracy than to our old Prussian royalism.' Like most other people Bülow was to admire Holstein less when he knew him better.

Eulenburg, perhaps the only man who ever loved William II, did his utmost to avert an explosion by argument and remonstrance. 'When through Bismarck's retirement the control of foreign policy passed into your hands,' he wrote to Holstein in February, 1896 'you, who are born to rule, found the Emperor in your way, since he developed contrary to your wishes and expectations. That must lead to differences. I have confidence in his shining gifts and in the lofty idealism which will win through—the confidence that you lack. We both serve him, I with love, you without.' Holstein replied that it was true that he felt himself *de facto* Director of the Political Department. His differences with the Emperor were in respect of method, not of policy, and he had once shared the hope that he would learn from life. 'To-day that hope is much weaker. I fear that if experiences are to have any effect they will have to be of a rough character, experiences in which the whole people will be involved.' Eulenburg was increasingly alarmed at the growing hostility of such an unscrupulous foe. 'I am horrified,' he wrote to Bülow in March 1896, in reference to the cabal against the Emperor; 'they stick at nothing.' The group, he added, consisted of Holstein, Marschall and Bronsart, whose tactics were to provoke difficulties in order to range the Chancellor against the ruler, and thus to confront the latter with a combined opposition before which he would have to give way.

Hohenlohe knew what was going on, and Eulenburg's conversations with him and the Emperor established full harmony between them. 'The Holstein system,' he concluded, 'feels itself threatened by Hohenlohe's pliability and my mediation.' The Chancellor expressed his gratitude. 'The dream of Holstein's heart,' wrote Eulenburg in 1902, 'was a tame Emperor living away from Berlin, affixing his signature to documents, with Hohenlohe and Marschall bending obediently before his will. Yet it was not I alone who felt his great diplomatic talent to be indispensable. He must be taken care of in the interest of the Emperor and the Government, as one takes care of an ill-tempered and even dangerous sporting dog for the sake of his excellent scent.' Holstein's position, in fact, seemed impregnable. 'He is in complete control of the Office,' reported Monts to Bülow in March 1896.[1] 'His capacity for work arouses admiration. Unfortunately his nerviness and touchiness grow on him.' He suffered under the coldness of the Emperor, added Monts; but so long as he and

[1] Bülow, *Denkwürdigkeiten*, i. 38–9.

Hohenlohe held the reins of foreign policy firmly in their hands, things would go fairly well.

One of Holstein's few friends was Schlieffen, the brilliant Chief of the General Staff. At some unspecified date during Hohenlohe's Chancellorship he asked Hutten-Czapski to sound Holstein and Hohenlohe on a vital but very delicate matter, since he did not wish to approach them directly.[1] In the event of a war on two fronts, ran the message, international treaties could not be kept. No country was mentioned, but the reference to Belgium was clear enough. 'And what is your opinion?' inquired Holstein. 'Any such breach,' replied the envoy, 'might have grave consequences.' Holstein was now ready with his answer. 'If the Chief of Staff, above all Schlieffen, believes this to be necessary, diplomacy must accept it.' On the following day Hutten-Czapski, accompanied by Holstein, visited Hohenlohe. The old Chancellor listened to their views but expressed none of his own. Hutten-Czapski reported to Schlieffen, who never recurred to the subject. Nor was it necessary, for the warning had been given, and, according to Monts, Bülow always spoke of a violation of Belgian neutrality in a war on two fronts as a settled thing. At this period, however, Holstein surveyed the European situation without much anxiety. In welcoming George Saunders, Chirol's successor as *Times* Correspondent in Berlin, in February 1897, he said that there were no objections to England making a clean sweep in Egypt if she desired.[2] Whatever happened, Germany stood to gain. 'Even should you choose to make friends with France, the result would only be that Russia would want *us* more than ever.' That England might one day make friends with Russia as well as with France crossed his mind.

VI

THE burly Marschall, nicknamed by Kiderlen the Hippopotamus, was not a man to make friends, and the Emperor had never liked him. His approaching fall was freely canvassed in 1896, and the aged Hohenlohe was expected to go too. Holstein was terrified lest Botho Eulenburg, over whom he had no influence, should be the next Chancellor. 'You know that I go if Hohenlohe and Marschall go,' he wrote to Philip Eulenburg early in 1897. He had suggested Miquel,

[1] *Sechzig Jahre*, i. 371–3.   [2] *History of the Times*, iii, 297–8.

the veteran Minister of Finance, on the ground that he could speak, but in reality because he knew nothing of foreign affairs and would therefore be as wax in his hands. In a memorandum to the Chancellor Count Hutten-Czapski designated Holstein as the best qualified for the post of Foreign Minister, but admitted that for obvious reasons he was unavailable. A middle way was found in the relegation of Marschall to an Embassy, the retention of Hohenlohe, and the appointment of Bülow as Foreign Minister. Early in 1895 Eulenburg had written to the Emperor: 'Bernhard is the most valuable official Your Majesty possesses, the predestined Chancellor of the future.' At the end of the same year William II was repeating the fateful words: 'He and no other shall be the future Chancellor, he shall be my Bismarck.'[1] Eulenburg was prompted not merely by personal friendship but by the conviction that Bülow alone could put an end to an intolerable situation in the Wilhelmstrasse and give the monarch the support he needed. In April 1897 the Emperor spoke of Holstein as 'an old man for whom I have broken many a lance; full of brains and full of hallucinations, who sometimes makes the Wilhelmstrasse even madder than it is already.' He never learned how Holstein used to speak of him. In a letter to Bülow of June 1, 1897, Eulenburg describes an evening in Holstein's room in the Foreign Office, when Kiderlen, who was half drunk, and Holstein denounced the ruler, the latter remarking that he must be treated as the child or the fool he was. The time was certainly ripe for a new broom, and Bismarck among others welcomed the change. 'He will be better than Marschall,' he observed; 'Holstein's influence at any rate will diminish.'[2] Unfortunately neither of these forecasts was fulfilled.

On his way from Rome to Kiel, where he was to meet his master, Bülow broke the journey at Berlin. He found an emotional letter from Holstein beseeching him to speak to no one in or out of the Foreign Office and to keep his hands free till they had a talk. 'I found him in a rather uncertain mood,' writes the prince in his Memoirs, 'in his celebrated room adjoining that of the Foreign Minister, on whom he used to burst at any moment, to the great distress of the latter's peace of mind and nerves.[3] He would have preferred to keep Marschall in office, in view of the commanding influence he exerted over him. That his position was badly damaged increased Holstein's

[1] Haller, *Eulenburg*, 225. [2] Bismarck, *Gespräche*, iii. 474.
[3] *Denkwürdigkeiten*, i. 6–7.

penchant for the Minister because he thereby became more dependent. Yet he preferred me to other possible successors. He made a clever remark that Kiderlen was impossible. "The Foreign Office puts up with Holstein or at worst with Kiderlen, but Kiderlen plus Holstein would be too much." I soon discovered that what he feared was the re-emergence of Berchem or the return of Herbert Bismarck, who, since his break with Friedrichsruh, appeared to him in sleepless nights as a nightmare with his angry colossus of a father behind him. While on the one hand he besought me not to give the Emperor a blank refusal, on the other he pictured the Foreign Office, the relations of the Ministers to one another, and the life in Berlin as a veritable Inferno. That was intended to make me anxious and uncertain at the start and thus to enhance my dependence on the great Geheimrat who under Hohenlohe, under Caprivi, or through his old and powerful influence on Herbert even in the last years of the Bismarck era, was the determining influence in the Foreign Office.' Bülow admits, however, that, though Holstein and Kiderlen had often intrigued, they were, despite their failings, primarily concerned with the welfare of the country. 'Holstein was a stiff Prussian. The idea that Prussia and Germany might lose their position and be damaged or misused by other Powers stirred him to the depth of his being. It could truly be said of him that zeal for our House consumed him, indeed often destroyed his sense of realities, and his watchfulness turned into an excess of mistrust. Kiderlen was to Holstein like Sancho Panza to Don Quixote.'

The father of the new Foreign Secretary had said to Holstein many years earlier, 'Look after my eldest son when I am gone.'[1] When, however, on the fall of the Bismarcks, Bülow was mentioned for the Foreign Office, Holstein declared that in that event he would resign. He secured his promotion from Bucharest to Rome in 1893 despite the opposition of Marschall,[2] but he had no wish to see him in the Wilhelmstrasse. When he learned of the Emperor's prophecy about his future Chancellor at the end of 1895, he tried to stave off the day of its fulfilment. To become Foreign Secretary, he told Bülow, would damage his chances of the Chancellorship, for Foreign Secretaries were not promoted. The new Minister was aware that his advent was a blow to the official who had held the rudder for seven years; and Herbert Bismarck, with whom he maintained friendly

[1] Bülow doubts the story, iv. 547. [2] *Ibid.*, iv. 650.

relations, repeatedly warned him against the malice and knavery of the man whom in Friedrichsruh they called the slow-worm. 'There were worse plans in the Foreign Office last winter than we imagined,' wrote Bülow to Eulenburg a few weeks after his appointment.[1] 'The Chief group, Holstein, Kiderlen, Pourtalès, display a bad conscience and great apprehension. Holstein is sentimental ("For twenty years I have felt like a father to you"), Kiderlen is like an earwig, Pourtalès like a submissive Attaché. Of course the group has not yet lost hope of regaining control. Their ideal is Hermann Hatztfeldt (Duke of Trachenberg) as Chancellor and Kiderlen as Foreign Secretary, with His Majesty to be treated as a minor.' Eulenburg, who knew the undercurrents of Berlin infinitely better than his friend, exhorted him to show his teeth when necessary. 'Good nature does not carry one far in the Wilhelmstrasse. Even the monster of the labyrinth begins to cringe at your feet.' Holstein knew a clever man when he saw him. 'With Bülow I am on excellent terms,' he informed his cousin in July 1897, and in October he reported to Kiderlen that he was threading his way very skilfully among the thorns.[2]

Strong in the support of his master, Bülow proceeded to assert himself. 'I must get into my hands the *personnel* and the press,' he observed to Hammann.[3] He knew, adds the head of the Press Department, that the first of these objects would involve friction, and when in 1898 he made the changes which he deemed necessary, Holstein stayed away from the office for two months and sulked. In the summer of that year the monarch expressed his delight to Eulenburg. 'The rule of the Privy Councillors is over. Who speaks now of Herr von Holstein? He occupies his proper position. When his foes tell me he had better go, I rejoin: "Is he still taking the lead?" Since Bülow has held the reins no one knows the names of the Councillors, so we need not trouble about them.'[4]

The Emperor was too sanguine, for 'the monster' was scotched but not killed. Hohenlohe warned Bülow on his appointment that 'dangerous and evil counsels usually come from Holstein,'[5] and indeed the game of intrigue never ceased. No sooner was the new Minister installed than he received from Holstein some of the Emperor's *marginalia* on Waldersee, of which 'traitor' was one of the

---

[1] Haller, *Eulenburg*, 240.   [2] Jäckh, *Kiderlen*, i. 169.
[3] Hammann, *Zur Vorgeschichte des Weltkrieges*, 4–5.
[4] Haller, *Eulenburg*, 240.   [5] Bülow, *Denkwürdigkeiten*, ii. 113.

mildest; for he feared that Bülow might become too friendly with the ex-Chief of Staff, who, though temporarily out of favour at Court, was not to be despised.[1] His maxim was *Divide et Impera*. At the end of his life Bülow confessed that Holstein was never sympathetic to him; but he added that his wide personal contacts, his knowledge, his great experience, his quickness of apprehension, his resolution and, last but not least, his cunning and his unscrupulousness made him one of the most powerful personages in the state. Everyone who worked with him had reason to complain. 'Our friend Holstein bombards me with excited letters and telegrams,' lamented Hohenlohe in March 1892. 'Now he is angry with the Emperor, now so full of suspicion of Goluchowski that I had to speak to him.'

A fresh revelation of abnormality was afforded by the death of Bismarck in the summer of 1898, which brought immense relief to his apostate *protégé*. The temptation to give a parting kick at the dead lion was irresistible. 'With fevered zeal,' writes Bülow, 'he tried to persuade me that Bismarck's death had provoked no emotion, still less sorrow.[2] He quoted Talleyrand's odious remark on the death of the great Napoleon: *Ce n'est pas un événement, c'est à peine une nouvelle*. He complained of the Under-Secretary Richthofen for hoisting the flag on the Foreign Office at half-mast. This demonstration of grief, he argued, would displease the liberal *bourgeoisie* and still more the working-classes, and, worst of all, would incur the wrath of His Majesty. In his blind yet petty animosity the old Geheimrat, who had stood closer to the great Bismarck for over thirty years than most other people, seemed to me like a malignant wolf who ought to be behind bars and not roaming at large.' The new Foreign Minister, however, was as incapable of caging the wild animal as his predecessors. Holstein's influence, he asserts, was less during his term of office than in the preceding decades,[3] but this judgment is not confirmed by those who saw them working together. Bülow told Raschdau, who complained of Holstein's intrigues, that he hoped to get rid of him within three months, but nothing more was heard of this audacious plan.[4]

Bülow became aware of the difficulties of his task in the first diplomatic problem by which he was faced. The seizure of Kiao-Chau,

---

[1] Bülow, *Denkwürdigkeiten*, i. 363.
[2] *Ibid.*, i. 229.   [3] *Ibid.*, i. 112.
[4] *Süddeutsche Monatshefte*, March 1931, 390.

while ostensibly the result of the murder of German missionaries, was the fulfilment of a secret deal with the Tsar, but it came as a shock to the uninitiated world. The handling of a delicate situation was complicated by the gymnastics of Holstein. 'Less positive than negative, more destructive than constructive,' complains Bülow in relating the incident, 'he felt himself more indispensable the less secure were his superiors.[1] From this point of view the Emperor's friendly feeling towards me worried him. The idea occurred to him to spur on the Chancellor in the Eastern question and to hold back the Foreign Minister. While he depicted all the dangers of the enterprise in excited private telegrams, he egged on Prince Hohenlohe to take a bold and confident line with the Emperor. I saw through his game and was much too convinced of the wisdom of my policy to be caught; and Prince Hohenlohe was too much of a gentleman and too old to lend himself to such intrigues. On this and on many later occasions Holstein resembled a watchdog who guards the house against robbers, but with whom one can never be sure that he will not bite his master in the legs.'

Holstein had received permission from Bismarck to correspond direct with the diplomatic representatives of Germany through private telegrams which were not entered in the file and not always shown to the Chancellor or the Foreign Minister. It was a dangerous precedent, but the privilege once granted could not be withdrawn. Like Louis XV he carried on a secret diplomacy of his own. He corresponded incessantly with Hatzfeldt in London, Radolin in St. Petersburg and Paris, Eulenburg in Vienna, Monts in Munich and Rome, while among the younger generation Eckardstein was the favourite. Radolin used to read Holstein's letters to young Bernstorff, later Ambassador at Washington. Sometimes he was told that his latest despatch was valueless and that the enclosed version must be substituted.[2] If certain members of the diplomatic service were thus privileged, others were punished or ignored. Radowitz had never been forgiven for his conduct in 1878. 'I do not know whom Holstein hates most, the French or me,' complained Münster, the veteran Ambassador at Paris, to Eckardstein in 1898; 'in recent months he has kept me without information except what directly concerns Paris. How he can take the responsibility of leaving me utterly uninformed in this important post, simply from personal pique, he

[1] *Denkwürdigkeiten*, i. 186–7.   [2] Bernstorff, *Memoirs*, 28, 31.

must reconcile with his conscience if he has one. It is good that Hatzfeldt at any rate is in touch with this unfathomable eccentric.' When Raschdau, his colleague in the Political Department, accepted a diplomatic post at Weimar in 1894 because he found Holstein intolerable, the latter revenged himself by cutting off the usual supply of despatches. Despite the protests of the old Grand Duke, who had long enjoyed the privilege of reading them, and despite the intervention of Marschall and Hohenlohe, the boycott continued, and the disgusted Raschdau left the diplomatic service in 1897.[1]

The animosities of the misanthrope were not confined to his own countrymen. 'Your Goluchowski is a sheep,' he wrote to Eulenburg in 1897. The Austro-Hungarian Foreign Minister was well aware of these sentiments, for the two men had been Secretaries of Legation in Paris in the early seventies. Goluchowski had displayed his sense of social superiority, and Holstein never forgave personal humiliations. At the end of 1898 the expulsion of some Austrian subjects from Posen provoked loud resentment in Austria, and he proceeded to launch an attack on the Ballplatz. 'The inspirer of this campaign,' wrote the distracted Eulenburg in February 1899, 'is our friend Holstein, who is slowly turning his back on me since I stuck up for Goluchowski because he is the only guarantee that Austria does not throw herself into the arms of Russia.[2] If His Majesty and Bernhard Bülow did not listen to me, we should soon be confronted by a Franco-Russo-Austrian alliance. The whole Triplice rests for the moment on Goluchowski, the Schratt and myself. It is maddening when Holstein carries a personal vendetta into politics.' The tension was relieved by a change of Ministry in Austria, but the uneasy friendship of Eulenburg and Holstein was at an end. The latter ceased to write, and when the Ambassador visited Berlin he was 'not at home.' 'I was deeply sorry,' comments the Prince; 'though he was half crazy, he was a lonely, unhappy nature, and my sympathy with him is great. The cause of the change was not only his partial exclusion by Bülow, but also my political "failure" in relation to Goluchowski. I put the interests of the Fatherland above his whims.' Two years later, when the enmity of 'the monster' assumed new forms, Eulenburg poured out his heart to Bülow. 'When I think that I have

[1] The correspondence was published by Raschdau, 'Zum kapitel Holstein,' in *Deutsche Rundschau*, December, 1924.
[2] Haller, *Eulenburg*, 262–6.

done him nothing but good, that I helped him whenever I could, that I have suffered much on his account—and now this enmity, this hatred! It is wholly inexplicable. I shall never lift a finger against him, because I am sorry for him and despite everything I cannot forget what we were to each other.' Holstein's feud with Goluchowski continued, and Eulenburg's retirement from Vienna and from public life in 1902 was due not merely to worsening health but to increasing friction with the Mystery Man of the Wilhelmstrasse.

VII

AT the opening of 1899 Holstein was tolerably satisfied with the European situation and not wholly dissatisfied with the ruler. 'The most interesting question for us is always the Emperor,' he wrote to Monts in January.[1] 'I watch him from a distance and therefore all the more objectively. With great gifts and little initial experience he has at times strange methods of doing business. But he recognises the right aims (I speak of foreign policy), though sometimes his temperament leads him to a zigzag course like a swimmer crossing the stream. The world has gradually realised that he intends a pacific honourable policy, and more is not needed at the present time for the safety of the Reich. The Powers which might be a danger to us are now so occupied with external or domestic cares that a coalition such as worried Bismarck or Moltke is unthinkable without great mistakes on our part.' Yet even at the best of times he was a *mauvais coucheur*, and threats of resignation continued throughout the Hohenlohe regime. 'He begs me to forward his request to retire to the Emperor,' noted the Chancellor in his diary[2] on June 26, 1899. 'I am doing so. He thinks the Emperor wants to get rid of him, but I do not believe it. He can only be reassured if he tells him he still requires his services.' No one now took these antics very seriously, for everyone knew that his post was his life. Yet he always repudiated the notion that he was fully in control. 'For the second time since Bismarck's withdrawal,' he wrote to his cousin on July 1, 1899, 'my advice was not taken.[3] The first was the Kruger telegram. The second was when Bülow was persuaded by the octogenarian Münster to support the Permanent Court of Arbitration. For nine years I have had the moral responsibility for the Political Department. Not everything has been done—

[1] Monts, *Erinnerungen*, 357-9.   [2] Hohenlohe, 509.   [3] *Lebensbekenntnis*, 194-5.

far from it—as I desired, but if I opposed anything it was not done. Even the anonymous rabble which shrieks that I betrayed first Arnim and then Bismarck cannot blame our foreign policy. I did not forward to the Emperor the memorandum recommending acceptance, and I sent in my resignation. Since Bülow would not forward it, I sent a duplicate to Hohenlohe, who forwarded it to the Emperor. To avoid scandal I attributed it to my eye trouble. The Emperor rejected it and said I should spare my eyes for a time. So be it, and I will see about resignation in two months.' When Hohenlohe, full of years and honours, resigned in October 1900, Holstein recalled the thirty years of their association, in which he could not remember any difference in regard to foreign affairs.[1] 'I am genuinely proud of the fact that my conception of the best interests of the Reich coincided with that of yourself, who will always stand out in history as one of the pioneers of the German idea and as a living bridge across the Main.' The association was continued during the few remaining months of the old statesman's life.

We owe an unusually sympathetic portrait of 'the omnipotent Holstein' at the turn of the century to Rosen,[2] subsequently Foreign Minister, who was summoned by him to the Political Department from his post in Jerusalem in 1900. 'His will shaped policy, not the Foreign Minister or the Chancellor. I felt that his benevolence sometimes went too far, as he demanded more than at first I felt able to perform. After receiving me most cordially on the first day, he seemed to forget me for the next three or four days, which made me a little uncomfortable. Then he came and said he had purposely left me alone so that I could settle down. To my gratitude to him for my promotion was added the highest admiration. His boundless political knowledge impressed everybody who saw him at work. His grasp of the whole subject, aided by an exceptional memory and astonishing industry, was unique. Yet he was not in the least bureaucratic. He set me some difficult tasks and was lenient to a beginner's mistakes. In such cases he gave me thorough instruction, and his talk made me forget all about time and place. If anything important or interesting occurred, he stayed on without thinking about meals or office hours. He was usually there at ten, and when I went home at nine in the evening he was still at work. If it got too late he sent

[1] Hohenlohe, 594–5.
[2] *Aus einen diplomatischen Wanderleben*, i. 7–26 and 38–45, abridged.

everybody away except one attendant and then locked up the papers in his desk. Even on busy days he would talk to me for an hour or more, also about things outside his official work. This remarkable man was interested in everything. I count these conversations among the pleasantest experiences of my career and, despite later differences, I retain my gratitude. The common notion that in his later years he shut himself up is only partially true. He had an exceptional knowledge and astonishingly correct judgment of a host of people he had never seen, and often surprised me by his verdicts on foreign diplomats I chanced to have known. Yet he was always ready to supplement or correct his opinions except of one of his *bêtes noires*. I never heard him talk of the Arnim trial, but his unsociable ways were generally attributed to this episode.' Only gradually, as his persecution mania increased, did Rosen fully realise that he was a pathological case. Among his worst traits were his readiness to take offence and his practice of withholding important information from German representatives abroad whom he disliked.

When Bülow followed Hohenlohe as Chancellor in 1900 he vainly pressed Holstein to accept the post which he vacated and which the colourless Richthofen was appointed to fill. 'A lonely old bachelor would have had to alter his scheme of life,' he explained to his cousin. 'I hope it will be all right with the new team and good will on my part will not be lacking.' 'In one of my first talks,' writes the Emperor of his new Chancellor,[1] 'I cautioned him against Holstein. He was endowed with great ability and a phenomenal memory. He could make or mar the career of all the young diplomats. At times he was the *Spiritus Rector* both of the Foreign Office and of foreign policy. The worst of it was that he evaded all official responsibility. He preferred to work in the dark. He declined every responsible post, though many were open to him. For long I tried in vain to make his acquaintance. I invited him to meals but he declined every time. Only once did he condescend to dine with me in the Foreign Office, where he appeared in morning coat and explained that he had no dress suit. His memoranda, though clever, were often as ambiguous as the Delphic oracle. This powerful influence, often exerted behind the back of the officials, seemed to me dangerous. It often happened, especially in the Richthofen era, that when I advised an Ambassador to discuss a question with the Foreign Minister I

[1] *Ereignisse und Gestalten*, 83–5.

received the reply "J'en parlerai avec mon ami Holstein." Thus he controlled a large part of foreign policy. He listened to the Chancellor, but what the Kaiser thought or said was a matter of indifference to him. If success was achieved it was claimed by the Foreign Office; if not, it was put down to the impulsive young ruler. For long he seemed to Bülow indispensable, but at length the pressure that this sinister man exerted on everyone became intolerable.'

'From month to month I watch the dependence of Bülow on Holstein with ever growing apprehension,' wrote Eulenburg in May 1902; and later he confessed that he had never dreamed that he could become so terribly dependent on Holstein, who had a rope round his neck. The recovery of power was observed by everybody. 'I do not understand how Bülow allows it,' noted Waldersee in his diary at the end of 1901, in reference to a press campaign against himself and the Emperor.[1] 'It is a subject of general comment that he keeps his place under Bülow, when one imagined he would promptly dismiss him. I think the Emperor supports him—the reason I cannot entrust to paper.' According to Arthur Zimmermann, Holstein used to stay away when Bülow opposed his suggestions, and Princess Bülow was despatched to his home to entice him back.[2] Bülow knew his deficiencies and complained of the unsteadiness of his nerves, of which the breakdown of tripartite rule in Samoa in 1899 provided one of the earliest examples. When the news arrived that British and American cruisers had bombarded Apia and that German colonists had been arrested, the Foreign Minister, who was in his Flottbek home, hurried to Berlin. 'Holstein was at the station to tell me in great but, as I thought, forced excitement, that the only possible way of getting out of this disagreeable situation was for me to resign after such a blow. I quietly replied to the incorrigible eccentric that I found his solution rather attractive. If I were to go I should recommend as my successor Prince Herbert Bismarck. Holstein, who since 1890 feared the Bismarck family as the devil fears holy water, at once took a calmer view of the situation.'[3]

The gossip of the capital at the turn of the century is reflected in the entertaining letters of Princess Anton Radziwill, *née* Castellane, to General de Robilant, formerly Italian Military Attaché in Berlin.

[1] *Denkwürdigkeiten*, iii. 171.
[2] *Süddeutsche Monatshefte*, March 1931, 391.
[3] Bülow, *Denkwürdigkeiten*, i. 282–3.

The Mystery Man was constantly in her thoughts and everywhere she found traces of the hidden hand. In the space of a single year we hear that he had made his friend Radolin Ambassador at Paris; that Mme Minghetti, the mother of Princess Bülow, had taken an aversion to him, which had made bad blood in the Chancellor's household; that he had procured the dismissal of Eulenburg from the Embassy at Vienna.[1] 'Holstein has succeeded in bringing him down. Though he never goes anywhere, he holds all the subterranean threads in his hands to such a degree that he always attains his goal.' At the end of 1902 she reported that Lanza, the Italian Ambassador, was so upset at the sudden and unexplained loss of his friendship on returning from a visit to Rome that he exclaimed that he would have to resign his post. 'This Holstein, for whom I have felt very little respect since he played such an execrable part in the Arnim case, remains omnipotent in the Foreign Office in spite of everything. He must possess some secret power, for all the Chancellors have been terrified of him, and those who do not cultivate him know they are risking their career.' 'Ce vilain homme,' 'cet horrible Holstein,' 'cet homme funeste,' the Fouché of his time; these missiles hurled at the head of a man she had never seen suggest that he had become an almost legendary figure in his lifetime.

It was with such a neurotic councillor at his elbow that Bülow was condemned to undertake negotiations of the most delicate character with Great Britain, Russia and France in turn. The cardinal problem of his twelve years of office was the relation between Germany and Great Britain. The anger created by the Kruger telegram, though never forgotten, was softened by Germany's steady support in Egypt, which was all the more welcome at a time when our relations with France in Africa and with Russia in the Far East were ominously strained. The agitating experiences of the year 1898, which opened with the seizure of Port Arthur and closed with the Fashoda crisis, raised the question whether the traditional policy of 'splendid isolation' provided Great Britain with the necessary security. The new orientation found a vigorous exponent in Chamberlain, who expressed his low opinion of France and Russia with his usual unreserve, and suggested a working partnership with Germany and the United States. The latter, as might have been foreseen, had no stomach for European entanglements, and anything in the nature of

[1] *Lettres de la Princesse Radziwill*, ii. 323, iii. 30–3.

an alliance with the former was at the moment out of the question; for Salisbury and the majority of his colleagues saw no reason for abandoning the policy of the free hand, and Germany was unwilling to compromise her friendly relations with Russia by close association with her hated rival. The approaches of Chamberlain, though approved by some of his colleagues, never amounted to a substantial offer, for it is the prerogative of the Prime Minister or the Foreign Secretary, not of the Colonial Secretary, to declare the policy of the British Government. Moreover Chamberlain's memoranda to Salisbury, published in the third volume of Garvin's biography, explain that the initiative had come from the German side.

Though an alliance was out of the question a rapprochement with Germany was the obvious course for British statesmanship at a time when war with France and Russia seemed by no means impossible. The secret treaty signed in August 1898, which divided the Portuguese colonies into British and German spheres of influence, registered the high-water mark of co-operation. The ensuing negotiations with regard to Samoa proved more difficult, and the stubbornness of the British Premier aroused resentment in Berlin. Holstein had no craving for a large-scale diplomatic partnership and was filled with distrust of Salisbury, but he was eager for regional agreements. 'Could not Salisbury be side-tracked by some of his colleagues in the questions which concern us?' he telegraphed to Hatzfeldt on February 24, 1899.[1] 'Chamberlain must have realised the gain to England in prestige, independence and power by the relatively unimportant Portuguese agreement, and he must be clever enough to see that similar special agreements would bring further strength. This inquiry is purely on my own. You alone can say if direct intercourse with him would do more harm than good. Another question. Cecil Rhodes wishes to come to Berlin. Is he a man with whom one could discuss the policy of compensation in the grand style? In other words, is his influence strong enough to push through an agreed settlement against the *vis inertiae* of Salisbury? Would he have a say in Moroccan questions? Would he consider the surrender of Zanzibar in return for railway and other concessions on the mainland? Would his influence tell in the Samoa question?' The Ambassador replied that it would be dangerous to go behind Salisbury's back, and that the Prime Minister had no present intention to make special agree-

[1] *Die Grosse Politik*, xiv. 580–3.

ments with Germany. The influence of Rhodes, he added, must not be overestimated since the Raid. A few weeks later, when the Samoa problem seemed as far as ever from solution, Hatzfeldt reported that Salisbury's earlier sympathy for Germany had ended, mainly for personal reasons. Under these circumstances it would be best neither to run after England nor to make binding agreements with other Powers which would prevent an understanding with the English if they came to their senses.

On receiving Hatzfeldt's rather depressing letter Holstein drew up one of the comprehensive memoranda in which from time to time he crystallised his thoughts.[1] 'To-day France cannot reach an agreement with England because the objects of compensation would not suffice to satisfy Russia, to say nothing of Germany, who would not be content merely to look on during the partition of the globe.' Harmonious relations between Russia and Germany, he added, were a vital interest of both, but there was no need for a binding agreement with a point against another state which would thereby become an opponent. 'The dangers which threaten us from Russia are too remote to compel us to bind ourselves to her natural antagonists.' France remained irreconcilable. 'But the possibility cannot be excluded that Germany, Russia and France, in the press of events, may one day form a League whose first article would be the mutual guarantee of their territories. Till then Russia and Germany will continue their present policy without any treaty agreement, namely the maintenance or peaceful modification of the situation. In this we are nearer to Russia than Russia, despite her alliance, to France. For the supreme aim of France is unattainable by peaceful means.' With such confidence in the moderation of Russia, Holstein saw no reason to jeopardise her goodwill by flirtations with her principal rival. Her ambitions and commitments in the Far East necessitated caution in Europe, and her agreement with Austria in 1897 had put the Balkan question into cold storage. There was, he believed, no need to abandon what Bülow always described as the independence of German policy. He was equally hostile to the ideas discussed at the Hague Conference during the summer of 1899. 'Arbitration,' he wrote, 'is all right for small states and small questions, not for large states and large questions.'[2]

[1] *Die Grosse Politik*, xiv. 534–8.
[2] Memorandum of May 8, 1899. *Ibid.*, xv. 188–9.

The outbreak of the Boer War in October 1899 weakened the bargaining power of Great Britain, and with Chamberlain's potent aid the dragging dispute over Samoa was settled by the division of the islands between Germany and the United States. If Eckardstein is to be believed, Holstein remarked on the eve of the South African conflict that it was naïve of him to imagine that England would risk a war, since the other Powers would intervene. When the storm broke he feared that Great Britain in her extremity would offer a bait which Germany might be tempted to swallow. The Emperor's visit to England in November, the first since the Kruger telegram, was a welcome sign that the barometer was rising, but Holstein's suspicious brain dwelt more on the pitfalls than on the prizes of the visit. 'Avoid all political conversations, especially with Salisbury, and treat him with cool courtesy,' he wrote in a characteristic memorandum for the Emperor which was approved by Hatzfeldt and Hohenlohe.[1] 'Be equally reserved but warmer in tone with Chamberlain, who will doubtless press for an agreement pointed against Russia. Say that you will carefully consider the proposal, but display no enthusiasm, and thus his offer will increase. Accept nothing positive and reveal no plans.'

Holstein, as Bülow points out, was never an Anglophobe. Like his friend Schlieffen, Chief of the Staff, he wished to concentrate on the army and not to drive England into the Franco-Russian camp by a programme of capital ships. 'He was not anti-British but pro-British, hotly, almost passionately as was his wont.[2] Though a Pomeranian Junker by birth, he was as anti-Russian as any Liberal. He was against accepting Chamberlain's proposals without firm obligations and guarantees, but he long cherished the hope that such guarantees would be forthcoming some day.' The whole Foreign Office, adds Bülow—Holstein, Richthofen and Mühlberg—were, like Hohenlohe himself, quite ready for a treaty with England if only the needed pledges were given. 'On our side everything was done to procure them.' Bülow did not believe, as Holstein used sometimes to suspect, that Chamberlain never seriously intended closer relations, but only talked of them in order to make the French and Russians pliable and to compromise Germany in the eyes of the latter. 'In my view he attempted to bind us at the moment when that

[1] Bülow, *Denkwürdigkeiten*, i. 311–3.
[2] *Ibid.*, i. 326–7.

course suited him, convinced that with a change in the situation he would easily escape from his promises.'[1]

The fruits of the visit of the Emperor and his Foreign Minister were disappointing. Salisbury had lost his wife and kept out of the way. Chamberlain's speech at Leicester, which he believed—wrongly, according to Bülow—to embody his visitor's ideas no less than his own, received a chilly response from the German Foreign Minister, who was convinced that public opinion, inflamed by detestation of the Boer War, would tolerate no intimacy with Great Britain. Bülow's *douche* was quickly followed by the seizure of German ships wrongfully suspected of carrying contraband to the Boers, which led to peremptory demands in Downing Street and smoothed the way for the Second Navy Bill. 'If England does not release the steamers and give us satisfaction or arbitration,' telegraphed Holstein to Hatzfeldt on January 7, 1900, 'a continental group will at once arise, primarily to consider the principles of sea-law.[2] As they are only waiting for Germany, the grouping could be affected in a few days. That would be a first step in a direction which Germany regrets to choose, but the blindness of the English statesmen leaves us no choice.' The plant which Chamberlain had sown and watered had soon withered away.

The second and far more important chapter of the negotiations for an Anglo-German partnership begins in January 1901.[3] During a visit to Chatsworth, the country home of the Duke of Devonshire, Eckardstein was assured by Chamberlain that for him and his friends in the Cabinet the time of 'splendid isolation' was over; that the choice lay between the Dual and the Triple Alliance; that, unlike some of his colleagues, he would prefer the latter; and that the first step should be a secret Moroccan agreement between England and Germany on the basis of previous discussions. The matter should be taken up when Salisbury left for the Riviera and the details discussed with Lansdowne and himself. So long as he felt convinced that a lasting co-operation with Germany was possible, he would stoutly resist an arrangement with Russia. If, however, it appeared that such co-operation was impracticable, he would turn to her, despite

[1] Bülow, *Denkwürdigkeiten*, i. 331.
[2] *Die Grosse Politik*, xv. 457.
[3] The documents quoted and summarised in the following pages are taken from *Die Grosse Politik*, xvii. ch. 109; Eckardstein, *Erinnerungen*, vol. ii; and *British Documents on the Origins of the War*, ed. Gooch and Temperley, ii. ch. 10, Cp. Hammann, *Zur Vorgeschichte des Weltkrieges*, ch. 5.

the high price England would have to pay, perhaps involving China and the Persian Gulf. These declarations, except as regards Morocco, were to be regarded for the present as purely academic.

On the same day that this significant news was telegraphed to Berlin, Hatzfeldt, the invalid Ambassador, sent one of his private wires to Holstein. Chamberlain's utterances, he observed, confirmed his old conviction that England would come to them when she felt the need of support. 'You and I agree that the idea of an alliance is premature. Chamberlain seems to share this opinion and to wish to lead up to the later definitive understanding by a special pact concerning Morocco. That we can accept.' Holstein was in no way impressed either by the prospect of a deal with Great Britain or by the warning that she might look elsewhere. 'The whole threat of disarming the enmity of Russia and France by yielding in China and the Persian Gulf,' he telegraphed to Eckardstein, 'is utter nonsense. In the first place France does not get enough out of it. Neither for this nor any other concession would she hand over Tangier and therewith the Straits of Gibraltar to England. If England made large concessions in territory and spheres of influence to Russia and France, she would whet their appetite and make the struggle for existence inevitable, even were it to be postponed: a weakened England against strengthened foes. A broader treaty with England is almost unthinkable for us, since it would almost certainly involve a danger of war. For this immense risk a corresponding payment will be forthcoming only when England forms a more correct, that is to say more modest, estimate of her achievements and of the friendship of America. Salisbury's words to Hatzfeldt: "You ask too much for your friendship" still hold good. This and the ill-treatment of Germany, which under Salisbury has become a habit, must be forgotten on both sides so as to make a fresh start. Meanwhile Kitchener is applying Salisbury's methods in South Africa.' Holstein spoke in the same sense to Richthofen, his nominal superior, who wrote to the Chancellor on February 5: 'Let England come to us. The spectre of a Russo-English alliance appears to me, after numerous conversations with Holstein, nothing but a spectre.'[1]

A shorter telegram to Metternich, who was attached to the Emperor during his visit to England on the occasion of the Queen's illness, reiterated his standpoint. 'I am particularly suspicious of the

[1] Bülow, *Denkwürdigkeiten*, i. 512.

present ardent wooing by Chamberlain & Co., because the threatened understanding with Russia and France is such an utter fraud. By yielding England would postpone the struggle for existence for a year or two, but make it all the more certain, since her foes would be strengthened and herself be weakened in power and prestige. We can wait: time is on our side. A sensible agreement with England, that is one which pays a fair price for the almost certain risk of war, is only to be expected when the feeling of insecurity becomes more general there than it is to-day.' The pundits of the Wilhelmstrasse were blind to the signs of the times, repeating like parrots that they had merely to wait till England was forced to feed out of their hand.

Three weeks after Chamberlain's unofficial conversations at Chatsworth, the question of Anglo-German co-operation was officially raised by the Foreign Secretary. In view of the rumours of a Manchurian agreement between Russia and China, reported Eckardstein on February 7, Lansdowne had informed him that Great Britain and Japan intended to protest to China, and inquired whether Germany would join in holding Russia in check. Two days later Holstein telegraphed to the Chancellor in Homburg his draft of a reply to the inquiry. Germany could not involve herself in so sharp an antagonism to Russia on account of Manchuria, but would be ready to declare: 'We desire the preservation of the peace of the world, as we wish to live in peace ourselves. If this proves impossible we intend to remain neutral; but we cannot foresee the extent and development of a conflict once begun nor what tasks the preservation of an equilibrium may impose upon us.' This declaration, he added, should limit the area of the war and indeed render it impossible, and he hoped that England would be content. 'I agree with your proposals,' replied Bülow; 'I hope indeed they will satisfy England, for in view of the present acute anti-English feeling in Germany too far-reaching demands for our support of English interests in China would render a subsequent understanding on a broad basis far more difficult.'

On February 11 Holstein explained his views in greater detail in an illuminating telegram to Eckardstein. 'You and I have often discussed the question of a German-English alliance. Such an alliance, in which each party deals with a single aggressor and the *casus foederis* only arises when there is more than one foe, has many attractions for the thoughtful statesman, but would unfortunately be in direct conflict with German opinion to-day. The systematic campaign against England, which began after Bismarck's retirement, is largely due to the intolerable personality of Salisbury, whose antipathy to the German Emperor and sympathy for France have shaped English policy during the last decade. This policy revealed itself as brutal and untrustworthy. The Chancellor, who bears the brunt of the attacks, will not be inclined to divert them in even greater strength against the Emperor, which would certainly occur if a German-English alliance were now to be made. It would then be said that England scores at our expense but would as usual slip out of her obligations. This conviction, which is shared by 99 per cent. of the German people, could not be altered by assurances but only by facts, namely if the defensive treaty, apart from a fully-secured reciprocity, carried with it direct advantages, not mere promises. I begin a new paragraph in order to emphasise that the offer of an alliance cannot proceed from Germany. For first, I do not believe that England will make acceptable concessions so long as Salisbury has a say, and I think it unworthy of a Great Power again to be told: You ask too much for your friendship. And secondly, after all our experiences with Salisbury, he could quite well inform St. Petersburg of our offer and its conditions and ask: What do you offer? England's position, owing to Japanese co-operation and the certainty of the neutrality of the Triple Alliance, is exceptionally good and can only become worse. Thus an alliance with Germany is unnecessary for the attainment of her present aims. The people could only be convinced by positive facts that a treaty did not serve English purposes.'

On March 18 a momentous conversation took place between Lansdowne and Eckardstein. According to the latter the Foreign Minister observed that he was considering the possibility of a long-term defensive alliance, which he believed that several of his most influential colleagues would approve.[1] According to Lansdowne's report, on the other hand, the suggestion was made not by himself but by his visitor.[2] The latter believed that the German Government, while averse from an agreement limited to the present situation in China, would entertain favourably the idea of an understanding of a more durable and extended character which might be described as a purely defensive alliance between the two Powers, directed solely against France and Russia. So long as Germany and England were attacked by one only of the other two Powers, the Alliance would not

[1] *Die Grosse Politik*, xvii. 41–2. [2] Gooch and Temperley, ii. 60–1.

operate; but if either Germany or England had to defend herself against both France and Russia, Germany would have to help England, or England Germany, as the case might be. After replying that the project was very novel and far-reaching and would require careful examination, the Foreign Minister proceeded to indicate some of the difficulties. 'Baron Eckardstein was careful to assure me that his suggestion was not made under instructions,' concluded the report, 'but I feel no doubt that he has been desired to sound me.'

Which of these versions are we to believe? Lansdowne was not only a man of spotless integrity and wide experience, but he was bound by every obligation of honour and precedent to provide the Cabinet with an accurate account of a conversation of such significance. Eckardstein's report, on the other hand, was conveyed in the form of a private telegram to Holstein, who in a letter of March 17, which reached him on March 19, sent a precise injunction: 'I expressly forbid you the slightest mention of an alliance. The moment, if it ever comes, has not yet arrived.'[1] How then, it may be asked, could Eckardstein venture to make such a proposal without permission? The probable explanation is that the ardent Anglophil, the husband of a wealthy English wife and with a pleasant position in society, was deeply convinced not only of the desirability but of the possibility of such a pact and was eager to reap the credit. Moreover he confesses that on March 16, when he was the guest of the Foreign Minister, he had given his host a broad hint to come forward with an offer of alliance, remarking: 'If there were a defensive alliance covering all eventualities, Germany would of course be in a position to localise a war between Russia and Japan by influencing France.' This passage, he adds, was omitted from his telegram to Holstein lest he should denounce him for going too far.[2] Holstein, in fact, was an impossible chief, and his letters and telegrams were the despair of his correspondents. 'I have often begun important negotiations at his order,' complains Eckardstein, 'and then been instructed to break them off as soon as the other party was ready for agreement. Directly negotiations began to go smoothly he became suspicious.'

Bülow replied on March 20 that the defensive arrangement which he believed Lansdowne to have proposed appealed to the German Government, which must however first consult its allies; meanwhile it would be well for England to approach Austria, though not Italy.

[1] Eckardstein, ii. 279.   [2] *Ibid.*, ii. 280.

If Goluchowski approved Germany would be ready for negotiations and perhaps Japan might be drawn in. In a conversation on March 22[1] Lansdowne is stated to have made some informal inquiries as to the nature and scope of a defensive alliance, to which the German representative was instructed to return informal replies. The best plan, he was to say, would be for England to connect herself with the Triple Alliance; the *casus foederis* would arise in the case of two or more enemies and the pact must be public. Japan, who pursued a policy of expansion, would find no advantage in a purely defensive alliance but might be glad to get into good company.

The position of Japan presented grave difficulties to the Wilhelmstrasse, for it was generally known that before very long she might be at war with Russia, with whom Germany was determined not to quarrel. 'Japan, who pursues an acquisitive policy,' wrote Holstein on March 27,[2] 'is a compromising comrade for Germany, who wishes to keep in with Russia. Even the fact that we were discussing common action with her would be taken by Russia as a sign that we wish to change from a purely defensive to an aggressive policy. It would be quite different if England would some day associate herself with the Triple Alliance, and if Japan could be brought in as an appendage of England. In that case England, who stands essentially on the defensive in Asia and Europe, would act as a make-weight against Japanese effervescence; and, if not, the new group would be so strong that the sentiments of other Powers towards us would be of less consequence. We have told Japan that we have no political arrangements with Russia, and that therefore we should remain neutral in a Russo-Japanese conflict and thereby in all probability secure the neutrality of France. Beyond that we cannot go.' Bülow expressed his gratitude for 'this masterly memorandum with which he agreed in every point.' The possibility of a struggle for the hegemony of the Far East seemed an additional reason for extreme circumspection in dealing with Great Britain.

On March 29 Lansdowne told Eckardstein that as Salisbury was ill he could not say much; that his colleagues were apprehensive of the vague and far-reaching arrangement suggested; and that it would be desirable to know for instance what would happen if Japan were at war with Russia and threatened by France. Eckardstein replied

[1] There is no record of this conversation in the British Foreign Office.
[2] *Die Grosse Politik*, xvi. 350–1.

that as Salisbury was ill and the Reichstag irritable, it would be best to defer the discussion till after Easter. During this interval the Wilhelmstrasse, conscious of the difficulties arising from the unpopularity of Great Britain, became ever more convinced that a purely Anglo-German arrangement was impracticable. In a telegram of April 14 from Richthofen, drafted by Holstein, Hatzfeldt was instructed to explain to Lansdowne, in case he recurred to the subject, that the foes of the Triple Alliance were trying to turn Austria against Germany by attributing to her plans of partition after the death of Francis Joseph. 'This suspicion can best be dispelled when it is seen that a leading *rôle* in the formation of the projected alliance is assigned by Germany to Austria. That is why we lay so much weight on Vienna being in some measure the centre of the negotiations.'

In proposing to substitute the Triple Alliance for Germany as a bargaining and contracting unit, the Wilhelmstrasse overshot the mark. According to Eckardstein[1] Lansdowne informed him on May 15 that he and some of his colleagues would welcome a defensive alliance with Germany. He had seen the Prime Minister, who approved the principle of mutual support against two or more assailants, but not of complicating the issue by including Germany and Italy. If the matter were to advance further both sides must now put their ideas on paper, though the drafts would still be of an academic character. Since no report of this interview has been found in the British archives, we may be allowed to doubt how far Eckardstein was correct in his account of the conversation, particularly with regard to the favourable attitude of Salisbury.

On May 23 Lansdowne discussed the alliance question for the first time with the Ambassador himself, who, though old and ill, retained his mental alertness. When the Foreign Secretary pointed out the difficulties and uncertainties involved in joining the Triple Alliance, Hatzfeldt replied that an alliance with Germany alone was impossible. He stressed the dangers of Britain's isolation, and argued that she would be wise to join one or other of the two European groups. If she approached Russia she would have to pay a high price. If nothing came of these discussions Germany might be driven to remove friction with Russia by a deal. The conversation did nothing

---

[1] Though the telegram bears Hatzfeldt's signature, the interview was between Eckardstein and Lansdowne.

to bridge the gulf, and Lansdowne wrote to Eckardstein that it in no way diminished his desire for the memorandum which he had been promised. No document was sent, for the Wilhelmstrasse intervened. 'I am suspicious of putting anything on paper at the present moment,' wired Holstein. 'When the first written document in the alliance question leaves our hands, the first formal suggestion of an alliance comes from us—exactly what we wish to avoid. To decide on the principle whether an attack on the Triple Alliance should raise the *casus foederis* for England the English require nothing in writing. When England has expressed herself on the principle, written notes, for instance on the meaning of the word Attack, can be exchanged. Till then, in my opinion, we should give nothing in writing.'

The failure to provide the memorandum was of little importance, for on the very day on which Holstein was warning Hatzfeldt of its perils Salisbury condemned the whole project root and branch.[1] 'It would hardly be wise to incur novel and most onerous obligations in order to guard against a danger in whose existence we have no historical reason for believing.' Moreover, it was impossible to promise aid, since the British Government could only wage a war supported by public opinion at the time. Holstein had proved right in his unvarying scepticism with regard to the Prime Minister, and Eckardstein, despite his boasted acquaintance with British statesmen, had deceived himself. Whatever life there had been in the plan was trampled out of it by Salisbury's uncompromising words.

On June 14 Holstein discussed the deeper issues of Anglo-German relations in one of the most elaborate of his memoranda. Salisbury's reply to Bismarck's celebrated letter of 1887, he declares, had been regarded by the Chancellor as a refusal of his advances. British policy, indeed, rested on the conviction that a continental struggle was inevitable, and that Great Britain would profit by a conflict in which she took no part. In other words it was the business of other Powers to pull the chestnuts out of the fire for her. 'This catspaw theory, which has gradually become a fetish for a certain school of English politicians, is beyond doubt the cause of the universal hatred of England to-day. No one likes being duped, and the people of the Continent have gradually reached the conviction that England is out to dupe them. Salisbury has carried out this policy more openly than any of his predecessors.' Turning to the project of an alliance he

[1] Gooch and Temperley, ii. 68–9.

reiterates the familiar arguments. 'If we assume the immense burden and responsibility of defending the British Empire with all its colonies against all comers, the Triple Alliance must be regarded as a whole, just like the British Empire, so that for instance an attack on Austria or Italy by two or more Powers would call not only the members of the Triplice but also England into the field. An alliance of England with Germany alone would make the position of the latter worse instead of better. For since the contents of the treaty would be published, her opponents would know that if they attack Austria, and Germany goes to her assistance, England will take no part. But the inclination to fight with Germany would be greatly enhanced when it was known that in certain eventualities she is pledged to support Great Britain. At present we feel strong enough not to hurry in the search for support. Moreover we believe that the current of events will probably one day bring Germany and England together. In times of excitement we have avoided building dams which would impede the flow of the stream, and we will retain our freedom as long as we can. Neither Yunnan nor Morocco are important enough for us to risk a war or seek support.'

The opposition of Salisbury and the German refusal to supply a written draft combined with the ill-health of Hatzfeldt to defer further discussion till the autumn; but when the summer holidays were over neither Metternich, the new Ambassador, nor Eckardstein reverted to the subject. Lansdowne agreed with the Prime Minister that to join the Triple Alliance was out of the question, but he was far less satisfied with the policy of isolation than his chief and was ready for a limited Anglo-German understanding without pledges of military support.[1] Even this appeared to Salisbury to be full of risks and to carry with it no compensating advantage. Yet what was too much for the British Premier was too little for the German Government, as Metternich frankly explained to Lansdowne in their first and last interview on the subject: if a defensive alliance between the British Empire and the Triple Alliance were ruled out in London, no minor proposal would be considered at Berlin.[2] Thus the conversations which began on March 18 ended on December 19, never to be renewed.

The failure of the discussions of an Anglo-German partnership caused Holstein no pangs, for he neither initiated them nor believed

[1] Gooch and Temperley, ii. 79–80.   [2] *Ibid.*, ii. 3.

in their success. Eugen Fischer is in error in arguing that 'Holstein's Great No'[1] had ruined a promising prospect; for the Wilhelmstrasse was agreed that the Triple Alliance must be treated as a unit, and Salisbury's consent was never won even to an Anglo-German defensive alliance or to a declaratory pact. No British offer of an alliance was refused for no official offer had been made. In a conversation with Chirol on October 31 Holstein explained his position to his old friend.[2] 'I wished to avoid treating the alliance question as actual. First, I did not believe that Salisbury would wish to change his cats-paw policy, though every one saw through it. Secondly, there was no reason for Germany to seek support, since our position had greatly improved in recent years. The German and Russian Emperors were convinced of each other's peaceful intentions, but I was one of those who felt that the tendency of the time would gradually bring together Germany and England, perhaps after I am gone. This view is shared by the Emperor and the Chancellor. The alliance question, in my opinion, could not be seriously discussed so long as Salisbury was at the helm. All that could be done was to leave the future open.'

Next day Holstein drew up a memorandum on what he intended to say when he saw Chirol again. 'Luckily Germany can wait, for with the paralysing influence of Salisbury nothing serious can be done.' Bülow approved the memorandum and added: 'We must display neither restlessness nor impatience but allow hope to glitter on the horizon. In that hope lies the safest guarantee against the capitulation of the English to Russia.' The two men had been in agreement throughout. If there had been a spark of vitality left in the project of an alliance, it would have been extinguished by the sharp exchanges between Chamberlain and Bülow at the end of the year on the conduct of British troops in South Africa and German troops in the campaign of 1870. A furious attack on the Colonial Minister was launched in the German press, and now even Chamberlain had had enough.

---

[1] His volume, *Holsteins Grosses Nein* is vitiated by his confidence in the testimony of Eckardstein.

[2] *Fifty Years*, 288–97. Chirol's statement that he visited Berlin at the pressing invitation of Holstein is contradicted by Rosen, *Oriental Memories*, 76–80. This interview, he declares, was sought by Chirol, and Holstein, who at first refused to receive him, only yielded to the representations of Mühlberg, the Under-Secretary. The Chirol visit to Berlin is analysed in *History of the Times*, iii. 810–819, and doubt is expressed as to the accuracy of his testimony.

On January 3, 1902, Holstein wrote a friendly New Year's letter to Chirol containing a few final reflections on the discussions of the past year. Since Salisbury was known not to share Chamberlain's views, he declared, the German representatives in London were instructed not to broach the subject but simply to receive any overtures. These directions had been followed except in one isolated case in the summer of 1901, when 'poor Hatzfeldt in an access of nervous overexcitement appears to have summoned Lord Lansdowne to come to terms then and there.' Hatzfeldt was thereupon disavowed and recalled. 'I was therefore somewhat surprised to hear about a week ago that Lascelles had informed the Chancellor that the British Government considered the present time unfavourable for further discussion of an Anglo-German agreement. Why not have let the matter rest since nobody—to my knowledge at least—had urged it?'

Whether the statesmen of Germany might have made better use of the friendly sentiments of Chamberlain and Lansdowne during the years of anxiety when we had South Africa on our hands will long remain a subject of debate.[1] It seems clear that the importance of British friendship was insufficiently recognised at Berlin and that no sustained attempt to achieve it was made; yet there is no ground for the wholesale condemnation meted out by certain critics on both sides of the North Sea. Even if Salisbury had been ready to meet the Germans half-way, the weakness of Russia had not yet been revealed on the Manchurian battlefields and her contingent estrangement might well seem a needless German risk. Equally the failure of the discussions of 1901 left no scars in Downing Street, where they were never taken very seriously. What angered British citizens was not the breakdown of the negotiations, of which they never heard, but the hostility displayed during the South African War. This it was which finally transformed Chirol, now Foreign Editor of the *Times*, into a Germanophobe. The hot resentment might gradually have cooled, as it had cooled with regard to the Kruger telegram, but, before the

---

[1] The best recent discussions are Willy Becker's *Fürst Bülow und England*, which follows Eckardstein and Fischer, and Gerhard Ritter's *Die Legende von der verschmähten Freundschaft Englands*, the argument of which is summarised in its title. Cp. Brandenburg, *From Bismarck to the World War*, chs. 5 and 7, and Meinecke, *Geschichte des Deutschenglischen Bündnisproblems, 1890–1901*. On the appearance of vol. ii. of the *British Documents on the Origins of the War*, edited by Gooch and Temperley, Meinecke surveyed the problem afresh in an article *Zur Geschichte der deutschenglischen Bündnisverhandlung von 1901*, in *Am Webstuhl der Zeit, Festschrift für Delbrück*.

mellowing influence of time had begun to act, German policy in Morocco and on the high seas chose a path which banished all hope of genuine reconciliation. In June 1902 George Saunders, the outspoken *Times* correspondent in Berlin, described Bülow as a mountebank and the Emperor as a wayward boy. Since neither side trusted the other progress was impossible.

Holstein placed the responsibility for the estrangement of England on the Chancellor. After his summer holiday in 1902 he used the visit of the Boer Generals to Berlin for the purpose of collecting funds to explain once more his attitude on Anglo-German relations. 'Since my return,' he wrote to his cousin in November, 'I have had much unpleasantness—I mean in my work, for I have hardly any personal life.[1] When I arrived the question of the audience was acute. It was a mistake of Bülow. He had tried for years to make the Emperor anti-English. England regarded him as chief foe because he had made two speeches against her and never said a word of blame for the miserable caricatures of the King and the army. Richthofen, Hammann and I vainly advised him against his anti-English demonstrations, but he took the advice of the Pan-Germans. He did not want to do anything against the English, only to demonstrate. Actually we greatly helped them during the war by declining a Russian plan of mediation. But by our friendly actions and unfriendly language we (i.e. Bülow) fell between two stools. Both sides blamed us, the one because we had done too little, the other because we had said and written too much. The Emperor reluctantly consented to receive the Generals, but when he learned the reaction of the English press he became uncomfortable. When I returned on September 30 I saw there was no time to lose. Happily the Boers, under the influence of Leyds, made a new condition, and I forced Richthofen to telegraph to the Hague that in consequence the audience could not take place. A copy was sent to Bülow who forwarded it to the Emperor. This crossed one from the latter, saying he could not receive them. Bülow thanked me for getting him out of a hole, but the incident left an impression on the Emperor. After his return from Kadinen he did not see Bülow for a week when he asked to be received. I gather that he had much to criticise. The press began to speak of a Chancellor crisis. That did not suit His Majesty who wished to give him a lecture but not to part with him. Thus the

[1] *Lebensbekenntnis*, 214–16.

journey to England took place under the best auspices, but one sees that Bülow is uneasy about the peace. He is too yielding in our negotiations with England about the evacuation of Shanghai and Venezuela. I fear that the English and the Emperor notice his uncertainty, but I can do nothing. By nature he is inclined to regard firmness as rudeness.' No one had ever accused Holstein of being too pliable.

The visit of the Boer Generals was not the only subject of disagreement with the Chancellor in the autumn of 1902. When the renewal of the Triple Alliance came up for decision Bülow was inclined to accept the Italian demand for a modification of the terms. To this Holstein was so strongly opposed that he became ill with the strain. 'My stomach trouble,' he reported to his cousin on September 25, 1902, 'I owe to the Triple Alliance.[1] When the negotiations began in January the Italian Government, at the suggestion of the French Ambassador, wished to add to the text a statement that the treaty contained nothing hostile to France. Wedel, the Ambassador in Rome, and Bülow wished to consent. I strongly urged renewal without change or not at all, for I felt sure Italy would give way. It almost came to a breach with Bülow, and for three weeks we did not meet. I was right, for the Italians yielded, to the fury of the French.' That it was only a paper victory Italy was soon to make clear.

In May 1903 Holstein explained once again that his power was limited. 'The work is eased by experience, and I only deal with the more important matters,' he reported to his cousin.[2] 'That does not mean that I make the policy. I regard my task as getting things straight or pulling back. That was the case since 1885, i.e. since Herbert Bismarck succeeded Hatzfeldt, for instance in the Caroline Islands and the Samoa conflict of 1889. For Bismarck after Schweninger was a different person. In the autumn of 1889 I said to Herbert, when the old man dealt with some affair in a frivolous way: "Without Schweninger your father would be dead, but he would have gone down like a big shining sun. He is still alive, but like other people he grows old." Herbert shrugged his shoulders.' Yet Holstein's position was impregnable even though he did not always get his way. 'I cannot make distant visits,' he wrote to his cousin in August 1903; 'the Chancellor feels uncomfortable when I am away.'

[1] *Lebensbekenntnis*, 212–13.
[2] *Ibid.*, 222–3.

VIII

WHILE Great Britain and Germany were drifting ever further apart, a vigorous but clumsy attempt was made to restore the wire to St. Petersburg which had been rashly cut in 1890. The approaching struggle in the Far East rendered the German attitude of vital importance to Russia, and busy brains in the Wilhelmstrasse began to assess the contingent benefits. In a closely argued memorandum dated January 16, 1904, on the eve of the war, Holstein discussed the price his country might exact for its support.[1] 'The Far Eastern policy of Russia,' he concluded, 'is in acute antagonism to that of Japan, America and England, while her Balkan policy, in its attempt to secure the latch-key of the Mediterranean, infringes the interests, not only of England, France and Italy, but also of Austria-Hungary and Roumania. It is not improbable that, if Russia becomes involved in hostilities over one of these questions, the Powers interested in the other will use the opportunity for a simultaneous attack. She must therefore reckon with the possibility that all the Great Powers except Germany may make a concentric onslaught either by arms or diplomatic pressure. Thus Germany is the only Power to which she can turn for help. An entente between Russia and England is impracticable for many grave reasons, especially the Russophobe attitude of America. Germany must therefore weigh the question whether and on what conditions she would join Russia against her foes. What would be the possible gain and the possible risk? This can only be answered after obtaining military and naval opinion.'

The Japanese victories on sea and land, and the friction with Great Britain arising from the seizure by Russia of her merchantmen, had enhanced the value of German friendship when the Dogger Bank outrage brought an alliance for the first time within sight.[2] On October 24 Holstein discussed an agreement with the Russian Ambassador, and a telegram from Willy to Nicky suggested that, in view of a possible joint protest from the Japanese and British Governments against the coaling of the Russian fleet, Russia, Germany and France should combine. The angry Tsar warmly approved such an arrangement 'to abolish Anglo-Japanese arrogance and insolence,' and in-

[1] *Die Grosse Politik*, xix. 37.
[2] *Ibid.*, xix. 303, note.

vited William II to draft it.[1] The Chancellor forwarded the draft of a defensive treaty to the Emperor; but after further negotiations, conducted through the latter in letters and telegrams drafted by Bülow and Holstein, the project foundered when Russia insisted that France must be informed before an agreement was signed.

The annihilation of the Russian fleet at Tsushima brought peace within sight, and encouraged the German Government to renew the offer of an agreement on the occasion of a meeting between the two monarchs in Finnish waters. In the preparations for the historic conference, and in the discussions which followed the signing of the Björko pact, Holstein's part was at least as important as that of the Chancellor who sought his advice at every stage. There is indeed no chapter in his long reign at the Foreign Office in which, to judge by the published documents,[2] his influence was so marked. Parts of the correspondence reveal the Chancellor as the pupil and the old Privy Councillor as the master.

On July 20, 1905, Bülow telegraphed to Holstein from Norderney that the Tsar had accepted the Emperor's offer of a visit, and that the latter wished for a copy of the defensive alliance proposed in the previous autumn. No one, he added, must know of the coming interview, which, he believed, would be useful. 'Wire me above all what you advise me to suggest to His Majesty in forwarding the text. I believe your inventive mind will know how to pick out the threads which may be of use to us.' Support for Russia in the peace negotiations, he concluded, was out of the question, but it would be advantageous if the Tsar could be so far won over that Witte and Lamsdorff on the conclusion of peace would be unable to engineer a Russo-Franco-British Entente. In forwarding the draft Holstein expressed a doubt about reopening the question of an alliance; the sentiments of

[1] On October 31 a meeting was held at the Chancellor's residence which Tirpitz has described in his *Memoirs* (i. 166–9). Holstein, at the instigation of the Emperor, advocated the offer of an alliance to Russia, adding that the two countries should press France to join the coalition. After some observations from Schlieffen, the Chief of Staff, the Admiral and Richthofen criticised the proposal and argued that Holstein's psychological calculations were mistaken. Pointing a pistol at her head, argued Tirpitz, would not persuade France to mobilise her army for German aims, while a Russian alliance would increase the danger of a war with England in which Germany would have to pay the bill since her fleet was in its infancy. Holstein, records Tirpitz, stoutly defended his plan; and the latter renewed his opposition in a letter to Richthofen, arguing that the true policy was to gain time in which to build a fleet.

[2] *Die Grosse Politik*, xix. ch. 138.

the Tsar were unknown and Lamsdorff would use the German suggestion and the possible Russian refusal to the detriment of Germany, according to his habit. On the other hand, if the adhesion of Germany to the Franco-Russian alliance brought Russia no direct military advantage in the Far East, the moral effect when the new grouping became known would be calculated to diminish Japanese demands. This indeed was the chief argument for Russia attaching Germany, not England, to the Dual Alliance, and in consequence the treaty would have to be published and must contain no secret articles. On the same day, after further consideration, he despatched a second telegram. 'If it is possible to stop His Majesty taking the initiative I think it would be better. He should wait till the other party, even though in quite general terms, displays a wish for co-operation.' Meanwhile the Emperor should renew his advice to the Tsar to grant a Constitution, since, if he did not, the Russian press would attribute it to the visitor's advice.

The conclusion of an agreement had been frustrated in 1904 by Russia's obligations to France, and the Chancellor sought Holstein's advice on this crucial issue. 'Shall I telegraph His Majesty that we cannot allow Russia to inform France and invite her to join before Russia has bound herself to us?' The demand that Russia must agree with Germany before she negotiated for the adhesion of France, replied Holstein, was out of date, for the Rouvier Cabinet would be less hostile than Delcassé; and Russia to-day was more dependent on France than six months ago, and therefore would never take a step of such importance without French consent. Moreover, Rouvier, Lamsdorff and Witte might say to the Tsar; 'Had we not better line up with England rather than Germany?' The only advantage of association with Germany was that it would improve Russian prospects in the peace negotiations, whereas England would only be of use on their termination. The Tsar would probably merely promise to consider the question and then telegraph to decline. It was therefore most important that the Emperor should wait for the Tsar to begin, since a Russian refusal would damage Russo-German relations. On commenting on the Chancellor's suggestions to his master Holstein advised some additional bait for the hook. If Germany joined the Dual Alliance, he should tell the Tsar, she would always side with Russia, who would thus have her way, whereas England as the third party would always go with France, especially in the Near East.

England was working for an Anglo-Franco-Russo-Japanese grouping, and Russia needed Germany if the equilibrium were to be preserved.

The Björko pact was signed on board the *Hohenzollern* on July 24, 1905, though not in the expected form. 'Do you think that the addition *en Europe*,' wired the horrified Chancellor to Holstein when he heard the news, 'renders the treaty useless? If so, shall I refuse my signature and thus cancel it, or would it even thus be valuable as loosening the Dual Alliance?' Its value, replied Holstein, was greatly diminished. The interpolation would be very welcome to Russia, who, in the event of an Anglo-German war, would not need to attack India. In Europe Russia would not be able to help Germany for years on account of the state of her fleet, whereas Germany was bound to attack England if Russia moved through Persia towards the Indian Ocean and was in consequence attacked by England. It would be fruitless, however, to ask Lamsdorff to remove words which were so useful to Russia and so detrimental to German interests, but the Emperor might mention it at his next meeting with the Tsar. 'The only positive advantage is that Russia cannot join the Quadruple group and the circle round Germany cannot close. That is something.'

When the Emperor defended his handiwork, the Chancellor explained that England was afraid of a Russian attack on India, and that, if that fear were removed, she was more likely to attack Germany. Bülow, indeed, took the matter more tragically than Holstein, and suggested that the Tsar should be invited to promise that Russia should fight on the whole line, despite the limiting words. Holstein stuck to his guns. Lamsdorff, he rejoined, would decline, and things would only be worse: it was premature to urge an alteration till his view of the treaty was known. Moreover, it was of use as a symbol of the Tsar's sentiments and as a possible instrument of pressure on France. The 100 per cent. pact had been reduced to 50 per cent., but the 50 per cent. remained. After an emotional interlude caused by the Chancellor's offer of resignation, the Emperor saw the error of his ways and desired to suggest a change in a telegram to the Tsar. But Holstein was still immovable. 'If we propose to alter the text Lamsdorff will also insist on changes, and we may lose the treaty. Use your whole authority to prevent any suggestion of a change and indeed any discussion. Remember that Lamsdorff is eager for an opportunity to water it down in its bearing on France, so do not give him that opportunity.' Holstein was right, for an approach to Lamsdorff would have been useless. He had not been consulted by his master, and when he saw the document he pointed out that it was incompatible with the Dual Alliance. Witte lent his powerful aid, the Tsar was converted, and the house of cards toppled down. The addition of the words *en Europe*, which had caused such a flutter, was of no real importance, for the project was doomed from its birth. The difficulty which had prevented success in 1904 proved insurmountable in 1905, for since 1891 Russia was no longer a free agent in her dealings with Berlin. An effective Russo-German partnership was equally impossible with or without France. It was a deep personal disappointment to William II, who had seen for a moment the mirage of a stabilised monarchical Europe under the control of himself and the Tsar. Holstein's expectations had been more modest, and the *débâcle* confirmed his opinion that it would have been wiser to leave the initiative to Russia. With the end of the war in the Far East her need for German support disappeared, the main obstacle to Anglo-Russian friendship was removed, and the road was clear for the creation of the Triple Entente.

IX

THE last chapter of Holstein's official career is headed Morocco, where he had long foretold an international crisis.[1] 'Like you,' he wrote to Bülow on August 24, 1900, 'I greatly fear the Morocco question will flare up one day. We must reckon with the fact that Salisbury may have to sacrifice to the French not Tangier indeed but the whole of the interior to the Atlantic, in order to make them pliable in other quarters such as China, or in the hope that a French advance on the Atlantic would make Germany attack her. I really do not know if we could accept that and if we should not take strong diplomatic action in Paris, either asking France's intentions or proposing an agreement on Morocco—the latter a fairly hopeless prospect. We shall not be able to wait too long with this move, for the longer the

---

[1] The fullest and fairest account is by Eugene N. Anderson, *The First Moroccan Crisis, 1904–6*. For the French side, in addition to the official publications, see G. Saint-René Taillandier, *Les Origines du Maroc Français, Récit d'une Mission, 1901–6*.

French Government is committed to an advance the more difficult it will be to retreat. The answer will of course depend on the relations of France and Germany to other countries, especially England, at that moment. Relations with England are just now more important than ever, and I would give a good deal if Salisbury's rule came to an end.'

The failure of the attempt to secure some kind of Anglo-German agreement at the turn of the century was logically followed first by an Anglo-French *détente* and later by an *entente cordiale*. Eckardstein reported in 1902 that he had seen Chamberlain and Paul Cambon in close conversation and had caught the fateful words Egypt and Morocco, but Holstein was blind to the trend of events. On the occasion of King Edward's visit to Paris in the spring of 1903 the Russian Ambassador in Berlin told the Emperor that he feared Delcassé would swing over to England at the cost of Russia and Germany. 'Osten-Sacken's fear of Delcassé is so exaggerated,' telegraphed Holstein to the Chancellor on March 30, 'that I regard it as a pose.[1] Delcassé has English sympathies and has probably often shown the Russians that he is not disposed to let them use him against England, but the Franco-English alliance is music of the future. This idea will only become practical politics when the *Revanche* idea has passed away. While it lasts France needs the backing of Russia, for only Russia, not England, could halt an invading German army.' That France might win the friendship of Great Britain without sacrificing Russian support had not crossed his mind. The spectacular triumph of the King's visit to Paris set the world talking, and on May 10 Eckardstein, now a free lance, wrote to the Chancellor that France and England were working for a solution of all their difficulties, and that a new Triple Alliance was in process of formation.[2] The shrewd warning fell on deaf ears. 'Eckardstein is alone in his view of the eventuality of a Franco-Anglo-Russian grouping,' wrote Bülow to his Ambassador in St. Petersburg on May 13; 'I see no reasons so far to concur in his view.' The cheers in the streets of Paris modified the ideas of Holstein as little as those of his chief. According to Eckardstein he declared that it was naïve to believe in the possibility of a Moroccan agreement between England and France. When it came a year later, on April 8, 1904, he realised

[1] *Die Grosse Politik*, xvii. 573, note.
[2] *Ibid.*, xvii. 567–70.

his error but disclaimed responsibility for the unwelcome development. 'I am not happy about the situation,' he wrote.[1] 'The mistaken attitude during the Boer War is bearing fruit in the partnership of England and France. Not I alone but other officials of the Foreign Office tried three years ago to make Bülow condemn the exaggerated Anglophobia and above all the shameful caricatures, but the good Bülow prefers to swim with the stream. England and France will scarcely attack us, but we cannot acquire territory overseas. I do not desire it, but many people clamour for it and wonder that Germany gets nothing. No overseas policy in opposition to England and France! We could go with England and occupy France's present position, i.e. be friends both with England and Russia. But we missed the chance and Delcassé scored. A year or two ago people were so crazy that if one did not join in the outcry one was attacked in the press for Anglophilism, as in the case of myself.' In July 1904, in offering his resignation owing to friction with Richthofen, he explained that he would be glad to be freed of responsibility owing to the decline of German prestige.

At the end of November 1904 occurred the well-known incident of the Imperial dinner-party.[2] The oracle of the Wilhelmstrasse was in his sixty-eighth year when he received an invitation to dinner at Potsdam. He replied that he had no evening clothes, but the excuse was brushed aside and he appeared in morning dress. 'The Emperor was friendly,' he reported to his cousin. 'On shaking hands he joked about the evening dress. "Yes, Your Majesty, I could not get one in six hours." We conversed for forty-five minutes; Bülow and Tirpitz were in the group, and the Emperor did most of the talking. I asked him several questions to which he gave detailed replies. He is a great conversational artist.' Unfortunately that is all we know of the meeting.

By the end of 1904 dark clouds were gathering in the sky, and German naval plans were beginning to fret British nerves. On December 26 Holstein discussed Anglo-German relations with the British Ambassador.[3] The alarm at the possible action of the German fleet, he argued, was absurd, but the British press had long carried on a regular campaign of which the Government could not disapprove since it did nothing to check it. The newspapers had created a

---

[1] *Lebensbekenntnis*, 231. [2] *Ibid.*, 236.
[3] Gooch and Temperley, iii. 58–9.

situation in which the nation might be involved in war by any untoward incident, though he personally shared Metternich's view that England had no intention of attacking Germany. Holstein, like most men of the older generation, was much more interested in the army than in sea-power, and he described the Chancellor's plan of building a formidable fleet without a collision with England as an attempt to square the circle.[1] Yet though he was alive to the dangers of *Flottenpolitik*, he had no hesitation in advising an equally risky policy in Morocco at a time when Anglo-German relations were showing signs of increasing strain.

A despatch from Bihourd, the French Ambassador at Berlin, to Delcassé, on January 25, 1905, described the old Geheimrat at the summit of his power.[2] 'Your Excellency is aware of the exceptional situation of M. de Holstein. This head of the Political Department of the Foreign Office lives in extreme isolation; receiving nobody, declining all invitations, even those from the Emperor, he spends his old age in a very small circle of old friends, one of whom is Prince Radolin. This *Éminence Grise* who despises the trappings possesses the power. He inspires if he does not direct the foreign policy of the empire and he dominates the staff. M. de Bülow, it is said, would not have accepted the post of Foreign Minister without the assurance of the support of M. de Holstein, an old friend of his father; and Baron Richthofen, who is on pretty bad terms with the omnipotent head of the Political Department, had awaited a superficial reconciliation before he accepted his post. This lack of confidence helps to explain the inability of the latter to give diplomatists any information.'

Germany had a good legal case in Morocco, and the action of France at the end of 1904 suggested that her treaty rights were in jeopardy. The first warning came in January 1905 from Kühlmann, Chargé d'Affaires in Tangier, who observed that his country was in no way bound by the Anglo-French agreement of the previous year; but a more public protest seemed to be required, and it was decided that the Emperor should visit Tangier on his Easter cruise in the Mediterranean. According to Hammann the idea emanated from Holstein, but it was approved by the Chancellor and forced on the reluctant ruler. Such a step required to be thought out to the last

---

[1] Bülow, i. 431.
[2] *Documents Diplomatiques Français*, 2nd series, vi. 60.

detail, yet by an extraordinary oversight the Imperial tourist was not provided with a text in which every word had been weighed. The Emperor's two speeches, writes Bülow in his Memoirs, were sharper than he intended—a result which he foolishly ascribes to the excitement of a rough landing and an unruly steed. The effect upon the highly-strung Holstein was to produce hemorrhage of the stomach, the first manifestation of the illness of which he died four years later.[1]

Holstein's reactions are mirrored in the letters to his cousin. 'I cannot get away, for the whole Morocco question is on my hands.[2] My attack was due to excitement because the Emperor for a time opposed our advice. Later he did his job well. Moments of tension will come before it is over. The English press is trying to intimidate us—a bad sign, for it shows they think it possible.' 'If you could see my life you would understand my silence,' he explained on June 16. 'The work is crushing. I was ill for a whole month. It was a political necessity for the Emperor to go to Tangier, but when an Englishman was nearly murdered there, he was disinclined to land and his entourage encouraged him in this attitude. Even when he was in Lisbon he objected. The excitement about whether he would land or not knocked me up. On March 30, the day before the landing, I was giddy and expected a stroke, but it was only a bad stomach attack. Politically we have achieved much. Delcassé, our cleverest and most dangerous enemy, has fallen. I think the Morocco question will go well. We do not want anything in particular: our aim was to show that we cannot be ignored and above all to overthrow Delcassé. Since our reconciliation last October Bülow has shown me full confidence in these eight months when one difficult question followed another. I have negotiated with him alone and without dispute. Richthofen, the Foreign Minister, is quite out of it, but he is useful to Bülow in Parliamentary matters and as a link with the Ministers. Now and again he asks me about the situation. I exchange ideas with Bülow alone, then I give orders or do the thing myself. My lonely responsibility causes me many a sleepless night. I helped Schiemann with his article this week, though that is not always the case.' Never before had he been so completely the fashioner of German policy.

[1] Holstein told Schwabach that the reading of the speeches made him ill and compelled him to take to his bed. Schwabach, *Aus meinen Akten*, 336.
[2] *Lebensbekenntnis*, 237–240.

When Delcassé sent his chief assistant at the Quai d'Orsay to Berlin to reconnoitre, since Bihourd, the French Ambassador, had lost his nerve, Paléologue reported that Holstein's influence was stronger than ever. The Emperor and Chancellor, if left to themselves, would favour a rapprochement; but the terrible *Éminence Grise* was always whipping them up, and whenever they seemed to be resisting Schlieffen intervened.[1]

The Tangier challenge was followed by the Sultan's invitation to a Conference of the signatories of the 1880 Treaty of Madrid. What seemed to the Wilhelmstrasse, which suggested it, the obvious way out of a dangerous situation appeared to Delcassé as a summons to surrender. Moreover he believed that Germany had no real grievance and no intention of going to war if the invitation were declined. But had he any grounds for assuming that Germany was bluffing? There was a difference of opinion in London. Eckardstein quotes King Edward's angry exclamation: 'Of course we know already from Lascelles that this infernal mischief-maker Holstein is at the bottom of the whole affair.'[2] Hammann pronounces a note drawn up by Holstein for the semi-official organ at the beginning of April to have been a summons to war, and he therefore substituted a milder version of his own. The document has not been found in the Archives, but the available material does not indicate that Holstein was bellicose at this stage and he angrily resented its suppression. 'Why did not my programme for the press, approved by the Chancellor, appear in the *Norddeutsche Allgemeine Zeitung* yesterday?' he complained. 'It was not at all sharp. Yesterday's article was in direct contrast, as it merely regretted that Delcassé had not invited us to share in the negotiations. That makes us look ridiculous, as if we are sulking. If France now proposes separate negotiations, we must reply: "only a general Conference of Treaty Powers;" otherwise we shall be considered as greedy as France. We should therefore say, if possible to-day: "Germany will not take part in any separate agreement in which the Morocco Government and all the Treaty Powers do not share." Our position will only be clear and impregnable when this is

[1] Paléologue, *Un Grand Tournant*.
[2] *Erinnerungen*, iii. 122. Von der Lancken, *Meine Dreissig Dienstjahre*, 57–60, suggests that Holstein's stiff attitude was partly determined by his old friend Schlieffen, Chief of the Staff, who, convinced that Germany would some day have to fight for her life, desired to utilise the Russo-Japanese war for the reckoning with France. See Hugo Rochs, *Schlieffen*, 43–4, 49–50.

the common property of the press. By our present attitude to the public we run the risk of seeming afraid and therefore may easily be compelled to take all the stronger action.'[1]

Hammann promptly counter-attacked. 'Till now our rule with the press was: We go direct to Fez, not *via* Paris. Now it is to be: We go neither to Paris nor to Fez, but to a Conference. The proposed repudiation of any separate agreement contradicts the announcement of the Emperor and the Chancellor that we negotiate direct with the Sultan. If this new idea goes out officially without the most careful preparation of the press, public opinion will be confused. The people, much more than the press, is opposed to a serious conflict with France and England about Morocco. We should therefore avoid everything which would diminish the confidence in the steadiness and coolness of German policy. If we nail our colours to a Conference in the official press we must see it through, else the Chancellor would get a slap in the face.' To this closing reflection Bülow appended the words: 'Quite right.' With Holstein, however, warnings fell on deaf ears. When Jagow, Secretary of Legation in Rome, visited Berlin and told him that the Italians would not co-operate he tartly rejoined 'They must.'

During the anxious weeks between the invitation to a Conference and the fall of Delcassé, Rouvier, who was determined to keep his country out of war, began to take the reins into his own hands. On May 1 Schwabach, head of Bleichröder's bank, was visited by an acquaintance named Betzold, a German residing in Paris, who informed him that the French Premier intended to dismiss Delcassé, and asked him to arrange for an interview with Holstein.[2] Holstein, who had known Betzold in his Paris days, agreed to receive him, and pointed out that in the previous year it would have been easy to reach a direct agreement between Paris and Berlin; now, having at last been compelled to take a stand on treaty rights, it would be difficult for Germany to change her course. He proceeded to accuse Delcassé of hostility and untruthfulness, and added that the only possible explanation of his conduct, now that Russia was temporarily out of action, was British encouragement. In suggesting that the *tempo* of the negotiations should be slowed down and that Delcassé should be

[1] *Die Grosse Politik*, xx. 297-301. Cp. Hammann, *Zur Vorgeschichte des Weltkrieges*, 136.
[2] Schwabach, *Aus meinen Akten*, 290-2.

removed he was forcing an open door, for Betzold replied that Rouvier entirely shared his view of his Foreign Minister.[1]

Rouvier's message about Delcassé enabled Bülow and Holstein to go ahead without fear of war, since they knew that his fall was desired by his own chief. The news of his resignation in June was received with delight in the Wilhelmstrasse, and the Chancellor blossomed into a Prince, but at this moment a slip of the Emperor reduced the dimensions of the victory.[2] Overjoyed at the fall of the obnoxious Minister, the impulsive ruler remarked to General Lacroix, who was representing France at the wedding of the Crown Prince, that all would now be well, that he had never cared about Morocco, and that he did not grudge it to the French. This Imperial impromptu complicated the task of the Wilhelmstrasse throughout the long negotiations that ensued. 'While we, in the sweat of our brow,' wrote Holstein despondingly to Bülow some months later, 'are fighting for a settlement of the Morocco question securing our economic and political interests, His Majesty had long given way. The French knew it, but our public did not, and therefore could not understand why the French Government was weak and yielding before the return of General Lacroix, but firm and self-confident afterwards. They held a direct acceptance from the Emperor.'

Satisfaction at the fall of Delcassé was qualified by the rumour that Great Britain had offered France armed support in the event of war. The story, though completely devoid of foundation, was believed both in Paris and Berlin, and the assumed revelation of British hostility increased the anxieties of Berlin. On June 10, four days after the resignation of the French Minister, the British Ambassador had earnest conversations with Bülow and Holstein.[3] If anyone had told him two years ago, declared the latter, that a war between England and Germany was within the bounds of possibility, he would have laughed; now things had reached such a point that it could no longer be considered impossible. What explanation could be given of the offer to conclude an offensive and defensive alliance with France against Germany? When Lascelles replied, as he had replied to the Chancellor a few minutes earlier, that he did not

[1] *Die Grosse Politik*, xx. 257–9. According to Eckardstein, Betzold carried away the impression that Holstein was determined on war, *Erinnerungen*, iii. 114.
[2] Bülow, ii. 123.
[3] Gooch and Temperley, iii. 80–2.

believe the story, Holstein rejoined that he feared there could be no doubt of its accuracy. He did not apprehend any immediate danger, and the Moroccan question would not lead to any serious complications. Germany's action had been most considerate and conciliatory. She desired no territory and no special privileges, merely commercial opportunity for all. The legend of a British offer of military support was promptly and emphatically denied by Lansdowne; but as it was reiterated by Delcassé and his friends, German statesmen could hardly be expected to believe the assurances of Downing Street.

Holstein's attitude at this moment was explained in a conversation with Chirol.[1] 'His object,' relates the latter, 'was to show me that no more on this occasion than on any other in the course of his long career had his policy been inspired by hostility to England. As it was a *conditio sine qua non* of German security to keep France isolated, Germany was bound to take the earliest opportunity to drive a wedge into the Entente before it had time to consolidate. That his policy had in this respect failed and would continue to fail he flatly refused to believe. It had, he said, succeeded in Paris since the French had already sacrificed Delcassé, who had signed the Anglo-French agreement, and England would very soon realise that she could never rely on the French. He was especially bitter against "the Admirals" who were exploiting the Emperor's mania for ships to drive Germany into a policy of naval expansion which could only be carried out at the expense of her land forces, and, worse still, at the risk of collision with England. He went very near to admitting that a war with France would not have been unwelcome to him, if only because it would have served to bring the Emperor back to the bed-rock of Germany's continental position in Europe from his dangerous vision of her future lying on the seas.'

The French Premier, it was quickly discovered, was not his own master. Rouvier, telegraphed Holstein to Radolin on June 28, was counter-working the Conference without wishing to do so.[2] 'I do not understand why France shirks the Conference, where she is sure to find more support than Germany, if Germany were bent—as she is not—on systematic opposition. On the contrary our plan is to use the opportunity to prepare the way for better relations. This is much more practicable in a Conference than in negotiations *à trois*, where

[1] Chirol, *Fifty Years*, 300–1. [2] *Die Grosse Politik*, xx. 490–3.

the third party is an Oriental. It is easier for Germany to make concessions to France in a Conference than direct.' Radolin showed the telegram to Jean Dupuy, who agreed with every word and promised to explain to Rouvier the gravity of the situation. A private letter of the same date (June 28) to the *Kölnische Zeitung* also shows Holstein in a conciliatory mood. 'I consider the danger of war at the present moment to be extremely small. It will be still smaller if our firmness is understood. Please keep this summary of the situation secret, spare French susceptibilities, and do not give the chauvinistic press (which is to be found rather in England than in France) any excuse for talking of the violence of the German press. If calmly but firmly handled, the French will eventually realise that nobody benefits from the economic paralysis but the English neighbour.'

After wearisome negotiations a preliminary agreement with France was reached on September 28, 1905. The Conference was accepted, and the three principles of the integrity of Morocco, the independence of the Sultan, and the economic equality of the Powers, were recognised as its basis. This left over the vital question of the control of the police in the ports which, as both sides well understood, was to dominate the debates. French policy would obviously depend in large measure on the attitude of Great Britain; and on January 3, 1906, Grey reiterated to the German Ambassador the informal warning, which Lansdowne had given in the previous year, that British opinion might demand intervention if France were to be attacked.[1] The Wilhelmstrasse naturally desired further light on this vital matter, and on January 12 the British Ambassador visited Holstein at the latter's invitation.[2] France, declared the latter, sought a mandate for the organisation of the police in Morocco, which Germany would strenuously resist. There was a danger that France, dissatisfied with the results of the Conference and relying on the support of England in anything she might do, might seek to create a *fait accompli* by invading Morocco; then the Sultan would appeal to the Emperor and war would result. What would England do? The danger would be averted if the British Government hinted that in such a case public opinion in England would probably refuse military aid. Lascelles rejoined that the danger of a French invasion of Morocco seemed very remote. Holstein's suggestion was forwarded to Sir Francis Bertie, British Ambassador in Paris, who

[1] Gooch and Temperley, iii. 209.   [2] *Ibid.*, iii. 222–5.

replied that he was convinced that France would not invade Morocco, and that any such hint to the French Government would shake its confidence in the British Government. Sir Frank Lascelles was accordingly instructed to tell Holstein that the British Government could not deprecate any action on the part of France which came within the terms of the agreement of 1904.

The anxious reflections suggested to Holstein by the British reply were embodied in a memorandum of January 18.[1] 'The outcome of the Conference depends on the way England supports France. The Anglo-French agreement of April 1904 only stipulates diplomatic support. But Lord Lansdowne told Count Metternich that in the event of a Franco-German war it would be difficult to prevent the English people giving military aid. Will England be content with fulfilling her treaty obligations, or will she cover the French flank with her armed hand in the conquest of Morocco and the ensuing complications? That would mean that England, after receiving compensation for her sacrifice, joins France in forcing the other Treaty States to yield without similar compensation. Who is then the attacking party? If England confines herself to her diplomatic *rôle*, France will follow a quiet policy, and the Conference will end in peace with honour for all parties. But if she holds out the prospect of armed support one cannot foretell whether France will resist the temptation once more to turn the world upside down. Some quarters are dissatisfied with the situation to-day and therefore desire such a catastrophe, but I do not think the game is worth the candle for England, Germany or even France.'

On the very day before the opening of the Conference a telegram from the French Minister at Copenhagen, long the whispering-gallery of Europe, encouraged the French Government to take a strong line.[2] 'Information reaching me from many quarters indicates a marked tendency towards a *détente* on the part of Germany, and the Imperial Government neglects no opportunity of displaying it. It is rumoured that a sort of reaction will appear in certain fields of German diplomacy against M. de Holstein, who is held largely responsible for the sharpness and above all the prolongation of tension between France and Germany. Some people attribute the illness of Baron Richthofen to the difficulties arising therefrom.' Holstein's

---

[1] *Die Grosse Politik*, xxi. 96–7.
[2] *Documents Diplomatiques Français*, 2nd series, viii. 547.

influence was more fully realised in the camp of the Western Powers than in his own country, but now at last there seemed a possibility that the man of Tangier might not have things all his own way.

The first month of the Algeciras Conference, which opened on January 16, 1906, revealed the gulf which separated the protagonists and indicated that Germany could rely on Austria alone. Baron de Courcel, ex-Ambassador to Berlin, visited the Wilhelmstrasse on his way home from representing France at the burial of King Christian in Copenhagen, and had three important interviews with Bülow and Holstein on the crisis.[1] The latter urged the internationalisation of the police for four or five years, after which Germany and France could, without a new Conference, make a fresh agreement, and Germany might perhaps hand over Morocco to France in return for concessions elsewhere. The Emperor, he added, would never demand any part of Moroccan territory. Courcel had no great opinion of the value of Morocco, but feared that Germany might drive a wedge between France and England. Of the second interview we know nothing. In the third Holstein declared that, in recognition of her privileged position, France might have exclusive control of one port. All others would be controlled by several states, including Germany and France, each state providing an equal number of officers. As compensation for the privilege given to France Germany must insist on the principle of equality in the Bank, though there also France might perhaps have a slight advantage. Courcel replied that the proposals were not unacceptable but that it was not for him to decide. 'Je suis arrivé a Berlin comme Ambassadeur de France, je pars comme Ambassadeur d'Allemagne.'

Summing up his impressions of the Courcel talks Holstein revealed the governing principle of his policy. 'The rapprochement with England began directly after Fashoda, when the French saw that they could achieve nothing in opposition to her. In the same way they will only begin to entertain the idea of a rapprochement with Germany when they see that the friendship of England—which since the last elections can only be Platonic—does not suffice to obtain Germany's consent to the occupation of Morocco, but that Germany wishes to be loved for her own sake.' Holstein had no preference for war, for he believed that France could be brought by steady pressure to

---

[1] *Die Grosse Politik*, xxi. 206–9. Cp. Tardieu, *La Conférence d'Algéciras*, 241–6.

recognise German rights. It was a tragic miscalculation, for at Fashoda she had stood alone and at Algeciras she was surrounded by friends. Moreover the Liberal victory in January 1906 left British policy entirely unchanged.

A week later, on March 1, General Swaine, who had been on friendly terms with Holstein during his residence in Berlin as Military Attaché, found him incensed against Delcassé and Révoil.[1] He regretted that Nicolson's instructions at Algeciras were blindly to support France instead of forming with his American, Austrian and Italian colleagues a Court of Arbitration to seek some means of satisfying both sides. He believed the Conference would end satisfactorily, but if not, and even if Germany were alone, this would not mean war. France would not attack Germany and Germany would certainly not attack France. Germany, however, had been much pained at the time of the Anglo-French Convention to be regarded as a negligible quantity, which no Great Power would tolerate. Throughout the conversation, reported General Swaine, there was a vein of bitterness in his manner, like a microbe trying to sting, but this was always his way.

So far there is no documentary evidence that Holstein differed from the Chancellor or that he was set on violent courses, though he was obviously willing to take great risks. Hammann complains that for months no one in the Foreign Office knew what he was after, and Rosen goes so far as to say that the whole Morocco chapter was primarily a campaign of revenge by Holstein against Delcassé.[2] The Chancellor now took frequent counsel with Hammann and Mühlberg.[3] The isolation of Germany became increasingly apparent: Austria indeed stood by her side, though without the slightest enthusiasm. The open defection of Italy was the surprise of the Conference, which knew nothing of the Tripoli-Morocco agreement of 1900; and Russia and England drew nearer to each other in their joint support of France. In the background Roosevelt worked for compromise and cautioned Germany not to press France too hard. On March 12, accordingly, the German Government accepted in principle a scheme for the control of the police proposed by Austria.[4]

[1] Gooch and Temperley, iii. 280. Révoil was the chief French representative at Algeciras.
[2] *Aus einem diplomatischen Wanderleben*, i. 42.
[3] Hammann, *Zur Vorgeschichte des Weltkrieges*, 148–51.
[4] *Die Grosse Politik*, xxi. 276–8.

Holstein, whose policy was based on the conviction that France would not fight, was staggered by the decision. 'The Emperor lacks perseverance, without which political successes are impossible,' he lamented to his cousin on March 17,[1] 'and he lacks his grandfather's nerves. That is the worst of it. Foreigners are learning that he yields to strong pressure, and that is a danger. Pressure will often be applied. This I have pointed out but I can do no more.' He took no further part in the negotiations, and, according to Harden, never again spoke of Morocco to the Chancellor.

There is nothing in *Die Grosse Politik* to suggest anything beyond a legitimate difference of opinion between the responsible statesman and his principal adviser. Both were playing with fire, but the Chancellor, like his master, was determined not to get burned. Bülow complains in his spiteful Memoirs, written twenty years later, that his old associate had not been playing the game, and the situation, he declares, was complicated by his relations with the Ambassador in Paris.[2] He had known Radolin since they were fellow students and had persuaded Bülow, against his better judgment, to transfer him from St. Petersburg to Paris in 1900 as Münster's successor. 'I have never asked you for anything,' he had pleaded, 'but to-day I have an urgent wish. I have only one really good friend and that is Radolin. Send him to Paris, if not for his sake, then for mine. As I want neither promotion nor Orders nor any of the honours most people covet, do this at any rate for my friend.' His wish was fulfilled, but when the Morocco crisis arose the Chancellor regretted his decision. For the Ambassador, he complained, looked rather to his patron, who corresponded with him by private cipher, than to the Chancellor, whose instructions were delayed, evaded or incorrectly carried out. Bülow, however, is an exceptionally untrustworthy witness, and the picture of Radolin as a mere tool of Holstein is a caricature. On one occasion, for instance, the Chancellor sent instructions to his Ambassador, relating to a possible meeting between the Emperor and President Loubet, without telling Holstein what he had done; and Radolin, as in duty bound, carried them out. When the suspicious old autocrat learned that his trusted *protégé* had taken independent

---

[1] *Lebensbekenntnis*, 245.
[2] *Denkwürdigkeiten*, i. 496–7. Radolin maintained in Paris that Holstein was pacifically inclined. Tardieu, *La Conférence d'Algéciras*, 74, note and 163, note.

action, he invaded the house of Princess Radolin, who happened to be in Berlin, and angrily declared that her husband would soon lose his post. His wrath only abated when he convinced himself that his sole friend in the diplomatic service had merely fulfilled the precise orders of his chief.[1]

According to Bülow, the end of Holstein's official career was due, not to the increased activity of the Chancellor nor to political disagreement, but to the accident of ministerial change. Richthofen, who had followed Bülow as Foreign Minister in 1900, had been treated throughout as a cipher by his nominal subordinate, and Holstein's career was nearly shipwrecked in 1904 by a particularly gross abuse of his position.[2] The Emperor's toast at the dinner to King Edward at the forthcoming Kiel regatta was drafted as usual in the Foreign Office, but on this occasion Holstein not only drafted but despatched it before it was approved by the Foreign Minister. When Richthofen entered the room and asked to see the draft, he was informed that it had been sent off. When he told Holstein what he thought of him, the offender urged his dismissal on the ground of laziness. The audacious request was refused by Bülow, who commissioned Hammann and Mühlberg, the Under-Secretary, to secure the withdrawal of the resignation he had sent in. The two men grudgingly resumed official co-operation, but the Minister remained a mere figure-head. Their relations are suggested in an anecdote of Eckardstein. When the ex-diplomatist explained the danger of the Morocco situation to Bebel on a visit to Berlin, Richthofen warned him to leave the capital lest the angry Holstein should arrest him, for in these latter days he was known in the Foreign Office as 'the mad hyaena.'[3]

When Richthofen died of a stroke in January 1906 Bülow sought a successor who was not *persona ingrata* to Holstein.[4] The choice fell on Tschirschky, whom the latter approved as a friend of his favourite Radolin. 'Since December 30,' he wrote to his cousin on January 20, 'I was ready to go, having sent in my resignation.[5] Bülow, whose weakness spoiled my game, would not let me. So I remain for the time and will see what happens with the new Minister.

[1] Information supplied by Princess Radolin.
[2] Hammann, *Zur Vorgeschichte des Weltkrieges*, 127–9, and *Bilder aus der etzten Kaiserzeit*, 29–34.
[3] Haller, *Die Aera Bülow*, 35.
[4] Bülow, ii. 214–5.   [5] *Lebensbekenntnis*, 224.

That post I could not take, but I have asked to be Director of the Political Department. I have done the work for decades and have hitherto declined all promotion, but now, with a new Minister, I must have a secure position or go. Bülow consents.' The new Foreign Minister was not expecting a bed of roses. 'The difficulties of my post I know better than anyone,' he confided to Monts on January 30.[1] 'His Majesty, Bülow and Holstein! Each is enough to frighten one, despite their talents and virtues. I hope Holstein will not prove too difficult.'

Tschirschky's hopes were disappointed, and on March 28 he confided to Monts that Holstein must be removed. 'He has become impossible. He no longer works, only butts in occasionally with some plan based on personal motives. His whole aim recently was that we should wreck the Conference.' For many years he had enjoyed the privilege of entering the room of the Minister unannounced. These sudden invasions proved too much for Tschirschky, who locked the door; and when the old Geheimrat entered from the corridor with a bundle of papers he was invited to lay them on the table and to wait till he was called. After ruling for sixteen years he was not content to serve a man whom he called a menial (Hausknecht). 'As I am nearly seventy,' he wrote to his cousin on March 17, 'I shall not be here long. And for an old man it is always difficult to obey. When I shall go I cannot say. Bülow does his utmost to keep me.' An official resignation was despatched on April 3, accompanied by a private letter to the Chancellor.[2] 'The Foreign Office is too small for Tschirschky and myself. Please accept my request to resign. It is best for my dignity and peace of mind to make an end.' According to Eulenburg it was the fifteenth time that he had played this card, according to Holstein himself only the fourth. 'He was convinced,' writes Bülow who knew his ways, 'that I should prevent acceptance,' but the old campaigner had not allowed for the chapter of accidents.

On April 4, the day after despatching his letter of resignation, Holstein described the crisis to his cousin.[3] 'Two days ago I gave the Chancellor my resignation. I was with him from 6.30 to 11, but could not persuade him to forward it. He locked it up and wished to think it over. So yesterday I sent the request to the Foreign Office.

---

[1] Monts, 439–44.
[2] See Holstein's account in *Die Zukunft*, October 18, 1907.
[3] *Lebensbekenntnis*, 245–7.

So it is settled. I withdraw not on account of the press articles, which I do not greatly mind, but because I conclude from the attitude of the new Minister that the Emperor wants me to go. In these long years it was often my fate to oppose his projects with solid arguments. Then people told him "Holstein is against that." Thus he gradually took a strong objection to me and used the Moroccan question to get rid of me and as a warning to all who might think of opposing him. In that matter I took the view that we should stand firm in the conviction that the neutrals would come forward with mediation plans. Russia needs a big loan, Italy is converting her debt, England wants to diminish the guilt of the Boer War. All need not only peace —which was never endangered—but settled conditions. They would certainly have come forward with proposals directly they saw the Conference was in danger. My view was shared by the Chancellor, the Foreign Minister, and the Under-Secretary. But the Emperor got a fright when the papers announced that Delcassé had been summoned to the King of England. Our most gracious Majesty has much imagination and weak nerves. He wrote to Bülow that we must yield. I regret it in view of the future, for the other Cabinets will remember that in similar circumstances Germany yielded to pressure. They will apply the same method and then there would be real danger, whereas the Morocco question was not at all dangerous. That I who for sixteen years have striven to avoid a threat to our safety should now be regarded as a warmonger is an irony of fate.'

On April 5 the Chancellor, worn out by the Moroccan crisis, fainted at the close of a speech in the Reichstag. On the same day the British Ambassador, who had received a note from Holstein stating that he had sent in his resignation on April 3, visited him at his request in the Foreign Office.[1] Lascelles found him greatly agitated as he had just heard of the Chancellor's seizure. 'He said he had asked me to call on him in order to speak about his resignation on account of his disapproval of the manner in which the business of the Press Bureau was conducted, but was induced to withdraw it at the urgent request of Prince Bülow who had assured him of his support. I had no doubt seen the recent attacks on him in the press, one of which had been directly inspired by a high official in the diplomatic service. This alone would not have induced him to resign; but he had received information, which he could not doubt, that the Emperor had been assured that the British Government regarded him as the

[1] Gooch and Temperley, iii. 332–4.

one obstacle to the establishment of friendly relations between England and Germany. I said that he had astonished me very greatly. I had always understood that he had desired a friendly understanding between our two countries, although we might have had considerable differences of opinion on certain points and perhaps on the methods of bringing it about, but I never doubted the sincerity of his wish for the maintenance of peace between the two countries. Herr von Holstein said that he was inclined to believe that the information given to the Emperor had been invented, but His Majesty seemed to believe it and would probably have dismissed him before long. There could be no doubt that the Emperor desired a friendly understanding with England. So far his attempts to bring one about had not been successful and he required a scapegoat, which he had now found. I said I understood that in the position which he held it was only natural that he should have made some enemies who were jealous of the influence he possessed. To this he replied that his influence had been very greatly exaggerated. It was true that he was consulted on all important matters of foreign policy, but he was in the position of the man whose advice was sometimes taken, sometimes rejected, and sometimes partly taken. His influence therefore could not be considered as very great, but such as it was it had no doubt created jealousies which had been employed with great effect against him. He was now sixty-nine years old. His eyesight was failing. He had done his work, at least his work was now finished, and in any case it could not have continued much longer; but it was hard that he should be misrepresented as an obstacle to a friendly understanding with England, when the cardinal point of his policy had been that a war between the two countries would be the greatest calamity that could happen to either. It would be a satisfaction to him in his retirement if he could think that his sovereign should some day know that he had been misrepresented, and he would be gratified, if the opportunity should arise, that I should tell His Majesty that in my opinion he ought not to be considered as an enemy of England.'[1]

[1] In a minute on this despatch Sir Eyre Crowe wrote: 'Herr von Holstein has not, I think, been a friend to this country. . . . It is not unjust that he should now pay the penalty of having persistently failed to appreciate the position which England really occupies in the world (so long as she is strong).'

Sir Eric Barrington wrote: 'Herr von Holstein is modest with regard to the influence he exercised, but members of the German Embassy here have always assured me that, no matter who was Foreign Minister at Berlin, the policy was invariably his.'

On the morning of April 5 Tschirschky informed William II of Holstein's request to resign. According to Hammann the Emperor congratulated the Foreign Minister, and the matter was officially concluded on April 16.[1] The victim believed that he had been sacrificed while the ailing Chancellor was unaware of events, for it seemed unthinkable that his old chief should let him go. He had been living, however, in a fool's paradise, and Bülow's Memoirs reveal what he had come to think of 'the incorrigible intriguer.' Two years earlier, wearied by the unceasing feuds between Holstein and the staff, he had told him that unless there was peace he would be regretfully compelled to dispense with his services.[2] Holstein immediately informed the Emperor of the warning through his friend Radolin, and at their next meeting the Chancellor was greeted with the words: 'I tell you, Bernhard, you must leave my good old Holstein alone. He was the only man who stood by me loyally in my fight against Bismarck.' The Emperor, however, who, like Bülow, wished to untie the Moroccan knot instead of cutting it, was now ready and indeed eager for the change. When shortly afterwards the Chancellor was dilating on the incapacity of the Foreign Minister, the monarch interrupted him: 'I must beg you, dear Bernhard, to leave Tschirschky alone. He was the only man who stood loyally by my side in my struggle against the diabolical Holstein.'[3] 'The Monster' had at last reaped what he had sown, for he was now without a friend in Berlin.

When it was all over, he despatched a long report to Monts dated April 22.[4] 'The two who shot me out were Hammann and Phili. Since April 1905 the former has been holding me up in all the papers as the enemy of France and a warmonger, and Phili sees they reach the Emperor. Moreover Phili and Radowitz have corresponded during the Conference. Finally there is an ominous intimacy between Phili and the French Councillor of Embassy Lecomte. That press campaign ruined my political reputation and also weakened Bülow's position. In my two previous conflicts with the Richthofen-Hammann group Bülow took my side and others had to give way. But this time, when I told him at the beginning of April that Tschirschky's attitude made it impossible to remain, we both felt that Tschirschky's side would win since the Emperor had been systematically turned against

---

[1] *Die Grosse Politik*, xxi. 338–9, note. The resignation was announced on April 18.
[2] *Denkwürdigkeiten*, ii. 216.
[3] Höllensohn.   [4] Monts, *Erinnerungen*, 358–60.

me. How could Bülow recommend my continuance in office after I had been held up in the press of every country as a light-hearted warmonger? Poor Bülow felt and saw he could drift no longer. Meanwhile he locked up my resignation which we had discussed 6.30–11.30 and wanted to think out a compromise. Next morning, on April 3, I read that the Order of the Black Eagle had been given to Phili and Radowitz. As this confirmed the rumour of a secret action against the Government policy I sent a duplicate of my resignation to the Foreign Office and so informed Bülow. He replied I must give him time: he would present it orally to the Emperor. He will have had some *modus vivendi* in mind, but next day he fell ill. On April 17 Tschirschky wrote that "in accordance with the instructions of the Chancellor" my resignation had been laid before the Emperor and accepted. "The instructions" is incorrect. Bülow could not issue them till April 16 even if he had so desired. They wished to end the matter so that nothing should intervene. Your old comrade Holstein.' Monts had earned the privilege of this detailed communication by a letter of condolence. 'After Bismarck's death you always seemed to me the embodiment of the great days that are gone, the living tradition of the statecraft which raised Germany so high. My confidence in you was like a rock.' In a subsequent letter to Tschirschky Monts described Holstein as an honourable man, 'whereas we know that Bülow treats truth as a navigator treats the pole-star, seeing where it is without always steering by it,' These eulogies, however, did not prevent Monts from describing Holstein after his death as half crazy.

The other side of the story is found in a letter of April 13 from Tschirschky to Monts.[1] 'I and all who have recently worked with Bülow are convinced that Holstein is chiefly responsible for his mental and physical collapse. You cannot imagine how ingeniously and unceasingly he has tormented poor Bülow. When I came here I had no notion, but I soon saw these conditions could not last. Owing to Holstein Bülow had to do four times the work. Rightly assuming that he never has solid reasons for his daily changing proposals, Bülow worried every time about what he was after, whether intriguing against him, or me, or someone else. No conversation was possible without endless speculation on his obscure designs. An impossible situation! He sent his resignation and Bülow resolved to present it to the Emperor. Then came the illness and it remained locked in his

[1] Monts, *Erinnerungen*, 442–4.

table. Though I know he was resolved to let him go, and I am also sure about the Emperor, I shall not act without Bülow or behind his back. So we must wait till he is well enough to deal with it. Holstein has asked for leave; he hardly worked all the winter. This does not prevent him coming daily to the office if no one is here and he summons journalists and even Ambassadors. Personally I have had no particular friction with him, but he saw I would not be his slave. I have discussed it all with His Majesty and I am convinced there was nothing else to be done, for the good of everybody, and above all Bülow.'

What was Bülow's real part in the catastrophe? 'Holstein had laid his plans carefully,' he writes in his Memoirs, 'but it had not occurred to him that I should fall ill and by doctor's orders be beyond the reach of interviews and documents at the very moment when his letter came into the hands of his enemy Tschirschky, who used the favourable opportunity to butcher him in cold blood.'[1] This was the version which Holstein believed or tried to believe[2] and which rendered possible their continued intercourse, but it is none the less incorrect. Holstein admitted that the Chancellor may have needed a scapegoat and he never again fully trusted his old chief, but, as Monts explains, he refused to admit Bülow's part in order to keep in touch with official circles. In January the Chancellor had yielded to his request to be made Director of the Political Department, but he assured the exasperated Hammann that he would part with him when the Conference was over.[3] Moreover we learn from *Die Grosse Politik* that in informing the Emperor of the letter on April 5 Tschirschky was acting in agreement with Bülow, and when the matter was formally dealt with on April 16 it was again with his knowledge.[4] For on April 14 Karl Ulrich von Bülow wrote to Tschirschky: 'I beg to inform Your Excellency that yesterday my brother requested me to ask Your Excellency to settle the affair of Herr von Holstein with His Majesty.' The Chancellor, it is perfectly clear, never lifted a finger to save his old subordinate, as William II revealed in his Memoirs.[5] His fall was hailed with delight in Paris, where the *Journal*

---

[1] Bülow, ii, 215.
[2] 'Briefe des Geheimrats von Holstein,' *Süddeutsche Monatshefte*, March 1919.
[3] The fullest account of the events which led to his resignation is in Hammann, *Bilder aus der letzten Kaiserzeit*, 29–39. Cp. Hutten-Czapski, i. 463–81.
[4] *Die Grosse Politik*, xxi. 338–9. This confirms Hammann's statements.
[5] *Ereignisse und Gestalten*, 86.

des Débats described him as France's most dangerous enemy since Bismarck; and no tears were shed in the Wilhelmstrasse at the disappearance of the capricious autocrat. The fiercest condemnation came from Maximilian Harden in the *Neue Freie Presse* on June 3. 'He had no idea that by his crazy rage he himself helped to create the new partnership of the Western Powers. When Bismarck went France was isolated; when Holstein went it was Germany. No realm had been conquered, no useful tradition bequeathed, no human heart won. Great and small breathed more freely at his dismissal, and he would have been quickly forgotten had not the survivors feared his wrath, some revelation, a bombardment with paper bullets.'

X

HOLSTEIN received brilliants of the First Class of the Red Eagle for his services, but the acceptance of his resignation filled him with the same incredulous fury that had maddened Bismarck sixteen years earlier, and he glared round for the snake in the grass. He knew that the Emperor was not his friend. On mentioning Holstein's name in conversation with William II at Homburg in August, 1906,[1] Lascelles was astonished at the outburst of indignation which it evoked. 'His Majesty said that he was a most dangerous man. He had, no doubt, great ability, but the influence he exercised over the German Foreign Office was a most pernicious one. Had Herr von Holstein had his way the Algeciras Conference would have broken down, and His Majesty himself had been obliged to intervene strenuously to prevent instructions being sent to the German representatives which would at once have brought the Conference to an end.' It was clear, commented the Ambassador, that Holstein was made the scapegoat for the failure of German diplomacy. In the following spring the Emperor's wrath was still hot. 'Herr von Holstein,' he minuted on a despatch describing Tardieu's history of the Algeciras Conference,[2] 'so altered my very definite instructions and arrangements with the Chancellor that finally the opposite was done. He has again and again stirred up and injected poison against France, and so worked on the Chancellor that to my intense astonishment he asked me on several occasions whether I wished for war with France, whereas my

[1] Gooch and Temperley, iii. 365-6.
[2] *Die Grosse Politik*, xxi. 566-7.

instructions were clear: The Algeciras Conference is to be the stepping-stone of the agreement between France and Germany.'[1]

Having assumed without the slightest reason that Eulenburg, who had lived in retirement since 1902, was the chief offender, Holstein wrote him a violent letter.[2] 'My eviction, which has been your goal for many years, is at last attained, and the low attacks on me have your approval.' He added that for certain reasons Eulenburg was a man whom it was best to avoid. The Prince read the letter with horror, hurried off to Berlin, sent a challenge to his tormentor, and reported to the Foreign Office. Tschirschky and the Under-Secretary Mühlberg, anxious to avoid a scandal, sent Geheimrat Kriege to tell Holstein that he must withdraw, and the infuriated old man was persuaded to sign the following apology: 'Since Prince Eulenburg has declared on his word of honour that he had nothing to do with my dismissal or the press attacks, I withdraw the wounding expressions in my letter on May 1.' Eulenburg had in fact learned of the resignation from the Emperor himself, who explained that it was impossible to keep him and that he was now quite mad.

The Prince knew his old associate well enough to realise that his apology was not a capitulation, and he foretold that the implacable eccentric would revenge himself. He had not long to wait, for on August 17 the *Zukunft* published a letter from Holstein defending himself against Harden's criticisms of his Moroccan policy, denying the assertion that he had controlled affairs since the fall of Bismarck, and attributing his resignation to departmental differences. The rapprochement of the two men who had long detested each other filled Eulenburg with dark foreboding. 'I consider the Holstein-Harden alliance an ominous affair, and not I alone,' he wrote; 'whoever knows these conspirators shares my opinion. What will they brew?' On November 24 the *Zukunft*, in a flamboyant article entitled 'Dies Irae,' denounced some of the closest associates of the Emperor—'the Liebenberg Round Table' [3]—as political mischief-makers and as a coterie in which spiritualism, faith-healing and other morbid tendencies were rife. A fortnight later Harden wrote that he would hesitate three times before declaring that any man was an intimate of Eulen-

---

[1] The last sentence is in English.
[2] Eulenburg's side of the story is told in Haller, *Eulenburg*, 313-63, and Muschler, *Philipp zu Eulenburg*, 605-61.
[3] Liebenberg was Eulenburg's country home.

burg. Finally, on April 27, 1907, he openly charged the Prince with sexual abnormalities. None of his ammunition, he declares, was supplied by Holstein, who always repudiated the charge.[1]

'Tschirschky has told the Emperor that all Harden's articles are inspired by me,' reported Holstein to his cousin on November 4, 1907.[2] 'My enemy Hammann, head of the Press Bureau, deals out the same story. His object is so to incense the Emperor against me that he forbids Bülow to consort with me, and I hear he has talked to the Chancellor in this sense. Bülow, who apparently has no wish for a break, replied that he had not broken with Herbert Bismarck. I am quite indifferent. Since Bülow so rarely follows my advice our association had only uncomfortable or disagreeable results for me. When I was reproached for helping to overthrow Bismarck it was hard to bear. But the reproach for getting rid of Phili Eulenburg and Lecomte does not worry me, even if it were all true. But I never mentioned Lecomte to Harden.' A few days later he wrote to Monts in a similar strain.[3] 'Bülow and his mother-in-law wrote to invite me, but I have politely declined. It is degrading to be treated with the greatest friendliness while one is attacked in the Chancellor's press during the last nineteen months. First I was blamed for Morocco, then for the Harden scandal. I know that Bülow told somebody that I stirred up Harden. I know also that Bülow and his press bureau is in touch with Harden. I think the latter's campaign a lesser evil than the continuance of the abominations he has exposed. Yet I gave Harden no material with which he could risk a lawsuit. I received material direct from Bülow, I suppose to forward to Harden, which I did not. I only told him what I told Eulenburg himself—that I regard him as a low and dangerous man. Bülow told me of the relations of Eulenburg and Lecomte, of which I knew nothing.' Eulenburg and Bülow, however, found his hand in the plot, and they used to call him the weasel since he never desisted till he had cleared out the hen-roost.

'I am wholly innocent,' wrote Eulenburg to Bülow, 'but I am afraid of false testimony as Holstein would not stick at 10,000 marks

---

[1] For Harden's side of the controversy, see his 'Holstein' in *Köpfe*, vol. i. and his 'Eulenburg' in *Köpfe*, vol. iii. For Holstein's share in a seemingly compromising document in the Foreign Office, see Muschler, pp. 465–8, 512, and Haller, 323–4. Eulenburg's two biographers have no doubt that Holstein supplied Harden with material. Trotha denies the charge, while admitting that he was a good hater.

[2] *Lebensbekenntnis*, 294–6.   [3] Monts, 297–8.

if he could find a good witness.' There is no need here to describe the unsavoury Harden and Eulenburg trials, for Holstein remained in the background. Count Kuno Moltke emerged unscathed; but as a breakdown of the Prince's health prevented the completion of trial for perjury, friends continued to assert his innocence and foes his guilt. After an exhaustive examination of the evidence his biographer, Professor Johannes Haller, a trained historian, pronounces him a deeply injured man who bore his sufferings with Christian resignation, and his judgment is confirmed by his later biographer Muschler. On the other hand, though only one of Harden's witnesses could be taken seriously, the evidence of the fisherman of the Starnberger See left an abiding impression on the public mind, all the more since there had been gossip of the sort for many years. Eulenburg's scutcheon was tarnished, and William II terminated the most cherished friendship of his life. Bülow acidly suggests that if Holstein's deathbed, like that of Richard III, was haunted by ghosts of his victims, the spectre of Eulenburg was in the van.

A series of letters to the editor of a South German paper during the spring of 1906 began the campaign of the fallen autocrat for the vindication of his policies.[1] The first, dated April 23, complained of the belief that he sought war with France. 'I am too much of a Royalist to say that His Majesty employed these rumours as a pretext, but that I had long been out of favour you know as well as I.' The chief author of his fall, he suggests, was Hammann, head of the Press Bureau, which he compares to a swollen liver. 'I shall not start a press campaign, partly in order not to damage the Chancellor. His position is not improved by my departure, which was forced through while he was ill.' Writing again on May 13, he thanks the editor for his support. The Moroccan question, he added, was never dangerous, for France would not have fought. First to threaten and then to climb down was a strategy which could lead to no good result, and German policy had suffered from a failure of nerve. A third letter, written a fortnight later, finds confirmation of his judgment in the aggressive attitude of the French press—the first manifestation of such a spirit since 1870. The surrender of Germany, he feared, would encourage France to put forward impossible demands, even perhaps for a revision of the Treaty of Frankfurt.

[1] The letters were subsequently published in the *Süddeutsche Monatshefte*, March 1919.

The apologia was developed at greater length in two unsigned articles in the *Schlesische Zeitung*, denying that a policy of firmness involved the risk of war, which he forwarded to his cousin with a covering letter on May 28.[1] 'I regard the efforts of the Flottenverein as foolish and dangerous. Experts recognise that since the Morocco Conference people talk to us in a different way. They see that His Majesty has weak nerves and therein lies grave danger. France fears a victorious General more than an enemy army. The English Jingo party was smashed at the election. England has only one cause of disquiet—the German fleet or rather the chauvinist tone of the press. While this lasts she will stick to France. So, if war comes, England and France will be allies. Our fleet would have to be as strong as theirs combined; if not, it would be an element of weakness. Too much attention is paid to the fleet, too little to the army. The fleet alarms neighbours and drives them to unite. So we must reckon with a French-English-Russian war.' This was a significant admission, but till the end of his life he argued that his Moroccan policy was perfectly sound and only needed to be carried out by men with strong nerves like himself. 'The cleverest living diplomatist is King Edward,' he wrote to his cousin on June 12;[2] 'our Emperor is not a politician.' A signed letter in Harden's *Zukunft* of August 18 corrected errors in recent articles by the Editor. That he had decided everything since the fall of Bismarck he denies. 'It is sufficiently known in and outside the Foreign Office that I had no share in the shaping of the political transactions which have often been regarded as causes of the Anglo-French rapprochement of April, 1904: I mean, the Kruger telegram, the Bagdad railway project, and the anti-English speeches in the Reichstag. In each case I was faced by a *fait accompli* or a decision on policy.' Like many other fallen autocrats he cherished the illusion of infallibility.

The end of Holstein's official career was not the termination of his influence, for he remained in close touch with Bülow till the day of his death. The Chancellor's position was rudely shaken by the Morocco crisis, but the Emperor had no other candidate in sight and he remained in office for another three years. In 1907 Lascelles reported that the two men were on the best of terms and met frequently at the Chancellor's house, whereas the door of the Foreign

---

[1] *Lebensbekenntnis*, 253–4.
[2] *Ibid.*, 258.

Office was closed to him.[1] The Chancellor explained to his friends that he continued to see him because he knew too much and might reveal secrets, and secondly because as a gentleman he could not cut a man with whom he had been associated for thirty or forty years.[2] Hammann was convinced that Bülow's sole motive was to avert the betrayal of diplomatic secrets. A very different explanation, offered by Johannes Haller after the Prince's death, asserts that the old Geheimrat had procured copies of letters compromising the reputation of Princess Bülow in her earlier years; and Raschdau, the last survivor of the Bismarckian Foreign Office, had received confidences from Holstein which, he declares, compromised the character of the Chancellor himself.[3] Whatever were the reasons for their continued association, Bülow kept him fully informed and freely sought his advice. 'He sees Bülow every day for hours,' reported Princess Radziwill in March 1907, repeating and exaggerating the gossip of the capital.[4] When Haussmann complained in the Reichstag on December 10, 1908, that he had played the *rôle* of 'a little Delcassé,' and had been in the habit of requiring German diplomatists to correct their despatches, the Chancellor threw his shield over his old subordinate.[5] He had grown grey in long and arduous service under four Chancellors; he was a man of strong and watchful patriotism, who had defended German interests for a generation; and his exceptional industry, outstanding political capacity and independent character had won the respect of all who knew him.

On the occasion of a visit of British journalists to Germany in the summer of 1907, Alfred Spender, Editor of the *Westminster Gazette*, called on the Chancellor in his official residence.[6] At the end of the conversation Bülow remarked: 'Come along, I must introduce you to Holstein.' He was sitting in an adjoining room—a stout, elderly man of rather forbidding appearance, who spoke perfect English without a trace of German accent. Bülow introduced his visitor as 'the editor of one of the friendly papers.' 'Pardon me, Prince,' came the sharp reply, 'one of the relatively friendly papers.' 'He seemed beside him-

---

[1] Gooch and Temperley, iii. 333, note. According to Hans von Flotow he arrived in the dark and was admitted through a special door, the servants being pledged to secrecy. *Süddeutsche Monatshefte*, March 1931, 399.
[2] *Denkwürdigkeiten*, iii. 48–9.
[3] *Süddeutsche Monatshefte*, March 1931, 390.
[4] *Lettres*, iii. 287. [5] Bülow, *Reden*, iii. 164.
[6] Spender, *Life, Politics and Journalism*, i. 210–1.

self with anger, and was about to display an intimate knowledge of a certain article I had written on the Morocco question nearly two years previously when the Prince turned the conversation to English books and literature. Holstein then recovered his temper, and quoted Kipling with much admiration. Then, as he seemed to be getting back to Morocco, the Prince said he must go and dress.' When Spender returned to London and reported the adventure to Count Metternich, the Ambassador bluntly exclaimed that it was impossible. Benckendorff, the Russian Ambassador, was almost equally sceptical. The unbroken intimacy with the Chancellor is confirmed by the biography of Kiderlen, with whom Holstein remained on excellent terms till his death, and by his letters to his cousin. It was natural that he should denounce the doings of Tschirschky, whom the Emperor, he bitterly observed, loved for his pliability; but the confidence of the highest official in the land was a compensation for the hostility of lesser lights. 'Aehrenthal's visit has made a good impression,' he wrote to Kiderlen in May 1907; 'Bülow told me all about it.' The Chancellor, he added, had talked to him the last two Mondays for two hours on each occasion.[1]

In the autumn of 1907 Holstein again addressed his countrymen in his own name. In a letter published in the *Zukunft* of October 18, after thanking the Editor for defending him against attacks on his Moroccan policy, he declared himself compelled to correct the misstatements which the Foreign Office had done nothing to rectify.[2] He denied that his resignation was due to difference of opinion with Tschirschky, for nothing was or could be settled without the concurrence of the Chancellor who maintained personal control throughout the negotiations. He was unaware of any difference with Bülow until 'the change of front' on March 12, after which he ceased to take any part in Moroccan affairs. 'That I ever pursued other aims in Morocco than his or employed methods not approved by him is an invention.' The statement may be true in the sense that Bülow on some occasions yielded to his arguments without being fully convinced, but the fact remains that the Chancellor at last found himself compelled to seize the rudder lest the ship should be steered straight into the rapids.

[1] Jäckh, *Kiderlen*, i. 225.
[2] The letter was summarised in a despatch from Sir F. Lascelles, October 23 1907. Gooch and Temperley, iii. 332–3, note.

The three main international problems during Holstein's closing years were the naval rivalry with Great Britain, the Bosnian crisis, and the Morocco problem. In regard to the first his record was good, though he had never thrown his whole weight against the dangerous Tirpitz policy. On one occasion he urged Schwabach to introduce a resolution in the Berlin Chamber of Commerce condemning excessive ship-building,[1] but as a rule he contented himself with grumbling. The fleet, testifies Harden, was the bitterest anxiety of his closing years. 'Navy fever,' wrote Holstein to a friend in December 1907, 'rages in Germany.[2] This dangerous illness is nourished by the groundless fear of an English attack. It produces three bad results—in domestic policy through the activities of the Navy League, in finance by the endless expenditure, in foreign policy by the mistrust that this arming provokes. England sees in it a threat which binds her to the side of France, and it is impossible, however we tax ourselves, to build a fleet equal to those of England and France in combination. The Liberal Ministry will not draw the logical conclusion from the menace which is universally recognised, but the Conservatives will do so. Many members of the Reichstag condemn the Navy fever, but nobody will take the responsibility of opposing the demand for ships. If one resists the fever one is denounced as unpatriotic, but in a few years the correctness of my view will be recognised. We must expose the lying phrase that every new vessel increases the power of the Reich, for every new ship causes England to build two.'

The Emperor's letter to Lord Tweedmouth in March 1908 moved Holstein to sarcastic comment in a letter to his cousin.[3] 'It amused me. Another proof of his resemblance to his mother, of whom Lord Ampthill said that she would write her head off! The letter is harmless in content, but the idea of writing to the Navy Minister about naval matters is utterly tactless. The discussion in Parliament was very correct, but the King answered rudely: 'This is quite a new procedure.' So long as the Flottenverein presents England to the German people as the hereditary enemy, we cannot wonder at the English distrust, and I am surprised it is not greater.' That Bülow attempted at the eleventh hour to slow down the pace

---

[1] Schwabach, *Aus meinen Akten*, 442–3.
[2] Hermann von Rath, 'Erinnerungen an Holstein,' in *Deutsche Revue*, October 1909, 17–18.
[3] *Lebenskenntnis*, 308.

may well have been partially due to the influence of his old adviser. According to the latter they usually met twice a week and corresponded almost every day. Unfortunately the Chancellor had waited too long, for his days were numbered and in naval affairs Tirpitz was now in control.

Holstein had always been anti-Russian, and when the Bosnian crisis broke over Europe his position was clear. From the lonely farmhouse in the Harz, where as usual he was spending his summer holiday, he wrote to the Chancellor urging him to support the annexation even though he had not approved it. In the British demand for a Conference he detected an attempt to break up the Austro-German alliance. Austria, he declared, would regard it as a deadly insult to be placed in the dock, and if Germany consented the friendship with Vienna would be at an end. 'If we hold fast, the object of the whole *Einkreisungspolitik* is frustrated.' The news leaked out that he was trying to regain influence, and his 'unofficial councils' were criticised in the Reichstag, but once again the Chancellor rallied to his defence.[1]

On October 19, 1908, Chirol had a long conversation with his old friend, and was struck by the tone of authority in which he surveyed German policy.[2] 'Had he been Foreign Minister he could not have spoken with more assurance. He was probably conscious of the impression he was making on me, for as we parted he said: "Of course I no longer speak as a responsible official, but I need not tell you that I still know perfectly well what I am talking about." ' After fighting the old battles of the Kruger telegram and the Tangier visit over again he passed on to the two burning issues of the time. He had always been opposed to excessive shipbuilding, he explained, not only because it would lead to ruinous competition but because it might involve the neglect of the army, which was a matter of life and death. He added that Bülow would strive against any further expansion and indeed would make a Cabinet question of it. He went on to complain that he was tarred with the brush of Anglophobia and that probably nothing he could say would destroy that legend. Passing to the Bosnian crisis he urged that Austria could not safely have postponed action. 'We might have used our good offices in Vienna had we been

[1] On December 10, 1908.
[2] Gooch and Temperley, vi. 158-61. His position was well understood in Downing Street.

consulted, but as usual we were not. You must not be under any misapprehension. We are not going to desert our ally.' The conversation ended with a warning against the danger of irritating Austria. 'Remember, there we come in too. I do not want to say too much about our Emperor and it is not for me to pose as his champion. He is only too much inclined to blow hot and cold, and his bark is worse than his bite. He too will never go to war if he can help it. But there are two things he could not stand: if France were to give any open provocation, or if Austria were threatened.' His last words to his visitor were that the Emperor would either die in a madhouse or destroy the German Empire.[1]

Holstein had constantly urged the Chancellor to summon Kiderlen from Bucharest to the Foreign Office, since Schön, who succeeded Tschirschky in 1907, was unequal to his task. Kiderlen, he had often remarked to Hutten-Czapski, was the only independent person in the diplomatic service. He was delighted that his old colleague was appointed Acting Minister in November 1908 when the Bosnian crisis was at its height, and the two men were in close contact during the five months of Schön's absence through illness. One of Kiderlen's first visits was to Holstein's flat, and his letters show that he found time for several more.[2] In February 1909 Holstein told his cousin that the Foreign Minister came to him twice a week. Advancing years had in no way diminished the feverish interest with which the old warhorse watched the swaying fortunes of the campaign. 'I had a very excited express letter from Fritz, whom the Emperor's New Year's language has robbed of his sleep,' wrote Kiderlen on January 10, 1909, in referring to the Imperial comments on Schlieffen's famous article on Germany's military prospects.[3] 'I am glad to have been there, for he was visibly relieved when I came, and repeatedly said that he could talk things out with me and could only be reassured about public affairs if he did. Recently he became so excited that he thought the Chancellor ought to threaten to resign. He had already drawn up an eight-page letter of resignation for him which he read to me. I talked him out of it, but I fear he is ill.'

Holstein warmly applauded the Chancellor's handling of the Bosnian crisis and was ever ready with advice. He was no friend of

---

[1] This item comes not from the report to the Foreign Office but from *Fifty Years*, 301.
[2] Jäckh, *Kiderlen*, ii. 2.   [3] *Ibid.*, ii. 21.

the Russians, testifies Trotha, thinking them deceitful and false. Indeed Hans von Flotow, at that time an official in the Foreign Office and later Ambassador at Rome, declares that the whole policy was his.[1] He denounced the pro-Turkish sentiment of the Foreign Office and ironically suggested that the gentlemen of the Wilhelmstrasse should all wear a fez. In an undated letter of November 1908 he urged Bülow to declare that Bosnia was an Austrian domestic question. England, he added, seemed to be making a last attempt to bring about a Turco-Bulgar war, which could easily be prevented by a reference to the Hague Court. 'Perhaps you will discuss with Kiderlen whether Rosenberg should speak to the Prince in this sense, if he is consulted, as is probable.' In the following month the Chancellor explained to Monts, the German Ambassador in Rome, the importance of keeping Aehrenthal in office, and for this purpose Austria should not be frightened by emphasising the Italian danger. 'If there was too much talk of Italian faithlessness it would confirm the tendency of Vienna to immobilise a needlessly large force on the Italian frontier, which, in the event of a war with Russia, would be a disadvantage to Germany as well as to Austria. I have discussed these questions fully with Holstein, Kiderlen and Jagow, and the military aspects with Moltke; all of them absolutely agree to this course.' With Bülow and Kiderlen in office, a first-class European crisis in full swing, and his counsel continually in demand, the last winter of Holstein's life was the happiest time of his failing years. 'People came to consult him,' remarks Trotha; 'he never ran after anyone.' He frequented one or two houses where he knew that he would not meet strangers, particularly that of Frau von Lebbin, widow of a Prussian official who had stood by him during the Arnim crisis. Paul von Schwabach, the well-informed head of Bleichröder's bank, wrote him long letters about high politics,[2] and Harden's friendship was a delight. Though he loved good literature, the conversation never strayed far from foreign affairs: of domestic politics, parties, finance, economics, administration, he knew nothing.

While the Bosnian crisis was dragging its weary length, Berlin and Paris sought and found a *modus vivendi* in Morocco. In an interview published in the *Matin* in May 1908 Holstein declared that his advice about Morocco had never been asked or given since his

[1] *Süddeutsche Monatshefte*, March 1931, 339.
[2] Paul von Schwabach, *Aus meinen Akten*, 147–51.

resignation;[1] but it is an eloquent testimony to his influence that the Chancellor did not decide on the final step before he had secured his approval. For this purpose he chose von der Lancken, who had carried on the negotiations in Paris and was a *persona grata* with the old recluse.[2] Bülow might well feel a little apprehensive, for Holstein had always scouted the notion of a rapprochement with France and Morocco was the chief cause of his fall. The only danger to friendly Franco-German relations, observed Aehrenthal to Sir Charles Hardinge in 1907, was the possible revival of Holstein's influence.[3] When, however, von der Lancken explained the situation he found that he was forcing an open door. 'You are surprised to find so little opposition,' he remarked to his visitor. 'I must confess that things have gone differently from what I intended and wished. We made a mistake in 1905 in working for a conference. I had already realised my mistake in believing that England would never associate herself with the Franco-Russian alliance. When this danger loomed up I felt we must break the ring, even at the risk of war, before it closed on us. Hence the Emperor's visit to Tangier. But there again I was wrong in my estimate of the leading actors. I ought to have known that Bülow would find it difficult, and His Majesty impossible, to decide for war.' He made the same *amende honorable* on the last visit of Monts. 'I must ask your forgiveness; you were right about Morocco and Algeciras.' The Franco-German agreement of February 9, 1909, however, which thus received a blessing from an unexpected quarter, merely brought a temporary *détente*, for the mischief of 1905-6 was too deep-seated to be undone. On October 11, 1909, Pichon, the French Foreign Minister, expressed the opinion to Mumm von Schwarzenstein, German Ambassador in Tokio, that Holstein's morbid distrust had been largely responsible for the misunderstanding between the two countries.[4]

No one in Germany felt keener satisfaction than Holstein when in March 1909 Izvolsky bowed to what the Wilhelmstrasse described as a friendly service, but what the victim declared to the British Ambassador to be a diplomatic ultimatum. Though signed by the Chancellor the despatch was suggested and drafted by Kider-

[1] Summarised in a report from its Berlin correspondent in the *Times*, May 27, 1908.
[2] Von der Lancken, *Meine Dreissig Dienstjahre*, 54-7.
[3] Lord Hardinge, *The Old Diplomacy*, 145.
[4] *Die Grosse Politik*, xxxix. 287.

len, who journeyed to the old hermit's modest flat to receive congratulations.[1] 'Fritz, who is still in bed with phlebitis,' he reported on March 29, 'said he admired my cheek in daring to inflict this humiliation on Izvolsky, especially as I had no one behind me.' It was the last gleam of sunshine for the man who had watched with satisfaction Bismarck make the Austrian alliance of 1879, and to whom that partnership had always remained the foundation of German policy.

When the end was in sight his old friends Frau von Lebbin and Count Hutten-Czapski were constantly at his sick-bed and the Chancellor paid his last visit.[2] The dying man was in bed with high fever, but he had prepared himself for the interview by a strong injection. His first question was whether Bülow would remain in office, to which the Chancellor rejoined that it did not depend on himself alone. Visibly excited and in the most emphatic tone he proceeded to argue that, in view of the foreign situation, it was his duty to remain with or without the confidence of the Emperor, whether or not the Finance Bill was passed. Bülow retorted that he must decline to accept laws or measures which he disapproved. 'You must remain, I tell you, you must remain!' cried the old man, whose words poured forth in a torrent. 'Who except you can steer our ship with such an impulsive Emperor, with an unpolitical people, and with a Reichstag immature as a child in foreign affairs? Stay on at any rate for four or five years. You have handled the Bosnian crisis with brilliant success, and at the same time you have established better relations with Russia than at any time since Bismarck. You must remain. Even your enemy Maximilian Harden says so. You ought at any rate to have time to reach a naval agreement with England. Then they may get rid of you. Till then you are indispensable.' As he left the room the Chancellor heard the husky voice: *Bleiben! Bleiben!* Bülow's fate, though Holstein did not know it, had been sealed by the *Daily Telegraph* incident, but he was spared the pain of seeing the pilot dropped. Among the mourners at the grave no one displayed more signs of grief than the Chancellor himself.[3]

'Vengeance was the mainspring of his activity,' commented

---

[1] Jäckh, *Kiderlen*, ii. 29.
[2] *Denkwürdigkeiten*, ii. 466–8. Bülow's reports of such interviews must be taken with a grain of salt.
[3] *Süddeutsche Monatshefte*, March 1931, 391.

Princess Radziwill.[1] 'He has been the evil genius of Germany, and we owe to him a large part of the misfortunes which have come to this country in the last five years. I wish I could think that all the consequences of his detestable influence were finished, but I fear that others may be in store for us. God knows what papers he has left and in whose hands they are.' A week later she reported that he had left them to Mme Lebbin, 'who boasts of it and goes about saying: That is my power! Bülow is so terrified that he redoubles his attentions to this intriguing woman, and no one doubts that there was a secret between Holstein and him.' On July 11 she reported that the Emperor was said to be immensely relieved. 'He was at Corfu when Wangenheim, German Minister at Athens, arrived. "Come and let me embrace you," he exclaimed, "I have just heard the news of Holstein's death. Ouf! C'était le cri du coeur." '

The eyes of the dying man were fixed to the last on the European chessboard over which he had brooded for half a century. Three weeks before the end on May 8, 1909, a telegram was sent at his wish by the Under-Secretary to the Chancellor in Venice, urging the addition of a sentence in the instructions to Metternich to prevent the raising of the subject of capture at sea leading to an increase of friction between the two nations.[2] For thirty years his aim had been the maintenance of the Austrian alliance and the benevolent neutrality of Great Britain. But the first was of limited utility if the smouldering wrath of the Russian people was its price, and a condition of the second was a *détente* with France. The various factors of the European situation were so closely interlocked that an error in judgment on one vital issue vitiated the whole scheme. The main diplomatic event of the first decade of the twentieth century was the birth of the Triple Entente, in the possibility of which he had obstinately refused to believe but which he had done as much as any other man to provoke.

No one ever doubted Holstein's patriotism, and he was wholly free from the Byzantinism of official circles; but the sixteen years of his quasi-dictatorship left Germany without a friend except Austria, whose strength was steadily ebbing as the tide of nationalism rose. He combined an incomparable knowledge of detail with a pathetic inability to forecast the trend of events or to measure the effect of his policy on the decisions of other Governments. His colleagues were

---

[1] *Lettres*, iv. 76–77, 84.
[2] *Die Grosse Politik*, xxviii. 156–7, note.

agreed that he was not quite right in the head; but if some excuse for his vagaries be sought in his pathological temperament, it was a costly error on the part of his superiors to allow him to win and retain such a commanding position in the state. Future generations, observed Count Lerchenfeld, the veteran Bavarian Minister at Berlin, would fail to understand that a people of sixty millions allowed itself to be led and misled by a lunatic. That, of course, is putting it too strongly. But if it was true, as Eulenburg declared and Brandenburg agrees, that he possessed the biggest brain since Bismarck, it was equally true, to borrow a witty phrase of Donna Laura Minghetti, the mother of Princess Bülow, who knew him well, that it was for men like him that the Bastille had been built. From the fall of the Iron Chancellor to the outbreak of the First World War the foreign policy of Germany lacked unity of control, for neither Holstein, the Emperor, nor any of his advisers held the rudder firmly in his grasp. The moral of this astonishing career is that power and public responsibility should always reside in the same hands.

Bibliographical Note

A large-scale biography must await the publication of Holstein's papers, which were bequeathed to Frau von Lebbin, who handed them over to Paul von Schwabach, head of Bleichröder's bank. See Schwabach, *Aus meinen Akten*, 446–8. *Friedrich von Holstein: Lebensbekenntnis in Briefen an eine Frau*. Eingeleitet und herausgegeben von Helmuth Rogge, 1932, contains interesting and important letters to his first cousin extending over half a century. *Fritz von Holstein als Mensch und Politiker*, by Friedrich von Trotha, with a valuable Introduction by Friedrich Thimme, 1931, a much slighter work, includes letters written to his devoted friend and hostess Frau von Lebbin, aunt of the author, in 1896 and 1908. *His Excellency the Spectre*, by Joachim von Kürenberg, with an Introduction by Wickham Steed, 1933, is a brilliant blend of fact and fantasy. A vivid and sympathetic portrait in his closing years is in Harden's *Köpfe*, vol 1. Of the many works which throw light on his activities the most important are the memoirs of Hammann, Eckardstein, Bülow, Rosen, Monts, Alexander Hohenlohe, Hutten-Czapski, Lerchenfeld, and Von der Lancken. *Die Grosse Politik der Europäischen Kabinette 1871–1914*, contains his official memoranda. Eugen Fischer's *Holsteins Grosses Nein* analyses his policy and influence during the Anglo-German negotiations at the turn of the century. Krausnick, *Holsteins Geheimpolitik in der Aera Bismarck 1886–1890*, is a useful monograph. The best German guide through the period of his greatest influence is Brandenburg, *From Bismarck to the World War*.

INDEX

AEHRENTHAL, 507–8
Alexander II, 368–72
Alexander III, 372–5, 419
Althusius, 4–5
Andreas, 342
Arndt, 73–4
Arnim, 363–4, 398–403, 415, 427–8
Augusta, Empress, 358–9

BALLHAUSEN, Lucius von, 317, 357–8
Barraclough, 338
Baumgarten, 295–6
Benedikt, 384–5
Beust, 276, 323
Bismarck, 24–5, 254, 275–448, *passim*
Bismarck, Herbert, 383, 396, 409, 413, 415, 418, 421, 423, 428, 446, 454
Boyen, 200–1
Brandenburg, Erich, 308–10
Brühl, Count, 44, 116
Brunswick, Duke Charles William Ferdinand of, 42–3, 81, 83, 86, 149, 153, 172–3
Bucher, Lothar, 311–12, 380, 397, 407–8, 416, 420
Bülow, 28–9, 318, 396, 444–510, *passim*
Bunsen, 260–2
Busch, Moritz, 317, 353–5, 375, 379–380, 397, 408

CAPRIVI, 383–5, 388, 417–30
Catherine the Great, 119–34, 136–7, 155, 251
Chamberlain, Joseph, 458–69, 447
Charles V, 215, 225–34
Chirol, Valentine, 436–8, 468–9, 484, 505–6

DAHLMANN, 20–22, 268
Dawson, 303–4, 331
Delbrück, 27–8, 333

Delcassé, 477–84
Dohm, 80
Droysen, 247–8, 293–5

ECKARDSTEIN, 401, 459–67, 477, 490
Eulenburg, 318, 413, 416–17, 426–8, 433, 440–51, 498–500, 511
Eyck, Erich, 302–3

FICHTE, 15–17
Forster, Georg, 74, 209
Francis Joseph, 379–80, 384
Frederick I, King, 244–5
Frederick the Great, 6–8, 40–2, 54, 77–84, 96–118, 119–45, 163–4, 241–253
Frederick II, Emperor, 227, 355–6, 375–6
Frederick, Empress, 359–60, 375–6
Frederick William I, 40, 243–6
Frederick William II, 84–95, 96–118, 144–60, 253
Frederick William III, 159–63, 297
Frederick William IV, 259–65, 270–1, 297, 321–2, 344
Freytag, Gustav, 273, 281, 285, 296

GIERS, 373, 419–20
Gneisenau, 201
Görres, 194, 202
Goethe, 10–11, 37, 39, 40, 44, 45, 53, 57, 64, 69, 72, 166–89
Gontaut-Biron, 329, 365–8
Gortchakoff, 364–5, 369–70, 373
Great Elector, The, 40, 99–100, 243–4
Grey, 485

HALLER, Johannes, 327, 334–5
Hammann, 421–2, 438, 479, 499
Harden, Maximilian, 333, 383, 498, 501, 504

INDEX

Hardenberg, 18, 154, 198–9, 254–9
Hatzfeldt, 408, 456–69
Haugwitz, 152, 158–63, 255
Hegel, 18–20
Henry, Prince of Prussia, 78–9, 82, 94–5, 119–65, 255–6
Herder, 1, 45, 48, 69
Hertzberg, 85, 86, 88, 95, 151
Herz, Henriette, 72, 192
Hitler, 33–4
Hohenlohe, Prince, 358, 363, 400, 406, 429, 430–53
Hohenlohe, Alexander, 401, 403, 430, 439–40
Holstein, 391–511
Humboldt, W. von, 11–13, 85
Hutten-Czapski, 431–3, 444, 409

IZVOLSKY, 508–9

JOSEPH II, 135–6, 250–2

KANT, 13–15, 73
Karl August, Duke of Weimar, 169–189, *passim*
Karl Friedrich of Baden, 47–8, 208
Keudell, 318, 343–4, 361
Kiderlen, 419, 421, 427–8, 444, 503, 506–9
Klopstock, 68, 72, 191
Knigge, 67–8

LAMSDORFF, 475–6
Lansdowne, 461–9, 485–6
Lenz, 301
Lerchenfeld, 379–80, 409, 511
Lessing, 41, 52, 56, 70–1
Li Hung Chang, 389–90
Loewenstein, Prince Hubertus, 335–6
Lorenz, Ottokar, 323
Luther, 2–4, 211–13, 223–35

MARCKS, Erich, 297, 301, 304–8, 312, 318–19, 323
Marschall von Bieberstein, 417–45
Mathy, Karl, 286–7
Mauvillon, 81, 96–118

Meinecke, 319, 339
Melanchthon, 4, 224–32
Mendelssohn, Moses, 55, 56, 81, 106–7
Metternich, Count, 467, 486
Meyer, A. O., 301, 318, 319, 328
Mirabeau, 43, 73, 75–118, 146–8, 193
Moeller van den Bruck, 32–3
Moltke, 374
Montgelas, 206–7
Monts, 402, 404, 508
Möser, Justus, 9–10, 37, 64–5
Moser, F. K., 8, 37, 49, 54, 58–60, 69
Moser, J. J., 47
Motley, 360–1
Müller, Johannes, 54, 74, 191
Münster, 408, 449, 451

NAPOLEON I, 181–6, 254–9
Napoleon III, 315, 324, 352
Naumann, 29, 30
Nicolai, 55, 56, 80
Niebuhr, 40, 54, 71, 211
Nietzsche, 27
Nowak, 332

ONCKEN, 310–11, 324, 326

PREUSS, Hugo, 30

RADOLIN, 484–5, 489–90
Radowitz, 318, 361, 380, 404–5, 416, 494–5
Ranke, 173, 210–66
Rathenau, 30
Ritter, Gerhard, 312, 326
Rosen, 402, 452–3
Rouvier, 482–8
Rudolph, Crown Prince, 372–5

SALISBURY, 458–69
Scharnhorst, 199–200, 257
Schiller, 45, 46, 57, 69, 73, 178–9
Schlieffen, 424–5, 444, 458, 506
Schlözer, 8–9, 49, 60–3
Schmitt, Carl, 34–5
Schweinitz, 411, 412, 418
Schubart, 63–4, 69, 74

Seckendorf, 5–6, 57–8
Spengler, 31–2
Srbik, 319–21
Stahl, 22–4
Stein, 18, 43, 44, 54, 196–8, 254–9
Steinberg, 336–7
Sybel, 322–3

TAYLOR, A. J. P., 337–8
Thimme, 314–15
Tirpitz, 389, 473
Treitschke, 25–6, 234, 252–3, 264–6, 267–99
Tröltsch, 29–30
Tschirschky, 490–6

VALENTIN, Veit, 319, 327, 335

WAHL, 332
Waldersee, 318, 374, 377, 398, 409–10, 413–15, 423–4
Wallenstein, 237–41
Ward, A. W., 303–4
Weckhrlin, 64
Weishaupt, 65–7
Wieland, 37, 41, 53, 192
William I, 323, 345–76, *passim*
William II, 322–3, 376–90, 410–11, 412–510, *passim*
Winckelmann, 55
Windthorst, 359–60
Witte, 473–6

ZIEKURSCH, 331–2